Asceticism
and the
New Testament

Asceticism
and the
New Testament

edited by

Leif E. Vaage
Vincent L. Wimbush

Routledge
New York and London

Published in 1999 by
Routledge
29 West 35th Street
New York, NY 10001

Published in Great Britain by
Routledge
11 New Fetter Lane
London EC4P 4EE

10 9 8 7 6 5 4 3 2 1

Library of Congress Cataloging-in-Publication Data
Asceticism and the New Testament/edited by Leif E. Vaage
    and Vincent L. Wimbush.
        p. cm.
    Includes bibliographical references and index.
    ISBN 0-415-92195-3.—ISBN 0-415-92196-1 (pbk.)
    1. Asceticism—History—Early church, ca. 30–6000—Congresses.
    2. Bible. N.T.—Criticism, interpretation, etc—Congresses.
    I. Vaage, Leif E.   II. Wimbush, Vincent L.
BV5023.A75 1999
248.4'7'09015—dc21   98-51082
                                                           CIP

Contents

⊶⊷

PART ONE
(*All About*) JESUS

PART TWO
PAUL (*The Real Thing*)

PART THREE
Imitatio PAULI

PART FOUR
UN-PAUL

Acknowledgments

Thanks are due to many institutions and individuals for their support, which included the convening of a conference in Toronto in October 1996 and the coordination and research and all other work that led to the publication of this book.

Thanks are due first to the Social Science and Humanities Council (SSHRC) of the Government of Canada for the grant that defrayed the cost of travel and accommodations of most of the participants in the October 1996 conference.

Thanks are also due to the Academic Initiatives Fund of Emmanuel College, which provided a generous supplement to the SSHRC grant. Principal Roger Hutchinson's support was especially important and critical.

Thanks also must go to the Academic Office and President's Office of Union Theological Seminary, New York City, and to President Roseann Runte and the President's Office of Victoria University for their moral and financial support.

Of great help in the planning and organization of the conference was Susanne Abbuhl, Ph.D. candidate in Old Testament at Emmanuel College, Toronto—our sincere appreciation goes to her. Also to be thanked are Theresa Moritz, independent scholar in medieval studies, Toronto, and Ph.D. students Stamenka Antonova (Early Christianity, Columbia University) and Nhai Khounvongsa (New Testament, Union) for their diligent copy-editing work. Khounvongsa deserves a special word of appreciation for preparation of the index.

Finally, our thanks to all contributors to the volume, who were willing with great *discipline* to entertain our question about asceticism and the New Testament.

List of Contributors

Batten, Alicia
University of St. Thomas
St. Paul MN

Castelli, Elizabeth A.
Barnard College
New York NY

Countryman, L. Wm.
Church Divinity School
of the Pacific
Berkeley CA

Eisenbaum, Pamela
Iliff School of Theology
Denver CO

Elliott, Neil
College of St. Catherine
St. Paul MN

Garrett, Susan R.
Louisville Presbyterian Theological
Seminary
Lousiville KY

Hock, Ronald F.
University of Southern California
Los Angeles CA

Keith, Alison
Victoria College
University of Toronto
Toronto ON
CANADA

Klassen, William
Kitchener ON
CANADA

Kloppenborg, John S.
University of St. Michael's
College
Toronto ON
CANADA

Knust, Jennifer Wright
Columbia University
New York NY

Love, Will
Orogi City
JAPAN

MacDonald, Margaret Y.
St. Francis Xavier University
Antigonish CANADA

Patterson, Stephen J.
Eden Theological Seminary
St. Louis MO

Rensberger, David
Interdenominational
Theological Center
Atlanta GA

Saldarini, Anthony J.
Boston College
Chestnut Hill MA

Scroggs, Robin, ret.
Union Theological Seminary
New York NY

Seim, Turid Karlsen
University of Oslo
NORWAY

Smith, Abraham
Andover Newton Theological
School
New Centre MA

Streete, Gail Corrington
Rhodes College
Memphis TN

Tolbert, Mary Ann
Pacific School of Religion
Berkeley CA

Vaage, Leif E.
Emmanuel College
Toronto
CANADA

Valantasis, Richard
Hartford Theological Seminary
Hartford CT

Wimbush, Vincent L.
Union Theological Seminary
New York NY

Introduction

Leif E. Vaage and Vincent L. Wimbush

I. ANTECEDENT QUESTIONS AND CONTINUING ISSUES

Was Jesus an ascetic? Did Paul teach contempt for the world? Does the New Testament model and therefore compel otherworldly orientations? Was Early Christianity a world-renouncing movement? If so, must contemporary Christianity be such? These questions were not necessarily the immediate impetus for the collection of essays that follow, but they do nevertheless get to the heart of some of the perduring basic and provocative issues that attend the modern and contemporary, academic and popular, religious and cultural engagement of the New Testament in general, and efforts to recover the historical Jesus and Paul and the primitive church in particular—all for the sake of understanding and finding compelling models for orientation to the increasingly complex world. These questions are addressed in the present collection of essays. As should be expected, different essays address the questions in different ways and differently assess the evidence. We think that the most important contribution of this collection lies in provoking thoughtful persons to come to more explicit terms with some of the complex presuppositions, practices, and issues that are involved in the study of the New Testament and the study of certain ancient forms of piety and world orientation.

This collection of essays is about the politics of two types of *disciplin(e)ary* practices, namely, ancient asceticism and world renunciations, and the arena of contemporary scholarship in the New Testament and early Christianity. The first set of disciplinary practices—ancient asceticism and world renunciations—refers to some clearly identifiable, intentional, often religiously inspired and religiously justified, and often absolutist orientations to and understandings of (a particular) society and culture and the enveloping natural order. The second set of practices—contemporary scholarship in the New Testament and early Christianity—refers to some clearly recognizable, academic/scholarly, sometimes absolutist, social-discursive formations and orientations. At different times or sometimes simultaneously and to different degrees, the latter has modeled, rationalized, and participated in, but also critiqued and sought to undermine, the former. It is the benefits to be gained by considering the complex and fascinating range of relationships between these two types of disciplin(e)ary practices that make opportune, and in our opinion compelling, the publication of this book.

II. HISTORY AND PROBLEMATICS BEHIND THE CONVERSATION AND THE BOOK

"Asceticism and the New Testament" was the topic of discussion for a small international group of scholars of the New Testament, early Christianity, and classics convened by the editors of this book at Emmanuel College, University of Toronto, 3–5 October 1996. Scholars in attendance had been asked to contribute to the discussion by taking responsibility for one or more New Testament text(s).[1] Responsibility entailed accepting the charge to interpret such texts with asceticism in mind, viz. to test what differences a focus upon ascetic practices, the rhetorics of renunciation, and ascetic ideologies and politics make for interpretation.

The Toronto conference was itself the logical and practical result of a long history of interfield and interdisciplinary discussions, research, and publications on asceticism. The editors and some of the conferees have long been members of the Asceticism Group, a diverse set of scholars in primarily religious and theological studies. Formed in 1985, the Asceticism Group has facilitated discussion, debate, and research and publications in connection with different conferences and colloquia. The group's activities have resulted in the appearance of several major publications: *Ascetic Behavior in Greco-Roman Antiquity: A Source Book*, ed. Vincent L. Wimbush (Studies in Antiquity and Christianity; Minneapolis: Fortress, 1990); *Discursive Formations, Ascetic Piety and the Interpretation of Early Christian Literature*, ed. Vincent L. Wimbush, *Semeia* 57–58 (Atlanta: Scholars, 1992); *Asceticism: Essays Originally Presented at an International Conference on the Ascetic Dimension in Religious Life and Culture, Held at Union Theological Seminary in New York, 25–29 April 1993*, ed. Vincent L. Wimbush and Richard Valantasis (New York: Oxford University Press, 1995); and *The Sexual Politics of the Ascetic Life: A Comparative Reader*, ed. Vincent L. Wimbush and Will Love *(Union Seminary Quarterly Review* 48: 3–4, 1994 [1995]).

Although at first constituted mainly of scholars of the New Testament and early Christianity, at each stage of its development the Asceticism Group has broadened and diversified its membership, agenda, and orientation. As the publications listed above reflect, in its agenda and orientation the group has moved from focus upon early Christian and Greco-Roman asceticisms to the comparative focus upon the ascetic dimension in religious life and culture. Each of the publications (with its antecedent conference or set of colloquia) represents a progressive widening of the field of vision within which the phenomenon of ancient asceticism is being viewed. The first book, *Ascetic Behavior in Greco-Roman Antiquity*, takes the discussion of ancient asceticism beyond the canonical boundaries of early Christianity and Judaism into the wider Greco-Roman world. The second publication, *Discursive Formations, Ascetic Piety, and the Interpretation of Early Christian Literature*, shifts the methodological parameters of the discussion beyond the boundaries of ancient history to include certain theoretical questions and perspectives posed by North Atlantic modernity and postmodernity. *Asceticism*, the collected essays from an international conference—a publication to which many of the essayists in this book refer—incorporates in the discussion of ancient asceticism cross-cultural and other religious perspectives beyond the boundaries of the "Western-Jewish-Christian" tradition. Finally, *The Sexual Politics of the Ascetic Life* continues the cross-cultural perspectives as it takes up the issue of gender in the politics of the ascetic piety.

With the present book, *Asceticism and the New Testament*, there is a sense in which the conversation has come full circle—with the changes in perspectives and approaches such a protracted return should entail. Notwithstanding the dangers of a fall into smugness and self-satisfaction, we are convinced that there is a pressing need for such a return. Traditionally shunted by mainline New Testament scholarship into the academic ghetto of "patristics," the study of asceticism can be shown to be both a fruitful and critical framework within which we can better understand the social-historical and politico-theological meanings of the collection of texts that constitute the New Testament. Despite the considerable, admittedly complex evidence that types of ascetic and world renunciatory behaviors can be argued to have defined the development of that part of Early Christianity that the New Testament texts illuminate, the ascetic dimension has historically for the most part been excluded from Western mainstream academic-scholarly-ecclesiastical-canonical exegetics and analytics and reconstructions of Christian origins, and thereby raises serious academic-political and ecclesiastical-political questions and suspicions.

Elaine Pagels, a well-known scholar of the New Testament and Early Christianity, as a member of a panel that focused upon asceticism in contemporary religious life and culture, dramatically stated the issue about the study of asceticism in connection to the politics of scholarly formation:

> Because my work is in the early history of Christianity and not in contemporary history, I want simply to state that the way I was educated involves a deep bias against recognizing asceticism as a fundamental part of Christian tradition.

I was actually surprised in graduate school—when I suggested at one point that the apostle Paul thought celibacy was definitely preferable to marriage—to be told by my German Lutheran professor that this was a complete misunderstanding of what Paul meant. And later, after writing *The Gnostic Gospels*, I found a scathing review by my former teacher Professor Henry Chadwick, who said that the Gnostics were not rejected from the early Christian movement because their movement involved a contradiction of its institutionalization, but rather because the Gnostics rejected the goodness of the body and the world. I thought that his was a remarkable statement, because this was the man with whom I studied patristics.

So this conference has made me aware of the difficulty, if one has been brought up in that kind of Protestant Christian environment, of actually uncovering what happens in the Christian gospels and what occurred in the early sources of this tradition. This has made me very grateful to the many people who have been doing that work of uncovering in the early Christian tradition. And, I am grateful to people like Brother Julian [another panelist who defined himself as a contemporary ascetic] because as I hear him, I remember the introduction that Thomas Merton wrote to the *Wisdom of the Desert Fathers* in which he says that the ascetic life offers the means of divesting oneself of the false, socially constructed, self to discover one's own true self.[2]

The experience Pagels describes will not, we suspect, be foreign to many other scholars in the field of New Testament and early Christian studies. As embodied discursive and social practices that both reflect and perhaps determine certain political and ideological positions and formations, asceticism focused upon as problematic in connection with the (hardly unproblematic ecclesiastical and cultural category) "New Testament" requires scholarly analysis to become equally concrete and politically engaged, perhaps even self-revealing.

As a specific mode of bodily resistance and as an analytical wedge for describing alternative or countercultural activity on the part of ancient "spiritual" and intellectual virtuosi, asceticism is a phenomenon recognized across conventional religious, cultural, and disciplinary boundaries; thus, it requires the scholar of Christian origins to appropriate an *askesis* of learning, to listen to and learn from others, to seek to contribute to what is otherwise known as the field of history of religions or comparative religions on terms that should transgress disciplinary boundaries and make the interpreter hypersensitive about, if not completely undermine, the history of Western Christian hegemony in the conceptualization of the subject. So, as a specific mode of cultural critique and resistance to the dominant—the socioeconomic, the ideological and theological, the cultural and political—asceticism has important hermeneutical potential, insofar as it provokes critical thinking regarding the New Testament as both window onto and mirror reflecting social dynamics. This would, of course, have the effect of taking the study of the New Testament far beyond the usually bounded interests of historical reconstruction and the aesthetics of the literary-rhetorical imagination or religio-theological applications. Asceticism assumes all such interests, approaches, and agenda; but it refuses to allow them to be separated, and it also forces them to mean differently as it shifts the bottom line of interpretation from the boundedness of text to the redescription and assessment of complex and fluid constructions of social texture(s).

III. OBJECTIVES

The principal objective of this book is to explore how the phenomenon of asceticism in Greco-Roman antiquity can serve as a theoretical framework or methodological wedge for redefining and redirecting scholarly interpretation of the New Testament and Early Christianity. We believe that some of the questions and problematics posed by the *ancient* practices of asceticism are significant precisely because of the ways in which they encourage further exploration of *contemporary* alternate social values implicit and/or requisite for such study. We have also dared to imagine that continued wrestling with the topic of asceticism can lead to a generation-specific, if not altogether fresh, reading of the New Testament as one of the complex constitutive elements in the ancient stream that has led to modern and late modern Western civilization and the formation of our local worlds.

By reframing the traditional object of inquiry of New Testament scholarship in terms of asceticism, we act on our conviction that not only will a better understanding of the primary social vectors of early Christianity be achieved, but even more important, the relationship between such historical study and the contemporary cultural context of the scholars who engage in it will be problematized. Thus, the topic "Asceticism and the New Testament" provides both a readily intelligible and an effective means of concretely redefining the interpretive practices of prevailing New Testament scholarship (and, by implication, other students of the ancient world, especially of the religions of the ancient world). It may even be possible, with the continuation in some modified forms of particular lines of traditional research, to contribute more directly and fully to the contemporary larger public conversation about what makes for a "good and healthy" human society, what renders a society bankrupt and liable to resistance of some sort.

IV. ORGANIZATION

This collection aims to cover all the New Testament texts. Yet as a reflection of our intention to be as honest as possible about the issues prompting the project in the first place, the reader will note that there is no attempt to force asceticism onto or out of any text. There is no obsession to find ascetics in every book, on every line. Some texts provide more material, more perspective and controversy than others. So not all texts require the same amount or type of attention; some texts with obvious literary and theological and other affinities are discussed as part of a cluster or grouping.

Each contributor was asked to submit an essay—not an exegesis paper or a mini-commentary. We intended the essays to use asceticism as a heuristic point of entry or methodological wedge into the different symbolic worlds. The essays are not intended to be the last words about either the respective texts of focus or about asceticism; they are intended only to demonstrate the different possibilities opened up for interpretation, including ideological implications and sociopolitical ramifications, by the question of asceticism.

There is no general definition of asceticism with which all contributors agree.[3] But each contributor has been asked to include a preliminary, operational construal of asceticism for the sake of engagement of particular texts. Many of the interpreters used Richard Valantasis' proposal for a more abstract definition in connection with performance theory as point of departure for discussion. Others followed Anthony Saldarini's proposal for a "vague" definition as starting point. Almost all essayists found both Valantasis' abstract and Saldarini's "vague" proposal wanting in some respects. This debate has not been settled. But all contributors to this book were asked to declare themselves by including at the beginning of their essay a clear indication of—and why—they understand asceticism as they do. Some may feel that our inability or unwillingness to define more narrowly, viz. universally, just what "asceticism" is must reflect a serious weakness in project conceptualization and design, or at least a problem for the possibility of finding asceticism in the New Testament.[4] But from our point of view, the value of the category of asceticism is not that it provides, at long last, *the* hermeneutical key with which to unlock the treasure chest—or prison house—of the text. The category of "asceticism" is useful not because it constitutes better *answers* to long-standing questions in the field of New Testament or any other type of scholarship, but because it provides an opportunity to ask new and, we think, better *questions* of the texts at hand. This is desirable if only in order to reconstitute through a different disciplin(e)ary practice what we think is the degenerating body of New Testament scholarship.[5]

As the table of contents indicates, we have followed a fairly well-recognized clustering of the texts (notwithstanding our panache with the characterization of categories and rubrics). This we have done in order to help readers see the larger literary, rhetorical, historical, and ideological-theological relationships that writers were intentional about first addressing and then problematizing. Some (major and minor) clusterings, readers will clearly note, asceticism as a wedge tends to scramble or render questionable.

NOTES

1. Not in attendance at the conference in Toronto but asked subsequently to contribute to this book were Ronald F. Hock, Robin Scroggs, and Neil Elliott.
2. See transcription of remarks of Elaine Pagels ("Asceticism and Scholarly Asceticism") as part of "Panel Discussion on Contemporary Religious Life and Culture," in *Asceticism*, ed. Vincent L. Wimbush and Richard Valantasis (New York: Oxford University Press, 1995), 599–600.
3. Many contributors did in fact use R. Valantasis' provocative essay "Constructions of Power in Asceticism," in the *Journal of the American Academy of Religion* 63 (1995), and "A Theory of the Social Function of Asceticism," in *Asceticism*, ed. V. L. Wimbush and R. Valantasis (New York: Oxford University Press, 1995), 544–52. Also, Anthony Saldarini's essay in this book includes arguments about points of departure for the interpretation of texts. This has fostered conversation and made this collection of essays far more coherent than the typical collection.
4. See, e.g., the remarks by Mary Ann Tolbert in her essay in this volume.
5. That a novel application of the category of asceticism to the New Testament would also entail further thinking and debate about the precise nature of the New Testament itself and "asceticism" itself should occasion no surprise. It is simply a standard feature of the enterprise of scientific research. Research tools must constantly be refined, research agenda and foci must be constantly examined.

Part One

(All About)
JESUS

Asceticism and the Gospel of Matthew

Anthony J. Saldarini

INTRODUCTION

Linking asceticism with the Gospel of Matthew sounds strange because New Testament scholars do not normally use asceticism as a descriptive or analytical category. Matthew's disciplined, focused way of life demands restraint and personal application, but is it ascetical? The stuff of developed Christian asceticism is prayer or meditation, fasting, vigils, celibacy, poverty, monastic or hermetic withdrawal, renunciation of the world, systematic rejection of bodily pleasures, penitential practices, and so forth.[1] This list of practices can be partially universalized, according to John Hick:

> It is probably a universal religious intuition that "true religion" is to be found within the wide spectrum that begins with commitment, dedication, singleness of mind, purity of heart, and self-discipline in prayer or meditation; that extends into practices of pilgrimage, fasting, vigils, celibacy, poverty and obedience; and that may go on to further and sometimes extreme austerities, which border in the end on pathological excesses.... It [asceticism] embraces the whole realm of spiritual method and discipline, including the solitude, silence, and devotions of monastics, the austerities of shamans, and the severe practices of ascetics seeking special insights and visions.[2]

This type of descriptive definition also calls to mind similar definitions of apocalyptic literature such as writings containing historical reviews, pseudonymity, eschatological thought, fantastic imagery, and so forth.[3] Both have a rich content with little structure or obvious intelligibility.

Traditional Christian ascetical practices have been linked hermeneutically with New Testament texts, but these practices are not explicitly described, praised, and recommended there. Traditional theology made the link between the gospels and the later ascetical tradition by imposing abstract categories that encompassed both: "In the gospels asceticism is presented under the concrete theme of following the historical Christ and thus sharing the hardships, dangers and penalties that loyal discipleship to Him exact"; following Jesus "implies an ascetic self-renunciation by the disciple."[4] According to this view, experiencing what Jesus experienced and participating in his fate mean denying self and all that separates oneself from Christ. While this approach may serve a relatively uncritical spiritual formation, it will not stand up to thorough analysis or support cross-cultural comparisons.

Recent work on the connections between the New Testament documents and Greco-Roman literature has stressed the common role of self-mastery and virtue in both. The mastery of oneself through control of the passions is a major concern of Greek and Roman philosophy and ethical literature.[5] The New Testament patently encourages self-control in the face of human passions and proclivity to sin and teaches about virtues and vices, but these topics do not receive the extended thematic attention characteristic of later Christian literature. In the gospels and in Acts, exhortations are brief and models of virtue implicit.

Some scholars define Christian asceticism by its worldview and motivations, which are based on a contrast between this world and a higher, more spiritual and more sacred world, a view that again can be partially universalized for the study of religion. As Walter Kaelber summarizes it:

> [Asceticism], when used in a religious context, may be defined as a voluntary, sustained, and at least partially systematic program of self-discipline and self-denial in which immediate, sensual, or profane gratifications are renounced in order to attain a higher spiritual state or a more thorough absorption in the sacred. Because religious man (*homo religiosus*) seeks a transcendent state, asceticism—in either rudimentary or developed form—is virtually universal in world religion.[6]

Certainly, some rudimentary comparisons among religions and their literatures can be made using these abstract categories. But such schemes tend to reinforce what we "already know" and hide the riches and particularities of the texts we read. For example, in the New Testament the oppositions between the physical and spiritual worlds, body and soul, self and God, and spiritual and worldly knowledge are either not explicitly thematized or are heavily qualified by the traditional Jewish insistence that "body and soul" form some kind of permanent whole. Behaviors and motives, attitudes and goals, and language and metaphors in the New Testament are significantly different from those in later Christian ascetical literature. A comparison of very different texts must lead to more flexible categories that enable us to encompass the varieties of attitude and behavior in a coherent but varied whole.

An adequate definition of asceticism involves epistemology, categorization, and the systematic comparison of texts that reflect diverse patterns of human thought and behavior. Categories of sameness or difference highlight certain aspects of the things to be compared and contrasted and allow us to relate them to one another positively or negatively. However, these same categories inevitably conceal and suppress other aspects of the things to be compared and contrasted and thus conceal and suppress other relationships that might be noted and evaluated. For example, a comparison that focuses on the presence or absence of life after death might ignore a religion's attitudes toward life and communal survival in this world.

Thus, more importantly, categories used in a comparison are implicit and must be thought of explicitly as part of a system or theory. When we describe, compare, and contrast, we do so against a whole field of experience and thought that is filled with potential similarities and differences. Trivial comparisons and distinctions endanger understanding every step of the way because they obscure the important and central aspects of a religion or text. Only a systematic comparison, which critically accounts for and evaluates its own procedures, categories, and conclusions, can claim to have grasped dissimilar phenomena with some kind of intelligibility. And, finally, the fashioning of theories and categories and the observation and description of phenomena in texts or experience must be ongoing processes that continually influence and modify one another. Thus a highly abstract, precise definition from which other definitions may be clearly deduced tends to obscure cogent, precise, and significant comparisons among different religions or different positions within a single religion. Similarly, a single, tight deductive scheme eliminates numerous perspectives and theories that might be useful for understanding a complex field of phenomena. The wrong kind of system may be reductionist in an epistemologically impoverished sense.

At this point, a type of vague abstraction may be helpful. Charles Sanders Pierce developed this notion to accommodate modern science and to supplement traditional Aristotelian logic. It has recently been used for the comparison of religions by Robert C. Neville.[7] According to this view, abstraction comes in two forms: general (the usual way we think of abstraction) or vague. General abstractions can be applied directly to a subject matter, for example, "human being." Vague abstractions can only be applied to a concrete subject matter through intermediate specifications and theories. The instantiations of a vague category may be very different from one another, mutually exclusive, or contradictory. Even so, they may still be intelligible instances of a vague category:

That the theory is vague means that it can be specified by two or more less vague theories or interpretations, that might not be compatible with one another or even commensurable except when reformulated as specifications of the vague theory. The theoretical elements are determinate with respect to one another, but indeterminate with reference to their applicability, depending on less vague determinations.[8]

In such a procedure, the highest-level categories are very important for the unity of the theory, but "the singularity of at least some of the elements in the subject matter is equally determinative. Both angles of determination are requisite for importance."[9] For example, in a discussion of ultimate realities, the figure of God would be central for West Asian religions, a harmonious universe for Chinese religions, and a critique of all "realities" or nothingness for the Buddhist tradition. The criterion for the relevance of items to a topic and for success in comparison is not a precise fit, as in a mathematical theory, or a conceptual similarity, as in logic, but the cogency of the comparisons within a theory of religions.

How then might a series of interrelated categories illuminate ascetical behavior and an ascetical outlook both in individuals and in communities? I shall argue for a set of categories different from, but not totally opposed to, those suggested in recent studies of asceticism. Ascetical attitudes, commitments, and behavior are a specification of the vaguer, more general, flexible category of "discipline," which may encompass activities and attitudes oriented toward virtue, knowledge, achievement, social standing, survival, religion, and productive activity, among others. Asceticism in this scheme would be a type of religious discipline.[10] Understanding asceticism as a specific kind of religious discipline implies inner human tensions among needs, passions, feelings, desires, thoughts, spiritual aspirations, and strivings for achievement. Kallistos Ware has captured this aspect of asceticism as a discipline well. In its most general sense,

> asceticism...leads us to self-mastery and enables us to fulfill the purpose that we have set for ourselves, whatever that may be. A certain measure of ascetic self-denial is thus a necessary element in all that we undertake, whether in athletics or in politics, in scholarly research or in prayer. Without this ascetic concentration of effort we are at the mercy of exterior forces, or of our own emotions, and moods; we are reacting rather than acting. Only the ascetic is inwardly free.[11]

This view of asceticism owes much to ancient Greco-Roman teaching on discipline, detachment, self-mastery, and striving for virtue and can be found in vestigial form in the New Testament documents.

Discipline, in turn, is a specification of an even vaguer category: education. Education, in its root sense, encompasses individual and social formation, which varies greatly according to factors such as culture, geography, history, and politics. According to Leif E. Vaage, the overall human enterprise of education is aimed at fashioning a mode of existence, one that would offer a higher or better way than the natural or fallen state.[12] Asceticism, in this case, is

> a certain disciplinary techne of the body as the specific means deemed most likely to permit the achievement of a stipulated end. All share, in other words, the same form of cultural "engineering," a discernible and distinct style of "crafting" the social self. Thus the pragmatic and theoretical wager that, through "asceticism," one can enjoy a still unrealized, but progressively anticipated, greater sense of personal well-being.[13]

I would add that the personal well-being sought in religious discipline and especially in asceticism is an ultimate or spiritually deep well-being, the type of "reward" designated as a general compensator by Rodney Stark. A general compensator actually substitutes for a greatly desired reward—eternal life, continual intimacy with a divine being, or complete happiness—that cannot be obtained in ordinary life. A general compensator is the promise of such reward, substantiated by some overarching worldview such as a religious system.[14] Thus Vaage's category of asceticism implies an underlying theory of human happiness or wholeness, whether religious or not, and, if religious, some greatly desired goal or reward that transcends the ordinary achievements of human life.

Thus far, the definition of asceticism has kept the social functions of asceticism in the background. Richard Valantasis, in his most recent effort to define the term, attempts to transform asceticism into a category of cross-cultural analysis, using social scientific theories of power. He stresses that power must be understood within the context of intentional human activities as a type of social relation.[15] Thus "asceticism may be defined as performances within a dominant social environment intended to inaugurate a new subjectivity, different social relations and an alternative symbolic universe."[16] Asceticism is a construction and expression of power within a social world. The new subjectivity created through ascetical practice may come about through a reaction against the prevailing culture (combative), a transformation or enrichment within the culture (integrative), an educative process, a search through pilgrimage, or a revelatory illumination. The new subjectivity results in new social relations and a new symbolic worldview, both of which resist and seek to transform the dominant culture and its characteristic subjectivity, social relations, and worldview.[17]

Valantasis' analysis of asceticism as an expression of power within the context of intentional human activities and social relations explains the powerful positive and negative social reactions provoked by ascetics, ascetical behavior, and the ascetic worldview. Asceticism implicitly challenges and criticizes the dominant social and cultural outlooks, practices, and norms and seeks to modify or overthrow them.

Vincent L. Wimbush has captured the negative or conflictive side of asceticism with a more limited definition: "Ascetic behavior represents a range of responses to social, political and physical worlds often perceived as oppressive or unfriendly, or as stumbling blocks to the pursuit of heroic personal or communal goals, life styles, and commitments."[18]

Just as the unusually rational, creative, altruistic, charismatic, or powerful human being stands out from ordinary life and society, the disciplined, determined, or persistent ascetic stands out through particular achievements that are either accepted or resisted by society. It is important to note, however, that the relationships between ascetics and society are manifold. They always involve tension, as do all social relationships, but do not always result in conflict. The changes in social relations brought about by asceticism may, in fact, support a culture and be accepted by it.

Walter Kaelber has developed a fivefold typology of asceticism's relation to culture that captures explicitly many elements of the previous definitions: "(1) asceticism against culture, (2) asceticism of culture, (3) asceticism beyond culture, (4) asceticism and culture in paradox, and (5) asceticism as transformer of culture."[19] Along with Valantasis, Kaelber stresses the rich and manifold functions and outcomes of ascetics, their behavior, and their outlooks in various social and cultural contexts.

Can all of these aspects of human behavior and what we have traditionally called asceticism be integrated into an empirically faithful and systematically useful theory of human behavior? And can the category of asceticism bear the weight put upon it by recent studies that see it as identifying a fundamental, cross-cultural human process? Asceticism has most frequently been used to describe a relatively narrow range of activities in both ancient Greek and Christian literature. In recent centuries in the West, asceticism has been understood as an aspect of Christian religious behavior and has been transferred to similar behaviors and outlooks in other religious cultures such as Hinduism and Buddhism. While an analysis of asceticism can illuminate cross-culturally many different processes, behaviors, and human goals, I do not think that, in the end, asceticism is a flexible enough category to bear the weight of the varied phenomena that create new subjectivities, social relations, and symbolic worlds.

I would suggest instead, therefore, a series of broadly inclusive, vague categories that allow for the comparison of very different and even contradictory religious and social expressions. I think that some work on asceticism implicitly defines its subject matter in wide-ranging terms but is hobbled by the single category "asceticism" into which all phenomena must fit or to which all must relate. The categories I list here are not related deductively to one another, but rather complement and specify each other. Provisionally, it seems to me that asceticism involves, at a very general level, the following features:

1. *Intentional, goal-oriented human behavior, both personal and communal,* is understood according to the various anthropologies of different cultures with their diverse views of human freedom or fate, of ultimate human goals, etc.

2. Intentional, goal-oriented human behavior works itself out in *social relations and personal subjectivity* related to those social relations. Modern Western culture, for example, stresses the individual, as opposed to ancient Mediterranean cultures, which emphasize kinship and community. Despite the bewildering array of social arrangements in world cultures, these competing understandings of human life share broad similarities that may be compared and contrasted.

3. The Gospel of Matthew understands all social relationships under the core symbol of the *kingdom (rule or reign) of God.*

4. Social relations involve constant interaction, change, and conflict. Thus, *power relationships,* understood in various ways, are fundamental and often constitutive of social relations and of the person within society. Change may be understood as growth, transformation, or revolution, but in all cases various power relationships are involved.

5. Social relations and power relationships within society necessarily imply and contribute to the *social construction of the self or a subjectivity.* Different cultures understand and evaluate the human person and the spiritual, intellectual, volitional, moral, and pragmatic activities of humans differently, according to their cultural worldview.

6. In the Gospel of Matthew, the dominant subject is Jesus, and the subjectivity he creates is most consistently expressed as *discipleship* or *following.*

7. More particularly, the cultural processes described here usually include and require some kind of *education* or socialization process for the young and continuing socialization and adaptation for adults and the culture as a whole. This broad sense of education recognizes that a culture with its views of self, society, and outsiders is constantly changing with circumstances or (re)constructing itself.

8. The educative process and the social construction of the self and viable social relationships ordinarily require some kind of *disciplined human behavior,* oriented toward a goal intentionally chosen by the culture or individual. Discipline is common in the religious sphere as well as in the political, social, educative, and family spheres of activity.

9. The program of disciplined behavior found in the Gospel of Matthew explicitly claims *the law and the prophets,* that is, the Hebrew Bible, as

its source. It has also been influenced by teachings about the two ways in Judaism and Christianity and by popular Greco-Roman ethical teachings.

10. Certain kinds of disciplined behavior in relationship to religion, along with their motivations and goals, are often referred to as *asceticism*.

Note that the categories in this list do not inevitably follow from one another, but describe only part of a very broad field of human activities. They can be related to one another, however, and the assumptions, theories, experiences, etc., that underlie them can be compared and contrasted productively, even when very different expressions of diverse social cultures are considered together. Many of the sayings and teachings in the Gospel of Matthew are enigmatic or underdetermined in their application. Nevertheless, they challenge conventional ways of living early Jewish and early Christian life, they relate in some way to following Jesus, and they are part of the long road that leads to developed Greek and Syriac asceticism of the third through sixth centuries.

THE GOSPEL OF MATTHEW

The teaching in the Gospel of Matthew may be linked with later Christian asceticism and with cross-cultural comparisons of asceticism by an analysis of Matthew's demanding way of life in a stressful social context.[20] Matthew's audience is a late-first-century CE group of Jews who are followers of Jesus.[21] For them, Jesus taught God's rule over the world through the central symbol of the kingdom of God, that is, of heaven. Attention and fidelity to God's rule demand obedience to God's commandments, which are found in the Bible but must be interpreted according to Jesus' teaching, as understood by Matthew. Thus, for Matthew, righteousness demands practicing the commandments and implies a disciplined pursuit of virtue. To encourage communal fidelity to God, Matthew draws upon biblical law and prophets, the wisdom tradition both in the Bible and in Second Temple Jewish literature, Second Temple apocalyptic literature, and topics found in Greco-Roman philosophical, ethical, and exhortatory literature.[22] The person who learns Matthew's teachings is a dedicated follower of Jesus and a seeker after the kingdom of God and its justice (see Matt. 6:33).[23] A person engaged in this kind of intentional, goal-oriented, disciplined behavior may thus be understood as a certain kind of ascetic.

The probable social context of the Gospel of Matthew also fits the ascetical enterprise. The gospel is filled with protests against persecution and with polemics against a variety of opponents, especially the leaders of the Jewish community.[24] Matthew's group is most probably a sect or a deviant association within the larger Jewish community. Alternatively, many hold that Matthew's group has just left or been expelled from the Jewish community.[25] In either case, the late-first-century CE tensions and conflicts mirrored in Matthew's narrative demand a pattern of resistant behavior and the construction of a revised subjectivity and identity for the deviant group. The stringent demands that Matthew makes on his audience are typical of new religious movements that meet social opposition and oppression.

Interestingly, recent sociological analysis by Stark explains how inhospitable circumstances, demanding behavior, and a high degree of commitment serve to constitute a new group and to attract recruits.[26] Religion in general and especially new religious groups provide a way to attain desirable rewards that are presently scarce or unavailable.[27] The difficulties associated with the pursuit of these goals require discipline, perseverance, suffering, and even death, that is, virtues and behaviors associated with asceticism in the religious sphere. The "high cost of admission" to Matthew's group makes it that much more attractive to many adherents. The asceticism, discipline, and intentional creation of a new subjectivity or new way of understanding and living out the biblical tradition and Judaism builds a strong group ethos with sharp boundaries, clear goals, and congruent demands. Stark's analysis confirms in many respects Bryan Wilson's now popular theory of sects, which categorizes them according to their responses to varied social contexts.[28] In most cases, intentional behavior under difficult circumstances and the creation of a new group under hostile conditions require the discipline and renunciation of normal desires characteristic of asceticism.[29]

Although later generations tamed the Gospel of Matthew by ignoring or modifying many of its teachings (a process that will be analyzed later in this chapter), the text retains a harsh integrity that testifies to the energy that Matthew's first-century group put into creating a new life and a new set of attitudes and commitments (that is, a new subjectivity). According to Matthew, the followers of Jesus must acknowledge God's rule (the kingdom of God) in contrast to the dominant Roman and Jewish worlds in which they live. They must strive for a new righteousness (5:20), that is, a way of thinking, judging, and acting that corresponds to the kingdom of God now and in the end. All must be perfect as God is perfect (5:48), without reserve or limit.

Matthew teaches these norms as necessary for anyone following Jesus. They do not form a special program for leaders or devotees, and they are subordinate to the explicit goals and master metaphors of the Matthean narrative, such as the kingdom of God, righteousness, judgment, and Jesus. In many cases these commands and practices are suggestive and indeterminate rather than explicitly worked out into a disciplinary or ascetical program in the usual sense. In response to Matthew's program we might say that his version of Christianity "has not been tried and found wanting. It has been found difficult; and left untried."[30] The teaching and way of life found in the Gospel of Matthew merge what later Christian writers would identify as asceticism and ordinary Christian life. We shall trace the demands of this commitment through the general theme of following Jesus as specified by the subthemes of poverty, sexual restraint, fasting, and leaving home.

The gospel narrative puts enormous stress both on following Jesus and on the disciples as sometimes successful, sometimes failed followers of Jesus.[31] Both John the Baptist and Jesus left their homes, and Jesus called his disciples to leave their homes, work, and family to follow him who has "nowhere to lay his head" (8:18–22; cf. also 4:18–22, and 9:9). Jesus' true family is a fictive kinship group, which includes those who do God's will and are with Jesus (12:46–50) rather than members of Jesus' blood kinship group or home village. Disciples will have conflict with their families and neighbors (10:34–37), as Jesus did in Nazareth (13:53–58). In a sense, the lonely wilderness, where John works (3:1; 11:7) and where Jesus is tempted by the devil (4:1), withdraws with his disciples, and feeds the crowds (14:13, 15), is symbolic of leaving home and family. By contrast, a scribe who wants to follow Jesus is bothered by homelessness, and another person refuses to abandon his father until he has buried him as the command to honor one's parents requires (8:18–22). Forced to choose, Matthew and his associates must go with their own group and not with their families, parents, or anyone who will impede their relationship with the teacher and master, Jesus. In this, they stand against the powerful Near Eastern cultural assumption that one's family and kinship group come first. Matthew seeks to create a new personal and communal subjectivity with altered relationships not only to families but to society at large. Leaving home changes the fundamental structures of political and familial society with economic, religious, and cultural consequences for all.

A willingness to leave home, the center of ancient economic life and security, and follow Jesus entails acceptance of poverty and requires both detachment from wealth and trust in God. Poverty of spirit in the beatitudes (5:3) requires loyalty to God rather than to wealth (6:24). This very impractical trust in God for life's necessities (6:24–34) in order to seek the kingdom of God and its righteousness (6:33) requires the follower of Jesus to give up his or her wealth in favor of eternal life. As a negative example, the rich young man's attachment to wealth keeps him from following Jesus and acknowledging the centrality of God's rule (19:16–30).

Poverty undercuts the drive to stabilize the family through acquisition of arable land, which was the ordinary form of wealth in antiquity. The state of mind and spirit that comes from poverty and meekness (5:3, 5) characterizes the kingdom of God as described in the Sermon on the Mount. Neither home nor family nor wealth nor the difficulties of life will distort a clear focus on God or impede a frank understanding of the human condition with its limitations and paradoxes.[32] The poor in spirit of the beatitudes will have nothing and need nothing to take on their journeys to spread Jesus' teachings, nor will they be deterred by rejection (10:7–15). What chokes the spread of the word are the anxieties of life and the seduction of wealth (13:22), which misdirect the heart to earthly rather than heavenly treasures (6:19–21). Poverty of spirit relativizes the human desire for security and wealth so that God becomes the center of consciousness and the goal of behavior (6:22–34).

Although Matthew warns against the dangers of wealth and preoccupation with the necessities of life in chapters 6 and 19, the evangelist does not balance these strictures with praise of poverty as a good in itself. He focuses rather on the metaphoric meaning and implications of poverty, the attitudes and outlooks fostered by it, and the behaviors consequent to these attitudes and outlooks. In general, the means used in the struggle against the passions and for the formation of correct attitudes and behaviors are firmly subordinated to the ends for which these efforts are undertaken, namely, the kingdom of God and following Jesus. The practices of detachment required by such poverty, loss of home, and following Jesus later supported the growth of monastic and ascetical ways of life that required poverty and celibacy.

The loosened ties of followers with their families in Matthew's gospel does not include abandonment of marriage. Matthew discourses on human sexual passions and opposes divorce in order to protect marriage, but does not encourage or praise celibacy as an ascetical practice. The Hebrew Bible assumes that men divorce their wives, just as they married them. (In the Near East a man took a woman as wife after family negotiations, and could dismiss her as well. Legally marriage was not a mutual contract.) The Hebrew Bible regulates the dissolution of marriage so that the woman is legally free to be taken in marriage again (Deut. 24:1–4), but it does not give reasons or set conditions for initiating a divorce, nor does it encourage or oppose it. Matthew follows early Christian teaching, perhaps from Jesus, in treating the marriage bond as inviolate, except for unspecified sexual irregularity (*porneia*), which dissolves the marriage (5:31–32; 19:1–9). The repeated prohibition against divorce emphasizes that, for Matthew, the danger is not so much to the human consumed by passion but to the marriage bond, which requires complete and permanent fidelity. Mary's "Joseph-less pregnancy" implies adultery and the destruction of the engagement/marriage contract until the situation is clarified and regularized in a dream (1:18–20).

To protect marriage further, Matthew not only repeats the commandment against adultery but also forbids inner lust, which can easily lead to marriage-destroying adultery (5:27–30).[33] The destructive power of passion and temptation, symbolized by sexual desire, must be combated by the most extreme means, even the removal of an eye or a hand. Biblical strictures against mutilation (Deut. 23:1; Lev. 22:24) forbid taking this hyperbolic counsel literally, but the metaphor encourages extreme effort to control human behavior. For example, when the disciples wonder who can accept Jesus' rigorous teaching about lifetime commitment to marriage without divorce, they are referred to the eunuch-sayings, which are ambiguous in meaning but clear in intent (19:10–12). The "eunuch for the sake of the kingdom of heaven" may be understood either as a celibate who spreads the news of the kingdom or as a separated married person who does not remarry. In any case, normal cultural practices have been rejected and the follower of Jesus must be ready to live without a sexual relationship if a marriage ends.

Consistent with the Jewish tradition, Matthew nowhere praises celibacy in itself. Unlike other writers in the Greco-Roman tradition, the evangelist does not encourage control of sexual passions for the sake of individual self-mastery: Lust is not presented as a threat to reason or the soul, nor is continence championed as a virtue that will benefit the whole person.

The gospel's approach to fasting, a traditional and widespread practice, is noticeably diffident. Even with its stringent teaching about following Jesus, leaving home, poverty, and marriage, the Gospel of Matthew takes fasting for granted, but does not promote it as an important part of Matthew's teaching and communal practice.[34] Jewish culture promoted or presumed fasting for a variety of purposes, some of which appear in Matthew's narrative. John the Baptist, for example, engages in what seem to be ascetical practices. He lives in the wilderness of Judea, eating locusts and wild honey and dressing in rough camel skin (3:1–4), so that Jesus may contrast John's hard prophetic life, similar to that of Elijah, with the luxuries of rulers (11:7–9). But despite Jesus' praise of John, people contrast Jesus and John (11:16–19) and their disciples (9:14–17) because Jesus and his disciples do not fast while John and his disciples do. Even though Jesus fasts when the Spirit leads him into the wilderness to be tempted (4:1–2), fasting is not a constant practice associated with Jesus in Matthew.

Matthew uses fasting and feeding as a metaphor to orient his listeners toward other fundamental values. In the fourth beatitude (5:6) the blessed hunger and thirst for justice and will be satisfied, most probably at the end of the world when God directly intervenes to correct the unjust workings of the world. Yet, despite the stern demands of the beatitudes, Jesus does not require either his disciples or the people following him to fast. When a crowd of 5000 men plus women and children join Jesus in a wilderness location (*eremon topon*) and lack food, Jesus feeds them. The model of God feeding Israel in the wilderness during the Exodus controls Jesus' action in the narrative. God's and Jesus' compassion for human needs concerns Matthew more than the necessity of human discipline and abnegation. Similarly, another group of 4000 men plus women and children had been with Jesus for three days in the wilderness and were fed so they would not become faint on the way. Finally, Jesus defends the picking of grain by his hungry disciples on the Sabbath (12:1–8).[35] Matthew either shows little interest in fasting or promotes other interests that involve being fed and cared for by Jesus.

Many motives and goals for fasting may be found in Jewish tradition, for example, repentance for sins, preparation for prayer or visionary experience, and petition or intercession with God. Matthew does not mobilize that rich tradition to support a regular practice of fasting, nor does he give fasting prominence in his community's life. (The statement that a particularly virulent type of demon could only be driven out by prayer and fasting [17:21] is a later manuscript tradition.) Jesus' private fasting before his temptations (4:2) seems to prepare him spiritually for combat with the devil, but this is not made explicit. The Sermon on the Mount instructs Jesus' followers to avoid ostentation when fasting as well as when giving alms and praying (6:1–18), but does not say why they fast. Fasting in Matthew speaks implicitly to the difficulties of following Jesus and to the threats and persecutions suffered by Matthew's late-first-century CE group. But the evangelist does not integrate fasting into a structured program of discipline or a coherent vision of communal relationships.

The mastery of oneself through control of the passions is a major concern of Greek and Roman philosophy and ethical literature. In Matthew's narrative Jesus is tempted by gluttony after fasting and by vainglory, power, and arrogance (4:3–10). His temptations typify the challenges facing followers of Jesus and model the self-denial necessary for obedience to God and God's commandments in the Hebrew Bible.[36] Matthew understands righteousness or justice (*dikaiosyne*) to be "the right conduct which God requires."[37] These just behaviors, including the attitudes and goals that are integral to them, demand a type of asceticism of the mind and body.[38] Thus human behavior and society in Matthew are based on justice, just as in the Hebrew Bible and in Greek literature. According to Stoic teaching, asceticism is a kind of practical training and education.[39] Discipline flows from the mind to the body, and goodness of character is determined by the nature of the soul.[40] Matthew does not thematize these Greek reflections or use the same terms, but righteousness is determined for Matthew by inner attitudes and corresponding behaviors (5:20–6:18), as found in the Sermon on the Mount, where teachings against anger, lust, divorce, oaths, retaliation, and hatred of enemies and instructions to give alms, pray, and fast without public display guide communal life. John the Baptist's teaching of repentance from sin, his ascetic life in the wilderness, and his death defending his teaching (3:15; 21:32; cf. 14:1–12) provide another model of fidelity to God. For the follower of Jesus, endurance of persecution "for righteousness' sake" (5:10–12; cf. also 10:16–39) is the highest test of virtue and fittingly the climax of the beatitudes.[41] Inevitably, control of the passions becomes associated with Jesus' overcoming the most basic passion, the desire for life. In summary, hunger for justice (5:6) and seeking the justice of God's kingdom (6:33) require a behavior and personal formation that may be called ascetic.

Paradoxically, nonetheless, Matthew does not recommend ascetical practice and discipline as good in themselves, but offers rest to those who take up Jesus' yoke (11:28–30). Taking up a yoke is a common metaphor for obedience to God's commandments. Despite the opposition that followers of Jesus will meet and despite the demands of the teachings found in the gospel, Matthew envisions the demands of God's kingdom to be nonthreatening and comforting through the mediation of Jesus. The picture may be too rosy, but it contrasts sharply with the later emphasis on the difficulties of the ascetical life.

CONCLUSION

Can we say that the Gospel of Matthew is ascetical in any sense? Clearly, the gospel reads differently from Christian ascetical literature of the third and fourth centuries CE. The laws and practices promulgated in the Gospel of Matthew are often underdetermined and suggestive rather than explicitly worked out into a disciplinary or ascetical program with practices fully explained and related to one another.[42] On the other hand, later Christians developed ascetical practices and programs after reflecting on Matthew and the other canonical gospels in order to follow Jesus more faithfully and zealously.

The broad, cross-cultural definitions of asceticism with which this study began certainly encompass the Gospel of Matthew. Matthew's discourse on persecution in chapter 10, his many conflict stories, and a plot that ends with the execution of the narrative's hero register various explicit and implicit responses to a social, political, and religious world perceived as hostile to the evangelist's community (cf. Valantasis). The author of the Gospel of Matthew seeks to "inaugurate a new subjectivity, social relations and an alternative symbolic universe" through instruction in the kingdom of God.[43] The five sermons in Matthew (5–7; 10; 13; 18; 24–25) and other teachings of Jesus endorse and initiate a sustained educative process that transforms the community and its members (cf. Vaage). Clearly, an affirmative response to Jesus' call in Matthew for people to embrace God's kingdom requires "a voluntary, sustained and at least partially systematic program of self-discipline and self-denial" oriented toward the spiritual and transcendent side of life (cf. Kaelber and Hick).[44] Thus, the Gospel of Matthew may be said to contribute to a discussion of both Christian asceticism and asceticism as a cross-cultural phenomenon.

We end, however, where we began, with doubts about using a historically narrow Western category as an encompassing cross-cultural category. Valantasis is correct that asceticism is a response to an often oppressive social situation; Vaage, that asceticism is part of an educative program; and Kaelber and Hick, that asceticism is often associated with a search for authenticity and for something beyond the ordinary and obvious. All acknowledge both social and personal aspects of asceticism and related topics. How, then, should we speak of humans and the ascetical process? Asceticism should be firmly situated within the intentional human processes that lead to the construction of society and what we call personal identity. The key relationships that guide that process relate people through individual and communal inquiries and exercises of power. Leadership, socialization and education, acknowledgment of obligation, and disciplined human behavior all contribute to the formation of a whole, or spiritual, or saved, or enlightened, or holy, or harmonious human being, which is the goal of ascetical practice in many cultures.

Notes

1. For a very traditional and concise definition and history of asceticism in Christianity, see "Asceticism," in *Oxford Dictionary of the Christian Church*, 3rd ed. (New York: Oxford University Press, 1997), 113–14.
2. See John Hick, "Foreword," in *Asceticism*, eds. Vincent L. Wimbush and Richard Valantasis (New York: Oxford University Press, 1995), ix.
3. D. S. Russell presents an unstructured list of phenomena in his standard treatment, *The Method and Message of Jewish Apocalyptic*, Old Testament Library (Philadelphia: Westminster, 1964), 105, and ascribes to them a distinct impression and mood. By contrast, John J. Collins has worked out a coherent morphology for the genre "apocalypse" in his "Introduction: Towards the Morphology of a Genre," in *Apocalypse: The Morphology of a Genre*, ed. John J. Collins (Atlanta, Ga: Scholars, *Semeia* 14, 1979), 6–8.
4. J. Lachowski, "Asceticism (in the New Testament)," in *New Catholic Encyclopedia* (New York: McGraw-Hill, 1967), Vol. 1:937–938.
5. For a cogent analysis of the role of self-mastery in Romans, see Stanley K. Stowers, *A Rereading of Romans: Justice, Jews, and Gentiles* (New Haven, Conn.: Yale University Press, 1994), 42–82. For a more general review of these materials, see Abraham J. Malherbe, *Paul and the Popular Philosophers* (Minneapolis, Minn.: Fortress, 1989); for a selection of texts, see idem, *Moral Exhortation: A Greco-Roman Sourcebook* (Philadelphia: Westminster, 1986).
6. Walter O. Kaelber, "Asceticism," in *The Encyclopedia of Religion* (New York: Macmillan, 1987), Vol. 1:441–45, esp. 441.
7. Robert C. Neville, *Normative Cultures* (Albany: SUNY Press, 1995), esp. chap. 3.
8. Ibid, 32.
9. Ibid, 32.
10. Asceticism is linked with the disciplinary teachings of the Pastoral Epistles by Lucinda A. Brown, "Asceticism and Ideology: The Language of Power in the Pastoral Epistles," in *Discursive Formations, Ascetic Piety and the Interpretation*

of Early Christian Literature, Part I, ed. Vincent L. Wimbush (Atlanta, Ga.: Scholars, *Semeia* 57, 1992), 77–94.

11. Kallistos Ware, "The Way of the Ascetics: Negative or Affirmative?" in *Asceticism,* eds. Wimbush and Valantasis, 3.

12. Leif E. Vaage, "Ascetic Moods, Hermeneutics, and Bodily Deconstruction: Response to the Three Preceding Papers," in *Asceticism,* eds. Wimbush and Valantasis, 260.

13. Ibid, 250–51.

14. Rodney Stark and William Sims Bainbridge, *A Theory of Religion* (New York: Lang, 1987), 36–42.

15. Richard Valantasis, "Constructions of Power in Asceticism," *Journal of the American Academy of Religion* 63 (1995), 779–80. Some theorists see social relationships as a whole as a construction of power (ibid, 782–87).

16. Ibid, 797.

17. Ibid, 800–4.

18. Vincent L. Wimbush, "Introduction," in *Ascetic Behavior in Greco-Roman Antiquity: A Sourcebook,* ed. Vincent L. Wimbush (Minneapolis, Minn.: Fortress, Studies in Antiquity and Christianity, 1990), 2.

19. Walter O. Kaelber, "Understanding Asceticism—Testing a Typology: Response to the Three Preceding Papers," in *Asceticism,* eds. Wimbush and Valantasis, 324–28.

20. J. Duncan M. Derrett, *The Ascetic Discourse: An Explanation of the Sermon on the Mount* (Eilsbrunn: Ko'amar, 1989), adopts Eastern Christianity's traditional reading of the Gospel of Matthew as a program of asceticism and mysticism. The effective history of the interpretation of Matthew runs in this direction, but the first-century CE author spoke in other accents about different concerns.

21. Anthony J. Saldarini, *Matthew's Christian-Jewish Community* (Chicago: University of Chicago Press, Chicago Studies in the History of Judaism, 1994).

22. Hans Dieter Betz, *The Sermon on the Mount: A Commentary on the Sermon on the Mount, including the Sermon on the Plain* (Minneapolis, Minn.: Fortress, Hermeneia, 1995), systematically parallels Jesus' teachings with Jewish and Greco-Roman materials.

23. Ibid, 482. Betz sees the Sermon on the Mount as a pre-Matthean composition, but most commentators think that the author of the gospel wrote the sermon using traditional materials from several sources.

24. See Saldarini, chap. 3.

25. For the best recent statement of the expulsion thesis, see Graham N. Stanton, *A Gospel for a New People: Studies in Matthew* (Edinburgh, Scotland: Clark, 1992). A more precise sociological analysis of deviance and sectarianism leaves Matthew still within the Jewish communities of the late first century.

26. Rodney Stark, *The Rise of Christianity: A Sociologist Reconsiders History* (Princeton, N.J.: Princeton University Press, 1996), chap. 8. For an analysis of the Gospel of Matthew using sociological categories, see Saldarini, chap. 5.

27. See Stark's more extended analysis of the compensators offered by religion for scarce but desirable rewards in Stark and Bainbridge, 36–42.

28. Bryan R. Wilson, *Magic and the Millennium: A Sociological Study of Religious Movements of Protest among Tribal and Third-World Peoples* (London: Heinemann, 1973).

29. Some scholars have claimed that Matthew softens the original demands made by Jesus. For example, Karl Kautsky, *Der Ursprung des Christentums* (Stuttgart, Germany: Dietz, 1908), 345–47, interpreted Matthew using Marxist theory and held that Matthew tamed the teachings of Jesus to make the church more socially acceptable. Thus, for example, the first beatitude, "Blessed are the poor in spirit," may be contrasted with Luke's version, "Blessed are you poor" and "Woe to you rich" (Luke 6:20, 24) in order to argue that Matthew mitigates the beatitudes to accommodate the prosperous (for more on this, see Betz, 115, esp. n. 169). However, the following review of Matthew's teaching testifies to their rigor.

30. G. K. Chesterton, *What's Wrong with the World* (New York: Dodd/Mead, 1910), part I, chap. 5.

31. Jack Dean Kingsbury, "The Verb *anakolouthein* ('to follow') as an Index of Matthew's View of His Community," *Journal of Biblical Literature* 97 (1978): 56–73; idem, *Matthew as Story*, 2nd ed. (Minneapolis, Minn.: Fortress, 1988), 129–45. Georg Kretschmar, "Ein Beitrag zur Frage nach dem Ursprung frühchristlicher Askese," 61 (1964): 27–67, esp. 49–64, isolates following Jesus as the theme that carries through from Matthew into ascetical theology and practices during the next three centuries in Syria.

32. Betz (*Sermon on the Mount*, 111–19) develops this line of thought, which is also found in Greco-Roman literature.

33. Matthew allows divorce because of *porneia*, a general term for any sexual irregularity. The meaning of *porneia* in Matthew has been argued extensively and inconclusively. In general, Matthew seems to understand marriage to be an exclusive sexual union between a man and a woman that comes to an end when the woman has had sex with a man who is not her husband. This notion incorporates the biblical notion of purity, not just as an ethical norm but also as a state of sanctity or a mode of acting properly and being as one ought to be. Thus adultery does permanent damage to the marriage bond, which cannot be repaired by repentance or forgiveness.

34. Betz, *Sermon on the Mount*, 419, n. 621.

35. See Saldarini, *Christian-Jewish Community*, 126–31, for the arguments over Sabbath observance presumed by the narrative.

36. W. D. Davies and Dale C. Allison, Jr., *A Critical and Exegetical Commentary on the Gospel According to Saint Matthew: Volume 1, Matthew I–VII* (Edinburgh, Scotland: Clark, 1988).

37. Ibid, 452.

38. For the common Stoic asceticism of the mind, see James A. Francis, *Subversive Virtue: Asceticism and Authority in the Second-Century Pagan World* (University Park: Pennsylvania State University Press, 1995), 11, 32–33.

39. Ibid, 11–19.

40. Ibid, 28–33.

41. Betz, *Sermon on the Mount*, 146.

42. See note 20. Derrett reads later theology and interests back into Matthew, but the interpretive trajectory of Matthew in some later Christian groups is clear.

43. Valantasis, "Constructions of Power," 779–80.

44. Cited in Kaelber, "Asceticism," 441.

2

Asceticism and Mark's Gospel

Mary Ann Tolbert

INTRODUCTION

When viewed through the lens of later Christian asceticism, the Gospel of Mark presents something of a conundrum. On the one hand, Jesus withdraws for periods of prayer (1:35; 6:4; 14:32–42) and commands those who would follow him to leave family (1:20; 10:28–29) and wealth (10:21), to be the slave of all others (10:43–44), and even to be willing to deny themselves and lose their lives for his sake and the gospel's sake (8:34–35), all commands with strong ascetic qualities. On the other hand, Jesus also declares all foods clean (7:19), refuses to require his disciples to fast (2:18–19), multiplies food for the multitudes (6:35–44; 8:1–8), regularly dines in the homes of followers (2:15–17; 14:3), curses a fig tree when it does not supply him with food out of season (11:12–14), blesses the bond of marriage as the purpose of God's creation (10:2–9), accepts children as part of the kingdom (10:13–16), and travels with and is ministered to by a company of women (15:40–41), all teachings and actions that seem to run counter to traditional ascetic practice. If Mark is portraying Jesus in any kind of ascetic mode, it is clearly of a very different character from that which later develops in Christian monasticism. In this chapter, I wish to explore this conundrum in the Gospel of Mark by analyzing both its seemingly ascetic and seemingly counterascetic qualities. On the basis of that analysis, I hope to propose some tentative hypotheses about the reasons for Mark's differences from later conventional ascetic practices. These differences, I will suggest, are related to differences between the social location of the Markan author and its first audience, a marginal group within a hostile dominant society, and the social location of the Desert Fathers and other cenobitic enthusiasts some three hundred years later, the often privileged and learned denizens of dominant parties within late antique society. Before beginning my textual analysis, however, I must deal with a prior and vexing issue that problematizes all discussions of asceticism, namely, how is asceticism itself to be defined?

DEFINITIONAL DYSFUNCTION

One of the most striking results of the work of the different (American Academy of Religion and Society of Biblical Literature) groups and other conferences on asceticism over the past decade is the failure to arrive at any generally accepted definition of asceticism.[1] While ambiguity and blurred boundaries may well be positive qualities and clear definitions are not always the great boon they are touted to be, some step beyond the intuitive "I know it when I see it" stance toward asceticism is necessary for textual or discourse analysis to proceed. Recent attempts at definition run across a spectrum from very narrow delineations that refuse to associate the term with anything other than the Christian exercise of renunciation developed in the hermitages and monasteries of the fourth century to very broad definitions that understand asceticism as "the primary system of formation within a culture," orienting "the person or group of people to the immediate cultural environment."[2] In my view, both ends of this spectrum raise serious historical or conceptual problems.

To assert that the term "asceticism" can only be applied accurately to the monastic movement in Christianity is not only to ignore the cross-cultural importance of asceticism in the great Far Eastern religions of Buddhism, Jainism, and parts of Hinduism, but also to overlook the ascetic streams already present in Jewish, Greek, and Roman culture prior to the fourth century CE. From the Rechabites of Jeremiah's day, who lived in the desert in tents and prohibited wine drinking, to the members of the Dead Sea Scrolls community or Philo's Therapeutes,[3] withdrawal from society and communal practices of renunciation for the sake of religious purity and occasionally protest is a clear, if not widely documented, option in ancient Hebrew and Jewish religious life. Similarly, although Greek philosophers are often generally characterized as purveyors of the virtue of moderation, the "middle way" between the extremes of renunciation and indulgence, important exceptions occur in the long (and mostly obscure) history of the cults of Pythagoras and Orpheus. Pythagoreanism, which decreased in popularity in Greece during the fifth and fourth centuries BCE but was revived strongly in the first century BCE, especially among the Romans, is an important witness to the ascetic impulse within the Roman empire. It even influenced early Christian views of asceticism through Iamblichus' popular *Life of Pythagoras* written in the early fourth century CE. Pythagoras, like Empedocles after him (who was probably influenced by Orphism), insisted on a practice of life founded upon

vegetarianism, which set his followers apart from most of the social intercourse of Greek and Roman towns.[4] While Greek and Roman religious practice in general sanctioned occasional days of fasting, withdrawal, and purification as the necessary preparation for cultic participation, in Pythagoreanism
(and possibly Orphism and some of the later Neoplatonists) that occasional
practice was championed as a way of life, a continuing exercise (*askesis*)
required for salvation. Hence, even if one confines one's gaze solely to
ancient Mediterranean culture, the Christian monasticism of the fourth century CE and later has obvious and significant antecedents. To limit the term
asceticism to later Christian monasticism is historically misleading and indeed
inaccurate.

At the other end of the spectrum, to define asceticism as "the primary
system of formation within a culture" is equally problematic, although for
different reasons. Here the term becomes a repository for practically any
form of behavior, from taking a canoeing vacation[5] to passionate gardening.
Although it may well be true, especially in modern society, that ascetic
behavior may be an end in itself and have no religious connotations, to
designate asceticism as any kind of cultural formation makes the term "a category of alarming and perhaps vacuous comprehensiveness," as Robert
Parker concluded about a similar broad usage of the term "pollution."[6] This
broad cultural exploitation of asceticism to describe any and all kinds of "discipline," from training for a physical contest to farming, and all kinds of
renunciation, from reducing the hours spent watching TV to anorexia, is, I
believe, really a metaphorical[7] use of asceticism that draws the power it has
from the concrete, historical phenomenon of ascetic practice found throughout many religious traditions of the world. The benefit of such a metaphorical use of asceticism is to draw attention to the fact that *any* process of
socialization into *any* distinct group or identity requires renunciation and
discipline, since some life options must be rejected for others to be embodied. However, to me the value of such a seemingly self-evident point appears
to be too modest a gain compared to the concomitant loss of historical and
cultural specificity for the term *asceticism* itself. The ascription of asceticism
to any kind of cultural formation stretches the reference of the word to a
level of generality that threatens to make the term both vacuous and useless.

Yet it may well be that the very vacuity of the term *asceticism* in some
scholarship is precisely what makes it an appealing choice for postmodern
exploration. It bears both the tradition of its historical past and the openness
of its modern usage in ways that can challenge and rechallenge the boundaries of both. Since neither arena can claim complete and final definitional
victory, the conversation continues, and, from a postmodern perspective,
that result itself is the real victory.

Nevertheless, if one assumes, as I do, that an ascetic discourse is a recognizable subset of discourse in general (accounting for the "I know it when
I see it" intuition), then for the sake of concrete textual analysis something

more discrete than "cultural formation" is needed to distinguish just what one is looking for in the discourse of a text. Because most narrative texts can be said to create their own fictional "world," the process of reading any text could be said to be a kind of "cultural formation," and thus, in its metaphorical sense, a type of asceticism. From this perspective, Mark, and every other narrative ever written, is an ascetical text. While that point may have some theoretical validity,[8] it does nothing to help explain the similarities and differences between Mark and other clearly ascetical texts such as, for example, the *Sayings of the Desert Fathers* or Athanasius' *Life of Antony* and *Life of Pachomius*.

THEORY AND CONTEXT OF INTERPRETATION

Even if we decide to refuse the broadest definition of asceticism as too general to be useful in textual analysis, the literary model of study we are drawing upon itself opens up additional complications for the discussion of asceticism and Mark. Textual meaning is construed by readers (or hearers) of a text out of complex systems of understanding and formation that include not only the conventions of reading they have been taught but also the specific social, historical, and cultural repertoire of views and beliefs they bring to the text.[9] Because the interpretation of any text is a collaboration between the reader and the text, multiple interpretations of any text are inevitable. While those interpretations may arise to some degree out of the indeterminacy that marks all narrative from the most mundane toy assembly instructions to the most complex surrealist novel, they also owe their existence to the diverse social, cultural, and historical locations of different groups of readers who co-create each text's particular meaning.

Consequently, were we to question whether or not Mark could be interpreted by some of its readers as an ascetic text, even within a narrower definition of asceticism, the answer must be in the affirmative. Not only theoretically but also historically, readers of Mark have seen in the text's many references to the suffering of Jesus and his followers and in the commands to lose one's life for the sake of the gospel and the renunciations of wealth, power, and status called for by faith in Jesus' message ample justification for viewing the text as ascetic. Other, more counterascetic tendencies in the text are then understood in light of its clear asceticism or are selectively ignored. Such interpretations of Mark are especially convincing to those readers, whether ancient or modern, whose own religious, social, or intellectual locations identify asceticism as an important cultural value. For other readers less interested in asceticism, such interpretations would in all likelihood appear less persuasive. Again, from the perspective of readers and their interpretations of texts, Mark can be (and has been) read as an ascetic text.

Without denying, therefore, the *possibility* of reading Mark as an ascetic text or denying the validity of readers reading Mark in their own way according to the conventions of their own eras and concerns, I want to direct this chapter on Mark and asceticism toward one particular set of readers, namely, the first readers or hearers of the gospel in their own historical context. While it is certainly not absolutely necessary to limit my purview to the historical milieu of Mediterranean antiquity, it seems thoroughly justifiable to do so, since I am looking specifically at an ancient Greek text. In the language of cultural theory, for a communicative event to take place, the production of a discursive form must be linked to its translation or decoding.[10] Or in the terms I used earlier, the reader must construe the meaning of a text. However, the practices of encoding and decoding "do not constitute an 'immediate identity'" because they are rarely "perfectly symmetrical."[11] The lack of symmetry between the encoding and decoding of a discursive form is thus yet another source of multiple meanings for the same text. The cultural, social, and linguistic codes used by the producer of the text, in our case by the anonymous ancient author we conventionally call "Mark," are historically distant from those of any modern interpreter, even an interpreter intent on pursuing a historical reading of the gospel, as I hope to do. The best that a historical reading can accomplish is to attempt to diminish the asymmetry between the encoding of an ancient text and the decoding of a modern interpreter by reconstructing as much as possible the historical and literary milieu of the author and using that reconstruction as the context of interpretation. While "perfect symmetry" will never be achieved, such being the distance and difference of antiquity from the present, some reduction in asymmetry may well be accomplished, allowing us to hear the ancient text in ways somewhat closer to the hearing of the original audience. To pursue the possible interpretations of the first hearers of Mark, then, what we know or can theorize about the ancient setting of Mark must become the context for our interpretation.

The Gospel of Mark was probably written around 70 CE in Greek for a Greek-speaking audience. Although the location of the production of the text and the original audience for whom it was produced are unknown, two major hypotheses, one from church tradition and one from modern scholarship, have been proposed concerning these issues. Most early church witnesses believed that the gospel was written in Rome by a follower of Peter during the period of Nero's persecutions of Christians and Jews. While some modern scholars follow this traditional view, others have suggested an alternative view that locates the production of the gospel somewhere in Palestine during the first Jewish-Roman War, close to the time of the destruction of the temple. While there are great differences between these two dominant viewpoints, what they have in common is their setting of the writing of the gospel in a time of persecution and destruction, a time in which the physical as well as spiritual survival of Christians and Jews was in jeopardy.

Both theories furthermore find supporting evidence for this under-standing of a dangerous original setting in Mark 13 or the gospel's "little apocalypse." In this chapter, Jesus predicts for his followers the destruction of the temple (13:2), wars and rumors of war (13:7), and constant persecu-tion by the world, both in its public forms (governors and kings, 13:9) and in its private forms (brothers, parents, and children, 13:12) even to the point where "you will be hated by all for my name's sake" (13:13). Either of these two dominant hypotheses about the original location of the writing of Mark provides a vividly real context for the dire warnings in Mark 13. What Jesus predicts in this chapter was, in fact, the present reality of the author and the first audiences of the gospel, and thus they may well have believed that they were living in the horrors immediately preceding the end of time.

It is against this context that the same persons' understanding of the ascetic and counterascetic themes in Mark needs to be evaluated. How might the earliest audiences of the gospel have decoded Jesus' commands and actions? Since the clearly identified ascetic texts that are still extant, even Iamblichus' *Life of Pythagoras,* all postdate the writing of Mark, there is no text with which to compare Mark that an ancient audience might also have known.[12] Nevertheless, understandings of asceticism were, as I have already argued, present in first-century Jewish and Roman society. How might we distinguish those ascetic understandings from those we and an ancient audi-ence might intuitively recognize as nonascetic?[13]

One attempt to describe ancient ascetic understandings can be found in the work of Averil Cameron.[14] Cameron has defined ascetic discourse as the "typical ways of expressing ascetic ideas,"[15] and for her, early Christian ascetic discourse

> can also evidently be identified where certain key terms and concepts are present, even where the text as a whole may not be concerned with advocating asceticism directly. Thus, the complex of ideas clustering round the themes of renunciation, temptation, denial, spiritual progress or ascent in the spiritual life, and the spe-cialized use of Greek terms such as *porneia, eros, logismoi, aktēmosynē* would be a fair indicator.[16]

The specialized use of the Greek terms Cameron lists are in short supply in the New Testament as a whole and especially so in Mark. Of the terms list-ed, only *porneia* appears in Mark, and it appears only once, at 7:21, although a verbal form also appears at 10:19 and, with an augment, again in 7:21. Mark 7:21, in which Jesus is listing the things that defile human beings, also contains a version of *logismoi,* namely, *dialogismoi,* to indicate the evil thoughts that can lead to defilement. Such a word search thus provides us with very little evidence for the suggestion that Mark as a whole is engaged in any kind of ascetic discourse, at least as Cameron has attempted to define it for early Christianity.

Since Cameron's work is based on a slightly later period of ascetic development than the time of Mark, we will need to augment her helpful suggestions with further historical possibilities. Thus, the themes of renunciation, temptation, denial, and spiritual progress (or formation), as well as several prominent themes that Cameron does not list but are also often present in ancient ascetic discourse, for example, withdrawal, purification, demonology, and suffering, may provide fruitful starting points for analyzing a narrative like Mark's gospel in its own historical period. Although thematic analysis is always more prone to the idiosyncrasy of an interpreter's imagination than is the delineation of vocabulary clusters,[17] in this case such a procedure seems the best avenue for reaching the nexus of ascetic and counterascetic elements in the Gospel of Mark. Thus, in the following section, I use these themes as guides to exploring the Gospel of Mark as ascetic discourse, keeping in mind how an ancient audience in the midst of persecution might have heard them.

MARK AS ASCETIC DISCOURSE

Although the Gospel of Mark is traditionally lumped with Matthew and Luke as one of the "synoptic gospels," all three gospels evince significant differences from each other. Exploring the possible ascetic dimensions of Mark highlights especially its paucity of teaching or parenetic material when compared with the other two synoptic gospels. In Mark, Jesus' "new teaching," as suggested in 1:27 and fulfilled throughout the rest of the gospel, amounts mainly to Jesus' actions and often to his action of healing. What parenetic material Mark does contain is usually found in the controversies Jesus has with the Pharisees, scribes, and Jerusalem religious leaders and the more extended battles in which he must engage due to his own disciples' lack of understanding. Consequently, in exploring possible ascetic themes in the Gospel of Mark, we must look at the actions of Jesus or the events he is involved in as well as at his words if we wish to sample the full range of the Markan material.

Withdrawal from the World

Withdrawal, or *anachoresis*, is one of the most common themes in ascetic practice.[18] The ascetic withdraws from the normal converse of daily life to devote his or her attention to the divine or some other "higher" goal. In Mark, the verb *anachoreo* appears only once, at 3:7, to describe Jesus' withdrawal with his disciples to the sea after a series of increasingly rancorous controversies with the Pharisees (2:15–3:6). This one occurrence in Mark of the technical word for ascetic withdrawal is particularly striking for its emphasis on the continued presence of "the world" with Jesus. Following Jesus in his "withdrawal" are not only the disciples but also a huge multitude from Galilee and "also from Judea and Jerusalem and Idumea and from beyond the Jordan and from about Tyre and Sidon" (3:7–8). Jesus is literally depicted as carrying the world with him in his withdrawal to the sea. The crowd is so great, in fact, that he must ask the disciples to prepare a boat for his escape in case the very size of the crowd crushes him. This hardly seems to be a typical image of ascetic withdrawal, even though some of the stories in the *Sayings of the Desert Fathers* indicate similar problems, on a generally smaller scale, with well-meaning followers. Usually these groups of visitors are quickly dispatched or craftily avoided altogether.[19] In Mark, the very size and geographical extent of the crowd seems to emphasize the failure of this withdrawal to bring ascetic solitude or quiet to Jesus and the disciples.

The motif of withdrawal, without the specialized vocabulary of *anachoresis*, does occur in other places in Mark. Jesus and his twelve disciples leave the crowds on several occasions for private conversation (4:10; 7:17; 9:28; 9:30–31; 10:10; 13:3) or less frequently for rest or solitude (6:31; 7:24). In the latter case, as with the incident in 3:7, which we discussed earlier, the context makes it clear that such solitary withdrawal is not to be allowed, for the crowds or a supplicant for healing always quickly disrupts the plan.

More in harmony with ascetic withdrawal are Jesus' three private prayer periods: 1:35; 6:45–46; 14:32–35. In each case Jesus either goes to a deserted place or sends everyone, including the disciples, away while he prays. None of the three incidents is of a very long duration, however, for in the first, Simon comes searching for him; in the second, Jesus must help the disciples to row against the wind; and in the third, Judas and the soldiers from the chief priest arrive to arrest him. Most interestingly, while Jesus does occasionally teach the disciples about prayer (11:20–26) or command them to pray (14:38), he never indicates in these teachings that they need to withdraw or be alone to pray. Jesus' own sporadic departure and return is all Mark offers to the tradition of ascetic withdrawal for prayer. Moreover, in striking contrast to the idea of withdrawal as the requisite discipline that following Jesus demands, the one task given to the followers of Jesus, which will hasten that glorious, saving end of the world, is to preach the gospel to all nations (13:10), a task that compels them to venture farther into the world rather than to withdraw from it.

One final instance of the motif of withdrawal, which actually comes at the very beginning of the gospel, is much closer to the recorded experience of later hermits and cenobites: the temptation in the wilderness. But this story belongs mostly to another major ascetic theme: temptation.

Temptation

When the ascetic withdraws into the wilderness or into the monastery, he or she begins the hardest battle of all: the battle to resist temptation. One episode in Mark depicts Jesus engaged in this war; however, unlike Matthew and Luke with their conversations between Jesus and Satan, Mark devotes only two verses to this remarkable story, 1:12–13. Jesus is driven into the wilderness by "the spirit" immediately after his baptism; he remains there the requisite forty days being tested (*peirazo*) by Satan. In addition to these tests, whatever they are (Mark gives no indication), Jesus is with the wild beasts, and the angels serve him. Whether these associations with Satan, beasts, and angels occur simultaneously or sequentially, neither the grammar nor the context makes especially clear. One might argue, I suppose, that concluding the story with the phrase about the angels suggests a victorious result to Jesus' interaction with Satan, but that argument is an inference that the gospel itself never bothers to make explicit.

Jesus is tested (*peirazo*) several other times in the narrative: at 8:11; 10:2; and 12:15. All of these, however, come in the midst of public debates at the hands of the Pharisees, Jesus' very human enemies.[20] *Peirazo,* in its noun form, occurs one other time, at 14:38, where Jesus warns the disciples to "watch and pray that you may not enter into temptation." This last allusion to testing may imply something of the battle with Satan or at least with one's own inner weaknesses more characteristic of ascetic testing. The disciples, of course, fail the test miserably by falling asleep, not once but twice more, demonstrating definitively the weakness of their flesh (14:37–42). This episode is the closest Mark gets to insisting that withdrawal for watchfulness and prayer stands as a defense against the weakness of the flesh in tests with Satan. Jesus' prayer, in both its admission of desire to avoid the coming evil and its firm commitment to do whatever is necessary to fulfill God's will, prepares Jesus for the passion to come, while the disciples' sleep leads inexorably to their flight and denial.

Although Satan explicitly tempts Jesus only once in Mark, the gospel is full of demons, which Jesus exorcizes, silences, or otherwise controls. A developed demonology is another common theme of ascetic discourse.

Demonology

One of the singular developments of Christian monasticism is the growth of demonology. Demons tempt, persecute, and harass the ascetic ceaselessly. All manner of physical and spiritual exercises is required to escape or at least to mitigate this constant barrage of evil. Demons (*daimonion*) and unclean spirits (*pneuma akatharton*) also play a major role in Mark (see, e.g., 1:21–28; 5:1–20; 6:7–13; 7:24–30; 9:14–29). In Mark, however, Jesus is the unchallenged master of the demonic forces. He harasses and persecutes them (e.g., 1:24; 5:7–8); moreover, they not only acknowledge his sovereignty (e.g., 1:34; 3:11), but they even beg his indulgence (5:10–13). Jesus is also able to convey this total power over the demonic forces, more or less successfully (see 9:28–29), to his disciples (3:15; 6:7,13) and even to others who simply invoke his name (10:38–39).

This serene dominance over the demons constitutes a kind of counterascetic theme in the gospel. While demons are the source of many human ills, Jesus and his followers are assured of victory in any contest with these forces. For Mark, just as it is not Satan who continues to test Jesus throughout the narrative but instead the Pharisees, it is not the demons who harass and persecute Jesus and his followers but instead the religious and political leaders of Jerusalem. What threatens Jesus and those who follow his way are the human powers of this generation, not the cosmic powers of evil.[21] In later centuries, when those human powers are all ostensibly Christian, ascetic Christians must find their persecution and harassment in the work of those demons, which Jesus and his followers in Mark so thoroughly control.

Purification

In Mark, the Greek words for demons (*daimonion*) and for unclean spirits (*pneuma akatharton*) seem to be basically interchangeable (see, e.g., 6:7 and 6:13; 7:25 and 7:26, 29, 30; and also, perhaps, 3:22 and 3:30). The acknowledgment of at least some of the demons as unclean spirits raises the possibility of recognizing Jesus the healer as a purifier of others. Purification of the body and spirit is clearly one important aspect of ascetic practice in Greek and Roman religions.[22] Jesus as the exorcizer of unclean spirits purifies the bodies of those who come to him for healing. Occasionally, Jesus requires some further exercise to accompany his healing purification (1:44; 8:26), but generally his single action is completely sufficient. Ascetic purification is, however, most often a self-purification, a discipline enacted on one's own body, but in Mark there is no indication of Jesus' self-purification unless the Transfiguration, in which Jesus' clothing becomes whiter than any human bleach could make it (9:3), should be interpreted in this way, which I doubt. So while we may have reason to see Jesus' healings as purifications, Mark cannot be said to advocate any particular practice of purification, especially of self-purification, other than having faith in Jesus' power to heal.

In addition to the purification of healing, purity issues are also at stake in a number of other episodes in the gospel. Several events can be seen as contrasts to the Holiness Code in Leviticus; indeed, Mark seems to depict Jesus as a consistent violator of the Levitical purity practices. Jesus touches the (apparently) dead (5:41) and a menstruating woman (5:27–30), he eats with sinners and other unclean people, and he declares all foods clean (7:14–23). This last element is part of a whole discourse on clean and unclean, 7:1–23, which is unique in the gospel, and it is a discourse that exemplifies some of the complexities of judging Mark's ascetic viewpoint.

The section (7:1–23) is set up by a complaint from the Pharisees that Jesus' disciples do not observe hygienic eating practices (7:1–5); the complaint is interrupted by a rather confused explanatory aside from the narrator on the washing rites of the Jews. Jesus replies to the complaint by first attacking the Pharisees (in 7:6–13) for their own violations of the tradition of Moses (presumably the rhetorical point of this ploy is to undermine the value of their washing tradition by showing that others of their traditions seem to violate the "word of God"). The second phase to Jesus' reply (in 7:14–23) is a crucial passage for our present purposes, in which Jesus redefines the nature of purity. First to the crowds (7:14–15) and then in an expanded form privately to his disciples (7:17–23), Jesus asserts that nothing from the outside (*exothen*) will make a person impure; only that which comes from within (*esothen*) or from the human heart causes defilement. The Markan narrator explicitly interprets Jesus' sayings to indicate that all foods are clean (7:19b), and the abrogation of Jewish dietary law may well historically have been the essential meaning of this discussion for the author of Mark and the original audience, as the narrator's intrusion into the story indicates.

Nevertheless, within the context of the Pharisees' complaint, Jesus' statements in 7:14–23 also have the effect of undercutting all manner of purity rites surrounding the preparation of the body before eating or before other ritual acts. If defilement comes only from the heart, then the condition of the body is of no account, and in fact, as later asceticism asserted, the actual polluting of the body with dirt, blood, lice, and so on, may provide a salutary discipline for purifying the heart. While explicit body/heart or body/spirit dualism appears fairly seldomly in Mark (see 7:18–23; 14:38)—the gospel generally provides a more holistic view of human beings, as the healing material suggests—in an atmosphere of greater dualism these sayings are fuel to the fire of bodily denial for the sake of heart-rightness. Consequently, although Mark itself uses these sayings by Jesus primarily to expand the food options of early Christians, certainly a counterascetic (but very much pro-Gentile[23]) interpretation, the sayings also lay the groundwork for the turning of purity codes on their heads that is so often characteristic of later Christian ascetic practice.

Renunciation

Probably no other theme is more closely associated with asceticism than renunciation or voluntary repression.[24] It may indeed form the most essential ingredient of the "I know it when I see it" intuition about asceticism. Renunciation of what society offers conventionally by way of food, clothing, sexual expression, shelter, social interaction, leisure, wealth, bodily comfort, and convenience generally evinces the presence of ascetic practice. Even though it is possible for these renunciations to become an end in themselves, most commonly they are directed toward some other particular goal; in Christian asceticism, that goal is often union with the divine or living the will of God or perfecting oneself to make oneself worthy of salvation.

The Gospel of Mark contains quite a few statements by Jesus on the importance of giving up conventional values and material resources to follow the way of the Cross. Here it would seem that we might find a rich harvest of ascetic ideas, but again Mark's way of putting the matter skews the argument. Jesus' teachings and actions in Mark consistently insist on the necessity of giving up conventional social standing, power, wealth, and even family relationships in order to "do the will of God" (3:34–35) or to follow Jesus truly (see, e.g., 1:20; 8:34–36; 9:34–35; 10:21–22, 42–45). Although Jesus' separation from his own blood family and kin appears to be based more on their unbelief and rejection than on his decision to leave (see 3:20–21 and 6:1–6), he clearly rebukes most public attempts to increase his status. Indeed, Jesus himself silences those unclean spirits who would make his own status known and orders secrecy about his divine identity throughout the early part of the gospel. Even Jesus' status as Son of God is to be denied, it seems, until after the resurrection (9:2–9) or at least until the beginning of the passion (14:61–62).

However, this "status" asceticism, as we might call it, stands in some contrast to Jesus' views on the more conventional bodily asceticisms related to eating, sexuality, comfort, and so on. Mark presents Jesus' relationship to food, for example, in a very positive, almost gluttonous, light: Jesus multiplies food for the multitude—twice (6:35–44; 8:1–10); he is often portrayed as dining in the homes of followers (2:13–15; 14:3–9; and perhaps, 1:29–31); he refuses to encourage his disciples to fast (2:18–22) and justifies their food-gathering in violation of the Sabbath (2:23–28); he curses a fig tree because it does not satisfy his hunger, even though it was not the season for fruit (11:12–14). Indeed, abstinence from food, a major marker of ascetic denial in Greco-Roman society as exemplified in the cult of Pythagoras, appears to be the opposite of Jesus' practice. For Mark, Jesus is a living symbol of plenty, just as the kingdom of God itself is the advent of the abundant harvest (4:8, 20). It may be that among the poor, the sick, and the outcast, whom Mark portrays as primarily attracted to Jesus' message, the real miracle was in being able to eat, not in being able to fast.

Other bodily expressions also seem to be encouraged or, at least, not discouraged. For later asceticism, sexuality became the foremost arena for ascetic denial,[25] and since the Gospel of Mark is mostly silent on the subject, that silence might be taken as providing some support for hiding or denying the importance of sexual activity. The problem with that view is that what little Mark does have to say about sexuality is basically positive or at least affirmative of its value. Most importantly, Jesus sanctions marriage as divinely mandated in creation by alluding to Genesis in his rejection of the practice of divorce (10:2–12). Although Jesus does indicate that marriage will not be a social union continued in heaven (12:18–27), on earth, whether married or not, close associations with women are part of Jesus' ministry and practice. He heals women, some in the privacy of houses (1:29–31; 7:24–30), a sexually provocative setting in ancient Mediterranean society, and some in the streets (5:25–34), hinting at women of possibly dishonorable status in ancient society. Moreover, Jesus appears to travel with a company of women and receive some kinds of service or ministry from them (15:40–41) on a regular basis. In a striking scene, he commends the actions of an otherwise unknown woman who anoints his head with costly oil at a dinner (14:3–9). Since usually the only women who frequented the dining rooms of men were family food-servers or prostitutes, and the woman's action itself smacks strongly of the latter, the entire incident is drenched in sexual intimations. Jesus' attitude to children is similarly positive: He receives children into the kingdom, making them, in fact, emblematic of those who can enter the kingdom (9:36–37; 10:13–16), and he acknowledges the responsibility of parents for the care and well-being of their children (5:21–24, 35–43; 7:24–30; 9:14–29).

Finally, when Peter asserts that the disciples have left everything to follow him, Jesus assures Peter that, "There is no one who has left house or brothers or sisters or mother or father or children or lands, for my sake and for the gospel, who will not receive a hundredfold now in this time, houses and brothers and sisters and mothers and children and lands, with persecutions, and in the age to come eternal life" (10:29–30). Although it is surely the case that ascetic renunciations were requited with definite rewards, mostly perhaps spiritual, the ascetic was not generally rewarded with exactly the things he or she renounced, as Jesus here says will be the case for his followers. Jesus' disciples will receive a "hundredfold now" the very social and material relations they had to give up to follow Jesus in the first place. Such a following thus seems to be more a wise investment, offering ample material reward, than a discipline of renunciation.

There is, of course, a "catch" in the assurance, a "catch" that in Mark eventually trips the twelve disciples into stumbling: These new relations come "with persecutions." The followers of Jesus will have to suffer in and for their new life. The importance of suffering and its close relationship to persecution in the gospel calls for further careful consideration.

Suffering, Persecution, or the Infliction of Pain

Suffering, most often as self-inflicted physical pain or as the sinful soul's sadness in the presence of the divine, is another characteristic theme of ascetic discourse. For the ascetic, suffering is required simply by virtue of the fallen nature of human life, and disciplines of physical discomfort, like flagellation, wearing a hair shirt or other uncomfortable clothing, sleeplessness, back-breaking physical labor, etc., are generally intended both to chasten the sinful desires of the body and to remind the soul of its profound flaws. The Gospel of Mark, too, has often been characterized as a gospel of suffering. Many of Jesus' sayings and especially his three predictions of the passion (8:30; 9:30–31; 10:32–34) emphasize the necessity of suffering for both himself and his followers (8:34–37; 13:9–13). However, suffering in Mark is not self-inflicted but comes rather as a result of powerful human opposition to the way of Jesus. Suffering in Mark is, then, really persecution.

In Mark's "little apocalypse" (chapter 13), Jesus warns that his followers will face the same "sufferings" he has predicted for himself in his passion: They will be "delivered up" to councils and kings to be put to death; they will be beaten and hated by all (13:9–13; cf. 10:33–34). The cross that the followers of Jesus in Mark are called upon to bear (8:34) is not like the cross of the Gospel of Luke, which one takes up daily (see Luke 9:23), but *the Cross,* the one instrument of death for both Jesus and anyone with the courage to follow him in the face of the certain persecutions of councils, kings, and chief priests. For Mark, denying oneself is the actual willingness to renounce one's claim to the continuation of one's physical existence, not simply the renunciation of conventional social relationships or bodily comforts.

The certainty of persecution for Jesus and for his followers explains why, throughout Mark, the contrast to faith is most often fear or cowardice (e.g., 4:40–41; 5:36; 9:32; 10:32) rather than doubt or uncertainty. What makes such courage possible is faith in the ample benefits of the gospel now ("houses and brothers and sisters and mothers and children and lands," 10:30) and the assurance of the coming of God's kingdom soon, since "the one who endures to the end will be saved" (13:13). Thus, faith in Jesus and preaching the gospel will reward the follower of Jesus now with healing, food, family, and possessions, as well as provide eternal life in the future; but the cost of this present abundance, a modest one perhaps in light of the gains, is incurring the wrath of those evil powers who respond—as they did to Jesus himself—with persecution and death. In its understanding of suffering, Mark stands far closer to the great martyr tradition of early Christianity than to the ascetic tradition, even though the ascetic tradition itself may be an adaptation for another age of the martyr's plight.[26]

Spiritual Formation

The final theme to be explored is the overarching idea of spiritual formation, the path or discipline of continuous exercise (*askesis*) that shapes the novice into the perfected state of divine union or grace. Many of the other themes, like renunciation, suffering, purification, withdrawal, and so on are the means by which this crucial spiritual formation is accomplished. The dedication to rigorous, constant practice is a major requirement for perfection in the disciplined life of the ascetic. Here, again, the Gospel of Mark depicts a counterstance, and here, again, Mark also stands in striking contrast to the other canonical gospels, and especially to Matthew.[27]

In Mark, those who stay with Jesus, travel with him, and hear his public and private teaching are the very ones who at the end, under persecution, show a complete lack of "perfection," readiness, or any kind of spiritual formation, much less spiritual ascent. The twelve disciples in Mark are the only characters to follow Jesus from the beginning until almost the end of the gospel. They are constantly instructed and often reprimanded about what following Jesus means and requires. Yet all of this practice and instruction falls on deaf ears, for their hearts are hardened to Jesus' words and actions (6:52). Their conduct of life, even a life lived literally in the footsteps of Jesus, does not fit them for the tests to come. The only characters Mark seems to present as real success stories are the ones whom Jesus heals, who then preach the good news long before the disciples are permitted to do so (1:40–45; 5:20); yet these healed ones Jesus almost invariably sends immediately away (5:20, 34; 8:26; 10:52) without any further efforts at spiritual formation, not even a "go, and sin no more" (see John 8:11).

In these portrayals, Mark seems to be proposing that faith in Jesus and his powerful word is all that is actually necessary for the Christian life. Teachings, pleadings, and daily examples are ineffective for Christian formation where fear rather than faith is the response of the heart, while, on the other hand, where faith is present, nothing else seems to be needed. The Gospel of Mark thus presents faith in Jesus as an immediate response of the heart and the Christian life as the courage to witness to that faith in the face of persecutions. This view may well depict a kind of spiritual formation, perhaps a charismatic one, but it does not seem to fit the theme of the continuing exercise of life that is more typical of ascetic formation.

The Gospel of Matthew, with its concern for the perfection of the Christian and the learning that fits one for the kingdom of God, is much more amenable to the picture of later ascetic spiritual formation than anything that can be found in Mark.

CONCLUSION

Spiritual formation may be viewed in another way when discussing Mark. The hearing of the gospel itself, its rhetorical effect on an audience, also works a kind of "formation" on the audience. How might Mark's early audiences have heard this complex of ascetic and counterascetic themes? How might they have been spiritually "formed" by this narrative?

The Gospel of Mark does not seem to present Jesus or his followers as "ascetics" in the way later monastic Christianity would understand and develop the idea. In Mark, for example, Jesus himself neither practices nor teaches any of the conventional disciplines of bodily renunciation. Nor does he really teach a practical ethics of behavior or action, except in the general terms of doing the will of God and loving God and loving one's neighbor. Jesus does suffer, but not through self-inflicted pain; his suffering is the result of persecution from those who oppose his way. Jesus purifies others, although he does not obey purity rules himself and even negates many of them for his followers. He does teach and instruct by both action and word, but his closest followers bear no fruit from having witnessed those things daily. He does call his followers to deny themselves and to take up their cross, but in the context of the gospel such an action is required by the persecutions that following Jesus' way inevitably entails. Mark's call is not a call for the daily renunciation of common social life but for the one moment of sacrificing one's life itself for the sake of the gospel.

Moreover, the Gospel of Mark also does not seem to present Jesus or his followers as "ascetics" in the way other ascetic behavior in Jewish, Greek, or Roman society was portrayed. This is not a group, like the Rechabites or the Qumran community, whose goal is to withdraw from society. While Jesus does withdraw for periods of prayer and begins his ministry with a stint in the wilderness being tempted, the mission Jesus is on—and which his followers must complete—demands that he go among the people, even when their sheer numbers threaten to crush him (3:9). Unlike the followers of Pythagoras, Jesus' disciples are not instructed to obey special eating restrictions or even to perform the periodic purifications and fasts expected for participation in ancient religious ritual. No John the Baptist eating locusts and wild honey (1:6) is Jesus; he is instead generally depicted as dining openly in the homes of his followers (1:29–31; 2:15; 14:3–9); indeed, Jesus' characterization at moments may even be understood as the embodiment of abundance in the midst of scarcity.

It is hard to believe that an ancient audience, hearing the Gospel of Mark, would identify the teachings or actions of Jesus and his followers as ascetic in any way conventional to that historical period. Following Jesus does require discipline, but so does following any other way of life, from thievery to farming. It also demands renunciation of other goals, but, again, so does every other distinctive way of life. It involves serious risk, and while not all other ways of life do that, stances that counter the current status quo always will, whether religious, political, or social.

Nevertheless, an ancient audience would be formed in a special fashion by listening to this story—formed, in fact, into "perfect disciples" who understand Jesus' parables, see his healings and feedings, stay awake at Gethsemane, watch the crucifixion, and hear the announcement of the resurrection.[28] This formation is not based on disciplined practice but on a willingness to listen and to believe. However, at the end of the gospel, for the listener to remain a "perfect disciple," he or she must begin to act on that belief in the midst of a very dangerous world, a world that murdered Jesus himself. And acting on that belief may well mean rejection by family, loss of status, loss of wealth, and renunciation of virtually all that conventional society values.

In acting on their formation by the rhetoric of Mark, early Christians accepted a life that we now would perhaps see as a kind of "asceticism." If we want to designate it as such, however, we must be careful to continue to distinguish it from the better-known asceticism of the later Christian monastic movement, for the first audiences of Mark's gospel lived in a very different world than their later successors.

The Gospel of Mark, with its view of the present evil powers in charge of the world, be they Jews or Romans, depicts the community of Jesus' followers as a beleaguered minority in a sea of hostility. The courage to lose one's life was necessary in such a situation for anyone who truly wanted to follow the path of Jesus. With such active persecution threatening the Christian, self-inflicted pain was hardly necessary. In such a marginal state of existence, the promise of abundance—material, social, and spiritual—was the heart of the good news, not a command to withdraw from the world and renounce common human needs or pleasures.

In reading the *Sayings of the Desert Fathers,* I find an ascetic impulse that seems to come out of a social location very different from the one that the Gospel of Mark implies, namely, a location in which Christianity has finally "triumphed" over its enemies. When Christians themselves become the ones in power, the active persecution of Christians by political and legal authorities, which plagued Mark's world, comes to an end. In this new world, if physical suffering for one's faith is to be found, it must be self-chosen.

Perhaps this aspect of direct self-choice of suffering is one of the sharpest ways to distinguish the "ascetic" themes of Mark from the asceticism of later Christianity. For Jesus and Jesus' followers in Mark, one's choice is to follow the will of God in abundance and health, but once that decision is made, persecutions, harassment, and death arrive inexorably at the hands of enemies. Suffering in that world comes from persecution. For the ascetic Christian of a later date, the rigors of denial, renunciation of bodily comfort, withdrawal, and suffering are all self-chosen by the individual, not imposed on him or her by uncontrollable external authorities. Suffering in this later world comes from self-inflicted discipline for the betterment of the soul. Even though some of the same language may be used both in the Gospel of Mark and in later ascetic discourses, the situation described by that language, it seems to me, is drastically different.

Notes

1. See Elizabeth Clark's excellent review of all the problems encountered in recent attempts at defining asceticism in "The Ascetic Impulse in Religious Life: A General Response," in *Asceticism*, eds. Vincent L. Wimbush and Richard Valantasis (New York: Oxford University Press, 1995), 505–10.
2. Richard Valantasis, "A Theory of the Social Function of Asceticism," in *Asceticism*, eds. Wimbush and Valantasis, 547.
3. While the debate continues over Philo's authorship of *De vita contemplativa*, I agree with those who hold for the probability of Philo as author. See the recent translation by Gail Paterson Corrington, "Philo, On the Contemplative Life: Or, On the Suppliants (The Fourth Book on the Virtues)," in *Ascetic Behavior in Greco-Roman Antiquity: A Sourcebook,* ed. Vincent L. Wimbush (Minneapolis, Minn.: Fortress, Studies in Antiquity and Christianity, 1990), 134–55.
4. For a fuller discussion of Pythagoreanism and Orphism as it relates to asceticism, see Robert Parker, *Miasma: Pollution and Purification in Early Greek Religion* (Oxford: Clarendon, 1983), 281–307. For an indication of Pythagoreanism in the early Roman empire, see Ramsay MacMullen, *Enemies of the Roman Order: Treason, Unrest, and Alienation in the Empire* (Cambridge, Mass.: Harvard University Press, 1966), 95–6.
5. As suggested by Peter H. Van Ness, "Asceticism in Philosophical and Cultural-Critical Perspective," in *Asceticism*, eds. Wimbush and Valantasis, 592. In this case, I find myself more in agreement with Gillian Lindt, who suggests that there is a difference between the periodic escapes of vacations and the practice of withdrawal that characterizes asceticism (see Gillian Lindt, "Asceticism in Sociological Perspective," in *Asceticism*, eds. Wimbush and Valantasis, 595).
6. See Parker, 5. See also the introductory section defining asceticism in Anthony J. Saldarini, "Asceticism and the Gospel of Matthew" (this volume, 11ff), for an attempt to define asceticism as a "vague category." Saldarini's definition certainly helps to associate asceticism with many other practices of life or action which are intentional, imply certain social and power relations, contribute to the construction of a (new) subjectivity, and require some type of education and discipline such as, for example, consumerism, materialism, or farming. What Saldarini's definition fails to do, however, is to provide any grounds for distinguishing asceticism from any of those other practices.
7. While all words can be called in some sense "metaphorical" and are certainly always contextual, what I am referring to here is the understanding of metaphor as the comparison of a better known with a lesser known. Asceticism in its historical, religious form is being used by way of comparison to illuminate the lesser-known patterns of "cultural formation."
8. Putting aside whatever theoretical validity the point may have, for me the point becomes *less interesting* than the alternative question it raises of what, then, if anything, could make a narrative text "nonascetic."
9. For general models of reading that take account of some of the complexity of this process in different ways, see, e.g., Wolfgang Iser, *The Act of Reading: A Theory of Aesthetic Response* (Baltimore: Johns Hopkins University Press, 1978);

Mikhail Bakhtin, *The Dialogic Imagination: Four Essays,* ed. Michael Holquist, trans. Caryl Emerson and Michael Holquist (Austin: University of Texas Press, 1981); Frank Lentricchia, *Criticism and Social Change* (Chicago: University of Chicago Press, 1983); Gayatri Chakravorty Spivak, *Outside in the Teaching Machine* (New York: Routledge, 1993). For a discussion of the social location of readers of the Bible in relation to the meanings they find, see Mary A. Tolbert, "When Resistance Becomes Repression: Mark 13:9–27 and the Poetics of Location," in *Reading from This Place: Social Location and Biblical Interpretation in Global Perspective,* eds. Fernando Segovia and Mary Ann Tolbert (Minneapolis: Fortress, 1995), 331–46.

10. Stuart Hall, "Encoding, Decoding," in *The Cultural Studies Reader,* ed. Simon During (London: Routledge, 1993), 91–92.

11. Ibid, 93.

12. The one possible exception might be Philo's *De vita contemplativa,* describing the community life of the ascetic Therapeutes. The authorship and dating of the text are disputed, in part because the otherwise unknown ascetic Egyptian community the text discusses embodies so very much the communal practices of later (third to fourth century CE) asceticism that it seems out of place in relation to other religious practices of the first century CE.

13. I take this to be one of the very important points made in Edith Wyschogrod, "The Howl of Oedipus, the Cry of Héloïse: From Asceticism to Postmodern Ethics," in *Asceticism,* eds. Wimbush and Valantasis, 16–19.

14. Averil Cameron, "Ascetic Closure and the End of Antiquity," in *Asceticism,* eds. Wimbush and Valantasis, 147–61.

15. Ibid, 150.

16. Ibid, 151.

17. See my own earlier concerns about this type of methodological procedure in Tolbert, *Perspectives on the Parables: An Approach to Multiple Interpretations* (Philadelphia: Fortress, 1979), 78–83.

18. Indeed, Kallistos Ware seems to understand it as one of the two defining characteristics of the ascetic life in "The Way of the Ascetics: Negative or Affirmative?" in *Asceticism,* eds. Wimbush and Valantasis, 3–8.

19. For a selection of sayings on the Fathers' ways of maintaining quiet and solitude, see Owen Chadwick, *Western Asceticism: Selected Translations with Introductions and Notes* (Philadelphia: Westminster, Library of Christian Classics 12, 1958), 40–43.

20. While I have never noticed this similarity before, the use of *peirazo* only for Satan and the Pharisees adds some additional weight to my claim that the Pharisees allegorically represent the type of the hard ground of the path, where Satan takes away the seed, in the parable of the sower (4:15). See Tolbert, *Sowing the Gospel: Mark's World in Literary-Historical Perspective* (Minneapolis, Minn.: Fortress, 1989), 153–54.

21. It might be argued that the cosmic powers of evil stand behind and provoke the human enemies of Jesus, and the parable of the sower suggests as much, but that suggestion is a very minor theme in Mark. Human agency in the exercise of evil power seems to be the predominant viewpoint of the gospel.

22. See Parker's full study of this theme in *Miasma*, especially chap. 10.

23. As with the vegetarian requirements of the Pythagoreans, the Jewish dietary restrictions were particularly burdensome to Gentiles because so much of urban social and cultural life was predicated on feasts and festivals, often featuring meats (commonly pigs!) sacrificed to deities or donated by important city patrons. The Corinthian Christian community was evidently caught in similar difficulties, as Paul's comments on meat-eating and meat offered to idols suggests (see 1 Corinthians 8, 10:14–30).

24. Ware ("Way of the Ascetics," 4, 8–12) identifies repression or self-control (*enkrateia*) as the second basic component of ascetic practice.

25. See the excellent discussion of the development of ideas on chastity in Christian practice in Peter Brown, *The Body and Society: Men, Women, and Sexual Renunciation in Early Christianity* (New York: Columbia University Press, 1988), 33–82.

26. Chadwick (*Western Asceticism*, 20–21) argues that the early Christian martyr tradition is at the roots of the development of later Christian asceticism, for the hermitage or monastery takes over the role of the prison cell in later periods as the heroic Christian martyr becomes the self-denying heroic Christian ascetic.

27. See, for example, Saldarini, this volume, 11–27.

28. See my full discussion of the rhetorical effect of Mark in Tolbert, *Sowing the Gospel*, 296–99.

3

Askesis and the Early Jesus Tradition

Stephen J. Patterson

Whoever finds his/her life will destroy it;
and whoever destroys his/her life will find it. (Q 17:33)

INTRODUCTION

When one thinks of the historical Jesus, one does not normally think of an emaciated bag of bones sleeping on a bed of nails and eating only bread and small grains. He was not, in the popular mind, an ascetic. But what was he? And what shall we call his earliest followers?

What shall we make of someone who leaves house and home to pursue the life of a mendicant holy man, eschewing family, village, economic stability, and religious acceptance? Whatever one might call this socially radical life, it has again not normally been seen as ascetic. Part of this has to do with our ideas about the historical Jesus; more than that, however, it has to do with our ideas about asceticism. We think of ascetics as strange—strange in a disturbed sort of way. Many think of Jesus as unusual, but not strange. Seldom is he described as disturbed. He is our Savior, after all. And whatever we might think of him, it would be nice to know that at least we could get along easily with him. It is hard to imagine an intimate walk in the garden with Simon Stylites.

These are, of course, the common stereotypes with which one must contend in any attempt to bring fresh insights about asceticism to bear upon New Testament texts. In what follows, I intend to look at the figure of Jesus and the early Jesus tradition, as represented especially by the sayings tradition shared by Q and the *Gospel of Thomas,* to see whether *askesis* proves to be a helpful category wherewith to understand the practice of earliest

Christianity. I will argue that indeed it does, but only when one moves beyond the stereotypes to consider what asceticism really represented in the ancient world. Drawing on a number of recent theoretical discussions of the phenomenon,[1] I will suggest that asceticism is an appropriate framework for understanding what the early Jesus movement was all about.

Q, THOMAS, AND THE SOCIAL RADICALISM OF THE EARLY JESUS MOVEMENT

Let us begin with the tradition among Jesus' early followers of cultivating and collecting sayings attributed to him. We know of two documents from the first century CE that represent the fruits of that labor, one lost but recoverable through careful research, the other lost but rediscovered by chance in 1945. The first, of course, is Q. Many scholars date Q in the 50s or 60s of the first century CE on the grounds that it betrays no knowledge of the destruction of Jerusalem, a fact that is so prominent in later texts like Mark, Matthew, and Luke. Many also follow the hypothesis of John S. Kloppenborg that Q passed through two major compositional phases: an early phase consisting of several sapiential speeches (Q^1) and a later phase in which severe words of judgment against "this generation" were added (Q^2).[2] In any event, Q is perhaps the earliest repository for material attributed to Jesus and cultivated by his initial followers.

The second "sayings-gospel" from this early period is the *Gospel of Thomas (Gos. Thom.)*, which cannot be dated with any certainty. However, the fact that the tradition it preserves is basically autonomous, that is, rooted in the oral traditions common to Q, Mark, and the later gospel writers and not literarily dependent on the canonical gospels means that *Gos. Thom.*, too, is a repository for material whose provenance is possibly very early.[3] Moreover, since it is an autonomous tradition, the overlapping material between Q and *Gos. Thom.* stands to be very old—older than the first editions of Q or *Gos. Thom.*—and potentially very revealing of the basic content and ethos of the early sayings tradition from which both the Q and *Gos. Thom.* trajectories originally emerged.

In an earlier essay, I assembled the material common to both Q and *Gos. Thom.* and examined it as a cross-sectional sampling of the earliest layer of the Jesus tradition.[4] Since I will here rely on that earlier work, a brief summary of the results is in order.

In the material shared by both Q and *Gos. Thom.*, there is a preponderance of wisdom forms of the sort that Bultmann listed under the category "Logia (Jesus as the Teacher of Wisdom)." There are, for example, numerous *maxims*,[5] some formulated on the basis of the natural world (*Gos. Thom.*

5:2 and 6:5–6//Q 12:2; *Gos.Thom.* 45:1//Q 6:44b); some formulated on the basis of human experience (*Gos.Thom.* 4:2//Q 13:30; *Gos.Thom.* 24//Q 11:34–36; *Gos.Thom.* 33:2–3//Q 11:33; *Gos.Thom.* 34//Q 6:39; *Gos.Thom.* 35:1–2//Q 11:21–22; *Gos.Thom.* 41:1–2//Q 19:26; *Gos.Thom.* 45:2–3//Q 6:45; *Gos.Thom.* 47:2//Q 16:13; *Gos.Thom.* 86:1–2//Q 9:58); and others formulated as macarisms (*Gos.Thom.* 54//Q 6:20b; *Gos.Thom.* 58//Q 6:22; *Gos.Thom.* 68:1–2//Q 6:22–23; *Gos.Thom.* 69:2//Q 6:21a; *Gos.Thom.* 103//Q 12:39).[6] There are also several *hortatory formulations*[7] (*Gos.Thom.* 14:4//Q 10:8–9; *Gos.Thom.* 26:1–2//Q 6:41–42; *Gos.Thom.* 36//Q 6:39; *Gos.Thom.* 94//Q 11:9–10; *Gos.Thom.* 95:1–2//Q 6:34–35a) and *sapiential questions* (*Gos.Thom.* 89:1–2//Q 11:39–41).[8] Finally, there are *six parables* (*Gos.Thom.* 20//Q 13:18–19; *Gos.Thom.* 63//Q 12:16–21; *Gos.Thom.* 64//Q 14:15–24; *Gos.Thom.* 76//Q 12:33–24; *Gos.Thom.* 96//Q 13:20–21; *Gos.Thom.* 107//Q 15:3–7).

This preponderance of wisdom materials suggests that those who cultivated this tradition had an interest in the questions posed by the ancient Near Eastern wisdom tradition.[9] Theirs was a quest for insight into the nature of human existence, of humanity's proper stance within the world and the ultimate reality that underlies the world and everything in it. Theirs was a theological quest rooted in the world of human experience and reflection.

But if the form of this material suggests roots in the wisdom tradition of the ancient Near East, its content betrays a markedly different orientation from that which one usually finds in ancient wisdom. Wisdom in the ancient Near East was, for the most part, a school tradition carried on by scribes and scholars working under official sponsorship. As such, it tends to be rather conservative in its approach to the ultimate questions it raises. Its values are those of the status quo: moderation, order, hierarchy, wealth as a sign of diligence and reward, and so on. The ancient sages were not especially interested in rocking the boat or agitating for social reform.[10]

In comparing the wisdom of Q with the broader tradition of ancient Near Eastern instruction, Kloppenborg has called attention to the fact that Q does not share the generally conservative orientation of ancient wisdom. Rather, "Q presents an ethic of radical discipleship which reverses many of the conventions which allow a society to operate, such as principles of retaliation, the orderly borrowing and lending of capital, appropriate treatment of the dead, responsible self-provision, self-defense and honor of parents."[11] What is true for Q is no less true for the early tradition shared by Q and *Gos.Thom.* Here, too, family life is eschewed (*Gos.Thom.* 55 and 101:2–3//Q14:26–27) or depicted as disintegrating (*Gos.Thom.* 16:1–4//Q 12:51–53); poverty and begging are embraced (*Gos.Thom.* 54//Q 6:20b; *Gos.Thom.* 69:2//Q 6:21a; *Gos.Thom.* 36//Q 6:39; *Gos.Thom.* 14:4//Q 10:8–9; *Gos.Thom.* 95:1–2//Q 6:34–35a); homelessness is lamented but accepted (*Gos.Thom.* 86:1–2//Q 9:58). More than that, the cultural codes that form the social boundaries between Jews and Gentiles here fall under attack (*Gos.Thom.* 89:1–2//Q 11:39–41; *Gos.Thom.* 14:4//Q 10:8–9).[12]

These are not ordinary sages. Despite the presence of a number of sayings of a more conventional quality,[13] they are here clearly not employed in the interest of preserving the status quo. At least two proverbs seem to imply conflict (*Gos.Thom.* 35:1–2//Q 11:21–22; *Gos.Thom.* 103//Q 12:39). There is criticism afoot (*Gos.Thom.* 41:1–2//Q19:26; *Gos.Thom.* 39:1–2//Q 11:52; *Gos.Thom.* 78:1–3//Q 7:24–26; *Gos.Thom.* 91//Q 12:56). Boat-rocking is in the air (*Gos.Thom.* 4:2//19:26; *Gos.Thom.* 10//Q 12:49; *Gos.Thom.* 16:1–2//Q 12:51). Persecution is welcomed as the legitimation of faithfulness in the face of a hostile and unfaithful world (*Gos.Thom.* 68:1–2//Q 6:22–23).

GERD THEISSEN AND WANDERRADIKALISMUS

The preceding litany of socially radical attitudes and behavior will no doubt call to mind the work of Gerd Theissen, who, in a series of publications in the 1970s, offered a social-historical description of earliest Christianity under the general rubric of *Wanderradikalismus.*[14] According to Theissen, at the center of the Jesus movement was a group of itinerant charismatic leaders, the likes of which we see in figures such as Peter, Stephen, Paul, Barnabas, and other less illustrious figures, such as Lucius from Cyrenacia or Agabus the prophet.[15] The role of the wandering radical was not institutionally grounded, but based on a call to a life "over which he had no control."[16] It was a charismatic role. To accept this role meant a life of homelessness (Mark 1:16–20; 10:28–31; Matt. 8:20; 10:5–15, 23; 23:34; Acts 8:1),[17] turning away from family (Mark 10:29–30; 1:20; 6:4; 3:32; Matt. 8:22; 19:10–11; 16:17; 10:24; Luke 14:26; 8:19–21; 11:27–28; 12:52–53),[18] shunning wealth and possessions (Mark 10:17–22, 25; Matt. 6:19–21, 25–34; 10:10, 42; Luke 16:13, 19–31; 6:24; 10:5–15),[19] and the rejection of any means of protection on the road (Matt. 5:39, 41; 10:17–23).[20] The picture Theissen offers is one of the itinerant preacher who wanders from place to place, offering preaching and healing in exchange for hospitality.

These wandering radicals did not carry out their mission alone. Theissen argues that they were supported by a network of communities to whom they could turn for support and hospitality. These persons he calls "local sympathizers."[21] One may see the imprint of these local sympathizers on the tradition in the form of a certain tension in the gospels between the material cited earlier that sanctions a wandering radical lifestyle and other material that seems rather to endorse a more settled and conventional existence. On the matter of the law, for example, Theissen observes:

Some communities wanted to see the law fulfilled down to the smallest detail (Matt. 5.17ff.) instead of criticizing it (Matt. 5.21ff.). They felt that scribes and Pharisees were legitimate authorities (Matt. 23.1ff.) instead of morally corrupt groups over which one could only throw up one's hands in horror (Matt. 23.13ff.). They recognized the temple and its priesthood through sacrifice (Matt. 5.23), paying the temple tax (Matt. 17.24ff.) and accepting priestly declarations of wholeness (Mark 1.44), instead of rejecting its cultic practices (Mark 11.15ff.). They accepted patterns of fasting practiced around them (Matt. 6.16ff.) and had a positive attitude towards marriage and the family (Mark 10.2ff.; 10.13ff.).[22]

There are similar tensions in the way in which authority is assigned in early Christian groups. For example, Matthew assigns all authority "to bind and to loose" to the early Christian community (Matt. 18:18), even while including a tradition that assigns authority to Peter (Matt. 16:19).[23] Or consider how community boundaries are policed. In Matt. 18:15–17, one learns of procedures for expelling persons from the community. But in the *Didache* (11:1) wandering prophets are exempted from any such provisions, for they are subject only to "the judgment of God."[24] To account for these tensions, Theissen imagines the situation to have been as follows:

> At first, wandering charismatics were the authorities in the local communities. In any case, local authorities were unnecessary in small communities. Where two or three were gathered together in the name of Jesus (Matt. 18.20), a hierarchy was superfluous. Problems were resolved either by the community as a whole or by wandering charismatics who happened to arrive.... The less the structures of authority in local communities had come under the control of an institution, the greater was the longing for the great charismatic authorities. And conversely, the greater the claim of these charismatics to authority, the less interest there was in setting up competing authorities within the communities.[25]

Yet, as such communities grew in size, becoming more complex and demanding more reliable and consistent forms of leadership, the older structure of authority gradually became obsolete. As Theissen points out, there inevitably arose the need to establish local authorities who quite naturally found themselves in competition with the wandering charismatics.[26]

If Theissen's thesis is essentially right, we have a framework within which to understand the social radicalism of the early sayings tradition common to both Q and *Gos.Thom.* These materials would come from that early period in which wandering radicals moved from community to community, cultivating a tradition of countercultural wisdom as a way of responding to their earlier experience of Jesus, who presumably was the originator of this tradition. Moreover, it would not be surprising to find in this early tradition a greater emphasis on the socially radical ethos of the itinerants than on the more conventional lifestyle of their supporters. The latter would have arisen later, as local communities began to form and to function between the occasional visits by the wandering charismatics. Indeed, I have attempted to demonstrate exactly this in a previous essay. There I argue that already in Q[1] one can begin tracking a shift from the itinerant social radicalism of the earliest tradition, shared by both Q and *Gos.Thom.*, to a perspective that is more centered on local, settled groups.[27]

RECENT CRITICISM OF THEISSEN'S THESIS

In recent years Theissen's hypothesis has been subject to criticism from many different angles. Out of this critical discussion, two correctives in particular are pertinent to the present discussion and should be noted at this point.[28]

The first corrective is that of Burton Mack. Mack's concern is primarily with the idea that the early itinerants described by Theissen were engaged in a mission to spread a word of repentance to an intransigent world standing on the edge of apocalypse.[29] This view, attributed to "many scholars" (it is not clear that Theissen himself holds to it), is, according to Mack, faulty in two ways. First, it assumes that all of earliest Christianity was apocalyptically oriented. Such a view does not (could not yet) take into consideration John Kloppenborg's redactional layering of Q into an early, sapientially oriented collection of speeches and a later, apocalyptically oriented statement of judgment against "this generation." When Kloppenborg's work is considered, it becomes much less likely that the earliest phase of the Q group's activity was apocalyptically motivated.

Second, Mack questions the sense of "mission" in the scenario of radical itinerancy, noting that some of the sayings Theissen uses to establish the itinerancy thesis in the first place are rather ambiguous and could be taken as addressing persons in settled communities rather than itinerants. Mack concludes, "Apparently radical itinerancy was not the only way, or not the way at all, in which the reign of God was talked about, practiced and announced by the tradents of Q[1]."[30]

Part of this critique is, in my view, valid, and part of it is not. Mack is right to call attention to Kloppenborg's work on Q and to the general collapse of the apocalyptic hypothesis of Christian origins as necessary correctives to Theissen's view. This is confirmed all the more when we broaden our view beyond Q and take into account the early tradition common to both Q and *Gos.Thom.*, which is devoid of apocalyptic interest.[31] Mack's related concern over the idea of an early Christian "mission" is also to be sustained, in the sense that when the urgency of apocalyptic catastrophe is removed from the picture, a mission to save the world from imminent doom is also removed. This is not to say, however, that what these early Christians were up to was entirely without purpose. How to name that purpose is the question—a question upon which I shall focus attention presently.

Where Mack's critique of Theissen's thesis runs aground is in moving beyond these observations to call into question the notion that early Christians were engaged in radical itinerancy at all. His conclusion that itinerancy was "not the only way, or not the way at all" is tenuously worded, and rightly so. It is true that some of the Q texts Theissen uses to substantiate his thesis are ambiguous and applicable to any number of situations and not just radical itinerancy (wisdom tradition is by nature malleable and adaptable to various life circumstances). But Theissen does not focus his thesis particularly on texts from Q, but rather cuts a wide swath through early Christian tradition, drawing from a wide variety of texts to substantiate his thesis, including Mark, James, the *Didache,* the Pauline texts, and Acts.[32] In this way, Theissen provides a broader context within which to understand the Q texts, and thus to clarify or to specify their ambiguity.

Herein lies the strength of Theissen's thesis. Critiques of it that focus too narrowly on Q fail to appreciate this. Mack's critique is typical in this respect. By focusing too narrowly on Q^1, Mack fails to provide a plausible early Christian context within which to understand the Q^1 material.

A second corrective to Theissen's thesis has been suggested by Kloppenborg.[33] Kloppenborg acknowledges that Theissen's basic scenario of wandering radicals moving among settled communities that supported them is essentially right, but argues that it needs certain qualification. First, lower Galilee was so densely populated in the first century CE that any program of itinerancy must be imagined as a series of short excursions, or quick moves from place to place, rather than as something approximating the long journeys of Paul. Second, in the Q texts dealing with itinerancy (especially Q 10:2–12), acceptance or rejection of the wandering radicals seems to depend as much on the village as on the individual household. This suggests that one might imagine a network of supportive villages rather than a network of supportive households. Third—and this is the most pertinent of Kloppenborg's observations for the work at hand—Kloppenborg sees little evidence in Q 10:2–12 that the wandering radicals were expected to function as "leaders" in those places they visited. Their position among those who might receive them, in fact, seems rather weak, and must be defended (Q 10:7). But if they were not the "leaders" of these communities, what, then, were they?

To summarize, recent criticism of Theissen's thesis cannot really dispute the presence of material in the early sayings-tradition that indicates that some of the early followers of Jesus were engaged in a lifestyle we shall still call wandering radicalism.[34] Some of these persons did leave house and home, abandoning family and village ties to live as mendicants moving from place to place, offering care for the sick in exchange for food. Their critique of local culture included attacks on the family, as well as on conventional codes of work and economic life, religion, and politics. They were itinerant social radicals. However, two critical questions have been raised concerning how one ought to regard this itinerant social radicalism and those who pursued it in the name of Jesus. First, from Mack: If these wandering radicals did not see themselves as carrying out a mission per se, how shall we describe what they were doing? Second, from Kloppenborg: If the wandering radicals were not leaders in the early Jesus movement, what, then, was their function?

RECENT THEORETICAL DISCUSSIONS OF ASCETICISM

To answer these two questions, I want to turn first to some recent discussions of the phenomenon of asceticism. In short, my thesis is that if we look at how ascetics understand themselves and what it is they are doing, we might have a viable paradigm for understanding the itinerant radicalism of the early Jesus movement. What these wandering radicals were doing was not so much a "mission" as it was *askesis*. They were understood by their contemporaries to be not so much "leaders" as "performers" exemplifying through their activity a new understanding of human existence and of human life lived faithfully to God.

Ware: Ascetics Are Not Sick

To think of Jesus and his early followers as ascetics will not come easily to many moderns, whose perceptions of asceticism will likely include suspicions of fanaticism, extreme austerity, even social pathology.[35] The harsh rigor most people associate with asceticism does not fit well with the figure of Jesus, who, in contrast to the austere John, came "eating and drinking," a reputed "drunkard and glutton" (Q 7:34). Of course, most Christians are not much predisposed to see Jesus as an overweight alcoholic, either. A moderate figure, one easily embraced by the moderate people we imagine ourselves to be, is probably the tacit assumption most people bring to the task of imagining Jesus. But Jesus and his early followers were not moderate people. They did embrace an unusual lifestyle that, in its own way, demanded a kind of mental and physical rigor that cannot be lost from sight if we are to appreciate what the early Jesus movement was about.

This does not mean, however, that we must think of the early Jesus movement as fanatical or pathological. Here our stereotypes of asceticism must give way to the ideas and attitudes ancient ascetics held about themselves. Common sense might tell us that those involved in *askesis* would not see their own activity as unduly extreme or pathological. Still, Kallistos Ware's study, "The Way of the Ascetics: Negative or Affirmative?", is a necessary reminder that the stereotypes we bring to this discussion may exercise a distorting effect.[36]

Ware shows that the basic impulse behind ancient ascetic practice was not negative but, by and large, positive. *Anachoresis,* or withdrawal from the world, was not usually carried out in a spirit of misanthropic pessimism, but out of a desire to help those who could not withdraw in the same way. With the words of St. Seraphim of Sarov, Ware summarizes: "Acquire the spirit of peace, and then thousands around you will be saved."[37]

Enkrateia, or self-denial, Ware argues, was not motivated by a deep desire to do violence to the flesh or to be at war with the body—or so one may say, at least, of "natural asceticism." Drawing upon the definition of Dom Cuthbert Butler, Ware agrees that what distinguishes natural from unnatural asceticism is precisely one's attitude toward the body. Unnatural asceticism, which assaults the body with pain and privation, evinces an implicit rejection of creation. Natural asceticism, on the other hand, aims to reduce life to its simplest form—plain clothing, basic shelter, moderate fasting, drinking only water, sexual abstinence—to reaffirm creation's basic goodness and adequacy. The point is not to destroy the body, but to free it from the passions and thereby to return it to health. "Natural asceticism," Ware argues, "is warfare not against the body, but for it."[38]

This is the first point to be drawn from current ascetical theory: The basic impulse of asceticism is not negative but positive. It is motivated by a sense of constructive purpose, not a desire to leave a cruel world behind or to do violence to one's bodily self. But what is the constructive purpose of *askesis*? How exactly does it work for its practitioners and those who observe them?

Malina: Shrinking the Self

In another helpful study, Bruce Malina offers several observations from the fields of psychology, social psychology, and cultural anthropology that may help clarify how asceticism actually functions.[39] The basic observation Malina makes runs the risk of anachronism, since it may rely too much on current psychological theories of how the modern self or "I" is formed. However, the main point still bears consideration.

According to Malina, if one looks at the various behaviors and activities one might call ascetical—dieting, vegetarianism, fasting, sexual abstinence, sexual control, virginity, retreat from society, neglect of the body, wearing rough clothing, etc.—one might well observe that they all entail "shrinking the self."[40] The phrase invoked is by Baumeister[41] and reflects the idea that persons begin life with a basic psychophysical self: a body-plus-consciousness. Gradually, this self is then built upon through interaction with others, assuming thereby an identity, roles, status, aspirations, definitions of meaning, and so on. In this way, a psychological socialized self is constructed onto the psychophysical self. Asceticism, insofar as it aims to disengage one from so many features of socialization—developing relationships, acceptable appearance, food and clothing, esteem-generating pursuits—has the result of shrinking the self back down to its basic psychophysical starting point: a body-plus-consciousness.[42]

Even though Malina's theory is grounded in observations about modern human consciousness, it may nonetheless be valid as a way of understanding some aspects of ancient social-psychological formation as well. If modern folk rely on a certain social engagement for the development of a "self" or "I," the same would only be truer for ancient folk, since one of the most important features distinguishing the modern from the ancient person is our modern predilection for social isolation and individualism.[43] If the sort of social engagement Malina describes is necessary for the formation of the modern, relatively isolated "self," how much more would this be true for ancient persons, whose identity was much more oriented toward a primary community, such as a village or kinship group? Thus, the sort of "self-shrinking" activities Malina describes would have been even more striking and effective in an ancient context than in the modern world. This would be especially true of ascetics involved in withdrawal from family and village life, eschewing the values commonly held by ordinary ancient society.

One part of this theory, however, does not fit so well with what we otherwise can say about ancient ascetics. Malina speaks of the indicated self-shrinkage again and again as escape or self-negation. This identification presumably comes from the contemporary psychological discourse upon which Malina relies for his theory. Modern psychologists, concerned primarily with various pathological manifestations of self-shrinking, such as anorexia, masochism, or even suicide, no doubt often find escape from the self, even the body itself, to be the ultimate motivation for such behavior. The problem with this vocabulary is that an ancient ascetic's explanation for what he or she did does not sound at all like a suicide note. Returning again to Ware, we might say that the ascetic's motivations are not, for the most part, negative but positive. If the effect of asceticism is indeed the shrinking of the self, the motivation for the same *askesis* may not be escape or flight from the self.[44] What, then, is the motivation?

Valantasis: Ascetic Power and the Construction of Reality

Perhaps the most ambitious attempt to arrive at an overarching theory of asceticism is that of Richard Valantasis.[45] His basic idea, however, can be summarized succinctly. "Asceticism," says Valantasis, "may be defined as performances within a dominant social environment intended to inaugurate a new subjectivity, different social relations, and an alternative symbolic universe."[46] Note, first of all, that, like Malina, Valantasis sees asceticism as having to do with the self, a "subjectivity." But rather than viewing the process as entirely negative, Valantasis sees the process as "inaugural." That is, one might still agree with Malina that, initially, the practices of asceticism have the effect of reducing the social self. But if one listens to the voices of ascetics themselves, one finds that the goal of such activity is not ultimately the elimination of the self, but the inauguration of a new self. When Abba Joseph, having successfully mastered the ascetic practices of the Desert Fathers, comes to Abba Lot and asks, in a sense, "What next?" Abba Lot answers, "If you wish, become entirely as fire."[47] The ascetic is to find a new "subjectivity" out of which to live.

Of course, one cannot simply define oneself in isolation. The power to be a self requires an "other," over against which and in relation to which one can be and become "oneself." The "self" is always to some extent, in this regard, a "*social* self." Also, the self receives its identity only within a structured universe, within which it has a place. Valantasis recognizes both of these insights from Berger and Luckmann.[48] Thus, his definition does not focus solely on the development of a new subjectivity out of which one might begin to live, but also includes the goal of constructing "different social relations" and an "alternative symbolic universe" as part of what the ascetic tries to achieve. In creating new associations of like-minded people and by articulating a new construction of reality, the ascetic works at building up a new social-psychological self to replace the old. Valantasis summarizes:

> Asceticism does not simply reject other ways of living (that is the misconception denoted by the negative implications of the word "asceticism"), but rather asceticism rejects precisely in order to embrace another existence, another way of living embodied in a new subjectivity, alternative social relations, and a new imaging of the universe. And this intentionality has power—power to create a new person, power to restructure society, power to revise the understanding of the universe.[49]

ASCETICISM AS PERFORMANCE

There is one more aspect of Valantasis' definition that deserves special attention. He refers to ascetic practices as "performances." This is an astute observation. There is a certain performative quality to asceticism that is easily overlooked if one only thinks of asceticism as withdrawal. The ascetic withdraws from the social mainstream, but in a way that calls attention to himself or herself. The ascetic does not go quietly. In its most dramatic form, asceticism can take on a quality that is almost exhibitionist. Simon Stylites stands on a stage large enough only for him, and elevated for all to see. What he does, he does for others to observe. By Richard Schechner's definition, this is a performance.[50]

What did ancient performers expect from their audiences? And what did ancient audiences expect from a performance? A performance in antiquity, whether it be a theatrical presentation, a dance, an exhibition of painting or sculpture, a poem, a musical performance, any fine art—was, above all, an attempt at "imitation." This much we learn from Aristotle's famous dictum, "Art imitates nature" (*he techne mimeitai ten physin*). This was true for the highest cultural expression of art as well as the most common. Among the fine arts, the most common and vulgar—street theater—was accorded the most mimetic quality; it alone was called *mimus*.[51] When someone stepped out of the crowd to perform, what the crowd expected to see displayed before it was an imitation, *mimesis*.

But so as not to misunderstand Aristotle's observation, we must note that what he means by the "imitation" of nature has nothing to do with realism, literalism, or simple copying, as we might presume. When a performer offered an imitation of human life, she or he did not aim simply to present life as it was, but to present it with large, recognizable strokes, so that the audience might easily see the ideals being advocated or the vices being scorned.[52] In *Poetics* 2.1, Aristotle writes:

> Since living persons are the objects of imitation, and since these are by necessity of higher and lower types (for moral character normally only answers to these differences, since all moral differences are distinguished by vice and virtue), then we must imitate people as better than in real life or as worse than in real life, or such as they are.

This is the basis for Aristotle's distinction between comedy and tragedy: "comedy imitates people as worse than in real life, tragedy as better than in real life" (*Poetics* 2.7). This sort of larger-than-life *mimesis* is not purposeless. An ancient performance usually did not have as its goal the simple entertainment of an audience. A performance exercised what power it had to move the audience to consider something anew. The source of this power lies in the largeness of the characters, their hyperbolized features, the extreme drama of their lives. Augusto Boal explains:

> [W]hat did "imitate" mean for Aristotle? To recreate that internal movement of things toward their perfection. Nature was for him this movement itself and not things already made, finished, visible. Thus, "to imitate" has nothing to do with improvisation or "realism," and for this reason Aristotle could say that the artist must imitate men "as they should be" and not as they are.[53]

These observations help to specify the performative aspects of ancient asceticism, especially its characteristic extremism or physical and psychological rigor. The ascetic makes a public display, a performance, of his or her take on life; thus, open withdrawal from the social and cultural mainstream is an implicit, but very clear, indictment of this world. The practices in which the ascetic engages and the newly emerging subjectivity out of which the ascetic begins to act are at once rejections of older, inadequate understandings of self and demonstrations of new, ideal possibilities for self-understanding. The new social relations forged in the solidarity of ascetic practice suggest a new way of ordering the world and being in relationship to one another. Such asceticism is *mimesis* in the Aristotelian sense. The ascetic aims to imitate life not as it is, but as it ought to be.

WANDERRADIKALISMUS AS ASKESIS

The itinerant social radicalism characteristic of the earliest sayings-tradition is a form of *askesis*. It is a series of performances, done for others to see. The aim of these performances is to separate those who participate in them from the dominant social ethos, to create a new network of social relations in which an alternative symbolic universe might be articulated. And out of that new combination of activities, relationships, and discourse, those who participate begin to develop of new sense of self, a new way of being in the world, to which others might be drawn.

Itinerancy

First let us consider the texts central to the itinerancy thesis itself. In Q 10:2–16 there is a rather elaborate discourse by Jesus, instructing his followers to fan out into the towns he intends to visit, go without the normal accouterments of travel (purse, bag, sandals), enter a house with a word of peace, eat whatever the householder offers, and care for the sick there. The exact wording of the Q-discourse is difficult to reconstruct, since Matthew conflates this Q-speech with a similar speech from Mark 6:7–13, leaving us overly dependent on Luke's wording for the original text of Q. Still, Arland Jacobson's reconstruction of the Q-text will serve us well enough:

> [And he said to them,]
> 10:2The harvest is great, but the laborers are few. Pray, therefore, the lord of the harvest to send out laborers into his harvest. 10:3Go! Behold, I send you out as lambs in the midst of wolves. 10:4Carry no purse, no bag, no sandals [and salute no one on the way]. 10:5And whatever house you enter, first say, "Peace to this house!" 10:6And if the house is worthy, your peace will rest upon it; but if it is not worthy, it will come back to you. 10:7And remain in the same house, eating and drinking what is provided by them; for the laborer is worthy of his reward. [Do not go from house to house.] 10:8And when you enter a city, and they receive you, eat what is set before you, 10:9and heal those sick within it, and say to them, "The Kingdom of God has come near to you." 10:10And whatever city you enter and they do not receive you, when you go into its streets, say, 10:11 "Even the dust of your city that clings to our feet we wipe off against you. [Nevertheless, know this, that the Kingdom of God has drawn near.]" 10:16Whoever hears you, hears me, and he who rejects you, rejects me; and whoever rejects me, rejects the one who sent me.[54]

This tradition is older than Q itself, as the very similar scene in Mark 6:7–13 demonstrates (presuming, of course, that Mark did not himself make use of Q at this point). And there are parts of the speech that are older still—sayings that circulated independently before they were incorporated into this speech. One such saying is found in Q 10:8–9.[55] An independent version of this saying is found in *Gos. Thom.* (14): "When you go into any region and walk about in the countryside, eat whatever they put before you, and care for the sick among them."[56] It is also a tradition known to Paul, who makes reference to it in settling a dispute among his followers in Corinth that arose over the eating of meat that had been offered to idols (cf. 1 Cor. 10:27).

How shall we regard the activity described in these texts and the persons who are engaged in it? As we have already noted, the idea that theirs is a mission to prepare the way of Jesus owes too much to the Q-context in which this tradition is found to be generally useful. Notice that in the *Gos. Thom.* version of the saying, no mission is implied; the itinerants are simply presumed to be "out there," at least some of the time. The itinerants also do not seem to be leaders. They are not guaranteed authority or even a kind reception in the places they will visit. So who are they, and what are they doing?

Recall, now, Valantasis' definition of asceticism: "Asceticism may be defined as performances within a dominant social environment intended to inaugurate a new subjectivity, different social relations, and an alternative symbolic universe." The aforementioned itinerants are engaged in a kind of asceticism. Itinerancy itself suggests social separation, stepping outside the societal mainstream. Insofar as social location means locale, they have none. In this sense, the itinerants, like ascetics, are shrinking their social self, as Malina describes. And yet, they do not remain isolated. They seek out new social relations—anyone who will receive their message of peace and take them in. A new community is formed, albeit on unusual terms.

The itinerants are dependent on other people, indeed, radically so, lacking even the basics for survival on the road. They need this new community. And they have nothing to offer in return but humane care—the most affordable, yet most valuable, of commodities. Then they speak: "The reign of God has drawn near to you." This naming of the activity asserts a new symbolic universe: God rules in this place and time. This is what caring and being cared for means.[57] The itinerants are no longer simple beggars, but agents of God's reign. They are no longer themselves—artisans, farmers, fishers, clerks, weavers, maids—but have constructed and/or been constructed into a new subjectivity.

Then they move on. This, too, is interesting. For it now becomes clear that they do not necessarily expect that all with whom they come in contact will join them on their journey. They leave their hosts behind, for the itinerants need local supporters. If everyone did what they are doing, who would feed them? Rather, who they are and what they do is to be seen and experienced. It is a performance of something—the reign of God. Who they are and what they do imitates life, life as it ought to be. The itinerants are not leaders but performers who, in their *mimesis* of real life, draw people forward into a new way of thinking about themselves and their social relationships.

Leaving Family

An aspect of the social radicalism of this early sayings-tradition is forsaking family ties. Perhaps this goes hand-in-hand with itinerancy itself. In an agrarian culture, all hands are needed to keep the family afloat. One could not leave home to wander among towns and villages without risking alienation from those left behind to carry on the work of the family alone.[58]

As with itinerancy, the tradition of leaving behind one's family is also very old. There are indications of the phenomenon in Q, *Gos.Thom.*, and Mark. A tradition found in both Q and *Gos.Thom.* bears examining more closely. The Q-version of the tradition may be reconstructed from Luke 14:26–27 and Matt. 10:37–39, but it probably represents a later, more developed form of the tradition than the one found in *Gos.Thom.* 55; or, at least, one may say that neither of the Q-derived versions can be considered very old.[59] *Gos.Thom.* 55 is representative of the earliest tradition: "Jesus said, 'Whoever does not hate his father and his mother cannot become my disciple. And whoever does not hate his brothers and sisters and take up his cross in my way will not be worthy of me.'" What is the point of hating one's parents, one's brothers and sisters? Is this really necessary? The same question must have occurred to Matthew. For, in the end, Matthew could not accept the idea, and so altered the tradition: "One who *loves* father and mother more than me is not worthy of me." It is not a question of hatred, but of priorities. Luke, too, must have winced at the tradition. He refuses to take it literally, adding "even one's own life" to the list of things one must hate. It is clear that Luke could accept the traditional saying only as hyperbole. But the *Gos.Thom.* version can be taken quite literally. And if one sees it as part of a package of ascetical practices centered around itinerant radicalism, it makes sense.

Gos.Thom. 55 is perhaps the best example of removing oneself from the context in which one's social-psychological self is formed and maintained. The family, with its extended kinship network, was the most significant context in which ancient identities were formed. In the ancient Mediterranean world, the redefinition of self must surely have meant removing oneself from one's family. This would have been a necessary part of any ascetical program.

But we must remember that withdrawal is not the ultimate goal of *askesis*. Withdrawal enables entry into a new set of social relations. The reintegration of the itinerant into a new social system is, to be sure, not entirely evident in this particular text. However, in a related tradition found in both *Gos.Thom.* and Mark, the ascetical paradigm is more nearly completed:

And his mother and his brothers came; and standing outside they sent to him and called him. And a crowd was sitting around him; and they said to him, "Your mother and your brothers are outside asking for you." He replied, "Who are my mother and my brothers?" And looking around at those who sat about him, he said, "Here are my mother and my brothers! Whoever does the will of God is my brother, and sister, and mother." (Mark 3:31–35)

Here is the introduction of the new set of social relations to which Valantasis refers, the alternative symbolic universe, and the inauguration of a new subjectivity. The rigorous follower of Jesus loses his or her family ties, but is integrated into a new kinship group, articulated in ideal terms and offered as a new construction of reality.

Finally, there is the performative aspect of leaving one's family. It would have been an extreme act, one that called attention to itself. What was the ideal it aimed to demonstrate? It demonstrates a fundamental connectedness, a kinship, that transcends familial bonds and relationships, that is mediated through a common relationship to God. With God as their Father, human beings are all siblings; this is the point of calling God Abba, according to Elizabeth Schüssler Fiorenza.[60]

This idea became so important in the early church that it was retained, even as communities were formed that did not necessarily reject conventional family life. Paul, for example, spiritualizes the concept: "For all who are led by the spirit of God are sons (and daughters) of God.... When we cry, 'Abba! Father!' it is the spirit itself bearing witness to our spirit that we are children of God" (Rom. 8:14–16).

Pauline Christianity even found a way to translate the performative aspect of this tradition, by associating it with baptism. The drama of this liturgical act means, says Paul, that all are counted as sons and daughters of God: "For in Christ Jesus you are all sons (and daughters) of God, through faith. For as many of you as were baptized into Christ have put on Christ. There is neither Jew nor Greek, neither slave nor free, no longer male and female; for you are all one in Christ Jesus." (Gal. 3:26–28). This was perhaps a better way of giving expression to the ideal. In Paul's communities, anyone willing to go through this ceremonial act, a "staged" event in many respects, might participate fully in the dramatic transfer from the old symbolic universe to the new. In the days of the early Jesus movement, this transfer was "performed" by the itinerant for others, in a radical display of the ideal world to which the followers of Jesus were drawn.

To Destroy One's Life

There is a saying in Q that may be used to summarize what the early sayings-tradition is talking about. The saying is found in Luke 17:33 and Matt.

10:39; the Q-version might have gone something like this: "Whoever finds his/her life will destroy it; and whoever destroys his/her life will find it" (Q 17:33). This saying is perhaps one of the oldest attested sayings in the Jesus tradition. In addition to Q, Mark also knew it (8:35), as did John (12:25). *Gos.Thom.* may have known it, too, if we can imagine the same sentiments lurking behind the following statement: "Jesus said, 'Whoever has found the world and become rich, let him/her renounce the world'" (*Gos.Thom.* 110). The paradox of the latter saying captures precisely the impulse that motivates the ascetic approach to life. Finding fullness of life involves leaving one's old life behind.

What the earliest followers of Jesus knew and, perhaps, what Jesus himself knew, was that life presents us with a script. We take our cues from the social world in which we are constantly immersed. This world has all the answers we need to life's most pressing questions: Who am I? What shall I do with my life? What shall I value? Whom shall I value? The world provides us with an identity and an agenda. The world can script our lives, if we let it. The ascetic is one who makes a conscious decision to lay down the script, to step outside of conventional roles, outside of the familiar world of commonly assumed values, activities, plans, agendas.

The ascetic is one who ventures the performance of a newly imagined reality, drawing others to it in a radical display of otherness. This is what the itinerant social radicalism of the early Jesus movement was all about. It is in this sense that we may usefully think of Jesus and his early followers as ascetics, and the early Jesus tradition in terms of *askesis*.

NOTES

1. I refer especially to the studies collected in Vincent L. Wimbush and Richard Valantasis, eds., *Asceticism* (New York: Oxford University Press, 1995).

2. See John S. Kloppenborg, *The Formation of Q: Trajectories in Ancient Wisdom Collections* (Philadelphia: Fortress, Studies in Antiquity and Christianity, 1987). Kloppenborg also discusses a third phase, relatively late, of little significance for this discussion.

3. For the autonomy of the *Gos.Thom.* tradition, see Stephen J. Patterson, *The Gospel of Gos.Thomas and Jesus* (Sonoma, Calif.: Polebridge, 1993), 9–110. An earlier helpful study is John Sieber, "A Redactional Analysis of the Synoptic Gospels with regard to the Question of the Sources of the Gospel of *Gos.Thomas*" (unpublished Ph.D. diss., The Claremont Graduate School, 1965). For a comprehensive review of the scholarly discussion of this issue, see Patterson, "The Gospel of *Gos.Thomas* and the Synoptic Tradition: A *Forschungsbericht* and Critique," *Forum* 8 (1992): 45–97.

4. See Patterson, "Wisdom in Q and Thomas," in *In Search of Wisdom: Essays in Memory of John G. Gammie,* eds. Leo G. Perdue, Bernard Brandon Scott, and

William Johnston Wiseman (Louisville, Ky.: Westminster/Knox, 1993), 187–222.

5. Bultmann's term was *Grundsäzte*. See Rudolf Bultmann, *Die Geschichte der synoptischen Tradition*, 9th ed. (Göttingen, Germany: Vandenhoeck & Ruprecht, 1979), 77.

6. The Q-version is probably secondary here; it has been reformulated to prepare for the hortatory conclusion appended in Q 12:40.

7. Bultmann's term was *Mahnworte*. See Bultmann, *Geschichte*, 80.

8. Q's polemical formulation is probably secondary; so Helmut Koester, *Ancient Christian Gospels: Their History and Development* (Philadelphia: Trinity Press International/London: SCM, 1990), 91–92. See also Kloppenborg, *Formation of Q*, 149–50.

9. This was the basic insight of James M. Robinson in "LOGOI SOPHON: Zur Gattung der Spruchquelle," in *Zeit und Geschichte: Dankesgabe an Rudolf Bultmann*, ed. Erich Dinkler (Tübingen, Germany: Mohr [Siebeck], 1964), 77–96; idem, "LOGOI SOPHON: On the Gattung of Q," in *Trajectories Through Early Christianity*, eds. James M. Robinson and Helmut Koester (Philadelphia: Fortress, 1971), 71–113.

10. See James L. Crenshaw, *Old Testament Wisdom: An Introduction* (Atlanta, Ga.: John Knox, 1981), 20 (also n. 20 for further literature).

11. See Kloppenborg, *Formation of Q*, 318.

12. This is implied especially by the last of these sayings. The issue of whether or not to eat what is offered would have arisen primarily as itinerants wandered among Gentiles (see Patterson, "Paul and the Jesus Tradition: It Is Time for Another Look," *Harvard Theological Review* 84 [1991]: 32–33).

13. The following sayings are more proverbial in character: *Gos.Thom.* 6:5–6//Q 12:2; *Gos.Thom.* 26:1–2// Q 6:41–42; *Gos.Thom.* 33:2//Q 11:33; *Gos.Thom.* 34//Q 6:39; *Gos.Thom.* 45:1–2//Q 6:44b–45; *Gos.Thom.* 47:2//Q 16:13; *Gos.Thom.* 94//Q 11:9-10; *Gos.Thom.* 24//Q 11:34–36; *Gos.Thom.* 35:1–2//Q 11:21–22; *Gos.Thom.* 103//Q 12:39.

14. The most important of these studies were collected and published together in Gerd Theissen, *Studien zur Soziologie des Urchristentums*, 2nd ed. (Tübingen: Mohr [Siebeck], Wissenschaftliche Untersuchungen Zum Neuen Testament 19, 1983). A more popular presentation of Theissen's theses appeared as idem, *Soziologie der Jesusbewegung* (München: Kaiser, 1977); idem, *The Sociology of Palestinian Christianity*, trans. John Bowden (Philadelphia: Fortress, 1978).

15. See Theissen, *Sociology*, 9.

16. Ibid, 8.

17. Ibid, 10–11.

18. Ibid, 11–12.

19. Ibid, 11–14.

20. Ibid, 14.

21. Ibid, 17–23.

22. Ibid, 18–19.

23. Ibid, 20.

24. Ibid, 21.

25. Ibid, 19–20.

26. Ibid.

27. See Patterson, "Wisdom in Q and Thomas," 208–12.

28. I leave aside criticism of those parts of Theissen's thesis having to do with later developments, which Theissen refers to as *Liebespatriarchalismus*. I also leave aside for now the broad critique by Richard A. Horsley, *Sociology and the Jesus Movement* (New York: Crossroads, 1989), 13–64; see also idem, "Questions about Redactional Strata and Social Relations Reflected in Q," in *SBL Seminar 1989 Papers,* ed. David J. Lull (Atlanta, Ga.: Scholars, 1989), 186–203, especially regarding the lack of attention to political matters. These criticisms I find largely valid, but not relevant to the topic at hand. Those criticisms by Horsley having a direct bearing on the itinerancy thesis itself will be dealt with as they arise in the discussion that follows.

29. See Burton L. Mack, "The Kingdom That Didn't Come," in *SBL 1988 Seminar Papers,* ed. David J. Lull (Atlanta, Ga.: Scholars, 1988), 620–21.

30. See Mack, "The Kingdom That Didn't Come," 623.

31. See Patterson, *The Gospel of Thomas and Jesus,* 168–70; also idem, "Wisdom in Q and Thomas," esp. 208–20.

32. Theissen overlooks *Gos.Thom.*, as does Mack, which only adds to the evidence for itinerant social radicalism. See Patterson, *The Gospel of Thomas and Jesus,* 121–57. Recently, William Arnal ("The Rhetoric of Marginality: Apocalypticism, Gnosticism, and Sayings Gospels," *Harvard Theological Review* 88 [1995]: 480–82) has questioned my analysis, relying on the criticisms of Theissen offered by Mack, Kloppenborg, and Horsley to argue that Theissen's hypothesis may now be dismissed. But of these three, only Mack actually rejects the itinerancy thesis itself. Neither Horsley nor Kloppenborg rejects the idea that there were people in the early Jesus movement who were itinerant. The way in which Horsley and Kloppenborg understand the phenomenon is simply different from Theissen's (for Kloppenborg, see my note 33; for Horsley, see his "Redactional Strata and Social Relations," 198). And of these three, none considers the evidence from *Gos.Thom.* Arnal's analysis is limited to *Gos.Thom.* 42 and 73, which Arnal considers too ambiguous on their own to suggest itinerancy. But this leaves aside *Gos.Thom.* 14, which presumes itinerancy, and *Gos.Thom.* 86, which justifies it. There are also the sayings that imply leaving behind one's family (see esp. *Gos.Thom.* 55; also *Gos.Thom.* 101, 99).

33. See Kloppenborg, "Literary Convention, Self-Evidence, and the Social History of the Q People," in *Early Christianity, Q, and Jesus,* eds. John S. Kloppenborg and Leif E. Vaage (Atlanta, Ga.: Scholars, *Semeia* 55, 1992), 89–90.

34. Recently, the basic view of Q-Christianity as including itinerant radicals has been reaffirmed by Leif E. Vaage, *Galilean Upstarts: Jesus' First Followers According to Q* (Valley Forge, Pa.: Trinity Press International, 1994), esp. 17–39.

35. See Wimbush and Valantasis, "Introduction," in idem, *Asceticism,* xx.

36. See Kallistos Ware, "The Way of the Ascetics: Negative or Affirmative?" in *Asceticism,* eds. Wimbush and Valantasis, 3–15.

37. Ibid, 8.

38. Ibid, 10.

39. See Bruce Malina, "Pain, Power, and Personhood: Ascetic Behavior in the Ancient Mediterranean," in *Asceticism,* eds. Wimbush and Valantasis, 162–77.

40. Ibid, 162.

41. Malina cites Roy F. Baumeister, *The Escaping Self: Alcoholism, Spirituality,*

Masochism and Other Flights from the Burden of Selfhood (New York: Basic Books, 1991).

42. See Malina, "Pain, Power, and Personhood," 162–64.
43. Ibid, 165.
44. See Elizabeth Castelli's critique, "Asceticism—Audience and Resistance: Response to the Three Preceding Papers," in *Asceticism,* eds. Wimbush and Valantasis, 181–82.
45. See Valantasis, "Constructions of Power in Asceticism," *Journal of the American Academy of Religion* 63 (1995): 775–821; also idem, "A Theory of the Social Function of Asceticism," in *Asceticism,* eds. Wimbush and Valantasis, 544–52.
46. See Valantasis, "Constructions of Power," 797.
47. The reference is to Valantasis' example ("Constructions of Power," 775) of Abba Lot and Abba Joseph taken from the *Apophthegmata Agion Pateron* (Athens: Aster, 1970), 53.
48. See Peter L. Berger and Thomas Luckmann, *The Social Construction of Reality: A Treatise in the Sociology of Knowledge* (Garden City, N.Y.: Doubleday, 1966). Valantasis also acknowledges Robert Hodge and Gunther Kress, *Social Semiotics* (Ithaca, N.Y.: Cornell University Press, 1988).
49. See Valantasis, "Constructions of Power," 799.
50. Ibid, 798, following Richard Schechner, *Performance Theory,* rev. ed. (London: Routledge, 1988).
51. See Allardyce Nicoll, *Masks, Mimes, and Miracles: Studies in the Popular Theatre* (New York: Harcourt, Brace, 1931), 80–81. Nicoll cites the telling passage from Diomedes, *Artis grammaticae libri III:*

> The mime is an imitation and irreverent [i.e., secular] expression of some dialogue, or the lascivious imitation of indelicate deeds and words; it is thus defined by the Greeks: "The mime is an imitation of life (mimesis biou)."… The word "mime" comes from *mimeisthai* ("to imitate") as if it had a monopoly of imitation, although other forms of literature are based on this. It alone, however, was granted this common quality as a privilege, just as the man who makes verse is called a poet (*poietes,* literally "a maker") while artists, who also make something, are not called poets.

The internal quotation is of uncertain provenance, although Nicoll speculates that Theophrastus is its source.
52. On mimesis and its meaning, especially in Aristotle, see S. H. Butcher, *Aristotle's Theory of Poetry and Fine Art* (New York: Dover, 1951), 121–22.
53. See Augusto Boal, *Theatre of the Oppressed* (New York: Theatre Communications Group, 1985), 8.
54. See Arland Jacobson, *The First Gospel: An Introduction to Q* (Sonoma, Calif.: Polebridge, 1992), 139–40.
55. I consider both verses to come from Q; Kloppenborg, *Formation of Q* 195 is in agreement; Jacobson, *First Gospel,* 142; Siegfried Schulz, *Q: Die Spruchquelle der Evangelisten* (Zürich: Theologischer, 1972), 406–7. Vaage, *Galilean Upstarts,* 128–31, omits v. 8 from his reconstruction.
56. See Patterson, *The Gospel of Thomas and Jesus,* 24–25.
57. This understanding of the tradition is indebted to John Dominic Crossan, *The Historical Jesus: The Life of a Mediterranean Jewish Peasant* (San Francisco: HarperCollins, 1991), 332–48.

58. See Theissen, *Sociology,* 12.
59. Both are younger than the *Gos. Thom.* version of the saying. *Gos. Thom.* 55 presents us with a difficult, but eminently realistic, statement. A young person drawn into the Jesus movement might well feel compelled to leave behind his or her family of origin: mother, father, sisters, brothers. Horsley ("Redactional Strata," 198) notices this and consequently dismisses the notion that this tradition was ever really taken literally. But Horsley overlooks the *Gos. Thom.* version of the saying, which could easily have been taken quite literally.
60. See Elizabeth Schüssler Fiorenza, *In Memory of Her: A Feminist Theological Reconstruction of Christian Origins* (New York: Crossroad, 1988), 140–51, esp. 150–51.

4

Beloved Physician of the Soul? Luke as Advocate for Ascetic Practice

Susan R. Garrett

*Jesus answered, "Those who are well
have no need of a physician, but those who are sick; I have come to call
not the righteous but sinners to repentance." (Luke 5:31–32; cf. 4:23)*

Introduction

For centuries readers have debated whether the traditional ascription of the Gospel of Luke to "Luke, the beloved physician" is a historically accurate reminiscence or merely a pious fiction. H. J. Cadbury dealt a serious blow to the claim of historical accuracy early in this century by demonstrating that the supposedly technical medical language in Luke's gospel could be found also in the LXX and in cultivated Hellenistic nonmedical writers.[1] Here, I am raising a different question: Does the author of this gospel—whether or not a medical physician—show particular attentiveness to questions regarding therapy or healing of the *soul or self*?[2]

The reigning paradigm in philosophical ethics from before the time of Aristotle to the time of Epictetus and beyond was a medical model, as classicist Martha Nussbaum has shown.[3] The medical model compared the work of the philosopher/ethicist to that of a physician; the symptoms such "physicians" treated were desire (*epithymia*) and other passions of the soul. The procedures advocated by these moral philosophers included various methods of *askesis* or training for the soul—what B. L. Hijmans describes as "methodical aids to moral (self-)education."[4] Such aids consisted of mental exercises designed to train one to assess sense impressions (*phantasia*) correctly and to make proper judgments. Persons might deliberately cultivate mental alertness, imagine themselves experiencing grievous personal loss, engage in daily and rigorous self-scrutiny, or reflect upon admirable personal examples. Such methods for "healing" the "diseases of the soul" did not necessarily require rigorous bodily disciplines such as those associated with the asceticism of a later era. Hijmans argues that the *askesis* advocated by Epictetus, for example, had nothing to do with methods employing actual degradation of the body: "In fact, Epictetus's *askesis* is wholly rational, involves the logos only and in practice is entirely conducted by means of words."[5] It may well be the case, however, that the roots of later Christian asceticism go back to just such philosophical practices of therapeutic *askesis*.

Richard Valantasis has defined asceticism as "performances within a dominant social environment intended to inaugurate a new subjectivity, different social relations, and an alternative symbolic universe."[6] In the following analysis of Luke's discourse vis-à-vis asceticism, I employ this definition, which has at least two strengths. One strength is that the definition is phrased in positive terms: The ascetic does not simply *reject* customary, culturally approved ways of living, "but rather asceticism rejects precisely in *order to embrace another existence,* another way of living embodied in a new subjectivity, alternative social relations, and a new imaging of the universe."[7] A second strength of Valantasis' definition is that it enables one to perceive how various cultural models of asceticism,[8] although different in significant respects, all implicitly *construct power*: power to overcome the old subjectivity, the old prescriptions for social interaction, the old ways of dealing with "the cycle of needs and desires that constitute this world."[9] Thus, the definition helps us discern similarities (analytically speaking) between the ascetic practices advocated by first-century writers such as Epictetus, Seneca, or Luke and the harsher punishments of the body practiced by later Christians such as the Desert Fathers. Cultural models of asceticism—whether they represent beliefs and practices of the first, the fourth, or the twenty-first century—seek to replace a more conventional way of looking at and relating to the self, others, and the world with a new vision of what we might call "the flourishing self." All such models assume that disciplined practice (*askesis*) will generate the power necessary to cast out the old and bring in the new.

I must, however, carefully specify how I shall interpret Valantasis' claim that ascetic practices inaugurate a new symbolic universe or worldview. In my interpretation and use of the definition, the "inauguration" of persons into a new, alternative symbolic universe (i.e., alternative to the dominant culture) is, in some sense, prior to their adoption of ascetic disciplines. Ascetic practices serve not so much to *inaugurate* a new symbolic universe, therefore, as they do to *establish more firmly* alternative subjectivities, patterns of social relationships, and ways of relating to the world that are consistent with an alternative symbolic universe already inhabited by the aspiring ascetic. In other words, conversion to an alternative symbolic universe is the presupposition that makes a person wish to establish and maintain (via ascetic practice) a new subjectivity, new social relationships, and new ways of relating to the world. Only from the vantage point of the new (countercultural) symbolic universe do the old ways appear problematic; only from this new vantage point can one discern a compelling need to take up ascetic practices so as to eradicate all vestiges of the old and more firmly entrench the new.[10]

The abstract definition of asceticism offered by Valantasis (and adopted here) permits one to see similarities between circa first-century CE philosophical "therapies of the soul" and other, later asceticisms. But any analysis of a *particular* cultural model of asceticism must carefully attend to the cultural and linguistic details of the discourse in which said model comes to expression. Evidence suggests that Luke's particular discourse of asceticism shared key assumptions with circa first-century CE philosophical discourse about disciplined practice (*askesis*) as the means to a flourishing self. Therefore, in this chapter I look at the Gospel of Luke with these philosophical views of *askesis* serving as a backdrop or point(s) of comparison in order to bring Luke's distinctive construction into sharper focus.

LUKE AND HELLENISTIC PHILOSOPHY

Clearly, Luke was familiar with some of the conventions of Hellenistic philosophy. In his gospel, Luke implicitly concurs with the widespread philosophical goal of mastering one's passions: The Lukan Jesus is less prone to emotions than his Markan counterpart.[11] Luke's excising of references to Jesus' emotions is particularly notable in the Gethsemane account, where he drops Jesus' reference to his own grief (cf. Mark 14:34) and portrays Jesus not as "falling to the ground" (cf. Mark 14:35) but as "kneeling" (i.e., maintaining a posture of dignity and control).[12] Thus Jesus demonstrates through his calm endurance of severe hardships that he is a match for the wise men of the age. Moreover, in Acts Luke positions Paul as a philosopher. A. J. Malherbe has demonstrated that in the discourse to the Ephesian elders at Miletus (Acts 20:17–35), Luke ascribes to Paul certain "psychagogical" techniques (that is, techniques pertaining to the training or discipline of the soul) "that were followed by responsible moral philosophers and were widely discussed."[13] Finally, as Abraham Smith demonstrates in his chapter in this volume, Luke presents Stephen as "a man of self-control," in accordance with first-century CE philosophical ideals.[14]

More direct evidence that Luke was sympathetic to contemporaneous philosophical views of ascetic practice is found in Acts 24:16, where Paul says to the governor Felix, "In this matter I myself strive [*asko*] always to have a clear conscience before God and before humans."[15] This verse reveals at least two of Luke's presuppositions about moral exertion. To begin with, the reference to striving for a "clear conscience" betrays an assumption that a person of integrity such as Paul would regularly engage in *self-examination* or *self-testing* with respect to moral accomplishments and moral failings; Stoics and other moral philosophers of the first century CE regularly advocated such self-examination as an aspect of ascetic practice.[16] Luke's use of the term *askein*—its only occurrence in the New Testament[17]—hints at his familiarity with this cultural model of asceticism, inasmuch as it reveals his assumption that exertion or striving in the ethical sphere can improve one's moral standing.

Yet another sort of evidence indicating that Luke was concerned with ascetic practice such as that advocated by contemporaneous philosophers is a collection of Jesus' teachings in the gospel on topics pertaining to moral character or to moral discipline. An important saying about the cultivation of moral character is Jesus' imperative to "Be careful lest the light in you be darkness" (Luke 11:35). This saying is uttered in connection with teachings on the urgency of being "single" or "single-minded" (11:34–6), clean on the inside as well as on the outside (11:39–41; cf. 44).[18] Sayings on moral discipline include Jesus' admonition to "bear one's cross" (9:23; 14:27), "deny oneself daily" (9:23), renounce family (14:26) or "all that one has" (14:33), and give up possessions through almsgiving (11:41; 12:33) or through the refusal to lay up earthly treasures (12:15–21). They include also Jesus' teachings about the need for mental or moral alertness or preparedness (12:35–47; 17:3; 18:1; 21:34, 36). Some of the themes touched upon in these sayings are also discussed in writings about *askesis* by moral philosophers. Luke may have intended for such teachings of Jesus to serve as educational tools or resources in Christians' ascetic practice, much as Epictetus exhorted students to have certain fundamental teachings "ready to hand."[19]

DISEASE, HEALTH, AND HEALING

Given this evident knowledge of and sympathy for the goals and methods of contemporary philosophy and given the predominance of the medical metaphor in such philosophy, we should not be surprised to find Luke portraying Jesus as the truly great physician: a healer not only of bodies but also of "diseased" or "sin-sick" souls. Luke has Jesus explicitly describe himself as a physician in one passage: In Luke 5:31–32, Jesus answers Pharisees and scribes who criticize his eating with tax collectors by saying, "'Those who are well have no need of a physician, but those who are sick; I have come to call not the righteous but sinners to repentance.'" Elsewhere in the gospel, Luke presents Jesus as one who—like the philosophers of his day—advocates certain ascetic techniques for the promotion and sustenance of health or "flourishing" in the soul or self, as I shall shortly demonstrate.

Building on Valantasis' aforementioned definition of asceticism, we can assert that any discourse of asceticism in Luke would presuppose the following:

1. A conception of the (problematic, rejected) subjectivity, prescriptions for social interaction, and ways of relating to the world (i.e., all those things that are to be replaced)
2. A conception of the flourishing self and its place in society and in the world
3. A conception of the "ascetic" methods or techniques that will empower their practitioner(s) to transform subjectivities, social relations, and ways of relating to the world from the old to the new (i.e., that which will empower the ascetic practitioner to replace [1] with [2])[20]

I shall proceed with my analysis of Luke's discourse by asking how he fills out each of these three conceptions. Throughout the analysis, I discern how Luke's discourse constructs the power that is necessary in order to effect personal healing or change. Where is this power located? Does the power made available through ascetic practices compete with Jesus' power to "save" or complement it?

In the narrative world of the Gospel of Luke, there are two irreconcilable character types: those who have repented of their sin, calling upon Jesus to help or to heal them, and those who refuse to repent. The physician-saying quoted earlier (Luke 5:31–32) occurs in all three synoptic gospels, but it is Luke alone who has Jesus specify that he has come to call sinners to repentance. In Luke's schema, this bringing of persons to repentance is essential for their healing. Repentant persons do not "trust in themselves" to be righteous (Luke 18:9; cf. 10:29; 16:15; 20:20) but recognize their own unworthiness before God. This confession of sin, in turn, prepares them to take the essential second step to salvation, namely, *calling upon Jesus* to help them in their need. These twin steps of *repentance* and *calling upon Jesus* change a person's relationship to the cosmic powers, both good and evil, that are operating in the world. Sinners who have repented and claimed Jesus' forgiveness constitute *the well* in Luke–Acts. Sinners who have not yet repented—or those who suppose themselves to be righteous and who therefore refuse to repent—constitute *the sick*.

Luke never uses rigorous analytical terms to describe the psychological make-up of either character type. There is nothing in Luke or Acts resembling Aristotle's precise analyses of the temperate person, the self-restrained person, or the profligate person.[21] What Luke does offer are characterizations of the unrepentant and the repentant in metaphorical terms: In addition to the metaphors of sickness and health, he uses the figures of "darkness" or "blindness" versus "light" and "sight," of "bondage" versus "freedom," and of "hypocrisy" or "duplicity" (i.e., division of the self) versus "integrity" or "singleness" of self. None of these sets of metaphors makes a consistent or tightly circumscribed point about the self that can then be restated in discursive language; rather, the metaphors typically overlap or mix with one another, functioning in an impressionistic way to convey the narrator's evaluation of persons' moral/spiritual standing. Those who are blind, who exist in darkness, who continue in bondage, who are hypocritical or divided in eye and heart—such persons stand on the side of death and Satan.[22] They are the sick whom Jesus calls to repentance and thereby to health. By contrast, those who see, who are bathed in light, who have experienced release from bondage, who are single in eye and in commitment to God—such persons stand on the side of God and God's salvation. They have been healed of their disease.

Next I trace Luke's construction of each of these psychological types in somewhat more detail. Afterward, I discuss the role that Luke assigns to ascetic practices in achieving a state of wellness or flourishing and how this role compares to the role played by Jesus.

The Sick Soul: Blind, in Bondage, and Divided

Luke repeatedly uses the intertwined metaphors of *darkness* and *blindness* to characterize the unrepentant. Those destined to hear the message of salvation are ones "who sit in darkness and in the shadow of death" (Luke 1:79); they require someone to "open their eyes" that they may "turn from darkness to light and from the authority of Satan to God" (Acts 26:18; cf. Luke 4:18). Jesus warns opponents that by putting him to the test they show that their "eye is evil" and their bodies "full of darkness" (Luke 11:34–35). When the authorities come to arrest Jesus, he informs them that the present hour is marked by "the authority of darkness" (Luke 22:53). When Bar Jesus is cursed by Paul and condemned as a "son of the devil," he is blinded for a time, made "unable to see the sun." The "mist and darkness" that come over him signify his alliance with the powers of darkness—as do the scales that come upon Paul's own eyes at the time of his encounter with Jesus on the Damascus Road (Acts 9:18).[23]

Luke also characterizes the unrepentant as being *in bondage*, either to sin or to Satan.[24] Satan is one who exercises authority over the kingdoms of the world (Luke 4:5–6). Probably Luke here reflects the Jewish notion that Gentiles, in their idolatry, are actually serving the devil.[25] But Luke contends that many Jews are likewise in bondage: Moses had led the Israelites out of physical enslavement to the Pharaoh, but afterward the people reverted to idolatry and hence to servitude (Acts 7:39–43). They are not truly free to worship God until they participate in the "new exodus" led by Jesus.[26]

Yet another way Luke characterizes the unrepentant is by alluding to their *lack of singleness* or "integrity." By putting Jesus to the test, his opponents reveal that their "eye"—symbolic of the whole person—is "evil" rather than "single" (Luke 11:34–36).[27] This image of the "singleness" of eye (or heart, or soul) is the most revealing of Luke's psychological metaphors. In using such language, Luke participates in the rich discourse about the self that was being carried out among various Jewish and Christian writers of his day. Such authors referred "singleness" and its opposite, "doubleness" or "duplicity," not only to the eye but also to the face (hence one can be "two-faced"), to the soul ("double-souled," in Greek, *dipsychos*), and especially to the heart ("double-hearted" or having a "divided heart").[28] The "single" person was viewed as entirely devoted to God, with no fraction of the self wavering or holding back in its commitment. By contrast, the "double" or divided person bore "a heart within their heart: at the very back of the self there lurked a shadowy enclave that nurtured guile, rebelliousness, resentment and hidden lust."[29]

Although Luke has only the one explicit reference to "singleness" (Luke 11:34), he likely presupposes the concept at Luke 17:7–10, where Jesus exhorts the apostles on the need for devoted service of God—service, that is, that is done without thought of reward (cf. the similar passage at Eph. 6:5–8).[30] Additionally, the concepts both of singleness and of its opposite (i.e., double-mindedness) underlie the Acts account of Ananias and Sapphira: When the duplicitous couple conceals part of the proceeds from the sale of their land, thereby "putting the Spirit of the Lord to the test" (Acts 5:9), they endanger the "oneness of heart and soul" (Acts 4:32) enjoyed by the Jerusalem church. Finally, Luke presupposes the notion of double-mindedness in his recounting of Jesus' accusations against the Pharisees in 11:39–12:3 (see, e.g., 11:39: "'Now you Pharisees clean the outside of the cup and of the dish, but inside you are full of greed and wickedness'"). The evangelist places these indictments immediately after the sayings about the single eye; thus the Pharisees provide a counterexample to the single-minded behavior that Jesus has just commended. Moreover, Luke has Jesus summarize these charges against the Pharisees by remarking to the disciples, 'Beware of the yeast of the Pharisees, that is, *their hypocrisy*'" (Luke 12:1; cf. 6:42; 12:56; 13:15; 20:20). In classical usage the terms *hypokrisis*, *hypokrineisthai*, and *hypokrites* are not inherently negative (although in certain contexts they may be); they derive etymologically from the world of the theater and mean something like "acting," "to act," and "actor." In the usage of diaspora Judaism (including the LXX), however, the words took on distinctly negative connotations, referring either to wickedness in an absolute sense or more narrowly to the wickedness of deception and pretense (i.e., pretending to be righteous, or peaceable, or repentant when one is not).[31] Clearly, Luke is influenced by the latter pattern of usage: In his gospel, the Pharisees are duplicitous or deceptive in that they pretend to be righteous but inwardly are full of wickedness. Thus for Luke the Pharisees represent the very opposite of "singleness" (*haplotes*).

The Flourishing Soul: Sighted, Free, and Whole

The repentant are those who have recognized their sin. In every respect they are the diametrical opposite of the unrepentant sinners described earlier. They have heard and believed Jesus' message that God anointed him "to bring good news to the poor," "to proclaim release to the captives and recovery of sight to the blind, to let the oppressed go free" (Luke 4:18–19). Hence they responded to John's "baptism of repentance for the forgiveness of sins" by asking how they might bear fruits worthy of repentance; they respond to Jesus himself (or to his authorized emissaries) by calling upon Jesus to help them in their hour of need.

In Luke's schema, flourishing souls have been *healed of blindness,* both physical (blindness of eye) and psychic (blindness of soul). The healing of physical blindness was already a significant component of Jesus' earthly ministry (Luke 18:41–42; cf. 7:21–22). In the era after Jesus' resurrection, those who call upon his name have their psychic blindness healed as well: They are blessed with superior insight into divine affairs. To the "seventy other disciples" (who symbolize spirit-anointed believers in the time of the church[32]), Jesus says: "'Blessed are the eyes that see what you see! For I tell you that many prophets and kings desired to see what you see, but did not see it, and to hear what you hear, but did not hear it'" (Luke 10:23–24).

Some of the first of the repentant to experience this gift of spiritual insight are Jesus' closest followers, whose eyes Jesus opens when he breaks bread with them after the resurrection (Luke 24:30–31, 35). In Acts, Jesus' giving of sight is illustrated above all by the triple account of Paul's conversion. Shortly after his encounter with Jesus, "something like scales" falls from Paul's eyes; thenceforth he himself is one whose eyes have been opened, who has "turned from darkness to light and from the authority of Satan to God" (Acts 9:8, 17–18; 22:11–13; cf. 26:18, 23).

The flourishing have also been *released from bondage.* Even before Jesus declares his ministry of "release to captives" in his sermon in Nazareth,[33] the canticle of Zechariah proclaims that God is raising up a mighty savior for his people who will save them from their enemies (Luke 1:68–71). In so doing, Zechariah proclaims, God is remembering the covenant oaths, fulfilling the promise to Abraham that the people "might serve God without fear, in holiness and righteousnesss before him all our days" (1:74–75). In the Acts account of Stephen's speech, Luke returns to this theme of the covenant promise of freedom. Stephen proclaims that the promise to Abraham of deliverance from oppressors and liberty to worship God (Acts 7:7; cf. 7:17) was not actually fulfilled in the Exodus led by Moses because after the first Exodus the people returned to their worship of idols (7:39–43, 53). As I have argued elsewhere, in Luke's salvation-historical scheme it was Jesus who finally fulfilled the divine promise to release persons from bondage—Jesus was the "prophet like Moses," who led the "new exodus" from bondage as foretold by Isaiah and other prophets.[34] Thus released from their servitude of wickedness and of idolatrous powers, persons helped by Jesus are, truly, free to worship God as God requires.

Finally, Luke portrays the flourishing as ones *who have been made single or whole*. Such persons have been empowered to worship God devotedly, with no hypocrisy, no reservation, no secret thought for power or gain. They do the will of God from the heart and say to their master at the close of the day, "'We are unworthy servants; we have done only what we ought to have done'" (Luke 17:10). When they give alms, they give them freely and generously, without reservation or doubt about either the worthiness of the recipient or the act of giving itself.[35] Moreover, the virtue of "singleness" characterizes not only their individual lives but also their lives as a fellowship: In the Jerusalem church, the believers share their possessions with one another and eat their food "with glad and generous—or sincere or single-minded—hearts" (Acts 2:44, 46). Thus they are truly "of one heart and soul" (4:32).

Power to Heal

Hellenistic philosophers regarded the "passions" or "emotions" (*pathe*) as "diseases of the soul" that must be cured through the studied use of philosophical words. Since before the time of Plato, philosophers had debated the precise nature of the passions, their locus or process of origin in the soul, and the appropriate means of treating them. Despite the range of nuances with which philosophers of the Hellenistic period addressed these and related questions, they generally agreed that there was a close relationship between *one's cognitive beliefs* on the one hand and *the arousal of the passions* on the other. Nussbaum remarks that, among all the Hellenistic philosophical schools,

> the cognitive dimension of the emotions is stressed, and, in particular, their close connection with a certain sort of ethical belief, concerning what has importance and what not. What I fear, for example, is connected with what I think worth caring about, with the degree of importance I ascribe to unstable things that can be damaged by the accidents of life. Passions may be "irrational" in the sense that the beliefs on which they rest may be false, or unjustified, or both. They are not irrational in the sense of having nothing to do with argument and reasoning.[36]

Accordingly, programs of philosophical *askesis* centered *on identifying and treating false and irrational beliefs*: on helping persons identify those elements in life that are under our control and those that are not, those elements that are important objects of our concern and those that are matters of indifference. For, it was supposed, if one changed a person's beliefs on such matters, one changed the frequency and intensity of his or her passions as well. Probably Luke (like the philosophers described by Nussbaum) perceived a connection between incorrect belief on the one hand and arousal of the passions on the other. Thus Luke could not show Jesus as grief-stricken in Gethsemane, for to do so would have been to suggest that Jesus held an incorrect belief: the belief that the preservation of his own flesh was as important as doing God's will. Jesus' followers thus also are counseled not to covet, for to do so would be to misjudge the value of earthly life with its material goods versus eternal life, which cannot be purchased (Luke 12:15, 33).

For the philosophers, *words* (spoken or written) were the chief means for correcting false beliefs and thereby for healing disease. The philosopher used words to chastise the immoral—to "diagnose" diseases of the soul. Words were also the medium by which the philosopher expressed correct beliefs about the value of externals, in hopes of replacing the false or irrational beliefs that were the cause of such diseases.[37] Persons convicted of their error surveyed the old way of looking at and relating to self, others, and the world and embraced a new, alternative way.[38] Because such persons could newly see the necessity of implementing change in all aspects of life, they willingly took on certain therapeutic (ascetic) disciplines. These disciplines reinforced philosophy's alternative construction of reality by training the aspirant to make correct judgments about sense impressions—that is, by accustoming him or her to making proper evaluation of the worth of externals.

Similarly for Luke, *words* are the means to convict persons of their disease—of their blindness, bondage, and duplicity. In his gospel, Luke places special emphasis on the *authoritative* and *healing* character of Jesus' word.[39] Jesus uses words to heal as well as to call persons to repentance and reform. In Acts, the apostles and other church leaders so fully embody Jesus that *their* words of summons to repentance virtually constitute a second "visitation" of the Lord. Persons convicted by Jesus or his emissaries are healed of their blindness: From a new vantage point they (like converts to philosophy) survey the old way of looking at and relating to self, others, and the world and recognize the need to embrace a new, alternative way.

Still, we should be wary of identifying Luke's view of disease and therapy too completely with that of the philosophers. In the moral philosophical writings (especially Stoic ones), the teacher offers advice and admonition but the student finally determines the well-being of his or her own soul.[40] For Luke, the unrepentant are in bondage not only to passions but also to a powerful being, and the one who enslaves them, who enters into the divided heart and controls it (see Acts 5:3), can be effectively mastered only by the personal agency of Christ. Thus it is not just words that convey power to change, but specifically the words of Jesus or words spoken *in Jesus' name:* "There is salvation in no one else, for there is no other name under heaven given among mortals by which we must be saved" (Acts 4:12; cf. 3:16).

When Jesus acts, or when others speak or act in his name, Jesus intervenes directly in the inner selves of those in bondage, releasing them from sin (and hence from enslavement) and enabling them to overcome Satan or any lesser powers who would lead them astray through seduction or affliction. This is what it means for Jesus to "heal" persons of their disease.

But is Jesus the only wielder of power? Or can believers' adoption of ascetic practices also mediate power to change—to break the bonds of old ways? Both answers are probably correct, although only when the matter is viewed from slightly different angles. As argued earlier, in principle Luke holds that it is Jesus and Jesus alone who has the power to effect healing or release. Jesus broke Satan's power through his death and resurrection; thenceforth Christians have nothing to fear from these forces, for Jesus' superior power is instantly mediated to them whenever they call upon his name (cf. Luke 10:19).[41] Luke understands repentance and conversion (i.e., movement from the "sickness" of unrepented sin to the healthy or flourishing state of Christian discipleship) within the context of this new world order.

The conversion of Saul (Paul) is paradigmatic in this regard. Prior to his encounter with Jesus on the Damascus Road, Saul served the devil's aims by persecuting the church.[42] Jesus convicts Saul of his blindness, his bondage to Satan, and then drives the point home with an object lesson: He makes Saul physically blind. Later, when Ananias lays hands upon Saul, *immediately* the scales fall from his eyes. Saul is baptized, having his sins washed away, calling upon Jesus' name (Acts 22:12-16; cf. 9:1-19; 26:12–18). The conversion is virtually instantaneous—completed at the moment when Saul calls upon the Lord. Thenceforth there is no need for him to undertake ascetic disciplines to reorient himself away from the devil or the world, for he has already "turned," decisively, at the time of his conversion and baptism. The devil will have no power over him any longer. Saul/Paul's example illustrates (three times) Luke's view that *believers who call upon Jesus' name partake of Jesus' own absolute power over all demonic or diabolical forces.* This view, if carried to its extreme, would seem to render ascetic disciplines superfluous, for theoretically there are no human needs or desires upon which the demons or their lord can successfully play in order to lead the believer astray.[43]

And yet, Luke does seem to make a place for ascetic disciplines within the Christian life, and presumably his readers did also. I have argued elsewhere that Luke emphasizes Christ's victory over Satan partly out of a pastoral motive: the evangelist endeavors to counter Christian fear of the devil's power.[44] This effort on Luke's part probably implies that he *knows of Christians who do, indeed, fear the devil.* In other words, Luke's strong protestations about the demise of the devil suggest that he and other Christians of his day did not *experience* the victory over Satan as already won. Luke knows that Satan is still at work in the world, and the evangelist as much as concedes that the devil may succeed in invading so-called believers if they permit him to do so: Witness the case of Ananias and Sapphira, whose heart Satan had filled so as to lead them astray (Acts 5:3, 9). Moreover, Luke knows that in the long days after Jesus' departure, the temptation to get caught up in daily living would grow strong, just as in the days of Noah and Lot (Luke 17:26–30; cf. 8:12–14). He therefore presents certain ascetic disciplines as desirable and effective protections against such dangers, even if *theoretically* they are redundant of salvation through Jesus' name. In other words, in Luke's scheme of salvation *Jesus has power* to heal and to reform, *but ascetic practices also convey such power.*

Indeed such practices would seem to be essential for those who aspire to remain faithful to Jesus over the long haul. In the period following repentance and baptism, Luke teaches, Christians encounter obstacles in the Way of the Lord. *Askesis* helps persons surmount these roadblocks in the Way. What, then, are the roadblocks, and how does *askesis* help persons overcome them?

Three Dangers and Three Disciplines

There are at least three sorts of dangers that threaten those who have repented and been baptized in Jesus' name during the period of the church. First is the continuing effort of Satan to disrupt the fellowship and impede the growth of the word, using whatever means are at his disposal. To cope with this threat, I suggest here, Luke teaches his readers that Satan is powerless against them when they call in faith upon Jesus' name *and advocates the discipline of prayer* as a guard against satanic temptation. A second sort of danger threatening believers' perseverance is the delay of the parousia, which may lead to apathy or doubt about its future occurrence and to easy distraction by the concerns of daily life. Responding to this threat, Luke teaches that the coming of the Son of Man will take place soon and *advocates the discipline of watchfulness or alertness* as a guard against the snares of daily living. A third sort of danger is constituted by specific elements of such "daily life" in the world, including especially the temptations of wealth and status. To guard against this sort of danger Luke *counsels followers to "deny themselves daily," to be on guard against covetousness, and to renounce all that they have, even family, in order to follow Christ.* The second and third of these procedures for dealing with threats to perseverance find parallels in the moral philosophical writings, and all may be viewed as forms of *askesis* or "discipline," as I now briefly demonstrate.

Ascetic Discipline #1: Prayer as a Guard against Satanic Temptation

Luke portrays Satan as active in the period of the church. Satan endeavors to undermine the church's growth by various means: for example, by prompt-

ing Ananias and Sapphira to act with duplicity (Acts 5:1–11) and by working through the false prophet Bar Jesus (13:4–12, esp. 10).[45] But prayer in
Jesus' name equips believers to conquer the threat of satanic temptations.
Already in his earthly ministry, Jesus had anticipated the ongoing activity of
Satan, "the Enemy," and promised his followers that the devil would be
powerless against them whenever they invoked Jesus' name (Luke
10:17–20).[46] Later Jesus had instructed the disciples that, in the period after
his earthly ministry, when God's elect "are crying to him day and night" for
divine vindication, they ought "always to pray and not to lose heart"
(18:1–8). He had told them that in the time of eschatological testing they
ought to "pray to have strength to escape all these things" (21:36). In the
so-called Lord's Prayer, Jesus had taught the twelve disciples that they
should pray not to be led into temptation (or testing: *peirasmous* [11:4]),
and in Luke's Gethsemane account this same exhortation to the disciples
occurs again, not one time (as in Mark) but twice (22:40, 46). Presumably
the added emphasis is necessary because Luke views the period of the passion as one of heightened satanic activity.[47]

Attention to the example set by Jesus suggests that Luke views prayer as
a form of discipline or *askesis*. As is well-known, Luke heightens the motif of
Jesus at prayer. Luke reports seven such instances, versus only three instances
apiece in Matthew and Mark (Luke 3:21; 5:16; 6:12; 9:18; 9:28; 11:1;
22:41 [cf. 44]). Two of these references deserve further comment.

First, Luke 6:12 reports that Jesus "went out to the mountain to pray;
and he spent the night in prayer to God." The duration of the prayer is noteworthy. Also significant is the reference to the mountain: Luke seems to have
picked up the motif of Jesus *praying* on the mountain from Mark 6:46, part
of the so-called "Great Omission," and he alone among the evangelists
repeats the motif later in his account by mentioning that Jesus prayed on the
mountain during the Transfiguration (Luke 9:28).[48] Thus Luke seems to
think of Jesus as having a designated place to engage in the discipline of
prayer.[49]

Second, Luke 22:41—part of the Gethsemane account—depicts Jesus as
"kneeling" in prayer. As noted earlier, this marks a change from Mark's portrayal, in which Jesus "falls to the ground" (Mark 14:35). Jerome Neyrey has
argued that Luke introduced the change so as to emphasize Jesus' control
over his emotions. Thus, prayer for Jesus is not an outpouring to God done
in desperation and grief, but an activity that illustrates Jesus' own self-mastery. Moreover, Neyrey has presented a convincing argument for the authenticity of Luke 22:44, Jesus' *agonia*, in which he "prays more earnestly" and
sweats great drops like blood. Neyrey contends that this picture of Jesus is
best understood against the background of the philosophical contest or gym-
nastic exercise, as known from Philo and other contemporary philosophical
authors. Jesus' prayer is thus the means by which he struggles against the

passion of grief and gains mastery over it.[50] Finally, Neyrey contends that Luke frames the incident with Jesus' two admonitions to "pray not to enter into temptation" (22:40, 46) in order to define the struggle or *agonia* of Jesus in the Garden as a confrontation with Satan. Thus, Jesus here models the ascetic procedure that the faithful will eventually use in their own confrontations with Satan.[51]

Ascetic Discipline #2: Watchfulness in Preparation for the Coming of the Son of Man
Luke is concerned about the problem (either real or anticipated) of *moral laxity* in a church that no longer expects the imminent coming of the Son of Man. To address this problem, Luke adjusts the eschatological traditions he takes over, endeavoring to persuade his readers that the day may indeed be imminent and rallying them to renew their vigilance in daily living.[52] Luke's Jesus repeatedly exhorts his followers to stay alert, lest they be ensnared by the temptations of everyday life and so be found to be unprepared on that day. The motif is a traditional one in Christian circles (see, e.g., 1 Thess. 5:1–11; Mark 13:33–37); Luke's treatment is more extensive than that of either Mark or Matthew.

The three short parables about alertness in Luke 12:35–48 all build on an assumption that no one can know the day or hour when the foretold events will take place.[53] In all three parables, Jesus insists that this universal ignorance of the hour necessitates vigilance and fidelity on the part of believers. Jesus exhorts his audience to "let your loins be girded and your lamps burning" (12:35),[54] and then proceeds with the series of parables:

1. Hearers should be like persons waiting to open the door when their master returns from the marriage feast (12:36–38).
2. They should eschew the example of the householder who, because he did not know at what hour the thief was coming, let his house be broken into (12:39-40).
3. They should imitate the faithful and wise steward, who is doing what is expected of him when the master arrives (12:42–48).

John Carroll writes that the last of the three parables "urges not a simple posture of readiness (which might be misconstrued as passivity), but a vigilant way of life oriented toward the duties assigned by God (= the 'master')."[55]

This theme of the need for readiness recurs in parenetic passages in Luke 17:26–30 and 21:34–36, where Jesus warns against getting so caught up in the routines of life that one fails to stay alert.[56] How easy it is for one to let his or her heart be weighed down with dissipation and drunkenness and the cares of this life! But "that Day" will come suddenly upon such a one, "like a snare." Hence Jesus commands, "Be alert at all times, praying that you may have the strength to escape all these things that will take place, and to stand before the Son of Man" (21:36). The use of a present finite verb and a present participle (*agrypneite, deomenoi*) and the temporal reference ("at all times") are suggestive of the ascetic nature of this requirement of vigilance or alertness. It is not a duty that can be met on an occasional basis, but one that requires constant, unrelenting effort or discipline.

The need for constant alertness is also a prominent theme in the moral philosophers. In a treatise entitled "On Attention," Epictetus remarks that the time to commence with alertness is not tomorrow but today:

> But now, when you say, "To-morrow I will pay attention," I would have you know that this is what you are saying, "To-day I will be shameless, tactless, abject; it will be in the power of other men to grieve me; I will get angry to-day, I will give way to envy." Just see all the evils that you are allowing yourself! But if it is good for you to pay attention to-morrow, how much better it is to-day![57]

What is the object or focal point of one's vigilant attention? Epictetus describes it as certain key principles, namely, that "No man is master of another's moral purpose; and: In its sphere alone are to be found one's good and evil" (Diss. 4.12.7). These principles are put into practice when one habitually scrutinizes the *phantasiai* and makes correct judgments about them (i.e., about what does and does not lie within the jurisdiction of the moral purpose).[58] Nussbaum calls such insistence that the pupil be ever watchful and critical in the use of appearances as "the most general strategy of Stoic therapy." She writes, "The job of living actively in accordance with one's own reason, rather than passively, in the grip of habits and conventions, requires vigilance and probing."[59]

Although the eschatological dimension is lacking in the philosophical discussions of alertness, the parallel such discussions offer to the Lukan treatment of the theme is still noteworthy. Despite their differences, for example, Luke and Epictetus share important ideas about the practical consequences of failure to remain alert. Both hold that the pleasures and the terrors of the world (that is, the material goods that the world values and the circumstances that it fears) distract one from knowing what is truly good, and hence from choosing and persevering in the approved manner of life. And, for Luke as for Epictetus, the time to commence with alertness is, most emphatically, "today."

Ascetic Discipline #3: Self-Denial to Ward Off Greed and Arrogance

In Luke's gospel, greed and arrogance characterize the unrepentant (see, e.g., Luke 16:14–15; 18:9–14), but the seeming benefits of wealth and status may also tempt those who have already received the word (8:14; cf. Acts 8:9–24). Accordingly, Luke portrays Jesus as teaching that his disciples must live a life characterized by *denial of self* (Luke 9:23). What does it mean to "deny one's self"? Other sayings about discipleship in this gospel help to interpret the admonition: To deny oneself is to follow Jesus, daily "bearing one's cross"—daily embracing, in other words, the possibility of suffering or even martyrdom because of one's allegiance to Christ (9:23; 14:27).[60] To deny oneself is to renounce one's possessions (14:33) and to give alms (12:33), refusing to be anxious about such indifferent matters as food and clothing (12:22–34; cf. 12:15–21). To deny oneself is to unloose the ties—and with them the security—of family (14:26). In short, to deny oneself is to relinquish any claim on external things, the things of this world—even life itself (9:24; 14:26)—and thereby to lay up for oneself "treasure in heaven."

Philosophers had for centuries taught that blessedness comes to persons who relinquish (or at least stand willing to relinquish) most of the goods and circumstances valued by the world. In Plato's *Apology* (29E), for example, Socrates chastised the people of Athens for "neglecting what is of supreme importance" and giving their attention to "trivialities." Because they expended so much effort trying to acquire material wealth and prestige, Socrates claimed, the Athenians had little time or energy to devote to worthier ends, such as "truth and understanding and the perfection of their souls." Socrates described his efforts to rectify this situation:

> For I spend all my time going about trying to persuade you, young and old, to make your first and chief concern not for your bodies nor for your possessions, but for the highest welfare of your souls, proclaiming as I go, Wealth does not bring goodness, but goodness brings wealth and every other blessing, both to the individual and to the state. [61]

For Plato, concern with bodies or with possessions easily spiraled into uncontrollable lusts, which in turn brought misery (see, e.g., Gorgias 493D–494A). The happy person was the just or temperate individual—the one whose desires "have been taught to flow in the channel of learning," who was concerned with the pleasures not of the body but of the soul (Plato, Republic 485D).[62] Later, Stoics regarded the capacity to distinguish between matters properly under one's control and those outside it as so crucial to personal well-being that they developed various ascetic practices to instill this ability; one such practice was to contemplate the loss of personal possessions or of loved ones. Epictetus compares the requisite attitude to that of someone on a voyage, who may go on shore when the ship anchors and pick up small items, but who must willingly give these up and run back to ship if the captain calls: "If there be given you, instead of a little bulb and a small shellfish, a little wife and a child, there will be no objection to that; only, if the Captain calls, give up all these things and run to the ship, without even turning around to look back" (*Encheiridion* 7).[63] The wise person must stand ready and willing to forfeit not only possessions or loved ones, but even life itself. Seneca, for example, exhorted Lucilius to contemplate regularly the possibility of death and to be ready to die, so as to banish the fear of death that would render life unhappy.[64]

One could argue that there are differences in function between Luke's and the philosophers' respective counsels to relinquish any claim on possessions, family, and life. For the Stoics, for example, the giving up of all claims on external goods is not, strictly speaking, a means of *denying* the self, but of declaring the autonomy of the self vis-à-vis all external encumbrances and vicissitudes of fortune. In Luke's gospel, by contrast, such relinquishment functions to express that one's primary commitment is to another being: One denies oneself, takes up one's cross, and *follows Jesus*. But there are also similarities between Luke and the philosophers on this issue of "self-denial." For Luke, as for the moral philosophers, the giving up of family, possessions, and life habituates the self to making right judgments about what truly matters in life:

> Do not be afraid, little flock, for it is your Father's good pleasure to give you the kingdom. Sell your possessions, and give alms. *Make purses for yourselves that do not wear out, an unfailing treasure in heaven,* where no thief comes near and no moth destroys. For where your treasure is, there your heart will be also. (Luke 12:32–34, italics mine; cf. 12:13–31)

For the Stoics and other philosophers, failure to break the grip of desire for possessions, family, and even life itself leads inevitably to a kind of enslavement and unhappiness. Similarly for Luke, refusal to deny oneself leads to enslavement and to the loss of one's very soul (Luke 9:24). Finally, for Luke as for his philosophical contemporaries, the breaking of the grip of desire for possessions, family, and life is a process requiring *daily* exertion or *askesis* (Luke 9:23).

CONCLUSION

"Asceticism" may be viewed as a system of measures or disciplines designed to inaugurate (or to establish more firmly) a new subjectivity, different social relations, and a symbolic universe alternative to that of the dominant culture. The disciplinary measures in a given cultural model of asceticism function as a medium of power, which enables practitioners to root out the old ways and to implant (or tend and nurture) the new. In this study I have examined the cultural model of asceticism that comes to expression in Luke's gospel, comparing this model to contemporaneous moral philosophical views. Luke seems to share certain key assumptions with the philosophers: notably, the notion that there are "sick" souls and "well" ones, and that certain measures must be taken to transform the former into the latter. Luke uses several parallel sets of metaphors to express these notions of the self's "sickness" and "health": The sick are the unrepentant and are characterized also as "blind," "in bondage," and "duplicitous" or "hypocritical"; the well are the repentant and are characterized also as "seeing," "released" or "forgiven," and "single" or "single-minded."

Luke's notion of how a person moves from sickness to health is somewhat different from the view of the philosophers; Luke places a strong emphasis (unparalleled in the philosophers) on *the agency of Jesus* in effecting personal change. It is Jesus' words, or words spoken in Jesus' name, that move persons from sickness to health, from darkness to light, from the authority of Satan to God. Such a strong emphasis on the personal agency of Christ would seem to leave no room for ascetic practices—and yet, Luke does make room. Perhaps he does so because Christians in the church of Luke's day experienced ongoing (postconversion) temptations contrary to perseverance and perfection as very real, and this needed effective countermeasures.

I have identified "three dangers and three disciplines" that Luke portrays in his gospel. The first danger is Satan's ongoing effort to obstruct the church; against this danger Luke advocates the discipline of prayer. The second danger is posed by the apathy, doubt, and distractions of daily living that come about as a result of the delay of the parousia; against this threat Luke advocates the discipline of watchfulness or alertness. A third danger that Luke highlights is the temptation posed by wealth, status, and other "worldly goods"; against this danger Luke advocates a discipline of self-denial. Luke seems to assume that these three practices (and one could perhaps identify others) will contribute to a believer's ability to endure, even in times of temptation. In other words, these ascetic practices are assumed to mediate power, just as Jesus does.

NOTES

1. Luke, the sometime companion of Paul, is mentioned in Philem. 24 and 2 Tim. 4:11 and is specifically identified as "the beloved physician" in Col. 4:14. See H. J. Cadbury's discussion of the medical question in *The Style and Literary Method of Luke* (Cambridge, Mass.: Harvard University Press, 1920), 39–64. Cadbury was responding to W. K. Hobart, *The Medical Language of St. Paul: A Proof from Internal Evidence that "The Gospel according to St. Luke" and "The Acts of the Apostles" Were Written by the Same Person, and that the Writer Was a Medical Man* (1882; repr. Grand Rapids, Mich.: Baker, 1954). The matter is discussed by J. Fitzmyer, *The Gospel According to Luke* (Garden City, N.Y.: Doubleday, 1981), Vol. 1:51–53.

2. Luke uses the term *psyche* to mean the human self or as a synonym for human person or human life. Plato and successors addressed the topic of the structure and functioning of the human *psyche* in their efforts to understand the nature and origin of the passions, viewed as "diseases of the soul." Plutarch's essay *On Moral Virtue* provides a late-first- or early-second-century CE critique of the different philosophical schools' respective views of the structure of the soul and the origin of the passions (the critique is anti-Stoic and favors Aristotelianism). On pyschology prior to Plato, see H. M. Gardiner, R. C. Metcalf et al., *Feeling and Emotion: A History of Theories* (New York: American Book Company, 1937); on Plato's construction of the soul, see T. M. Robinson, *Plato's Psychology* (Toronto: University of Toronto Press, 1970).

3. See M. C. Nussbaum, *The Therapy of Desire: Theory and Practice in Hellenistic Ethics* (Princeton, N.J.: Princeton University Press, 1994); on the medical model, see 48–53 and passim. Nussbaum argues (316) that the medical analogy is more pervasive and more highly developed in Stoic texts than in those of any other Hellenistic school. See, for example, Cicero, *Tusculan Disputations* 3.6, 13; Seneca, *Ep. Mor.* 8.2.

4. B. L. Hijmans, *[ASKESIS]: Notes on Epictetus' Educational System* (Assen, The Netherlands: Van Gorcum, 1959), 54.

5. Ibid, 91. On the other hand, it was widely assumed that proper philosophical training would enable the *sophos* to endure the physical hardships brought about by fortune or providence; indeed, such hardships were often looked upon as part and parcel of philosophical training (much as physical rigors were part and parcel of athletic training). On philosophical teachings about the endurance of physical hardships, see especially V. C. Pfitzner, Paul and the Agon Motif (Leiden, The Netherlands: Brill, 1967); J. T. Fitzgerald, *Cracks in an Earthen Vessel: An Examination of the Catalogues of Hardships in the Corinthians Correspondence* (Atlanta, Ga.: Scholars, 1988). The *locus classicus* for Epictetus' view of the necessity and means of *askesis* is Diss. 3.2.1–6, discussed in Hijmans, *[ASKESIS]*, 64–68.

6. See Richard Valantasis, "Constructions of Power in Asceticism," *Journal of the American Academy of Religion* 63 (1995): 797. In this article, Valantasis explores and expounds upon the various elements of the definition.

7. Ibid, 799 (italics mine). Cf. Leif E. Vaage, "Ascetic Moods, Hermeneutics, and Bodily Deconstruction: Response to the Three Preceding Papers," in Asceticism, eds. Vincent L. Wimbush and Richard Valantasis (New York: Oxford University Press, 1995), 252.

8. The expression "cultural models of asceticism" is my own. "Cultural models" are socially transmitted, taken-for-granted mental representations of different aspects of the world, "shared cognitive schemas through which human realities are constructed and interpreted" (cited from the back cover of R. D'Andrade and C. Strauss, eds., *Human Motives and Cultural Models* [Cambridge, England: Cambridge University Press, 1992]; an earlier collection of essays that has especially influenced my thinking on the topic of cultural models is that of Dorothy Holland and Naomi Quinn, eds., *Cultural Models in Language and Thought* [Cambridge, England: Cambridge University Press, 1987]). Cultural

models shape human experience by imposing culturally distinct patterns of order on the world. They supply interpretations of events and inferences about them and provide a framework for remembering, reconstructing, and describing experiences. For further discussion of "cultural models" and an application of the notion to the study of another ancient text, see my essay "Paul's Thorn and Cultural Models of Affliction" in *The Social World of the First Christians: Essays in Honor of Wayne A. Meeks,* eds. M. White and L. Yarborough (Minneapolis, Minn.: Fortress, 1995).

9. The phrase is taken from Vaage, "Ascetic Moods," 258.

10. Valantasis, by contrast, emphasizes the conscious intentionality of the ascetic's effort to develop an alternative symbolic universe (see Valantasis, "Constructions of Power," 796–97). He cites Philo's treatise *On the Contemplative Life* as an example in which an author "consciously projects an alternative symbolic universe"; Philo uses traditional imagery "in an entirely new way." I myself perceive a greater continuity between this treatise and (counter-?) cultural trends exhibited in other literature of Philo's day than does Valantasis; see my essay, "The 'Weaker Sex' in the *Testament of Job,*" *Journal of Biblical Literature.* 112 (1993): 58 (cf. ibid. 66–68, in which I briefly discuss the Philonic text). But even if Philo was as innovative as Valantasis suggests, any *reader* of *On the Contemplative Life* would have to become persuaded of the legitimacy of Philo's "symbolic universe" before he or she would take on ascetic disciplines in imitation of the Therapeutae. Not every scholar can effect a paradigm shift, and not every ascetic can create a whole new symbolic universe.

11. See the table of passages where Luke has eliminated or otherwise modified Mark's portrayal of Jesus' emotions, in Fitzmyer, *Luke,* Vol. 1: 572. On the pervasiveness in first-century CE society of the goal of self-mastery (i.e., mastery over the passions) see S. K. Stowers, *A Rereading of Romans: Justice, Jews, & Gentiles* (New Haven, Conn.: Yale University Press, 1994), 42–82.

12. See J. Neyrey, *The Passion According to Luke: A Redaction Study of Luke's Soteriology* (New York: Paulist, 1985), 49–68, for these and other arguments that in Luke's Gethsemane account the evangelist took pains to show Jesus' mastery over his emotions, in keeping with contemporary philosophical ideals.

13. See A. J. Malherbe, "'Not in a Corner': Early Christian Apologetic in Acts 26:26," in *Paul and the Popular Philosophers* (Minneapolis, Minn.: Fortress, 1989), 152–53. For the argument that Luke presents Paul as the ideal philosopher, see also K. L. Cukrowski, "Pagan Polemic and Lukan Apologetic: The Function of Acts 20:17–38" (Ph.D. diss., Yale University, 1994), esp. 230–65. Cukrowski summarizes conventional portraits of the "ideal philosopher," and also discusses in more detail the psychagogical themes of the Miletus discourse as highlighted by Malherbe, pp. 247–50. Further, Cukrowski (pp. 63–78) identifies (but carefully avoids overstating) philosophical motifs in Luke's portrait of Jesus.

14. See Abraham Smith (this volume, 97–114).

15. Biblical quotations follow the New Revised Standard Version, modified occasionally to bring out particular aspects of the Greek.

16. See the "Golden Verse" ascribed to Pythagoras, as quoted in Epictetus, *Diss.* 3.10.2–3 (trans. W. A. Oldfather, Loeb Classical Library):

Also allow not sleep to draw nigh to your languorous eyelides,
Ere you have reckoned up each several deed of the daytime:
'Where went I wrong? Did what? And what to be done was left undone?'
Starting from this point review, then, your acts, and thereafter remember:
Censure yourself for the acts that are base, but rejoice in the goodly.

See, further, Hijmans, *[ASKESIS]*, 88–90, for discussion and additional citations from Epictetus. See also Cicero, *Cato Maior* 38; Seneca, *De Ira* 3.36. In his letters, Paul likewise counsels persons to engage in self-examination or self-testing; see, e.g., 1 Cor. 11:28, 31; 2 Cor. 13:5; Gal. 6:1, 4. Nussbaum sees the origin of such Hellenistic philosophical techniques as memorization, confession, and daily self-examination in a new recognition during this era of the "depth and complex interiority of the personality" (see Nussbaum, *Therapy of Desire*, 40; also 340–41, 348).

17. The nominal form, *askesis,* does not appear in the New Testament at all.
18. On these sayings, see also my essay, "'Lest the Light in You Be Darkness': Luke 11:33–36 and the Question of Commitment," *Journal of Biblical Literature* 110 (1991): 93–105.
19. The *Encheiridion* of Epictetus, which is full of examples of moral exercises, includes six uses of the term "ready to hand." Hijmans, *[ASKESIS]*, 69, counts seven references here. A search of the *Discourses* (in the *Thesaurus Lingual Graecae: Canon of Greek Authors and Words* corpus) turned up twenty-three occurrences; see, e.g., Diss. 1.27.6; 3.10.1; 3.21.18; 3.22.95; 3.24.103.
20. Nussbaum, *Therapy of Desire*, 28–29, offers a similar list of three conceptions intrinsic to the medical metaphor: (1) a conception of "disease" (the factors, especially socially taught beliefs, that prevent people from living well); (2) a conception of "health"; and (3) a conception of the therapeutic techniques (the proper philosophical method and procedure) to "heal" the soul's diseases. See 45–47 for the "schematic enumeration of likely characteristics of 'medical' argument," which Nussbaum uses to organize her investigations of the various philosophical thinkers and schools.
21. See Aristotle, *Nichomachean Ethics*, esp. book 7.
22. Cf. my discussion of how to interpret the metaphoric language of Luke 11:33–36, in "'Lest the Light in You Be Darkness,'" 95–96; also 100, n. 23, and 103, n. 29.
23. See my discussion of Luke's characterization of Paul as servant of Satan in ibid, 104; also later in this chapter, 81.
24. See, e.g., Acts 8:22–23, where Peter admonishes Simon Magus to repent, saying, "For I see that you are in the gall of bitterness and the chains of wickedness"; on this passage, see my book, *The Demise of the Devil: Magic and the Demonic in Luke's Writings* (Minneapolis, Minn.: Fortress, 1989), 70–73. Not only the unrepentant are in bondage to Satan, but also some of the sick or infirm: see esp. Luke 13:16.
25. Such a notion is certainly evident at Acts 26:18 (in which Jesus commissions Paul to turn the Gentiles from darkness to light and from the authority of Satan to God). For further support of this contention, see Garrett, *Demise of the Devil*, 40; also 129, n.12, and 130, nn. 17–19.

26. See my discussion of Luke's view of the Israelite people as "in bondage" prior to the "new exodus" led by Jesus in my article, "Exodus from Bondage: Luke 9:31 and Acts 12:1–24," *Catholic Biblical Quarterly* 52 (1990): 660–61.

27. On how the sayings in Luke 11:33–36 respond to opponents' testing of Jesus, see Garrett, "'Lest the Light in You Be Darkness,'" 102–3.

28. For citations of early Jewish and Christian texts that use these and related terms, see H. W. Hollander and M. de Jonge, *The Testaments of the Twelve Patriarchs: A Commentary* (Leiden, The Netherlands: Brill, 1985), 340–41. Such texts include, for example, T. Iss. (regarding which, see ibid, 233–34); T. Asher; Philo, *Quaest. In Gen.* 4.165; James; 1 Clem. 23.1-2; Hermas, Sim. 9.21.1; Vis.. 2.2.4. Secondary discussions include J. Amstutz, *[HAPLOTES]: Eine begriffgeschichtliche Studie zum jüdisch-christlichen Griechisch* (Bonn, Germany: Hanstein, 1968); Hollander and de Jonge, *Testaments of the Twelve Patriarchs,* 233–34 (on T. Iss.); O. J. F. Seitz, "Antecedents and Signification of the Term *Dipsychos,*" *Journal of Biblical Literature* 66 (1947): 211–19; idem, "Afterthoughts on the Term *'Dipsychos',*" *New Testament Studies* 4 (1957–1958): 327–34; Garrett, "'Lest the Light in You Be Darkness'" (on Luke); J. Marcus, "The Evil Inclination in the Epistle of James," *Catholic Biblical Quarterly* 44 (1982): 606–21. There are important antecedents to the notion of double-mindedness already in the Hebrew scriptures; see Seitz, "Antecedents." On notions of double-mindedness and hypocrisy in the Dead Sea Scrolls, see Marcus, "The Evil Inclination"; U. Wilckens, "[*hypokrinomai*]," *Theological Dictionary of the New Testament,* ed. G. Friedrich (Grand Rapids, Minn.: Eerdmans, 1972), 8: 565–66. Hollander and de Jonge argue that the idealizing of simplicity in the *Testaments of the Twelve Patriarchs* (and, one could add, in other Jewish and Christian writings of this era) parallels the appreciation for this virtue in contemporary Cynic and Stoic thought. See Hollander and de Jonge, *Testaments of the Twelve Patriarchs,* 234, who cite as definitive the studies by H. Hommel, "Das hellenistische Ideal vom einfachen Leben," *Symbola* 1 (1976): 256–73; and R. Vischer, *Das einfache Leben: Wort und motivgeschichtliche Untersuchungen zu einem Wertbegriff der antiken Literatur* (Göttingen, Germany: Vandenhoeck & Ruprecht, 1965).

29. See P. Brown, *The Body and Society: Men, Women, and Sexual Renunciation in Early Christianity* (New York: Columbia University Press, 1988), 36.

30. Note that a discussion of single-mindedness makes good sense in the Lukan context: The apostles have just asked the Lord to "increase our faith"; he in turn responded with a metaphor illustrating single-minded faith (Luke 17:5–6; cf. Mark 11:22–24). The problem of doubt (inadequate faith) was associated with double-mindedness by some authors; see, e.g., James 1:6–8; Hermas, Vis. 4.2.6.

31. Ulrich Wilckens considers the discontinuity between classical and diaspora Judaism's respective usages of the *hypokrinomai*-word group to be quite remarkable: See Wilckens, "[*hypokrinomai*]," 565. In using this verb, some biblical authors reflect knowledge of classical usage of the word group (see, e.g., 2 Macc. 6:21; 4 Macc. 6:12; Luke 20:20). But even here the words are used with distinctly negative implications.

32. On this passage as prefiguring the period after the resurrection, see Garrett, *Demise of the Devil,* 46–55.

33. Ibid, 141–42, n.17, regarding how Luke conflates scriptural passages to heighten the emphasis on "release" in this sermon.

34. See Garrett, "Exodus from Bondage." Other secondary discussions of the Lukan motif of "release" include M. H. Miller, *The Character of Miracles in Luke-Acts* (Ann Arbor, Mich.: University Microfilms, 1971), 155–71; S. H. Ringe, *Jesus, Liberation, and the Biblical Jubilee: Images for Ethics and Christology* (Philadelphia: Fortress, 1985), esp. 65–80.

35. According to R. H. Charles, ed., *The Testaments of the Twelve Patriarchs* (London: Black, 1908), 105, *haplotes* and related words were originally used in connection with gift-giving to describe the giver's singleness of purpose and freedom from motives such as display or ostentation (see, e.g., 1 Chron. 29:17 LXX [cf. 29:9]; T.Iss. 3:8; Rom. 12:8; Herm. Man. 2.4–6; Herm. Sim. 9.24.2,3). Charles claims that eventually this older usage gave rise to a derivative application of *haplous* to mean "generous" or "liberal."

36. See Nussbaum, *Therapy of Desire*, 38, 91–93, 359–401. The cognitive dimension of the passions in Stoic thought is examined very thoroughly in B. Inwood, *Ethics and Human Action in Early Stoicism* (Oxford: Clarendon, 1985).

37. See Nussbaum, *Therapy of Desire*, 34–35, for a description of medical moral philosophy's very high assessment of the efficacy of argument. Such a high opinion, Nussbaum writes, "is only natural, given its diagnosis. For if the diseases that impede human flourishing are above all diseases of belief and social teaching, and if, as they hope to show, critical arguments of the kind philosophy provides are necessary and perhaps even sufficient for dislodging those obstacles, then philosophy will seem to be necessary, perhaps even sufficient, for getting people from disease to health."

38. Here I write as if conversions to philosophy were always instantaneous and complete. Certainly they were sometimes portrayed that way; see, e.g., Lucian, *The Double Indictment* 17; *Nigrinus* 3–7, 35–37. For a recognition that progress in philosophy will take time, see Plutarch, *On Listening to Lectures*, 46D–47D.

39. Note how Luke has changed Mark's "he taught as one who had authority" (Mark 1:22) to "his word was with authority" (Luke 4:32).

40. Nussbaum (*Therapy of Desire*, 328) discusses Stoicism's "symmetrical anti-authoritarian account of the teacher–pupil relationship." This relationship was somewhat different from the one in, for example, Epicureanism, whose practitioners revered Epicurus as almost akin to a God (see ibid, 130–31). For an example of Stoic conviction that persons determine the well-being of their own soul, see Epictetus, *Diss.* 4.9.11–18, esp. 4.9.16: "You have but to will a thing and it has happened, the reform has been made; as, on the other hand, you have but to drop into a doze and all is lost. For it is within you that both destruction and deliverance lie."

41. Luke's portrayal of how Jesus' death and resurrection effected "the demise of the devil" is the topic of my book *Demise of the Devil*. For an analogous argument about the pastoral function of the christology and eschatology in Ephesians (i.e., to combat fear of demonic powers), see C. E. Arnold, *Ephesians: Power and Magic: The Concept of Power in Ephesians in Light of Its Historical Setting* (Cambridge, England: Cambridge University Press, Studiorum Novi Testamenti Societas Monograph Series 63, 1989).

42. For fuller development of the thesis that Luke presents Saul/Paul as a servant of Satan prior to his conversion, see my article "'Lest the Light in You Be Darkness,'" 104–5.

43. Contrast the function of language about Satan and demons in later monastic ascetic discourse as described by Valantasis, "Daemons and the Perfecting of the Monk's Body: Monastic Anthropology, Daemonology, and Asceticism," in *Discursive Formations, Ascetic Piety and the Interpretation of Early Christian Literature, Part I,* ed. Vincent L. Wimbush (Atlanta, Ga.: Scholars, *Semeia* 57, 1992), 47–79: In this monastic discourse, demons are constructed "not as forces exterior to the self, but as elements closely aligned with the formation and manipulation of the body itself" (47). Ongoing interaction with the adversarial demons constitutes the process by which the monk de/reconstructs the body. "Monastic daemonology...revolves about an intense relationship between monks and the daemons which rule over the monks' bodies and who also regulate the development of virtue for the monks through a continual process of testing" (68–69).

44. See Garrett, *Demise of the Devil,* 105–6; also note 23, this chapter.

45. On these incidents, and in general on the theme of the activity of Satan in the period of the church, see Garrett, *Demise of the Devil.*

46. In *Demise of the Devil,* 46–57, I argue that this passage foreshadows events to come in the period of the church.

47. See ibid, 54–55.

48. Mark 3:13–19a, which is the true parallel to Luke 6:12–16 (the account of Jesus' choosing of the Twelve), mentions Jesus' location on the mountain but says nothing about his praying there; again, Luke has apparently picked up this prayer motif from Mark 6:46.

49. Fitzmyer, Vol. 1, 616, observes that the motif of the mountain as a regular place of prayer is continued also in Luke 19:29; 21:37; and 22:39.

50. See Neyrey, *Passion According to Luke,* 53–54 (on Jesus' emotional state in the Garden); 55–57 (on the authenticity of Luke 22:43–44); 58–65 (on Jesus' *agonia* as a victorious struggle, including a discussion of *agonia* as philosophical combat in Philo). On the philosophical notion of the *agon,* see also Pfitzner, *Paul and the Agon Motif.* Prayer is not a prominent theme in the moral philosophical writings, but it does occur occasionally: See P. Rabbow, *Seelenführung: Methodik der Exerzitien in der Antike* (Munich, Germany: Kösel, 1954), 305, n. 33, citing Epictetus, *Diss.* 3.5.8; 3.22.95; 3.24.95; 4.4.34; Marcus Aurelius, *Meditations* 9.40. All of these passages indicate, with varying nuances, that the function of prayer is to express (or to aid one in expressing) conformity to the divine *logos.* Thus, prayer does not change the external circumstances precipitating temptation, but rather it prevents the passion that would otherwise arise in response to it. Marcus Aurelius writes, "If they [the gods] have power, why not rather pray that they should give thee freedom from fear of any of these things and from lust for any of these things and from grief at any of these things [rather] than that they should grant this or refuse that" (trans. C. R. Haines, Loeb Classical Library).

51. One could make the case that *the positing of personal examples for contemplation* is another ascetic practice that Luke supports. Besides the Gethsemane account, the most obvious advocacy for this practice occurs in Acts 20:17–38, where Paul

holds up the example that he himself set as a standard against which to measure the "savage wolves" who will enter the flock after his departure. On the use of Paul as an example in this passage, see Cukrowski, "Pagan Polemic and Lukan Apologetic," esp. 230–65. On the use of personal examples in ancient moral exhortation, see B. Fiore, *The Function of Personal Example in the Socratic and Pastoral Epistles* (Rome: Biblical Institute Press, 1986); Hijmans, *[ASKESIS]*, 72–77; Nussbaum, *Therapy of Desire*, 338–40.

52. On Luke's eschatology, see esp. J. T. Carroll, *Response to the End of History: Eschatology and Situation in Luke–Acts* (Atlanta, Ga.: Scholars, 1988), who stresses the importance of distinguishing between Luke's narrative setting and Luke's own social setting, and argues that the narrative motif of delay in Luke–Acts serves the opposite function of that identified by H. Conzelmann, *The Theology of St. Luke,* trans. Geoffrey Buswell (Philadelphia: Fortress, 1961). Carroll (*Response,* 166) writes: "Delay does not oppose but undergirds expectation of an imminent End in Luke's own situation," for Luke has shown that delay and duration were the "orders of the day" throughout his narrative.

53. Matthew has a partial parallel in 24:42–51; cf. Matt. 25:1–13 and Mark 13:33–37.

54. Carroll (*Response,* 55, n. 63) notes that the exhortation picks up the wording of Exod. 12:11.

55. Ibid, 56.

56. Matt 24:37–39 is a partial (shorter) parallel to Luke 17:26–30. There is no parallel to Luke 21:34–36 in either Matthew or Mark.

57. Trans. W. A. Oldfather, LCL.

58. On the proper assessment of *phantasiai,* see, for example, Epictetus, *Diss.* 1.27.1–6. On the importance of constant alertness for Epictetus, see, further, Hijmans, *[ASKESIS]*, 68, 87. Also pertinent to the theme of alertness in Epictetus are the philosopher's numerous exhortations to have certain teachings "ready to hand" (see note 11, this chapter).

59. See Nussbaum, *Therapy of Desire,* 327–28.

60. The qualifier "daily" is unique to Luke among the evangelists. (Some manuscripts lack this qualifier, though ancient and early witnesses support it; the qualifier may have been omitted by scribes so as to bring the passage into line with its parallels in Mark and Matthew.) This reference to denying oneself *daily* suggests that Luke views the action of "taking up one's cross" as a form of *askesis:* It is a discipline in which one willingly and regularly engages.

61. See Plato, *Apology* 30B (trans. H. Tredennick, in *The Collected Dialogues of Plato,* eds. Edith Hamilton and Huntington Cairns [New York: Pantheon, 1961]).

62. Trans. P. Shorey, in *Collected Dialogues of Plato,* eds. Hamilton and Cairns.

63. See also Epictetus, *Encheiridion* 3; 15. For a further list of citations from Epictetus (on free meditation designed to master desire), see Hijmans *[ASKESIS]*, 86.

64. Cf. Seneca, *Ep. Mor.* 61; 101.7, 10; Marcus Aurelius, *Meditations* 2.11; 7.56.

5

"Full of Spirit and Wisdom": Luke's Portrait of Stephen (Acts 6:1–8:1a) as a Man of Self-Mastery

Abraham Smith

INTRODUCTION

The term *askesis* (literally "practice" or "exercise"), from which the word "asceticism" is derived, appears only once in Acts.[1] Before Felix, in a defense-speech, Paul states, "I do my best (*asko*) always to have a clear conscience before God and all people" (Acts 24:16).

The kind of *askesis* of which Paul speaks belongs to a network of diction found in the philosophical schools and movements of the Hellenistic era.[2] Of course, before the writing of Acts, the term had evolved from a Homeric athletic art to a Platonic training of the body for the soul's freedom within the civic order and then to a strategy of interior freedom from vices in the later moral discourse of the Hellenistic era.[3] After the writing of Acts, the language of *askesis* became the diction for Christian asceticism of the second and third centuries CE (e.g., in the writings of Clement of Alexandria and Origen) and for monasticism in the fourth century CE.[4]

To expose an intersection between asceticism as moral discourse and the book of Acts, I propose to examine Luke's portrait of Stephen (Acts 6:1–8:1a) as one of several protagonists whose sagelike colors are drawn from the palate of moral discourse.[5] More specifically, I propose to show that Luke portrays Stephen as a man of self-mastery vis-à-vis his opponents, who, despite their prestigious status, demonstrate ignorance, injustice, obstinacy,

and uncontrollable rage. To do this, this chapter proceeds through four dis-
crete discussions: (1) Acts and the Philosophical Ideal, (2) The Philosophical
Ideal of Self-Mastery, (3) Comparison as a Rhetorical Strategy for Character
Portrayal in Acts, and (4) Stephen as a Man of Self-Mastery. In conclusion,
I will pose a fifth topic, an ideological critique of Luke's acceptance of self-
mastery as an ideal worthy of emulation.

ACTS AND THE PHILOSOPHICAL IDEAL

A list of philosophical ideals could include such traits as wisdom, righteousness, courage (in the face of grave danger),[6] *parresia* (openness or coura-
geous speech), "disregard for personal gain,"[7] and self-mastery.[8] Among
scholars of Acts, a few (Stanley Morrow, Abraham Malherbe, and John
Lentz) have noted that Luke portrays the protagonists of Acts (e.g., Peter,
Stephen, and Paul) as men of philosophical ideals, including the ideals of
parresia, disregard for personal gain, and self-mastery. Stanley Morrow
asserts that the word *parresia* was often used in Cynic literature to indicate
an important philosophical ideal, namely, the philosopher's "boldness and
openness of speech."[9] Similarly, Abraham Malherbe argues that Luke's contemporaries saw fearless speech as a philosophical ideal worthy of imitation.
Furthermore, Malherbe contends that the term *parresia* in Acts is used as
part of Luke's apologetic to show that the church's leaders (but especially
Paul), far from exhibiting characteristics of morally irresponsible charlatans,
actually manifested philosophical ideals, particularly in their willingness to
speak publicly without fear.[10] Indeed, the word *parresia* is used in Acts several times (Acts 9:27; 13:46; 14:3; 19:8; 26:26) to define Paul's frankness or
openness of speech. Moreover, John Lentz follows the life of Paul in Acts
and avers that Luke portrays Paul as one who incorporated the cardinal
virtues of courage, justice, self-mastery, and wisdom.[11] In fact, Acts portrays
Paul using the two lexical expressions most often associated with self-mastery: *enkrateia,* or self-control (Acts 24:25), and *sophrosyne,* or restraint (Acts
26:25).[12]

Other scholars have noted Luke's use of philosophical diction to describe
the Christian community in Jerusalem. Eckard Pluemacher notes connections
between the summaries of the Jerusalem church in Acts and the ideal *polis* in
philosophical tractates.[13] Alan Mitchell finds connections between the summaries and philosophical friendship traditions.[14] Gregory E. Sterling, observing connections in content, form, and function between the summaries and
the literary depictions of other religious and philosophical groups,[15] avers
that the summaries constitute an indirect apology, that is, a group's own affirmation that the Jerusalem community is not an inferior group, for it possesses the noblest philosophical ideals of Hellenistic philosophy.[16]

Some scholars also note other connections between the persons or groups mentioned in Acts and various philosophers or philosophical communities. Charles Talbert argues that Luke drew on the popular images of the philosopher for all of Luke–Acts.[17] Robert Brawley finds a number of connections between Paul and Socrates (e.g., use of dreams and oracles as a justification for one's behavior, acceptance of hardships, and disregard for personal gain).[18] Steve Mason suggests that the text of Acts itself equates the Christian community (or the Nazarenes) and others in the narrative groups (e.g., Pharisees, Sadducees) with philosophical schools or *haireseis*.[19]

Given these connections between Acts and philosophical ideals, communities and *dramatis personae,* is it possible that a key philosophical ideal, self-mastery, courses through the veins of the narrative? Is it possible, furthermore, that Luke exploits this ideal to characterize Stephen, the first martyr? To answer these questions, it is necessary initially to explore the philosophical ideal of self-mastery more carefully.

THE PHILOSOPHICAL IDEAL OF SELF-MASTERY

Among the aristocratic literati, moral excellence was often achieved through an ethic of self-mastery, that is, control of passions.[20] Life was viewed as a constant battle, the moral problem of which was excessive pleasure, that is, enslavement to desire,[21] and the moral aim—as reflected in several antipassion *topoi* [22]—was mastery[23] over one's own desires, although not total abstinence.[24] Moreover, a sign of moral virtue was one's ability to endure hardships without giving way to one's passions.[25] This ethic, first advanced by the philosophers, was soon adopted and proliferated to serve the elite ends of the Augustan revolution[26] and was co-opted by elite Jews.

The Philosophers

Among the philosophers, self-mastery was actually a matter of "taking care of one's soul," a theme found among the Epicureans and among the Stoics, from Zeno to Marcus Aurelius.[27] It appears that the "care of the soul" through the rigors of self-mastery was an adult, largely male enterprise. That is, self-mastery was defined in androcentric terms, and even the women who possessed it were considered not "feminine."[28] Toward proper care of the soul, moreover, philosophers of various stripes advocated a therapeutic model.[29] For most of the philosophies at the time of the Roman empire, "human misery was largely the result of anxiety and disturbance in the soul, which was caused by false beliefs about the nature of the world."[30] These false beliefs caused endless quests for "all sorts of objects of desire: wealth, luxury, power, love."[31] The therapy needed was something to extirpate those false beliefs that caused the soul to become diseased.[32] That is, if one could remove the beliefs that made the soul sick, one could render the soul healthy.[33]

Augustus and His Culture-Shapers

Augustus and his propagandistic culture-shapers deemed an ethic of self-mastery to be necessary for a superpower that claimed mastery and superiority over the "others who were, it was implied, unable to control themselves."[34] Long before Augustus, Greek writers saw self-mastery as an ideal for rulers. Xenophon's words are typical: "If we classify those who have control over all these things [i.e., bodily needs] as those who are fit to govern, will we not place those who cannot do them with those who have no claim to rule?"[35] Throughout the imperial period, moreover, moralizing rhetoric was exploited to emphasize one's own continence and to accuse "one's opponents for alleged sexual and sumptuary excesses."[36] The writings of Greco-Roman moralists were replete with the rhetoric of invective against excesses and against the corollary of incontinence, that is, lavish display or conspicuous consumption.[37]

The Jewish Elite

The ethic of self-mastery was also co-opted by the Jewish elite in its presentation of the Jews as "a uniquely self-mastered people."[38] Philo (e.g., in *Legum Allegoriae* 3.156), the *Testament of the Twelve Patriarchs, Testament of Job,* Ben Sira, and Baruch all speak of self-mastery as an ideal, with each viewing it as a masculine characteristic.[39] So prevalent was the ideal among the Jewish elite that Stowers considers Jewish elite writings to be "a philosophy for the passions, a school for self-mastery."[40]

For the Jewish elites, self-mastery brought a sense of honor. That is, Jewish dietary and Sabbath regulations,[41] idolatry prohibitions (cf. Wis 14:22–29; Philo, *Vita Mosis* 1; Josephus, AJ IV.6.6-12), and other purity codes[42] signaled not only Jewish self-definition,[43] but moral superiority as well.[44] For the Jewish elite, Jewish law includes all of the ideals of the philosophers. In effect, it "is superior because it better produces self-mastery."[45] As Philo notes, "The law requires that all who live according to the sacred constitution [*politeuma*] of Moses must be free from every unreasoning passion and every vice to a higher degree than those who are governed by other laws."[46]

In sum, three key points may be made about self-mastery in the ancient world: (1) It was cast in androcentric terms; (2) it exemplified one's "care of the self" in the face of external circumstances beyond one's control; and (3) it brought a sense of honor, as one or more groups compared themselves to others.

COMPARISON AS A RHETORICAL STRATEGY
FOR CHARACTER PORTRAYAL IN ACTS

Acts not only presents its protagonists with the philosophical ideals, but it also, as John Lentz has noted, employs *synkrisis* to highlight the virtuous character of the protagonists.[47] *Synkrisis*, or comparison and contrast, was a key literary convention.[48] As William Batstone has noted, it is "agonistic, it is used for competitive comparison and to praise or blame."[49] In his dramas, Sophocles often contrasted heroes and lesser beings "by playing them against one another."[50] As John Darr suggests, "Often, biographers paralleled the lives or exploits of famous persons so that the audience would compare and contrast—and ultimately rank—them in terms of their significance and continuing influence."[51] The erotic novels also featured *synkrisis*, moreover, as a key technique for their complex, dual plot structure, that is, a structure in which "one plot follows the heroine, the other the hero in their various separate adventures."[52]

Several scenes involving Paul illustrate Luke's use of *synkrisis*. After Saul's (Paul's) conversion, the narrator contrasts Paul with his opponents. Repeatedly, the narrator describes Paul's opponents, whether Jews or Gentiles, as an attacking or stirred-up mob (Acts 16:22; 17:13; 21:34, 35). In the dungeon in Acts 16, when the earthquake shakes the foundations, the jailer—completely out of control and in the dark about the whereabouts of the prisoners—draws his sword to kill himself and is only saved by Paul, who (perhaps without even seeing him) says: "Do not harm yourself, for we are all here" (Acts 16:29). And in the famous storm at sea (Acts 27), not only does the account vindicate Paul as innocent, but it also demonstrates his self-mastery and, by contrast, the lack of control of others. The narrator relates that the Roman centurion and everyone else except Paul are afraid (Acts 27:17) and give up hope (Acts 27:20). Indeed, were it not for the calmness and self-mastery of Paul, death would surely have come to the others.

The narrator, moreover, establishes a contrast between Paul's former life and his present one.[53] In his *former* life, Paul hears a voice telling him: "It is hard to kick against the goads." According to Lentz, this is a well-known proverb that, in effect, means that "opposition to God is worthless and impossible."[54] Furthermore, in relating the story of his *former* life, Paul uses a form of the word for "madness" (*emmainomenos*) to describe his rage against the church (Acts 26:11). This expression means to be mad against or to be furious with. It is a cognate form of the word *mainomai*, and it seems to anticipate Festus' response to Paul's defense: "Too much learning is driving you insane (*manian*)" (Acts 26:24). Yet, Paul in his *present* life insists that he is not "out of his mind" (*mainomai*) and that he speaks with *sophrosynes* (sobriety or self-restraint, Acts 26:24,25).[55]

Through *synkrisis*, then, Acts clarifies the self-mastery of Paul. On the one hand, the narrative of Acts portrays Paul's opponents as foils whose own lack of control reveals—in stark contrast—Paul's self-mastery. On the other hand, the narrative of Acts depicts Paul's former life as a foil against which to characterize Paul's present life as he stands before prestigious figures.

STEPHEN AS A MAN OF SELF-MASTERY

Given these examples of *synkrisis*, in Acts and elsewhere, the task that remains is to explore Luke's use of *synkrisis* to portray Stephen as a man of self-mastery. Appreciating Luke's portrayal of the self-mastery of Stephen requires two steps. First, because Acts is an agonistic narrative, the portrait of Stephen must be viewed as a strategically placed image designed to contrast the demeanor of the early Christian witnesses and their opponents. That is, in one sense, Stephen's self-mastery is linked to the self-mastery of other witnesses in the book of Acts. Second, because Luke casts Stephen as one who bore striking similarities to Jesus, Stephen must be seen as one whose self-mastery is linked to Jesus who also demonstrated incredible self-mastery in a climactic *agon*.

Strategic Placement of Stephen

In Acts, leading characters (Stephen, Peter, and Paul) are strategically cast as mediating authorities whose generosity is practiced without seeking or requiring reciprocity, whose inclusiveness has no limitations, and whose benefactions result in a series of adventurous *agones*. Furthermore, Acts includes a brief but telling introduction (1:1–11) and the adventurous journeys of beneficent witnesses to and beyond Jerusalem.[56]

Architectonically, the journeys take place in a series of narrative movements, each extending the geographical reach of the witnesses and each building toward a pivotal *agon,* that is, a death or a near-death escape. Accordingly, in the first movement (limited to Jerusalem, Acts 1:12–8:1a), the powerful oratory and deeds of both the Twelve and the seven confirm them as authorized cosmic power brokers,[57] but not long afterwards, honor-sensitive opponents are struck by the heroes' influence among the people and seek, in turn, the heroes' arrest and destruction. The movement ends, however, not with the arrest of the apostles, but with the death of Stephen.[58]

A second movement (in and around Judea and Samaria, Acts 8:1b–12:25) features telltale signs of shifts in heroic leadership and of the divine patron's cosmopolitan influence.[59] The second movement virtually ends with a study in contrasts: One angel rescues Peter from death row near the Passover season; another angel brings the *hybris* and life of Herod Agrippa I to a horrifying end (Acts 12:1–23).

A third movement (Acts 13:1–28:31) follows the adventures of (Saul) Paul as the hand of God guards him from envious opponents in Asia Minor,

Europe, and Asia and from dangerous forces of nature on land and sea. After a near-death escape from a horrendous shipwreck, Paul preaches at Rome, the imperial center, whose shadow of influence never completely leaves the story. In the end, however, the authorial audience knows that the real power is the one that has given the witnesses boldness and stamina both to speak about the divine patron's universal generosity and to influence all levels of society in every place.

Thus, within Acts' agonistic narrative, Stephen is one of several leaders who herald the Jewish deity's claim to be the universal patron or benefactor.[60] These leading characters, while repeatedly stylized in the patterns of suffering-yet-steadfast Septuagint prophets,[61] journey everywhere with the paradoxical news of God's vindication of the humble and destruction of the proud.[62] Moreover, the movements to and beyond Jerusalem provide settings for the protagonists to meet the significant figures of the *oikoumene* and for the deity to exert a powerful influence over every level of society.[63]

Placed at the end of the first narrative movement, the fate of Stephen reveals the Council's intensifying lack of control, despite the fact that it represents the Jewish elite and has earlier castigated the witnesses as "uneducated and ordinary" people (Acts 4:13). Like a crescendo, the early portion of the Acts narrative moves with a series of three arrest scenes: first, of Peter and John (Acts 4:3); next, of all the apostles (Acts 5:17); then, of Stephen (Acts 6:12). In the first arrest scene, the Council responds with a warning (Acts 4:18). In the second, it responds by whipping the apostles (Acts 5:40). In the third—and by now the audience expects something worse—it responds by stoning Stephen (Acts 7:58). Stephen's words seem to capture the Council's obstinacy (Acts 7:51): "You stiff-necked people, uncircumcised in heart and ears, you are forever opposing the Holy Spirit, just as your ancestors used to do."

Given the oppositional and violent character of his opponents, Stephen, by contrast, remains calm. The Freedmen demonstrate their lack of control when they work surreptitiously, like the Council in the previous chapters, to bring about Stephen's demise (Acts 6:11).[64] The Council, true to (its stylized) form, demonstrates lack of control. That is, after Stephen's speech (and because the Freedmen have already stirred up the people against Stephen, Acts 6:12), the Council's fury (*dieprionto*), once exhibited behind closed doors for the sake of the people (Acts 5:33; cf. 5:26) is now openly displayed as it joins the rest of Stephen's opponents (cf. *dieprionto*, Acts 7:54). The Council's desire (*eboulonto*) to kill (*anelein*, Acts 5:33) the apostles also finally leads to the murder (*anairesei*, Acts 8:1) of Stephen.

Furthermore, the actions of Stephen's opponents are characterized in ways proverbially linked to a lack of self-mastery. Plutarch's description of angry people is typical: They grind their teeth (*Moralia* 458B), and they are so full of confusion that they cannot see or hear what would help them (*Moralia* 454F). From beginning to end, however, Stephen, who was called to assist widows (Acts 6:1–6), demonstrates his concern for others. Even as he dies, he prays that God will not hold "this sin" against his enemies (Acts 7:60).

Thus, like the earlier witnesses, Stephen possesses self-mastery.[65] Just as the earlier witnesses faced hardships without ceasing to "teach and proclaim Jesus as the Messiah" (Acts 5:42), Stephen faced hardships—even the loss of favor among the people—without renouncing his convictions.

Stephen and Jesus: A Pattern of Suffering

As a number of commentators have noted, both Stephen's speech and his martyrdom reflect a general pattern of prophetic suffering.[66] That is, the speech speaks of leaders rejected by the people for whom they care; likewise, Stephen faces rejection, although he seeks to offer God's beneficence through signs and wonders (Acts 6:8). It is also true, moreover, that Stephen's life, trial, and fate resemble Jesus' life, trial, and fate in Luke's earlier text. In their lives, for example, both Jesus and Stephen possess wisdom (Acts 2:40, 52; 6:3, 10), an attribute often associated with *sophrosyne*.[67] Both are full of the Holy Spirit (Acts 4:1; 6:3; 7:55). Both offer benefactions to others. Similarly, their trials and fate manifest parallels.

At their trials, both suffer travesties of justice. In the case of Jesus, as Douglas Edwards has noted, the Council "omits the call of witnesses, abbreviates the trial procedures, and fails to include the religious as well as political accusations before Pilate."[68] In the case of Stephen, trumped-up charges are brought against him, and, as Richard Pervo notes, the Council "reconstitutes itself as a lynch mob, forgoing such technicalities as the delivery of a verdict and a sentence."[69]

It is also the case, moreover, that both Stephen and Jesus meet the same fate of losing the favor of the "people" (*laos*). As Robert Tannehill has noted:

> Stephen's opponents are able to poison the minds of sufficient numbers that the people's sympathy begins to shift. This development parallels the shift in attitude of the people in the passion story, for after supporting Jesus and preventing his enemies from acting, they join in shouting for Jesus' death before Pilate (cf. Luke 23:13–25).[70]

Against this fate, both Jesus and Stephen ask God to receive their spirits (see Luke 23:46; Acts 7:59).

What is often missed in comparisons of the two figures, however, is the irony that pervades their closing moments. Obviously, the Gospel of Luke saturates Jesus' closing moments with irony. One instance is based on the mockery of Jesus as a prophet (Luke 22:64) or as a Messiah-king (Luke 23:11). The request for a prophecy (Luke 22:64), the offer of an elegant robe (Luke 23:12), feigned homage (Luke 23:11), and the inscription at the top of his cross ("This is the king of the Jews," Luke 23:38)—all are false ascriptions of Jesus' greatness, with respect to the mockers. They are simply mocking him. Yet, because the authorial audience knows that Jesus is indeed a prophet (Luke 7:16) and the Messiah-king (Luke 1:33; 9:20; 19:38), the mockers are cast as victims of irony.

A second instance more specifically features the mockers' request for prophecy. That is, the scene of the mocking soldiers who ask Jesus to prophesy (Luke 22:63–64) comes directly after Peter remembers Jesus' prediction of his denial. Thus, the words of the mockers ironically victimize them. Unknown to them, one of Jesus' prophecies has just come true.

Yet a third instance of irony is seen in the precision with which Jesus' earlier prophecy (Luke 18:31-33) comes to pass. With almost nauseating accuracy, the particular elements of Jesus' last passion prediction come true. He is turned over to Gentiles (Luke 18:32; 23:1), he is mocked (Luke 18:32; 22:63; 23:11, 36), and he is flogged (Luke 18:32; 23:16, 22). The irony, then, is that Jesus' accusers have no idea that their hostile and forceful actions actually fulfill Jesus' prophecy. Thus, even if the accusers think they are in charge, Jesus' authority is revealed in the fulfillment of his prophecy. The accusers are not in charge. Jesus' words are.[71]

Similarly, the whole of Acts 6:1–8:1a is full of irony. First, although the Council considers itself to be in charge, the entire thrust of the closing scenes of Acts' first movement appears to turn on the responses people make to Stephen's powerful words on several occasions. Initially, the Freedmen, unable to withstand Stephen, plot against him (Acts 6:9–11). Next, the Council members, after hearing Stephen's speech, grind their teeth (Acts 7:54). Then, to make matters worse, when Stephen speaks of the vision he sees ("the glory of God and Jesus standing at the right hand of God"), all of his opponents (including the Council) cover their ears, rush against him, drag him out of the city, and pound him with stones (Acts 7:57–58). The Council is not in charge. Stephen's words are.[72]

Second, Stephen's speech itself sets up the scaffolding for ironic construction. Although Stephen's listeners would not see themselves as those who reject their leaders (as Stephen's speech suggests), the movement of the cases of rejection in the speech builds in intensity (from tension with Joseph to the point of killing the prophets and the Just One), in a manner similar to the movement of the plot in the first movement of Acts (1:12–8:1a). Furthermore, Stephen's speech attributes to certain opponents (Joseph's brothers, the new Pharaoh, or the people themselves) the characteristic blunders of opponents to Jesus or to the witnesses—indeed, characteristic blunders of persons with false beliefs about power: They are jealous (Acts 7:9; cf. 5:17), they seek to contain the growth of a group despite the divine promises granted to that group (Acts 7:17–19; cf. 4:17; 5:16–18), and they reject the one sent or selected by God (Acts 7:35; cf. 3:13).

Third, one of those attending the stoning of Stephen, namely, Saul (Paul), will later confirm Stephen's self-mastery in a speech that draws on the lexical expressions of the closing scenes from the first movement. Speaking about his former life, Paul notes the times when he cast a vote against the witnesses as they were being condemned to death (*anairoumenon;* Acts 26:10). He speaks about the madness that so characterized his life that he tried to force the witnesses to blaspheme (*blasphemein;* Acts 26:11). He also notes how he pursued or persecuted (*ediokon;* Acts 26:11) them. Earlier, Stephen is killed (*anairesei*) while Saul (Paul) guards the stoners' coats (Acts 8:1; cf. 22:20). Stephen is charged falsely for speaking blasphemous (*blasphema*) words (Acts 6:11). Furthermore, Stephen's speech closes with a biting barb that borders on hyperbole (Acts 7:52): "Which of the prophets did your ancestors not persecute (*edioxan*)?"

The similar diction suggests that Paul admits his own lack of self-mastery[73] in his former days. By contrast, he also acknowledges Stephen's self-mastery. The irony, then, is the utter futility of those who seek to stop the Christian witnesses through acts of persecution (cf. Acts 5:38–39). He who stands as the most vehement and violent persecutor of the witnesses at the end of the first narrative movement will himself stand as the most assertive defender and victim of persecution at the end of the third narrative movement.

Finally, yet another way in which Stephen's self-mastery is evinced is in the similarities between Stephen and Jesus, for both exhibited dauntlessness and resoluteness of character in the face of an ignominious *agon.* Because of the fair number of similarities, readers or listeners familiar with the earlier story would see Stephen as a steadfast figure in the same way that they could view Jesus in that light. Both are men of self-mastery because both are able to endure hardships in the face of excruciating—even if ironic—circumstances.

CONCLUSION

Given Luke's portrait of Stephen's self-mastery, a self-mastery similar to that possessed by the other witnesses in Acts and by Jesus in the Gospel of Luke, two final issues must be raised. First, what end did such a portrait serve? Second, given the way self-mastery is constructed as a masculine trait, what are the ethical implications of embracing Luke's acceptance of this philosophical ideal?

The first issue is really a matter of exigence. Without clear information about the real Luke or Luke's real audience, all that we can do is press for a reconstruction of Luke's purposes in the most general of terms. That is, we can speak only of what may have been the general concerns of most early Christians.

In the case of Luke's real audience, we need not know for certain that they experienced persecution (cf., however, Luke 8:13; 12:4–12; 21:12–17; and all of Acts). As a part (or a potential part) of the early Christian movement, Luke's audience would have needed only to fear or remember persecution and the real likelihood of betrayal and defection.[74] The fear and memory of trial alone is enough to warrant the Acts of the Apostles.

Aside from the fear of persecution and trial, the early Christians likely faced social criticism. The social critiques leveled at Christianity by Celsus, Lucian, and others in the second century CE were ready polemics even in the first century CE. The charges, admittedly more hyperbolic than true, viewed Christianity as "a lower class movement...as uneducated and socially insignificant, if not downright irresponsible or dangerous."[75]

Luke's audience, at whatever point they heard Acts, may have feared trial, persecution, and social criticism. Given the context of social criticism, Acts appears to be a document written to offer assurance. Acts argues that the right course for "Israel" is transcendence over the circumstances of change, chance, and coincidence (essentially, the cultivation of a philosophical ideal) through the imitation of paradigmatic leaders, that is, suffering-yet-influential prophets or *cosmic* power brokers, including the key cosmic power broker, Jesus. Accordingly, Acts develops pronouncements about such paradigmatic leadership through a series of *agones*.

The indicated *agones* chart the course of the paradigmatic leaders' *cosmic* power brokering despite the opposition of stylized opponents who futilely seek to limit access to power to a select, exclusive few. As spirit-filled cosmic power brokers, these leaders, including Stephen, dramatically illustrate Jesus' prophetic posture of transcendence over agonistic circumstances, even over the strictures of unjust circumstances, including death. Thus, for Luke, the solution to both the possibility of enduring persecution and social criticism is a prophetic (philosophical) posture in which fully informed witnesses announce God's beneficence (or judgment for the impenitent) to everyone, despite conflict, including death.

The second issue is actually a feminist ideological critique of Luke's acceptance of the philosophical ideal of self-mastery. The broadening of feminist research beyond the terrain of "compensatory scholarship" has led a number of scholars of Greco-Roman antiquity to focus not exclusively on "woman," but on "the entire spectrum of Greco-Roman gender assumptions, not excluding men's image of themselves as males."[76] In so doing, they have rendered the category of "man" just as problematic as the category of "woman," that is, as a site governed by gender relations and the hegemonic assumptions that order those relations.[77] It is well known now, for example, that "Greco-Roman sexual relations were organized as patterns of dominance-submission behaviors that ideally replicate and even confirm social superiority or inferiority."[78] Put another way, human sexuality was a nonmutual act "by one person upon another" and a classifying symbol of the dominance of the "active" male over the "passive" female, boy, or slave.[79]

Within New Testament studies, some scholars are beginning to consider how masculinity was constructed in the Greco-Roman world. For example, Stanley Stowers reads masculinity within the Greco-Roman "discourse of self-mastery."[80] For ancient audiences, then, Luke's acceptance of the philosophical ideal of self-mastery, construed as a male activity, was, in effect, acquiescence to a patriarchal point of view. And to the extent that contemporary audiences accept Luke's rhetoric for its "collective defenses and ideological constructions," they are, in effect, perpetuating patriarchy in (perhaps) an unwitting way.[81]

NOTES

1. On the word *askesis*, see G. W. H. Lampe, *A Patristic Lexicon* (Oxford: Clarendon, 1961), s.v.

2. On the language of *askesis* and the philosophical life, see Vincent L. Wimbush, "Introduction," in *Ascetic Behavior in Greco-Roman Antiquity: A Sourcebook*, ed. Vincent L. Wimbush (Minneapolis: Fortress, 1990), 1–11, esp. 3.

3. For a summary of the importance of *askesis* in Hellenistic times, see John T. Fitzgerald, *Cracks in an Earthen Vessel: An Examination of the Catalogues of Hardships in the Corinthian Correspondence* (Atlanta, Ga.: Scholars, 1988), 90–100.

4. On the continuation of *askesis*, in one form or another, see the essays in Vincent L. Wimbush and Richard Valantasis, eds., *Asceticism* (New York: Oxford University, 1995).

5. Under the previously prevailing paradigm of rigorous historical inquiries, scholarship on Stephen was usually directed toward the determination of Luke's sources and of Luke's editorial hand in the final form of Stephen's speech. Differences of opinion about Luke's sources, however, have suggested the need for alternative methods to investigate Luke's earliest witnessing martyr (without losing the vital contributions of historical inquiries). On the source problems, see John Kilgallen, "The Function of Stephen's Speech (Acts 7:2–53)," *Biblica* 70 (1989): 173–93, esp. 173–74.

6. Epictetus lauds Diogenes as a model philosopher because he "disdained death and hardship." See Robert L. Brawley, *Luke-Acts and the Jews: Conflict, Apology and Conciliation* (Atlanta, Ga.: Scholars, 1987), 60; cf. Epictetus, *Diss.* 1.24.3.10.

7. Socrates best demonstrates this ideal. As Brawley notes (*Luke–Acts*, 61), "Part of Socrates' defense is that he does not profit from his philosophy (Plato, *Apology* 19D–E), and he denounces those who do (Xenophon, *Memorabilia* 1.2.6–7)."

8. On the cardinal virtues, see John C. Lentz, *Luke's Portrait of Paul* (Cambridge, England: Cambridge University Press, 1993), 62. Also, see Cicero, *Inv.* 2.157 ff.; *Off.* 1.15 ff.; Diogenes Laertius, 7.92.

9. Stanley Morrow, *"Parresia* in the New Testament," *Catholic Biblical Quarterly* 44 (1982): 434.

10. See Abraham Malherbe, "'Not in a Corner': Early Christian Apologetic in Acts 26:26," *Second Century* 5 (1985): 197.

11. See Lentz, *Luke's Portrait,* 62.

12. On both expressions, see Helen North, *Sophrosyne: Self-Knowledge and Self-Restraint in Greek Literature* (Ithaca, N.Y.: Cornell University Press, 1966).

13. See Eckard Pluemacher, *Lukas als hellenistischer Schriftsteller: Studien zur Apostelgeschichte* (Göttingen, Germany: Vandenhoeck & Ruprecht, SUNT 9 1972), 16–18.

14. See Alan Mitchell, "The Social Function in Acts 2:44–47 and 4:32-37," *Journal of Biblical Literature* 111 (1992): 255–72.

15. See Gregory Sterling, "'Athletes of Virtue': An Analysis of the Summaries in Acts (2:41–47; 4:32–35; 5:12–16)," *Journal of Biblical Literature* 113 (1994): 679–96. Sterling (694) asserts: "The presence of these proverbs [having 'all things in common' and having 'one soul'] suggests that readers should think of the community in philosophical terms."

16. Ibid, 696.

17. See Charles Talbert, *Literary Patterns, Theological Themes, and the Genre of Luke–Acts* (Missoula, Mont.: Scholars, 1975), 89–98.

18. See Brawley, *Luke's Portrait,* 58–59.

19. See Acts 5:17; 15:5; 26:5; Steve Mason, "Chief Priests, Sadducees, Pharisees and Sanhedrin in Acts," in *The Book of Acts in its Palestinian Setting,* ed. Richard Bauckham (Grand Rapids, Mich.: Eerdmans, 1995), 133, 153.

20. See Stanley K. Stowers, *A Rereading of Romans: Justice, Jews, and Gentiles* (New Haven, Conn.: Yale University Press, 1994), 57; cf. Plato, *Republic* 430E–431A.

21. As Xenophon asserts, "Or what man who is the slave of his pleasures (*hedonais douleuon*) is not in an evil plight, body and soul alike.... Every man who is a slave to such pleasures (*douleuonta de tais toiautais hedonais*) should entreat the gods to give him good masters; thus, and only thus, may he find salvation" (*Memorabilia* 1.5.5).

22. A *topos* is a stock type of material frequently used to argue a point. See Burton Mack, *Rhetoric and the New Testament* (Minneapolis, Minn.: Fortress, 1990), 32.

23. As Epictetus asserts: "And it is our nature to subordinate pleasure (*hedinen*) to these duties [of being noble, self-respecting men] as their servant, their minister, so as to arouse our interest and keep us acting in accordance with nature" (*Diss.* 3.7.28). Also, note Plutarch's remark: "to rule pleasure (*hedonon*) by reason marks the wise man, and not every man can master his passion (*orges*)" ("The Education of Children," 7F).

24. Note the following apology for hedonism given by Aristippus: "I have Lois, not she me, and it is not abstinence from pleasures that is best, but mastery over them without ever being worsted." See Diogenes Laertius, 2.75. On the care with which one needs to assess philosophical responses to the passions, see Kallistos Ware, "The Way of the Ascetics: Negative or Affirmative?" in *Asceticism,* eds. Wimbush and Valantasis, 3–15; John M. Dillon, "Rejecting the

Body, Refining the Body: Some Remarks on the Development of Platonist Asceticism," in *Asceticism*, eds. Wimbush and Valantasis, 80–87.

25. This was especially the case for Seneca, whose essay, *De constantia sapientis,* portrays the *sapiens* (or "wise man") as one able to remain steadfast in the face of severities (1.1.658).

26. See Stowers, *Rereading,* 57.

27. On this theme, see Michel Foucault, *The Care of the Self, vol. 3: The History of Sexuality,* trans. Robert Hurley (New York: Pantheon, 1978), 46.

28. So, when a woman (e.g., Marcia in Seneca's *ad Marciam*) was praised for her stability and maturity in the tradition of consolatory material, she is so praised for "possessing the qualities which were defined in that society to be the natural prerogative solely of males." See Abraham Smith, *Comfort One Another: Reconstructing the Rhetoric and Audience of 1 Thessalonians* (Louisville, Ky.: Westminster/Knox, 1995), 103. As Satlow notes, a woman was deemed a sexual equal in the eyes of Musonius Rufus only when she "abandoned those traits that were gendered as feminine." See Michael L. Satlow, "'Try To Be a Man': The Rabbinic Construction of Masculinity," *Harvard Theological Review* 89 (1996): 21, n. 7.

29. See Margaret Nussbaum, "Therapeutic Arguments: Epicurus and Aristotle," in *The Norms of Nature* (Cambridge, England: Cambridge University Press, 1986), 31–74, esp. 36. On Hellenistic medical discoveries as the cause for the philosophical interest in the medical model, see Julia E. Annas, *Hellenistic Philosophy of Mind* (Berkeley: University of California Press, 1994), 20. On the use of the medical model by the Stoics, see Stowers, "On the Use and Abuse of Reason," in *Greeks, Jews and Romans: Essays in Honor of Abraham J. Malherbe,* eds. David Balch, Everett Ferguson, and Wayne A. Meeks (Minneapolis, Minn.: Fortress, 1990), 274.

30. See Stowers, "On the Use and Abuse of Reason," 275.

31. See Nussbaum, "Therapeutic Arguments," 33.

32. See Stowers, "On the Use and Abuse of Reason," 275.

33. See Nussbaum, "Therapeutic Arguments," 33.

34. See Catherine Edwards, *The Politics of Immorality in Ancient Rome* (Cambridge, England: Cambridge University Press, 1993), 25.

35. See Xenophon, *Memorabilia* 2.1.1–7; cf. Erwin R. Goodenough, "The Political Philosophy of Hellenistic Kingship," *Yale Classical Studies* 1 (1928): 95.

36. See Edwards, *Politics of Immorality,* 26.

37. On the rhetoric of invective, see Jacqueline Long, *Claudian's In Eutropium, or, How, When and Why to Slander a Eunuch* (Chapel Hill: University of North Carolina Press, 1996); also Phillip DeLacy, "Cicero's Invective Against Piso," *Transactions of the American Philosophical Association* 72 (1941): 49–58.

38. See Stowers, *Rereading,* 57.

39. For the references, see Satlow, "'Try To Be a Man,'" 22–26.

40. See Stowers, *Rereading,* 58.

41. On the Jewish dietary regulations, see Baruch Bokser, *Philo's Description of Jewish Practices* (Berkeley, Calif.: CHS/HMC, Protocol of the Thirtieth Colloquy, 1977).

42. On the Jews' presentation of themselves as morally superior because of their "proper" sexual relations, see S. C. Barton and G. H. R. Horsley, "A Hellenistic

Cult and Group and the New Testament Churches," *Jahrbuch Für Autike und Christentum* 24 (1981): 40. On the Jews' cultic purity, see Philo, *Spec. Leg.* II.145–8; 1QSa, col. 2.

43. See, for example, Philo, *Spec. Leg.* II.145–8.

44. Purity was also a concern for other groups, for, as Stowers (*Rereading*, 94) has noted, many subcultures of the Greco-Roman world represented others "as less pure and less self-controlled than themselves."

45. See Stowers, *Rereading*, 59.

46. Ibid. See Philo, *Spec. Leg.* 4.55; cf. Josephus, *Apion* 2.168–171; 2.221–235.

47. See Lentz, *Luke's Portrait*, 84.

48. Not only did Menander Rhetor and Theon recommend it, but it was considered basic to the *progymnasmata,* or the elementary exercises for student composition.

49. See William Batstone, "The Antithesis of Virtue: Sallust's *Synkrisis* and the Crisis of the Late Republic," *Classical Antiquity* 7 (1988): 3.

50. See Ann Francis De Vito, "Characterization in Greek Tragedy" (Ph.D. diss., University of Toronto, 1988), 202.

51. See John Darr, *On Character Building: The Reader and the Rhetoric of Characterization in Luke–Acts* (Louisville, Ky.: Westminster/Knox, 1990), 58.

52. See Mary Ann Tolbert, "The Gospel in Greco-Roman Culture," in *The Book and the Text: The Bible and Literary Theory,* ed. Regina Schwartz (Cambridge, Mass.: Blackwell, 1990), 266.

53. From virtually the very beginning of Paul's performance on the narrative stage, the narrator of Acts describes the preconversion Saul as one "ravaging the church" (Acts 8:3) and dragging off people (Acts 8:3). Moreover, the narrator speaks of Saul as one who breathes threats and murder (Acts 9:1). Ananias evidently fears him so much that he gives the Lord a "reality check" in his vision: "You know I have heard from many about this man" (Acts 9:13). And the fear and disbelief of other Christians shows that Ananias was not entertaining a private phobia (Acts 9:26).

54. In Euripides' drama *Bacchae,* for example, it means *hybris.* For the citation and the illustration from Euripides, see Lentz, *Luke's Portrait,* 84.

55. Lentz (*Luke's Portrait*) understands Paul's defense before Festus and King Agrippa II in light of the contrast Paul draws between his former and present life.

56. The introduction is a plot synopsis, roughly depicting the geographical areas (Jerusalem, Judea and Samaria, and the ends of the earth) into which Jesus' mediating authorities (the apostles and disciples) will go to herald the divine patron's good news of universal accessibility. It should be obvious now that the geographical markers do not represent "realistic" spatial demarcations in the modern sense. What is basic to the schema is the symbolic grouping into three distinct areas—one, the center of Jewish power; a second, the area in and around Judea and Samaria; and finally, the ends of the earth, that is, as far as human beings can reach.

57. For the term "cosmic power-brokers," I am indebted to Doug Edwards. In the first century CE, according to Randall Clark Webber, both oratorical ability and miraculous power were deemed to be confirmations of one's prestige. See Randall Clark Webber, "An Analysis of Power in the Jerusalem Church in Acts," (Ph.D. diss., Southern Baptist Theological Seminary, 1989), 173, 185, 206.

58. I partially agree with the observation of John Polhill ("The Hellenist Breakthrough: Acts 6–12," *Review and Expositor* 71 (1974), 475–86) that the first five chapters of Acts present "a picture of a Christian community in Jerusalem which is closely bound to Judaism." I differ only in positing an even larger unit (1:12–8:1a), as Stephen's speech is still given in Jerusalem. Of course, it should be clear that Stephen's speech sets the stage for movement beyond Jerusalem; cf. Richard Pervo, *Luke's Story of Paul* (Minneapolis, Minn.: Fortress, 1990), 29.

    In my estimation, Acts 1:12–8:1a is divided into three large parallel units (1:12–4:31; 4:32-5:42; 6:1–8:1a), each with two distinctive subunits recounting the validation of the witnesses' brokering authority, even in the face of increasing conflict. Each unit begins, thus, with the resolution of an internal brokerage problem (1:12–26; 4:32–5:11; 6:1–7), a resolution portraying the witnesses as fostering a virtually idyllic political community; and each unit concludes by illustrating the beneficent deity's vindication of the community's leaders, past and present (2:1–4:31; 5:12–42; 6:8–8:1a), despite the escalation of conflict to near-violent or violent ends.

    The parallels between the first and second units extend even further, for in both units scenes of the deity's benefactions (2:1–3:26; 5:12–16), along with episodes of arrest(s) and imprisonment (4:1–4; 5:17–26), precede a lengthy sequence of trial episodes (including the witnesses' defense, the Council's deliberation, and the release-vindication of the witnesses, 4:5–31; 5:27–42). Of course, the third unit also includes arrest and trial episodes, but here there is no private Council deliberation, for the people, before whom the Council always guards its image, are finally stirred up against one of the protagonists, namely, Stephen (6:12). For more on the similarities among the three units, see Pervo, *Luke's Story of Paul*, 18–23.

59. On the shift in power and the "waning role" of the Twelve, I am indebted to Robert W. Wall, "Successors to 'the Twelve' according to Acts 12:1-17," *Catholic Biblical Quarterly* 53 (1991): 628–43; cf. also Pervo, *Luke's Story of Paul*, 44–45.

60. See F. W. Danker, *Benefactor: Epigraphic Study of a Greco-Roman and New Testament Semantic Field* (St. Louis, Mo.: Clayton, 1982); Halvor Moxnes, "Patron–Client Relations and the New Community in Luke–Acts," in *The Social World of Luke–Acts: Models for Interpretation,* ed. Jerome Neyrey (Peabody, Mass.: Hendrickson, 1991), 244.

61. On Luke's dependence on the LXX for character scripts (especially, the suffering-prophet typologies mediated through Isaiah), see Prescott Williams, "The Poems about Incomparable Yahweh's Servant in Isaiah 40–55," *Southwestern Journal of Theology* 11 (1968): 73–87; James Sanders, "Isaiah in Luke," *Interpretation* 36 (1982): 144–55.

62. On paradox as a theme throughout the Gospel of Luke and in Acts, see Robert Tannehill, "Attitudinal Shifts in Synoptic Pronouncement Stories" in *Orientation by Disorientation: Studies in Literary Criticism and Biblical Literary Criticism,* ed. Richard A. Spenser (Pittsburgh, Pa.: Pickwick, 1980), pp. 183, 197; Carol Joan Schers Lahurd, "The Author's Call to the Audience in the Acts

of the Apostles: A Literary-Critical-Anthropological Reading" (Ph.D. diss., University of Pittsburgh, 1987), 127.

63. Cf. Douglas Edwards, "Acts of the Apostles and the Graeco-Roman World: Narrative Communication in Social Context," in *1989 Annual SBL Seminar Papers*, ed. David Lull (Atlanta, Ga.: Scholars, 1989), 371, 372. Obviously, the most impressive setting is Rome. Rome, however, is not the end of the earth. With Paul and the gospel in Rome, however, one can say that the gospel has a fair chance to get to the end of the earth.

64. Note that the Council is drawn as morally surreptitious, for its "private" deliberations during the earlier trials stand in contradistinction to the "openness" of the protagonists (Acts 4:10). James Allen Walworth ("The Narrator of Acts" [Ph.D. diss., Southern Baptist Theological Seminary, 1984], 138, 139) has noted the general tendency of the narrator in Acts to "construct the narrative such that the characters he favors are always performing public acts, while the disfavored characters are presented in private and clandestine activity." Walworth goes on to note: "The narrator often pairs these two contrasting modes of characterization in close proximity so the readers will not miss the contrast" ("Narrator of Acts," 139).

Furthermore, the Council officials constantly worry about their image before the people (4:22; 4:26). The Council's apprehension about its image before the people leads the Council, therefore, to maintain two different impressions of itself—one of nonviolence before the people (4:26) and one of mounting fury inside its closed Council chambers (5:33, 40). Worse than that, however, the Council, twice desiring to assure itself of *totally* concealed deliberations, orders the witnesses out of their chambers (4:15; 5:34).

65. My goal has not been to show how Stephen acquired self-mastery, nor does the text of Acts seem so inclined. For the text to show the process of gaining self-mastery, Stephen's time on the narrative stage would need to be longer and more of the technical terms would be used to describe the process. The text of Acts does reveal Stephen, however, to be one who *already* has achieved self-mastery in his readiness for martyrdom. On self-mastery as a "preparation for death," see Lentz, *Luke's Portrait,* 76; cf. Clement, *Stromateis* IV.8.58.2–4.

66. See Kilgallen, "Function of Stephen's Speech," 174–76; Walworth, "Narrator of Acts," 134; Luke Timothy Johnson, *The Literary Function of Possessions in Luke–Acts* (Missoula, Mont.: Scholars, 1977), 52.

67. See Lentz, *Luke's Portrait,* 76; cf. *Wis* 8:7; Xenophon, *Memorabilia* 3.9.4f.

68. See Douglas Edwards, "Acts of the Apostles and Chariton's *Chaereas and Callirhoe*: A Literary and Sociohistorical Study" (Ph.D. diss., Boston University, 1987), 171–72.

69. See Pervo, *Luke's Story of Paul,* 30.

70. See Robert Tannehill, *The Narrative Unity of Luke–Acts: Vol. 2. The Acts of the Apostles* (Minneapolis, Minn.: Fortress, 1990), 84.

71. For a different but supportive catalogue of irony in the closing scenes of Luke's gospel, see John Paul Heil, "Reader-Response and the Irony of Jesus before the Sanhedrin in Luke 22:66–71," *Catholic Biblical Quarterly* 51 (1989): 271–81. Jesus' words about his death, of course, are based on a keen insight about God's

will as revealed in Scripture. As he asserts later to his disciples: "Thus it is written that the Messiah is to suffer and to rise from the dead on the third day" (Luke 24:46).

72. Stephen's powerful words, moreover, are themselves a fulfillment of Jesus' prophetic words: "I will give you words and a wisdom that none of your opponents will be able to withstand or contradict" (Luke 21:15; cf. Acts 6:3, 10). The following prophecy is fulfilled as well: "When they bring you before the synagogues and the rulers and the authorities, do not worry about how you are to defend yourselves or what you are to say; for the Holy Spirit will teach you at that very hour what you ought to say" (Luke 12:12; cf. Acts 6:3).

73. Obviously, there are also other narrative motivations for the story about Stephen. As Balch has noted, "The Stephen story is both the climax of the persecution in Jerusalem and the transition point for it to move outward from Jerusalem in mission." See David Balch, "The Genre of Luke–Acts: Individual Biography, Adventure Novel, or Political History," *Southwestern Journal of Theology* 33 (1990): 12.

74. On the possibility that some of the authorial audience were already Christians while others were only potentially so, see John Darr, "'Watch How You Listen' (Luke 8:18)," in *The New Literary Criticism and the New Testament*, eds. Edgar V. McKnight and Elizabeth Struthers (Valley Forge, Pa.: Trinity Press International, 1994), 91.

75. See Malherbe, "'Not in a Corner,'" 196.

76. On the shift from "compensatory scholarship" to the entire spectrum of Greco-Roman gender assumptions, see Marilyn B. Skinner, "Ego Mulier: The Construction of Male Sexuality in Catullus," *Helios* 20 (1993): 107.

77. See Skinner, "Ego Mulier," 107.

78. Ibid, 111.

79. See Christine Downing, *Myths and Mysteries of Same-Sex Love* (New York: Continuum, 1989), pp. 134–36; David Halperin, *One Hundred Years of Homosexuality and Other Essays on Greek Love* (New York: Routledge, 1990), 29.

80. See Stowers, *Rereading*, 45.

81. See Lennard J. Davis, *Ideology and Fiction: Resisting Novels* (New York: Methuen, 1987), 15.

6

Children of the Resurrection: Perspectives on Angelic Asceticism in Luke–Acts

Turid Karlsen Seim

Among ascetics in the early Syrian church, Luke's gospel was favored for its encouragement of their choice of life.[1] Their appreciation was particularly due to the fact that this gospel took a critical stance on marriage and also attested that the unmarried children of God are "*isangelloi,*" like angels, and thus share in the "*angelikos bios.*"[2]

The anti-Marcionite prologue to the Gospel of Luke assumes a similar position in terms of the biographical notice that Luke "*agynaios, ateknos...ekoimethe.*"[3] The historical accuracy of this rather late piece of information remains an open issue. But it captures the ascetic inclination of the profile of Luke better than many modern commentators who, rather, commend Luke for his apologetic ability in establishing the Christian movement in the Roman world and in replacing eschatological excitement with paraenetical reasoning and philosophical patterns, convinced that the end no longer is near.

From one possible perspective, Luke's writings represent a unique merger of synoptic traditions about Jesus[4] and a fascination with Paul and his mission. With regard to the obvious ambivalence of the Pauline tradition concerning asceticism, Luke supports and intensifies Paul's ascetic preference in ways that are opposed to the domestic accommodations of the Pastoral letters.[5] In Luke's portrayal and advocacy of Paul, the latter becomes not the defender of conventional household ideals, and his preaching is once summarized by the phrase, "*peri dikaiosynes kai enkrateias kai tou krimatos tou mellontos*" (Acts 24:25).[6] This is later echoed in the Acts of Paul and Thecla, where the main topic of the apostolic preaching is *enkrateia.*[7]

Correspondingly, the common synoptic ethos of voluntary dispossession and of spiritual discipline is, in Luke, intensified by an ascetic emphasis. This emphasis exceeds the accommodation of the philosophical ideal of a disciplined pursuit (*askesis*) of certain acclaimed virtues to achieve well-being. It helps explain why some controversial virtues figure more prominently in Luke–Acts and how well-being here is qualified.

My interpretation of Luke–Acts assumes the understanding that asceticism in early Christianity, whatever else its *enkrateia* and discipline might imply, was marked by chastity or celibacy. John of Ephesus, for example, may have confronted ascetic dualism and withdrawal into the wilderness, he may have insisted on remaining involved in human affairs, he may have defined asceticism as utter devotion to God and to God's commandments alone, but he quite simply took for granted that the ascetic was a celibate.

It is, of course, possible to reactivate the wider and more general meaning of the Greek term "*askesis*" and thus to embrace as "asceticism" any and all disciplined, goal-oriented behavior or crafting of the social self or instrumental practice in the service of social formation or cultural engineering. Formal and abstract definitions like these run the risk, however, of becoming all-embracing and thereby stating only the obvious wisdom that a certain command of oneself and a certain measure of self-denial is an element in everything we undertake as socialized human beings. Such a statement would certainly accommodate most early Christian discourse and therefore needs further substantiation, not least to clarify the various and even conflicting positions with regard to ascetic practices in the different early Christian communities.

Luke's ascetic profile has sexual renunciation as a prominent feature, and this reflects the radical requirements of discipleship in the Jesus tradition and the eschatological impetus that is evident also in Paul's preference for an unmarried life. This is not to exclude the intriguing insights of other contributions in this volume that trace the possible patterns of a more philosophically determined discipline (*askesis*) in Luke–Acts.[8] The well-informed author of Luke–Acts undeniably explicates and defends the Christian movement by presenting it as a justifiable and good philosophy.[9]

Since the popular philosophy of Hellenistic and Roman times, even among some elite Jews, was coined in a Stoic mold, it is certainly worthwhile to explore whether or not Luke reflects an understanding of moral excellence as self-mastery or the control of passions to overcome the temptations of excessive pleasure and the enslavement to desire that such passion induces. This philosophical ideal was one of temperance and moderation or self-control by *apatheia*. It did not demand total abstinence, and by its very nature it does not invite the extreme.

Luke makes both Jesus and the protagonists of the apostolic period meet such philosophical ideals; they are prototypes of self-control, not giving in to

emotion and desire, even in times of trial, hardship, and excruciating circumstances. Luke's temperate heroes are successful in their various *agones* as
they remain in control of themselves, in contrast to the passionate expressions of their opponents.[10]

There is, however, a remarkable absence in Luke of the common philosophical terms for such asceticism. The ascetic "coinage" is missing. This is
all the more remarkable when one compares Luke–Acts with the writings of
Philo and also 4 Maccabees, which are crowded with such philosophical
terms as they attempt to express and to promote a Jewish position in the language of Hellenistic philosophy. In Luke, the one occurrence of the otherwise rather common and generally applicable word "askein" (Acts 24:16) is
hardly enough to make the case. The adoption by Luke of such a pattern can
therefore only be discerned indirectly in terms of undergirding paradigms
and, as mentioned earlier, in the literary characterization of the main figures.

Passion or desire (*pathos*) is not a category whereby Luke would name
what is wrong or evil in the world. Evil, rather, is named in mythological
terms, so that only by the intervening action of Jesus, his healing touch, can
the selves of those in bondage be released from sin or enslavement to the
power of Satan and the demons. This is a different worldview from the preceding philosophical one, marked as it is by a primary cosmological dualism
rather than the indicated anthropological tension.

Such a worldview registers a relocation of the role of *askesis*, specifically,
the Stoic paradigm.[11] Well-being in Luke–Acts is not achieved by *askesis* per
se, but by divine intervention. Personal discipline does not help one achieve
salvation, but is a matter of ongoing self-care or self-maintenance. By means
of daily exertion, the repentant sinner may counter the many threats to perseverance. The list of such disciplines is a fairly traditional one: prayer, alertness, and breaking the grip of desire for possessions, family, and even life
itself.

However, does this disciplinary practice have a purpose beyond persistent steadfastness? What are the anthropological implications of Luke's
mythological-cosmological outlook? Perseverance is different from obstinate
persistence because it ultimately makes sense only when it leads somewhere.
Perseverance is in itself not a sufficient reason to persevere, even if survival
might be. But, then, survival is the goal, and in Luke ultimate survival is
achieved by giving up one's present life in order to gain life immortal. Thus,
in the case of Stephen's "stoic" death, he sees finally the heavens opened and
beholds the glory of God (Acts 7:54ff.).

The ultimate purpose of asceticism in Luke–Acts, therefore, reflects an
eschatological dimension that is lacking in the philosophical discussions.
Many of the same ascetic practices may be observed, but their purpose and
thereby their motivation would still be different. This means, furthermore,
that asceticism in Luke–Acts cannot be reduced to a disciplined, intentional,

goal-oriented human behavior. The ascetic ethos of abandonment rather represents the way in which the goal itself may be proleptically reflected and realized. The ascetics express a chronic liminality,[12] already embodying what the kingdom of God requires; they are "the children[13] of the resurrection."

From this perspective, some ascetic features, more than others, represent specific signs of the heavenly life, that is, immortality. As part of a longer discourse in Luke 17:20–37, for example, Jesus admonishes the disciples about the concerns or lack of concerns demanded in the "days of the Son of Man."[14] The instruction is undergirded by examples from history illuminating significant aspects of the future day of judgment: It will happen suddenly and violently, and many may not be prepared.

Before their destruction, the people of Noah's generation were eating and drinking, marrying and being given in marriage, until the very day when Noah entered the ark and the flood came and all was destroyed. Despite the efforts of many interpreters to read the text differently,[15] the conduct of Noah's generation described in this passage is, in fact, not marked by any excessive concern for bodily needs; it is not characterized as wicked or lecherous (even though that was a well-known theme); heedlessness is not an issue, even though the example conveys an implicit call to alertness and preparedness.[16]

The question still remains as to what these particular examples in Luke 17:20–37 communicate not only about the need to be constantly alert, but also about how one can be prepared. What did the people of Noah's generation do wrong? They were engaged in normal, everyday activities, in seemingly irreproachable deeds that aim at preserving life and securing the future. If this is subject to judgment, the implication must be that the usual strategy for survival is inadequate as eschatological readiness.

In the following paraenesis (Luke 17:33), Luke has included a special variant of the logion about winning life by renouncing it. There is here no concern for future generations, for the survival of the species, for upholding this world. Human beings can ultimately not secure their life; only those who lose it will keep it.

In certain Jewish texts, some ideas about prelapsarian human existence were developed. According to *Vita Adam et Evae* 4, for example, eating, drinking, and procreating belong to the "animal" side of human beings. In their prelapsarian existence, Adam and Eve did not have such physical needs. These arose after the fall. Sexuality or marriage and procreation were not part of the original divine plan, but are secondary circumstances and a reminder of the fall and loss of original, angelic perfection and integrity.[17]

This can also be expressed in the categories of life and death; the body Adam received at creation was a living body, and he was able to live from "the food of angels" or nothing at all. After the fall, Adam and Eve are dead, or perhaps mortal, and the body of death needs earthly food and drink; it also procreates in order to overcome its mortality.

Anthropologically, this tension between the prelapsarian potential and the postlapsarian reality means that the human person lives with both predispositions and can choose either to be controlled by bodily needs or seek to overcome them. The latter choice enables one to realize one's likeness with the image of God. This likeness is often transcribed through the mediating concept of similarity to the angels. Thus, the first virgin creatures in Paradise before sin were characterized by such a similarity.[18] This original state means that the human person possesses the potential for angelic life and that certain epistemological and moral qualities reveal this, such as the ability to remain upright, to speak in language, and to reason, as well as to observe the Law.[19] It is a short step from here to an ascetic program meant to control one's "animal" nature, through which death demands that certain physical needs be met, and to foster those qualities reflecting a "*bios angelikos.*"[20]

In the eschatological discourse of Luke 17, such ideas are merely echoed in the disparagement of seemingly necessary lifesaving activities. But another passage explicitly introduces the term "*isangelos.*" In the Lukan version of Jesus' dispute with the Sadducees about the resurrection (Luke 20:27–40), Jesus' answer is made into a treatise on the ethos of the resurrection and immortality.[21] The treatise exhibits an almost pleonastic compilation of terms, indicating that Jewish concepts are here being interpreted in Hellenistic terms.[22] Resurrection has been recast as immortality.

In all the synoptic versions of this dispute, the different nature of the resurrected life is emphasized. After the resurrection, marriage is irrelevant; it has no further role to play when all have become like the angels. In Mark and Matthew, this is spelled out in temporal categories as a dichotomy between the present world and the afterlife. In Luke, however, temporal categories are not totally abandoned, but the antithetic layout transposes the contrast between the present time and the future to an already existing distinction between those who belong to this age or world and those who are considered worthy of a place in the other age and the resurrection from the dead.[23] Whether or not one now enters into marriage reveals to which group one belongs. Like Noah's generation, which perished in the flood, it is characteristic of the "sons (both women and men) of this world" that they marry or submit to marriage. A certain ascetic discipline is used to characterize the group in opposition to these "others."

Over against the Sadducean position that a man should *anistanai sperma* and gain immortality by posterity,[24] Jesus in Luke holds that marriage (and procreation)[25] is no longer necessary in order to survive death; instead, there is resurrection and immortality. It is possible that a verse like Luke 9:27 has been retained by Luke not as an outdated statement about the early parousia but in order to claim the immortality of those who are worthy to reach the world to come and the resurrection from the dead. Even if they die, they do not perish (cf. Acts 13:37). Being the children/sons of the resurrection, they are sons of God and are like the angels. Their likeness to the angels is manifest in the fact that they cannot "really" die.

This likeness to the angels is often described or visualized through the concept of the radiant glory, *doxa*, that is distinctive of the heavenly life and sphere. The risen ones are transfigured by light; they shine brightly.[26] So Stephen's face is like the face of an angel (Acts 6:15), and when he "falls asleep," the heavens open to receive his spirit. He both beholds and reflects the glorious quality of the heavenly life. In this story, a spatial framework or cosmology rather than the temporal one of history is predominant.[27]

Immortality therefore takes priority over asexuality,[28] but they are as intimately connected as are marriage and death. Death necessitates marriage.[29] It is therefore characteristic only for the present age/world and a mark of those who belong to this age/world. Only the lack of immortality makes marriage and procreation a security measure for the future. When the promise of immortality abolishes the need for this measure, marriage may be abandoned and procreation with it.

A more sinister version of the same idea, mirroring the judgmental orientation of Luke 17, may be found in Jesus' words to the daughters of Jerusalem in Luke 23:27–30.[30] In the coming days of tribulation, women with children will praise as blessed those who never gave birth.

This is an extreme expression of hardship, but even so it reflects the same criteria of how one may be prepared for "the days of the Son of Man," as we have seen earlier. Furthermore, it is a negative version of what is elsewhere stated in positive terms, when motherhood is transferred from the biological function to a fictive role of discipleship (Luke 8:19–21; 11:27ff.). Luke's portrayal of the virgin mother, Mary, and of her role as an ideal disciple also gains new significance in light of this transfer.[31]

Matthew may liken the feast of the kingdom to a wedding, but in the Lukan version matrimony prevents attendance at the great banquet (Luke 14:20). In the following list of the costs of discipleship (Luke 14:25–27; cf. also 18:28), Luke is less interested in property such as fields and cattle. The focus is on the required abandonment of family relations. The explicit inclusion of "wife" in these lists makes it clear that Luke does not necessarily share Mark's and Matthew's concern about the inviolability of cohabitation in marriage. There is in the Gospel of Luke no parallel to the positive instruction about marriage and the rejection of divorce in Mark 10:1–12 (cf. Matt. 19:1–12), and even though the well-attested logion about divorce and remarriage is included in Luke 16:18 from Q, it represents a puzzle in that context. The thrust of the saying is to discourage remarriage rather than forbid divorce.[32]

The transformation of temporal categories into categories whereby a distinction is revealed between two different groups could be subsumed under Luke's alleged tendency to weaken the eschatological expectation and to compensate for this with a paraenetical interest and investment. To some extent, this is the case. Attention is transferred from the future to the present, and in the present the marks of the resurrection are effectively discerned even before the telos comes. The time and the hour of the eschaton, whether it be early or late, does not really matter from this perspective; what matters is to be prepared through assimilation to the life of the resurrection. Thereby eschatological expectation and ascetic zeal are made to nurture one another constantly.[33] The proleptic realization of the angelic life is both a condition and an effect of eschatological salvation.

The criticism of marriage in Luke is not due to the pragmatism of practical considerations; it is not because the demands of marriage are burdensome and render concentration diffuse. The emphasis on sexual renunciation and celibacy marks an asceticism that is eschatological in its orientation and constitutes its core characteristic. As other articles in this volume demonstrate, Luke is an early representative of the Christian adaptation of philosophical ideals of self-control and temperance, and he may well wish to advocate a Christian discipline that accommodates traditional philosophical models, methods, and ideals. But Luke combines this interest with ideas common to Hellenistic Judaism about the angelic life in paradise, which may be rehearsed ascetically. Thus, an asceticism marked by sexual renunciation "embodies both the purity of prelapsarian creation and the immortality of angelic life; it brings the paradise lost and the paradise to come into the present."[34] The promise of resurrection delivers immortality such that the life-securing measures made necessary by the threat of death no longer are relevant and, indeed, distract and mislead and are therefore subject to judgment.

Such an eschatological orientation has its correlate in protological reflection, and both dimensions hermeneutically converge and constitute asceticism's utopian impulses. An ascetic life expresses the meaning of human existence doubly defined by its mythological origin and its eschatological culmination, the *telos* invoking the *arche*[35] and thus providing a means whereby the contingency of human reality that occupies the space in between may be overcome. As a rehearsal of the heavenly life or the life to come, asceticism enables the human person to function within the world as re-envisioned or re-created,[36] that is, a world where death no longer prevails. In the case of Luke, this means that asceticism becomes a way of life whereby eschatological excitement is both suspended and maintained.

NOTES

1. Cf. S. Brock, "Early Syrian Asceticism," *Numen* 20 (1973): 5–6; T. H. C. van Eijk, "Marriage and Virginity, Death and Immortality," in *Epektasis: Melanges patristiques offerts au Cardinal Jean Danielou,* ed. Jacques Fontaine and Charles Kannengiesser (Paris: Beauchesne, 1972), 212.

2. For the significance and development of this idea in early Christian asceticism, cf. K. S. Frank, *Angelikos Bios: Begriffsanalytische und Begriffsgeschichtliche Untersuchung zum "Engelgleichen Leben" im frühen Mönchtum* (Münster, Germany: Aschendorff, 1994); R. Lane Fox, *Pagans and Christians in the Mediterranean World from the Second Century A.D. to the Conversion of Constantine* (London: Viking, 1986), 336–74.

3. A text-critical version of the full Greek text may be found in *Die antimarkioni-tischen Evangelienprologe,* ed. J. Regul (Freiburg, Germany: Herder, Vetus Latinale, 1969), 16. This is the only prologue in Greek. DeBruyne and Harnack both suggested an earlier date, which Regul refutes by dating the prologue to the mid–fourth century CE.

4. This more open expression is used, since the specific question of exactly which sources these are does not need to be resolved here.

5. On the discussion about the relationship between Luke and the Pastoral Letters, cf. J. D. Quinn, "The Last Volume of Luke: The Relation of Luke–Acts to the Pastoral Epistles," in *Perspectives on Luke–Acts,* ed. C. H. Talbert (Danville, Va.: Association of Baptist Professors of Religion, 1978), 62–75; S. G. Wilson, *Luke and the Pastoral Epistles* (London: SPCK, 1979). Their suggestion of shared authorship is highly unlikely.

6. Most interpreters attach little importance to the content of this summary and discard it as a contextually polemical variant, well designed to infuriate Felix, who had offended moral standards by taking Drusilla as his wife; cf. the commentaries by Conzelmann, Haenchen, and Schneider, *ad locum.*

7. On this, cf. D. R. MacDonald, *The Legend and the Apostle: The Battle for Paul in Story and Canon* (Philadelphia: Westminster, 1983), who explores whether the oral traditions on which the Apocryphal Acts are based might reflect the circles critically addressed by the Pastoral Letters; cf. also V. Burrus, *Chastity as Autonomy: Women in the Stories of the Apocryphal Acts* (Lewiston, N.Y.: Mellen, Studies in Women and Religion 23, 1987).

8. See the chapters by Susan Garrett (this volume, 71–95) and Abraham Smith (this volume, 97–114).

9. Cf. A. J. Malherbe, "Not in a Corner: Early Christian Apologetics in Acts 26.26," *Second Century* 5 (1986): 193–210; W. A. Meeks, *The First Urban Christians: The Social World of the Apostle Paul* (New Haven, Conn.: Yale University Press, 1983), 28; S. K. Stowers, "Social Status, Public Speaking and Private Teaching: The Circumstances of Paul's Preaching Activity," *Novum Testamentum* 26 (1984): 61.

10. Cf. esp. Smith (this volume, 97–114), who makes a good case for Stephen in Acts 6–7.

11. Cf. Garrett (this volume, 71–95).

12. Cf. E. A. Clark, *Jerome, Chrysostom and Friends: Essays and Translations* (New York/Toronto: Mellen, Studies in Women and Religion 1, 1979), 49–50, who applies Victor Turner's concept of liminality to understand the Christian ascetics of the third century CE.

13. The term *huioi* is not necessarily inclusive of women, but women still feature prominently in Luke's ascetic vision; cf. T. K. Seim, *The Double Message: Patterns of Gender in Luke–Acts* (Nashville, Tenn.: Abingdon, 1994), 185–248.

14. The speech is a redactional combination of various sources, with substantial Q-material. In Luke's redaction, the remark about Lot's wife in Luke 17:32 plays a key role; cf. R. Geiger, *Die lukanischen Endzeitreden: Studien zur Eschatologie des Lukas-Evangeliums* (Bern/Frankfurt a.M.: Publisher, 1973) 118ff., 142–49.

15. See J. A. Fitzmyer, *The Gospel according to Luke I–II*, The Anchor Bible 28/28a (New York: Doubleday, 1981–1985), 1170; F. W. Horn, *Glaube und Handeln in der Theologie des Lukas* (Göttingen, Germany: Vandenhoeck & Ruprecht, Göttinger theologische Arbeiten 26, 1983), 201; Q. Quesnell, "Made Themselves Eunuchs for the Kingdom of Heaven (Mt 19.12)," *Catholic Biblical Quarterly* 30 (1968): 345; K. H. Schelkle, "Ehe und Ehelosigkeit im Neuen Testament," in *Beiträge zur Auslegung und Auslegungsgeschichte des Neuen Testaments* (Düsseldorf, Germany: 1966), 189. Especially for Horn and Schelkle, it is important to rescue "die bürgerlichen Lebensformen an sich" as acceptable and good.

16. Geiger, *Lukanischen Endzeitreden*, 95, holds this to be a remarkable difference vis-à-vis other Jewish parallels which emphasize the necessity of God's judgment on human sinfulness. J. T. Carroll, *Response to the End of History: Eschatology and Situation in Luke–Acts* (Atlanta, Ga.: Scholars, SBLDS 92, 1988), 90ff., regards this as an implicit instruction that also what is not directly evil may be judged. Both Geiger's and Carroll's interpretation of Luke here make the Lukan position match Paul's concern in 1 Cor. 7:32–43. However, the Pauline key word *merimnao* is absent in Luke 17, which means that Luke does not seem to identify the problem in the same way as a matter of divided attention.

17. L. Troje, *ADAM und ZOE: Eine Szene der altchristlichen Kunst in ihrem religionsgeschichtlichen Zusammenhänge* (Sitzungsberichte der Heidelberger Akademie der Wisssenschafter, Philosophisch-historisch Klasse 17; Heidelberg, Germany: C. Winter, 1916), 31ff. This has been further explored by G. Sfameni Gasparro in a series of publications, mainly in Italian, but cf. "Asceticism and Anthropology: Enkrateia and 'Double Creation' in Early Christianity," in *Asceticism*, eds. Vincent L. Wimbush and Richard Valantasis (New York: Oxford University Press, 1995), 127–46. With regard to the impact of the same on patristic writers such as Tatian, Julius Cassianus, and Origen, cf. idem, "Image of God and Sexual Differentiation in the Tradition of Enkrateia: Protological Motivations," in *Image of God and Gender Models in Judaeo-Christian Tradition*, ed. Kari E. Börresen (Oslo, Norway: Solum, 1991), 38–171; cf. also E. Pagels, *Adam, Eve and the Serpent* (New York: Random House, 1988), 12ff.

18. See Sfameni Gasparro, "Asceticism and Anthropology," 135; cf. also J. Jervell, *Imago Dei: Gen. 1.26f im Spätjudentum, in der Gnosis und in den paulinischen Briefen* (Göttingen, Germany: Vandenhoeck & Ruprecht, Forschungen zur Religion und Literatur des Alten und Neuen Testaments 79, 1960), 86–89.

19. Jervell, *Imago Dei*, 40ff.

20. G. Stemberger, *Der Leib der Auferstehung: Studien zur Anthropologie und Eschatologie des palästinensischen Judentums im neutestamentlichen Zeitalter (ca. 170 v. Chr.-100 .n. Chr.)* (Rome: Biblical Institute, Analecta biblica 56, 1970), 116; Troje, *ADAM und ZOE*, 32.

21. O. Schwankl, *Die Sadduzäerfrage (Mk 12,18–27 parr): Eine exegetisch-theologische Studie zur Auferstehungserwartung* (Bonner biblische Beiträge 66, Frankfurt

am Main, Germany: Arhenaum, 1987), pp. 448, 464. The differences are such that T. Schramm, *Der Markus-Stoff bei Lukas: Eine literarkritische und redaktionsgeschichtliche Untersuchung* (Cambridge, England: Cambridge University Press, Studiorum Nori Testamenti Societas Monograph Series 14, 1971), 170ff., argues that the Lukan version is based on a tradition different from Mark.

22. For Schwankl, *Sadduzäerfrage*, 451, this is primarily a pedagogical strategy of little consequence for content.

23. Most interpreters prefer to minimalize the implications of the comprehensive changes in the Lukan version and read Luke as a slightly hellenized commentary on Mark. My reading is supported by van Eijk, "Marriage," and Gasparro, "Asceticism and Anthropology," 134ff. Cf. also P. Nagel, *Motivierung der Askese in der alten Kirche und der Ursprung des Mönchtums* (Akademie, Texte und Untersuchungen zur Geschichte der altchristlichen Literatur 95, Berlin, Germany: 1966), 35ff. It is noteworthy that all three of these scholars are concerned with the immediate *Wirkungsgeschichte* of the Lukan text, suggesting that this interpretation offered itself early on.

24. See van Eijk, "Marriage," 21ff. The use of the reference to Gen. 38:8 plays on resurrection terminology.

25. Procreation is implied as the very purpose of marriage. Codex D and some Latin and Syrian translations that add "*gennontai kai gennosin*" make this explicit.

26. Cf. Stemberger, *Leib der Auferstehung*, 89.

27. While our sources operate with both temporal and spatial categories, modern interpreters tend to speak more exclusively in temporal/historical terms, which are felt to be less problematic for a modern worldview and are sometimes defended as a Hebrew versus Greek perspective. Even though this position has been seriously modified, it still colors the exegetical language.

28. B. Witherington III, *Women in the Ministry of Jesus: A Sudy of Jesus' Attitudes to Women and Their Roles as Reflected in His Earthly Life* (Studiorum Nori Testamenti Societas Monograph Series 51, New York: Cambridge University Press, 1984), 34ff., takes this to deny that asexuality is an issue at all in the passage. In Witherington's opinion, Luke assumes that all existing marriages will continue into eternity.

29. See van Eijk, "Marriage," 215; cf. also B. Lang, "No Sex in Heaven: The Logic of Procreation, Death and Eternal Life in Judaeo-Christian Tradition," *Alten Orient und altes Testament* 215 (1985): 237–53.

30. M. L. Soards, *The Passion according to Luke: The Special Material of Luke 22* (Journal for the Study of the New Testament Sup. 14, Sheffield, England: Journal for the Study of the Old Testament, 1987), 222–43, gives a good overview of the extensive discussion of this passage.

31. For further argumentation, cf. Seim, *Double Message*, 66ff., 198–208.

32. For further discussion, cf. ibid, 223ff.

33. This supports the view by Carroll, *Response*, 166ff., who accepts Conzelmann's theory about *Parusieverzögerung* but argues that Luke's adjustment does not contradict a strong expectation of the end of time, but rather helps keep it alive at a time when a prolonged period of waiting was already a fact.

34. See E. Castelli, "Asceticism—Audience and Resistance," in *Asceticism*, eds. Wimbush and Valantasis, 182.

35. Ibid, 180ff.

36 Cf. Valantasis, "A Theory of the Social Function of Asceticism," in *Asceticism*, eds. Wimbush and Valantasis, 544–52.

7

Asceticism and the Gospel of John

David Rensberger

INTRODUCTION

The Gospel of John has never been a focal point of research on early Christian asceticism. There are good reasons for this, as we shall see, yet there are also points at which John's interests and those of the ascetics do at least run parallel. Before I enter into this analysis in detail, let me make some preliminary observations about asceticism, my own relationship to it, and the Gospel of John.

Growing up Mennonite, I had little sense of what asceticism was; the term was not in our religious vocabulary. Yet the Mennonite understanding of Christianity as countercultural, of martyrdom as a natural consequence of belief, and of discipleship as self-effacement and service to others might well be considered to have ascetic features. At any rate this background may have predisposed me to fall in love (there is really no better way to put it) with the spirituality of *The Imitation of Christ* when I discovered it in the midst of the spiritual melting pot of California and New Mexico in the 1960s. Reading the *Imitation* in the foothills of the Sangre de Cristo Mountains activated a kind of inner compass for me, and subsequent readings of Brother Lawrence, Thomas Merton, the ascetics of the Egyptian desert, and others have served to confirm the direction in which it pointed. Of course, academic preparation in graduate school and a position on the New Testament faculty of a Protestant seminary have tended to pull in other directions, and I have often lived in a kind of tension (not always a creative one) between these two forces during the last twenty-five years.

My relationship to asceticism is thus much more personal than academic (even if it also remains much more a matter of nostalgia than of observance), and I fear that this circumstance is felt in this chapter. Add to this the fact that I have always found less enlightenment overall in theoretical frameworks than in the details of texts and lives, and it will be apparent why the reader will not encounter as profound an engagement with the theory of asceticism here as in some other places in this volume. But after all, such a diffidence may not be entirely inappropriate in the context of asceticism. "The psychological heart of asceticism seems to lie in a reaction against the purely theoretical, the doctrinal, or the abstract. Above all, the ascetic wishes to know through experience."[1]

Nevertheless, one must indicate some working understanding of asceticism before attempting to relate it to a particular text. Richard Valantasis has discussed asceticism in terms of performances designed to inaugurate individuals into a new culture, alternative culture, or counterculture.[2] He defines it succinctly as "performances within a dominant social environment intended to inaugurate a new subjectivity, different social relations, and an alternative symbolic universe."[3] As a purely functional definition, this works well enough, and Valantasis' discussions of the social functions, power relationships, and typology of asceticism make a noteworthy contribution to the subject. However, I think it is confusing and far too sweeping when he also speaks of asceticism as "the primary system of formation *within* a culture" that equips people to live in the culture.[4] He is closer to the mark when he limits this universal function by describing it as beginning in "the arenas of personal, social, and intellectual *opposition*."[5] Asceticism as specifically *counter*cultural will prove to be very important when inquiring into the Gospel of John.

Valantasis draws on the work of Geoffrey Harpham, for whom "asceticism is the 'cultural' element in culture," and "the mark of culture is the conviction of the value and necessity of self-denial."[6] The latter statement seems to me highly debatable, but Harpham's main interest is in asceticism as both condemning and endorsing culture, in "its capacity to structure oppositions without collapsing them,[7] to raise issues without settling them." Thus he defines asceticism in its broadest sense as "any act of self-denial undertaken as a strategy of empowerment or gratification."[8]

Raising issues without settling them, of course, is the academic's own stock-in-trade, and we should perhaps apply a hermeneutics of suspicion, or at least a grain of salt, to Harpham's interpretation at that point. Some ascetics seem intent on settling some issues with vivid finality, Origen's self-castration furnishing an obvious example. But what of Harpham's (and Valantasis') notion of asceticism as the driving force in the formation and transmission of culture? Despite Harpham's references to self-denial, it is hard to see what is specifically *ascetic* about asceticism so conceived. It is at this point that Anthony J. Saldarini's appeal to the concept of "vague categories" seems to me to provide the necessary corrective.[9] By these means Saldarini is able to *distinguish* asceticism as only one among a number of human socializing activities so that it need not be the only process that functions to produce personal, social, and cultural transformation. Harpham and Valantasis, by contrast, seem to have expanded an *instance* of the larger category of "disciplined human behavior" into the entire category. Even the understanding of asceticism as culturally formative through its opposition to culture casts too broad a net, in my opinion. Valantasis' definition, quoted here, seems to define all countercultural activity as such as "ascetic." In so doing, it leaves out precisely the element of self-denial that seems essential to me as marking off asceticism from other types of cultural opposition.

Leif E. Vaage emphasizes that asceticism is not an end in itself, but a means toward achieving some other purpose.[10] Vaage thereby underlines the nature of asceticism as something fundamentally constructive, and not merely negation for its own sake.[11] But what does it construct? Valantasis speaks of a new subjectivity with new social relations and a new symbolic universe, and this certainly points to something important in the aims and results of ascetic practice. I wonder, however, if it does full justice to those aims and results as articulated by early Christian ascetics themselves. Their goal, as I understand it, was a self that had utterly abandoned itself, whose own interests were lost in devotion to and knowledge of God. Ascetic practice was not its own end, but neither was self-creation as such. The remaking of the self, like the development of new communities with new cultures, was part and parcel of achieving the larger purpose of abandonment to the service of God and to communion with God. Perhaps the point that needs to be emphasized is that this *was* seen as a larger purpose, not simply as the same purpose under a different name.

In the present context, then, I could make do with the Ethiopian Orthodox understanding of asceticism quoted by Ephraim Isaac: "Self-denial in lawful things enables us to turn with great earnestness to spiritual things."[12] This is obviously not a comprehensive definition, since it does not include those kinds of asceticism that consider the "things" renounced to be not "lawful" but deleterious in and of themselves. Nevertheless, it does underline the fundamentally theological purpose of any kind of asceticism to which the Gospel of John might be related. More fully and more formally, Walter O. Kaelber suggests that asceticism "when used in a religious context, may be defined as a voluntary, sustained, and at least partially systematic program of self-discipline and self-denial in which immediate, sensual, or profane gratifications are renounced in order to attain a higher spiritual state or a more thorough absorption in the sacred."[13] The reference to "a religious context" reminds us that the category of asceticism can be applied to other contexts as well, without making universal claims for it. Like Valantasis, Kaelber stresses the often countercultural nature of ascetic activity, citing the ascetic inclination to reject the given in favor of the possible.[14]

As a means of further clarifying my own working understanding of asceticism, I set out simply to identify the assumptions that I seemed to be making about asceticism in connection with the fourth gospel and to test these against the approaches cited herein. What I found, and what appears in this chapter, is a conception of asceticism as consisting of specific, repeatable practices and behaviors intended to result in a transformed identity and consciousness and in relationships repatterned to form an alternative cultural milieu, a spiritual counterculture where life is lived in communion with God. These practices and behaviors typically require humility, renunciation, self-denial, and a self-abandoned submission and devotion to the will of God. Bodily self-denial is important, but, at least with regard to John, it is not the only kind. The lowering of social standing also involves renunciation, a restriction of the self, especially in an honor/shame society like that of the ancient Mediterranean world.[15] The devotion of the will, the intention to God rather than to the self, including the social self, seems to me a fundamental factor in ascetic practice so understood.

Admittedly, this can hardly be considered a scientific definition of asceticism. It is limited to a theistic religious domain, and perhaps also to the cultural milieu of early Christianity, and so it is not broadly cross-cultural. Nevertheless, it shares important features with the definitions of both Valantasis and Kaelber. Like them, I emphasize the aim of transformation and the countercultural nature of asceticism. Like Valantasis, I include transformation of social relationships as well as of the self, but unlike him I posit a counterculture whose central values are explicitly theological or spiritual. Rather more like Kaelber than Valantasis (or especially Harpham), I regard asceticism as setting its practitioners apart from society at large, or at least as marking them out. There are types of asceticism that are integrated into the larger society,[16] but even such ascetics are identifiable as *ascetics*, as people following something other and more restrictive than the normal course of life in society.

All of these understandings of asceticism point to the centrality of activities, performances, *practices*. Asceticism, whatever theory or theology may lie behind it, does not exist in the realm of the abstract but in that of concrete daily life. The same may be said of the Christianity attested by the Gospel of John, but this fact is by no means so self-evident. Long regarded as the "spiritual gospel," John has often seemed to reside entirely in the theological and abstract. It is important, then, to remind ourselves of the social location of Johannine Christianity before going further.[17] This gospel, it now seems clear, was written in and for a Christian community primarily of Jewish origin whose members were faced with expulsion from their local synagogue because of their confession of Jesus as Messiah (9:22; 12:42; 16:2). The location of the community is unknown, as are the geographical extent of the threatened expulsion and the reasons behind it. John's exalted christology of the divine Son of God come down from heaven may have provoked the threat, but expulsion may also have driven the Christians to higher levels of christological confession. The community was evidently open to Samaritans and Gentiles and was willing at least to portray women as disciples whose competence is equal or superior to that of men. The gospel also shows a tendency to identify the Christian community with marginalized or oppressed groups and to depict groups and individuals in positions of power as hostile or at least doubtful.[18] Such social factors may have been irritants alongside the theological ones, especially to Pharisees in leadership positions who sought both to stabilize the synagogue community and to eliminate rival parties in the aftermath of the revolt against Rome in 66–70 CE. Under these circumstances, there was strong pressure on Jewish-Christian believers to conceal or tone down their belief. Particularly those in higher social positions found themselves forced to choose between concealment and the loss of status that open confession, and subsequent expulsion, would bring. The gospel writer more than once calls forcefully for precisely this downward social mobility (3:1–21; 12:42–43).

The Gospel of John is thus very much concerned with drawing people into a new social as well as theological reality. Its counterculture involved not only rejection of and rejection by "the world" in the abstract, but also the concrete alienation and dispossession of a community from the social and cultural reality that had once given meaning to its members' lives. This gospel thus seems to offer fertile ground for exploration in relation to asceticism, at least in the terms suggested by Valantasis. Employing my own less global conception, however, and keeping in mind the centrality of ascetic *practice* renders the situation more complex. Moreover, the task at hand is not only to discover whether John is or is not an ascetic document, but also to ask how ascetic categories and interests might shed light on the reading of John and how John might help in the understanding of ancient asceticism. In what follows, then, I consider first the presence or absence of typical ascetic practices in John and then examine some Johannine countercultural activities to determine whether they should be considered ascetic. Finally, I will explore several other features of this gospel that, while not directly involving ascetic practice, may offer openings to ascetic interpretation.

JOHN AND ASCETIC PRACTICE

The first thing to be noted is that there are no overt references to ascetic practice in the Gospel of John. There are no sayings or stories concerning fasting, celibacy, or vigils, for instance. Jesus is evidently unmarried, but the gospel writer never remarks on this. Several times Jesus withdraws from public view (7:1–9; 8:59; 10:39–40; 11:53–54; 12:36). However, this is never an ascetic *anachoresis,* nor even a retreat for prayer such as those in Mark (1:35; 6:45–46; 14:32–35), which are discussed by Mary Ann Tolbert elsewhere in this volume. Instead, Jesus' withdrawals in John always represent an attempt to escape persecution (or, in 6:15, to avoid being made king; contrast the parallel Mark 6:45–46). When John does depict Jesus at prayer, it is always in the presence of others (6:11; 11:41–42; 12:27–28; chapter 17); but in contrast with the synoptics, and especially Luke,[19] John lays little emphasis on Jesus praying and never uses the word "prayer" at all. As already indicated, John tends to identify with those of lower economic, religious, and social standing. Yet it also shows Jesus associating with people who are not marginalized, at least economically (2:1–11; 12:1–8); he even performs a miracle for a royal official (4:46–54). He does not overtly call on these people to renounce their property or positions, nor does it appear that he or his disciples live in poverty (note 12:6; 13:29). They eat and drink normally (2:1–11; 13:23–26; 21:9–13), and in fact Jesus miraculously provides food for a crowd of 5000 (6:1–13). The fact that he willingly shares food and drink with Samaritans (4:4–9) actually implies a rejection of some physical regulations and restrictions, although this does not represent a critique of asceticism so much as a lowering of boundaries between Jews and Samaritans within the Christian community. Finally, although distinctions between Jesus and John the Baptist are important in the fourth gospel (1:6–8, 15, 19–34; 3:23–30; 5:33–36; 10:40–41), the contrast between John as ascetic and Jesus as eating and drinking (Mark 2:18–19 and parallels; Matt 11:16–19 = Luke 7:31–34) does not appear. The reason for this may be that the gospel writer insistently presents John the Baptist as pointing away from himself toward Jesus, perhaps in view of ongoing competition between the Johannine Christian community and disciples of the Baptist. Therefore the gospel's narrative might avoid anything that would put the spotlight on John himself. Only the humility with which the Baptist diverts attention, and followers, away from himself and toward Jesus might be considered ascetic; in 3:30, indeed, he allows himself to "decrease" to such an extent that he disappears from the narrative entirely.

The surface of John's text thus gives no indication of any interest in asceticism. It does not portray Jesus as teaching or practicing asceticism on the one hand or as criticizing ascetic practice on the other. Yet the surface of the text is only a beginning point in any interpretation of John. We must go on to consider deeper ways in which asceticism and the characteristic features of this gospel might be mutually enlightening. In the course of this, we will see that several of the facts just mentioned also have other meanings in relation to asceticism.

COUNTERCULTURAL PRACTICES IN JOHN

It is by now widely, although not universally, acknowledged that the Johannine community must be considered a sect.[20] This is not meant pejoratively, but in the relatively neutral sociological sense, focusing on the group's relationship to the larger society. A sect in this sense is a group that has rejected the world in order to establish a separate community, a community that is voluntary but requires total commitment. Such a community becomes the exclusive locus of salvation, and cultivates intimate relationships of mutual love among its members. All these features characterize the Gospel of John as sectarian, as does its pervasive dualism and its use of language to sustain a counterreality against that of the dominant society.[21]

The culture of a sect, the system of symbols that give meaning to its members' experiences and actions, is thus necessarily a counterculture. Having defined itself against a society, the sect naturally opposes, or at least reinterprets, many of the symbols and meanings of that society's culture. This is seen repeatedly in John. How God is known and who knows God, what is sin and who is a sinner, are pointedly redefined (7:28–29; 8:19, 54–55; 9:1–41). Jewish holy days and the symbols associated with them are given new meaning in Jesus (e.g., the bread of Passover in 6:1–59; the water and light of Tabernacles in 7:1–10, 37–39; 8:12). This act of breaking down the symbolic universe of the old culture and forming the reader in the new one has obvious parallels with asceticism as defined by Valantasis.[22] Like withdrawal into a hermitage or cenobium, where fasting, celibacy, prayer, and vigil form one into a new self and a new life lived with God and for God, reading the Gospel of John plunges one into a new reality, where symbols both novel and familiar, endlessly repeated and surprisingly varied, condition one in a life so new that it can only be seen as the result of being "born again, born from above" (3:3–8). Yet there is an all-important difference. Valantasis speaks of "*performances* that aim toward establishing a counter-cultural or alternative cultural milieu…the careful repatterning of basic behaviors and relations."[23] It is precisely such ascetic practices and behaviors that we do not find in John. Indeed, John is notoriously short on specific ethical and behavioral instruction of any sort.[24] In a sense, of course, given the parallels just described, the reading of John itself might be considered functionally "ascetic." However, I have argued that it is just at this point that the global, functional understanding of asceticism misses the mark. Not everything that is formative and countercultural is ascetic, and there is no indication that reading John is intended to be a praxis of self-denial. Perhaps, then, in this regard John is "parallel" to asceticism in a fairly literal way: They are two lines that run in the same direction but never meet. Reading John forms the reader in a new symbolic universe but does not appeal to specifically ascetic categories in doing so.

There are some particular actions that appear in John, however, even if only by way of allusion. The same passage that speaks of being "born from above" says that this is a birth "of water and Spirit." There can be little doubt that this is a reference to baptism, and baptism is thereby specified as a boundary marker between the old world and the new, or rather between the world and those who are "from above." Christian baptism is nonrepeatable, however, and thus not the type of performance or practice that can rightly be considered ascetic. John also alludes to the other primary Christian sacrament, the eucharist, in speaking grotesquely of eating the flesh and drinking the blood of the Son of Man (6:51–58).[25] This is a repeated action, and clearly it also seems to be part of what sets the believing community apart from "the world." The Eucharist is true food and drink that offers true life, eternal life, precisely because it is the flesh and blood of the divine Son of Man. But only those who believe this, that is, who believe the Johannine christology of incarnation, receive this life. Thus participation in the Eucharist not only brings the individual into relationship with the divine life giver, but also affirms her or his membership in the countercultural community. It is part of what forms the believer's new identity within the new social and cultural context.[26] It thus has the same function as ascetic practice, but lacks the essential element of self-denial. I will have more to say about the significance of eating and drinking in the fourth gospel later on. What we have seen here reminds us once more that, while asceticism does have the function of inaugurating individuals into an alternative culture, this function is not exclusive to it.

When speaking more explicitly of conduct that distinguishes believers from the world, John has only one category to offer, namely the "new commandment" to love one another. It is by their practice of mutual love that Jesus' disciples will be identified (13:34–35). This love is further characterized as being like that of Jesus for the disciples, and so having one very concrete property, that of laying down one's life for one's friends (15:13). Jesus' sacrifice of his own life, like a good shepherd laying down his life for his sheep (10:11–18), provides the model for believers. Here we do have a repeatable type of behavior that manifestly involves self-denial and is expressly said to be part of the repatterning of relationships to form the alternative cultural milieu. If this love were put into practice in a definite set of actions (as in Luke 6:27–36), we might very well call those actions ascetic. Yet even love remains a *category* of action more than a praxis specific enough to be fully recognizable as ascetic in John. The gospel does not, for instance, speak of renouncing one's possessions in order to sustain one's brothers and sisters, although something like this is found in 1 John 3:16–17. Once again we seem to have a phenomenon that runs parallel to asceticism rather than actually crossing its path.

There is, however, one action that John calls for that should probably be considered ascetic. This action is the open confession of belief in Jesus as Messiah, particularly on the part of those for whom such a confession would be costly. John presents this cost in terms of expulsion from the synagogue, implying a loss of relationship with family and community as well as a loss of the symbols and activities that had given life meaning. For those who had significant standing within the synagogue community, it would mean down-

ward social mobility as well, including the loss of status and honor. The call
to open confession is thus a call to social renunciation, a kind of social asceticism. This can be illustrated by several specific examples, bearing in mind in
each case that in view are the circumstances of the time when the gospel was
written, not the lifetime of Jesus.

In 9:18–23, the parents of a blind beggar healed by Jesus refuse to admit
knowing anything about the circumstances of his healing because of their
fear of expulsion from the synagogue. Such is their terror that they direct the
hostile inquisition back onto their own son. He, however, under the prod-
ding of the authorities,[27] responds spiritedly, accepts his expulsion, and so
comes truly to "see," to recognize Jesus and believe in him (9:24–39). The
beggar, of course, has little to lose socially by his forthright acknowledgment
of Jesus; yet, having so little, he willingly and courageously abandons even
that. John 12:42–43 speaks of people who did have something to lose. These
are the *archontes*, the "rulers" or authorities of the local Jewish community.
Some of them have believed in Jesus, but they will not confess it, fearing the
loss of honor, of "human glory," that would come if they were expelled from
the synagogue community that gave them their status. So successful are these
rulers in concealing their faith that the Pharisees, who apparently wield the
actual power in these matters, can confidently question whether any of them
believes (7:47–49). One particular figure who seems to represent the
faint-hearted *archontes* is Nicodemus. He is described as both an *archon* and
a Pharisee and as one who acknowledges Jesus as a teacher, but only under
cover of darkness. Among his fellow Pharisees he raises only a timid legal
objection in defense of Jesus; after Jesus is safely dead he appears with Joseph
of Arimathea, who is pointedly characterized as a fearful secret disciple, to
bury the dead teacher with honor but also with finality. Although some see
this as equivalent to an open confession, it more likely represents the climactic failure of this ruler to make more than a subdued and ambiguous
acknowledgment of his faith.[28]

John clearly would have the *archontes* in the social context of the
Johannine community follow the path of the beggar rather than that of
Nicodemus. It is this call for downward mobility through confession that can
be seen as ascetic.[29] It amounts to a renunciation of social status, and as such
requires both humility and self-denial. The aim of this renunciation is faithful testimony to the one sent from God, the kind of self-abandoned obedience and devotion to divine will and divine calling that is the aim of Christian
asceticism, a willingness to risk all and to have nothing for the sake of God.
Indeed, according to 16:2, life itself was at risk. Such a willingness to lay
down one's life for one's friends represents faithful discipleship to and imitation of Jesus (15:13), another important ascetic theme. In this respect, christological confession might be compared to Jesus' washing of his disciples'
feet, which is both a symbol of Jesus' sacrificial and life-giving love and a

deliberate renunciation of status that is to be imitated by the disciples (13:3–15).

Open confession of faith in Jesus, risking loss of social context and, for some, loss of honor and status, perhaps even of life, is thus in a real sense an ascetic act in the Gospel of John. It also resembles ascetic practice in its character as a performance, an activity with an audience.[30] Indeed, the public character of the desired confession is stressed by contrast with the fearful secrecy of those who fail to make it (9:22; 12:42–43; 19:38). While not inevitably a *repeated* action, confession of Jesus is a practice that has enduring consequences for those who undertake it. It implies their abandonment of the society they have known, and in this way it resembles ascetic *anachoresis*, withdrawal into the wilderness. Although there is no evidence in John of *physical* withdrawal or relocation, the enforced separation from roots and the loss of status were evidently traumatic enough in themselves that the threat of them intimidated some believers. Willingness to undergo this separation and loss therefore reflects a kind of ascetic self-denial.[31] Of course, such a willingness to suffer for one's confession of faith is really more at home in the Christian martyr tradition than in asceticism strictly construed, a point that is as relevant for John as it is for Mark.[32] However, later Christian asceticism was understood in part as "white martyrdom," the path of suffering open to those for whom, after Constantine, "red martyrdom" was no longer an option.[33] If later Christian asceticism seems more a self-chosen course *within* Christianity, we must remember that it was the choice of Christianity as such in earlier times that led to suffering. To choose Christianity was to choose a way of suffering, and to persevere in that way required discipline, so that conversion itself might be interpreted as an ascetic choice. At any rate, what we find in John is the motivation underlying both asceticism and martyrdom, namely the readiness to renounce one's own interests out of devotion to God.

The author of the fourth gospel seems to regard this self-denial as absolutely essential for both individuals and the survival of the Christian community. Those who shrink back from it demonstrate an unwillingness to be "born from above," since this birth involves baptism into the confessing community (3:3–8). The community itself can only exist by the willingness of its members to undertake this renunciation. The intent of the gospel as a whole seems to be to encourage its readers to maintain the confession, and therefore the renunciation (20:31).[34] Despite the absence of typically ascetic behaviors, then, there is at the heart of John a call to renunciation, to risk-laden abandonment of self-interest, that at least bears a resemblance to ascetic self-denial. Openness to God at all costs underlies much of later Christian asceticism, and John shares precisely this openness, so that in John we may at least tentatively identify the confession of Jesus as Messiah as an ascetic practice.

POSSIBILITIES FOR ASCETIC INTERPRETATION IN JOHN

This is the closest approach we find in John to an ascetic discipline being urged on readers of the gospel. It is worth asking, however, whether there are other characteristics of the fourth gospel that leave it open to ascetic interpretation. In what follows, I consider some ways in which ascetic categories could generate meaningful interpretation of John. I am not claiming that early Christian ascetics actually read the fourth gospel in these ways, however; it would be up to those who are expert in the ascetic texts to answer that question.[35]

The most obvious path to an ascetic understanding of John lies through its dualism. Sharp contrasts between light and darkness, above and below, spirit and flesh, those who are of God and those who are of the world pervade this gospel. They certainly provide an opportunity to think in terms of resisting the flesh and abandoning the world for the sake of God and life in the Spirit, even if the gospel itself does not overtly call for such actions. In this way it may be said that John lays a potential foundation for asceticism, while making hardly any move to build on that foundation.

"The world" is a kind of summary term in John for the religious, social, and political structures against which the Johannine Christian community struggled for self-definition. It does not refer to the created universe, the physical world as such, which John never disparages as material, changeable, or transient. Consistent with biblical monotheism in general, John regards creation as the work of God, accomplished indeed through the *logos,* the "Word," who was made flesh in Jesus of Nazareth. When the *logos* entered the world, it was thus only coming to what was its own (1:1–5, 9–11). It is this world that is the object of God's love, a love that desires to save it, not condemn it (3:16–17; 4:42; 6:63, 51; 12:46–17). Yet when the *logos* enters the world, it meets with both belief and rejection, and it is these responses that establish the two classes of those who are "born of God" and those who are "of the world," that is, the *human* world hostile to God and to the one whom God has sent (1:9–13). Those who belonged to the *logos* rejected the *logos* and refused to come to the light, and thereby proved that they were of darkness (3:18–21). The world hates the one who demonstrates that its deeds are evil (7:7), and so Jesus can say that he, his disciples, and his kingship are not of this world (8:23; 14:17–19, 27; 15:18–25; 16:8–11, 33; 17:6, 9, 14–18, 25; 18:36), whose ruler is the devil (12:31; 14:30; 16:11). This typically sectarian appraisal of "the world" is of course derived from the typically sectarian experience of the Johannine Jewish-Christian community in its rejection by the synagogue authorities.

John's dualism is thus not an absolute cosmological one, but a dualism of ethics or of decision. Even so, indeed *precisely* so, John calls on Jesus' followers to become ever more attached to him and detached from the world.[36]

This general movement of detachment from the world provides a point of contact between Johannine Christianity and asceticism. If it is hard to identify specific actions by which the Johannine community and its members defined themselves in resistance to the world, we have nevertheless seen that John's call for open confession of Jesus is itself one such action. Confession fulfills the ascetic function of detaching believers from the world, including their own social standing in the world. At this one point, then, John's modified dualism does lead to something resembling ascetic action.

The Johannine treatment of "flesh" also presents us with some complexities. On the one hand, flesh is contrasted with God and with Spirit. It is not the locus of evil, of *opposition* to God; rather, it represents the *merely* human, as against and inferior to the divine. Thus "judging according to the flesh" in 8:15 means judging by human standards, and "authority over all flesh" in 17:2 means authority over the human race. "Birth from the flesh" is birth in the ordinary human course of life. Birth from God, from water and Spirit, from above, is given to believers, to those who voluntarily cross over into the new community of Jesus the Messiah (1:12–13; 3:3–8). It is this birth that is entry into true life, eternal life, the divine life that Jesus brings to the world. The flesh, which cannot confer this birth, is useless by comparison (6:63).

On the other hand, the entry of the *logos,* the "Word," into the world is characterized precisely as "becoming flesh" (1:14). Following immediately on the contrast between birth from human flesh and birth from God, this can only mean that the divine *logos* truly became a human being, with all the uselessness, the futility, that "flesh" implies. We must bear this in mind, then, when we read that the life-giving bread that Jesus gives to the world is his flesh, which brings eternal life to those who eat it (6:51–58). It is not only Jesus' body and blood, consumed in the eucharist, but also his human life, his humanity as such, that he sacrifices to bring life to the world. If this were *only* a human life, only one more victim of cruel oppression among so many, it would be as "useless" in giving divine life as any other flesh. *This* flesh, however, the humanity of Jesus of Nazareth, is the flesh that the divine *logos* had become, and because it is the incarnation of the *logos,* of Spirit, it is able to give life (6:63).

Here again we do not find a cosmological dualism (between matter and spirit, for instance) or one between body and soul. John's dualism of flesh and spirit is a dualism of decision, like its dualism regarding the world, but a different sort of decision. Instead of a human decision to reject, which split humanity between those who are "of God" and those who are "of the world," this is first of all a divine decision to give life, which unites human flesh with divine *logos.* Although "world" and "flesh" seem to belong to the same negative dualistic pole, "the world" in the negative sense is in fact conquered by the *logos'* becoming flesh (John 16:33). Flesh in general remains flesh, even after the incarnation, and remains powerless by itself. But the decision to believe gives the believer new access to Spirit, new birth not of the flesh, and so new life, all made possible by the *logos'* becoming flesh.

Incarnation has several implications for asceticism. First, incarnational christology clearly would favor a kind of asceticism that seeks to train or discipline "the flesh" over one that regards "the flesh" as evil in itself, an opponent of everything spiritual that must be destroyed.[37] Second, incarnation implies that the flesh, the human realm, can be the realm of divine activity and revelation. This is not a claim that the material always and everywhere opens out onto the spiritual. It is focused on this one eschatological event. Nevertheless, it suggests that for those who believe in the incarnate *logos*, flesh is a vehicle for the creation of the counterculture of the Spirit. Third, the claim that the *logos* became flesh is countercultural, since it announces the penetration of an established barrier that had cultural meaning beyond the philosophical and spiritual. *Logos*, spirit, and intellect were associated in antiquity with free, upper-class males, while flesh, matter, and body were associated with the lower classes, women, and slaves. The assertion that the *logos* became flesh therefore represents a challenge to established social and ideological hierarchies. Incarnation implies resistance to "the world," a resistance that includes John's call to downward social mobility.[38]

The Gospel of John is permeated by the incarnational view of revelation and reality. This is why it contains physical symbolism that is sometimes within the bounds of reasonable expectation (light, water, vine), but sometimes wildly beyond them (eating Jesus' flesh and drinking his blood). If asceticism involves the use of the human body in creating a countercultural spiritual reality, then the incarnation of the *logos* has meaning for asceticism. The physical body of Jesus was indispensable for God's ultimate revelation; the bodies of his disciples are equally necessary to continue this revelation in the Christian community, for they will do his deeds and even greater ones (14:12) and will suffer as he suffered (15:12–13, 18–20; 16:2). Despite the absence of ordinary ascetic practices from John, its incarnational christology could lend sanction to an asceticism that sought to create a counterculture of spirit by devoting the flesh to God.

If the flesh of the incarnate *logos* is the site of divine revelation, then John's references to Jesus' body and bodily activities ought to be of interest.[39] Nearly every chapter of John contains such references. There is nothing particularly marvelous about this, but it reminds us that the "spiritual gospel" does attend to Jesus' physical nature. Some basic physical actions appear throughout John: traveling, seeing and being seen, and, above all, speaking. Jesus expels the money-changers and the sellers of cattle, sheep, and doves from the temple with more bodily vigor than in the synoptics, chasing the animals with a whip, pouring out the money, and overturning the tables (2:14–16). Jesus sheds tears (11:35); he looks upward in prayer (11:41; 17:1); he rides a young donkey into Jerusalem (12:12–16); one of his disciples leans on his chest while reclining to eat (13:23–25); he dips a piece of bread into the common dish and gives it to Judas (13:26). Physical means are involved in several of Jesus' miracles, and John seems to emphasize this physicality (distributing bread and fish in 6:11 [cf. 21:13], walking on the sea in 6:16–21, making mud from saliva to heal the blind man in 9:6, 11, 14–15). Jesus' body requires care: He grows tired and thirsty from travel (4:6–7); Mary anoints his feet and wipes them with her hair in anticipation of his burial (12:3–9). Jesus also cares for other people's bodies, putting on a towel and washing his disciples' feet (13:3–5).

In particular, Jesus' return to God has a bodily means, namely death by crucifixion (13:1–3; 14:12, 28; 16:10, 28).[40] It is "the temple of his body" that is destroyed and resurrected (2:18–22). His departure is spoken of several times as "being lifted up," a reference to the bodily reality of crucifixion (3:14–15; 8:28; 12:32–33). Not surprisingly, there is a heightening of bodily references in the crucifixion narrative. Jesus' body is vulnerable here. He is bound, struck on the face, flogged, and dressed in a crown of thorns and a purple robe (18:12, 22, 24; 19:1–4). He carries his own cross to be crucified (19:17–18). On the Cross, he is thirsty and is given sour wine to drink (19:28–29). After his death, his legs are not broken, but his side is pierced with a spear, and blood and water pour out (19:31–37). Finally, Joseph of Arimathea and Nicodemus take Jesus' body and bury it in an unused tomb, wrapped in linen cloths with seventy-five pounds of myrrh and aloes (19:38–42). This is the climax of Jesus' bodily vulnerability, for here he is utterly powerless, literally in the hands of those whose faith is most questionable (compare 19:38 with 12:42–43). The incarnation of the *logos* reaches its intended goal through the utter abjection of the body of Jesus. But this abjection is not passive: It is deliberately undergone. Jesus intentionally gives himself over to those who will hurt and kill him, who have no power over him otherwise (10:17–18; 14:30–31; 18:4–11; 19:11). Power thus belongs to the one who lays down his life, not to the one who takes life, an understanding of power quite at odds with that of "the world" (18:36).

Bodily references continue in the resurrection story. At first Jesus' body is absent, having disappeared from the tomb, leaving the linen wrappings and the head cloth behind (20:5–7). Mary Magdalene sees two angels sitting where his body had been (20:12); when she encounters the risen Jesus himself, she is not allowed to keep touching him, since he is ascending to God and she is to go on a mission (20:17). Afterward, Jesus enters a locked room and shows the disciples his hands and side, then breathes on the disciples to give them the Holy Spirit (20:19–20, 22). A week later he again enters a closed room and invites Thomas to see and touch his wounded hands and side (20:26–27).

Thus the body of Jesus, the flesh of the incarnate *logos*, is noted and sometimes emphasized in John. It is by means of his body that he makes God known, in miraculous acts; in spoken words; on the Cross, where the work of God that he came to do is finished (19:30); and in the resurrection. Not everything said about Jesus' body in John is ascetic, but the body of Jesus as the locus of divine revelation opens up the possibility of bodily practice as a means toward divine communion. The emphatic physicality of his death and resurrection, in particular, fits the paradigm of ascetics who seek to have the will of God carved into their bodies. Like them, Jesus offers "the temple of his body" to wounding and destruction for the sake of God's encounter with the world.

This voluntary bodily vulnerability on the part of Jesus belongs to his utter submission to God, his obedience to God in everything that he has been commanded to do (5:19, 30; 6:38; 7:16–18; 8:28–29; 12:49–50; 14:10, 24; 17:7–8). He does not seek glory for himself, but only seeks to glorify God by doing God's will (5:41–44; 7:18; 8:49–50, 54–55; 13:31–32). Jesus' own glorification, and his ultimate glorification of God, is the crucifixion itself (7:39; 12:16, 23–28; 17:1, 4-5). His abnegation of glory, that is, of honor within human society (12:42–43), provides a model for those in the Johannine environment whose own confession of Jesus threatened the loss of social status and honor, as discussed earlier. Moreover, the *logos'* becoming flesh in itself implies the overturning of social hierarchies, also noted earlier. The climax of the incarnation on a Roman cross makes it decisively clear that God is revealed not in the traditional domains of power and status, but in mortal weakness and vulnerability.

A similar claim is made by asceticism as well, that divine communion is found in humility, hunger, and solitude, in suffering that is, like that of the Johannine Jesus, deliberately chosen. Jesus' submission to God, even at the cost of his life, which can be characterized in terms of self-denial (5:30; 6:38; 12:27–28), thus resembles that of later Christian ascetics.[41] The involvement of his body in this submission increases the resemblance, although with Jesus the focus is primarily on a single event rather than on a continuing practice. It should also be noted that the goal of Jesus' submission is not a transformation of his own identity or consciousness; rather, his submission *proceeds from* his awareness of himself as the Son of God come down from heaven (5:19; 6:38; 12:49–50). Nevertheless, it seems possible to speak of Jesus' self-sacrifice in John as ascetic, not simply because it involves suffering, but because it is suffering voluntarily endured for the sake of doing God's work and making God known. We have here perhaps an asceticism of the will more than anything else. Yet every asceticism involves the disciplining of the will, and the goal of this discipline is often that the ascetic may achieve what Jesus simply does in John, namely the perfect submission of his will to God's. Thus it might be possible for Christian asceticism to look to the Johannine Jesus for its inspiration.

Two final aspects of the fourth gospel offer possibilities for ascetic interpretation. Ascetic practice often includes restraint of appetites for sex and food. The treatment of sexual and marital imagery and of food and drink imagery in John thus might give an opening to ascetic thinking.

Sexual and marital imagery is found primarily in John 3 and 4.[42] In 3:3–8, as already noted, birth into new life comes from above, from the Spirit, rather than from the flesh (see also 1:12–13; 6:63; and note 16:20–22). Although the flesh of Jesus and of the believing community is indispensable for this spiritual birth, the contrast with birth from the flesh does at least lower the estimation of physical birth. This could be taken to imply that those who seek to bring others to birth from the Spirit have a more important role than those who physically engender and bear children. If such a conclusion were drawn, it would affirm the work of celibate spiritual "athletes" and guides and might be particularly significant for women, as providing them a divinely given task outside the realm of motherhood and child-rearing.[43]

In 3:29, Jesus is the bridegroom come into possession of his "bride," the people who have believed in him. This imagery is continued in chapter 4, where the bride is personified in the Samaritan woman at the well. As is generally recognized, her encounter with Jesus reflects a genre of betrothal scene found several times in the Pentateuch. In these stories, a betrothal is initiated by the meeting of a foreign man with a woman at a well outside a town: Gen. 24:10–52 (Abraham's servant, representing Isaac, and Rebekah), Gen. 29:1–20 (Jacob and Rachel), and Exod. 2:15–21 (Moses and Zipporah). The dialogue about water, which suddenly shifts to the topic of the woman's marital status (John 4:6–18), seems designed to lead up to precisely such a betrothal. Yet just at the crucial moment, the woman's insight into Jesus' identity leads instead to a discussion of spirit and truth, and ultimately to her recognition of him as the Messiah. The woman's relationship with Jesus thus becomes a metaphor for his "betrothal" to the believer. Sexual ascetics might see in this complex a validation of their choice to pursue a spiritual marriage with God or with Jesus, who is often spoken of as the bridegroom of celibates. Again, women ascetics in particular might find encouragement in this woman whose marital and sexual status, suddenly introduced, is immediately rendered meaningless in comparison with her task of bringing news of the Messiah to the people of her town.

We have already had occasion to note various occurrences of food and drink imagery in John: the banquets and meals in 2:1–11; 13:23–26; 21:9-13; Jesus' and his disciples' sharing of food and drink with Samaritans in 4:4–9; the feeding of the 5000 in 6:1–13; and Jesus' body and blood as true, life-giving food and drink in 6:51–58. It is noteworthy in how many cases Jesus is the provider of what is eaten and drunk, not only the miraculous wine and food in chapters 2 and 6, but also the breakfast in chapter 21, and even the morsel of bread given to Judas in 13:26. In all cases, including the last (see 13:18), the emphasis is on Jesus as the giver of life and sustenance to his disciples, just as in 7:37–39 he offers the living water of the Spirit to thirsty believers. Only in 4:31–34 does Jesus himself receive food. This food, however, is not physical nourishment but the carrying out of the work that God has given him to do. The reference here to "the will of the one who sent me" makes a strong connection with the numerous passages noted above that speak of Jesus' submission to the will of God, which leads him to lay down his life. The ascetic traits of those passages, and of the crucifixion motif throughout John, are thus drawn into this discussion of food. We may also note an unmistakable similarity between Jesus, whose food it is to do God's will, and the fasting ascetic, who is nourished by the service of God. Thus John's overall portrayal of Jesus' asceticism of the will is brought into connection with a more overtly ascetic neglect of food, all of which might serve as a model for later ascetic imitation.

What is most characteristic of the Johannine food and drink imagery, however, is the portrayal of Jesus as provider. Even his request for water from the Samaritan woman quickly turns to an offer of "living water" to her (4:10–14). For asceticism, which practices "self-denial in lawful things" in order to "turn to spiritual things,"[44] the image of Jesus as the giver of true food and drink, the food and drink that yield real, eternal life, would surely be an encouraging and strengthening one. Fasting from "the food that perishes," the ascetic is sustained by "the food that endures for eternal life," given by the Son of Man (6:27)—by Jesus, that is, who turned plain water into the best wine and a few poor loaves into a banquet. Ultimately, indeed, it is Jesus himself who is the spiritual sustenance sent from God. He is the bread of life that comes down from heaven and gives life to the world, the bread that one may eat and never hunger, never thirst, never die (6:32–35, 48–51). Moreover, as noted earlier, consuming his flesh and his blood in the eucharist is part of what separates the believer from the world. Consistently with this, if more subtly, John also presents Jesus as the Passover lamb: He is condemned at the very hour when the lambs are being slaughtered, and like the lambs he dies with no bone broken (19:14, 31–36; see Exod. 12:46). Thus Jesus is the true food at the banquet of salvation, and could therefore be seen as the true sustenance of the ascetic.

There are thus points of attachment in John for ascetic practices regarding sex and food. The Johannine understandings of Jesus as the believer's bridegroom and the spiritual bread on which the believer feasts offer clear possibilities for interpretation in ascetic terms, even if the gospel itself does not make any moves in this direction.

CONCLUSION

The Gospel of John, paradoxical in so many ways, is also paradoxical in being a dualistic text that is hostile to the world but takes no apparent interest in asceticism. Generally speaking, the Johannine Jesus, even as he inveighs against the world and those who belong to it, neither encourages nor discourages ascetic practice in any direct and overt way. Only the saying in

4:31–34 presents Jesus as neglecting or refusing ordinary food in favor of the nourishment of doing God's will. Otherwise, apart from his apparent but unemphasized single marital status, he and his disciples lead normal lives among the Jewish people.

Thus, although the countercultural fourth gospel is in some ways parallel to countercultural asceticism, it does not inculcate any of the common ascetic practices of self-denial as a means of creating and sustaining its counterculture. Instead, the reading of the gospel itself serves this purpose, as apparently do the Christian sacraments of baptism and especially the eucharist. The Johannine love ethic offers a general basis for self-denying action, but no specific, regular acts of renunciation are demanded. The closest that the Johannine ethos comes to ascetic renunciation is the summons to open confession of Jesus as Messiah, which leads to the risk of expulsion from the synagogue, ostracism, and loss of social status and honor. To confess Jesus is implicitly to renounce one's standing in the world and to abandon one's place in society in favor of a new community. Yet even if confession, in such circumstances, should properly be considered ascetic, John gives no hint of other, more overtly ascetic practices accompanying this social "withdrawal."

Some aspects of Johannine theology, however, may offer openings toward an ascetic interpretation of this gospel. John's call for detachment from the world and attachment to Jesus, based on the world's rejection of its Savior and not on a rejection of matter or creation, could support an ascetic withdrawal based on a similar assessment of the world. The incarnation of the divine *logos* implies that human flesh can be the realm of divine revelation and redemption, opening up the possibility of ascetic action that seeks to create a spiritual counterculture by means of human bodies. In particular, John's presentation of Jesus as deliberately offering his body to torture and death in order to do God's will and to make God known bears a resemblance to ascetic self-denial. Even specific ascetic practices not encouraged by the gospel itself, such as celibacy and fasting, receive some support from John's presentation of Jesus as the spiritual bridegroom and the true bread from heaven.

The main thrust of the fourth gospel is neither ascetic nor antiascetic in the usual sense. Instead its concern is with eschatological life in the Spirit, the eternal life that begins here and now for the believer. For those who abide in Jesus as he abides in them (6:56; 15:4–10), who are guided by the Spirit of truth (16:13), there is an immediacy of divine presence, a life lived in communion with God. This presence itself creates a counterculture detached and in some respects withdrawn from the world, an alienated community that refuses allegiance to the world's orders of every sort. It would seem that this counterculture could live with or without the typical practices that made divine communion, the "angelic life," available to later Christian ascetics. Yet the gospel's portrayal of Jesus' self-sacrificing submission to the will of God, and its call for believers to sacrifice their own social well-being in their confession of him, partake of some of the essential characteristics of ascetic practice. They open up the possibility of an asceticism compatible with John's contest with the world, which is based on self-abandoned adherence to the giver of life, the divine *logos* made flesh, Jesus the Messiah.

NOTES

1. W. O. Kaelber, "Asceticism," in *The Encyclopedia of Religion* (New York: Macmillan, 1987), Vol. 1: 445.
2. R. Valantasis, "A Theory of the Social Function of Asceticism," in *Asceticism*, eds. V. L. Wimbush and R. Valantasis (New York: Oxford University Press, 1995), 547–51.
3. Valantasis, "Constructions of Power in Asceticism," *Journal of the American Academy of Religion* 63 (1995): 797.
4. Valantasis, "A Theory of the Social Function of Asceticism," 547 (italics mine).
5. Valantasis, "Constructions of Power in Asceticism," 795 (emphasis mine).
6. G. G. Harpham, *The Ascetic Imperative in Culture and Criticism* (Chicago: University of Chicago Press, 1987), xi, xii.
7. Ibid, xii.
8. Ibid, xiii.
9. See Saldarini (this volume, 13ff.).
10. L. E. Vaage, "Ascetic Moods, Hermeneutics, and Bodily Deconstruction," in *Asceticism*, eds. Wimbush and Valantasis, 250–51.
11. Ibid, 252. See also K. Ware, "The Way of the Ascetics: Negative or Affirmative?" in *Asceticism*, eds. Wimbush and Valantasis, 3-15.
12. E. Isaac, "The Significance of Food in Hebraic-African Thought and the Role of Fasting in the Ethiopian Church," in *Asceticism*, eds. Wimbush and Valantasis, 337. Isaac is quoting from *The Ethiopian Orthodox Church*, eds. A. Wondemagegnehu and J. Motovu (Addis Ababa: Ethiopian Orthodox Church Mission, 1970), 63.
13. Kaelber, "Asceticism," Vol. 1: 441.
14. Ibid, 444.
15. B. J. Malina, "Pain, Power, and Personhood: Ascetic Behavior in the Ancient Mediterranean," in *Asceticism*, eds. Wimbush and Valantasis, 168.
16. Valantasis, "Constructions of Power in Asceticism," 803; W. O. Kaelber, "Understanding Asceticism—Testing a Typology," in *Asceticism*, eds. Wimbush and Valantasis, 326–27. On Syriac-speaking Christianity, see S. A. Harvey, *Asceticism and Society in Crisis: John of Ephesus and the Lives of the Eastern Saints* (Berkeley: University of California Press, 1990), 43–56.
17. On the following, see D. Rensberger, *Johannine Faith and Liberating Community* (Philadelphia: Westminster Press, 1988), 15–36.
18. D. Rensberger, "Oppression and Identity in the Gospel of John," in *The Recovery of Black Presence: An Interdisciplinary Exploration: Essays in Honor of Dr. Charles B. Copher*, eds. R. C. Bailey and J. Grant (Nashville, Tenn.: Abingdon Press, 1995), 77–94. See also R. J. Karris, O.F.M., *Jesus and the*

Marginalized in John's Gospel (Collegeville, Minn.: Liturgical Press [Michael Glazier], Zacchaeus Studies: New Testament, 1990).

19. See Susan R. Garrett (this volume, 71–95).

20. W. A. Meeks, "The Man from Heaven in Johannine Sectarianism," *Journal of Biblical Literature* 91 (1972): 44–72; F. Segovia, "The Love and Hatred of Jesus and Johannine Sectarianism," *Catholic Biblical Quarterly* 43 (1981): 258–72; B. J. Malina, *The Gospel of John in Sociolinguistic Perspective* (Berkeley, Calif.: The Center for Hermeneutical Studies in Hellenistic and Modern Culture, Protocol of the Colloquy of the Center for Hermeneutical Studies in Hellenistic and Modern Culture 48, ed. H. C. Waetjen, 1985); J. H. Neyrey, S.J., *An Ideology of Revolt: John's Christology in Social-Science Perspective* (Philadelphia: Fortress Press, 1988); Rensberger, *Johannine Faith and Liberating Community*, 27–28.

21. N. R. Petersen, *The Gospel of John and the Sociology of Light: Language and Characterization in the Fourth Gospel* (Valley Forge, Pa.: Trinity Press International, 1993).

22. See especially Valantasis, "Constructions of Power in Asceticism," 811–13.

23. Valantasis, "A Theory of the Social Function of Asceticism," 549 (italics mine).

24. Contrast this with the lengthy list of behaviors to be cultivated or avoided that Anthony J. Saldarini finds in the Gospel of Matthew (this volume, 18ff.).

25. The question as to whether these verses are authentic to this gospel is treated in the commentaries; see also Rensberger, *Johannine Faith and Liberating Community*, 71–77.

26. Rensberger, *Johannine Faith and Liberating Community*, 77–81.

27. The synagogue authorities are referred to either as "the Pharisees" or, more commonly, as simply "the Jews" in John. The latter designation reflects the Johannine community's alienation from their roots but is not to be taken as indicating a general persecution of Christians by Jews.

28. On Nicodemus, see Rensberger, *Johannine Faith and Liberating Community*, 37–51; idem, "Oppression and Identity in the Gospel of John," 88–91. For a contrasting view, see, for example, R. E. Brown, *The Gospel according to John*, Anchor Bible 29–29A (Garden City, N.Y.: Doubleday, 1966–1970), Vol. 2: 959–60; R. Schnackenburg, *The Gospel according to St John* (New York: Crossroads Publishing, 1968–1982), Vol. 3: 296–97.

29. Compare Mary Ann Tolbert's remarks on "status" asceticism in Mark 10:34–35; 10:42–45 (this volume, 39–41).

30. Valantasis, "Constructions of Power in Asceticism," 797–98.

31. Compare Susan R. Garrett's discussion of self-denial as an ascetic discipline in Luke (this volume, 85–87).

32. See Mary Ann Tolbert's remarks on suffering, persecution, the cross, and ascetic choice in Mark (this volume, 41–42).

33. G. Wainwright, "Types of Spirituality," in *The Study of Spirituality*, eds. C. Jones, G. Wainwright, and E. Yarnold, S.J. (Oxford: Oxford University Press, 1986), 593; cf. Pseudo-Athanasius, "*The Life and Activity of the Holy and Blessed Teacher Syncletica* 8, 106," trans. E. A. Castelli, in *Ascetic Behavior in Greco-Roman Antiquity: A Sourcebook*, ed. V. L. Wimbush (Minneapolis, Minn.: Fortress, Studies in Antiquity and Christianity, 1990), 269–70, 308.

34. Reading the present subjunctive *pisteuete* with P[66], etc., rather than the majority-text aorist subjunctive *pisteusete* read by the NRSV.
35. See, for example, D. Burton-Christie, *The Word in the Desert: Scripture and the Quest for Holiness in Early Christian Monasticism* (Oxford: Oxford University Press, 1993), 226, 264–65. The latter discussion is especially interesting, treating Abba Poimen's interpretation of John 15:13 (love as the laying down of one's life for one's friends) in terms of refusing to repeat slander or to retaliate for wrongs in the monastic setting.
36. Meeks, "The Man from Heaven in Johannine Sectarianism," 67–72.
37. J. M. Dillon, "Rejecting the Body, Refining the Body: Some Remarks on the Development of Platonist Asceticism," in *Asceticism*, eds. Wimbush and Valantasis, 80–87; G. P. Corrington Streete, "Trajectories of Ascetic Behavior," in ibid., 121–22.
38. See, further, Rensberger, "Sectarianism and Theological Interpretation in John," forthcoming in a volume of the Society of Biblical Literature Symposium Series, ed. F. F. Segovia (Atlanta, Ga.: Scholars Press).
39. I was stimulated to consider this theme by some of John S. Kloppenborg's remarks in his response to this paper at the Toronto conference.
40. This implies that his coming from God was by means of physical birth, but John shows no interest in this.
41. See, for example, *The Wisdom of the Desert Fathers: Systematic Sayings from the Anonymous Series of the Apophthegmate Patram*, trans. B. Ward, 2nd ed. (Oxford: The Sisters of the Love of God, 1986) 21 (no. 60), 27 (no. 81).
42. John 7:53–8:11, a much later non-Johannine addition to the text, is not considered here.
43. See G. Clark, "Women and Asceticism in Late Antiquity: The Refusal of Status and Gender," in *Asceticism*, eds. Wimbush and Valantasis, 33–48. Compare the analysis of early Christian chastity stories concerning women in V. Burrus, *Chastity as Autonomy: Women in the Stories of Apocryphal Acts* (Studies in Women and Religion 23, Lewiston, N.Y.: Mellen, 1987), 87–103; R. S. Kraemer, *Her Share of the Blessings: Women's Religions among Pagans, Jews, and Christians in the Greco-Roman World* (Oxford: Oxford University Press, 1992), 154–55. Rather more speculative is A. C. Wire, *The Corinthian Women Prophets: A Reconstruction through Paul's Rhetoric* (Minneapolis, Minn.: Fortress, 1990), 82–97.
44. See discussion above re: E. Isaac, 129.

—⟨∞∞∞⟩—

8

Making Sense of Difference:
Asceticism, Gospel Literature,
and the Jesus Tradition

John S. Kloppenborg

The chapters in this section all engage in the intriguing exercise of setting canonical gospel literature alongside ascetical literature and observing similarities and differences. Of course, the gospels are not normally considered under the rubric of asceticism, and none of the writers argues herein that any of the gospels is a strong instance of an ascetical text. Nevertheless, each is prepared to venture that there are some points of convergence between the Jesus tradition and ascetical literature.

What is to be applauded from the outset is the fact that none of the chapters succumbs to the customary bad habit of New Testament scholars arguing about the genealogy of seemingly ascetic elements in the gospels: whether these early Christian writings could have been "influenced" by asceticism and whether asceticism was present in sufficient densities in the first century CE to have accounted for such "influence." Instead, the exercise is comparative and analogical: To quote Jonathan Z. Smith,

> comparison, in its strongest form, brings difference together solely within the space of the scholar's mind. It is the individual scholar, for his or her own good theoretical reasons, who imagines their cohabitation, without even requiring that they be consenting adults—not processes of history, influence, or diffusion, which all too often, have been held to be both the justification for and the result of comparison.[1]

I have chosen to concentrate not on the fine details of each chapter but to ask about what one learns from such a project of comparison. Each chapter includes serious reflections on the definition and scope of asceticism, and it is only by means of such a reflection that the comparison can be ventured at all, since, on the face of it, none of the characters of the Jesus tradition—except for John the Baptist—seems remotely ascetic. Accordingly, a fairly generous definition of asceticism is needed to allow ascetic elements in the gospels to be discerned. None of the writers is evidently prepared to widen the definition too far, lest the act of comparison become vacuous.[2] Tolbert and Rensberger register the greatest hesitations about calling the gospels ascetic; only Patterson is willing to use a broadly conceived notion of asceticism as "an appropriate framework for understanding what the early Jesus movement was all about."

This leaves us with three main options. First, one might simply be content with the rather uninteresting conclusion that the gospels are only weakly ascetic (if at all) and leave matters at that. Second, one might conclude that the documents could after all be peripheral examples of asceticism. This could be achieved by broadening the definition of asceticism to the point where the canonical gospels would thereby be let in. But such a strategy is not, I suggest, very enlightening, for in effect it compares various sets of "strong texts" by setting them on a weak or diffuse comparative grid. It is better, in my view, to pursue a third option and adopt a narrower and more restrictive definition of asceticism that precisely *excludes* the canonical gospels but excludes them in a disciplined, and therefore illuminating, manner.

Tolbert cautions against limiting our gaze to fourth-century monasticism when defining asceticism and rightly notes the important antecedents in Pythagoreanism, Philo's Therapeutae, and, one might add, John the Baptist. Her point makes all the more interesting the question: Why, at a time when asceticism was a cultural option and becoming an important element in antique religious practice, does it fail to appear in the gospels? Rensberger's approach is equally helpful. He does not limit himself to asking whether John is or is not an ascetic document—a question he answers in the negative—but proceeds to ask "how ascetic categories and interests might shed light on the reading of John and how John might help in the understanding of ancient asceticism." What makes reading John (or any of the other documents of the Jesus tradition) through ascetic lenses interesting are not only the similarities present but equally the dissimilarities, for the latter require us to give an account of the significance of difference.

Each author provides or assumes a working definition of asceticism and, using such a measure, discerns the extent to which the gospels reflect or fail to reflect ascetical practice and discourse. It is striking how influential Valantasis' discussion of asceticism has been for all of the writers—and I, too, assume a definition of asceticism that begins with Valantasis. Valantasis defines asceticism as "performances within a dominant social environment intended to inaugurate a new subjectivity, different social relations, and an alternative symbolic universe."[3] As the endeavor to create a new subjectivity and to affect the environment in which such a creation becomes possible, asceticism entails a specific construction of power. Valantasis identifies several aspects of this construction:

> the construction of reality and truth, which embraces a wide spectrum of intellectual, theological, literary, and political knowledge, as well as specific ideological and logonomic features; the social situation of asceticism in which the practice and teaching of the ascetic distinguishes itself from the practice and lives of the non-ascetic; the importance and centrality of practices and technologies to the ascetic program in which the practices at once construct power and modulate social concerns; the critical linking of solidarity/sociality with power as inverse descriptions of one another; and, finally, the production of systems that support the ascetic's subjectivity, social relations, and symbolic universe. The capacity to change and the capacity to affect the productive environment of another subject (even when that "other subject" is simply a redefinition of one's own self) implicate a wide assortment of human activity.[4]

Valantasis is reluctant to identify the definition of asceticism too closely with specific practices—fasting, sexual abstinence, self-denial, poverty, etc.—even though such practices may characterize asceticism. Instead, following Geoffrey Harpham, he underscores the role of asceticism in cultural diversity and resistance: "Asceticism *raises the issue* of culture by structuring an opposition between culture and its opposite."[5]

This rather abstract definition is useful as a starting point, for it indicates both the critical and the constructive dimensions of asceticism, functioning both at the level of the self and at the level of society. As a particular construction of power, asceticism intends the creation of a new subjectivity and does so by the articulation of a new self, toward which the ascetic moves, and an other self, which is abandoned or dominated. At the same time, Valantasis argues that asceticism involves a "delimitation and restructuring of social relations" and "the construction of a symbolic universe capable of supporting these subjectivities and social relationship."[6]

It is perhaps stating the obvious—but it is an important obvious fact—that in asceticism the *human body* is the particular site where power is displayed. Ascetical practices aim at the mastery of the appetites, whose locus is the body, and display that mastery by means of various performances. It is in these acts of displaying mastery or control that the new self is articulated and the oppositions to the dominant social environment become most obvious. Both the (interior) self-mastery and the demonstrative or performative aspects are essential to asceticism. It is the body itself that provides the particular "surface" of performance, whether in a dramatic form, such as Symeon Stylites' act of touching his toes 1244 times (Theodoret, *Historia religiosa*, PG 82.1481A) or in the more "passive" form of Thecla's refusal to marry—and hence, her choice to appear in public space without the usual markers of marriage; whether asceticism involves the performance of unusual or exaggerated actions or the abstinence from usual or expected behavior. I do not mean to suggest that *particular* bodily practices are normative; only that the deployment of power in asceticism always concerns the human body, however much the "body" itself is socially constructed.[7]

Several of the contributors to this section comment on the motif of self-mastery. Both Garrett and Smith note how the heroes of Luke–Acts are represented as having gained self-mastery in contrast to opponents who act in irrational and uncontrolled ways. The Lukan Jesus enjoins prayer, vigilance, and self-denial as part of the care of the self, and the dying Jesus displays the characteristics of self-control, temperance, clemency, and fortitude.[8] Similarly, the Matthaean Jesus displays self-mastery in the Temptation story and teaches self-denial and disciplined attention to inner attitudes (Saldarini). Such practices are part of ascetic discipline. Yet for both Matthew and Luke, it is not the body of Jesus that becomes specially visible as a result of his self-mastery, as it is, for example, in the case of Symeon. Apart from the Lukan Gethsemane scene (22:40–46) and Matthew's penchant for having Jesus touch people, Jesus' physical gestures go mostly unreported.

Rensberger notes the fact that the Gospel of John has remarks about Jesus' body in almost every chapter: Jesus sheds tears, looks up in prayer, is tired, eats, drinks, spits, wraps his body in a towel, and offers his hands and side for inspection. Rensberger is also correct that John has discourses that invoke marital, sexual, and alimentary images in his description of the alternate reality brought about by Jesus. But here too the body is not a site where self-mastery is displayed. That Jesus is flesh is theologically important to John and is signaled variously in the text, but there are almost no textual markers that draw specific attention to Jesus' body apart, perhaps, from the injunction to Mary Magdalene to "stop clinging, for I have not yet ascended to the Father" (20:17).

Asceticism is, of course, not the only construction that involves the human body as its specific locus. The body is also the site of the discourse on power that occurs in torture and the resistance to torture. A comparison of asceticism with torture may be instructive. Brent Shaw draws attention to Jerome's description of the martyrdom of a young woman of Vercellae about 370 CE, falsely accused of adultery.[9] When, under torture, her alleged lover confesses and "lies against his own blood," as Jerome puts it,[10] the woman was left no opportunity to deny the charge. Her only means of resistance was her body. But in contrast to the failed strength of her alleged lover, she refuses to be reduced by displays of power and in doing so rewrites the maps of power. This map, as Peter Brown describes it, involves a "time-worn polarity between 'male' self-control and its opposite, a convulsive violence, associated with 'womanish' lack of self-restraint."[11] Jerome comments expressly on the way in which her resistance challenged the sexual division of virtue: "But the woman for her part showed a courage superior to her sex."[12] Her invitation, "strike me, burn me, cut me in pieces. I did not do it" (*caede, ure, lacera; non feci*), disassembles her tormenters' construction of power, reducing the torturer to groans and gasps and turning the governor to irrational frenzy.[13] The governor then threatens the executioner with death "unless he can make the weaker sex confess what manly strength had been unable to conceal."[14] Again her body defeats this intention. Even the final attempts to behead her are variously thwarted: The executioner's "well-trained arm" only scratches her neck, and a second and a third stroke from the now-enraged executioner likewise fail. A newly appointed executioner succeeds—but only after the third attempt—in delivering the *coup de grace* from which, however, she later miraculously recovers. As Shaw notes, "the whole tale is replete with discourses of power that flow through her body and that are clearly understood to have political significance."[15]

The story in 2 Maccabees of the torture and killing of Eleazar (2 Macc. 6:18–31) and the mother and her seven sons (2 Macc. 7) evinces the same dynamics of the contrast between the "manly virtues,"[16] including self-mastery, rational speech, and indifference to pain, displayed by the martyrs, and the irrational fury that infects the Seleucid king and his torturers. Like the account of the killing of the woman in Jerome, the account in 2 Maccabees recounts in horrifying detail the violence inflicted to the bodies. But such attention is necessary, for the body of the martyr is precisely the locus where power is displayed—where the oppressive, dominating, invasive power that seeks to reduce the subject to a docile and malleable object meets the resistant subject. Ironically, it is through a surplus of the virtues promoted by the dominant power—self-mastery, *andreia*, indifference to pain—that the martyr is able to stop the invasion. The resistant body of the martyr becomes the rock upon which the conventional world founders and where the power of Empire is shattered.

Although in a less—but at times only slightly less—theatrical mode, ascetic performances also deconstruct the usual arrangements of power and articulate a new subjectivity. Valantasis notes three key aspects of asceticism: performance, intention, and novelty.[17] Accounts of the resistant body of the martyr involve the same three aspects, but they have inverse functions. Novelty in the first instance pertains to the instruments of torture, whose very novelty and incongruity with the human body are underscored in the typical action of displaying them to the crowd and to the victim.[18] At the most obvious level, both the performance and the intention also belong to the torturer. But both become the occasion of the martyr's own performance of self-control and the perfecting of a new subjectivity.

Even the novelty of the instruments of torture succumbs to redefinition by the martyr. The torturers' power is blunted in the speech of the

Maccabean martyrs, who declare that the pain they suffer is the purgative and redemptive discipline imposed by God (2 Macc. 6:32). Prudentius' account of the martyrdom of Eulalia has Eulalia announce that the wounds made by iron hooks are letters recording Christ's triumphs inscribed upon her body.[19] The gendered distinctions in the articulation of power and virtue are expressly deconstructed in a stream of ironic, even oxymoronic, statements:

> The holyspirit of Eulalia
> roared, and her bold nature
> prepared to shatter the violent onslaught;
> and with a breast panting for God,
> woman that she was, she challenged the weapons of men.[20]

In the case of the ascetic, the self-inflicted discipline and even pain is likewise resignified; it is not masochism, but portends a new subjectivity that is "bodied forth" through the ascetic practices. Insofar as this new subjectivity is at odds with ordinary cultural values, this display is likewise an act of studied resistance.

What does this have to do with asceticism in the gospels of the New Testament? In the first place, it should be clear that all three sets of documents—ascetical documents, martyrological stories, and the canonical gospels—involve discourses on power framed in opposition to conventional discourses. Opposition to conventional power is obvious in the case of the early Jesus tradition that Patterson discusses, where itinerancy confronts the ordinary world of "artisans, farmers, fishers, clerks, weavers [and] maids," and where the abandonment of kin groups signals a new kinship that "transcends familial bonds and relationships." The deliberate *sygkrisis* between the self-mastery of the Lukan Jesus and his followers and the irrationality of their opponents, discussed by Garrett and Smith, is not unlike the contrast that is deliberately structured into the martyrological accounts noted here or the confrontation with gendered power relations that occurs in Thecla's renunciation of marriage and her cutting her hair to look like a man.

Turning to John, one can readily agree with Rensberger that the fourth gospel is engaged in a project of deconstructing one culture and forming the reader in a new one. This entails the promotion of a resistance to the world and indeed an "innerweltliche Entweltlichung," to use the felicitous phrase of Luise Schottroff.[21] Might this also be called "inner asceticism"? Rensberger's answer, that John is "parallel" to asceticism insofar as the author forms the reader in a new symbolic universe without resorting to properly ascetic categories, seems on the right track. Like the martyrology that resignifies the instruments of torture, or the ascetic who resignifies self-imposed discipline and pain, John resignifies an externally imposed ostracism as something to be embraced as essentially salvific. Exclusion from the synagogue is a good thing, and holding back is to be discouraged.

But in John, unlike ascetical discourse and martyrologies, the body of Jesus goes largely unnoticed, an extraordinary feature of the gospel, given the fact that the author has to narrate that most extravagantly somatic form of execution—crucifixion. Not unlike Eulalia some centuries later, John redraws and inverts the maps of power associated with crucifixion, interpreting it as glorification and exaltation. But the body of Jesus is hardly noticed in all this. Even the piercing of the body (after his death!) is not treated as the moment of the deconstruction of the world, but is apparently quarried for some (obscure) allegorical significance. John is obviously interested in Jesus' death. But the body of Jesus is not a resistant body; on the contrary, it is completely amenable to death once the "hour" has come. The site of resistance is not Jesus' body, but the reader/hearer, who knows perfectly well that crucifixion is dishonor and humiliation but who is asked to imagine it otherwise. Perhaps we might think of John as *Schreibtischaskese*.

While similarities may be identified between the Jesus tradition, ascetical discourse, and martyrological stories, it seems to me to be fundamentally unhelpful to resort to a weak definition of asceticism that would allow one to embrace the gospels as ascetic. Similarly, while ascetic literature and martyrdoms share some of the same dynamics, it would hardly be an advance to treat martyrdom as a subdivision of ascetical literature.

To return to the opening methodological point: What is illuminating (for me) about the comparison of ascetical and martyrological documents with the early Jesus tradition is not that the gospels can be seen as ascetic. That would be to conceive the goal of comparison to be the creation of homologies. Instead, comparison discloses the significance of silences and lacunae and provokes the question: Why are the elements that are so key to the way in which asceticism or martyrological schemata visualized the loci of power so conspicuously absent from the Jesus tradition? I do not have a clear answer, but I suspect that body symbolism in general and the notion of a resistant, disciplined body in particular are key.

NOTES

1. Jonathan Z. Smith, *Drudgery Divine: On the Comparison of Early Christianities and the Religions of Late Antiquity* (London: The School of Oriental and African Studies; Chicago: University of Chicago Press, Jordan Lectures in Comparative Religion 14, 1990), 115.
2. See especially the comments by Rensberger on Geoffrey Galt Harpham, *The Ascetic Imperative in Culture and Criticism* (Chicago: University of Chicago Press, 1987).
3. Richard J. Valantasis, "Constructions of Power in Asceticism," *Journal of the American Academy of Religion* 63/64 (1995): 797.
4. Ibid, 793.

5. Harpham, *The Ascetic Imperative*, xii, italics in original.

6. Valantasis, "Constructions of Power," 796.

7. On the social construction of the monk's body, see Valantasis, "Daemons and the Perfecting of the Monk's Body: Monastic Anthropology, Daemonology, and Asceticism," in *Discursive Formations, Ascetic Piety and the Interpretation of Early Christian Literature, Part 2*, ed. Vincent L. Wimbush (Atlanta, Ga.: Scholars, *Semeia* 58, 1992), 47–79.

8. See John S. Kloppenborg, "*Exitus clari viri*: The Death of Jesus in Luke," *Toronto Journal of Theology* 8 (1992): 106–120.

9. Brent D. Shaw, "Body/Power/Identity: Passions of the Martyrs," *Journal of Early Christian Studies* 4 (1996): 269–312, at 272–73, citing Jerome, *Epistulae* 1.3–14 (*Corpus Scriptorum Ecclesiasticorum Latinorum* 54.1–9).

10. Jerome, *Epistulae* 1.3: *dum in suum mentitur sanguinem*.

11. Peter Brown, *The Body and Society: Men, Women and Sexual Renunciation in Early Christianity* (New York: Columbia University Press, Lectures on the History of Religions 13, 1988), 12.

12. *Epistulae* 1.3: *at vero mulier sexo fortior suo*.

13. Ibid. The governor, who initially "feasts his eyes on the spectacle," began gnashing his teeth in fury [*saevum dentibus frendens*] like some wild beast that had his taste of blood.

14. *Epistulae* 1.4: *nisi confiteretur sexus inferior, quod non potuerat robur virile reticere*.

15. Shaw, "Body/Power/Identity," 274.

16. Gendered language is expressly used to describe the mother, whose "womanly heart is stirred with manly courage" [*ton thelyn logismon arseni thymo diegeirasa*].

17. Valantasis, "Constructions of Power," 798–99.

18. See Seneca, *Epistulae morales* 14.4–6.

19. Prudentius, *Peristephanon* 3.135–139: "See, my Lord, you are writing on me. How I love to read these letters which, my Christ, record your triumph. The dark scarlet of my blood pouring out speaks your holy name" [*scribere ecce mihi, Dominie, iuvat hos apices legere qui tua, Christe, tropaea notant! nomen et ipsa sacrum loquitur purpura sanguinis eliciti*]. See John Petruccione, "The Portrait of St. Eulalia of Mérida in Prudentius' Peristephanon 3," *Analecta Bolladiana* 108 (1990): 81–104, esp. 98.

20. Prudentius, *Peristephanon* 1.31–35: "*Infremuit sacer Eulaliae/spiritus, ingenique ferox/turbida frangere bella parat/et rude pectus anhila Deo/femina provocat arma virum.*"

21. Luise Schottroff, "Heil als innerweltliche Entweltlichung: Der gnostische Hintergrund der johannischen Vorstellung vom Zeitpunkt der Erlösung," *Novum Testamentum* 11 (1969): 294–317.

Part Two

———❊❊❊———

PAUL
(The Real Thing)

9

God's Will at Thessalonica and Greco-Roman Asceticism

Ronald F. Hock

Introduction

Putting new questions to a familiar text often allows it to be seen in a fresh
way, as the questions reveal dimensions of the text not previously considered.
Paul's ethical instructions in 1 Thess. 4:3–8 have received considerable attention, but they have not been read in light of the ascetic trends that were gaining influence at the time that Paul founded a Christian community at
Thessalonica. Accordingly, this chapter evaluates 1 Thess 4:3–8 in terms of
these contemporary ascetic trends.

Both asceticism and 1 Thessalonians have been the object of considerable scholarly attention of late, and the present investigation must be situated within these discussions. 1 Thessalonians, always an item on the scholarly agenda, has nevertheless received even more than the usual attention, as
scholars are taking a new look at long-held views regarding the letter, such
as its date and where Paul wrote it, as well as applying new methods, such as
rhetorical criticism. The interest in asceticism, at least among New Testament
scholars, is more recent and limited. Vincent Wimbush's book on Paul as a
worldly ascetic raised the subject,[1] but it was put on hold until he, together
with a team of scholars from various disciplines, could conduct a broader
methodological and historical discussion of the subject. With those goals
achieved,[2] attention has returned to the New Testament and to the question
of whether asceticism is in any sense an illuminating category for analyzing
the forms of earliest Christianity.

To answer this question for Pauline Christianity, and especially for 1
Thessalonians, we begin with a definition of asceticism arising from the dis-

cussions initiated by Wimbush. Richard Valantasis' formulation, which will allow for a sophisticated and incisive analysis in 1 Thessalonians of possible ascetic identity and behavior, reads as follows: "Asceticism may be defined as performances within a dominant social environment intended to inaugurate a new subjectivity, different social relations, and an alternative symbolic universe."[3]

Valantasis elaborates further on key points in the definition, specifically on what he means by performances, intention, and novelty, as well as on how power is shown in an ascetic subjectivity, ascetic social relations, and an ascetic symbolic universe,[4] but the specifics on the relevant issues of this defintion can await their proper place in the analysis of 1 Thessalonians. The definition itself is sufficient to begin the analysis of this earliest of Paul's letters.

PAUL AND CHRISTIAN IDENTITY AT THESSALONICA

During Paul's initial missionary visit to Thessalonica (cf. Acts 17:1–9), he not only preached his message of salvation from the coming wrath of God but also formed a new assembly from those who had turned from idols to the living and true God (1 Thess. 1:1–10).[5] Some months later, with news from Timothy about this new assembly (3:6), he wrote the letter now called 1 Thessalonians. Of special interest to us among the contents of this letter are the ethical instructions Paul repeats from his initial missionary teaching, which were intended to guide them in living out lives that would be pleasing to God (4:1–8; cf. 2:12).

These verses are particularly important because they provide clues about the formation of a new, or Christian, identity among the Thessalonians and their possible differentiation from other groups in the city. To be sure, these instructions, as we have them, are only a brief summary and probably preserve only a portion of what Paul had said in Thessalonica. Nevertheless, since they function in the letter as a reminder to the Thessalonians (cf. 4:2, 6), they must also contain what was essential in those instructions. At least, this analysis proceeds on that assumption, that is, that enough of Paul's instructions are preserved in the letter to allow a meaningful description of the Thessalonians' new identity and way of life.

Paul identifies these instructions as the will of God (4:3) and illustrates what God's will entails by including three specific admonitions, all concerned with sexual morality (4:4–8), an intriguing choice, given our interest in asceticism as an analytical tool. At any rate, before proceeding with the analysis of these verses and their relation to asceticism, we need to pause briefly and address the relevant scholarly issues that affect the interpretation of these instructions.

EXEGETICAL AND THEORETICAL PRELIMINARIES

No one who comes to the ethical instructions in 4:3–8 is long unaware of the number of issues that swirl around the interpretation of these verses. The most intractable of the issues is, of course, the meaning of the word *skeuos* in v. 4.[6] Ever since the patristic period and continuing up to the present, interpreters of 1 Thessalonians have vacillated between rendering *skeuos*—literally "vessel," but clearly intended in a metaphorical sense here—as "wife" or "body" (or, as a specification of the latter, as "penis").[7] The former choice, "wife," has usually been preferred,[8] but recently the latter, especially in the sense of "penis," has received strong support.[9] Resolution of this issue is not possible here, but, as will become clear later, the arguments for "wife" appear stronger.[10]

Another linguistic problem concerns the meaning of *pragma* (matter, affair) in v. 6. Does it continue the subject of sexual morality, or does it introduce a new subject, such as greed, suggested by the verb *pleonektein*, meaning "to take advantage of"? That Paul continues here with the subject of sexual morality is increasingly the consensus, although scholars differ over whether the subject is still sexual immorality, as in v. 3,[11] chastity, as in v. 4,[12] or some new topic, such as adultery.[13] The last named is most likely, since *pragma* can be used for all sorts of sexual "affairs," including adultery,[14] as can *pleonektein*.[15]

Another issue revolves around whether Paul intended these instructions on sexual morality to address a specific situation in Thessalonica—one possibly brought to his attention by Timothy's report (cf. 3:6–7) but one surely thought to have arisen because of the Thessalonians' coming from a background of lax, pagan morality[16]—or whether he responded to a more generally positive situation, but one that still concerned Paul, given the newness of the Thessalonians' faith and the typical pressures of day-to-day life that they faced, thus making moral reminders necessary.[17] Related to this issue is the formal one of whether 1 Thessalonians, when considered rhetorically, is closer to a deliberative speech (and hence directed at getting the Thessalonians to act in a certain way)[18] or an epideictic speech (and hence aimed at praising the Thessalonians for doing as Paul had instructed them).[19] Evidence suggesting the overall confidence and joy that Paul had toward the Thessalonians (1:3, 7; 2:19–20; 3:6), plus his explicit statements about the Thessalonians doing well and needing only to do better (4:1, 10; 5:11), tip the scale in favor of Paul's responding to a generally positive situation that called for an epideictic rhetoric.

The last issue that need concern us here is in fact the most important: the background of Paul's instructions in 1 Thess. 4:3–8. Do they derive principally from Jewish moral teaching, or do they reflect a more broadly based

Greco-Roman ethic? Here scholarly preference clearly favors the former, indeed consistently seeing "a distinctively Jewish flavor"[20] in Pauls instructions on sexual morality. Parallels from various Jewish texts are cited,[21] and, what is more, this Jewish background is then used to contrast the morality Paul is inculcating with the virtual lack of any morals in the pagan environment that surrounded the fledgling Thessalonian assembly of Christians. Such a reading of pagan morality is often justified by appeals to Paul's own statement about the lustful passion of Gentiles who do not know God (4:5).

At any rate, this low view of pagan conduct and ideals is especially frequent in scholarly literature, as a few examples will show. J. B. Lightfoot notes: "[C]onverts had as pagans looked upon sexual immorality as a matter of indifference."[22] A. Plummer concurs: "Among the heathen sensual indulgence was regarded very lightly and was treated almost as a matter of course.... [T]he heathen...had lost sense of the difference between right and wrong, especially as regards chastity, purity, and honesty."[23] Likewise, Martin Dibelius:

> Nicht einheitlich ist die Frage zu beantworten, ob diese Mahnungen den wurdenden Christen neu waren. Der bisherige sittliche Stand der Neubekehrten war gewiss nicht gleichartig gewesen; für die meisten von ihnen aber mag es die Annahme einer strengeren sittlichen Lebensfhrung bedeutet haben.[24]

Also Beda Rigaux:

> C'est un grand changement dans la vie des néo-convertis. Sur la moralité des païens, Paul ne se faisait païs d'illusion.... Les païens considéraient ces actes comme tout à fait normaux.[25]

And such views continue up to the present, as seen in this statement by G. P. Carras: "[T]he application of Jewish ethics to Gentile converts...helped to distinguish these converts from the morals of their non-Christian contemporaries.[26]

The importance of this understanding of Paul's essentially Jewish sexual morality as contrasting so sharply with pagan conduct and norms is that, if true, it is evidence of Paul's intention to form an ascetic community in Thessalonica, since we would then have, to recast Valantasis' definition somewhat, an intention to inaugurate a new subjectivity as well as different social relations and an alternative symbolic universe that stand against, indeed reject, the dominant social values of Thessalonica and of Greco-Roman society in general.[27]

Such a possibility, however, retreats quickly from view once we realize that the sharp contrast between Paul's sexual ethic and that of Greco-Roman society all too readily assumes that Paul's ethnocentric attitude toward pagan morality was, in fact, descriptive of actual pagan behavior and ideals. Nothing, however, could be further from the truth. Indeed, as the following collection of evidence shows, Paul's concern for sexual morality and his emphasis on it as a defining characteristic of the Thessalonians' identity match the concern and emphasis of Greco-Roman society in general.[28] The implications of this thesis for placing Paul on an ascetic trajectory must await the presentation of the evidence.

To return to the text: Given this rehearsal of the most important issues affecting the interpretation of 1 Thess. 4:3–8, we can now summarize what Paul's missionary instructions about the will of God and the Thessalonians' sanctification (v. 3a) entailed. In a word, these instructions dealt with a single subject, sexual morality, divided up into three specific admonitions: (1) to abstain from *porneia*, or sexual immorality (v. 3b); (2) to acquire a wife in purity and honor, and not in the passion of sexual desire (v. 4); and (3) to avoid taking advantage of a brother, or fellow Christian, by means of an adulterous affair (v. 6). Divine sanctions round out the instructions (vv. 7–8).

SEXUAL BEHAVIOR AND NORMS IN THE GRECO-ROMAN WORLD

Why, then, did Paul reduce the will of God to sexual morality in his missionary preaching at Thessalonica and in his later letter to the Thessalonians, especially if these instructions, as this thesis proposes, differed little from the Thessalonians' previous ethics, Paul's unfortunate slip about Gentiles (v. 5) notwithstanding? A survey of Greco-Roman sexual behavior and norms allows us to set Paul's instructions in their social and intellectual context and hence permit a better historical assessment. Such a survey would involve a longer discussion than is permitted in this context, but a brief summary should suffice to show that, while sexual conduct and misconduct were indeed very public and pervasive, the moral standards regarding sexual conduct were exacting and high—and, as we shall see, the same as Paul's.

First, then, a review of typical sexual activity in the Greco-Roman world: Dio Chrysostom comments that brothels could be found everywhere in a city,[29] and Athenaeus cites a comic fragment that has prostitutes (*pornai*) posted outside a brothel, breasts uncovered and calling out to men, both young and old.[30] In addition, female escorts (*hetairai*) were a common feature of urban life, attending symposia[31] or waiting for their lovers to stop at their door on a revel after a symposium and be invited in for the night.[32] Being locked out only prompted larger gifts from a young man, and many *hetairai* soon ran through a lover's inheritance[33] or became rich through many lovers, as indicated, for example, by the famous Phryne, who, it is said, was able to dedicate a gold statue of Aphrodite to the goddess.[34]

Religious festivals were also noted for their sexual activity,[35] and weddings, at least for members of leading families, were often very large events.[36] In addition, stories abound of wives admitting lovers into their rooms, usually aided by a slave, flatterer, even by an unsuspecting husband![37] Indeed, one comic fragment boasts that no carpenter has made a door so stout that an adulterer could not get in.[38] Household slaves were often assumed to be sexually available,[39] even to visiting guests.[40]

Finally, sexual activity was especially associated with symposia, where we find a *hetaira* kissing her lover's friend,[41] *hetairai* competing to see who has the most beautiful breasts or hips,[42] parasites seducing their host's concubine,[43] a cook seducing the host's wife,[44] a Stoic gazing at a handsome cupbearer,[45] a Cynic stripping a flute girl,[46] an Epicurean grabbing a harp girl,[47] and a Stoic outbidding everyone in order to take home a flute girl.[48] The evidence of such sexual immorality is endless: One could also point to tourist attractions like Praxiteles' nude statue of Aphrodite at Cnidos,[49] as well as to love messages written on walls,[50] wedding and adulterers' songs in the air,[51] and foods believed to be aphrodisiacs on the menu,[52] but it should be clear by now that sexual activity and references to sex were pervasive in Greco-Roman society.

It should also be emphasized, however, that such conduct was not a matter of indifference, as Lightfoot says, and certainly was not the norm. Indeed, the evidence condemning such behavior is just as fulsome, whether we note a peasant farmer reviling a group of *hetairai* and their lovers on their way to a country symposium[53] or the philosopher Crates writing on the base of Phryne's golden statue of Aphrodite: "[Paid for] by the lack of self-control (*akrasia*) of the Greeks."[54] But opposition went beyond condemnation as various strategies for controlling sexual immorality were developed: architectural barriers in houses to separate men and women along with elaborate locking-up procedures at night,[55] the seclusion of women in the women's quarters and their careful monitoring when outdoors,[56] the provision of *paidagogoi* for boys to see that they behaved themselves as they went to and from school or the gymnasium,[57] to name just a few.

In addition to strategies like these, however, there developed an intellectual tradition, developed by philosophers, poets, orators, and novelists, that spoke out against sexual immorality of all kinds. This tradition, moreover, articulated the majority view, not just the view of intellectuals. At any rate, urban householders as well as peasant herders and fishermen speak out against sexual immorality,[58] finding allies in the moralizing of Cynics and Stoics in particular. The Cynic Crates, for example, was remembered for his constant attacks on prostitutes and *hetairai*,[59] views consistent with those of his teacher Diogenes and many later Cynics.[60] Similarly, Stoics attacked fancy clothes and unguents,[61] cookbooks,[62] pederasty,[63] adulterers,[64] and even all premarital relations.[65] Other philosophers joined in, such as the Platonist Nigrinus, who denounced adultery and disapproved of men who fought outside brothels on their way from symposia,[66] or the Pythagorean Apollonius, who criticized the youthful Bassus for associating with go-betweens.[67] Not all philosophers were themselves above criticism on these charges, as Lucian's many philosophic frauds exemplify,[68] but, on balance, philosophers had a reputation for resisting temptation and exercising self-control. Indeed, the Platonist Xenocrates was celebrated for resisting the likes of Phryne and Lais.[69] Consequently, the reputation of philosophers was such that Achilles Tatius frequently uses the verb *philosophein*, to act like a philosopher, as a synonym for *sophronein*, to exercise self-control.[70]

With the mention of *sophrosyne*, or self-control, we can shift from the voices raised against sexual immorality to the values that grounded their criticism, for their principal value was indeed *sophrosyne*, defined as the capacity to control one's desires, not to be enslaved by any pleasure, but, on the contrary, to live in an orderly way.[71] Desires (*epithymiai*) could be numerous, but sexual desire is so frequently meant that the principal connotation of *epithymia* was sexual desire.

Examples of this restricted but typical meaning are legion,[72] but the best examples come from the romances. Xenophon of Ephesus is typical. He frequently comments on the *sophrosyne* of his protagonists Habrocomes and Anthia. They pledge on their wedding night to remain faithful, promising to exercise self-control toward all others; their pledges are tested not only by prolonged separation but also by threats and temptations. Still, at the conclusion of the story Anthia, reunited with Habrocomes, can affirm to him: "No one has persuaded me to sin—not Moeris in Syria, not Perilaos in Cilicia, not Psammis or Polyidos in Egypt, not Anchialos in Ethiopia, not my master in Tarentum; no, I remain pure for you, having done literally everything to maintain my self-control [*sophrosyne*].[73] She then asks Habrocomes whether he also exercised self-control while they were apart, and he says: "No young girl seemed beautiful to me, nor did any other woman I saw please me. Indeed, you have Habrocomes back as pure as when you left me in prison in Tyre."[74] In short, what makes Habrocomes and Anthia worthy of their role as protagonists is precisely their commitment to *sophrosyne*. Xenophon has a memorable way of underscoring Habrocomes' commitment, saying that Habrocomes had *sophrosyne* as his *syntrophos*, or slave-companion, since childhood.[75] Thus one strongly held value to emerge from the concern about sexual immorality is self-control.

But another value also emerges. If a husband were to yield to temptation to a slave, *hetaira*, or to someone else's wife, he would display a lack of self-control (*akrasia*). From his own wife's perspective, however, his adulterous action would have been regarded as an injustice (*adikia*). In Chariton we can see the emergence of justice as a value in sexual matters: The eunuch Artaxates encourages his king's desires for Callirhoe by pointing out that, technically speaking, she was not married, since her marriage, whether to Chaereas or to Dionysius, was still to be decided by the king. Accordingly, Artaxates argues as follows: "Do not fear that you are committing adultery (*moicheia*). For there must first be a husband who is being treated unjustly (*adikeisthai*) and then one who is acting unjustly (*adikein*).[76] Similarly, Dio, commenting on men getting marriage partners through adultery, says: "No one, if he were a virtuous man, would dare to take a wife through adultery (*moicheia*), because then he would have acted unjustly (*adikein*) toward her former husband."[77] Finally, Musonius Rufus puts it succinctly: "The man who commits adultery acts unjustly (*adikein*) toward the husband."[78]

In sum, the concerns over sexual morality gave prominence to two virtues: self-control (*sophrosyne*) and justice (*dikaiosyne*). Far from losing a sense of right and wrong, as Plummer says, Greco-Roman society promoted sexual morality. Self-control and justice are the virtues that governed life, especially sexual behavior, in the Greco-Roman world of Paul's day and, presumably, in Thessalonica as well.

PAUL'S INSTRUCTIONS ON SEXUAL MORALITY AND ASCETIC SUBJECTIVITY

The very values that Greco-Roman society upheld turn out to be the same values that Paul inculcates in his missionary instructions in 4:3–8: *Sophrosyne* is the implicit value in Paul's first two admonitions, to abstain from *porneia* (v. 3) and to acquire a wife in holiness and honor (v. 4), whereas *dikaiosyne* is the implicit value in Paul's third admonition, his demand that no one wrong his brother in an adulterous affair (v. 6). The former is a personal virtue designed to define sexual morality before and within marriage, and the latter is a social virtue designed to protect the sanctity of others' marriages.

In other words, Paul's admonitions regarding sexual morality, which may well have paralleled Jewish views on the subject, matched the Thessalonians' own earlier values as well. Indeed, they had probably accepted Paul's missionary appeal and turned toward the living and true God because Paul addressed *their* concerns about sexual morality and affirmed *their* values of *sophrosyne* and *dikaiosyne* as being nothing less than the will of God, precisely what would assure, with the power of the Holy Spirit, their sanctification.

The implications of this interpretation of 4:3–8 for assessing the relevance of using ascetic categories for Thessalonian identity or subjectivity are, at first glance, negative. Precisely because Paul's understanding of God's will entailed the concerns and values of the larger Greco-Roman culture, it is difficult to argue that the Thessalonians' subjectivity was new, its social relations very different, or its symbolic universe much of an alternative to that of the dominant culture. Valantasis' emphasis on ascetic subjectivity as in opposition to the dominant subjectivity becomes problematic when looking at Thessalonian identity. If ascetic categories are to prove useful for Paul and the Thessalonians, it seems necessary to look at the two types of ascetic sub-jects Valantasis delineates as not necessarily opposed to dominant values, the integrative and the educative types.[79] Also, it seems odd that a text so focused on control and sexual matters should not be of relevance to a tra-jectory of asceticism. Perhaps the definition needs to be a little less formal and, when applied to Western asceticism, a little more material, namely, in allowing sexual *askesis* to be one principal sign of ascetic mentality, an *askesis* not in conflict with dominant values but rather one that saw itself as the best way of achieving those values.

NOTES

1. Vincent L. Wimbush, *Paul: The Worldly Ascetic* (Macon, Ga.: Mercer University Press, 1987).
2. See Vincent L. Wimbush, ed., *Ascetic Behavior in Greco-Roman Antiquity: A Sourcebook* (Minneapolis, Minn.: Fortress, 1990); Vincent L. Wimbush and Richard Valantasis, eds., *Asceticism* (New York: Oxford University Press, 1995).
3. Richard Valantasis, "Constructions of Power in Asceticism," *Journal of the American Academy of Religion* 63 (1995): 775–821, esp. 797.
4. Ibid, 797–814.
5. For discussion of Paul's founding of the Thessalonian church, see Abraham J. Malherbe, *Paul and the Thessalonians: The Philosophic Tradition of Pastoral Care* (Philadelphia: Fortress, 1987), 5–33.
6. For full discussion of the options, see Raymond F. Collins, "'This Is the Will of God, Your Sanctification' (1 Thess. 4:3)," in *The Thessalonian Correspondence,* ed. R. F. Collins (Leuven: Leuven University Press, Bibliotheca ephemeridum theologicarum loveniensium 87, 1990), 299–325, esp. 311–13.
7. For the patristic evidence, see Collins, "Will of God," 311.
8. For the meaning "wife," see, for example, Ernst von Dobschütz, *Die Thessalonicher Briefe,* 9th ed. (Meyer Kommentar, Göttingen, Germany: Vandenhoeck & Ruprecht, 1909), 163–65; James Frame, *A Critical and Exegetical Commentary on the Epistles of St. Paul to the Thessalonians,* International Critical Commentary (Edinburgh, Scotland: T&T Clark, 1912), 149–50; A. Oepke, *Die kleineren Briefe des Apostels Paulus,* (Das Neue Testament deutsche 8, Göttingen, Germany: Vandenhoeck & Ruprecht, 1959); Christian Maurer, "[*skeuos*]," *Theological Dictionary of the New Testament* 7: 358–67, esp. 365–67; O. Larry Yarborough, *"Not Like the Gentiles": Marriage Rules in the Letters of Paul,* (Society of Biblical Literature Dissertation Series 80, Atlanta, Ga. Scholars, 1985), 68–76; Traugott Holtz, *Der erste Brief an die Thessalonicher,* 2nd ed. (Evangelische—Katholischer Kommentar zum Neuen Testament 13, Zurich, Switzerland: Benziger, 1990), 157; Collins, "Will of God," 313.
9. For the meaning "body," see, for example, Martin Dibelius, *An die Thessalonicher I-II, An die Philipper,* 3rd ed. (Handbuch zum Neuen Testament 11 3rd ed., Tübingen, Germany: Mohr, 1937), 21; Beda Rigaux, *Saint Paul.*

Les Epîtres aux Thessaloniciens (Paris: Gabalda, Ebib, 1956), 504–6; O. Merk, *Handeln aus Glauben: Die Motivierungen der paulinischen Ethik* (Marburg: Elwert, 1968), 46–47; K. Staab, *Die Thessalonicherbriefe, Die Gefangenschaftsbriefe* (Regensburger Neues Testament 7, Regensburg: Pustet, 1969), 29. For recent proposals to translate *skeuos* as "penis," see, for example, J. Whitten, "A Neglected Meaning for SKEUOS in 1 Thess. 4:4," *New Testament Studies* 28 (1982): 142–43; Charles A. Wanamaker, *The Epistles to the Thessalonians* (Grand Rapids, Mich.: Eerdmans, New International Greek Testament Commentary, 1990), 152–53; and esp. Torlief Elgvin, "'To Master His Own Vessel': 1 Thess. 4:4 in Light of New Qumran Evidence," *New Testament Studies* 43 (1997): 604–19.

10. Among the typical arguments used, the most compelling is the material parallel of 1 Cor. 7:2. For uses of *skeuos* in this sense, see also Chariton, 1.14.9; Alciphron, *ep.* 3.16; Plutarch, *Praec. coniug.* 138E. This interpretation also requires an ingressive sense for *ktasthai*, that is, meaning "get" or "acquire" (cf. Longus, 3.15.1–2; Menander, *Mon.* 398–99 [p. 81, Jaekel]; and Chariton, 2.6.4) and receives confirmation from the context, esp. from the word *time*, or honor, used of another person (cf. von Dobschütz, *Thessalonicher Briefe,* 166), a usage illustrated by Alciphron, *ep.* 2.31; Xenophon of Ephesus, 5.10.12; and Chariton, 3.1.6; 2.7.

11. See, for example, Plummer, *Thessalonians,* 62; Rigaux, *Thessaloniciens,* 509–10.

12. See esp. Collins, "Will of God," 318–19.

13. So, for example, Lightfoot, *Notes,* 57; Staab, *Thessalonicherbriefe,* 30; and I. Howard Marshall, *1 and 2 Thessalonians* (New Century Bible Commentary, Grand Rapids, Mich.: Eerdmans, 1983), 111. H. Baltensweiler ("Erwägungen zu 1 Thess 4:3–8," *Theologische Zeitschrift* 19 [1963]: 1–13) has proposed the specific legal question of the marriage of a daughter that involves a family inheritance.

14. See Philostratus, *ep.* 7 (pederasty); Alciphron, *ep.* 2.35 (rape); and Plutarch, *Am.* 754E–F (revel). For adultery, see Chariton, 2.8.3; Alciphron, *ep.* 3.33; Epictetus, 2.4.4; 3.3.12; and Athenaeus, 13.590c.

15. See Dio, *Orat.* 17.10.

16. For a specific problem or crisis at Thessalonica, see, for example, Frame, *Thessalonians,* 145; Karl P. Donfried and I. Howard Marshall, *The Theology of the Shorter Pauline Letters* (Cambridge, England: Cambridge University Press, 1993), 49: "Paul is…dealing with a situation of grave immorality, not too dissimilar to the cultic temptations found in Corinth."

17. For Paul's instructions intended for a general situation, see, for example, Dibelius, *An die Thessalonicher,* 19–20; Collins, "Will of God," 323.

18. See, for example, George A. Kennedy, *New Testament Interpretation through Rhetorical Criticism* (Chapel Hill: University of North Carolina Press, 1984), 142.

19. See esp. F. W. Hughes, "The Rhetoric of 1 Thessalonians," in *Thessalonian Correspondence,* 94–115.

20. Collins, "Will of God," 324.

21. For details, see G. P. Carras, "Jewish Ethics and Gentile Converts: Remarks on 1 Thess. 4:3-8," in *Thessalonian Correspondence,* 306–15, and G.

Schimanowski, "Abgrenzung und Identitätsfindung: Paulinische Paränese Wissenschaffliche im 1. Thessalonicherbrief," in *Die Heiden*, ed. R. Feldmeier (Wissensduft liche Untersuchungen zum Neuen Testament 40, Tübingen, Germany: Mohr [Siebeck], 1994), 297–316.

22. J. B. Lightfoot, *Notes on Epistles of St. Paul*, ed. J. R. Harmer (London: Macmillan, 1895), 55.
23. A. Plummer, *A Commentary on St. Paul's First Epistle to the Thessalonians* (London: Roxburghe, 1918), 58, 61.
24. Dibelius, *An die Thessalonicher*, 20.
25. Rigaux, *Thessaloniciens*, 502.
26. Carras, "Jewish Ethics," 314. See also Holtz, *Der erste Brief*, 160, and Donfried and Marshall, *Shorter Pauline Letters*, 49: "Paul's severe warnings in this section...is [sic] intended to distinguish the behavior of the Thessalonians as Christians from that of their former life which continues to find ritual expression in the various cults of the city."
27. See esp. Valantasis, "Constructions of Power," 800.
28. For an emphasis on the appropriateness of using Greco-Roman backgrounds, including ethical traditions, in interpreting 1 Thessalonians, see the various studies of Abraham J. Malherbe, esp. "'Gentle as a Nurse': The Cynic Background to 1 Thessalonians 2," *Novum Testamentum* 12 (1970): 203–17, and "Exhortation in First Thessalonians," *Novum Testamentum* 25 (1983): 238–56 (both reprinted in *Paul and the Popular Philosophers* [Minneapolis, Minn.: Fortress, 1989], 35–48, 49–66). See also Yarborough, *Not Like the Gentiles*, 31–63.
29. See Dio, *Orat.* 7.133.
30. Athenaeus, 13.569b-c; cf. also DL 7.187–188; Dio, *Orat.* 33.60; and Xenophon of Ephesus, 5.7.1–3.
31. Lucian, *D. Meretr.* 6.2–3.
32. Alciphron, *ep.* 1.6.2; cf. Chariton, 1.3.2.
33. Athenaeus, 4.168d; cf. also Alciphron, *ep.* 3.14; Aelian, *ep.* 10; Lucian, *D. Meretr.* 12.1.
34. DL 6.60; cf. Athenaeus, 13.567e.
35. Menander, *Epitr.* 377–78; Aelian, *ep.* 15; Alciphron, *ep.* 1.11; Chariton, 1.1.6; and Xenophon, 1.3.
36. Xenophon of Ephesus, 1.7.3–8.1, and Chariton, 1.1.13. Even rural weddings might be large affairs (so Longus, 4.38, and Dio, *Orat.* 7.79).
37. Chariton, 1.4.1–2; Philostratus, *ep.* 7; Dio, *Orat.* 7.145.
38. Stobaeus, 3.6.11 (p. 282 Hense).
39. Lucian, *Gall.* 32; Herodas, 5.1–3; and Xenophon of Ephesus, 3.12.3–4.
40. Lucian, *Asin.* 1, 8–11.
41. Lucian, *D. Meretr.* 3.1.
42. Alciphron, *ep.* 4.14.4–6.
43. Alciphron, *ep.* 3.16.
44. Athenaeus, 12.542f.
45. Lucian, *Symp.* 15.
46. Lucian, *Symp.* 46.
47. Alciphron, *ep.* 3.19.8.

48. Athenaeus, 13.607b–e.
49. Ps.-Lucian, *Am.* 14–16.
50. Lucian, *D. Meretr.* 4.3.
51. Athenaeus, 14.619b; Dio, *Orat.* 33.56 (wedding song); Athenaeus, 14.638d–f (adulterer's song).
52. Athenaeus, 2.63d–64b; 7.316c; 9.371b.
53. Alciphron, *ep.* 11.
54. DL 6.60.
55. Achilles Tatius, 2.19.2–6.
56. Plutarch, *Praec. coniug.* 139c; Lucian, *Asin.* 5; and Chariton, 1.1.5.
57. DL 6.30-31. Cf. Aphthonius, *Progymn.* 3 (p. 5 Rabe).
58. Longus, 4.31.3; Achilles Tatius, 1.3.6; Aelian, *ep.* 9; and Alciphron, *ep.* 1.4.
59. DL 6.85–86, 89, 90.
60. DL 6.61, 63, 66; ps.-Socrates, *epp.* 8–9; Athenaeus, 13.566f–570f.
61. DL 7.17, 23.
62. Athenaeus, 10.457d–e; Musonius Rufus, *frag.* 12 (p. 86, 1–20 Lutz).
63. DL 4.40.
64. Epictetus, 2.4.1–11.
65. Epictetus, *Ench.* 33.8.
66. Lucian, *Nigr.* 16, 23.
67. Apollonius, *ep.* 74.
68. Lucian, *Fug.* 18; *Icar.* 21; and *Tim.* 54–55.
69. DL 4.7.
70. Achilles Tatius, 5.16.7; 6.21.3; 8.5.7. Note also Chaereas' selection of the philosopher Demetrius to accompany Queen Statira back to the King (Chariton, 8.3.10)
71. DL 3.91; 7.126.
72. See, for example, Athenaeus, 14.619e; Lucian, *D. Meretr.* 2.4; 7.4.
73. Xenophon of Ephesus, 5.14.2.
74. Ibid., 5.14.3–4.
75. Ibid., 2.1.4.
76. Chariton, 6.4.7; cf. Chariton, 5.4.1, and DL 6.54.
77. Dio, *Orat.* 31.42.
78. Musonius Rufus, *frag.* 12 (p. 86, 21 Lutz). Cf. Chariton, 5.4.1; Dio, *Orat.* 7.142; and Lucian, *Bis acc.* 32.
79. See Valantasis, "Constructions of Power," 802–4, 808–9.

Disciplines of Difference: Asceticism and History in Paul

Elizabeth A. Castelli

Introduction

In calling for a new model of writing history that highlights both historio-graphical operations and the *space between* the historian in his/her place and the object of study in its own, Michel de Certeau remarks, "The past is first of all the means of *representing a difference.*"[1] What de Certeau is trying to place before his readers is, in some measure, the radical impossibility of the historian's task—the deferrals implied in any re-presentation of the past, the condemnation of the historical writer to a certain kind of failure. At the same time, de Certeau also seeks to elaborate a set of interpretative operations whereby the ineluctable distance between the historian and her or his sub-ject matter becomes itself a part of the story: "The historian travels along the borders of his present; he visits those beaches where the other appears only as a *trace* of what has *passed*. Here he sets up his industry. On the basis of imprints which are now definitively mute (that which has passed will return no more, and its voice is lost forever), a literature is fabricated."[2]

Difference itself has already more often than not been a major charac-teristic in renderings of asceticism across cultures, in the fabricated literature of asceticism and its pasts. That is, asceticism is frequently distinguished from other behavior, whether religious or not, by its unsettling and often extreme difference—its refusal of the ordinary, the contingent, the quotidian. Asceticism's difference may be lauded as the manifestation of a peculiar spir-itual capacity or rendered by a skeptical judgment as the baleful product of psychological disturbance. Asceticism's difference inspires a fullness of inter-pretations, a paradoxical worrying about the difference—an admiration and a suspicion. Consider, for example, the classic nineteenth-century work *Varieties of Religious Experience,* by American pragmatist William James.

There, James calls asceticism a "further symptom of saintliness." Variously inspired by "organic hardihood" or a "love of purity," asceticism may be a happy sacrifice on the part of the practitioner inspired by love for the divine, or perhaps the product of "pessimistic feelings about the self," or rather the result of an "obsession" that "must be worked off" so that "the subject gets his interior consciousness feeling right again," or most extremely physical manifestations of "genuine perversions of bodily sensibility" in which pain is experienced as pleasure. Indeed, as he collects his examples of such saintliness, James assures his readers that the illustrations he will display before his audience will most certainly "make us rub our Protestant eyes."[4]

Of course, James is writing—as de Certeau and others will remind us that we all do—from a particular place and in response to the constraints and possibilities of his historical moment: For James, this was a moment characterized by the embrace of science in the study of human institutions and practices, the influence of evolutionary theory on the narrative *longue durée* of history, the use of the exotic as a transhistorical cultural emblem by which the self could be described most easily through recourse to a discourse of the other. For its location in this historical frame, James' project is striking for its remarkable openness to a range of experiences and its valuation of the very category of "religious experience" itself. For the heirs of James at work on more recent scholarly projects, the constraints he faced have been replaced by a different set of intellectual conditions characterized by an impulse to render ascetical practices in a wide range of historical and cultural locations both legible and intelligible—to supply the unfamiliar with a reassuring gloss of the familiar. The scholarly turn has been away from viewing asceticism as just so many examples of the spectacular and the exotic.

Yet, for whatever its time-bound shortcomings, James' grappling with the problem with the "other" of asceticism is nevertheless in some ways illuminating, for it points to a broader interpretative problem in the exploration of asceticism across scholarly disciplines, especially those tied to history. The problem has to do with the question of distance and its bridging. How do we as writers about the past, about asceticism's past, confront the historiographical challenges of asceticism's otherness and its deferrals? How do we, in de Certeau's terms, fabricate a literature about the past that foregrounds both its traces and its estrangements? How do we, in dealing with biblical texts, which possess a clarified immediacy because of their repetitions and their familiarities, insist upon the highlighting of their distance and their difference? How, moreover, do we think about the question of ascetical motive?

The question of distance, of separation, of getting from here to there, is one that asceticism in many respects is itself asking. Ascetics may be better at recognizing the otherness of their own objects of contemplation than are historians of religion. But indeed, the challenges facing each may be in some measure analogous. And they may best be met through the examination of strategies of discipline.

What I want to suggest in this chapter is that the call to bring asceticism into conversation with New Testament studies has really been a call to think about two different historicized disciplines—the disciplines of ascetical practice and subject formation, on the one hand, and the disciplines of scholarly investigation, on the other. What I hope then to do is to consider the ways that asceticism and interpretation come to engage one another around the problem of history and, moreover, to consider whether asceticism and history do not only raise the question of the "other" but also raise each other as questions. To do this, I begin by focusing on four different recent readings of Paul's ascetic impulses, specifically those impulses embedded in the ascetical advice found in his first letter to the Corinthian churches. This is advice that has been the subject of long, complex, and often contradictory exegetical debates.[5] It is advice already overinterpreted in discussions of asceticism, advice whose reading demands an ascetics of interpretation, as Harpham calls it—a text whose reading demands resistance.[6] My goal is not to hold up any one of these approaches as a singular model of how to read Paul and his asceticisms, but rather to ask how certain disciplinary assumptions come into play in the reconstruction of this one aspect of asceticism's past. I will then return to the broader theoretical concerns raised by the intersections of asceticism and history and raise some further questions.

DEFINING ASCETICISM

Part of my argument is rooted in the observation that asceticism and the writing of history are both characterized, in part at least, by the impossibility of ever fully achieving their aims. Such an impossibility has also characterized the study of asceticism itself, especially whenever anyone tries to offer a comprehensive and fully satisfying definition of what it is we think we're talking about when using the term "asceticism." Yet, however risky, it seems important to align myself with some approximation of what I mean when I speak of "asceticism" or the "ascetical" in this context. I begin with Richard Valantasis' programmatic definition of asceticism as consisting of "performances within a dominant social environment intended to inaugurate a new subjectivity, different social relations, and an alternative symbolic universe."[7]

This broad, maximalist definition disrupts ordinary assumptions that characterize asceticism as mere renunciation and negation. According to Valantasis' definition, the ascetical cannot so easily be reduced to the elements of an abstracted phenomenology, but rather must be situated simultaneously and concretely in relation to self, society, and the symbolic. In this view, asceticism has precise motives and clear goals; asceticism is geared toward transformation.[8]

By casting the net so widely, Valantasis' definition possesses rhetorical strength but also lays itself open to critique. The strength of the definition is that it requires us to think again about what we think we know about asceticism, to resist a complacent, I-know-it-when-I-see-it engagement with asceticism. This definition invites us to look again at practices long recognized as ascetical—fasting, for example, or sexual renunciation—and to evaluate them not only as practices of denial and negation but also as creative acts ("performances") that transform the material world as well as the spiritual. This definition shifts the ground from description to analysis and, as a consequence, may include within the framework of the "ascetical" both practices and modes of being in the world that exceed the recognizable domain of asceticism. Echoes of Geoffrey Harpham's ascetics of reading may be heard here.

One might complain that Valantasis' definition is too broad and sweeping to be useful in the task of identifying asceticism in texts and practices or, indeed, in applying "asceticism" as a lens through which to read. Are there significant arenas of human existence that would fall outside of such a broad definition? The definition also privileges the oppositional qualities of asceticism—its power as a form of cultural critique, as when Valantasis asserts that asceticism is "by nature" both "avant garde" and "transgressive"[9]—without necessarily fully exploring asceticism's potential for conservatism, its capacity to keep certain things (notions of the self, particular social relations, symbolic arrangements) firmly in place. And Valantasis' definition may not pay full attention to historical questions of change over time, although perhaps his situating transformation at the heart of the ascetical project links it to history in ways salutary to my own analysis.

These critical caveats aside, it strikes me that the broad definition he presents is nevertheless especially helpful for looking again at texts and practices whose "asceticism" is already too familiar—and certainly Paul's first letter to the Corinthians would fall into this category. Reading Paul's pronouncements there as calls to a performativity of transformation, one moves beyond already existing understandings to something new.

ASCETICISM AS PROPHYLAXIS IN 1 CORINTHIANS 7

In his recent book, *The Corinthian Body*, Dale Martin argues that Paul's asceticism is a manifestation of thinking about the body as the potential locus of pollution and the threatened object of invasion.[10] Like numerous critical interpreters of 1 Corinthians, Martin emphasizes the importance of reconstructing the rhetorical framework for the letter as well as attempting to flesh out the figures of Paul's Corinthian interlocutors, whose independent voices are not preserved. Martin begins from the common premise that the letter is written, not as a general theological treatise on matters ascetical and otherwise, but as an attempt to intervene in a concrete social situation where specifiable conflicts and problems require resolution. Paul writes in response to a group Martin and others call "the Strong," a group Martin reconstructs as representing the upper-class and educated elite within the Corinthian Christian community. Paul's attempt to persuade this group to view the situation from his own point of view assumes a complex ideological framework that Martin maintains must remain constantly in the foreground of any reconstruction. Martin's insistence on the centrality of ideology as an analytic category is a salutary corrective to the matter-of-factness of some discussions of Paul's letters, which invoke a slippery notion of "common sense" to account for Paul's arguments and proclamations.

Ideology is a term at once rhetorically charged and overdetermined, and Martin seeks to contain its potential unruliness by defining it concretely in terms of power and persuasion. "*Ideology*," he writes, "refers to the relation between language and social structures of power. It is the linguistic, symbolic matrix that makes sense of and supports a particular exercise of power and the power structures that exist."[11] Ideology as an analytic concept allows Martin to avoid the potential interpretative obstacles embodied in questions of agency and questions of ultimate truth value because, as he notes, ideology neither implies anything about conscious authorial intent nor requires an invocation of the traditional Marxist principle of false consciousness.[12] Rather, ideology helps to explain how certain relationships of power are rationalized, naturalized, and held in place—often through the unconscious acquiescence and/or collusion of everyone involved in a power relationship.[13]

In analysis of Paul's ascetical understanding in 1 Corinthians 7, ideology is a crucial notion because it highlights the contested character of Paul's point of view, radically destabilizing his repeated assertions of his own authority. Indeed, Martin argues that Paul's writing and the social conflict it presupposes suggest a bitter contest over ideology. For Martin, the dominant ideological framework that needs to be taken into account in this context is Greco-Roman medicine. As he reads the ancient corpus of medical literature, Martin discerns two competing ways of imagining the body's relationship to disease and illness. Since any relief or cure of physical distress emerges out of the interpretative framework out of which the distress is diagnosed, it matters a great deal how one thinks about the etiologies of bodily suffering.

The conflict between Paul and Corinth's "strong" Christians is a confrontation, Martin argues, between the two different medical models available in antiquity. Put simply, in this framework, disease derives either from an imbalance of the elements (heat/cold, wetness/dryness) in the body or from the invasion of the body by malignant forces.[14] These two medical views extend beyond the arena of medicine into the realm of the body politic. Radically divergent etiologies give way to equally different notions of prophylaxis and cure. In the case of a medical model that assumes that imbalance is the cause of sickness, physical boundaries are less important than internal equilibrium. For a model in which illness is seen as the result of invasion, impenetrable physical boundaries are the most significant protection against danger. Martin translates these medical models into the religious realm of the Christian churches in Corinth, arguing that the "strong" advocate asceticism as a balancing response to the threat of the absence of self-control while Paul's asceticism is a response to the dangers of cosmic pollution. Moreover, Martin argues that the performances of sexual acts or ascetical resistances are not themselves what is at stake; rather, what motivates these acts or resistances ("desire") is the relevant interpretative key. Differing interpretations of desire, inflected through two divergent medical models, propel the two ascetical possibilities to be found in 1 Corinthians. Put most simply, Martin argues that sex for the "strong" is a yielding to desire while for Paul sex is a prophylaxis against desire.[15]

Martin's rendering of Paul encourages his readers to look at the distance between their own circumstances and those of the first-century Greco-Roman world. Since many readers of Paul turn precisely to Paul's writings on embodiment in an interested and ahistorical search for a sexual ethics for their own time, they have tended to collapse the space between themselves and Paul's world or have brought (post)modern categories anachronistically to bear on the Pauline worldview. Martin is insistent—and rightly so, I believe—that such a gesture does not take adequate account of the radical otherness of the first-century Mediterranean world. Martin's interpretative stance places him on one side of a gaping abyss that separates his own world and circumstances from those of Paul and his readers.

Yet Martin continues to hold on to the ideal that one can mediate the radical separation of "there" from "here," and at times his own rhetoric betrays a nostalgic and idealized wish for a conceptual link, a way across. At one point in his reading of 1 Corinthians 7, Martin expresses a kind of resignation tinged with disappointment when his careful exegesis and philological investigation does not give way to a transparent Pauline text. He writes, "Perhaps this is another occasion on which our modern categories, indeed our language itself, simply fails us—by failing to bridge the categorical chasms of cultural difference."[16] One hears a nostalgic wish in this near-admission of failure, a deeply understandable longing (have we not all ourselves experienced this longing?) for a way to escape the confines of disciplinary inadequacy. It is in some important ways an ascetical admission of failure—the disciplined reader tries to bridge a gap, to establish union with the object of contemplation/study through disciplined performances, to focus on the embedded otherness of history while at the same time giving in to the desire to transcend it. The ideological ambiguities of asceticism and history-writing become visible at such a rhetorical moment. The vagaries of asceticism and its study reflect each other in such textual details.

ASCETICAL DIFFERENCE AS SEXUAL DIFFERENCE IN 1 CORINTHIANS 7

Martin's text displays this momentary, probably unconscious, and certainly paradoxical ascetical longing to escape historical difference, to achieve an impossible bridging of the distance segregating the historical narrator from the historically narrated, to traverse the abyss of cultural incommensurability and the lack of mutual intelligibility. As with asceticism itself, this longing coexists with a clear-eyed recognition of the inevitability of the separation and, indeed, with an implicit ethical claim of the desirability of the critical and irresolvable difference. Meanwhile, by placing a different kind of difference at the center of her investigation, Antoinette Clark Wire performs a distinctive reading of Paul's asceticism: It also undertakes rhetorical analysis and tentative historical reconstruction, but through a disciplined and rapt listening to the text's absent voices.[17] Placing gender at the center of her analysis, Wire insists that her readers keep their attention focused on a particular kind of difference—sexual difference—in evaluating and interpreting Paul's ascetical impulses. The specificity of women's experience of marriage in first-century Mediterranean culture requires that historians who track the personal, social, and symbolic transformations inaugurated by Paul's ascetical discourse keep in mind the precise character of the dominant social environment in which such transformations might take place: "the radical systematic disadvantages of women in that society as a whole—inferiority by age and possible slave heritage in marriage, dependency on men in all civil and judicial matters, and special vulnerability to death at birth and again at giving birth."[18]

Wire argues that the practice of sexual renunciation cannot have meant the same thing for women as for men either in the Corinthian community or in the world of first-century CE culture in general. What Martin characterizes as "the [singular] Corinthian body," Wire argues explicitly must be carefully specified since the lived reality of gendered bodies insists upon a differentiated analysis.[19] This differentiated analysis is called for precisely at points when women's historical and embodied experience is most veiled by the text's discourse. Probably the poignant and chilling moment for Wire and other feminist interpreters of 1 Corinthians lies in the syntactical parallelism of 7:4, where Paul asserts that "the woman does not have authority over her own body, but the husband has" and "likewise the husband does not have authority over his own body, but the wife has." What this parallelism obscures is the radically uneven distribution of power between women and men in first-century Mediterranean marriage, an uneven distribution of power that renders the claim of men's authority over their wives' bodies simultaneously redundant and menacing.

Wire's achievement in reconstructing a historical framework for 1 Corinthians lies in her plausible presentation of a female religious agency at the root of Paul's ascetical teachings. Of particular concern to Wire is the question of the relationship of ascetical practice to prophetic activity in Corinth, particularly among women. She provides ample evidence, derived from other biblical texts as well as a variety of Jewish, Greek, and Roman sources, to demonstrate the widespread associations between sexual renunciation and prophetic power for women in a variety of ancient Mediterranean contexts.[20] This concern over the sexual status of prophets seems not to have existed equally for men, with occasional exceptions; hence, the tie between asceticism and religious authority was especially significant for women. As a consequence of this link, Wire reads what some have seen as Paul's middle-of-the-road and conciliatory rhetoric in 1 Corinthians 7 as exacting a far greater price from these women than from the men in their community.

In some ways, Wire's historical practice in her book comes closest to the practice de Certeau advocates as he presses historians to recover the voices and echoes of the past, even while admitting the ineluctable impossibility of doing so. Indeed, Anglo-American feminist scholarship has long embraced this auditory metaphor, understanding the gesture of hearing lost, muted, or silenced voices as a practical form of resistance to dominant ways of telling the story. But even here, there are different forms of resistance. Some feminist readers, like Wire, approach the problem of the silence of the past by trying to construct an interpretative sound chamber that will block out at least some of the historical static. The project then takes on an ascetical dimension in its reiterated discipline of radical stillness, of simply listening. Others have found the silence too deafening and have in essence begun to speak for those lost voices of the past. This ascetical practice is less contemplative than performative, as it embarks upon writing the stories of the past in imagined voices, a midrashic intervention into the silent echoing space between the present and the past. Both strategies recognize the gap of difference and the desire it inspires: One meditates on the absence it represents; the other attempts a utopian restoration of presence.

ASCETICISM AS PAUL'S FATAL LEGACY

Biblical scholars like Martin and Wire are, of course, not the only interpreters who have undertaken to read the traces of Pauline asceticism in the New Testament. In what has widely been acknowledged as the now classic account of early Christian asceticism, historian Peter Brown offers a rendering of Paul's asceticism as an almost inadvertent and clearly overdetermined historical beginning.[21] By Brown's account, Paul's advice concerning asceticism functions as the historical foundation for Christianity's subsequent romance with renunciation as well as the cornerstone for a complex edifice of interpretation and theology. Paul's asceticism starts something, fabricates out of particular social conflicts in particular communal settings a pattern of spiritual and corporeal practice that will also lay the groundwork for thinking about the human condition itself. "The charged opacity of his language faced all later ages like a Rorschach test: it is possible to measure, in the repeated exegesis of a mere hundred words of Paul's letters, the future course of Christian thought on the human person," Brown writes.[22]

According to Brown, Paul is ultimately struggling against the implications of his own message, almost as though he were Dr. Frankenstein and asceticism his monster: "In his letters to the churches, we meet a man hurriedly placing sandbags along the bank of a potentially devastating torrent whose impetus, he knew only too well, owed much to his own previous message and example."[23] In this reading, Brown draws attention to the deepseated ambivalence that numerous other commentators have diagnosed in Paul's discourse in 1 Corinthians at the same time as others have been able to use this ambivalence to underwrite utterly divergent readings of Paul's views on marriage and asceticisms.[24]

Brown's own discipline in writing about ascetical disciplines is decidedly narrative and largely linear. He tells the story of Christian sexual renunciation as one of men and women whose ideas and practices respond to the constraints of the past and the pressures of the present. Remarkable individuals come sharply into view; we are really operating with Brown in the framework of religious biography, a disciplinary space where personal impulse and religious experience propel a historical narrative. Paul is, in this story, an innovator, an inventor, a creator of a radically changed future. His asceticism is a strategic by-product of a bigger project: inaugurating a new creation in response to his own personal transformation.

Brown's discussion also emphasizes Paul's asceticism as a rupture with the past and with his own present. While other authors (including others considered in this discussion) may emphasize the continuity of Pauline asceticism with other ideas and practices surrounding it, Brown focuses on Paul's asceticism as itself a manifestation of radical cultural difference.

> What was notably lacking, in Paul's letter, was the warm faith shown by contemporary pagans and Jews that the sexual urge, although disorderly, was capable of socialization and of ordered, even warm, expression within marriage. The dangers of *porneia*, of potential immorality brought about by sexual frustration, were allowed to hold the center of the stage. By this essentially negative, even alarmist, strategy, Paul left a fatal legacy to future ages. An argument against abandoning sexual intercourse within marriage and in favor of allowing the younger generation to continue to have children slid imperceptibly into an attitude that viewed marriage itself as no more than a defense against desire. In the future, a sense of the presence of "Satan," in the form of a constant and ill-defined risk of lust, lay like a heavy shadow in the corner of every Christian church.[25]

Brown's identification of the function of 1 Corinthians 7 as a kind of theological and interpretative Rorschach test is illuminating and on target. Readers of this chapter have long asserted with equal measures of certainty and myopia that Paul is the unambiguous champion of marriage and family on the one hand or celibacy and renunciation of passions on the other. Brown's own reading of the Rorschach infuses the chapter with an almost menacing cast. The "potentially devastating torrent" and the "fatal legacy" of Paul's unambiguous critique of desire found in Brown's rhetoric invite one to consider the question: "Devastating or fatal to whom?" Brown's Paul is an innovator, a founder, a leader whose legacy is the profound break with the past and the establishment of something new, something discontinuous, some lasting alternative. As a consequence, the historicity of Paul's asceticism produces a deep ambivalence in Brown's own reading of it: Paul's break with his past, his midwifery on the part of a new creation, his incipient institution-building are all caught up in a tensive and equivocal message that may well threaten the stability and longevity of the new social invention.

ASCETICISM AND THE END(S) OF HISTORY

In one version of his essay on Pauline asceticism, Talmud scholar Daniel Boyarin opens his discussion with the same lengthy quotation from Brown that I cited earlier.[26] In explicit contrast to Brown, Boyarin argues that Paul's asceticism does not break with a salutary and benign cultural embrace of human sexuality but rather, in some striking and important ways, punctuates an ongoing struggle within first-century Judaism in which "sexuality had become so problematic that totally escaping from it—as Paul himself claimed to have done—seemed the best possible solution."[27] Whereas Brown's reading of Paul's asceticism configures it as a discontinuity and a historical beginning, Boyarin's reading suggests that Paul's asceticism punctuates or culminates an ongoing interpretative struggle about the meanings of bodily impulses and divine prescriptions. In other words, according to Brown, Paul's asceticism begins something; according to Boyarin, it brings something to an end.[28]

Boyarin's discussion of Pauline asceticism rejects Brown's implication that sexual renunciation was an accidental by-product of Paul's attempts to find solutions to pressing social conflicts among a particular set of Christians.[29] He also implicitly rejects Brown's assertion that "in his other letters [those besides 1 Corinthians], sexual renunciation played no part in Paul's message or in his presentation of his apostolic mission."[30] Rather, Boyarin argues strongly for the view that Paul's discourse in Romans, 1 Corinthians, and Galatians embodies a "body politic" in which sexual asceticism becomes the unambiguous theological resolution of the vexing problem of "the inescapable dilemma of Adamic humanity."[31] No inadvertent residue in the struggle to

produce a new social formation inflected through the language of new creation, sexual asceticism in Boyarin's view is theologically central to the entire
project of Paul's cultural critique within first-century Judaism.

Central to Boyarin's interpretation is the recognition that Paul is situated *within* a historical discussion within Judaism and consequently that Paul's
discourse implies a continuity with his own cultural past even as he disrupts
his relationship to it in very striking ways. As Boyarin puts it,

> Paul lived and died convinced that he was a Jew living out Judaism. He repre-
> sents, then, one option which Judaism could take in the first century....
> Assuming, as I do, that Paul was motivated not by an abnormal psychological
> state but by a set of problems and ideas generated by his cultural, religious situ-
> ation, I read him as a Jewish cultural critic, and I ask what it was in Jewish cul-
> ture that led him to produce a discourse of radical reform of that culture.[32]

Paul's asceticism emerges, then, in direct conversation and debate with
the ideological world of first-century Judaism, a world in which embodiment
was not only a human condition but also a complex site of relationship to the
divine. Boyarin argues that in ancient Israel human reproduction was a highly valued ethical and religious good, but that by the first century CE a growing anxiety emerged surrounding the practice of sexuality.[33] Pauline asceticism responded to this sense of dis-ease within first-century Judaism.

Boyarin situates this asceticism within the broader framework of concerns over the flesh, both ritually and genealogically. Paul's emphasis on the
controversies surrounding circumcision, he suggests, does not approach circumcision as a simple synecdoche for "the law" in general, but rather draws
attention to the foundational links between circumcision (both as ritual
enactment and as bodily signifier) and generation as bodily practices and
divinely ordained obligations. The inversion of the traditional oppositions
that many commentators have seen in Paul—between flesh/letter/law and
spirit—here requires a foundational transformation of ideology and practice.
Paul's radical reform in the severing of the traditional genealogical specificity of Judaism disrupts a whole series of conceptual relationships—and asceticism becomes one bodily practice that reinscribes that disruption.

Boyarin's characterization of Paul as a "proto-encratite"[34] raises the
question of history in two different but related ways. Whereas Brown's
account of Paul's ascetical impulses posits Paul as the newly hapless founder
of an ascetical movement that got out of control somehow in a singular and
continous history beginning with Paul, Boyarin implicitly positions Paul as
one historical actor at a moment of historical fragmentation—one possible
resolution of one set of historical problems. Boyarin's history is less linear
than Brown's, less narrative and more tentative. It also emphasizes the myth-
ic demands of Paul's own situation, the need to account for and respond to
inherited myths of origins.

If Paul is a proto-encratite, then one needs to explore the relationship of Paul's asceticism to his notion of history, for encratism (small "e") itself emphasizes both the necessity and the contingency of history. Within the context of encratism, the *need* for asceticism is rooted in historical exigencies (what has happened in the past of human history) while the *goal* of asceticism is to render history irrelevant (by bringing it to an end). Boyarin reads Paul as advocating an asceticism that, among other things, interrupts genealogy and thereby brings history to an end. Many interpreters of Paul have diagnosed such a (small "e") encratism in the way that his asceticism is inflected through apocalyptic sensibilities and eschatological expectations. Equally significant, I think, is the tension between asceticism taking place in history—a set of performances that inaugurate personal, social, and ideological transformations—on the one hand, and asceticism's utopian impulses and suspicions of history on the other.[35] This tension requires elaboration and further reflection because it points to the space where ascetical disciplines and historical ones come into closest alignment, where our interpretative questions and our subject matter and our theoretical orientations and operations converge.

CONCLUSION

What do asceticism and history, in the end, have to do with each other? Asceticism consists of repeated disciplinary performances inspired by a desire for something other, while at the same time it embodies a resistance to desire—a resistance that aims at reconfiguring the self, relationship, and meaning itself. Asceticism is a radical response to knowledge, to some recognition of otherness and completeness; it is a radical response to desire, the desire to possess and to embody otherness and completeness. Asceticism's relationship to history is complex and not unitary. Paul's disciplinary performances intentionally disrupt history by interrupting genealogy, turning their back on the past, intervening. Paul's asceticism—perhaps asceticism in general—is deeply ambivalent toward history and its own possibilities. It is forward-looking and nostalgic at once, utopian in its impulse toward an unachievable perfection outside time, enacting its resistances to history within an endless repetition taking place one day after another. The disciplines of asceticism leave their traces almost imperceptibly, not through radical conversion, but through disciplined transformations. The practice of history-writing is caught up in a similar set of ambivalences and tensions requiring a kind of ascetical resignation to the conditions that render unrealizable any utopian dream of bridging the abyss between the present and the past. Both kinds of discipline, ascetical and historical, function in the space in between, as much a space characterized by the utopian language of "as if" as a space characterized by the Pauline language of "as if not."

NOTES

1. Michel de Certeau, *The Writing of History*, trans. Tom Conley (New York: Columbia University Press, 1988), 85.
2. Michel de Certeau, *L'absence de l'histoire* (n.p.: Mame, 1973), 8–9. Cited and translated by Jeremy Ahearne, *Michel de Certeau: Interpretation and Its Other* (Stanford, Calif.: Stanford University Press, 1995), 10.
3. William James, *The Varieties of Religious Experience: A Study in Human Nature* (New York: Penguin, 1982; orig. pub. 1902), 296–97.
4. Ibid, 330.
5. In addition to the four scholarly discussions discussed in detail in this chapter, the commentary literature on 1 Corinthians, and general histories of early Christian asceticism that include discussions of Paul, see also David L. Balch, "Backgrounds of I Cor. vii: Sayings of the Lord in Q; Moses as an Ascetic [THEIOS ANER] in II Cor. iii," *New Testament Studies* 18 (1971–1972): 351–64; idem, "1 Cor 7:32–35 and Stoic Debates about Marriage, Anxiety, and Distraction," *Journal of Biblical Literature* 102 (1983): 429–39; David R. Cartlidge, "1 Corinthians 7 as a Foundation for a Christian Sex Ethic," *Journal of Religion* 55 (1975): 220–34; Will Deming, *Paul on Marriage and Celibacy: The Hellenistic Background of 1 Corinthians 7* (Cambridge, England: Cambridge University Press, Stududiorum Novi Testament; Societas Monograph Series 83, 1995); Darrell J. Doughty, "Heiligkeit und Freiheit: Eine exegetische Untersuchung der Anwendung des paulinischen Freiheitsgedankens in 1 Kor 7" (Ph.D. diss., Göttingen, 1965); J. K. Elliott, "Paul's Teaching on Marriage in I Corinthians: Some Problems Reconsidered," *New Testament Studies* 19 (1972–1973): 219–25; J. Massyngberde Ford, "St. Paul, the Philogamist (I Cor. vii in Early Patristic Exegesis)," *New Testament Studies* 11 (1964–1965): 326–48; David E. Garland, "The Christian's Posture toward Marriage and Celibacy: 1 Corinthians 7," *Review and Expositor* 80 (1983): 351–62; Xavier Léon-Defour, "Mariage et continence selon S. Paul," in *A la recontre de Dieu: Mémorial Albert Gelin*, ed. A. Barucq, A. George, and H. de Lubac (Le Puy, France: Mappus, Bibliothéque de la Faculté Catholique Théologie de Lyon 8, 1961), 319–29; Margaret Y. MacDonald, "Women Holy in Body and Spirit: The Social Setting of 1 Corinthians 7," *New Testament Studies* 36 (1990): 161–81; Thaddée Matura, "Le célibat dans le NT d'après l'exégèse recente," *La Nouvelle Revue Théologique* 97 (1975): 481–500, 593–604; Helmut Merklein, "'Es gut für den Menschen, eine Frau nicht anzufassen': Paulus und die Sexualität nach 1 Kor 7," in *Die Frau im Urchristentum*, eds. Gerhard Dautzenberg, Helmut Merklein, and Karlheinz Müller (Freiburg, Germany: Herder, Quaestiones Disputatae 95, 1983), 225–53; Jeremy Moiser, "A Reassessment of Paul's View of Marriage with Reference to 1 Corinthians 7," *Journal for the Study of the New Testament* 18 (1983): 103–22; Elaine H. Pagels, "Paul and Women: A Response to Recent Discussion," *Journal of the American Academy of Religion* 42 (1974): 538–49; Benedetto Prete, *Matrimonio e continenza nel cristianesimo delle origini: Studio su 1 Cor. 7, 1-40* (Brescia, Italy: Paideia, Studi Biblici 49, 1979); W. E. Phipps, "Is Paul's Attitude Toward Sexual Relations Contained in 1 Cor. 7.1?" *New Testament Studies* 28 (1982): 125–31; Vincent L. Wimbush, *Paul the Worldly Ascetic: Response to the World*

184 Elizabeth A. Castelli

and *Self-Understanding according to 1 Corinthians 7* (Macon, Ga.: Mercer University Press, 1987); O. Larry Yarbrough, *Not Like the Gentiles: Marriage Rules in the Letters of Paul* (Atlanta, Ga.: Scholars, Society of Biblical Literature Dissertation Series 80, 1985).

6. Geoffrey Galt Harpham, *The Ascetic Imperative in Culture and Criticism* (Chicago: University of Chicago Press, 1987).

7. Richard Valantasis, "Constructions of Power in Asceticism," *Journal of the American Academy of Religion* 63 (1995): 797.

8. On intentionality as a component of asceticism, see ibid, 799; on the role of transformation or change in asceticism, see ibid, 793.

9. Ibid, 799–800.

10. Dale B. Martin, *The Corinthian Body* (New Haven, Conn.: Yale University Press, 1995), 198–228.

11. Ibid, xiv (italics mine).

12. Ibid, xiv–xv.

13. Ideological criticism has become an important contributor to biblical studies more generally, often with more explicit political aims than Martin's project betrays. See, for example, Roland Boer, *Jameson and Jeroboam* (Semeia Studies, Atlanta, Ga.: Scholars, 1996). For an overview of the field, see Bible and Culture Collective, *The Postmodern Bible* (New Haven, Conn.: Yale University Press, 1995), 272–308. For recent ideological interventions into biblical texts and biblical studies, see David Jobling and Tina Pippin, eds., *Ideological Criticism of Biblical Texts* (*Semeia* 59, Atlanta, Ga.: Scholars, 1992). A recent general treatment of ideology as a political and interpretative category may be found in Slavoj∂iñek, *Mapping Ideology* (London: Verso, 1994).

14. Martin, *The Corinthian Body*, 139–62. Martin depends to a certain extent on anthropological theories of disease and healing, although he perhaps unduly simplifies the matter. Recent anthropological literature has made careful distinctions between categories of "disease," "sickness," and "illness," as well as between the categories of "cure" and "healing"—all terms that Martin routinely collapses into one another. Moreover, anthropologists "after the linguistic turn" have tended carefully to the metaphoric character of this language, while Martin moves back and forth between real bodies and metaphoric bodies without always distinguishing them. See Allen Young, "The Anthropologies of Illness and Sickness," *Annual Review of Anthropology* 11 (1982): 257–85; Arthur Kleinman, *Patients and Healers in the Context of Culture: An Exploration of the Borderland between Anthropology, Medicine, and Psychiatry* (Berkeley: University of California Press, 1980); Loring M. Danforth, *Firewalking and Religious Healing: The Anastenaria of Greece and the American Firewalking Movement* (Princeton, N.J.: Princeton University Press, 1989), esp. 50–63.

15. Martin, *The Corinthian Body*, 217.

16. Ibid, 216.

17. Antoinette Clark Wire, *The Corinthian Women Prophets: A Reconstruction through Paul's Rhetoric* (Minneapolis, Minn.: Fortress, 1990), 72–97.

18. Ibid, 75.

19. Martin is not unaware of the challenges of gender for reading 1 Corinthians, which he deals with extensively in chapter 9 of his book (229–49) and which he

acknowledges explicitly in his discussion of Paul's sudden abandonment of the rhetorical strategy of status reversal when it comes to discussions of the relationship of males and females (198–99). For his disagreement with Wire's reconstruction of the "women prophets" as the group in Corinth especially promoting sexual renunciation, see 290, n. 27.

20. Wire, *Corinthian Women Prophets*, 83, 237–69.
21. Peter Brown, *The Body and Society: Men, Women and Sexual Renunciation in Early Christianity* (New York: Columbia University Press, 1988), 44–57.
22. Ibid, 48. See also Brown's characterization of 1 Corinthians 7 as "the chapter that was to determine all Christian thought on marriage and celibacy for well over a millennium" (54).
23. Ibid, 50.
24. See the literature cited in note 5 for some of this variety.
25. Brown, *The Body and Society*, 55.
26. Daniel Boyarin, "Body Politic among the Brides of Christ: Paul and the Origins of Christian Sexual Renunciation," in *Asceticism*, eds. Vincent L. Wimbush and Richard Valantasis (New York: Oxford University Press, 1995), 459–78; quotation 459. This essay, with some changes (including the exclusion of the quotation from Brown), also appears as "Brides of Christ: Jewishness and the Pauline Origins of Christian Sexual Renunciation," in Daniel Boyarin, *A Radical Jew: Paul and the Politics of Identity* (Berkeley: University of California Press, 1994), 158–79. Subsequent citations of Boyarin's essay are derived from the first essay in *Asceticism*, unless explicitly stated otherwise.
27. Boyarin, "Body Politic," 459.
28. It is important to note that this comparison is not strictly exegetical, for Brown and Boyarin use different texts to draw their conclusions about Paul and the historical significance of his asceticism. Brown's focus is on 1 Corinthians 7, while Boyarin treats several texts: Romans 5–8, 1 Corinthians 6, and Galatians 5–6. The comparison, rather, has to do with views of history and disciplinary strategies for dealing with distance and difference. The choice of emblematic texts (both those of these authors and my own) is simply one disciplinary strategy.
29. See Brown, *The Body and Society*, 52: "In [1 Corinthians], we can glimpse a church where issues of sexual control and sexual renunciation condensed anxieties about the entire structure of the communities that Paul had wished to found."
30. Ibid, 53.
31. Boyarin, "Body Politic," 473.
32. Boyarin, *A Radical Jew*, 2.
33. Boyarin, "Body Politic," 461.
34. Ibid, 472–73.
35. Here, "history" overlaps in significant ways with Wimbush's use of the term "world" in *Paul the Worldly Ascetic*.

Paul the Prisoner: Political Asceticism in the Letter to the Philippians

Robin Scroggs

INTRODUCTION

If, for the purposes of this chapter, asceticism is defined as a *negative response to a dominant culture*,[1] then the situation that lies behind Paul's letter to the Philippians is indeed ascetic. As usual, Paul does not tell us all we would like to know, but the basic fact is clear. The Apostle (although he chooses not so to identify himself in the letter) has been arrested by a Roman official on some charge—which would have been brought against him by private citizens and whose successful prosecution carried a penalty of death. At the time he writes the letter, Paul does not know what the result of the trial will be. The desperate ambiguity of life or death explicitly permeates the first section of the letter and must infiltrate every topic Paul addresses; however, some commentators seem to think Paul was on a Sunday outing while he wrote.

The purpose of this chapter is, then, to look for Paul's stance toward the "world" (that is, the dominant culture) and to be sensitive both to Paul's own self-awareness and to how that informs his directives to his beloved church at Philippi. I argue that his stance involves both a kind of withdrawal from the dominant political structures as well as an alternate reconstruction of a reality Paul considers true. Paul speaks about what this reality is and how it should affect the corporate—that is, political—lives of believers. Hence I think it fair to label Paul's thinking here "political asceticism."

To say that a group sees itself as distinctive (or unique) vis-à-vis the larger cultural organization(s) may say little. *Any* group formed has to have some purpose its adherents think is not simply met by other groups (or not available to them). This does not in and of itself imply a negative response toward the dominant culture, since features of the dominant culture may be emulated and copied within the group. In fact, at least some such features *have* to be so emulated, or else the group could not exist. Every group is a combination of like and unlike. It may be that the group stresses what is unlike, but what is like may be the major portion of the iceberg.

On the other hand, by "negative response" I presume that the group not only highlights its differences with the larger culture, but also explicitly or implicitly avows that some parts, at least, of the dominant culture are hostile to the vision of the group. Implicitly, perhaps explicitly, the group is creating an alternative vision to the reality that the dominant culture thinks to be true.[2] One of the "judgment calls" in this kind of analysis is to determine just what counts as an alternative vision, since inevitably features of the dominant culture will also appear and, somehow, be made to fit into the alternative vision. That is, even oppressed groups may try to co-opt some structures of the very culture that is the cause of the oppression. Most communities probably live in tension, trying to juggle both sides. Paul's churches—and no doubt Paul himself—reflect such tension.[3]

Surprisingly little attention has been devoted to the situation of the author of Philippians. Yet Paul's situation in prison, on trial for his life, along with the the attendant uproar among interested groups, must impinge upon his thinking about Christ and culture. Thus it is crucial to illuminate as much as possible just what that situation was.

PAUL'S SITUATION IN PRISON

It is hard to imagine a person arrested on a capital charge, especially if the person believes the charges are false, not taking a dim view of the structures (government, laws concerning charges, prison, etc.) that have forced him to his present, desperate straits.[4] Given his situation, Paul's letter is amazingly irenic. He says nothing about prison life and speaks of the uncertain outcome of his trial at times as a matter of indifference, at times as if he had control over the outcome himself![5] What Paul does say is vague (his readers/hearers doubtlessly knew what we would like to know), indeed, perhaps ambiguous. Some things can be said, and upon them I will build a hypothesis.

The Cause of Paul's Imprisonment

Paul is in a Roman prison (1:13). Death by execution is possible.[6] Since there is no evidence that being a believer in Jesus was at that time a capital offense, the charge against Paul must be a political, "secular" one, recognizable as serious by Roman authorities.[7] Could the charge have been treason (*maies-*

tas)? If treason, was the charge false (i.e., would no reasonable person have adjudged Paul an enemy of the emperor or empire)? If the charge was false, what could have been the evidence that private individuals brought to the Roman authority that made that authority think the situation serious enough to justify arrest? Was it something in Paul's preaching that made the charge sensible? Were those making the charge concerned for the safety of the province, or were they, for other reasons, trying to get Paul out of the way? If the latter, were they believers, nonbelieving Jews, or nonbelieving Gentiles?

These are all questions that cannot be answered without speculations that, perhaps, go beyond scholarly etiquette. The *lex maiestatis*, according to Richard Bauman, was supported and used by Tiberius, largely under the influence of Sejanus.[8] The misuse during Tiberius' reign became so obvious that the immediately succeeding emperors tended to put the law on the back burner. Caligula suspended the *lex maiestatis* for the first two years of his reign.[9] About Claudius, Bauman is unequivocal: "Claudius' first act on his accession was to suspend the *lex maiestatis;* it remained in abeyance for the whole of his reign,"[10] even though he devised substitutes and the death penalty was carried out on occasion. Nero kept the suspension of the law during the first eight years of his reign.[11] Thus, according to Bauman's evidence, the *lex maiestatis* was not invocable from 41 to 60 CE. This means that one may not make an appeal to this law as the law of Paul's arrest, unless one argues for a Roman imprisonment in the early 60s as the historical situation. It will not work for an Ephesian imprisonment.

The questions posed here, however unanswerable, are nevertheless reasonable and suggest something of the complexity that lies below the surface of Paul's text. In the provinces Roman law was in part at the mercy of the Roman officials. What the law was supposed to be is not necessarily what happened (anymore then than now).[12] The haunting suspicion remains that the charges had something to do with words or acts that seemed inflammatory against established orders. Without in any way defending Acts' story of Paul's arrest in Philippi as historical, the charge made there seems apropos: "These men are disturbing our city; they are Jews and are advocating customs that are not lawful for us as Romans to adopt or observe" (Acts 16:20–21).

Paul immediately muddies the water, however, by adding the elusive phrase: "It has become known through the whole imperial guard and to everyone else that my imprisonment is for Christ" (1:12).[13] I take it that this expresses a change in the perception of the outsiders as to the "real" reason for Paul's arrest. That is, they first had assumed that the official charge was the reason for the arrest. Now they have come to the perception that the actual reason for the arrest lies behind the official one. The real reason must have something to do with Paul's activity as a founder of churches and/or proclamation of the resurrected Christ. The persons who brought the political charges were really interested in getting rid of Paul because of his religious confession or activity. Since being named a "Christian" was not at that time a crime, such persons must charge him with something else.[14]

To sum up: We cannot know the exact charges brought against Paul or who brought them. We can, I believe, safely conclude that the official charge was "political," a capital offense on conviction, but that Paul affirms that behind the public charge lies the "real" one of his proclamation and/or activity in the communities he founds. He, or somebody, has been able to convince some of the surrounding nonbelieving audience that this is the case. In any event, Paul is in a life-or-death situation. While he may have "religious" enemies, the enemy that can execute him is the state. Given this situation, it is crucial to be sensitive to what he may be saying about "political asceticism."

Paul's Relationship with Other Believers in the City of Imprisonment

Paul causes another insoluble problem for exegetes when he says in v. 12: "I want you to know, beloved, that what has happened to me has actually helped to advance the gospel." This is further specified in v. 14: "Most of the brethren having become emboldened in the Lord by my imprisonment dare even more fearlessly to speak the word." Indeed, this outburst of preaching seems to be what constitutes the advance of the gospel due to his imprisonment. On the surface this is a remarkable claim. One would think that arrest of a leader would spread unease and fear among the followers. It would seem less likely that arrest would spur public preaching of the point of view of the person arrested than it would shut up such preaching.

To this problem must be added Paul's interpretation of the motivation of such preachers. There are some who preach out of good will (*eudokia*), out of love (for Paul, presumably) on the grounds that they know Paul is here destined for the defense of the gospel. Others preach from envy and rivalry, out of selfish ambition, with the intent to increase Paul's affliction (*thlipsis*) in prison. This strikes me as an equally remarkable judgment.

Scholars seem to agree that there must have been no difference in the *content* of these different preachers, since otherwise the Apostle would call attention to some error in the teaching of the "bad" side. But how does Paul *know* which preachers have bad intentions, and which good? Does the preaching of *both* sides create greater affliction for Paul, the difference being that for one side it is intentional, for the other not? Or does some preaching lead to affliction and the other not? Is the affliction Paul speaks of the mental one of knowing that the proclamation of the gospel does not always stem from pure motivation, or is it physical—greater abuse or torture that he has to endure as he awaits trial, or a greater threat as to the outcome of the trial?

The problems are truly unsolvable, but I think the issues at least justify raising the possibility that some conflict in *content* is the point of difference. What this difference might be cannot be solved by imposing the opponent(s) of chapter 3 into the picture, even if ultimately there might be some justification for so doing. A reasonable hypothesis, if one can be forthcoming, would better arise from acknowledging the political situation in which Paul seems to be. If it is the case that Paul's arrest has ultimately to do with the content of his proclamation, then is it possible to imagine a proclamation of the gospel that did not contain whatever elements considered offensive by those who caused Paul's arrest? If so, those who made such an apolitical proclamation could, by their example of proclamation, communicate that the gospel is not in itself subversive, that it is *Paul* who has "corrupted" the gospel by altering it in a subversive manner. The "political" charges against Paul are thus legitimate. It is not the proclamation about Jesus that need be subversive; it is Paul.

Such preaching could be a real affliction to Paul, not only because Paul might think it took the necessary offense out of the gospel, but also because it would make his own defense more difficult. Of course, such preaching might easily stem from sincere motives, and we must be careful not to take Paul's reading of motivation uncritically. It was certainly possible to conceive the gospel in a manner acceptable to state authorities (as shortly the author of Luke–Acts would try to do). Even Paul seems to make that point in Rom. 13:1–7:[15] Everything would depend upon how one expressed the meaning of the resurrection.[16]

Equally political was the relation of a missionary like Paul to the Jewish community. Did the formation of groups believing in Jesus, but who claimed to be Jews, threaten the stability of the Jewish relationship with civic and Roman authorities? How the resurrected Jesus was proclaimed must have been of interest to Jewish groups concerned about their own political situation. Now it was certainly possible to conceive the gospel in a way that comported with Jewish sensibilities (as the Galatian opposition to Paul makes clear), and how one decided on such issues also had political implications. It seems to me very likely that those who advocated circumcision and Torah obedience as essential elements in addition to believing in Jesus were not unaware of the political repercussion of their point of view.[17] Judaism had been given legal sanctions by the Romans. To claim that believing in Jesus did not in any way obviate Jewish customs enabled one to claim those sanctions. If the Romans cared (as I suppose they did) about the preaching in the synagogues, they must have known that Yahweh was proclaimed as cosmic *kyrios* and had acclimated themselves to such language without considering it dangerous. On the contrary, for someone to proclaim that a human had been exalted to the status of *kyrios* and was *isa theo* (2:6) might well seem less reconcilable to the lordship (and deification) of the Caesar.[18]

Paul certainly considered himself an authentic Jew. In my judgment, he assumed that the congregations he formed, however made up of Gentiles, were the congregations of Yahweh. It is not just the Gentile believers in Jesus who are not obligated to the law as necessary to full relation to God; Jews also, in Paul's thinking, are released from obligation to Torah (as necessary to full relation to God—Gal. 2:15–16). Yet whatever Paul's judgments, his position led ultimately to a make-up of communities into which Jews refused to enter[19] and which could not claim Judaism as a protective umbrella.[20] Already during his life, Jewish opposition to him certainly must have sensed keenly the political ambiguity and volatility of his position.

Thus there are at least two possibilities for a kind of preaching of Jesus that could cause affliction to Paul. One would be a presentation of the resurrected Jesus in clearly nonpolitical terms. The other would be a presentation of belief in Jesus that "tacked" Jesus onto a traditional Jewish system. Even the latter might have political undertones.

To understand the preaching of those to whom Paul ascribes positive motivations is actually more difficult because such preaching would be similar to that which presumably got Paul into trouble in the first place. It would have been politically dangerous and can best be understood as coming from those who are willing to put their own life on the line.

The volatility of the various proclamations can only have contributed to the volatility of Paul's situation. Paul was in a vulnerable position with regard to the state. He proclaimed a deified, resurrected human as *kyrios*.[21] He formed communities of Gentiles without official sanction from the Romans.[22] He had enemies among both Jews who did not believe in Jesus as well as those who did.[23] Whether in some way he also had Gentile enemies, we do not know—he certainly got in trouble with civic and Roman authorities (e.g., 2 Cor. 11:25–26). That his enemies could and would exploit his vulnerability seems a reasonable thing to expect. Just that exploitation may be the background of Paul's arrest.

It is out of this tense situation that the Letter to the Philippians emerges. I have so stressed the likely situation of incarceration because I cannot imagine that it has not left its imprint upon Paul's thinking. Despite his surface serenity, despite the fact that he applauds both kinds of preaching (1:18), one wonders if he is whistling in the dark.[24] Given what has happened, and what may happen, how might Paul's situation affect what it is that he wants to say and how he dares to say it?

The Letter from Prison

I focus on only a few passages, those that seem to me most centrally to deal with a suggestion of alternative structures.[25] The issue is not whether the alternative structures mirror or do not mirror the "outside" structures. Some such mirroring is, perhaps, almost inevitable.[26] The key factor is whether the alternative structures indicate an "ascetic withdrawal" from participation in the larger cultural and political realities, whether in actual practice or in attitude (that is, due to an alternative perspective on what is real and true). It is this latter possibility that I explore.

It should be noted that I am not suggesting in any way that the thrust toward "political asceticism" explains everything in the letter (or letters) to the Philippians. Paul's anxiety about life or death has to be deflected in part (or sublimated, as the emphasis on rejoicing implies—e.g., 4:4–7). Paul cares for the Philippians—so the letter is one of friendship;[27] he hopes for continued missionary activity—hence he lays plans for the future (e.g., his use of Epaphroditus and Timothy).

The Community Faces a Crisis

Stand Firm (1:27-2:4)

What seems to be primary on Paul's mind is the political situation of the church. By "political situation" I mean *both* the relations of the church to outside structures *and* the internal governance.

"Be worthy citizens under the gospel of Christ" (1:27a). Paul's choice of *politeuomai* in the opening command has evoked much recent discussion. While translators still give a general, ethical meaning to the term (e.g., "conduct yourselves," NIV; "Live your life," NRSV; "Let your conduct be worthy," NEB), many contemporary commentators tend to give prominence to the specific political nuance in the word.[28] The word here has something to do with participation in a political structure. The question is then *which* structure Paul has in mind. Since it can hardly refer to civic, much less Roman structures,[29] the simplest solution is to see Paul speaking of the internal government of the Philippian church. Wiles translates: "Govern yourselves according to the standard of the gospel of Christ."[30]

Thus the "gospel" is the constitution, the *politeuma*. Here the "political asceticism" is not found in the alternative structure itself but in the fact that that structure has a different "constitution," that is, an alternative "world" out of which it lives, one that is contrary to the "world" created by the larger society. In this sense the community is called to withdraw (at least in its commitment) from the "reality" claimed by society and to create in its own structure and life an alternative reality.

In 1:27b Paul exhorts them to be united in fighting together for "the faith of the gospel" (*te pistei tou euaggeliou*). If "gospel" is the constitution that provides the reality structure for the life of the Philippians, what then does "faith" mean in this context? Paul uses the word for "faith" (*pistis*) four times elsewhere in the letter. Two of them are in 3:9, in the familiar construction with *dikaiosyne*. Of the remaining two instances, one occurs in the sentence immediately preceding 1:27, that is, 1:26; the second, in the concluding remarks of this section (2:17).

In these three instances (1:26, 27; 2:17), *pistis* is a characteristic that does or should belong to the community. The only time *pistis* is qualified it is with *euaggelion*—thus it is something other than faith in Christ, although that would be a consonant term. Interestingly, and perhaps significantly, in 1:25 Paul writes of the "advance" of *pistis*, while in 1:12 he uses the same term, "advance," to refer *to* the gospel. That might suggest that the advance of the gospel is related to the advance of *pistis*, especially since in 1:27b those two terms are closely related. I suggest that *pistis* in these three instances can best be translated by "faithfulness" or "commitment," referring to commitment to the constitution that provides the members with their reality structure. Thus in 1:27b the Philippians are called to struggle to exhibit commitment to that reality which is the gospel.

This struggle for an alternative reality is now set against opposition to it (v. 28). Those opposing the community are the citizenry of Philippi who are offended (and threatened?) by the absurdity of the community's claims. This offense leads to action against the community that is strong enough to cause fear among the believers. While it is impossible to imagine the precise nature of the action, the fact that it causes fear makes it certain that the conflict has reached a volatile stage. As so often happens, political asceticism, however much it may tend toward a withdrawal from the larger structures of society, is sufficiently threatening that the society may devise punitive measures hoping to destroy the signs of any alternative reality. Hence Paul acknowledges that the community is suffering from those punitive measures (vv. 29–30). Indeed, at least in the present situation one sign of its loyalty to its constitution is that it does suffer.

The correct translation of 1:28b is almost certainly that of Collange and Hawthorne. It requires some additions, but no more so than the traditional one, and it makes much more sense. The former translates: "What is for them a sign of perdition is in fact your salvation"; the latter: "For although your loyalty to the faith is proof to them that you will perish, it is in fact proof to you that you will be saved—saved by God."[31] *Apoleia* and *soteria* thus do not refer to eternal states, but to the resolution of the present conflict. For the outsiders, commitment to the gospel can only lead to the destruction or dissolution of the group; Paul sees, on the other hand, that that commitment is precisely what will lead to a positive resolution, a deliverance from the present conflict. One problem with the traditional reading is that Paul seems to think it necessary to say that *soteria* is from God—certainly a redundant phrase if *soteria* is given its usual theological meaning. Paul surely uses *soteria* in a political sense in 1:19, which the NRSV correctly translates as "deliverance." In that case, *kai touto apo theou* in 1.28 is not redundant but refers to the conviction that the deliverance of the church from its current endangered position will be due to God.

Given the fragility of the political situation, where one reality is pitted against another, it is not surprising that the leader of the minority group would make a strong appeal for unity within the ranks. A breakdown in the unity of commitment can mean fragmentation, factions, and ultimate dissolution of a sectarian community. Paul has appealed to unity in 1:27 and returns to the appeal in 2:1–4. Phil. 2:1–4 also describes just what he thinks it means to "govern yourselves," that is, what sort of communal regulations are appropriate under the constitution that is the gospel. While there are uncertainties about the appropriate translations, the general idea is clear. The *euaggelion* permits no individualistic manipulation of the community for purposes of personal glory or ambition. Rather, the *euaggelion* expects a group of members to act out governance by caring for others rather than themselves. Here we find a classic expression of the sectarian ideal of mutuality, where *all* are leaders; thus no one is superior to another.[32]

Many scholars go further, however, to maintain that the ideal stated here is not mutuality but the first clear example of the ideal of humility (which is by definition *not* mutual), which later so captivated Christian theology and ethics. Only v. 3b can be read in this way, but it is almost universally so read. So powerful is this pull toward the ideal of humility that it becomes the point of interpretation for the entire passage and for at least the *Pauline* interpretation of the hymn that follows.

In her thesis V. Wiles argues strongly against the usual interpretation of v. 3b.[33] She begins with the observation that in Greek literature the basic term *tapeinos* has a primary meaning denoting humiliation and inferior station. While Paul's use of the derivative *tapeinophrosyne* in v. 3 is apparently the first extant appearance in Greek literature, for him to have assigned a positive meaning to it would hardly communicate with his readers. Indeed, for Paul to have called the Philippians to such a status, without some warning that he is changing the values placed on such status, would have been highly offensive. Wiles' own translation reads: "Do nothing on the basis of competitive self-promotion or the assumption of a false glory, but, mindful of your present humiliation, regard one another as your own leaders."[34] Not only is this a cogent interpretation, it is consonant with the political context I am suggesting.

Thus in 1:27–2:4 Paul pleads for a unity of mind about governance, based on a commitment to the constitution, the *euaggelion*. It is an alternate political structure, based on a sectarian sense of equality and mutuality, against what Paul seems to see as happening in the outside political structures, namely "selfish ambition and conceit." Perhaps he worries that the decision of the community to have specific leaders also endangers the sectarian drive toward mutuality.

But does Paul give any sense for what he means by *euaggelion* here? What *is* the constitution to which the church should commit itself and which should engender mutuality in leadership? For a possible answer to this question it is necessary to turn to the hymn.

The Constitution (2:6-11)

While I firmly believe that vv. 6–11 are a non-Pauline liturgical piece, almost certainly a hymn to be sung antiphonally,[35] a contrary opinion would not basically change exegesis of the passage for purposes of this chapter. Paul *does* dictate the lines, whoever "wrote" them, so he could not have been in any basic disagreement with the thought expressed.[37]

In any case, the lines are remarkable, the more so because of Paul's incarceration. Here he uses language that could almost have come from the very charges against him. One immediately thinks about censorship in Roman prisons; did the officials not care what prisoners wrote to the outside world? How did such a letter escape the eyes of the guards?[38]

Do these verses tell us anything about Paul's "political asceticism?" E. Heen, in his thesis about early Christian claims for the enthronement of Jesus, uses the schema of James C. Scott to provide a background for these claims and for 2:6–11 in particular.[39] Scott contrasts a "public" transcript (language and interpretation stemming from those in power) with a "hidden" transcript (language used in subordinate social levels covertly to subvert the public one). Heen argues that early Christian enthronement language is such a hidden transcript, designed to present an alternative view of reality against the dominant one of the empire and the civic self-understanding of the local elite. The local elite are involved because they had so much invested in the imperial ideology.[40] If this is the case, then an anti-imperial hymn is equally an anti-civic one, perhaps particularly in a Roman colony.[41]

Heen argues that the phrase in v. 6, *to einai isa theo*, should be understood against the public transcript of the emperor, who is also said to be "equal to God."[42] If Heen is correct, then whether that verse refers to a preexistent possession of such a status or to a refusal to seek such status as an obedient human (which is Heen's own view), the phrase presents an alternative (whether similar or contrasting) figure, against the emperor and the local elite.

The last verses of the hymn are, however, the crucial ones with regard to their possible political implications. Vv. 9–11 can be divided into three two-line formations:

> *dio kai ho theos auton hyperypsosen*
> *kai echarisato auto to onoma to hyper pan onoma*
> *hina en to onomati Iesou pan gony kampse*

[epouranion kai epigeion kai katachthonion]
kai pasa glossa exomologesetai hoti Kyrios Iesous Christos
[eis doxan theou patros].[43]

As has long been recognized, what is portrayed is an enthronement ceremony.[44] God exalts (the resurrected) Jesus, gives him *the* name (=crowns him), and presents him to his new subjects, who perforce do obeisance to him and acclaim him as the ruler. The extent of the lordship depends upon the extent of the new subjects. Are they the cosmic forces that have previously ruled the world?[45] Are they people? If so, who—rulers, everybody, members of the church? Without specification, the "every knee and every tongue" would presumably be universal in scope, in which case this is a cosmic enthronement ceremony. It names the whole world as ascribing obeisance to the new lord.[46] For a deified human to be given cosmic lordship is at least a *parallel* to the political ideology in the imperial realm. Whether the parallel could be taken more ominously as *opposing* that realm would depend upon the interpreter.[47]

To this possibility must be added a striking fact, little noticed by scholars, that there is no "eschatological reservation" to the claim in vv. 9–11.[48] It is *not* said that Jesus *will* reign in a future time of bliss. The reign is a present fact. While many scholars read in an implied eschatology, it is a characteristic of most liturgical materials that proclaim the resurrected Jesus (at least in the Hellenistic environs of the early churches) that in them there is silence about an eschatological future just as there is in 2:6–11.

Thus the enthronement is, in this respect, like that of any monarch, and the "every knee and every tongue" is like the political hyperbole associated with ancient enthronement liturgies—for example, "O King, live forever!"[49] Put into this context, the hymn affirms that there is a new cosmic lord, on the analogy of a new earthly emperor. It speaks of the hoped-for unity and peace under the new monarch. But just as there are areas of life that lie outside of or refuse to do obeisance to the new lord, despite the hyperbole the hymn does not necessarily anticipate a perfect obeisance and thus does not speak of a perfect world, present or future.

This is not to say that a "present eschatology" is implied by the hymn. Yes, it does proclaim a *new reality* brought by God in the midst of the continuation of the present world. Since I have serious questions about the ability of Greeks and Romans to "think eschatologically," I would propose that if one has to create a title for the phenomenon pointed to by the hymn (and other such liturgical materials in the New Testament) it might be a *new politics*. The lord is cosmic, not cultic. What the church does is sing a hymn about a lord who affects the entire world. This, I would suggest, is how Hellenistic believers would have interpreted the hymn. This is what it meant to them.

The absence of an eschatological future surely influences how the hymn would be taken by outsiders. What the lack of a future does is take away the safety that lies in the claim: "We're not singing about something that is now; we are singing about a future, final end of the world." The political order is not as threatened by a utopia (although it can be) as it is by assertions about *present* realities. That is, a non-eschatological portrait of the resurrection of Jesus can be more inflammatory and more suspicious to outside authorities than one that safely puts off any potential conflict until some future day (which the outsider doesn't think will come anyway).

Now we must return to the question with which this discussion opened. What is the *euaggelion*, the constitution, to which the Philippians are to commit themselves? If, as surely the entire context suggests, the hymn *is* the *euaggelion*, what is the good news? It is that the world is restored to its rightful ownership, that *kyrios Iesous Christos*, that in this world believers are cognizant that they *can* work out their own salvation, that options and possibilities are available that were not theirs previously, at least of which they were not aware. The constitution is *not* focused on Jesus as a suffering servant, but on a restored world led by the enthroned Jesus. Thus the implied message (if we must seek for one) for the singers of the hymn is not to humbly emulate a suffering servant, but to live a new freedom before the enthroned Jesus.[50]

The Difference a Lord Makes (2:5, 12-13)

We are now in a position to understand better the entire sequence of the passage, 1:27–2:13. Paul began with the exhortation to be worthy citizens under the constitution, the *euaggelion*. The Philippian believers were urged to be united in commitment. The reason for this call to unity is harrassment and/or persecution by outsiders. The possible results of this conflict are said to be either destruction (*apoleia*) or salvation (*soteria*). I argued earlier in this chapter that these terms do not refer to eternal determinations but rather to the historical situation of existence in Philippi. The issue is the life or death of the community. The distress caused to the community by this conflict is not to be seen as negative: It is a sacred *agon*.

This crucial moment is no time for division within the community. Everything depends upon unity. And on what does this unity rest? It is faith as commitment to the gospel. The gospel is the good news that God has restored the cosmos to its rightful ownership, reigning through *kyrios Iesous Christos*. Unity rests in the confident belief that God, not malevolent powers, reign—and reign even over the conflictive situation at Philippi.

Vv. 12–13 then express what Paul wants the oppressed community to think about that conflict *in light of the gospel*. Given the reign of God through *kyrios Iesous Christos*, what can be done? The believers are not to despair but are to work confidently themselves (in Paul's absence) toward a solution of the conflict. They are to "work out their own *soteria*." Here that word, just as in 1:19 and 28, refers not to eternal destiny but to a concrete, earthly event in the political realm. They are not helpless or alone in the conflict. They are empowered by God, who works in them (v. 13), to reach a successful resolution. In the midst of danger, Paul sees God working in his own situation for a determination that will further God's own purpose (1:19); likewise, Paul believes the same thing can happen in the Philippian conflict. And the reason Paul can be confident about this is his faith in the gospel, which portrays God's victory over God's world.

Paul is thus not a believer simply in passive withdrawal from the world. He advocates a withdrawal from commitment to the world's sense of what is real. But he believes that, because God has restored the world to its rightful ownership, that world can be confronted and defeated. God's power, manifested by the enthronement of Christ, now is at work in believers to effect God's will (*eudokia*) in the midst of opposition. To participate in working out that will is to participate in the lordship of Jesus Christ.

This participation is, I believe, pointed to by one verse in this section we have not looked at, namely, 2:5, the line of introduction to the hymn. The Greek is terse and requires expansion: *touto phroneite en hymin ho kai en Christo Iesou;* literally, "Think this in you which also in Christ Jesus." I propose the following expansion: "Commit yourselves to that reality which is based in Christ Jesus."[51] It is really the same thing as "the faith of the gospel" in 1:27. The hymn describes, then, just what the reality *en Christo* is, that is, just what the good news is.

Eschatological Offensiveness

If one thing is clear, however, it is that a non-eschatological view of the lordship of Christ is not completely adequate to Paul—which is as good a reason as any to think that Paul was not the author of 2:6–11. 1 Corinthians 15 and many other passages demonstrate that, for Paul, God's final victory over the cosmos was still outstanding. A present political interpretation of that lordship might be acceptable, but Paul would have had to "think" that reality in a larger eschatological context.

Indeed, 3:20–21 expresses a confident expectation for a victorious future, not yet visible, however much the power of God through the present lordship of Christ could change the old rule. Many have seen in these verses also a non-Pauline formulation,[52] and for the sake of convenience I lay out the lines as Becker has proposed:[53]

hemon gar to politeuma en ouranois hyparchei
ex hou kai sotera apekdechometha kyrion Iesoun Christon
hos metaschematisei to soma tes tapeinoseos hemon
symmorphon to somati tes doxes autou
kata ten energeian tou dynasthai auton
kai hypotaxai auto ta panta

There is a certain plausibility to the proposal for a non-Pauline origin, but for our purposes the issue is not crucial. The lines certainly express that eschatological future so essential to Paul's own Jewish thinking.[54]

"For *our* citizenship is in heaven." *Politeuma* has a number of nuances, and a full, if awkward, translation here could read: "For the political institution in which we have our citizenship is in heaven."[55] Commentators usually connect this phrase with what they presume is the legal situation of the church at Philippi; that is, they assume the members are citizens of the city. Since there were no doubt many noncitizens living there, I am not sure on what grounds civic citizenship is so easily assumed. It *may* be that the heavenly *politeuma* is to be contrasted to civic citizenship held by members of the church; it may equally be that it contrasts the primarily noncitizenship status of the members with "real" citizenship in the heavenly community. In any case, Paul says that the ultimate political attachment is not with the irreality of human establishments but with the real community of the faithful in heaven.

To soma tes tapeinoseos: "the body of our humiliation." Most interpreters (including myself) have taken *soma* here to be the individual self of the believer, similar to its use in 1 Corinthians 15.[56] It would be more consonant with the present interpretation, however, to consider that *soma* may not be the individual body but the corporate body of the *politeuma* referred to in the previous verse. In that case, the "body of our humiliation" would point to a community, that is, the church, whose status in the political order was one of *tapeinosis*—that is, of low status. That would then fit with the reading of *tapeinophrosyne* as negative status in 2:3. The church, harassed or persecuted by outsiders, feels painfully its outcast status.

Supporting this interpretation, perhaps, is the appeal to the kind of power that brings the transformation of the body. It is that which "enables him to subject all things to himself."[57] The power is not just the ability to change the reality of individual bodies. It is rather that cosmic power that gives Christ control over *all* reality, including corporate and political realities (cf. 1 Cor. 15:24-28). Phil. 3:21 is in many ways parallel to 2:9–11; in both cases *kyrios Iesous Christos* is the cosmocrator. The latter, however, speaks of a present lordship in the midst of present ambiguity; the former, of the ultimate resolution of that historical ambiguity.

Thus 3:20–21 describes an alternate reality to that espoused by the world. The church does not belong to this order, where it lives in humiliation, but to the heavenly *politeuma,* where ultimately it will be transformed into a body of glory by the lord of the cosmos.

Do the eschatological dimensions in this instance mute the political asceticism that may be more obvious in a non-eschatological description such as the hymn in 2:6–11? I have suggested that in a typical future-oriented statement, the political implications could be avoided. In this specific case, however, the use of the political term *politeuma* contrasts what is real citizenship with what is otherwise. Paul does not say the citizenship will be; it already is. Yet the coming eschatological transformation will be victorious over all realities in this world that have created a body of humiliation for the church. Thus Paul, caught personally in life-or-death political distress, cannot let go of a political reading of even traditional eschatological affirmations.

CONCLUSION

To conclude is to repeat. The Letter to the Philippians is shot through with political perspectives and innuendos. Given the author's situation this is not surprising. He faces the possibility of death, and, like any human, he expresses anxiety about his fate, however much he sublimates. He sees in the Philippians' distress a situation parallel to his own and attempts to get them to exhibit the same kind of stance toward political establishments and God's victory over them that he himself has (however ambiguously). He calls them to commit themselves to the gospel, the constitution of their faith, a constitution that affirms that God has restored control over the world through the Lord Jesus Christ. He urges them to believe that with God's help they can work out their own resolution to their conflict. In any event, they are to be confident that their citizenship exists in heaven, not in earthly realities, and that ultimately their humiliation will be overcome with God's glory. Paul's political asceticism is both a negative withdrawal from allegiance to earthly political structures and a positive faith that just as God triumphs through Christ so too can believers exercise God's power to influence historical events.

It was then, as now, an audacious claim, and we do not know whether the Philippians could have confidence in it any more than we can today. But, then, Paul's model of commitment was that of Abraham, who trusted that what was impossible was, in fact, going to happen (Rom. 4).

NOTES

1. I take my cue from a definition by Richard Valantasis: "Asceticism may be defined as performances designed to inaugurate an alternative culture, to enable different social relations, and to create a new identity." See Valantasis, "A Theory of the Social Function of Asceticism," in *Asceticism*, eds. Vincent L. Wimbush and Richard Valantasis (New York: Oxford University Press, 1995), 548. His emphasis on the activity is instructive. An alternative culture is called into being by acts, not by wishful thinking. Cf. K. Mannheim, *Ideology and Utopia* (San Diego, Calif.: Harcourt Brace Jovanovich, 1936), 192–211. In the case of Paul in Philippians, the acts he calls the church to are "political" acts, that is, activity that results in change in the internal structure of the church and,

perhaps, even in relation to outside society. The usual definition of asceticism as avoidance of certain bodily acts is not represented in our text, unless as a reverse image it appears in 3:17–18—but this is a stock phrase, and the attack is too vague for us to be able to know just what Paul is opposing.

2. I assume throughout that worldviews are socially constructed givens or creations, a view that has been popular since the publication of P. Berger and T. Luckmann, *The Social Construction of Reality* (Garden City, N.Y.: Anchor Books, 1966).

3. As far as I can judge, "political asceticism," as I have defined it, is but another term for "sectarianism," a phenomenon that has been applied to early Christianity for many years. Cf. my early paper "The Earliest Christian Communities as Sectarian Movement," now in my collected essays, *The Text and the Times: New Testament Essays for Today* (Minneapolis, Minn.: Fortress, 1993), 20–45. More precisely the term "counterculture" could be applied to movements within early Christianity. Of the three terms, this last seems to me to be most useful and accurate, but I will not use it in this chapter, in honor of the term that brings together the essays in this volume. Valantasis, however, does use this term in his description of asceticism in "Theory," 549, 551.

4. If one thinks they were not desperate, one needs to read about life in ancient prisons in C. Wansink, *Chained in Christ: The Experience and Rhetoric of Paul's Imprisonments* (Sheffield, England: Sheffield Academic Press, 1996), 27–95.

5. In an interesting article written not long after World War II, Gerhard Friedrich pointed out how little concerned Paul seems to be about the suffering and indignities of prison life and compares the Letter to the Philippians with ancient letters from prison, as well as sample letters from prison camps in World War II. See Friedrich, "Der Brief eines Gefangenen: Bemerkungen zum Philipperbrief," now in *Auf das Wort kommt es an: Gesammelte Aufsätze zum 70. Geburtstag,* ed. Johannes H. Friedrich (Göttingen, Germfany: Vandenhoeck & Ruprecht, 1978), 224–35. It is certainly true that Paul never complains explicitly in his correspondence. Paul is too subtle a writer to do that. I do think that he shows some justifiable anxiety over the outcome of the trial.

6. In 1:20, where the possibility of death is explicit, the terms clearly point to his defense speech at the trial. *Aischynomai* and *epaischynomai* already in early Christian literature can refer to refusal to confess the faith, either before earthly officials (Mark 8:38; probably also 1 Pet. 4:16) or in God's heavenly court (Mark 8:38, 1 John 2:28). *Parresia* also can be used in a legal or semilegal context, meaning frank, honest, and bold statement of the truth (Acts 4:13, 29; 28:31; and, by implication, in other passages of the Gospel of John). In 1 John 2:28 both *parresia* and *aischynomai* appear in reference to the heavenly judgment.

7. Evidence of charges brought against believers *qua believers* by the Romans does not antedate the date one assigns 1 Peter (= last decade of the first century CE?). Nero's executions were an ad hoc reaction and do not negate the judgment herein. Pliny (X.xcvi) in 110–111 CE is ignorant of whatever official charges might be encoded in Roman law, although he seems to think that capital punishment is appropriate. Even the term "Christian" seems to have been a late-first-century CE coinage, perhaps created as a derogatory term by outsiders.

8. Cf. Richard Bauman, *Crime and Punishment in Ancient Rome* (London: Routledge, 1996), 62.

9. Ibid, 66.

10. Ibid, 71.

11. Ibid, 83.

12. Bauman (*Crime and Punishment*) well shows the ambiguity about charges and decisions that runs through the Roman execution of justice. If the charge were not *maiestas*, then what other kind of charge would justify a capital punishment?

13. Of the several issues of translation in this passage, the only one that can concern us here is the meaning of *en Christo*. Does it carry the "mystical" sense, or is it simply to be seen as a reference to attachment to a movement, a perspective, a cause? G. Fee tries to have it both ways in *Paul's Letter to the Philippians* (Grand Rapids, Mich.: Eerdmans, 1995), 112–113, but this is probably to overread what may simply be a casual reference. Not all of Paul's sentences need to be given profound theological weight.

14. When I was growing up in the southern United States, I learned how easy it was to strip a person of power by the label of "communist." One should, on the other hand, consider the possibility that persons hearing Paul's confession about the lordship of Christ may have honestly thought he was preaching insurrection.

15. Rom. 13:1–7 is a critical text, given the interpretation I am here suggesting. Either Paul did not sense the political implications of his proclamation of the resurrected Jesus or the passage in Rom. 13:1–7 (assuming an Ephesian imprisonment) represents a change in his thinking, having recognized in the imprisonment the dangers of his earlier perspective.

16. It is conceivable, but unlikely, that the arrest of Paul had to do with the charge that he was creating illegal organizations, without official approval. It is my judgment that he considered himself to be forming communities that were legal under the protection granted assemblage of Jews. The fact that there are no hints elsewhere in this period of *legal* pressure on the community as such suggests that such communities at this time escaped the eyes of Roman authorities, perhaps because they were indeed seen as Jewish.

17. If the males in the community are circumcised, then they are full proselytes and are, in fact, Jews. Then the question about Roman protection of the community need not arise. It is only later that Romans moved toward suspicion against the circumcision of Gentiles. Cf. M. Smallwood, *The Jews under Roman Rule: From Pompey to Diocletian* (Leiden, The Netherlands: Brill, 1981), 378–83, 428–31, 467–72.

18. For a discussion of the term in 2:6 in relation to claims for the emperor, cf. E. Heen, "Saturnalicius Princeps: The Enthronement of Jesus in Early Christian Discourse" (Ph.D. diss., Columbia University, 1997), 177–93. I will return to Heen's argument later in the chapter.

19. Already this has happened by the time of the writing of Romans (cf. chaps. 9–11).

20. Heb. 13:10–14 suggests, however, that some did claim that protection.

21. While he may—and I believe he did—understand Jesus as preexistent, he does not seem to have emphasized this in his teaching. And while *Paul* may not have been happy with the term "deification" with regard to the resurrected Jesus, this

is almost certainly how pagan outsiders (and maybe some Jews as well) would have understood his proclamation. Whether Paul did think of Jesus as preexistent is, of course, disputed, and turns on how certain non-Pauline liturgical citations in his letters are to be interpreted. Of these the hymn in Phil. 2:6–11 is the key passage.

22. He boldly sent money out of the province to Jerusalem, as, apparently, only Jews could legally do. Cf. Smallwood, *Jews,* 125–27, esp. 126. This can only mean that Paul believed he could do this under the legal sanction of the Roman permission to Jews.

23. He is aware that when he goes to Jerusalem, he cannot necessarily count on the support from Jewish believers in Jesus; see Rom. 15:30–32.

24. Even though I have emphasized the crucial importance of Paul's legal situation, I think that I have made it clear that I differ essentially from E. Lohmeyer's perspective, that martyrdom is the great theme of the letter, in *Die Briefe an die Philipper, an die Kolosser und an Philemon* (Göttingen, Germany: Vandenhoeck & Ruprecht, 1964). What Paul says in Philippians is, in my judgment, much too ambiguous (and healthy) to force him into a grand march toward martyrdom.

25. My thought has been informed by many discussions over the last few years with Prof. Virginia Wiles, of Muhlenberg College, as we discussed the ideas that then appeared in her "From Apostolic Presence to Self-Government in Christ: Paul's Preparing of the Philippian Church for Life in His Absence" (Ph.D. diss., The University of Chicago, 1993). I refer frequently in what follows to this thesis, but it is difficult to be sure that I acknowledge everything that I have learned from her.

26. Perhaps the existence of bishops and deacons (1:1) attests to this mirroring.

27. As is emphasized by S. Stowers, "Friends and Enemies in the Politics of Heaven: Reading Theology in Philippians," in *Pauline Theology. Vol. 1. Thessalonians, Philippians, Galatians, Philemon,* ed. J. Bassler (Minneapolis, Minn.: Fortress, 1991), 105–21. This perspective has been accepted by Fee, *Paul's Letter to the Philippians,* 2–7.

28. See, for example, Fee, *Paul's Letter to the Philippians,* 161–62; R. Martin, *Philippians* (Grand Rapids, Mich.: Eerdmans, 1976), 82. J.-F. Collange, *The Epistle of Saint Paul to the Philippians* (London: Epworth, 1979), 73, seems to straddle the issue. In his recent thesis, B. Blumenfeld, "Classical and Hellenistic Sources for the Political Paul" (Ph.D. diss., Columbia University, 1997), 365–66, also urges the political sense, as does Wiles, "Apostolic Presence," 38–44.

29. It is a citizenship according to the *euaggelion.*

30. Wiles, "Apostolic Presence," 38. For her defense of this interpretation, see ibid, 38–45. Wiles takes *axios* to function as a noun, meaning "rule" or "standard." Fee (*Paul's Letter to the Philippians,* 162) also sees this: "With the modified, 'worthy of the gospel of Christ,' Paul defines both the parameters and the nature of the new 'polis' of which they are citizens and to which they have obligation."

31. See Collange, *Philippians* 72; G. Hawthorne, *Philippians* (Waco, Tex.: Word, 1983), 54. There are nearly unsolvable grammatical problems in vv. 28–29, which cannot adequately be discussed here. Hawthorne, in my judgment, correctly sees that *pistis* is the antecedent of *tis.* The contrast thus does not lie in some eternal reality, but in the differing perceptions about what faithfulness (or

stubbornness) to the *euaggelion* will result in. A second problem has to do with the antecedent of *touto* in the phrase *kai touto apo theou*. Strictly speaking, it cannot refer to the feminine *pistis,* but then it has no recognizable, grammatically correct antecedent. Many commentators, I think correctly, take the nearest antecedent, in this case, *pistis.* See, for example, most recently, Fee, *Paul's Letter to the Philippians,* 169ff.

32. Yet there are bishops and deacons! Is there an implicit critique of how locally elected leadership can go astray, from the standpoint of a sectarian ideal? Does Paul think that the Philippian bishops and deacons are actually engaged in behavior that is counter to the *euaggelion*? Cf. Wiles, "Apostolic Presence," 69–70, who concludes that our passage may be a "subtle critique of or at least a caution to the Philippians regarding their emerging polity."

33. Ibid, 49–67.

34. It seems clear to me that her reading of *tapeinophrosyne* is compelling, and it legitimates a rereading of the difficult *hyperechontas.* Taking her cue from the use of the definite article before the participle by P[46] and B, she argues that this shows at least how some early scribes read the passage. There also seems to be no doubt that as a substantive participle her translation is possible. Given what I am arguing as the general "political" context, this would favor the political rather than the ethical interpretation of *hyperecho.* As far as I can see, there is nothing in the word or the grammar (even without the definite article) that makes Wiles' reading improbable.

35. Cf. my article "Christ the Cosmocrator and the Experience of Believers" in *The Future of Christology: Essays in Honor of Leander E. Keck,* eds. A. J. Malherbe and W. Meeks (Minneapolis, Minn.: Fortress, 1993), 160–61. I will consistently use the word "hymn" as shorthand to refer to 2:6–11, simply as a reference to the verses in question, without investing in the notion that it is a non-Pauline creation.

36. I do argue later that the hymn is completely and non-eschatologically oriented to the present. Paul, on the other hand, retains an eschatological future, as 3:20–21 reminds us. In fact, it is possible to see 3:20–21 as something of a correction to the hymn; Paul, however, occasionally cites other liturgical material that is non-eschatological (see, e.g., Rom. 1:3–4). In fact, I argue that *most* liturgical material is non-eschatological (cf. "Christ the Cosmocrator," 166). Paul is clearly familiar with the non-eschatological orientation of non-Jewish believers, and he has thus come to terms with this inability to appreciate Jewish eschatology. He no doubt supplies for himself what is lacking in the liturgical material, and certainly has no compunction against sharing it with his pagan believers. Of course, it may also be that 3:20–21 is itself a liturgical formula; in this case, Paul "corrects" one formula with another.

37. I make no apology for ignoring the vast amount of scholarship poured out on these verses. For a recent and convenient summary, cf. J. Habermann, *Präexistenzaussagen im Neuen Testament* (Frankfurt, Germany: Lang, 1990), 91–157. Since our focus is on the enthronement section (vv. 9–11), even the current dispute about the issue of preexistence or a possible Adamic reference in v. 6 is not pertinent for us.

38. D. Georgi, *Theocracy in Paul's Praxis and Theology* (Minneapolis, Minn.: Fortress, 1991), 74, states that in citing the hymn Paul "introduces into the text

an affront that would be transparent to anyone familiar with Roman ways." On the other hand, it is also possible that we are oversensitized to such language, perhaps much more so than the actors themselves. Pliny (X.xcvi), for example, apparently finds the Christian hymn "to Christ as to a god" inoffensive. It is Christian obstinacy, not their theology, that bothers him.

39. Cf. Heen, "Saturnalicius Princeps," 10–13; James C. Scott, *Domination and the Arts of Resistance* (New Haven, Conn.: Yale University Press, 1990).

40. Cf. Heen, "Saturnalicius Princeps," 44–122.

41. Evidence for the prominence of the imperial cult in Philippi seems ambiguous. L. Bormann, *Philippi: Stadt und Christengemeinde zur Zeit des Paulus* (Leiden, The Netherlands: Brill, 1995), 41–60, stresses the omnipresence of the imperial cult in the first century, which then leads him to conclude (224): "Die paulinische Mission befindet sich nicht in erster Linie in der Offensive gegen einen wie immer gearteten religiösen Pluralismus. Sie gerät in Konflikt mit der offiziellen, gesellschaftstragenden und herrschaftlegitimierenden religiös-politischen Ideologie des frühen Prinzipats in der Phase der julisch-claudischen Dynastie." On the other hand, H. Hendrix, "Philippi," *Anchor Bible Dictionary*, ed. D. N. Freedman (New York: Doubleday, 1992), 5: 316, seems to choose religious pluralism as the dominant feature of the day.

42. Heen, "Saturnalicius Princeps," 177–93: The use of "equal to God" "appropriates for Jesus the honorific tradition of the ruler cult" (191–92). Heen cites Georgi in support of Heen's reading of the hymn. Georgi (*Theocracy,* 73) states: "For Paul (the Roman citizen) as well as for the citizens of Philippi (a military colony of Rome) the description of Jesus' exaltation and entrance into heaven must have suggested the events surrounding the decrease of a *princeps* and his heavenly assumption and apotheosis by resolution of the Roman senate, ratified in heaven."

43. To rehearse the scholarship on the verses is impossible here. Many scholars take the words enclosed in brackets to be Pauline additions to an original hymn, in which case there would be two verses of two lines each. It is sufficient for our purposes to deal with the text as Paul wrote it, without engaging in debate about this possibility.

44. Cf. my "Christ the Cosmocrator," 161–62. Needless to say, it is not (as far as anyone knows) an "Egyptian enthronement ceremony," which was a figment of scholarly imagination.

45. So E. Käsemann, "Kritische Analyse von Phil. 2,5–11," in *Exegetische Versuche und Besinnungen,* vol. 1, ed. E. Kasemann (Göttingen, Germany: Vandenhoeck & Ruprecht, 1964), 85–86.

46. I think it likely that the text of Daniel 7 lies behind this scene of cosmic enthronement. Certainly Isa. 45:23 is essentially quoted here, which, in the original, referred to God's ultimate lordship over God's world.

47. One sticky point in the presumed analogy has always been that the earthly emperor has the power, while the dead emperor only has divinity. In the case of the hymn (and others like it in early Christianity) the earthly Jesus has no power, while the resurrected Jesus has both power and divinity. The figures are, nevertheless, opposed to each other, and the logical problems are probably a modern scholarly refinement unobserved by people involved in the politics of that day.

48. In vv. 10–11, Isa. 45:23 is cited. The LXX has both verbs in the future. Phil. 2:10 reads *kampse*, i.e., in the subjunctive, and in v. 11, the textual evidence for *exomologe* is mixed, the better texts (P46, H, B) reading the subjunctive. It seems reasonably clear that the original text of Philippians read both as subjunctive, thus *deliberately* changing the LXX.

49. See, for example, Psalms 2 and 110—both psalms that influenced early Christian enthronement liturgies. For a Roman example, cf. Virgil's fourth Eclogue.

50. So also Wiles ("Apostolic Presence," 178–87), although she uses the motif of "change of lordship."

51. *Phroneo* means more than just "intellectually to perceive"; it also involves the direction of the will. "Incline," which is often used, is too weak. There is involved a commitment to what one perceives. *En Christo Iesou* must refer to that sphere of reality in which the resurrected Christ is present. It is hardly just a reference to a past historical series of events.

52. Cf. Fee, *Paul's Letter to the Philippians*, 377, n. 9, for a list. Fee himself rejects the liturgical origin of these verses. They are "vintage Paul."

53. Cf. J. Becker, "Erwägungen zu Phil. 3, 20-21" *Theologische Zeitung* 27 (1971): 16–29. He gives the lines in German, but makes no suggestion for a modification of the present Greek text.

54. Clearly the passage goes beyond the horizon of the hymn in 2:6–11. The question is whether one could suggest that 3:20–21 is a *deliberate* "corrective" to or an expansion of that horizon. That suggestion would have more plausibility on the assumption of a unified letter than it would if 2:6–11 and 3:20–21 belonged to different occasions.

55. Georgi (*Theocracy*, 76) labels *politeuma* a "highly political term."

56. Christ transforms the earthly body into a body of glory. In 1 Corinthians 15, it is a "spiritual body," but it is assumed that the meaning is the same.

57. The language is reminiscent of 1 Cor. 15:28, which is explicitly dependent on Psalm 8:6, which was applied by early believers to the resurrected and exalted Christ (see, e.g., Heb. 2:5–9).

The Letter to Philemon
and Asceticism

Robin Scroggs

Philemon is usually linked to Philippians on the assumption that, since both letters were written from prison, the imprisonment must have been the same. At any rate, the Letter to Philemon, which is a delightful piece of correspondence and shows Paul at his ingratiating best, does not contribute to the subject of asceticism, either political or otherwise. The political judgments and innuendos I have found in Philippians do not emerge in Philemon. The author seems entirely focused on his task of repairing the relationship between Philemon and Onesimus.[1] Perhaps this shows in a negative mirroring that what Paul does say in Philippians is not simply his own anxiety and projection but is thought out with the Philippian situation in mind.

NOTES

1. Were Philemon evidence that Paul favored a societal system without slavery, then much more could be said. While it is my judgment that Paul is urging Philemon to free Onesimus, to generalize from this one concrete situation is hardly justified. Not everybody even thinks Paul is suggesting that Onesimus be liberated.

Competing Ascetic Subjectivities in the Letter to the Galatians

Richard Valantasis

INTRODUCTION

In 1989, Victor Paul Furnish could report about the state of Pauline studies that the analysis of the Pauline congregations had finally displaced "biographical" questions about Paul. He wrote:

> Although the standard "biographical" questions about Paul are still debated, these have in general been subordinated to questions about the Pauline congregations and his interaction with them as apostle. One may judge this to be an altogether proper and indeed overdue refocusing of questions about Paul's life and ministry. It is Paul's interaction with his congregations, after all, for which his letters supply primary data—not for the reconstruction of his pre-Christian life, or for his theology in some systematic sense, or even, in the first instance, for his missionary preaching.[1]

A few years later in his Society of Biblical Literature Presidential Address of 1993, Furnish continued to emphasize how difficult it was to put Paul in his proper place in the historical context of the first century. Furnish argued that the more scholars learn about nascent Christianity, Rabbinic Judaism, and the Hellenistic and Greco-Roman worlds, the more difficult it has become to place Paul precisely in any one of these categories. In addressing this persistent problem, Furnish proposed both a historical and a theological interpretation of the Pauline letters in which the specificity of their historical context and theological content receive correlative and serious attention.[2]

Neither of these suggestions has yet been able to break through the persistent tradition of Pauline scholarship: Neither the discursive practices of the community to which the letters stand as witness, nor the theological statements outside the parameters of later theological categories have received primary scholarly attention. Pauline studies seem to revolve about the same scholarly questions without any attempt to shift the investigation or adjust the categories of research. The recent work of Daniel Boyarin, E. P. Sanders, James D. G. Dunn, Alan F. Segal, and the SBL Paul Group attests to this situation.[3] Paul holds scholarly fascination because he seems to beg to be explicated as the constructed "mind" or "personality" or "perspective" behind the letters. Pauline scholarship, even when oriented toward uncovering the historical context or the rhetorical strategies of the letters, has focused on the person, the mental processes, or the attitudes and theology of Paul in relationship to others.[4] "Paul," as constructed person, has remained the operative category of research. Furnish himself, in evaluating the scholarly production of recent years, returns to the historical and theological investigation of *Paul* as the primary factor in understanding the historical context of the letters. This chapter accepts Furnish's assessment and responds to his call for refocusing attention by moving in yet another direction, away from the psychotheological construction of the person Paul and toward the analysis of the discursive practices embedded in the Pauline letters.

Let me further explain my perspective. I wish to move the focus from Paul to the letters so that the center of attention becomes not "what Paul thought" but the evident and material discourse inscribed within the letters. This shift in focus emphasizes the discursive interaction of a community by contextualizing the narrative voice as only one aspect of the discursive field. I am interested in the Pauline letters as sites of discourse, as *loci* of conversation recorded in the early period of formative Christianity, in which the narrative voice of the author opens out discursively with the lives and interests of the recipients of the letters as one factor among many. The narrative voice, not the personality or thought of Paul, receives the attention that focuses on the discourse that this voice articulates.[5] Here, in this discursive practice, not in the mind of Paul, will scholars discover the dynamic of formative Christianity.

So far I have presented the problem and the method of analysis: The problem revolves about redirecting the attention of the Pauline epistles away from the psychological and religious characterization of the author, and the method uses a kind of discourse analysis to investigate the dynamic discursive practices that these letters embody.[6] There is, however, one more factor in this discourse analysis that will aid me in my project of recovering the discursive practices of these early Christian communities—a theory of asceticism.

I have been intrigued over the years with the peripheral suggestion by scholars of the connection between early Christian literary traditions and asceticism. This connection has been proposed regarding the early Syrian traditions of the sayings of Jesus, the trajectory of the *logoi sophon* into the *apophthegmata patrum* of the desert monks, the theological orientation of the *Gospel of Thomas*, and many other sites of suspected ascetical influence.[7] My recent research and publication revolves about the definition and role of asceticism in the religious literature of first-century Christianity, Second Temple and Pharisaic Judaism, and Greco-Roman religions and philosophy. I propose that what made Christianity advance so quickly through the first century revolves about a complex interaction of formative and ascetical practices, social and political experimentation, religious redefinition, and theological and biblical ingenuity focused upon the teaching and work of Jesus Christ. It is not primarily a personality cult, either of Jesus or of Paul, although certainly such cannot be ruled out, but the performance of a new way of living inaugurated by Jesus and extended by those captivated by the alternative that Jesus offered. The performances of formative Christianity, I argue, established an alternative way of living that included both a subversive set of redefined social relationships and an alternative way of thinking about the world.[8]

In a recent article I offered the following definition of asceticism: "performances within a dominant social environment intended to inaugurate a new subjectivity, different social relations, and an alternative symbolic universe."[9] Within the scope of this definition, the performances of Christianity, which set it apart from the dominant social and religious cultures of both first-century CE Judaism and the Greco-Roman world, demanded the formation of a new kind of person, living in an alternative society with its own standards and ordering of social relationships and in a symbolic universe that emerged to support both this alternative kind of person and these new social arrangements. I call this whole process "asceticism."[10] The theory explains four elements: intentional performances, the articulation of a new subjectivity, the reorganization of social relationships, and the reorientation of the symbolic universe.

The term "subjectivity" probably requires some preliminary discussion. By "subjectivity" I refer to the person that a society authorizes and designates as an agent, an actor, and a subject. A "subject" is the socially designated and authorized person within a cultural frame. I use this formal (and somewhat foreign) term to stress that people (especially ancient people and people from different modern cultures) are "not the same," that is, that social and political agency and authorization differ in every concrete circumstance, so that it becomes necessary to construct the authorized agents of a given society, both historical and modern. "Subjectivity" denotes the historically and culturally determined status of human identity. A construction of such a subjectivity includes those people who are considered capable of being agents in a particular society (on the analogy of the subject of a sentence being capable of relating to a verb), as well as those who have a unified psychological identity (although that psychology does not imply that it is according to modern or Western psychology), and those who participate in systems of the mediation of power (as in a political subject, or someone subject to the law).[11] I understand asceticism as the means of creating alternatives to the subjectivities promulgated by dominant social groups.

Of all of the Pauline letters, the Letter to the Galatians most directly and persistently raises the question of the promulgation of a new subjectivity.[12] If, however, one begins with the usual categories of identity (Paul the Christian, fighting the Jewish-Christian missionaries, about the role of Jewish Law for the newly emergent Christian sectarians), one very quickly (as the secondary literature attests) becomes enmeshed in a hopeless morass of conflicting categories attempting to explain the relationship of law to faith and Jew to Christian to Jewish-Christian. The point of the Letter to the Galatians begins with the articulation of a "new creation" in contradistinction to those who are circumcised and those who are not: "for neither is circumcision anything, nor is uncircumcision, but (only a) new creation" (6:15). The construction of this new person, this new identity, defined against the background of these two alternatives organizes the rhetoric and discourse of the letter.[13] Galatians articulates the relationship of these three subjectivities.

My thesis, stated simply and boldly, then, is that this letter organizes three different sorts of subjectivities: The first defines the natural subject,[14] the second defines the culturally dominant subjectivity of first-century Judaism, and the third develops the spiritual or pneumatic subjectivity of a Jewish sectarian group within the larger dominant Jewish religious and social culture. In this letter, the character "Paul" functions as an exemplar[15] of the third (or spiritual) category in an argument intended to solidify the continuing development of this subjectivity among people who cannot distinguish it properly from the perspective of the culturally dominant and Jewish subjectivity. These subjectivities compete because they are organized into a hierarchy in which the natural and traditional Jewish subjectivities must be left behind both to develop the spiritual and because there is conflict within the community itself as to the understanding of these subjectivities. Inasmuch as that "new creation" becomes real through the exercise of freedom, it constitutes an ascetical process intended to bring into existence the pneumatic person.

THE "NATURAL" SUBJECTIVITY

Two factors hinder the definition of the "natural" subject: First, the writer says very little about it, and second, what the writer says about it betrays his objections to it and bias against it. So, this subjectivity must be defined from a "hostile witness." Only one section of the letter (4:8–11) provides information regarding it, and what it conveys can only provide us with the contours of the subjectivity.

The reference to this subjectivity emerges from a comparison. The writer describes it as the recipients' "former" one. Paul, the narrator of the letter, does not participate in this subjectivity because he uses the second person plural ("you") as referring only to the recipients of the letter. We can, therefore, conclude definitively that this subjectivity does not reflect either the customary Judaism of the day or the Christian sect of Judaism that Paul advocates.[16] This subjectivity functions as a point of comparison with these others.

Three rather sketchy characteristics define this subjectivity: These people (1) submit to "beings that are by nature not gods," (2) are oriented toward "elements" (*stoicheia*), and (3) "observe (*paratereisthe*) days, months, seasons, and years." The last two factors, the "elements" and the cyclical calendrical observations, seem to imply a deterministic symbolic universe in which the person is subject to cyclical determinative interactions of the cosmic elements.[17] This assumption of the cosmic dimension has guided Betz to include the descriptor "elements *of the* world" in his translation.[18] From the narrator's perspective, this kind of subjectivity constitutes an enslavement: The deterministic perspective that "I" perceive here relates to that characterization of this "former" subjectivity as "slaves," of people "enslaved…to beings that are by nature not gods." This subjectivity, then, articulates a kind of person who reverences the cosmic deities, who observes the calendrical and cyclic organization of the universe and the effect these cycles have on the "elements" that constitute creation.[19] Betz concludes that "the opponents [of Paul] understand their religion as a cultic-ritualistic system of protection against the forces of evil."[20]

Although the narrator's perspective portrays the chronology of this subjectivity negatively in relationship to the recipients' current way of living, the distinction between their former and their current understanding is based also upon their knowledge of God. The narrator insists that this subjectivity chronologically preceded the time when they knew God and remains chronologically distinct from their current knowledge of God and God's knowledge of them. Its status as "former" and "prior" relates also to a quality or level of theological understanding. This former way of life, their chronologically prior way of living, was marked as theologically deficient, so that their current status in another subjectivity includes an increment of theological formation involving both knowing and being known by God.

Sketchy as this characterization remains, the writer does present us with enough information to outline the subjectivity. These persons, in a kind of subjectivity characterized as primitive or natural, acknowledge the cosmic elements and forces of the universe as deterministic of their lives, and they worship these elements according to the natural cycle of months, days, and years. So, this first subjectivity may be called a natural subjectivity, whose "natural" status becomes clearer in relationship to the next subjectivity.

THE "TRADITIONAL" OR CULTURAL SUBJECTIVITY

The natural subjectivity just defined stands in distinction to one characterized by a relationship to "law" (*nomos*). Although the word "law" also has a specific bifocal reference to the Torah and to the customs of Jewish religion,[21] I will employ periphrastic phrases and circumlocutions to avoid the technical theological language that has become the mainstay of both theologians and Pauline scholars.

In its dictionary meaning, *nomos* denotes habitual practice or custom(s), as well as statute and ordinance, or, generally, "law."[22] For *nomos* to have the force of law, it must dominate within its social environment. It connotes, therefore, the prescription of cultural dominance; that is, it suggests the hegemony of custom, practice, habit, the legislated and regulated ways of the majority or dominant group of people in a given cultural frame.

This culturally dominant subjectivity revolves about the engagement with *nomos* or (as I will call it here) "performing dominant religious culture."[23] In the context of Galatians, to become and remain a participant in this cultural subgroup, the person must perform the dominant religious culture in its entirety: A person may not choose parts of the custom and ignore others, but must perform it all. Speaking to those who are circumcised, the narrator writes, "he is obliged to perform the entire law" (5:3). The requirement of complete observance and performance enforces the totalizing thrust of the cultural system. Cultural hegemony is precisely that, hegemonic power, so that this subjectivity defines itself in relationship to this dominant perspective and acts fully in accord with it, without the leeway either to ignore or to transgress its prescriptions.

This cultural dominance of religious habit encloses all things under the rule of "trespass" (3:22). "Trespass" or sin establishes the limit of acceptability, a move that enforces dominance within the religious system. In this letter, strong boundaries produce clear delineations of acceptability and propriety, and these culturally dominant patterns are clearly delineated because "the writings enclosed all things under the category of sin" (3:22). The combination of a complete system and a clear articulation of boundaries creates an inflexibility about the cultural performances. The inflexibility relates not so much to specific performances, but rather to the need carefully and clearly to define and sustain cultural dominance.

This inflexibility finds expression in the dual role of the curse in this discourse. First, Paul invokes the curse upon those who would follow any other gospel than the one that he preached to them (1:8–9). The curse in the *exordium* of the letter expresses the clear and inflexible limits of the narrative perspective. This inflexibility mirrors the inflexibility within the dominant cultural subjectivity that the narrator opposes because the penalty for trespass against the dominant perspective is a curse. Everyone who does not conform to the dominant perspective and who does not perform all the elements of the customs is cursed: "For as many as exist from deeds of custom (*ex ergon nomou*) live under a curse" (*hypo kataran eisin*, 3:10).

The customs provide the education and induction of the person in the cultural sphere and provide guidance for the person living the traditional life in order to keep the subject safely within the confines of the dominant sphere (*hypo nomon ephrouroumetha sygkleiomenoi*—3:23). This subjectivity emerges, then, from some sort of education in which the subject learns the culturally dominant performances. Teaching inducts subjects into the dominant culture, and it is to this teaching that Paul objects, saying that he did not learn his gospel from anyone (1:12). By distancing himself from those who receive agency through teaching, Paul suggests that he is to be distinguished from this subjectivity. The centrality of the educative function to the articulation of this subjectivity emerges also from the mocking statement, "all I want to learn from you" (3:2): The process of teaching and learning (although not the perspective advocated in the letter) characterizes this subjectivity.[24]

This traditional Jewish subjectivity with its observance of cultural and religious codes stands in marked contrast with the natural subjectivity and with the pneumatic subjectivity that Paul develops. The traditional subjectivity orients itself toward the culturally dominant religious perspective in which the subject embraces the traditions or customs as a sure guide to living and finds fulfillment by becoming subject to the habitual mode of living. The hegemonic system guards the subject from trespass in that it functions as enclosure, as protector, and as guide. It remains a complete system that must be accepted fully to ensure success and fulfillment to the subject; therefore, personal freedom and creativity are subordinated to the dominant construction and understanding.

THE PNEUMATIC OR SPIRITUAL SUBJECTIVITY

This last subjectivity, the spiritual subjectivity, operates in a decidedly different way from these first two. The difference relates to two important shifts. In the first place, the person, the subject, receives definition only as part of a larger body of people, so that the individual becomes a member of a corporate body. In the second place, this corporate body becomes the place in which God dwells.

Baptism, apparently a ritual inaugurating the new corporate subjectivity, defines the spiritual subject: "As many as have been baptized into Christ have been clothed with Christ" (3:27). Baptism bestows identity, and the reference to "clothing" signifies the social markers for that identity. The corporate identity is that of Christ, into whose identity the subject has been incorporated. Moreover, that corporate identity leaves behind the old markers of ethnicity, social status, and gender precisely to create a new corporate and unified subjectivity: "There is neither Jew nor Greek, there is neither slave nor free person, there is no male and female, for all of you [plural] are one in Christ Jesus" (3:28).[25] This subjectivity exists as a plural unity, as a multiple one, whose unity destroys the traditional distinctions of ethnicity, social status, and gender. The corporate Christ-identity unites the plural membership into one, a unity that displaces old markers of identity.

This corporate subjectivity expresses a particular relationship with God: On the one hand, these corporate ones understand themselves as children of God, and, on the other hand, God's own spirit is made to dwell within them. The metaphor employed to define the new subject's relationship to God is that of parent to child, as stated in 3:26: "You are all sons of God through the confidence found in Jesus Christ." The familial relationship maintains a hierarchy of parent to child, of God to God's children. Through that hierarchical relationship, however, the distance between the child and God collapses. Precisely because the hierarchical relationship has been familialized, the spirit of God enters into the person: "And because you are sons, God sent his spirit into our hearts crying, 'Abba, Father'" (4:6, reading with P46, which does not designate the spirit as the spirit of the Son but as the spirit of God). This strategy both collapses the hierarchy through the work of God's spirit by locating the spirit within the subject and also maintains the transcendence of God outside the corporate subject by metaphorizing the conferral of the spirit through a hierarchical family relationship.

The instrument of this new subjectivity comes as a revealed confidence in Jesus Christ. Faith, *pistis*, or, as I call it, "confidence," is something revealed. The letter explains the revelatory quality of this confidence in the following way: "Before the coming of this confidence, we, being enclosed (in them), were guarded by the customs until the coming confidence should be revealed" (3:23). This confidence, or faith, comes by revelation, and it chronologically follows the traditional subjectivity that operates through the dominant cultural modes. In fact, this confidence stands in marked contrast, if not opposition, to the culturally dominant subjectivity because vindication[26] will come to this subject through this confidence, not through any cultural performance: "We are Jews by nature and not trespassers from the other cultures, and we know that a human being is not (finally) vindicated (*ou dikaioutai anthropos*) from cultural performance (*ex ergon nomou*), but through the confidence (based upon) Jesus Christ (*ean me dia pisteos Iesou Christou*), and we came to believe in Christ Jesus so that we might be (finally) vindicated out of Christ's confidence (*hina dikaiothomen ek pisteos Christou*) and not from cultural performance (*kai ouk ex ergon nomou*), because all flesh is not (finally) vindicated from (its) cultural performance" (*hoti ex ergon nomou ou dikaiothesetai pasa sarx*, 2:15–16). In the discourse of this letter, the revelatory basis of the subjectivity follows upon the educative basis, so that revelation follows teaching. Baptism inaugurates the corporate Christ-subjectivity, and confidence based in Jesus Christ accompanies it.

Three performances construct this subjectivity: God's provision of the spirit to the subject, God's performance of mighty acts among them, and freedom. The first two performances receive passing treatment, while the third, freedom, receives extensive treatment. According to 3:5, God provides the spirit to this subjectivity and also performs mighty acts among them, not by virtue of cultural performance, but by virtue of the subject's confidence in hearing about Jesus Christ (*ex ergon nomou e ex akoes pisteos*). Although God performs these activities, the subject is filled with the spirit and experiences mighty deeds. Both of these become guarantors of the new subjectivity as people both spiritual and powerful; power and spiritual fullness characterize the corporate Christ-subjectivity.

The most significant performance of this subjectivity, however, relates to the performance of freedom. This freedom emerges as the primary marker of those who have withdrawn from the dominant culture to create, as written in the postscript, "a new creation" (6:15). "Christ has set you free for freedom, so stand up and do not again be engaged with the yoke of slavery" (5:1); this statement marks slavery as everything not performative of freedom and underscores that the Christ-subject lives without any customary constraint. In this context, freedom posits a hierarchy in which the natural and the cultural subjectivities take a lower place because both the cosmic elements of the natural subjectivity and the cultural requirements of the traditional subjectivity enslave, while the higher subjectivity, the one found to be "clothed in Christ," has freedom.

The performance of freedom also undergirds the development of new social relationships: "For you were called to freedom, brethren, only [do] not [let] the freedom [become] a starting point for the flesh, but through love become slaves to one another" (5:13). This performance of freedom gathers all the elements of the *exhortatio* of the letter: Freedom means, among other things, rejecting vices (5:16–21) and developing virtues (5:22–26), helping those who have fallen (6:1–5), guiding one another in the new life and mores (6:6), and positively developing other performances indicative of this new subjectivity (6:7–10). The Christ-subject exercises freedom precisely to redefine the social, ethical, and religious living of the community, and since this Christ-subject exists as a corporate body, such ethical and moral elements establish the interior dynamic of corporate relations.

The pneumatic subjectivity developed in the discourse of this letter, then, portrays the person as a member of a corporate body beyond the limits of race, class, or gender. The touchstone for this subject revolves about a dual performance of freedom and confidence in which freedom activates the new status of the subject and confidence enables the subject to live outside the dominant cultural sphere. The confidence and freedom testify to the presence of Jesus Christ within the subject and confirm the corporate "co-inherence" of subjects within a larger body. This subjectivity would eventually become the one marked as "Christian," while the traditional would be marked as "Jewish" and the natural as "pagan."

THE RELATIONSHIP OF THESE SUBJECTIVITIES

How are these subjectivities related to one another? Although the narrator portrays himself as primarily oriented toward Gentiles (2:7–9), he expends little discursive energy on the articulation of the "former" or natural subjectivity. It seems as though this understanding of subjectivity stands as a foil to the articulation of the other two subjectivities (the traditional and the pneumatic) and does not really represent a viable subjectivity in the discourse of the letter. The narrator even characterizes the return to this subjective stance in the world as a return to "enslavement" to these "weak and poor elements" (4:9). Discursively, this subjectivity does not play an important role in the letter.

The next two subjectivities (the traditional and the pneumatic) have a specific relationship to one another. First, both of these subjectivities originate in the promise to Abraham. Both originate in a gospel (note the language) announced previously to Abraham: "The writings, seeing in advance that the other cultures are being vindicated by their confidence, announced the gospel in advance to Abraham that 'in you all the cultures will be blessed'" (3:8–9). This common origin receives allegorical treatment in the children of the two wives of Abraham, Sarah and Hagar (4:21–31). Both the common origin and the allegory of Abraham's sons imply an increment of equality in their difference. The narrator recognizes, on the one hand, that the promise to Abraham precedes the establishment of the cultural system and that the same father had two different, but equal, children, based on an agreement that God made with all humanity and that cannot be annulled (3:15–18).

This second aspect of the relationship of these two subjectivities significantly disrupts this relative equality. The traditional subjectivity stands in a chronologically subordinate position to the pneumatic. The narrator posits the relationship in questioning the function of the traditional customs: "Why then the custom of performances? Until which time the seed to whom it was announced should come."[27] The customary subjectivity functioned provisionally until the pneumatic subjectivity could develop, that is, until the Christ whose identity marks the corporate body should come. As indicated earlier, the traditions and customs provided the guardianship, the parameters, and the revelation that established the pneumatic subjectivity. So, although these subjectivities find equality in their origins, they do not find equality in their chronology. The pneumatic subjectivity takes precedence over the customary.

The references to the various gospels preached support this simultaneous equality and subordination of the traditional to the pneumatic subjectivity. The letter's discourse actually differentiates three gospels: one gospel announced in the scriptures beforehand to Abraham (3:8), the gospel to the uncircumcised to which Paul was called and which he was authorized by the other apostles to fulfill (1:15–16), and the gospel to the circumcised for which Peter was responsible (2:7–9) and which seems to have captivated the Galatians. Their inherent equality finds expression in their mutual concern for the poor (2:10); the subordination of one to the other finds expression both in the allegory of the slave-son persecuting the free (4:29–30) and in the apostolic conflict in Antioch. Despite their equality and the problems inherent in it, however, the discourse in this letter emphasizes the subordination of the customary ways to the pneumatic. The provisional status of the traditional subjectivity receives constant attention: Although it is equal to the pneumatic subjectivity, final vindication does not come through cultural performance, but through the confidence inspired by Jesus Christ. Paul further emphasizes his own perspective in the *exordium* of the letter by placing a curse on those who follow any other gospel except the one he advocates (1:6–9).

PAUL AS THE EXEMPLUM

Paul's autobiographical example demonstrates[28] this peculiar relationship of the two primary subjectivities. He expressed his own relationship to them in two different ways. First, Paul emphasizes the revelatory aspect of his own pneumatic subjectivity, and second, he establishes himself as a fully entitled member of the traditional, Jewish variety of subjectivity.

Most interpreters understand Paul's reference to these revelations as part of his apology for his apostolic ministry, so that he is understood to be promoting the validity and authority for his own ministry. Given the distinctions made earlier between the traditional and pneumatic subjectivity, however, it seems more consistent that Paul wants a clear distinction drawn between the Paul formed in the traditional subjectivity and the Paul living in the pneumatic. Paul emphasizes the revelatory quality of his message to underscore that it is the pneumatic Paul speaking: "It is not based on human things," he writes, "nor did I receive it from any human, nor was I taught (it), but (I received it) through a revelation of Jesus Christ" (1:11–12). Here the threefold subjectivities (the natural one received from a human being, the traditional one taught to its members, and the revelatory one) are distinguished one from another. Paul's was not the first two, but only the third. His particular pneumatic subjectivity may be more properly described as pneumatic-revelatory, because within the sort of pneumatic subjectivity he commends to his readers, he emphasizes that he is guided by the revelations. These revelations, that is, not only provide the origin of his apostolic mission ("Paul, an apostle not from human beings nor through any human being, but through Jesus Christ and God the Father" [1:1]), but also guide his major activities ("I went up [to Jerusalem] according to a revelation" [2:1]). One subjectivity, for Paul, functions around education, being taught, and the other subjectivity operates according to revelation. For Paul, this clearly marks the distinction between one subjectivity and the next, for "confidence," or "faith," is something revealed to those who were "guarded and enclosed by the customs until the coming confidence should be revealed" (3:23). Revelation here distinguishes itself from education, or cultural formation. Paul establishes himself solidly in the camp of the pneumatic subjectivity.

This same set of distinctions emerges in the second factor that Paul develops about himself: his credentials both in the traditional subjectivity and in the pneumatic. After characterizing himself as a persecutor of the assembly of God, as someone who wanted to destroy the assembly (1:13), Paul establishes himself as one well-versed in the tradition: "I succeeded in Judaism beyond many of the people of my own age in my ethnic race, having a greater zeal for the traditions of my fathers." This defines the traditional subjectivity for Paul as one that is caught up in the cultural dominance and cultural performance that younger people may learn. But Paul distinguishes it from the emergent subject constructed through revelation: "God was pleased...to reveal his son in me" (1:15–16). The reference to "revealed in me" no longer sounds problematic: Like the revealed confidence and the internalized presence of the deity, the revelation becomes internal, and that internal quality differentiates it from the external one that needs to be learned. In this section, Paul emphasizes that, until his revelation, he had all the necessary credentials for the traditional subjectivity; now that the revelation has come, however, that subjectivity no longer applies to him. His autobiography exemplifies the relationship of subjectivities in the letter.

THE COMPETING ASCETICAL SUBJECTIVITIES

Betz has rightly claimed that the "hermeneutical key" to the letter may be found in the epistolary postscript (6:11–18),[29] where Paul writes in his own hand. Three elements in this postscript stand out: (1) the conflict between representatives of the different missionary groups, (2) Paul's personal attestation that he boasts only in the Cross of his Lord Jesus Christ through which "the world has been crucified to me, and I to the world," and (3) his affirmation that the "new creation" takes precedence over circumcision and uncircumcision. All three of these elements point to an ascetical discourse within this letter.

Asceticism can only emerge from conflict with a dominant perspective. This relationship with a dominant perspective provides the impetus, the yearning or desire, to create "someone" different. The ascetic impulse begins when the person discovers that the "old way," the "former way," no longer satisfies and something else begins to draw the person forward into another mode of existence. This means that asceticism begins not with withdrawal itself, but with the dissatisfaction with the dominant perspective that leads to withdrawal. Asceticism, that is, begins when the *desire* for some alternative way of living emerges. The performances that create that new identity constitute the practice of asceticism, so that asceticism may be understood as the means of creating a subversive subjectivity within the dominant sphere. Without the strongly articulated dominant subjectivity, an ascetical alternative cannot be defined. But as the person begins to live into the new understanding of self, society, and world, that is, as the person begins to "perform" that new subjectivity, the new person begins actually to come to life, to exist. The performances (intellectual, ritual, social, political, or of any nature) call that subjectivity into being, define its social dimension, and construct the symbolic universe that will legitimize and explain the new being.

The conflict of perspectives on subjectivities and their proper performances in the Letter to the Galatians portrays the simultaneous affirmation of the dominant perspective and dissatisfaction with it that characterizes Paul's letter. Another way of saying this is that the discursive problem of the Letter to the Galatians revolves about the clear delineation of these subjectivities with a demand that the recipients choose which one they will follow. The pneumatic subjectivity, however, does not emerge in a vacuum: As the subversive subjectivity within a dominant culture, it expresses the conflict between the traditional articulation of the Jewish subjectivity and the emergent subjectivity of the ascetical pneumatic. The curse in the *exordium*, invoking the curse that accompanies all those who do not perform all of the cultural prescriptions (as stated in 3:10), demands just such a choice based not so much on the question of the variety of Judaism that will be lived out, but on the desire, if not the need, to create a subjectivity entirely different from the one advocated by the traditionalists. The choice, that is, revolves about the commitment to a subversive asceticism that constructs an alternative subjectivity. The conflict in the Letter to the Galatians, then, does not relate primarily to Paul, or to his theology, or even to his relationship with the traditional Judaism of his day, but to the right articulation of the pneumatic subjectivity among a group of people in Galatia who seem (to Paul, at least) not properly to understand it. In language typical of all ascetical literature, Paul insists that the old self must die for the new subject to be born: He "mortifies" himself, killing the world to him and him to the world, even bearing Jesus' *stigmata* on his body.[30] The old self must be repudiated, mortified, so that the new one may come into existence, and conflict remains endemic to this process.

I should be clear, however: The distinction between the old self and the new self finds clear articulation and delineation, but it does not imply an outright rejection or condemnation of the dominant view. One need only look at the relationship of monastic cultural withdrawal to the "great Church" to see that "difference" does not mean "repudiation." The difference expresses the subject's disillusion and dissatisfaction with the dominant perspective, a perspective without which the ascetical subject could not exist. Paul wants the church in Galatia to follow his way, but his way cannot exist divorced from the dominant perspective, and he affirms this coexistent interdependence in the allegory of Hagar and Sarah while posting his own preference in the hostile relations of their sons.

The difficulty is that the alternative subjectivity advocated in this letter may only be sustained by the performances proper to it. Tradition and the new subjectivity do not mix easily. To establish "the new creation" beyond circumcision or uncircumcision (here Paul lays out the three subjectivities clearly), the ascetic must live freely. The performance of freedom from traditional hegemonic Jewish practice inaugurates the pneumatic Christ-subjectivity of their Jewish sectarian subgroup organized around the confidence they experience through Jesus Christ, a confidence that comes to them by revelation, not by any dominant cultural performance or teaching.

The performance of freedom also reorganizes their social lives.[31] Their new identity emerges from performances structured in their becoming "slaves" to one another (5:13), as opposed to being slaves either of the cosmic elements or of the dominant culture. Their reorganized social life, moreover, demands that they live in the spirit (5:22–26) and reject the works of the flesh (5:19–21), while carrying one another's burdens and helping one another live the new life (6:1–10). The rejection of social vices, the development of social virtues, and the embracing of weaker members of the community pattern the new social organization. The confidence found in Jesus Christ frees them to structure a new society, a new ethic, and a new way of living.

The symbolic universe, which explains and legitimizes the subversive identity, receives significant attention. The discussion of the promise made to Abraham, and of Abraham's two wives and the sons of each wife, redefines the theological perspective away from the dominant and traditional categories of the law to provide the space for another understanding. Three gospels (one proclaimed in the scriptures to Abraham, one to the circumcised, and one to the uncircumcised) also explain the difference and locate the pneumatic subjectivity in relationship both to the past and to the future. The promise to Abraham confirms the relationship of the two major subjectivities by providing them with a common origin, and these subjectivities get organized into (as Boyarin argues convincingly) a hierarchy of spirit over flesh, of freedom over slavery, so that, although both are vindicated by the promise, priority of the pneumatic subjectivity is maintained.

The formation of this Christ-identity locates as primary the ascetical project found in the Letter to the Galatians. It also mirrors the ascetical agenda of formative Christianity. The often conflicting literature of formative Christianity, like Galatians, exposes the energetic experimentation and reconsideration of human subjectivity, social relations, and theological formulations. Christian literature from even before the creation of the texts enshrined in the canon forcefully posits the question of human existence and human social relationships. Wandering prophets, purveyors of wisdom, apocalyptic seers, healers, and magicians, and even heroes and divine figures point to the extensive range of human possibilities explored and modeled in formative Christianity. When the social context of this experimentation is considered—all varieties of Judaism, Samaritans, Romans, peoples of Phoenicia, Palestine, Arabia, Egypt, as well as people from all around the known world—the scope of the experimentation reaches monumental proportions. At its heart stands the consideration of a new subjectivity in Jesus Christ: in other words, early Christian asceticism.

The alternatives presented to the earliest followers of Jesus were complex and involved a wide spectrum of possibilities, each demanding its own formative processes. Each formative process, however, meant clear delineation and definition of its distinctiveness from the other options, which means that conflict and conflicting articulations form an essential aspect of the process. This is what we find in Paul's Letter to the Galatians: three options, clearly articulated and compared, but with a strong affirmation and choice of only one. With that choice and affirmation develop systems for the creation of people in the subjectivity; that is to say, with each choice comes an ascetical system that enables the new subjectivity, the yearned-for subjectivity, to become real. Asceticism, enshrining the conflict of differences, pervades the discourse of this letter and of all other aspects of early Christian formation.

NOTES

1. Victor Paul Furnish, "Pauline Studies," in *The New Testament and Its Modern Interpreters,* eds. Eldon Jay Epp and George MacRae (Philadelphia: Fortress, 1989), 321–50; quotation, 329.
2. Victor Paul Furnish, "On Putting Paul in His Place," *Journal of Biblical Literature* 113 (1994): 3–17.
3. Of all of these scholars, the work of Daniel Boyarin, *A Radical Jew: Paul and*

the Politics of Identity (Berkeley: University of California Press, 1994), stands out as the most significant attempt to restructure Pauline scholarship, although it continues in the tradition of discovering the Pauline mentality. See also Alan F. Segal, *Paul the Convert: The Apostolate and Apostasy of Saul the Pharisee* (New Haven, Conn.: Yale University Press, 1990); E. P. Sanders, *Paul and Palestinian Judaism: A Comparison of Patterns of Religion* (Minneapolis, Minn.: Fortress, 1977). The work of the Pauline Theology Group of the SBL has begun the shift in paradigm, although many of the resulting papers remain connected to the older patterns of scholarship: *Pauline Theology: Thessalonians, Philippians, Galatians, Philemon*, ed. Jouette M. Bassler, vol. 1 (Minneapolis, Minn.: Fortress, 1991); *Pauline Theology: 1 & 2 Corinthians*, ed. David M. Hay, vol. 2 (Minneapolis, Minn.: Fortress, 1991).

4. See, for example, Dieter Georgi, who, in constructing Paul's opponents, still relates them primarily to Paul's own attitudes.

5. The strategy exactly parallels the strategy in the study of the historical Jesus in which the narrative voice of the evangelists has been problematized to understand the underlying perspectives of the original source material separate from that of the evangelists.

6. To accomplish this analysis of discourse deflected from the traditional constructions of Pauline theology, I have purposefully chosen nontheological language from modern discourse to explain the discursive practices in this Pauline letter; the language of "law and faith" or "Judaism and Christianity" has been suppressed from my discourse to highlight more vividly the discourse the letters themselves develop.

7. The Syrian tradition of asceticism has been located at the very earliest tradition of the Jesus movement, so that the early itinerant followers of Jesus were considered ascetic; see Helmut Koester, *Introduction to the New Testament*, vol. 2 (Philadelphia: Fortress, 1982), 156; Stephen J. Patterson, *The Gospel of Thomas and Jesus* (Sonoma, Calif.: Polebridge, 1993), 166–68. See also Sidney H. Griffith, "Asceticism in the Church of Syria: The Hermeneutics of Early Syrian Monasticism," in *Asceticism*, eds. Vincent L. Wimbush and Richard Valantasis (New York: Oxford University Press, 1995), 220–45; Cyril C. Richardson, "The Gospel of Thomas: Gnostic or Encratite?" in *The Heritage of the Early Church: Essays in Honor of Georges Florovsky* (Rome: Institutum Studiorum Orientalium, 1973), 65–76; and A. Vööbus, *History of Asceticism in the Syrian Orient: A Contribution to the History of Culture in the Near East*, vol. 1 (Louvaine, Belgium: Secrétariat du Corpus Scriptorum Christianorum Orientalium, Corpus Scriptorum Christianorum Orientalium 184, 1958).

8. I would also argue that Pharisaic Judaism developed in a parallel fashion with the asceticism of the observance of the law constructing an alternative to the temple cult after the destruction of the temple in 70 CE.

9. This latest definition may be found in my article "Constructions of Power in Asceticism," *Journal of the American Academy of Religion* 63 (1995): 775–821; also idem, "A Theory of the Social Function of Asceticism," in *Asceticism*, eds. Wimbush and Valantasis, 544–52; idem, "The Stranger Within, The Stranger Without: Ascetical Withdrawal and the Second Letter of Basil the Great," in *Christianity and the Stranger: Historical Essays*, ed. Francis W. Nichols (Atlanta, Ga.: Scholars, 1995) 64–81.

10. Although my theory emerged from an analysis based entirely on Greco-Roman and late antique literature, it does not purport to be a definition from antiquity, but a modern scholarly focus through which to interpret the ascetical activities of ancient people. It provides a critical framework through which to define both what is ascetical and categories through which to compare various ascetical trends or activities.

11. My description of subjectivity summarizes, perhaps too simply, an extensive scholarly discussion focused on Michel Foucault, *The Order of Things* (New York: Vintage, 1973). For our purposes here, Elizabeth A. Castelli, *Imitating Paul: A Discourse of Power* (Louisville, Ky.: Westminster/Knox, 1991), 40, has worked through this concept in reading Foucault for Pauline studies, where she writes that Foucault's "very use of the name 'subject' for the modern individual is a play on the various significations associated with this word: one is a subject in the grammatical sense (as in the subject of a sentence), in the psychological sense (as possessing a unified identity), and in the political sense (as being subject to dominant powers)."

12. Beverly Gaventa, "The Singularity of the Gospel: A Reading of Galatians," in *Pauline Theology*, ed. Bassler, 147–59, has argued similarly that Galatians articulates "a new identity in Christ" that "results in the nullification of previous identifications" (149). Our end points are similar, while our methods of interpretation vary.

13. Gaventa ("Singularity," 149) calls this discourse a "christocentric" one because the new subjectivity revolves about a particular understanding of Christ. I argue later in this chapter that the pneumatic subjectivity is the emergent one, but I agree with Gaventa that this pneumatic subjectivity, particularly in its corporate dimension, revolves about christological theologoumena.

14. I call this the "natural" subjectivity because I want to set it in contrast to the "traditional Jewish" subjectivity that carefully and clearly distinguishes itself from those with foreskins (the translation "uncircumcised" already prejudices a perspective) and in contrast to the Jesus-Christ Jewish sectarians, who also embraced both those with and without foreskins. I am aware that this characterization has serious gender implications, identifying women with those lacking foreskins (i.e., circumcised Jews). In fact, Boyarin, *A Radical Jew*, 224–27, argues for the identification of "women" and "Jew" in Western discourse.

15. On this aspect of Pauline writing, see Castelli, *Imitating Paul*, 119–36.

16. James D. G. Dunn, "Echoes of Intra-Jewish Polemic in Paul's Letter to the Galatians," *Journal of Biblical Literature* 112 (1993): 459–77, understands this reference to refer to specifically Jewish customs: "Paul clearly has particularly Jewish festivals in mind" (470). His argument is that everything except the years has a clear reference to contemporary Jewish practice (470–73). Because he views the entire letter within the context of intra-Jewish polemic, he fails to see the sorts of contrasts in practices which the letter displays. Troy Martin, "Apostasy to Paganism: The Rhetorical Stasis of the Galatian Controversy," *Journal of Biblical Literature* 114 (1995): 437–61, argues that the primary problem with the Galatians is their supposed return to paganism. Martin's argument proceeds through an analysis of the rhetoric (stasis theory) of the letter, but his argument fails to convince me that the Galatians are indeed apostatizing. As will be seen in this analysis, the natural subjectivity does not receive suf-

ficient attention to pose a real threat to the primary two subjectivities that the letter develops.

17. Martin, "Apostasy to Paganism," 449–50, argues for the "pagan nature of this list" and refers the reader to his article entitled "Pagan and Judeo-Christian Time-Keeping Schemes in Gal 4:10 and Col 2:16" in *New Testament Studies* 42 (1996), 105–19. Betz, Galatians, 217, observes that "the cultic activities described in v. 10 are not typical of Judaism (including Jewish Christianity), though they are known to both Judaism and paganism" and are akin to pagan superstition (218).

18. Ibid, 215–17.

19. Betz (ibid, 214–15) rightly observes that the enslavement to beings that are not gods emerges from two potential discourses, namely, either that of hellenistic Judaism or that of Euhemerism, and that, in any event, it articulates the perspective of the narrator and does not provide an unbiased description of this subjectivity. This element may positively be understood: This subjectivity finds its orientation in subservience to gods who are believed to be gods by nature, at least by the people who fit into this category.

20. Ibid, 217.

21. See *Theological Dictionary of the New Testament,* ed. G. Kittel and G. Friedrich, tr. G. Bromiley (Grand Rapids, Mich.: Eerdmans, 1985), s.v. "law"; Stendahl, *Paul Among Jews and Gentiles.*

22. See *A Greek-English Lexicon,* ed. H. G. Liddell and R. Scott, rev. Sir Henry Stuart Jones (Oxford: Clarendon Press, 1968), s.v. *nomos.*

23. My conceptualizing of "performing dominant religious culture" stands in marked contrast to what E. P. Sanders calls "covenantal nomism" in his *Paul and Palestinian Judaism,* 75, 420, 544. See also James D. G. Dunn, "The Theology of Galatians: The Issue of Covenantal Nomism" in *Pauline Theology,* ed. Bassler, 125–46. Although I think that their cultural construction of Judaism at the time of Paul may have validity, I want to bracket the explicitly theological interpretation that both these scholars have placed on the "law." This is not because I reject their theological interpretation, but because I want to start fresh in understanding the theology present in the letter without the necessity of beginning with an artificially constructed theological category gleaned from all of the Pauline corpus as well as first-century CE Judaism.

24. The theorists who have most assisted me in understanding these systems of cultural formation are Robert Hodge and Gunther Kress, *Social Semiotics* (Ithaca, N.Y.: Cornell University Press, 1988). The process of such cultural formation has in itself been studied. Hodge and Kress have documented the formative interaction of dominant and minority culture in Australia. It does not surprise one to find such a process of teaching and learning, whether oriented toward schools or just passed on through living in a society, present in a subjectivity oriented toward a specific, dominant culture.

25. Wayne A. Meeks, "The Image of the Androgyne: Some Uses of a Symbol in Earliest Christianity," *History of Religions* 13 (1974): 165–208, explores the performative basis of this. See also the creative work of Boyarin, *A Radical Jew,* on gender and the androgyne.

26. Here I am following Boyarin's explanation of the term in *A Radical Jew,* 117–18.

27. There are a number of interesting textual and translation problems here. I am reading, as I consistently do, with P46, which has a significant variant merely acknowledged by Betz and by Bruce M. Metzger, *A Textual Commentary on the Greek New Testament*, 3rd ed. (London: United Bible Societies, 1971), 594. P46 simply reads: *ti oun ho nomos ton praxeon,* which I have translated earlier in the chapter. This reading with the addition of *etethe* is supported by other witnesses as well. Betz interprets the sense of the verse in relationship to a parallel in Romans. I am unwilling to make that assumption.

   The second problem relates to the translation in the passive of *diatasso*, which properly should mean "bequeath," not "ordain" (which is its active meaning). It certainly implies a "setting in order" or in the passive a kind of "having been set in order and passed on" or "bequeathed" into the hand of an intermediary.

28. Note that I am using Paul to demonstrate the different subjectivities: This is the reverse of most scholarship on the Pauline literature, which tries to define Paul by the evidence of his discursive practice.

29. Betz, Galatians, 313.

30. On the *stigmata*, see Gregory J. Riley, *Resurrection Reconsidered: Thomas and John in Controversy* (Minneapolis, Minn.: Fortress, 1995).

31. See Richard B. Hays, "Christology and Ethics in Galatians: The Law of Christ," *Catholic Biblical Quarterly* 49 (1987): 268–90.

Asceticism among the "Weak" and "Strong" in Romans 14-15

Neil Elliott

THE ROLE OF ROMANS 14-15 IN DETERMINING THE LETTER'S PURPOSE

"After centuries of neglect, Rom 12:1–15:13 is now recognized as crucial to our understanding of the letter. In particular, one's reading of Rom. 14:1–15:13 certainly affects how one construes Paul's theology in the rest of the letter."[1] Thus Mark Reasoner notes the modern shift toward a more thoroughly historical reading of Romans, in contrast to the sixteenth-century reformer Philip Melanchthon's assessment of the letter as a *compendium doctrinae Christianae*. In recent years, the later chapters of Romans have proven "foundational" for interpreters seeking to establish specific historical circumstances in Rome that occasioned the letter.[2]

Those efforts have met with controversy. Several scholars have protested that there is an insufficient basis in Romans 14–15 for describing circumstances in Rome.[3] They object that the earlier chapters of Romans give no indication of actual parties of "weak" and "strong" and that the efforts to read chapters 14 and 15 as a series of admonitions addressed alternately to "weak" and "strong" factions—or even to distinct congregations—so fragment Paul's rhetoric as to make it virtually unintelligible.[4] These scholars propose that the language of "weak" and "strong" here has simply been taken over and generalized from Paul's earlier controversy with the Corinthians, as reflected in 1 Corinthians 8 and 10.[5]

On some of these readings, Romans remains a rather tentative presentation of Paul's theology, his apostolic "last will and testament,"[6] intended for an audience with whom Paul is not well acquainted; his "oblique" language here indicates how "unsure" he is of their response.[7] The admonitions appearing in Romans 14 and 15 are "general paraenesis," bearing an "illustrative" value in "a letter which sums up Paul's missionary theology and paraenesis,"[8] showing "in behavioral terms the outworking of the main themes" of the letter as Paul's "great protreptic exhibition of 'his gospel.'"[9] Such phrases reflect an understanding of Romans as an epistolary showpiece, a theological "white paper" from Paul's apostolic portfolio, submitted for evaluation by the Roman congregation to garner their support for Paul's work—functioning, that is, in a way not unlike modern fundraising letters.[10]

This interpretation can have the effect of shielding the letter's inscribed audience from the letter's rhetoric. That is, although Paul speaks from the start of the "power of God" manifest in his *euaggelion* (1:16), he means only to "describe" or "present" this *euaggelion*, not to "evangelize" the Roman Christians themselves.[11] However useful such an interpretive strategy may have proved in delivering the letter over as raw material for dogmatic theology, it blatantly contradicts the plain sense of what Paul says about his purpose toward the Romans (*kai hymin tois en Rhome euaggelisasthai*, 1:15).[12]

In contrast, a growing number of interpreters recognize the character of Romans, no less than Paul's other letters, as a "word on target" to a specific historical situation.[13] Debates regarding what Paul could have known of the Roman situation, and when he could have known it, have given way to closer attention to the rhetorical coherence of the letter itself. One important consequence has been growing recognition that the letter makes sense as argumentation directed to its inscribed readers—the predominantly *Gentile* Christian community in Rome—whom Paul warns against an overweening arrogance vis-à-vis their Jewish neighbors (11:13–36).[14] In this climate, chapters 14–15 emerge as a key element within the letter, "where the main thrust of chaps. 12–16 undoubtedly lies."[15]

THE ROLE OF TORAH OBSERVANCE IN THE SITUATION ADDRESSED IN ROMANS 14-15

Recognizing that "weak" and "strong" do not appear as partisan designations earlier in the letter does not remove the interpretive burden of identifying the social realities to which these terms refer. Once we leave aside the overly specific determination of "weak" and "strong" as *labels* for distinct factions within Roman Christianity, we can see indications that Paul's exhortations address real tensions between Roman Christians who are more and less scrupulous in their observance of Jewish dietary practices and of "days"

(14:5, 6). At issue here is not the eating of idol-meat (*eidolothyta*) per se, as in Corinth; rather, the issue is eating "common," that is, profane food (*koinon*, 14:14).[16] Against Käsemann's objection that the vegetarianism to which Paul refers (14:2) cannot mean orthodox Jewish dietary observances, since "general abstinence from meat and wine is not found there,"[17] and against Karris' verdict that the history-of-religion search for an asceticism corresponding to Paul's remarks was "bankrupt,"[18] there is abundant evidence that, within an indifferent or hostile Gentile environment, observance of *kashrut* often required Jews to practice de facto vegetarianism.[19] Further, the caricatures drawn by Roman satirists show that Jewish observances, including vegetarianism and the observance of days, could be seen by Roman contemporaries in a thoroughly unfavorable light,[20] indeed, as "weakness."[21]

Establishing that the observance of *kashrut* is at issue does not resolve all the exegetical and historical problems in these chapters, however. First, nothing in the text allows us simply to equate "the weak" with Jewish Christians and "the strong" with Gentile Christians. Indeed, Paul readily enough aligns himself with "the strong" (15:1).[22]

Further, determining that the issue between "weak" and "strong" had to do with the observance of the *kosher* laws raises urgent questions about Paul's attitude to Jewish observance within the *ekklesia*. As Mark D. Nanos has compellingly argued, the conventional (Christian) presumption that the "weak in faith" (14:1) were "*Christian Jews* who still practiced the Law and Jewish customs" implicitly equates their "deficiency" of faith with "their failure to realize the full measure of their freedom in Christ from the practices of the Law."[23] Käsemann puts it bluntly: "The 'weak in faith' form the problem," specifically by keeping alive "the observance of a fixed tradition," that is, the *kosher* laws.[24] The consequence, Nanos argues, is that Christian interpreters of Romans constantly "find themselves trapped, as was Luther, into dealing with the admonition not to judge the opinions of the 'weak' (14:1), when by definition, their hermeneutical presuppositions necessarily engage them in the very process of judging their opinions."[25] Luther's own characterizations of "the weak" of Romans 14 were pejorative enough: They represented "the Jewish error," "superstitious piety," "gross ignorance." Nanos provides a telling survey of Luther's heirs, prominent modern scholars who perpetuate similarly prejudicial assessments of "the weak" as Jewish Christians who "fail to trust God completely," "over-sensitive Jews" with "'hyper-halakhic' anxieties," whose "scrupulosity" in Torah observance constitutes nothing less than "narrow-minded cowardliness."[26]

But, Nanos asks pointedly:

> [W]ould Paul have considered it a sign of weakness for Jews, in this case Christian Jews…if they continued to embrace the Law? Does keeping the Law really lie behind the "weaknesses of the weak" (15:1)? And if it does, why doesn't Paul

seek to correct such a view on the part of the "weak" or urge them on to a supposedly more mature position? In fact, why does he insist that the "strong" not judge such opinions if he felt they were the cause of "weakness" (14:1)?... And why would Paul instead insist on the "weak" being "fully convinced" in their own mind that their practices of the Law are "for the Lord" (14:5ff.)?[27]

William S. Campbell also warns against the "anti-Jewish" implications of equating the "weak in faith" (14:1) with Jewish Christians, whose "weakness" consists precisely in their inadequate independence from Torah observance: "An even greater consequence of this theology is that theologically Judaism, as such, and Jewishness—even in its manifestation as an element within Christianity—has no longer any actual right to exist."[28]

While at this point both Nanos and Campbell draw back from the implications of identifying the "weak" with Torah-observant Jewish Christians,[29] other interpreters have insisted that these implications follow naturally from Paul's language. John M. G. Barclay identifies "the weak" as Christians who "maintain Jewish kosher laws and observe the sabbath; the 'strong' do not."[30] However disagreeable the theological implications might seem to modern interpreters, Barclay observes that Paul "is in fact quite unashamed to declare that 'I know and am persuaded in the Lord Jesus that nothing is unclean of itself.'... This constitutes nothing less than a fundamental rejection of the Jewish law in one of its most sensitive dimensions." The laws of *kashrut* "are here so summarily dismissed as not even to receive mention."[31]

Thus, while the immediate intent of Romans 14–15 is "that those Jewish Christians in Rome who wished to retain their links with the Jewish community in Rome were enabled to do so," at least temporarily, the long-term social consequence of Paul's theoretical alignment with "the strong" means that "*Paul effectively undermines the social and cultural integrity of the Law-observant Christians in Rome.*"[32] Paul expresses the sort of toleration of individual conviction that "would surely have been castigated by Josephus as a crude example of autexousion, that self-defined liberty which he considered the root of apostasy (*Ant.* 4:145–49)."[33] While Josephus admits that Moses "did not admit casual visitors to join in our common life" and that consequently Jews "do not wish to associate with those who choose to live according to a different mode of life" (*Contra Apionem* 2:210, 258), Paul "requires of Christian members of the Jewish community a very significant depth of 'association' with those declining to live according to the same mode of life."

The Apostle thus created "tensions which were likely to grow to the point when a difficult social choice would have to be made between the Jewish and Christian community."[34] Francis Watson goes even further, arguing that this consequence was Paul's intention in the letter. While Gentile

Christians are urged not to despise Torah-observant Jewish Christians, it remains true that

> in their case nothing of fundamental importance has been sacrificed, whereas for the Jewish Christians a radical change of outlook is required. Paul's aim is thus to create a single "Paulinist" congregation in Rome—"Paulinist" in the sense that the Pauline principle of freedom from the Law is accepted. To put it another way, he wishes to convert the Jewish Christian congregation to Paulinism.... Paul's purpose in writing Romans was to defend and explain his view of freedom from the Law (i.e. separation from the Jewish community and its way of life), with the aim of converting Jewish Christians to his point of view so as to create a single "Pauline" congregation in Rome.[35]

Here we confront interpretations in clear conflict. Nanos and Campbell, among others, see the whole of Romans written to counter the incipient anti-Judaism of Gentile-Christian arrogance in Rome.[36] Paul does not mean to compromise the legitimacy of Jewish observance within the community of faith in Jesus. For scholars like Barclay and Watson, on the other hand, that is the inescapable sense of what the Apostle says. Clearly much is at stake in determining who is being characterized as "the weak" and what Paul understands to be the status of Torah observance among those who believe in Jesus.

WHAT CONSTITUTES THE "WEAKNESS" OF "THE WEAK?"

On one point the scholars just discussed agree: "The issue that arises here is a typical problem of commensality—how observant Jews (and perhaps Law-observant Gentiles) can participate in a meal hosted by those who do not scruple to observe the Law."[37] The immediate social context is the practice, assumed by Paul and his audience alike, of common meals at which those who observe *kashrut* and those who do not come together. But who, precisely, is seated at the table (or reclining upon the triclinium)?

When interpreters have assumed that Paul addresses intrachurch tensions along "ethnic" or "cultural" lines, that is, between "*Jewish Christians*" and "*Gentile Christians*,"[38] they have imagined "the table" as a Christian space at some remove from either the synagogue or Jewish private homes. This corresponds to the common assumption that the period of close ties between believers in Jesus and the synagogues of Rome has passed, not least as the result of the much discussed expulsion of at least some Jews, including some Jewish believers in Jesus, from the city of Rome in 49 CE.[39] James C. Walters sets out these assumptions quite schematically in a chart, adapted here:[40]

49 CE	55–58 CE	64 CE
Christians are:	*Paul's Letter Arrives*	*Christians are:*
Synagogue based		No longer synagogue based, but meeting in house-churches of their own
Predominantly Jews and Gentiles who live like Jews		Mostly Gentiles
Jewish in their socialization		Distinct from Jews in certain pronounced ways

As Nanos has convincingly argued, however, the assumption that "the weak in faith" in 14:1 are specifically *Jewish Christians* is unwarranted. Nothing in the text requires us to restrict the commensality in question to "Christian" meals. References to the "weak" as "brothers" (14:10, 13, 15)—even the reference to "the brother for whom Christ died" (14:15)—do not necessarily indicate *Christian* "brothers," for Paul speaks elsewhere of his (non-Christian) fellow Jews as "brothers" (9:3–5).[41] Nor do references to the "faith" of the weak (14:1), or to the intent of those who eat (or abstain) "to the Lord" (14:6), indicate *Christian* faith, for "Paul regarded the practices of non-Christian Jews as the result of faith, and therefore unquestionably acceptable to God."[42]

Christian interpreters have routinely seated Jewish and Gentile *Christians* at the disputed Roman tables[43] on the assumption that non-Christian Jews would ordinarily have had no occasion to sit at meals with Gentiles, let alone Gentile Christians. Barclay is representative of this viewpoint when he cites Josephus to the effect that Moses "did not admit casual visitors to join in our common life" (*Contra Apionem* 2:210) and that Jews "do not wish to associate with those who choose to live according to a different mode of life" (2:258).[44] On this assumption, Jewish *Christians* who participate in ethnically "mixed" meals such as Paul encourages are assumed *already* to have compromised their observance of Torah. But this conclusion is unwarranted. Against Josephus' sweeping generalizations about Jewish *amixia* we should place the evidence of the Mishnah that by exercising appropriate diligence, Jews could routinely shop in Gentile markets and eat with Gentile neighbors (*Abodah Zarah*), and the evidence of the *midrashim* that Jews contemplated a halakically appropriate diet for Gentiles who did not keep kosher. These Tannaitic traditions are often cited as possible deposits made by *earlier* currents of Jewish thought on relating to Gentiles in the Roman diaspora. Whether or not such currents flowed along strong, regular channels prior to the movement of which Paul was a part, and whether or not they could have informed a practice like that described in Acts 15 as the ruling of the "Apostolic Council,"[45] they reflect a principled willingness on the part of diaspora Jews occasionally to eat meals with sympathetic Gentiles, *under the right circumstances.*[46]

Paul's exhortations in Romans 14–15 readily can be read as efforts to secure just these "right circumstances"—the willing renunciation of non-kosher foods on the part of Gentile Christians—in Rome. *In principle*, he declares his opinion that "nothing is common in itself" (14:14); he immediately continues, however, that "it is *common* for anyone who thinks it is common." He thus implicitly recognizes that his audience includes those who do and do not observe *kashrut.* For those who have accepted the obligations of Torah, some foods are *koinon*, but "Christian Gentiles are not Jews, and thus are theoretically free of purity laws."[47] *Nevertheless, Paul bids his audience not to eat food that will "harm" their observant brothers and sisters.* It is therefore too strong, I think, to declare with Barclay that Paul's statement "constitutes nothing less than a fundamental rejection of the Jewish Law."[48] *The law remains valid for the Jew*, and the Gentile is asked to respect the Jew's sensibilities.[49]

Nanos' most important observation regarding Romans 14–15 is that *nothing in these chapters hints that Paul considers the practice of "the weak" to be deficient in any way.* It is not Paul's concern to characterize some Christians as "weaker" than others. To the contrary, Paul instructs the strong "to recognize that the practices of the 'weak' are *just as valid before God* as those of themselves, and that they spring from the *same* faith and thanksgiving toward God as their own practices (14:3–13, 14ff.)."[50] The "strong" may not have respected the practices of the "weak" as acts of faith—but "Paul did." Paul urges "the strong" not to dispute the opinions of "the weak"—"an instruction that has apparently been lost in Christian theology, even among those who make this very point"—and Paul urges the "weak" and "strong" alike to continue their respective practices "fully convinced" in their own minds (14:5, 22–23).[51] In whatever way the "weak" manifest their "weakness," it is *not* through scrupulosity or indecision.[52]

What, then, constitutes the "weakness" of the weak? Nanos argues that "Paul and his audience would have understood the phrase usually translated 'weak in faith' to be a highly nuanced and respectful reference to the Jews in Rome who were not Christians...those Jews who do not yet believe in Jesus as the Christ of Israel or Savior of the nations."[53] Such "weakness" is jeopardized by Gentile neglect of *kashrut*, according to Nanos, insofar as non-Christian Jews may have been "scandalized" by "Gentiles asserting that they are now part of the people of God, co-participants in Israel's salvation, yet with no regard for the minimal requirements of Law and Jewish custom."[54] Nonobservant Gentile Christians thus threaten to repel these Jews from considering the *christological* claims made for Jesus. "Paul's intention toward the 'weak' was to change their 'faith' to faith in Jesus as the Christ."[55]

While (as Nanos shows) nothing in these chapters indicates that "the weak with regard to faith" are *inadequately convinced* of their freedom from *kashrut*, neither do these chapters give any explicit hint of Paul's hope of bringing "the weak" to faith in Jesus. Nanos has effectively expelled the notion that "weakness in faith" has to do with abstemiousness. I want to bring into question the assumption that the phrase *asthenoi te pistei* refers to *any* deficiency of "faith." The "weak" apparently are characterized by the careful observance of *kashrut*, in conditions that may restrict their acceptable diet to a limited selection of vegetables (14:2). In surprising contrast to much interpretation of this passage, however, Paul never links "the strong" (15:1) with those who eat regardless of *kashrut* (14:2–3). I conclude that there is no reason to connect being "strong" with a particular diet (or lack of one). Paul simply says that the strong "should bear with the weaknesses of the weak and not please ourselves" (15:1), implying that the strength of "the strong" consists simply in their ability to support "the weak." In fact, we should more naturally align "the strong" with those to whom exhortations are addressed earlier in the letter—to "not regard themselves as higher than they ought" (12:3), to use their God-given gifts of service, liberality, and acts of mercy and aid (12:6–8), to contribute to the needs of the saints and practice hospitality (12:13), and to associate with the lowly (12:16).[56]

I have argued elsewhere that the situation Paul addresses in Rome may have been shaped by harsh social forces, both imperial and popular, that eroded the stability of the Jewish community. Beyond particular sharp attacks on the community itself, such as the expulsion of some Jews under Claudius in 49 CE, were the lasting deleterious effects of such attacks on the common life of Jews in their homes, neighborhoods, marketplaces, and places of assembly. Whatever the scope of anti-Jewish sentiment abroad in Rome at this time—it is clearly more virulent in the intellectual elite of the capital a few decades later[57]—Paul's rhetoric suggests that he regarded the predominantly Gentile Christian assemblies in Rome as susceptible to a *theological* anti-Judaism that read the Jewish community's misfortune as an indication of their lapse from God's favor. Such is the import of the rhetorical questions Paul raises, and rejects: "What advantage has the Jew? Or what is the value of circumcision?" (3:1). Has the word of God failed? (9:6). "Has God rejected his people?" (11:1). "Have they stumbled so as to fall?" (11:11).[58]

Other scholars have suggested that the characterization of some Torah-observant individuals as "the weak" may reflect power relationships that left some "considerably more vulnerable" than others; "weak" and "strong," it

has been suggested, may represent people occupying "differential social locations."[59] Mark Reasoner has illuminated the context of this language in the
imperial ideology of the period, which attributed "strength" to the power-
holding classes within the empire and derided the "weakness" of the lower
classes, especially caricatured as predominantly of foreign extraction and
given over to "superstition" and sinister religious practices.[60] Appealing to
the derogatory images of Jews routine in the satirists, he argues that "the
weak" in Romans 14 may reflect Roman perceptions of poorer individuals
observing a foreign religion—for example, Torah-observant Jews—perceptions in line with the popular stereotypes of the day.

I suggest that these chapters provide a glimpse of the Apostle battling
what may well have been the first occurrence of anti-Judaism within the early
Christian movement. Significantly, this is not yet the theological anti-
Judaism of the Gospel of Matthew or the Gospel of Mark, for example,
which is clearly entwined with reactions to the traumatic events of 66–70
CE.[61] What the Apostle seeks to confront is rather a more banal projection
into the heavens of the balance of misery on earth, a scapegoating of relatively dispossessed people that relies on an appeal to the divine will. By identifying himself among "we who are strong" or "powerful" (15:1), Paul lays
down an implicit honor challenge to his Christian listeners in Rome: to live
out "strength" or power not by abandoning "the weak" to their supposedly
God-ordained fate, but to "bear the weaknesses of the weak."

THE AUTHENTIC ASCETICISM OF "THE WEAK"

I have delayed until this point consideration of the categories at the heart of
this book, in part because the exegetical and historical issues involved in
Romans 14–15 remain a matter of contention among interpreters, and in
part because presenting one clear understanding of what is at issue in Paul's
letter is a prerequisite for understanding the role that asceticism may play in
the Roman situation.

We face a new set of questions as we turn to discuss asceticism in these
chapters of Romans. In the first place, despite widespread agreement that the
characteristic defining "the weak" is more-or-less scrupulous observance of
the Jewish kosher laws, there is no agreement whether something called
"asceticism" is involved here. Ernst Käsemann speaks readily of "religious
asceticism for the sake of maintaining purity," derived from "observance of
a fixed tradition which is related ultimately to the law of holiness" and sharp-
ened "in the daily confrontation with the Gentile environment" in the
Roman diaspora.[62] Francis Watson, on the other hand, declares that the
abstention of "the weak" from meat and wine is "*not* evidence of syncretistic or ascetic tendencies, but is fully compatible with the situation of Jewish
Christians who wished to remain faithful to the Law in difficult circum-

stances."[63] Neither of these authors presents a definition of asceticism, nor do most of the interpreters who have written on Romans 14–15.[64]

Obviously, the question of definition is important if we wish to determine whether or not the observance of *kashrut* in an unforgiving Gentile environment constitutes "asceticism." In an encyclopedia article on "Ascetical Aspects of Ancient Judaism," Steven D. Fraade notes that modern scholars disagree widely on their assessment of the range and prevalence of early Jewish asceticism. His own operating definition of asceticism within ancient Judaism includes "two main components":

> (1) the exercise of disciplined effort toward the goal of spiritual perfection (however understood), which requires (2) abstention (whether total or partial, permanent or temporary, individualistic or communalistic) from the satisfaction of otherwise permitted earthly, creaturely desires.[65]

Obviously the issue of the social construction of "asceticism" emerges at once from this definition: "otherwise permitted"—*by whom?* Hellenistic Jews such as Philo and the author of the *Letter of Aristeas* recognize that Jews are commanded to abstain from pleasures (such as the eating of pork) that are permitted Gentiles. Does this mean that observant Jews *as such* should be considered "ascetics"? Fraade seems not to think so, talking of "ascetic impulses *within* Judaism," which suggests that "asceticism" refers to the voluntary abstention from the satisfaction of desires otherwise permitted *within one's society*. Thus the Pharisees, who (on the widely accepted theory of Jacob Neusner) sought to practice in their homes and associations the same level of purity required of priests in the temple, would qualify as an ascetic movement; so would the Therapeutae. On the other hand, Fraade regards the (originally separatist) practice of the Pharisees to be the source of the ideal of "abstention," *perishut*, that appears in the rabbinic literature as "the holy vocation of Israel as a *people*," at once both "a 'kingdom of *priests*' and a 'holy *nation*,' sanctified to God while living among yet apart from the nations and their ways."[66] Here an "ascetic" ideal has become a premier value for an entire culture.

I note, further, that Fraade seeks to emphasize this "native" wellspring of Jewish asceticism. He argues that ancient Jewish ascetical practices can neither be interpreted "simply as a reflex of specific historical events," such as the Hellenistic crisis of 167–164 BCE, nor be attributed to putative "foreign influences" such as Platonism or Pythagoreanism. Rather, asceticism is "*a perennial side of Judaism* as it struggles with the tension between the realization of transcendent ideals and the confronting of this-worldly obstacles to that realization."[67] Curiously, such language implicitly construes the generation of ascetical impulses as an almost wholly inner development of the Jewish religion. Fraade speaks of "general developments" in the Second Temple period, including "an increasing preoccupation, among individuals and religious groups, with the dichotomy of this-worldly life and other-worldly demands and hopes; and, second, an increasing resort to ascetic practices as responses to that tension."[68] The resulting implication here is that asceticism arises within the tension between ideals generated by a culture itself on the one hand and natural or ontological limits on the other:

> Late biblical and postbiblical Judaisms, by increasing the ethical, pietistic, and legal expectations placed on the *individual*, had to find ways of dealing with the psychic and social pressures thereby created. Ideals of perfection are one thing; dealing with an individual's and a religious society's continuing failure to realize them is another. One of the ways in which asceticism deals with this problem is by defining discrete areas of self-control in which the individual's (and society's) will can be exercised successfully in fulfillment of transcendent purposes.[69]

In contrast to Fraade's essay, which implies that asceticism is a "perennial" aspect of Judaism *as such*, recent scholarship on Romans has usually understood the increased prominence of ritual "boundary markers" such as *kashrut*, circumcision, and Sabbath observance in the Hellenistic and Roman diaspora as a response to the social pressures brought to bear upon Jewish identity by an often coercive pagan environment.[70] On similar lines, as we have seen, interpreters have emphasized the social disarray occasioned in the Jewish community of Rome by the expulsion under Claudius. These proposals suggest that *specific and occasional social pressures from the environment,* pressures antagonistic to a particular distinctive (sub)cultural identity, have much to do with the heightened ascetical practices apparently in view.

In asking whether the abstention from meat and wine on the part of Roman Jews constitutes "asceticism," we touch at the heart of definitional questions that continue to preoccupy the academic investigation of asceticism in antiquity. Responding to the article on "Asceticism" in the *Encyclopedia of Religion,* William E. Deal notes that an attempt to provide a single, universal definition of asceticism valid across various cultures

> suggests...that no society allows free reign of expression and action, that there are always controls, restrictions, and limitations placed on what we can do with our bodies or on bodily functions and that these can be expressive of other meanings. When does self-discipline or self-denial become ascetic?[71]

Within a *particular* culture, Deal suggests, it might be instructive to ask which acts of self-denial were and were not construed by participants in the culture as "ascetic." But this intracultural approach brings into question the very possibility of a universal or cross-cultural definition. In fact, Deal suggests, the effort to arrive at such a universal definition of "asceticism" tells us more about "the logics and concepts of the tradition out of which the term originally comes"—the culture of the nonparticipant observer.[72]

At this point, I find Richard Valantasis in "A Theory of the Social Function of Asceticism" particularly instructive. Valantasis relies on Michel Foucault's understanding of asceticism as a dimension of "the relationship to oneself," within the larger context of self- and culture-formation. Asceticism is thus "self-forming activity (that is, the changes that one makes to oneself in order to become an ethical subject)." Valantasis also appeals to Geoffrey Harpham's theory of asceticism, which focuses upon the dynamic of desire and resistance, arguing that "there is an inherent level of self-denial necessary for a person to live within a culture so that the resistance to appetites and desires is at the heart of cultural integration and functioning."[73]

Valantasis proposes his own theory of asceticism focusing on the integration of an individual person, and of groups of people, into a particular culture: "At the center of ascetical activity is a self who, through behavioral changes, seeks to become a different person, a new self; to become a different person in new relationships; and to become a different person in a new society that forms a new culture." Asceticism at once "functions as a system of cultural formation" and "initiates a person or group into the cultural systems that enable communication" and empower people to live within the culture.[74] "Asceticism may be defined as performances designed to inaugurate an alternative culture, to enable different social relations, and to create a new identity."[75] It bears emphasis that this understanding of asceticism does not focus upon delimiting "ascetic" and "nonascetic" practices within a particular culture, but rather sees "ascetic" behavior as continuous with cultural formation itself. An analogy deriving from ritual theory may be appropriate. Just as ritual action, by virtue of its stylized, "theatrical" heightening of normal cultural acts, at once "embodies" the values of a culture and also "ritualizes" bodies by a choreography in sacralized space and time,[76] so ascetic action heightens normal cultural routines of self-restraint in such a way as to represent specific values within the culture as paramount in significance and importance. As Valantasis declares, ascetic actions "function as signifiers in a semiotic system, in that they carry meaning within the context of their performance"; asceticism "provides the method for translating [the] theoretical and strategic concepts [upon which culture relies] into patterns of behavior."[77] This means that whether ascetic action is construed (by other members of the culture) as "orthodox," radical, or even deviant will depend on the relative importance these values are given in the cultural environment.[78] Thus the interpretation of ascetic activity must be contextualized within a "thick description" of the culture(s) in which the ascetic activity takes place.

Elements of Valantasis' theory allow us to highlight certain aspects of ascetic practices among the Roman Christians and Paul's responses to them, which have often gone underappreciated. First, Valantasis points out that since ascetic acts function as "signifiers in a semiotic system," a practice such as fasting "bears no inherent and self-evident meaning except that which is assigned it in the system." Ascetic performances "include an element of intentionality," in that they "displace attention from themselves to a larger referential arena, and their purpose relates at once to an alternative culture and to the potential of a new subjectivity."[79]

As we have seen, Paul clearly understands the actions of the "weak" to be intentional: "Those who observe the day observe it to the Lord; those who eat, eat to the Lord, giving thanks to God; those who abstain, abstain to the Lord, giving thanks to God" (14:6). Once we get beyond the conventional prejudicial characterizations of their actions as "weak," that is, as somehow deficient "in faith," we may recognize that the ever more stringent efforts of Jews in Rome to keep *kashrut* under ever more straitened circumstances do indeed point "toward the successful creation of a larger frame of reference and of meaning that supports the ascetic manner of living." That is, they point toward the fulfillment of human life as promised in Israel's scriptures and, in Paul's view, reconfirmed through the resurrection of Jesus: "If we live, we live to the Lord, and if we die, we die to the Lord; so then, whether we live or whether we die, we are the Lord's. For to this end Christ died and lived again, that he might be Lord both of the dead and of the living" (14:8–9).

This "semiotic" understanding of asceticism also allows us to read the issue in Romans 14–15 as occurring at the point of contact (or collision) between two cultural systems, one—that of diaspora Judaism—which relies upon ascetic practice to point toward a particular vision of human fulfillment, another—that of (pagan) Rome—which sees in Jewish asceticism only the irrational idiosyncrasies of "the weak."[80] Paul clearly sympathizes with the viewpoint of the weak: He disallows "disputing over opinions" with the weak (14:1), "despising the one who abstains from food" (14:3, 10), or scandalizing the (abstaining) brother or sister (14:13). Though he affirms that "nothing is unclean of itself" (14:14), he insists on respect for the ascetic (i.e., in this case, *kashrut*-observant) subject: "It is unclean for anyone who regards it as unclean" (14:14). Paul consistently rejects a perspective in which the observance of *kashrut* could be dismissed, suppressed, or regarded as mere cultural idiosyncrasy.[81]

Valantasis highlights other aspects of his theory. Ascetic performance aims at "the articulation and construction of a new subjectivity"; at the center of ascetic activity "is a self who, through behavioral changes, seeks to become a different person, a new self."[82] Paul's repeated reference to the conscious intentionality of the ascetic practitioner emphasizes and honors this subjectivity: "Let all be convinced in their own minds" (14:5). "The faith that you have, keep between yourself and God; happy are they who have no reason to judge themselves for what they approve" (14:22–23). Valantasis also emphasizes the significance of social relationships for ascetic practice: "Culture becomes concrete at the level of social relationships," and so therefore must ascetic practice as well.[83] While it is widely recognized that Paul's concern in 14:1–15:13 is for the "unity" and "harmony" of kosher-observant and nonobservant Jews and Gentiles gathered at common meals (14:3, 13–15), it bears particular emphasis that *unity for its own sake is not Paul's goal.* He requires a "new perspective" among his audience that, in Mark Nanos' words, "respects the integrity of the Law and the Jewish practice of faith, and equally respects the integrity of Paul as a Jew, as well as a Christian, who deeply loved his Jewish brothers and sisters and who was concerned to correct behavior in Rome" that might have scandalized them.[84]

Just here our recognition of the semiotic function of ascetic behavior provides an important insight into Paul's theology and apostolic practice. Paul respects the "asceticism" of *kashrut*-observant individuals in Rome, but does not require *kashrut* observance of Gentile Christians as well. Paul respects the freedom Gentile Christians enjoy *individually* regarding *kashrut* observance, but requires their respect for Jewish sensibilities *at common meals* and, by implication, in assemblies in which Gentiles join their voices with the people of Israel in praise of Israel's God, the God of all creation (15:7–13).

In effect Paul encourages *two* strategies of asceticism, side by side, in the congregations he addresses. From the observant, Paul expects continued *conscious, intentional* observance of *kashrut* as an authentic "living to the Lord" (14:5–9, 22–23). From the nonobservant, Paul requires, *at common meals,* the renunciation of the freedom to "eat anything" (cf. 14:2), the renunciation of attitudes of judgment or indifference to the observant brother or sister (14:3–4, 13–16). *Both* "asceticisms" are to be conscious, intentional strategies of living before the same Lord (14:4), recognizing the same accountability toward God (14:10–12), the same valuation of "justice and peace and joy in the Holy Spirit" (14:17), the same renunciation of any action that injures or destroys "the work of God" (14:20). Of this common, overlapping asceticism Christ himself is the model, "for Christ did not please himself," but suffered reproach (15:3)—as *both* the observant Jew *and* the respectful Gentile Christian may expect for themselves in Neronian Rome.

A scholarly preoccupation with identifying the abstention of "the weak" and characterizing it as *weak,* that is, *deficient,* has generally obscured the importance of this genuinely Pauline asceticism, this self-restraining "pursuit of what makes for peace and for mutual up-building" (14:19) that unites *observant* Jew and Gentile alike. Significantly, the vision of human fulfillment toward which Paul imagines the faithful living is not a community in which differences between Jew and Gentile have been effaced, but one in which Jew and Gentile together praise God—tellingly, a vision set out gloriously in Israel's scriptures (15:5; in the "promises given to the patriarchs" and declared by the prophets, 15:8–12). The premier value represented by this

"Pauline asceticism" is not *unity*, to be achieved through the erasure of difference, but *hope* (15:4, 12–13).

Although Paul's identification with "the strong" (15:1) has led many interpreters to conclude—without warrant, as I have argued here—that he embraced a Gentile-Christian view of the *kosher* laws as no longer valid, careful attention to Paul's rhetoric in these chapters shows, to the contrary, that Paul calls on the Christians of Rome to honor the diligent observance of a beleaguered Jewish community, injured by imperial edict and insulted by an intellectual elite, as genuine faithfulness to God. It is *the asceticism of "the weak"* that points reliably toward "the successful creation of a larger frame of reference and of meaning," an "alternative culture and the potential of a new subjectivity"[85]—"the *basileia* of God, justice and peace and joy in the Holy Spirit" (14:17). The "weak" are, in this sense, *strong* in their deliberate living out of the values of the *basileia*, in hope of which the Gentiles alike are called to live (15:12–13).

NOTES

1. Mark Reasoner, "The Theology of Romans 12:1–15:13," in *Pauline Theology III: Romans,* eds. David M. Hay and E. Elizabeth Johnson (Minneapolis, Minn.: Fortress, 1995), 292.

2. Mark D. Nanos, *The Mystery of Romans: The Jewish Context of Paul's Letter* (Minneapolis, Minn.: Fortress, 1996), 86. Romans 14 and 15 have played a significant role in several reconstructions of the historical situation behind the letter: See Paul S. Minear, *The Obedience of Faith: The Purpose of Paul in the Epistle to the Romans* (London: SCM, 1971), 9; Francis S. Watson, *Paul, Judaism, and the Gentiles: A Sociological Approach* (Cambridge: Cambridge University Press, Society for the New Testament Studies Monograph Series 56, 1986), 94–98; A. J. M. Wedderburn, *The Reasons for Romans* (Edinburgh, Scotland: T. & T. Clark, 1991), 29–37, 59–65.

3. See Robert J. Karris, "Romans 14:1–15:13 and the Occasion of Romans," *Catholic Biblical Review* 25 (1973): 155–78; repr. in *The Romans Debate,* ed. Karl P. Donfried, 2nd ed. (Peabody, Mass.: Hendrickson, 1991), 65–84, whence I quote below; Günther Bornkamm, "The Letter to the Romans as Paul's Last Will and Testament," *Australian Biblical Review* 11 (1963): 2–14; repr. in *The Romans Debate,* ed. Donfried, 16–28; J. Paul Sampley, "'The Weak and the Strong': Paul's Careful and Crafty Rhetorical Strategy in Romans 14:1–15:13," in *The Social World of the First Christians: Essays in Honor of Wayne A. Meeks,* eds. L. Michael White and O. Larry Yarbrough (Minneapolis, Minn.: Fortress, 1995), 40–52; Wayne A. Meeks, "Judgment and the Brother: Romans 14:1–15:13," in *Tradition and Interpretation in the New Testament: Essays in Honor of E. Earle Ellis,* eds. G. F. Hawthorne and O. Betz (Grand Rapids, Mich.: Eerdmans, 1987), 290–300. Ernst Käsemann, *Commentary on Romans,* trans. G. W. Bromiley (Grand Rapids, Mich.: Eerdmans, 1980), 366,

warns that we must proceed "with great caution" to extrapolate information about the Roman congregation from these chapters.

4. Watson, *Paul, Judaism, and the Gentiles*, 97–98, argues that Romans 14–15 "*presupposes two congregations, separated by mutual hostility and suspicion over the question of the law*"; Paul's purpose in the letter was to convert the Jewish-Christian congregation "to his point of view so as to create a single 'Pauline' congregation in Rome."

5. Karris, "Occasion of Romans."

6. Bornkamm, "Paul's Last Will and Testament."

7. Sampley ("The Weak and the Strong," 40–52) declares that "Paul is an outsider to the Roman churches, without any basis for the friendship necessary for frank speech." James C. Walters (*Ethnic Issues in Paul's Letter to the Romans: Changing Self-Definitions in Earliest Roman Christianity* [Philadelphia: Trinity Press International, 1993], 84–92) speaks similarly of Paul's "oblique," general approach here to issues of *kashrut*.

8. Karris, "Occasion of Romans," 83–84. Meeks ("Judgment and the Brother" 292) insists that "there is no evidence…of any present crisis around this issue in the Roman groups."

9. Meeks, "Judgment and the Brother," 292, 297.

10. I discuss, and strive to refute, this understanding of Romans as a showpiece letter in my book, *The Rhetoric of Romans: Argumentative Constraint and Strategy and Paul's Dialogue with Judaism* (Sheffield, England: Journal for the Study of the Old Testament, Journal for the Study of the New Testament Supp. 451990), 60–66.

11. Käsemann, for example, can blithely declare that since "the epistle is clearly addressed to a community whose firm status as Christians is not in doubt," Paul's admonitions "are not directed against them and are not meant to stir them to repentance" (*Commentary on Romans*, 34).

12. See Elliott, *Rhetoric of Romans*, chap. 1; idem, *Liberating Paul: The Justice of God and the Politics of the Apostle* (Maryknoll, N.Y: Orbis, 1994), 73–75.

13. This is, above all, the legacy of J. Christiaan Beker, *Paul the Apostle: The Triumph of God in Life and Thought* (Philadelphia: Fortress, 1980). See also the essays gathered together in Donfried, ed., *Romans Debate*, and Wedderburn, *Reasons for Romans*.

14. For a discussion of the "double character" of the letter (as concerned with "Jewish" topics, yet addressed explicitly to Gentiles) see my *Rhetoric of Romans*, 9–42. Recent monographs that take the inscribed Gentile-Christian audience seriously include Stanley K. Stowers, *A Rereading of Romans: Justice, Jews, and Gentiles* (New Haven, Conn.: Yale University Press, 1994); William S. Campbell, *Paul's Gospel in an Intercultural Context: Jew and Gentile in the Letter to the Romans* (Frankfurt am Main, Germany: Lang, 1991); and Nanos, *Mystery of Romans*.

15. N. T. Wright, "Romans and the Theology of Paul," in *Pauline Theology*, eds. Hay and Johnson, 62. Elsewhere Wright argues (*The Climax of the Covenant* [Minneapolis, Minn.: Fortress, 1992], 235) that Romans 14–15 cohere nicely with the argument of the letter and that "the climax of the latter passage (15:7-13) can be seen in fact as the climax of the entire epistle." Nanos declares

(*Mystery of Romans*, 159) that these chapters express "the essential intention of the letter."

16. The terms used here for foods, "common" (14:14) and "pure" (14:20), are "characteristic of Jewish purity concerns." See John M. G. Barclay, "'Do We Undermine the Law?' A Study of Romans 14:1–15:6," in *Paul and the Mosaic Law*, ed. James D. G. Dunn (Tübingen, Germany: Mohr [Siebeck], 1996), 290. The use of *koinon* in the sense of "profane" "seems to have developed on Jewish soil. At any rate, there are no instances in non-Jewish secular Greek." See Friedrich Hauck, "koinos," *Theological Dictionary of the New Testament*, vol. 3, ed. G. Kittel and G. Friedrich, 791.

17. Käsemann, *Commentary on Romans*, 367.

18. Karris, "Occasion of Romans," 66–70.

19. Writings from the Hellenistic diaspora show abstinence from meat and wine as a routine expression of Jewish observance: See Dan. 1:3–16; Esth. 3:28; 4:16; Jdt. 12:1–2. Securing civic permission to prepare and sell kosher foods was a regular concern for diaspora communities (see Josephus, *Ant.* 14.185–267). In relation to Rome in particular, Josephus tells us that "certain priests" from Judea, being bound over to face charges before Caesar, "had not forgotten the pious practices of religion and supported themselves on figs and nuts" (*Vita* 3). Strabo speaks simply of Jewish "abstinence from flesh" (*Geography* 16:2:37). The Therapeutae, admittedly not representing routine Jewish practice, avoided meat and wine (Philo, *On the Contemplative Life*, 73–74); so did the Patriarch Isaac, according to the *Testament of Isaac* 4:5. See my *Rhetoric of Romans*, 52–57; Reasoner, "Theology of Romans 12:1–15:13," 288–90; Wedderburn, Reasons for Romans, 31–34; Barclay, "'Do We Undermine the Law?,'" 294–95.

20. In a long satirical lament about the decline of Rome, Juvenal's friend Umbricius, who is packing up to leave the city for a more traditional, if humbler, life in the countryside, describes the risks run by the poor in the rougher neighborhoods of the city. Umbricius contrasts the relative safety enjoyed by the wealthy, who can afford to travel about with armed escorts, with the constant threat of assault that the poor faced in the streets each day. He describes a mugger adding insult to injury by mistaking his indigent victim for a Jew reeking of vinegar, beans, and leeks. See Juvenal, *Satire* 3.278–301, in *Juvenal and Persius*, trans. G. G. Ramsay, Loeb Classical Library (Cambridge, Mass.: Harvard University Press, 1957), 53–55.

21. Horace describes turning to a passing friend when he wants to be rescued from a bore. His friend declines conversation, pleading that he is observing the "thirtieth sabbath" as "a somewhat weaker brother, one of the many" (*sum paulo infirmior, unus multorum*). See Horace, *Satire* 1.9.68–72, trans. H. R. Fairclough, Loeb Classical Library (London: Heinemann, 1929). Note that the observant Jews in the book of Daniel run the risk of appearing "weaker" than their Chaldean fellows (Dan 1:10). See my *Rhetoric of Romans*, 55; Reasoner, "Theology of Romans 12:1–15:13," 290; Barclay, "'Do We Undermine the Law?,'" 297, 302.

22. Wedderburn, *Reasons for Romans*, 59–60; Walters, *Ethnic Issues*, 57; Barclay, "'Do We Undermine the Law?,'" 293.

23. Nanos, *Mystery of Romans*, 87–88.

24. Käsemann, *Commentary on Romans*, 369.

25. Nanos, *Mystery of Romans*, 91.

26. Ibid, 92–94. Nanos' survey includes interpreters as diverse as Karl Barth, James D. G. Dunn, Peter Tomson, and Peter Stuhlmacher.

27. Ibid, 94–95.

28. Campbell, "Rule of Faith," 272–73.

29. Reasoner ("Theology of Romans," 289) declares Campbell's reticence to be "methodologically suspect, since our goal in interpreting this section of the letter is to determine what sort of social division Paul is describing within the Roman churches, regardless of how biased or prejudiced its basis might seem to us. All of us want to avoid anti-Semitism, but many people in first-century Rome had no such concern."

30. Barclay, "'Do We Undermine the Law?,'" 293.

31. Ibid, 300.

32. Ibid, 303, 305.

33. Ibid, 308.

34. Ibid, 307.

35. Watson, *Paul, Judaism, and the Gentiles*, 97–98.

36. Campbell sums up his assessment of Romans: "Paul, because of nascent anti-Judaism among the Roman Gentile Christians, finds himself cast in the role of defender of Israel against Gentiles, probably for the first time in his apostolic career." See Campbell, "Rule of Faith," 260; idem, *Paul's Gospel in an Intercultural Context*, 201 and passim. Nanos (*Mystery of Romans*, 10) declares that "the Paul we meet in this letter is engaged in confronting the initial development of…a misunderstanding of God's intentions in Rome manifest in Christian-*gentile* exclusivism." Stowers (*Rereading of Romans*, 289–93) observes that the Jewish persona who admonishes Gentile arrogance in Romans 9–11 comes at the climax of the letter's rhetoric. My own work on Romans is clearly in sympathy with these approaches: See idem, *Rhetoric of Romans*, 42–43, 290–99; idem, *Liberating Paul*, 175–80, 214–16.

37. Barclay, "'Do We Undermine the Law?,'" 291.

38. Ibid: "The controversies reflected here are easily imagined among Christians with different perceptions of the Jewish Law"; Watson, *Paul, Judaism, and the Gentiles*, 94–95; Walters, *Ethnic Issues*, 67–94.

39. Even Campbell, who has taken pains to insist against Watson that Paul did *not* advocate Christian separation from the synagogues ("Did Paul Advocate Separation from the Synagogue? A Reaction to Francis Watson," *Scottish Journal of Theology* 42 [1989]: 457–67), considers it "fundamental to the Roman situation…that political factors may have been instrumental in encouraging a rupture in relations between the Gentile churches and the synagogues," so that we must presume "a period of relative separation of Gentile Christians from the synagogue." See Campbell, "Rule of Faith," 264–65).

40. Walters, *Ethnic Issues*, 56.

41. Nanos, *Mystery of Romans*, 110–14.

42. Ibid, 113. Barclay ("'Do We Undermine the Law?,'" 292) considers the phrase "in honor of the Lord" (14:6) to indicate *Christian* faith, but Nanos (*Mystery of Romans*, 113–15) is able to show that the faith in question is Israel's faith in the one God of the *Shema*.

43. See Barclay, "'Do We Undermine the Law?,'" 291: "The question is simply whether or not the meat on the table in a Christian's house was considered pure by those observing the Jewish Law on this matter."

44. Ibid, 306–7.

45. Nanos (*Mystery of Romans*, 169; 50–57) describes the Apostolic Council (which he accepts as largely historical) as "a first-century development that stands somewhere between the ancient Mosaic model for governing the behavioral requirements for the 'stranger within your gates,' that is, of the non-Jew living in the land of Israel (Lev. 17–18), and the later rabbinic model of the Noahide Commandments that addressed the paradoxical issues that arose in Diaspora contexts." The basis for common fellowship sketched out in Paul's exhortations represented "the dominant notions of Diaspora Judaism" in Paul's day (ibid, 174). See also Peter Tomson, *Paul and the Jewish Law: Halakha in the Letters of the Apostle to the Gentiles* (Minneapolis, Minn.: Fortress, Compendia rerum Iudaicarum ad Novum Testamentum 3/1, 1990), 271–74. Against Nanos' reading (*Mystery of Romans*, chap. 4) on this point, Paul's references to the "obedience of faith" (Rom. 1:5) and to the "doctrine which you have been taught" (16:17) are too oblique to be perceptible references to the Apostolic Council. If Paul had meant to appeal to such an authoritative decision by his fellow apostles, surely he could have done so more clearly.

46. See Paula Fredriksen, *From Jesus to Christ: The Origins of the New Testament Images of Jesus* (New Haven, Conn.: Yale University Press, 1988), 151: "Jews could and did eat with Gentiles. The discussions preserved in the Mishnah that detail the correct procedure on such occasions attest to the frequency with which they occurred." See also Nanos, *Mystery of Romans*, 50–57; E. P. Sanders, "Jewish Association with Gentiles and Galatians 2:11–14," in *The Conversation Continues: Studies in Paul and John in Honor of J. Louis Martyn*, eds. Robert T. Fortna and Beverly R. Gaventa, (Nashville, Tenn.: Abingdon, 1985), 170–88.

47. Nanos, *Mystery of Romans*, 197.

48. Barclay, "'Do We Undermine the Law?,'" 300.

49. Neither is it obvious that Paul "could see no objection to eating shellfish, hare or pork" (ibid, 301). Paul identifies himself as one of "the strong" (15:1), but this alone does not indicate whether or not Paul considers himself free from the obligation of Torah; to the contrary, he may well number himself among those who exclude certain foods from their own diets as "common" (14:14). Nanos (*Mystery of Romans*, 96–97, 196–97) quite rightly points out that Rom. 14:14a does not exhaust Paul's judgment regarding *kashrut*.

50. Ibid, 96.

51. Ibid, 104–5.

52. "The 'weak' are not uncertain or wavering" (ibid, 135).

53. Ibid, 139, 143. Nanos observes that "weakness in terms of faith" (*ton asthenia te pistei*, 14:1) is immediately linked with the danger of putting a "stumbling block or hindrance [*proskomma e skandalon*] in the way" of another (14:13). Not only is the contrast of "faith" and "stumbling" or "falling" prevalent in the latter part of the letter (9:30–33, 11:9–11); in the biblical texts upon which Paul draws here for his imagery, ατθενια *asthenia* and its cognates were *synonymous* with verbs of stumbling. "In a manner quite different from the ordinary Greek usage for natural weakness, *astheneo* and *asthenia* developed a special character

in the prophetic literature of the Septuagint with respect to the divine judgment that would fall upon those who rebelled against God: *astheneo* was seldom used to translate the Hebrew verbs *rapa* ('to be weak') or *hala* ('to be sick'), but instead was frequently used to translate verbal forms of the root *kashal* ('to stumble, to stagger'), and for the corresponding noun *mikshol* ('hindrance,' 'stumbling block')" (ibid., 119–23). To these resonances we might add the assurance in 14:4 that "the weak" will be able to stand, being upheld by the Lord "who is able to make them stand," which echoes the promise in 11:23 that the "cultivated" olive branches (i.e., Jews who have declined to accept Jesus as messiah) "will be grafted in, for God has the power to graft them in again."

54. Ibid, 133.

55. Ibid, 151.

56. Nanos links "the strong" with "the state of mind that Paul confronts as unacceptable throughout this letter," concluding that "these are clearly characteristics of the 'strong' that Paul distances himself from and confronts as unacceptable on their part" (ibid, 98–99). I would say, rather, that in Paul's only explicit exhortation to "the strong" (15:1) he identifies himself with them; it is not clear to me that "the strong" as such is meant as a derogatory label.

57. John G. Gager, *The Origins of Anti-Semitism* (New York: Oxford University Press, 1981), 63–88.

58. I have pursued this interpretation in *Rhetoric of Romans;* idem, *Liberating Paul,* 221–26; idem, "Figure and Ground in the Interpretation of Romans 9–11," in *The Theological Interpretation of Scripture: Classical and Contemporary Readings,* ed. Steven Fowl (Oxford: Blackwell, 1996), 371–89; idem, "Romans 13:1-7 in the Context of Imperial Propaganda," in *Paul and Empire: Religion and Power in Roman Imperial Society,* ed. Richard A. Horsley (Philadelphia: Trinity Press International, 1997), 184–204.

59. See Barclay, "'Do We Undermine the Law?,'" 302; Campbell, "Rule of Faith."

60. See Reasoner, "Honores and Potentes in Roman Ideology," in *SBL Seminar Papers 1993,* ed. K. Richards (Atlanta, Ga.: Scholars, 1993), 1–15. See also Campbell, "Rule of Faith," on "Social Factors."

61. See the essays collected in Peter Richardson and David Granskou, eds., *Anti-Judaism in Early Christianity: Vol. 1, Paul and the Gospels* (Waterloo, Ontario, Canada: Wilfrid Laurier University Press, 1986).

62. Käsemann, *Commentary on Romans,* 369.

63. Watson, *Paul, Judaism, and the Gentiles,* 95–96 (emphasis added).

64. On problems of definition and the lack of clarity regarding asceticism in the Pauline letters, see the introduction in Vincent L. Wimbush, *Paul the Worldly Ascetic: Response to the World and Self-Understanding according to 1 Corinthians 7* (Macon, Ga.: Mercer University Press, 1987); on issues of definition and interpretation more broadly, see the conference papers gathered together in Vincent L. Wimbush and Richard Valantasis, eds., *Asceticism* (New York: Oxford University Press, 1995).

65. Steven D. Fraade, "Ascetical Aspects of Ancient Judaism," in *Jewish Spirituality from the Bible through the Middle Ages, World Spirituality: An Encyclopedic History of the Religious Quest,* vol. 13 (New York: Crossroad, 1989), 257.

66. Ibid, 270, 277.

67. Ibid, 260 (italics mine).
68. Ibid, 261.
69. Ibid, 276.
70. This is a particular emphasis in the work of James D. G. Dunn, *Jesus, Paul, and the Law* (London: SPCK, 1990); idem, *Romans* 9–16, Word Biblical Commentary 38B (Dallas, Tex.: Word, 1988), 795–806.
71. William E. Deal, "Toward a Politics of Asceticism," in *Asceticism*, eds. Wimbush and Valantasis, 426.
72. Ibid, 426–27.
73. Richard Valantasis, "A Theory of the Social Function of Asceticism," in *Asceticism*, eds. Wimbush and Valantasis, 544–52. Valantasis relies upon Michel Foucault, "On the Genealogy of Ethics: An Overview of Work in Progress," in *The Foucault Reader*, ed. Paul Rabinow (New York: Pantheon, 1984), and Geoffrey Harpham, *The Ascetic Imperative in Culture and Criticism* (Chicago: University of Chicago Press, 1987).
74. Valantasis, "Theory," 547.
75. Ibid, 548.
76. Valantasis relies on the theory of culture offered by Clifford Geertz, *The Interpretation of Cultures* (New York: Basic Books, 1973), for Valantasis' understanding of asceticism. I wish to highlight Geertz's understanding of the function of ritual action within culture as well. See also Catherine Bell, *Ritual Theory, Ritual Practice* (New York: Oxford University Press, 1992).
77. Valantasis, "Theory," 548, 550.
78. Deal, "Politics of Asceticism," 427.
79. Valantasis, "Theory," 548.
80. Reasoner, "Honores and Potentes."
81. Again, Nanos' forceful insistence on this point is particularly valuable: "The 'strong' are Paul's target, and the entire paraenesis is concerned with convincing them to accept the 'weak' without 'judging their opinions,' and further, to accommodate the sensibilities of the 'weak' by modifying their behavior to mirror that of the 'weak,' even as Christ had." See Nanos, *Mystery of Romans*, 147.
82. Valantasis, "Theory," 549, 547.
83. Ibid, 549.
84. Nanos, *Mystery of Romans*, 154.
85. Valantasis, "Theory," 547.

Part Three

Imitatio
PAULI

2 Thessalonians and the Discipline of Work

Jennifer Wright Knust

INTRODUCTION

2 Thessalonians does not easily lend itself to a discussion of "asceticism." No certain reference to ascetic practice is present. The document itself is concerned primarily with issues of eschatological doctrine as well as the importance of "work" (*ergon*) and "tradition" (*paradosis*). Yet examining 2 Thessalonians in light of discussions of asceticism has proven helpful in isolating the orientation and practices of competing world-critical groups. Although 2 Thessalonians bears no apparent trace of the types of disciplined actions commonly associated with asceticism, it hints at a world in which asceticisms are possible but not, in this case, clearly recommended or rejected. Reading 2 Thessalonians as a Deutero-Pauline letter that reflects competition among groups whose different views and practices may or may not be ascetic has led me to conclude that the author, his supporters, and his rivals may not have been as far apart as I originally thought.[1] While the author and those whom he opposed may have differed in terms of specific practices and emphases, they were both engaged in a world-destroying and world-inaugurating project. They both sought, with words, images, and rejection of the "things of the world" (*ta tou kosmou*), to attain fulfillment and transformation.

The author of 2 Thessalonians worried that the Thessalonian *ekklesia* might be persuaded by a rival Pauline group that was misusing a "letter purportedly from us" (2:1–2). The author, writing as Paul, warned the *ekklesia* "not to be quickly shaken in mind or alarmed, either by spirit or word" or

by the spurious letter (2:2a). To which "letter" the author might be referring has been widely disputed. Some have suggested that the "false" letter is
1 Thessalonians, while other scholars have proposed that the author is referring to Colossians or Ephesians.[2] In either case, in the view of the author, an
authentic Pauline letter has been falsely understood or a rival pseudonymous
letter has led some astray. As the self-proclaimed bearer of authentic Pauline
doctrine and practice, therefore, the author sets out to clarify the views and
practices of Paul to challenge the views and practices of his rivals.[3] Some set
of disputants have argued that "the day of the Lord has already come" (2:2).
The author disagrees, offering an eschatological timetable that would make
such a belief untenable (2:3–12). Never mind that the justification for the
"false" doctrine is Paul or another pseudo-Paul: Those who hold such views
must have misunderstood him. A further concern is that "false" leaders are
accepting bread without paying (3:6). Paul and his companions never
engaged in such a practice, the "Paul" of 2 Thessalonians argues, so neither
should they (3:8–12). God called the Thessalonians, the author reminds
them, through "*our* gospel," so the writer encourages them to "stand firm
and hold the traditions you were taught by us, either by word or by letter"
(2:14–15). Live only "in accord with the tradition that you received from
us" and "imitate us" (3:6–7). Any other practice or belief is to be rejected,
even if such a practice is justified by persons claiming Paul as their authority.

Despite their disagreements, "Paul" and his opponents share a similar
distrust of those who are outside of the faith. To both the author of 2
Thessalonians and his rivals the world is a bitterly hostile place. The present
time is characterized by falsehood and delusion, which leads, inevitably, to
persecution and trouble for those who know "the truth" (1:4–5; 2:6–7,
14–15; 3:2). The author expresses his discontent through repeated use of
apocalyptic motifs: There will be a judgment at the end of time in which the
afflicted will be vindicated and those who afflict will suffer (1:5); a "man of
lawlessness" will proclaim himself as god only to be slain by the breath of the
Lord (2:6–7); yet the righteous who stand firm and hold to tradition will
obtain the glory of the Lord Jesus Christ (2:14–15). Similarly, the "false"
viewpoint that the author attempts to counter also included apocalyptic
themes. A group of Pauline "brothers" have proposed a "realized eschatology"[4] that claims that "the day of the Lord has already come" (2:2).
Although their apocalyptic timetables are different, the author and his rivals
agree that the world is hostile and must be rejected. The shared "anti-world"
orientation of the author and his opponents raises the question of asceticism.
Vincent L. Wimbush has observed that an anti-world orientation is a hallmark of asceticism:

> Ascetic behavior represents a range of responses to social, political and psychical
> worlds often perceived as oppressive or unfriendly, or as stumbling blocks to the
> pursuit of heroic personal or communal goals, life styles, and commitments.[5]

To the author and his Pauline rivals, the world is perceived as unfriendly. The world persecutes and the *ekklesia* must stand firm.[6] A world-critical orientation, however, is not enough to suggest that either the author of 2 Thessalonians or those he criticized held an ascetic worldview or that they were practitioners of a type of asceticism.[7] A pessimistic view of the world is an oft-noted feature of apocalyptic ideology as well as asceticism. The close connection between apocalyptic and ascetic practice has been noted by Wimbush. Apocalypticism and gnosticism, he argued, "legitimized the retreat from a world deemed evil and a prison."[8] Thus, a descriptive definition of asceticism that highlights the anti-world orientation of ascetic literature alone has not been adequate for an analysis of 2 Thessalonians. The differences between anti-world groups in 2 Thessalonians lie not only in competitive eschatologies with a shared disdain for the world but also in differences of practice.

Richard Valantasis has argued that asceticism "may be defined as performances within a dominant social environment intended to inaugurate a new subjectivity, different social relations and an alternative symbolic universe."[9] Asceticism as performance set Christianity apart from the world around it, offering an alternative world with changed standards of social life and relationships.[10] Ascetic practices construct new subjectivities by means of disciplined actions with intended social implications and consequences.[11] Practices commonly associated with asceticism include forms of self-discipline (*enkrateia*), withdrawal (*anachoresis*), and self-control (*sophrosyne*), practices that may be described as limiting the self in some way. Ascetic dispositions and behavior are therefore a subset of the larger category of "discipline," which may include activities directed toward virtue, the self, knowledge and training.[12] Asceticism, therefore, involves more than orientation. Asceticism implies disciplined practice.

We have already observed that the author of 2 Thessalonians and his competitors presupposed a symbolic universe that perceived the surrounding world to be antagonistic. The true world, they believed, is available only to those who know God, believe the gospel, and obey "Paul." The disputes reflected in 2 Thessalonians have more to do with practice than orientation, however. On the one hand, the author, his supporters, and his rivals presupposed that the world was hostile to their interests and shared an assumption of the importance of practice. On the other hand, they differed considerably over what specific practices were legitimate and "according to Paul."

The author considered the practices of his rivals to be disturbing, labeling his opponents "busybodies" (*periergazomenoi*) who failed to "imitate us" (3:7, 11). The Thessalonian *ekklesia* was therefore warned to keep away from any brother who conducted himself in a disorderly manner (3:6), a manner contrary to the practice of Paul. Paul and his companions, the author insisted, were not disorderly (3:7). By labeling his rivals as behaving *ataktos*, that is, in a "disorderly" or "insubordinate" manner, the author accused them of obstinate resistance to legitimate authority.[13] Although many translations prefer "idle" to "disorderly," the basic meaning of the term is "undisciplined" or "disobedient."[14] The disorderly and insubordinate "brothers" stand accused of neglecting real work in favor of acting like busybodies. The author's problem with his rivals was not that they were doing nothing, but rather that their activities were not "according to Paul." Those who, in the estimation of the author, violated the example of Paul were disorderly and disobedient, not lazy.

Paul and his company, the author insists, were not disorderly (*ouk etaktesamen*) when they were among the Thessalonians (3:7), nor did they accept material support from them. Rather, "with toil and labor we worked night and day" so that the *ekklesia* might not be burdened (3:8). Rejecting the rebellious work of the opponents, for which they have received material support (3:8–9), "Paul" commands the members of the *ekklesia* to practice good works, to be obedient, and to reject the false views of the *ataktoi* while earning their own living (3:13, 14). Thus, both the author and his rivals were involved in particular practices of some kind. Whether or not these practices may be characterized as ascetic, however, is less certain.

Asceticism has been defined according to its characteristic anti-world perspective and as a set of disciplinary practices that offer transformation of the self and the community. Asceticism may also be viewed as an attempt to escape from the hostile world even while continuing to live within it, often at great cost. Asceticism, Harpham has argued, is grounded in resistance.[15] Resistance and opposition imply cost, yet another assumption shared by all parties to the dispute reflected in 2 Thessalonians. The *ekklesia*, "Paul" argues, must attempt to remain steadfast "in all your persecutions and in the afflictions which you are enduring" (1:4). The content of the *thlipseis* is undefined by the author, although the interpretation of it is in contention. The author claimed that the *thlipseis* represent the testing of God (1:5). His rivals suggested that *thlipseis* are evidence that the day of the Lord is either imminent or has already arrived (2:1–3).[16] In response, the author insisted that the *thlipseis* must not be understood as the final afflictions associated with the day of the Lord, but rather as intermediate troubles that the *ekklesia* must face for a while longer.[17] "Paul" and his Thessalonian rivals agree, however, that *thlipseis* are to be expected given the hostility of the corrupt world to the truth. Resistance is therefore a central theme of "Paul" and his rivals. The opposition that community members are facing in some ways proves the validity of their position, no matter when they expect the day of the Lord to arrive. They are living in a corrupt world and therefore the world does not accept them, the bearers of truth, whatever apocalyptic timetable they adopt.

Relating 2 Thessalonians to discussions of asceticism has suggested that, despite the author's rhetoric to the contrary, "Paul," those who supported him, and those he denounced shared a great deal. All participants in the con-

tentious Thessalonian *ekklesia* shared an anti-world orientation that demanded resistance to the world that persecuted them, two features often associated with asceticism. 2 Thessalonians is a short letter, however, and there is a
danger in reading too much asceticism into it. Clearly, "Paul" in 2
Thessalonians desires a transformation that will enable him and those like
him to escape from a corrupt world. A similar orientation has been detected
among those whom the author would censure. The most tantalizing difference between the author and his rivals, however, is over what sort of practices are to be encouraged. What must a person do to be transformed? The
author and his rivals seem to have answered this question differently. The
author, his supporters, and their opponents shared attitudes that could be
identified as ascetic, but orientation alone has not convinced me that the category of "asceticism" offers a satisfactory description of the author or his
competitors. A more careful examination of the dispute over practice is
required. Since 2 Thessalonians is such a brief letter, I have compared the
battle over practice in 2 Thessalonians with the conflicts reflected in other
Deutero-Pauline letters.

ASCETICISM, "PAUL," AND THE ATAKTOI

The *ekklesia* is threatened by those who do not know God or the Lord Jesus
Christ (1:8). The Thessalonian Christians are facing persecution and trouble,
although the content of that trouble is unspecified (1:4–5). They will be
rewarded for enduring their present afflictions, and those who afflict them
will suffer eternal destruction (1:6–9). Given their current distress, "Paul"
praises them for steadfastness and faith (1:4). They must remain resolute,
holding fast to tradition, engaging in good works, guarding against false
teaching, and obeying "Paul" (2:15, 17; 3:4, 12–14). The hostile world is
dangerous and threatening, as are "false" teachers who speak or act in a way
contrary to "Paul." "Every good resolve and work of faith in power" is
required to combat threatening falsehood and delusion (2:11). Moreover,
such a serious threat demands a firm grasp on "tradition" (2:15; 3:6),
engagement in "good works" (2:17; 3:13), care in interpreting "word" and
"spirit" (2:2, 17), and, most of all, obedience (3:4: "you are doing and will
do the things which we command"; 3:10: "we gave you this command";
3:14: "If anyone refuses to obey what we say in this letter, note that man,
and have nothing to do with him").

The emphasis on tradition and obedience as correctives to perceived disorder is found in the Pastoral Epistles as well. Given the danger of "false"
speech, Titus and Timothy are warned to listen only to disciplined, orderly
speech transmitted by approved authorities.[18] Particularly interesting is Titus
1:10–11: "Paul" warns Titus to avoid the "many rebellious persons" (*anypotaktoi*, a cognate of *ataktos*) who are "empty talkers and deceivers"

(*mataiologoi kai phrenapatai*) and guilty of "upsetting entire households" (*holous oikous anatrepousin*) by usurping authority that is not properly theirs. The author's interest in the controlling possibilities of tradition is a feature of what Gail Corrington Streete has called "householder asceticism." The Pastoral Epistles reflect, in her interpretation, a competition between, on the one hand, "true" or "sound" asceticism characterized by discipline of the self for the sake of social harmony and, on the other hand, "false" asceticism designed to provoke.[19] "True" ascetic practice is founded in tradition and order. "False" ascetic practice is associated with itinerancy and challenges to accepted social roles. Both asceticisms promote discipline of the self, but their social strategies and goals are different.

2 Thessalonians, like the Pastoral Epistles, is concerned with the disorder caused by "rebellious brothers." A "false" doctrine has spread that has caused the community to be "shaken in mind" and "excited" (2:2). This upsetting doctrine, spread by "spirit, word or letter supposedly from us," is false and deceptive (2:2–3). The author urges the *ekklesia* to accept his authority and return to his gospel, a gospel that precludes that of his competitors. Apostolic authority, the author hopes, will control community upheaval and delimit truth (2:13–15). The author of 2 Thessalonians, therefore, like the author of the Pastoral Epistles, emphasizes "tradition" as the appropriate source of authority. Unfortunately for the author of 2 Thessalonians, his opponents claimed that they too were inspired by Paul. The battle for Paul—a battle waged not only by 2 Thessalonians but also by other Deutero-Pauline letters—was, in many ways, a battle for "tradition": Which words, letters, and teachings should be considered authentic and on what basis?[20] The strategy employed by the author of 2 Thessalonians was to argue that his words were in fact Paul's words. Indeed, the careful imitation of the vocabulary of 1 Thessalonians by the author testifies to just how seriously he set about his task.[21] Perhaps the author's emphasis on "tradition" and careful speech implies a related interest in disciplined, socially acceptable ascetic practice, an association more clearly made in the Pastoral Epistles.

Margaret MacDonald observes that the authors of Colossians and Ephesians also shared an interest in socially acceptable forms of disciplined practice. Like the Pastoral Epistles, Colossians and Ephesians sought to encourage practices that promote social harmony and protect the community from hostile outsiders. The endorsement of a strict household code found in these two Deutero-Pauline epistles was an "invisibility strategy" designed "to ensure that church members exceeded the most conservative standards of the day. Such measures would be especially important if a group was being criticized as a social irritant."[22] Abiding by overly rigid household codes, therefore, would allow the "social irritant" congregations to stay out of harm's way, at least to some extent. The apparent compromise with the world recommended by Colossians and Ephesians enabled the community to remain in "the heavenly body" while acting "like an invisible body."[23] This strategy contrasts, however, with the more provocative practices adopted by their opponents, especially sexual asceticism and a challenge to marriage. Colossians, Ephesians, and the Pastoral Epistles exhibit, therefore, a competition over discipline and authority that may be viewed as a battle about asceticisms. A comparable rivalry may have been present in the Thessalonian *ekklesia* as well.

Perhaps the author of 2 Thessalonians would have favored "household asceticism" over practices that overtly challenged social arrangements. He clearly demonstrates a concern for tradition and obedience. Nevertheless, unlike Ephesians, Colossians, and the Pastoral Epistles, the author of 2 Thessalonians makes no explicit reference to the household norms. He is specific, however, about the need for work and practice. Hearts are established by "every good work and word" (2:17). "Paul" has confidence in the *ekklesia*, for "they are doing and will do" the things he commands (3:4). He reminds them that "with toil and labor we worked night and day" to support ourselves (3:8). Thus, those who do not work cannot possibly be living up to the example of Paul. On the contrary, everyone who aspires to authentic faith must "do their work in quietness" and "earn their own bread" (3:12).

To the author of 2 Thessalonians, good work seems to include both work within and on behalf of the *ekklesia* as well as working for one's own living. Believers must not, the author argues, refrain from their regular labor. Some within the community are doing just that. These "false brothers" have stopped working for their bread, receiving bread from the *ekklesia* instead. Their activity—the "work" that keeps them from truly working and thus earning their own bread—is characterized as useless, the "work" of "busybodies" (3:11). Why is work such a problem, especially worldly work, work that enables one to earn a livelihood? If the group that had claimed that the day of the Lord had already come is the same group that here refuses regular work, then perhaps we can surmise something about the "useless" work in which they were engaged.

According to Helmut Koester, the belief in the nearness of the day of the Lord led to behavior that "is characterized by the turning away from the pursuits of the world to the enthusiastic expectation of a change that is to come soon." [24] The author of 2 Thessalonians introduces discussion of the day of the Lord in the following way: "We beg you, brothers, concerning the coming of our Lord Jesus Christ and our meeting him, not to be quickly shaken in mind or excited by spirit, word or letter supposedly from us, that the day of the Lord has come" (2:1–2). Could those who believed that the day of the Lord has come have attempted to avoid work on the premise that they would soon be meeting him (the Lord)? Koester has suggested as much. On the other hand, perhaps those who were engaged in "useless" work and accepted payment for it saw themselves as spiritual leaders, worthy of their keep.

The suggestion that the *ataktoi* were spiritual enthusiasts who accepted payments for their services is often made.[25] A fitting comparison may be the "super apostles" of Corinth who so upset Paul. They accepted payment from the Corinthian churches in return for some kind of spiritual service (2 Cor. 11:1–15; 12:13).[26] In response, Paul calls them "false apostles" and "deceitful workers." Dieter Georgi considers the opponents of Paul to be spirit-filled leaders who demanded monetary compensation from their admirers as an acknowledgment of their transcendent spirituality.[27] Such a practice was not uncommon at the time.[28] Thus, two plausible explanations of the "work" of the *ataktoi* are available: First, that they, along with others, had exempted themselves from daily labor due to the belief that the parousia was imminent, and second, that they were spiritual adepts who were paid for their services. A third possibility is that the *ataktoi* adopted the stance of itinerant Cynic-type philosophers who begged for their support.[29] Lack of specific evidence makes it difficult if not impossible to conclusively determine the practical content of their behavior. Yet, they were clearly engaged in a set of activities that brought them material support and that the author found tremendously disturbing.

The rivals of the authors of the Pastoral Epistles, Colossians, and Ephesians probably did engage in "disturbing" practices commonly labeled "ascetic." Interpreters of the Pastoral Epistles frequently assume that the group or groups being attacked by the author were ascetics, persons who encouraged itinerancy, discredited marriage, avoided certain foods, promoted household upset, and included women who were not married.[30] Using Valantasis' definition of asceticism, Streete characterizes the asceticism of the opponents of the "Paul" of the Pastoral Epistles as "combative." [31] This type of asceticism is vehemently opposed by the same "Paul." "True" asceticism, according to the Pastoral Epistles, is "integrative." It resists not society or authority but individual desire, stressing self-control and socially useful self-discipline.[32] MacDonald discovered a similar dynamic in Colossians and Ephesians, although she views the emphasis on household order in these two letters as a survival strategy rather than a straightforward move toward social accommodation. Colossians in particular, she argues, "wages a battle on two fronts, rejecting one type of asceticism while fervently propounding another." [33] Unfortunately, the author of 2 Thessalonians did not offer enough of a description of the "useless" work of his rivals to call comfortably their activity "ascetic." Perhaps it is not too much of a stretch to imagine, however, that a conflict between combative and integrative ascetics may lie behind some of the rhetoric present in 2 Thessalonians. The author's repeated insistence on the value of work is suggestive in this regard.

Although work in the form of physical labor or the plying of a trade was considered demeaning by many Greco-Roman moralists, it was recommended for those in financial need.[34] Moralists such as Dio Chrysostom and Musonius Rufus encouraged the poor to work with their own hands. In some circumstances, even philosophers were urged to work.[35] As the author of 2 Thessalonians attempted to remind his readers, Paul himself emphasized the value of work, both on behalf of the community and to meet one's own material needs (1 Thess. 1:3; 4:11). Thus, by insisting on the importance of work, the author of 2 Thessalonians agreed with the moralists of his day, including the "authentic" Paul. Perhaps the author wanted to avoid an association by hostile outsiders between the Thessalonian *ekklesia* and social misfits, such as Cynics, who opted out of traditional work in favor of an assertive world-critical lifestyle and rhetoric.[36] Such a hypothesis may help explain the author's insistence that authentic faith necessarily includes work, both on behalf of the *ekklesia* and to earn one's own living. Still, can the work that the author of 2 Thessalonians recommends be considered "ascetic?"

Drawing upon Valantasis, I argued earlier in this chapter that ascetic practices construct subjectivity by means of disciplined actions with intended social implications and consequences. Working, earning one's own living, requires, it seems, a type of discipline. The believers in Thessalonica, finding the world utterly corrupt, enduring some kind of trouble, waiting for an end-time reversal when they will be finally vindicated, were instructed to continue their regular daily work, adding to it meeting and working on behalf of their "brothers." Could such work legitimately be considered a type of ascetic discipline? If it is the case that living according to a rigid household code or affirming the importance of careful control of speech and tradition are types of asceticism, then why not include work among the list of ascetic disciplines?

Members of the Thessalonian community were exhorted, even commanded, to participate in disciplined daily work. As we have seen, asceticism, that is, disciplined practice aimed at the transformation of the self and the world, can serve as a social survival strategy and as social critique.[37] Perhaps, in the context of 2 Thessalonians, the work that the author demands was a type of ascetic practice aimed at survival. In a context in which the world is so thoroughly denied, the daily toil of working for a living takes on the character of an ascetic discipline.[38] By challenging the value of socially acceptable work, the opponents may have favored an alternative, more combative approach to daily living. By insisting that daily work must continue, the author advocated a less overt critique of the corrupt world. If so, then the battle over work reflected in 2 Thessalonians may be another example of the competitive asceticisms apparent in other Deutero-Pauline letters.

CONCLUSION

A reading of 2 Thessalonians in light of asceticism has called to our attention the range of possible responses to a world that was condemned as corrupt. In her study of Colossians and Ephesians, MacDonald remarked that the question of asceticism enabled her "to see more clearly how traditional ethics allowing for the preservation of many aspects of conventional life may work in conjunction with an ethos where the world is nevertheless rejected in a profound sense."[39] Such is the perspective of the author of 2 Thessalonians. Although the author encourages members of the Thessalonian *ekklesia* to continue their usual work, avoiding the "false" view that the day of the Lord has come, he certainly does not expect the Thessalonians to embrace the world. On the contrary, the world is characterized by falsehood and delusion, a corruption that will only get worse as the day of the Lord gets closer and the "man of lawlessness" is revealed (2:3–12). Both the author of 2 Thessalonians and his rivals reject the world, but they choose different strategies for living in it. Like the author, the opponents have adopted for themselves an alternative symbolic universe, which includes a belief in the corruption of the present time. The issue between the author and his opponents revolves around the relative nearness of the final vindication rather than the proper orientation to the world. Both author and opponents may be described as proponents of new subjectivities that challenge previous social arrangements and reject previous modes of existence to some degree.

Nevertheless, the lack of detailed evidence regarding the actual practices of either the author or his opponents makes us reluctant to speak of 2 Thessalonians as a representative of ascetic literature and thought. As noted earlier, the close relationship between asceticism and apocalyptic thought has already been recognized. Wimbush suggested that apocalyptic thought "represented an unstudied response on the part of some who defined themselves as outsiders, as enemies of the prevailing order."[40] Apocalyptic thought rejects the present world as corrupt. Asceticism, on the other hand, both rejects and seeks to transform. Ascetic behavior, therefore, may be viewed as an attempt to convert a perceived rejection *by* the world into a rejection *of* the world through disciplined practice. By rejecting the perceived rejecters, asceticism turns rejection on its head. Ascetics do not simply reject the world, they seek to provoke it, challenge it, and force it to change, albeit in small, individual increments.[41]

A study of 2 Thessalonians vis-à-vis the question of asceticism has demonstrated to me just how complex varieties of world-critical practices and strategies can be. Whether or not the author of 2 Thessalonians or his rivals should properly be considered ascetic, their shared desire for transformation and escape from the present world is clear. Both the author and his opponents sought a new world and a new self in which the "saints" would be glorified in Christ and Christ in them. To that end, they developed eschatological timetables, sought to represent the "true" Paul and the different signs that he left them, and either challenged or affirmed the value of work "for now" in anticipation of a final vindication that would turn their perceived rejection into a magnificent affirmation of the fact that they, and they alone, knew the truth.

NOTES

1. For the view that 2 Thessalonians is pseudo-Pauline, see W. Trilling, *Der zweite Brief an die Thessalonicher* (Zürich, Switzerland: Benziger, 1980); W. Marxsen, *Der zweite Thessalonicherbrief* (Zürich, Switzerland: Theologischer, 1982); F. W. Hughes, *Early Christian Rhetoric and 2 Thessalonians* (Sheffield, England: Journal for the Study of the Old Testament, 1989); F. Laub, *Erster und zweiter Thessalonicherbrief* (Würzburg, Germany: Echter, 1985); M. J. J. Menken, *2 Thessalonians* (London: Routledge, 1994). For the argument that Pauline authorship must not be discounted, see R. Jewett, *The Thessalonian Correspondence* (Philadelphia: Fortress, 1986). Helmut Koester directly refutes Jewett's argument in "From Paul's Eschatology to the Apocalyptic Schemata of 2 Thessalonians," *The Thessalonian Correspondence,* ed. R. Collins (Leuven, The Netherlands: Leuven University Press, 1990), 441–58.

2. In a recent article, F. Laub has argued that the identity of the letter must be 1 Thessalonians, which the author of 2 Thessalonians carefully imitates in order to correct and clarify the proper understanding of Pauline eschatology. See F. Laub, "Paulinische Autorität in nachpaulinischer Zeit," in *Thessalonian Correspondence,* ed. Collins, 403–7. For an alternate view, see Hughes, *Early Christian Rhetoric,* 86–95, who concludes that the "letter purportedly from us" may well be Colossians or Ephesians. These letters, with their theology of fulfilled eschatology, represent something like the view that 2 Thessalonians is interested in disputing.

3. The author of 2 Thessalonians invokes the authority of Paul repeatedly: 2:5, 15; 3:4, 6-10. The epistolary postscript is most striking: "The greeting is in my—Paul's—hand, which is the sign in every letter of how I write" (3:17). By emphasizing that Paul himself has signed this letter in, as Menken puts it, a "somewhat overdone" manner, the author of 2 Thessalonians further insists that it is his view, his letter, that truly reflects the intentions of Paul himself. See Menken, *2 Thessalonians,* 35–36, 144–45. For a discussion of the use of the apostolic authority of Paul in 2 Thessalonians, see also G. Holland, "A Letter Supposedly from Us," in *Thessalonians Correspondence,* ed. Collins, 401; A. G. van Aarde, "The Struggle Against Heresy in the Thessalonian Correspondence and the Origin of the Apostolic Tradition," in *Thessalonian Correspondence,* ed. Collins, 423; Trilling, *Der zweite Brief,* 39–68.

4. Hughes, *Early Christian Rhetoric,* 57ff.

5. Vincent L. Wimbush, "Introduction," in *Ascetic Behavior in Greco-Roman Antiquity: A Sourcebook,* ed. Vincent L. Wimbush (Studies in Antiquity and Christianity, Minneapolis, Minn.: Fortress, 1990), 2.

6. The nature of the *diogmoi* or *thlipseis* referred to by the author of 2 Thessalonians is not clear. What is important is that the author perceives the world as eminently hostile to his community.

7. Cf. David E. Aune, *Prophecy in Early Christianity* (Grand Rapids, Mich.: Eerdmans, 1983), 107–21.

8. Wimbush, "Introduction," 4.

9. Richard Valantasis, "Constructions of Power in Asceticism," *Journal of the American Academy of Religion* 63 (1995): 775–821.

10. Valantasis (this volume, 211–230).

11. Cf. Anthony Saldarini (this volume, 11–28).

12. See Geoffrey Galt Harpham, *The Ascetic Imperative in Culture and Criticism* (Chicago: University of Chicago Press, 1987), xiv–xv, 27–28; Michel Foucault, *The Care of the Self*, trans. R. Hurley (New York: Random House, 1988), 64–68; Peter Brown, *The Body and Society* (New York: Columbia University Press, 1988), 179–84, 210–338; Wimbush, "*Sophrosyne*: Greco-Roman Origins of a Type of Ascetic Behavior," in *Gnosticism and the Early Christian World* (Sonoma, Calif.: Polebridge, 1990), 91–101; also Saldarini (this volume, 11–28).

13. Jewett, *Thessalonian Correspondence*, 104.

14. C. Spicq, "Les Thesalonicians," *Notes de Lexicographie Neo-Testamentaire* (1978) 1:159.

15. Harpham, *Ascetic Imperative*, xv–xvi.

16. Koester, "From Paul's Eschatology," 456.

17. Trilling, *Der zweite Brief*, 39–68.

18. Gail Corrington Streete (this volume, 299–316).

19. Ibid.

20. See C. Vander Strichele, "The Concept of Tradition and 1 and 2 Thessalonians," in *Thessalonian Correspondence*, ed. Collins, 499–504. Cf. Dennis R. MacDonald, *The Legend and the Apostle: The Battle for Paul in Story and Canon* (Philadelphia: Westminster Press, 1983).

21. See Franz Laub, "Paulinische Autorität in nachpaulinischer Zeit," in *Thessalonian Correspondence*, ed. Collins, 403. Cf. Mark Kiley, *Colossians as Pseudepigraphy* (Sheffield, England: Journal of the Study of the Old Testament, 1986), 76–91.

22. Margaret MacDonald (this volume, 269–298).

23. Ibid.

24. Koester, "From Paul's Eschatology," 456.

25. Jewett, *Thessalonian Correspondence*, 144–53.

26. See Dieter Georgi, *The Opponents of Paul in Second Corinthians* (Philadelphia: Fortress, 1986), 243–44.

27. Ibid.

28. See Ronald F. Hock, *The Social Context of Paul's Ministry: Tentmaking and Apostleship* (Philadelphia: Fortress, 1980), 50–59.

29. See James A. Francis, *Subversive Virtue: Asceticism and Authority in the Second-Century Pagan World* (Pennsylvania: Pennsylvania State University Press, 1995), 60–66; Ramsay MacMullen, *Enemies of the Roman Order* (Cambridge, Mass.: Harvard University Press, 1966), 59–61.

30. Streete (this volume, 299–316).

31. Ibid.

32. Ibid.

33. MacDonald (this volume, 269–298).

34. Hock, *Social Context*, 44.

35. Ibid. 44–47. On the disdain of daily, practical labor by Stoics in particular, see MacMullen, *Enemies*, 50–54.

36. See Leif E. Vaage, "Like Dogs Barking: Cynic *parresia* and Shameless Asceticism," in *Discursive Formations, Ascetic Piety and the Interpretation of Early Christian Literature,* ed. Vincent L. Wimbush (Atlanta, Ga.: Scholars, *Semeia* 57, 1992), 25–40.

37. Saldarini (this volume, 11–28).

38. Cf. James E. Goehring, "The World Engaged: The Social and Economic World of Early Egyptian Monasticism," in *Gnosticism and the Early Christian World*, eds. James E. Goehring, C. W. Hedrick, and J. T. Sanders (Sonoma, Calif.: Polebridge, 1990), 134–44, esp. 135, who noticed that in early Egyptian monasticism monks worked in ways that made the supposed gap between the desert and the inhabited world more rhetorical than actual. Monks were engaged in agriculture, handiwork, crafts such as shoemaking, and the selling of their wares at neighboring villages.

39. MacDonald this volume, 269–298).

40. Wimbush, "Introduction," 4.

41. Elizabeth Castelli (this volume, 171–186).

Citizens of Heaven and Earth: Asceticism and Social Integration in Colossians and Ephesians

Margaret Y. MacDonald

PAST APPROACHES AND NEW DIRECTIONS SUGGESTED BY CURRENT STUDIES OF ASCETICISM

My first reaction to the invitation to write this chapter was one of enthusiasm. The topic of asceticism is a fascinating one, and the thought of participating in a small conference with many opportunities for meaningful discussion was appealing. But as the conference date approached, my enthusiasm was replaced by some uncertainty. Asceticism has not figured prominently in discussions of Colossians and Ephesians to date, which inevitably raises the question of whether asceticism as a category of analysis sheds light on these documents. There is clearly an ascetic component in the false teaching of the Colossian "errorists," but it has received attention mainly in attempts to locate the origins of the false teaching in syncretistic or mystery religions, Judaism, or philosophical schools.[1] It remains to be seen whether, considered on their own terms, the brief references to ascetic elements can elucidate problems in Colossae. With very few exceptions, commentaries and articles on Ephesians ignore asceticism or mention it only in passing. Asceticism is most frequently discussed there as a historical catalyst to the strong reinforcement of traditional marriage arrangements in Eph. 5:22–33. Ascetic "false teaching" is proposed as forming part of the background leading to these instructions. But unlike the Pastoral Epistles, where marriage is also encouraged, Ephesians contains no clear indication of an attempt to respond to ascetic currents (cf. 1 Tim. 5:3–16). Narrow definitions of asceticism appear to have very little bearing upon our understanding of Ephesians.

However, as I began to familiarize myself with some of the current scholarship, it became clear to me that the study of asceticism in the ancient world involves much more than identifying specific ascetic practices and teachings. My fears about an inappropriately short chapter were largely alleviated as I started to think about asceticism as a multifaceted phenomenon that must be broadly defined. For example, in his introduction to *Ascetic Behavior in Greco-Roman Antiquity: A Sourcebook*, Vincent Wimbush states: "Ascetic behavior represents *a range of responses* to social, political, and physical worlds often perceived as oppressive or unfriendly, or as stumbling blocks to the pursuit of heroic personal or communal goals, life styles, and commitments."[2] (italics mine). The response(s) to the world demonstrated in Colossians and Ephesians was one of the main issues that occupied my attention in *The Pauline Churches*.[3] Thus, working on this chapter has offered me an opportunity to revisit some of my earlier conclusions.

Athough interpreters of Colossians and Ephesians have tended to restrict the use of the concept of asceticism to the labeling of particular practices of "opponents," recent scholarship on asceticism calls for a much broader application of the concept. We might, for example, consider the following definition of asceticism by Richard Valantasis, which, together with the complementary definition by Vincent Wimbush just cited, has informed my analysis in this essay: "Asceticism may be defined as performances within a dominant social environment intended to inaugurate a new subjectivity, different social relations, and an alternative symbolic universe."[4] As will be illustrated in this chapter, when asceticism is defined in this way, it is evident that the concept can elucidate not only the perspectives of the opponents of the authors of Colossians and Ephesians, but also the perspectives of the authors themselves. It is especially clear that the author of Colossians rejects a specific type of ascetic performance, one that involves physical indicators of world rejection and visible signs of identity. But the author clearly also has in mind a particular type of ascetic performance that should be embraced by the community. The author wages a battle on two fronts, rejecting one type of asceticism while fervently propounding another, intentionally directing the audience "toward an alternative mode of existence within a dominant social environment."[5]

For me to be as clear as possible about the approach I am adopting in this chapter, it is valuable for me to explain in what sense I am building on previous work. I considered Colossians and Ephesians together in the *The Pauline Churches* because they seemed to reflect similar stages of development, including similar responses to the dominant social environment. The close connection is, no doubt, the result of the probable dependence of Ephesians on Colossians.[6] But even at points where the documents differ we see evidence of a similar ethos: one that favors unity, integration, cosmic harmony, and participation in divine fullness. During the course of my previous work on Colossians and Ephesians I found it useful to imagine these letters as belonging to an intermediate stage in the institutionalization of the Pauline communities.[7] Using sociological analysis of sects as a tool for analysis, I identified a tension visible in Paul's communities between the desire to win new members and the desire to remain separate from the evil world.[8] In the trajectory extending from the undisputed letters to the Pastoral Epistles, I noted evidence of increased hostility between the church and the Greco-Roman world, yet a growing interest on the part of the church in social respectability. Although I recognized in Colossians and Ephesians some of the strong sense of opposition to the world that is characteristic of Paul's earlier letters, these later writings struck me as moving in the direction of the Pastorals with respect to the desire to appease tension in relation to outsiders. I judged the introduction of the household code into Pauline literature via Colossians (subsequently taken up in Ephesians) to be an especially strong indication of this tendency. Household codes offer indisputable evidence of the merging of traditional Greco-Roman ethics with early church exhortation. Moreover, there is significant evidence contemporary with Colossians and Ephesians to support the theory that New Testament household codes served an apologetic function. Traditional household ethics appear to have filled an apologetic purpose in some Jewish texts in the ancient world, and the household code of 1 Peter offers clear evidence of church ethics being shaped by a desire to appease strained relations with the outside world (1 Pet. 2:18–3:7; cf. 2:15; 3:15–16).[9]

I have not completely abandoned all of my earlier conclusions. However, working with the category of asceticism has enabled me to gain a greater appreciation of what is distinctive about the response(s) to the world exhibited by Colossians and Ephesians. For example, it has enabled me to see more clearly how traditional ethics' allowing for the preservation of many aspects of conventional life may work in conjunction with an ethos that nevertheless rejects the world in a profound sense. Not only do I feel that I have a greater understanding of how Colossians and Ephesians together constitute a particular strain of the Pauline heritage, but I also believe that working with the category of asceticism has alerted me to subtle differences in the patterns of life recommended by these documents.

I will begin my treatment of the individual documents with an analysis of texts indicating how one should deal with outsiders and the world (the dominant social environment). Both the scope of my previous work on attitudes to the world in Colossians and Ephesians and the fact that using asceticism as a category of analysis invites a focus on the encouragement of acceptance of "an alternative mode of existence" have led me to choose this starting point. In setting forth "an alternative mode of existence," Colossians and Ephesians employ many of the terms commonly associated with the identity of the Pauline churches.[10] Language of belonging works together with language of separation in the process of creating self-definition.[11] In Colossians and Ephesians the language of separation primarily takes the form of a remembrance of "conversion"—transference from the evil world outside into the "body" where salvation is found (e.g., Col. 1:13–14, 21–23; Eph. 4:17–24). Typically, remembrance of acceptance of the gospel and baptism is followed by ethical exhortations that set church members' behavior apart from the behavior of others. Because characterizations of the outside world take place within discussions of the dangers of church members' slipping back into evil ways rather than within explicit analyses of the outside world, it is easy to underestimate the strength of the opposition to the outside world. In fact, the allusions in Ephesians to the nature of existence outside of the body of Christ are among the most pessimistic in all of the New Testament.

COLOSSIANS

At one point Colossians reveals an explicit interest in relations between church members and nonbelievers. In Col. 4:5–6 the term "outsiders" (*tous exo*) is employed, drawing a definite line between those inside the community who are being saved and those outsiders who are not. In Paul's letters this term serves a boundary-drawing function, as part of a call for members to focus on internal matters concerning morality (1 Cor. 5:12ff.). Ethical exhortation includes the recommendation that one behave in a manner that commands the respect of outsiders (1 Thess. 4:12). Paul certainly believes that the community's interaction with outsiders can lead to the expansion of the church, as his description of the possible outcome of unbelievers' observing the worship of the Corinthians makes clear (1 Cor. 14:23-25). The missionary potential of social interaction probably also inspires Paul's recommendations that aim to strike a balance between idolatry on the one hand and complete dissociation from nonbelievers on the other (e.g., 1 Cor. 10:14–33).

Dealing with Outsiders

As in the undisputed letters, Col. 4:5–6 combines a strong sense of distinction from outsiders, an interest in the expansion of the church, and a plea for appropriate behavior in relation to nonbelievers. The prayer for the success of Paul's mission (Col. 4:2–4) supports the contention that the call in v. 5 for believers to make the most of time (or to use every opportunity) refers to evangelism (cf. 2 Thess. 3:1–2).[12] Indeed, Colossians depicts the church-in-Christ as an entity expanding to fill the world (Col. 1:6, 18–20, 23; 2:9–10, 19). However, in comparison to the undisputed epistles, Col. 4:5–6 displays a stronger awareness that relations with outsiders can be perilous. Conducting oneself wisely toward outsiders necessitates a prudent choice of words—speech that is "seasoned with salt."[13] The aspiration of knowing proper or effective responses to others is a tacit acknowledgment that wrong responses can lead to jeopardy, and it also may imply an atmosphere of competition between groups (cf. Col. 2:4; 1 Tim. 5:13–15). Here, the church at Colossae is being instructed to take every advantage of the opportunity for dialogue, but to take care not to harm delicate relations with outsiders. The sentiments expressed in Col. 4:5–6 are similar to those of 1 Pet. 3:15–16, where even more perilous relations with outsiders are in view. The community is instructed to always be ready to make a defense (*apologian*) to anyone who challenges them concerning their faith, although their dealings with nonbelievers still should be characterized by gentleness and reverence.

Col. 4:5–6 reveals an attitude to the world that is cognizant of the expansion of the church and is open to new members, but invites caution in dealing with outsiders. It seems likely that tension between the church and the world is on the rise. It is interesting to consider whether such tension has anything to do with the nature of the author's response to the Colossian false teaching—a problem that is usually identified as being at the heart of the document's purpose. Chapter 2 reveals that the author of Colossians is deeply concerned about deviance from the gospel that had been delivered to the community by Epaphras (cf. Col. 1:5–8). One may debate whether the Colossian false teaching involves the influence of an external group or groups or is largely an intrachurch phenomenon, but from the perspective of those labeling their opponents, deviance is most often perceived as moving people from inside to outside. This, at least, is how the author of Colossians sees the situation. Adherence to false teaching is depicted as regression into the world. The author asks a pointed question designed to warn recipients of the consequences of deviance: "If with Christ you died to the elemental spirits of the universe, why do you live as though you still belonged to the world?" (Col 2:20, NRSV). In essence, adopting the various rites and practices that are condemned in chapter 2 means no longer living in Christ (Col. 2:6), but living in the world. The teaching that can take one captive is further described in Col. 2:8 variously as philosophy, empty deceit, according to human tradition (cf. Col. 2:22), according to the elements of the universe, and not according to Christ. This broad generalization also effectively labels all that is outside of the church (or outside of the author's vision of the church) as evil, despite the possibility that the adherents to the "philosophy" themselves may have insisted upon the centrality of Christ to their experiences.

The references in v. 20 to the "elements of the universe" (*ta stoicheia tou kosmou*) have been extensively discussed and variously interpreted in the context of attempts to categorize the false teaching (Col. 2:8, 20; cf. Gal. 4:3,

9).[14] The elements of the universe have sometimes been equated with the "powers and principalities" (Col. 2:10, 15) and associated with the worship of angels (Col. 2:18). It has been suggested that the opponents sought to establish a proper relationship with spiritual beings by means of certain ritual and ascetic acts, in the hope of participating in divine fullness. But scholars have noted that philological evidence from the first century supports a straightforward understanding of these "elements" as the four elements of the universe (i.e., earth, water, air, fire).[15] Furthermore, a survey of the evidence has convinced Eduard Schweizer of the existence of a widespread conviction in antiquity that "the four elements, though originally in a harmony of equilibrium, were continually threatening the existence of the world by their 'mighty strife'...and their unending interchange."[16] Against such perceptions, the Christ hymn (Col. 1:15–20) proclaimed the once and for all reconciliation of all things on heaven and earth through Christ. In other words, in referring to the elements of the universe, the author might be stressing the error of the false teaching by exaggerating its connection with worldly (or cosmic), unstable, and, in the author's opinion, ultimately base phenomena. Against the notion that the *stoicheia* play a central role in the rituals of the Colossian opponents, it has been noted that the author of Colossians assumes that his audience will share his negative evaluation of life according to the elements of the universe; the point needs no justification.[17] Whatever the precise meaning of the *stoicheia*, it is clear that they figure in the author's polemic to reinforce the message that "shifting from the hope promised by the gospel" (Col. 1:23; NRSV) means the acceptance of worldly teaching against Christ (cf. Col. 2:20).

The depiction of acceptance of false teaching as a kind of regression into the world is found elsewhere in Paul's letters. Gal. 4:3–11, for example, where life outside of the church also is associated with the elements of the universe, speaks of a turning back to erroneous ways. In Galatians it is evident that the problem involves Judaizing teachers who have infiltrated the community and are instructing Gentiles to accept aspects of the Mosaic law. But in the opinion of some commentators, the dispute in Colossians is unlike the conflict with opponents in Galatians, and in other letters, in that Colossians fails to reveal the fire of a particular historical battle. In addition, the confidence in the faith of the community that is expressed in Col. 2:5 (cf. Col. 1:3–8) has struck some scholars as inconsistent with the kind of crisis situation underlying Galatians. Thus the question has arisen of whether Colossians is responding to a particular group of false teachers who have infiltrated the community.[18] The problem with a negative answer to this question is of course that it makes identifying the purpose of the letter much more difficult. After years of careful analysis scholars have failed to arrive at a consensus about the false teaching in Colossae as the product of Judaism, paganism, or a syncretistic combination of these or as inspired by gnosticism, mystery religions, or such philosophical traditions as Stoicism and Pythagoreanism. This lack of consensus precludes narrow solutions to the problem of determining the purpose of the letter.[19] In my view, the author's response leaves little doubt that the threat of false teaching is real, and the document reflects grave concern about the problem of deviance. Nevertheless, decades of examination of the supposed Colossian heresy against the background of the ancient world has made it seem increasingly clear that the heresy might not have been the position of one particular party, but rather "a set of traditions widely affirmed and practiced."[20]

Asceticism and False Teaching

So much concern about attaching the correct label to the problem in Colossae in fact may have blinded scholars to certain consistent elements in the false teaching that actually cut across the categories we usually employ to make sense of the ancient world. If we consider those texts that we are confident contain explicit statements about the content of the false teaching as opposed to possible allusions to it,[21] a sustained interest in discouraging ascetic practices emerges. Significantly, the ascetic tendencies of the supposed Colossian heresy are a unifying element among otherwise quite diverse practices and traditions. The presence of an ascetic component in the Colossian false teaching has consistently been recognized, but it has not received the detailed attention one might expect.[22] In particular, scholars have not fully explored the role played by asceticism in generating the negative reaction of the author of Colossians to the false teaching.

Scholars are confident that we may draw information about the content of the false teaching from Col. 2:16, 18, 20–23. The ascetic component of Col. 2:16 is perhaps least obvious. It provides evidence that the teaching critiqued by the author of Colossians includes Jewish elements: dietary regulations and observances of the Sabbath and festivals.[23] However, the reference to passing judgment on matters of food and drink also invites comparison to possible references to fasting in Col. 2:18 and 2:23. It is also important to note that what is being opposed here involves visible markers of identity, including food taboos and ritual celebrations. I will make clear later the significance of this aspect of the false teaching in relation to asceticism.

Col. 2:18 contains a term (*tapeinophrosyne*) that scholars consistently identify as part of the vocabulary of the false teachers. Although it can be used by the author of Colossians in a positive way to refer to the virtue of humility (cf. Col. 3:12), this term is usually understood here in a technical sense as referring to self-abasement or self-denial, which the author judges negatively. Early church authors use the term specifically to refer to fasting (e.g., Herm. *Vis.* 3.10.6; *Sim.* 5.3.7). The connection of "self-abasement" with visions and worship in this passage has suggested comparison to Jewish texts where fasting (or other rigors of devotion) is linked to visions.[24] The expression "angel's worship" (*threskeia ton aggelon*) has received significant attention. Traditionally, the expression has been translated (as an objective genitive) to mean "worship directed at angels." But, in light of literary evidence, some scholars translate the phrase (as a subjective genitive) as "angelic worship," that is, participation in some type of angelic liturgy.[25] Practitioners of the supposed Colossian heresy may have sought to participate in, or behold, angelic liturgies in the heavenly realm.[26] It would be going beyond the constraints imposed by the ambiguities in the evidence to say that Col. 2:18 refers to fasting as a method of inducing visions of worshiping angels, a worship in which practitioners believed they also shared. But the studies of this verse against the Jewish and pagan background of the ancient Mediterranean world have meant that we can be confident in seeing a connection between ritual, visionary experience, and ascetic practices in the Colossian false teaching.

Col. 2:20–23 adds support to the notion that the ascetic practices critiqued by the author of Colossians involve fasting and/or food and drink taboos. Community members are said to be submitting to regulations that the author describes sarcastically as a series of don'ts. Among the regulations is the command not to taste. It is interesting to note that the command not to hold (or touch: *haptesthai*; cf. *hapto*) employs the same terminology as the slogan of the Corinthian ascetics: "It is well for a man not to touch a woman" (1 Cor. 7:1).[27] I am convinced that the possibility that sexual asceticism is in view in Colossians should be considered seriously, although this assessment has not yet won wide approval by scholars. It is true that there is no explicit internal evidence that links the supposed heresy with the avoidance of sex, but the terminology is often broad enough to allow for sexual asceticism. This is particularly true of Col. 2:20 and of the reference to the severe treatment of the body in Col. 2:23. It is widely recognized that in the early church—and the ancient world generally—fasting and sexual asceticism frequently occur together. Deutero-Pauline literature provides a fine example of this conjunction of practices in the form of a reference to the false teaching combated by the author of the Pastoral Epistles (1 Tim. 4:3).[28] On the question of sexual asceticism in Colossians it is also worth reflecting upon the implications of the unmistakable legitimation of Christian marriage that occurs in the household code (Col. 3:18–4:1) and is made even stronger by the author of Ephesians (Eph. 5:21-6:9). In the Pastoral Epistles there is a direct relationship between strong encouragement of traditional marriage ethics and the curtailing of certain ascetic currents (e.g., 1 Tim. 5:11–16). There is perhaps not enough evidence to postulate that sexual asceticism is at the heart of the Colossian false teaching, but it may well have formed part of the "set of traditions" that the author of Colossians sought to counter.

Col. 2:23, a notoriously difficult verse to translate,[29] includes a second reference to humility or self-abasement (*tapeinophrosyne*; cf. Col. 2:18) and to severe treatment of the body (*apheidia somatos*). This last notion is a general reference to austerity, and it leaves open the possibility of a variety of ascetic performances involving physical renunciation. The author of Colossians understands these as threatening to the life of the community.[30] "Severe treatment of the body" may represent the author's own characterization of what those who accepted the regulations were doing, or it may be a label that the practitioners employed to express confidence in their own pursuits. The reference to severe treatment of the body invites comparison with Col. 2:11, where believers are said to have put off the body of flesh in the circumcision of Christ. This putting off of the body of flesh figures in an argument designed to convince the Colossians to remain faithful to Christ and not to be taken captive through "philosophy" (Col 2:8ff.). I will discuss Col. 2:11 in further detail later in this chapter, but the similar terminology raises questions about possible points of contact between the attitude of the author of Colossians toward renunciation and that of the opponents. It is clear, however, that the author disapproves of some means of renouncing or severely treating the body. They are mentioned in Col. 2:23 in conjunction with *ethelothreskia*, a term that may be translated somewhat awkwardly as "self-imposed or self-chosen worship or piety." As in Col. 2:18, asceticism appears to be directly related to ritual. Once again it is not certain whether this designation is being applied sarcastically by the author against those who accept false teaching to label their worship as purely human and worldly or whether it captures the group's self-designation, echoing their confidence in their achievements.[31] However, the author's judgment with respect to the opponents' claims and achievements is made clear by the evaluation underlying the subsequent phrase, *"hatina estin logon men echonta sophias"*—"these things [only] have the appearance of wisdom."

An intriguing phrase at the end of v. 23 offers the reason why the author judges the false teaching so negatively and may also shed light upon the motives of the opponents: "They are of no value in checking self-indulgence" (NRSV).[32] A more literal translation makes clear that the problem under dispute involves the containing of sensuality. The false teaching is of no value in checking the indulgence of "the flesh" (*tes sarkos*). It is important to recall here that the author of Colossians previously has described baptism (spiritual circumcision) as leading to the removal of the body of flesh (Col. 2:11). It seems likely that the containing of the indulgence of the flesh is something that both the author of Colossians and those who might be attracted to false teaching would desire. But the author clearly disagrees with the methods of containment recommended by the opponents. The author's main point seems to be that acceptance of the gospel and baptism are the basis of a life that holds the dangers of the flesh at bay. Measures recommended by the false teachers are not necessary and are, in fact, useless in checking the indulgence of the flesh. By no means, however, does the author of Colossians state that the struggle to separate from the evils of the world has been completely accomplished among believers. In chapter 3 the notion that church members have been raised with Christ (in baptism) provides justification for the appeal to believers to put to death all that is earthly, including a list of the vices associated with the children of disobedience (Col. 3:5ff.). In essence, life according to Christ involves participation in teaching, worship (including psalms, hymns, and spiritual songs; Col. 3:16), prayer (Col. 4:2–3), and an ethical stance that includes the household code (Col. 3:18–4:1).

Concerning Col. 2:23, two further points need to be considered that have to do with the attempt to draw the boundary between those who have been raised with Christ and nonbelievers. First, it is interesting to note that the term that is usually translated as "value" in Col. 2:23 is "honor" (*time*). Given the significant work of scholars concerning the importance of the categories of honor and shame in the biblical world, we should consider how our understanding of the text might be broadened by the concept of honor. For people in the ancient Mediterranean world, personal identity is connected to social identity: It is inextricably bound to public appraisal and concern for reputation.[33] Even the process of separating oneself from the outside world (cf. Col. 3:5) might still be validated to some degree by the judgment of outsiders. Certainly for Paul, the ritual setting seems to have been a place where concern for reputation was particularly acute. The eyes of witnesses could condemn or glorify (1 Cor. 14:23–25; cf. 1 Cor. 11:2–16).[34] The ritual and ascetic practices encouraged by the false teachers were visible markers of identity, and thus may have been treated by the author of Colossians as particularly strong indicators of the values of honor and shame to the outside world.

The problem of containing the indulgences of the flesh, which is raised by Col. 2:23 and may have been of concern to both the author of Colossians and to the opponents, also calls to mind Paul's recommendations in 1 Corinthians 7. Paul approves of celibacy for those who, like him, possess it as a special gift, and he connects the celibate state with freedom from the things of this world and the form of the world that is passing away. However, it is marriage that he recommends as a means of containing immorality. Passion clearly can corrupt the purity of the church (1 Cor. 7:2–9, 36–38).[35] Marriage keeps the line strong between what should be kept outside and what is inside the group. It is interesting to reflect on the question of whether the acceptance of the traditional arrangements of the household (Col. 3:18-4:1) is part of the solution that the author of Colossians offers to the problem of containing the indulgence of the flesh. A comparison of Colossians with 1 Corinthians 7 reveals definitively, however, the very strong stance of the author of Colossians against an asceticism involving physical signs of world rejection and visible markers of identity. In Colossians, such asceticism does not receive even qualified approval. As I will explain later, however, the author of Colossians nevertheless recommends a type of ascetic response to the world; it is one that calls believers to participate in "an alternative symbolic universe," but which insists that believers be physically integrated within the dominant social environment.

Heavenly Exaltation and Ritual

A survey of the explicit references to the content of the false teaching by the author of Colossians reveals a consistent critique of certain ascetic practices. We have very little information about what these practices specifically involved. They probably included some type of fasting, but they may also have involved sexual renunciation and other means of austerity. It is also clear that ascetic practices were linked to ritual observances in the supposed Colossian heresy. In fact, ritual is not only central to the conflict at Colossae, but also to the very shape of the text of Colossians. It is widely recognized that the Christ hymn of Col. 1:15–20 was a traditional hymn (an independent unit) that was inserted into the letter to reinforce its main argument. Occupying a central position in the letter, the hymn, with its accompanying interpretation in Col. 1:21–23, sets the stage for launching the attack on the content of the Colossian philosophy (Col. 2:8ff.). In essence, the combined effect of Col. 1:9–14 (a thanksgiving passage that also has a hymnic flavor) and Col. 1:15–23 is to remind the Colossians of what they already know. Words are proclaimed that they probably have often heard or sung. It is a strategy of remembrance and familiarity, a strategy designed to thwart deviance. It takes believers back to the beginning and reminds them of a particular worldview. The author presents a vision of the supremacy of Christ that is fundamentally related to the very process of separating from the evil world. This process involves being rescued from the power of darkness and being transferred into the kingdom of the beloved Son (Col. 1:13).[36] As the strategy of remembrance is put forth, frequent allusions to baptism work in conjunction with the hymnic influences (Col. 1:12–14; 2:11–15; 3:1–3, 10–11). Of particular importance for this discussion is Col. 2:11–15 because with this argument the author hopes to dissuade the Colossians from adopting the ascetic false teaching by appealing to the meaning of baptism.

Reference to the common experience of baptism reminds believers that they have already put off the body of flesh in the circumcision of Christ (Col. 2:11–12).[37] Although circumcision already had been discussed in a figurative sense in the Hebrew Bible (Deut. 10:16; Jer. 4:4; Ezek. 44:7) and in Paul's letters (Rom. 2:28–29; Phil. 3:3), the specific association of circumcision with baptism is made in Colossians.[38] This may be a sign that "circumcision" was a term employed by the opponents to refer either to a certain rite of initiation or to an alternate understanding of baptism.[39] Whatever the precise nature of the rites in question, the points of contact between the way baptism is described in Col. 2:11–15 and the criticism of the ascetic measures in Col. 2:16–23 make it appear highly likely that the significance of, and regulations surrounding, the removal of the "fleshly" body (Col. 2:11) were under dispute. The false teaching under attack in Colossians appears to envision a process whereby the removal of the "fleshly" body is continuously being realized or enacted by means of rituals closely associated with ascetic practices. An appeal to the members' experience of baptism serves the author of Colossians well as a refutation of this false teaching because it allows the author to instill a sense of finality and completion among the recipients. The description of baptism as burial and resurrection with Christ comes as a reminder that in this early church setting baptism could be understood as a dramatic reenactment of a once-and-for-all saving event. According to the author of Colossians, baptism marks the forgiveness of sins, the end of regulations (*dogmata*), and the ultimate triumph over principalities and powers (Col. 2:13–15; cf. 3:1–4).

Early Christian literature provides ample evidence that baptism was a powerful but somewhat ambiguous ritual that was variously interpreted in the early church. For example, comparison of Col. 3:10–11 with Gal. 3:27–28 and other texts (e.g., Clement of Alexandria, *Strom.* 3.13.92; *2 Clem.* 12.2; *Gos.Thom.* 37, 21a, 22b) that appear to draw upon the same (or a similar) traditional baptismal saying illustrates the wide range of possibilities.[40] In some cases the ancient baptismal formula is used in conjunction with garment imagery, which describes the removal of evil flesh in exchange for a transformed body. Dennis MacDonald has illustrated that in documents rooted in Valentinian gnosticism and early Syrian Christianity, the ancient baptismal saying was employed in conjunction with efforts to return to the perfect state of an androgynous creation where there would no longer be male and female.[41] The call for an ascetic departure from the world was proclaimed with such strong language as "tramping upon the garment of shame" (Clement of Alexandria, *Strom.* 3.13.92) and "destroying the works of the female" (*Strom.* 3.9.63). In everyday life, this state was acted out by means of the avoidance of sex altogether.

Despite the use of the baptismal tradition in Galatians to justify an innovative notion of the relation between Jews and Gentiles, 1 Corinthians 7 and 11:2–16 make it clear that Paul did not view incorporation into Christ as a return to androgynous perfection, nor did he support those in the community who pressed for complete avoidance of sex.[42] In Col. 3:10–11 there is no mention of the male/female pair, and some scholars have understood this omission as a sign of an attempt to harmonize the baptismal teaching with the traditional ethics of the household code.[43] But an understanding of the various permutations of the traditional baptismal saying leads to the suggestion that the absence of the male/female pair in Col. 3:11 may actually be due to the tendency for such language to be used in some circles as justification for severe treatment of the body (cf. Col. 2:23). It is interesting to note that despite the absence of the male/female pair, Col. 3:10–11 in some respects displays greater contact with the more ascetic versions of this formula than does Gal. 3:27–28. Col. 3:9–10 speaks of believers' having stripped off the old self with its practices and having clothed themselves with the new person (*ton neon*). There is clearly a connection here with the notion in Gal. 3:27 of putting on Christ. The new person is being renewed in full knowledge according to the image of his and/or her creator; in Col. 1:15, Christ is identified as the image of God. But the description of the new self also appears to be influenced by Gen. 1:26–27, where the human being is created in the image of God.[44] Putting on the new humanity in Colossians means sharing in (perhaps returning to) the perfection of creation. But it is clear that this new identity is to be lived out by means of a virtuous life that includes harmony among various cultural groups (Col. 3:11-15), and not severe treatment of the body.[45] Thus it is possible that underlying Col. 3:9–11 is a further attempt to respond to certain ascetic currents.

The appeal to baptism in an attempt to quell the false teaching in Colossians comes as a reminder that rituals could figure prominently in early church disputes. Against an earlier tendency to view doctrines at the center of religious controversy, more and more scholars are looking toward ritual and social life to explain aspects of early Christianity such as the conflict at Colossae. Questioning the supposition that the false teaching was necessarily less "christocentric" than Colossians, scholars are identifying the center of the author's objections as ascetic practices and visionary experiences.[46] The social order was threatened "because it offered the alternative of 'living like the angels' as a result of the visionary initiation."[47] In line with these scholars, I believe that the focus on christology forms part of the author's strategy to prevent deviance, especially deviant praxis, by reminding community members of what all hold in common and what is most important. In fact, there are indications in the text that the "Paul" of Colossians shares much of the same understanding of Christ as the opponents. Because of Christ believers have put off their bodies of flesh (Col. 2:11); they have triumphed with Christ over all cosmic powers (Col. 2:12–15), and the true focus of their longing is the heavenly realm (Col. 3:1–4). Both the stance of the author and of the opponents display a strong commitment to world rejection and to living out an alternative mode of existence. The "for or against Christ" choice presented by the author in Col. 2:8 to the recipients of the letter is, on the surface, doctrinal, but it should be understood as part of a larger strategy to outlaw specific ritual and ascetic practices as being incompatible with life in Christ.

As indicated earlier, there is good reason to suspect that the specific ritual and ascetic practices attacked by the author of Colossians were related to a particular vision of baptism. Social scientific studies of ritual are useful for understanding how ritual can figure so prominently in social conflict. Victor Turner's concept of *communitas* is especially helpful for shedding light upon the situation in Colossae:

> The bonds of communitas...are anti-structural in the sense that they are undifferentiated, equalitarian, direct, non-rational (though not irrational), I–Thou relationships. In the liminal phase of the [African] Ndembu rites of passage, and in similar rites the world over, communitas is engendered in ritual humiliation, stripping of signs and insignia of preliminal status, ritual leveling, and ordeals and tests of various kinds, intended to show that "man thou art dust!" In hierarchical social structures communitas is symbolically affirmed by periodic rituals... in which the lowly and the mighty reverse social roles. In such societies, too...the religious ideology of the powerful idealizes humility, orders of religious specialists undertake ascetic lives, and per contra, cult groups among those of low status play with symbols of power and authority.[48]

Turner's thought sheds light on the connection between baptism (a rite of passage), other rituals, and ascetic practices. It also helps locate what I believe to be at the root of the conflict in Colossae: the transition from anti-structured liminality back to social structures. The ascetic practices and ritual observances of the Colossian opponents are visible signs of their identity, indicators of their communitas. In social scientific thought, ritual action has been understood as fundamental to the process of creating the boundaries of a social group. In Turner's opinion, "one would not be stretching language unduly to say that its [ritual action's] symbolic behavior actually 'creates' society for pragmatic purposes—including both structure and communitas."[49] It is not surprising, therefore, that despite the indications of considerable convergence between the false teaching and the author's position, the opponents can be condemned as essentially belonging to another society: They are associated with human tradition and belong to the "world" (Col. 2:8, 20–23). Similarly, while it may first appear as a standard manner of chastising opponents, the charge of arrogance in Colossians is probably rooted in a fundamental threat to group identity (Col. 2:16–18).

Social Integration and Household Ethics

At this point, it is valuable to return to a question raised earlier: Does the evidence for rising tension between the church and the world revealed by Col. 3:5–6 have anything to do with the nature of the author's response to the Colossian false teaching? An understanding of the ritual observances and ascetic practices of the Colossians as visible signs of identity suggests that there may well have been a connection. First, it is important to note that ritual and asceticism are closely related to visionary experience in the Colossian false teaching. Paul's treatment of his opponents in 2 Corinthians and his attempts to control the enthusiastic worship of the Corinthians reveal a good deal of ambivalence about visions and ecstatic phenomena and an awareness that such displays were subject to misunderstanding both inside and outside of the church (cf. 1 Cor. 14; 2 Cor. 5:11–13; 12:1–7). Believers could lose sight of their priorities and outsiders could be turned away. The risks may have seemed even greater to one who subsequently wrote in Paul's name. Second, scholarly work on early Christian women has revealed that asceticism in church circles could act as an irritant in Greco-Roman society.[50] If the asceticism that is rebuked in Colossians was rooted in a conviction that to remove the body of flesh meant a return to a primordial state of perfection when there was neither male nor female, we can only imagine that the controversy would have been heightened. Such a view may be implied by the use of the ancient baptismal teaching in Col. 3:11. Indeed, the risks of public visibility may have contributed to Paul's negative response in 1 Cor. 11:2–16 against women symbolically acting like men. Finally, it is important to remember that in the social world, there is a connection between a person's social visibility and social ranking. The criticism of ascetic measures in Colossians invites comparison to Ignatius, *Pol.* 5.1–2. There, in the context of marriage instructions that resemble the household codes of Colossians and Ephesians, the bishop is warned of the dangers of physical renunciation leading to arrogance. In fact, those who boast of their continence may well perish! While Ignatius' response to physical renunciation is not as negative as that of the author of Colossians, I suspect that some of the same social forces are at work. Polycarp is instructed to test the motives of those who remain continent to the honor of the Lord's flesh by requiring of them the ultimate sign of discretion: silence. If these acts were unknown, any social advantage normally gained through the admiration by others of one's heroic asceticism would be thwarted.

In my view Colossians is best understood against a social background that included not only the problem of false teaching but also increasingly tense relations between the church and the outside world. Fundamental to the distinctive vision of church identity put forth by the author is the transformed notion of the body of Christ. Explicitly equated with the church (Col. 1:18, 24), the "body" in Colossians is ruled by its head, who is Christ (Col. 1:18, 2:10, 19). Christ is head not only of the church but also of every power and principality (Col. 2:10). In essence, Christ rules the universe. He holds all things together and restores cosmic harmony (Col. 1:18–20). The body-of-Christ symbolism in Colossians clearly articulates a vision that the church is a spiritual and cosmic assembly.[51] Scholars frequently have noted the probable correlation between hierarchical authority structures and the head/body language in Colossians.[52] However, according to Averil Cameron, it is important not to overlook the integrative function of this correlation. She notes that since human society was presented as naturally ordained according to hierarchical principles, in a context in which the same ordering, with Christ as the head, was seen as analogous to the human body, it provided the potential for a totally integrated rhetoric of God, community, and individual.[53]

In speaking of the asceticism of later periods of early Christianity, she states that the body became less a symbol of integration than an obstacle to overcome.[54] In many respects the conflict between the author of Colossians and the opponents has to do with rival understandings of the physical body. According to the author, the body is no longer an obstacle to overcome, but has been transformed to such an extent that believers have been exalted already (Col. 2:12–13; 3:1–4). With their new bodies believers participate in the new cosmic harmony. On the social plane this integrative view works in conjunction with traditional ethics to provide a pattern of life that allows for the preservation of many aspects of conventional life, while at the same time reinforcing convictions about ultimately belonging to another world. Although visible signs of departure from the world in the form of rituals and ascetic practices of various kinds are denounced, ultimately the world is rejected in a profound sense.

In studying Colossians we sense a peculiar tension between a symbolism that implies an ultimate rejection of the standards and priorities of society and an ethic that encourages acceptance of these same standards and priorities. Mary Rose D'Angelo alludes to this tension when she states:

> Three images "Paul" uses to illustrate the effect of baptism deserve attention: spiritual circumcision as putting off the fleshly body (2:11), canceling a debtor's bond (2:14), and stripping the rulers and authorities and displaying them as captives (2:15). These images are likely to have encouraged double consciousness in women and slaves, demanding that they deny their subjected status in the religious realm while submitting to it in the social world.[55]

According to D'Angelo, the use of this symbolism to serve the interests of the existing social order represents a missed opportunity. There is much in the symbolism that might have combined into "a message of empowerment," but instead, "these elements have been redirected to proscribe the addressees' visionary and ascetic yearnings and to submit them to the social order."[56] I agree with D'Angelo's conclusions about the direction of the developments in Colossians and support her attempt to elucidate "ways that slavery and the subjugation of women collaborate in sustaining the patriarchal order."[57] However, given the strong evidence for an integrative function of the symbolism, I would like to consider whether what D'Angelo identifies as a "double consciousness" played a part in a strategy for survival among early Christians.

The effect of combining symbols of heavenly exaltation and of the spiritual body with the traditional ethics of the household code in Col. 3:18-4:1

is the creation of a church that, on the historical plane, acts very much like an invisible body. In daily life believers would not act in a way that would appear distinctive to onlookers. The ascetic response would very much resemble the "inner asceticism" described by Walter O. Kaelber:

> More difficult to define, but perhaps also more significant, is what may be termed an "inner asceticism," consisting essentially of spiritual rather than physical discipline. Such asceticism involves not detachment from or renunciation of any specific worldly pleasure but rather detachment from or renunciation of the world per se. It is reflected in the biblical attitude of being "in the world, but not of it," or in the Bhagavadgita's "renunciation in action, rather than renunciation of action."[58]

In calling members to take their place in an ordered household that included subordinate women, children, and slaves, the author of Colossians is insisting that ethical ideals in the church match those of the world and that believers who are not "of this world" nevertheless be firmly rooted "in this world." In fact, recent scholarship suggests that the prescribed ethics of Christian household codes were even more conservative than what was commonly being lived out in Greco-Roman society.[59] Thus, these household codes may represent an attempt to ensure that church members exceeded the most conservative standards of the day. Such measures would be especially important if a group was being criticized as a social irritant.[60] Whatever the particular social forces at work, there is an unmistakable sanction in Col. 3:18–4:1 of existing societal structures and an encouragement for church members to continue to live within those structures.

Despite the harmony presented in the "Christianized" household of Col. 3:18–4:1, however, it is by no means clear how many church members actually belonged to such an integrated whole. There are indications within the New Testament household codes that church membership of slaves and women in pagan households was a source of tension between the church and the world (1 Pet. 3:1–6; 1 Tim. 6:1–2).[61] It seems probable that a desire to limit the potentially controversial visibility of these members by keeping them in place, combined with an awareness of their strategic opportunities to evangelize within the home, resulted in the reinforcement of the structures of the patriarchal order—structures that were later legitimized by canonization. Perhaps nowhere is the role of the household code in rendering church members invisible more clearly evident than in 1 Pet. 3:1–6. Here model, obedient Christian wives are instructed to display a modest silence so that their pagan husbands might "be won over without a word by their wives' conduct" (1 Pet. 3:1, NRSV). But invisibility is always qualified—and to a certain extent temporary—in a group that seeks to transform the world. An examination of this passage in light of the prerogatives of the head of the household in matters of religion has led me to recognize that early Christian authors could recommend subservience, while at the same time indirectly legitimating subversion of the traditional household by encouraging women to act as evangelists in their own homes.[62] Ultimately, it is important to remember that the household codes represent ideals and are not perfect mirrors of history: They must be interpreted critically against a background of competition and tension between social groups.

Rather than simply forming part of a general ethical exhortation, the household code of Colossians should probably be viewed as fundamental to the response against the false teaching. The spiritual body is not only a body that can become secretly integrated within household quarters, it is a place where attention-drawing acts of asceticism such as fasting and sexual renunciation have no place. Rituals associated with these practices must also be carefully circumscribed. The visible (i.e., physical/social) boundary markers of religion are to a large extent eradicated by the author of Colossians. However, given the importance of ritual action in the social world, one wonders whether the ritual invisibility that appears to be the outcome of the author's stance against the false teaching would have created new problems in maintaining the integrity of the group. It is worth citing Turner once again to understand the potential loss that accompanies the abolition of regulations concerning food and drink and the cancellation of festivals, new moons, and Sabbaths (Col. 2:16):

> [R]itual symbols are "multivocal," susceptible of many meanings, but their referents tend to polarize between physiological phenomena (blood, sexual organs, coitus, birth, death, catabolism, and so on) and normative values of moral facts (kindness to children, reciprocity, generosity to kinsmen, respect for elders, obedience to political authorities, and the like). At this "normative" or "ideological" pole of meaning, one also finds reference to principles of organization: matriliny, patriliny, kinship, gerontocracy, age–grade organization, sex-affiliation, and others. The drama of ritual action ... causes an exchange between these poles in which the biological referents are ennobled and the normative referents are charged with emotional significance.... Symbols, under optimal conditions, may reinforce the will of those exposed to them to obey moral commandments, maintain covenants, repay debts, keep up obligations, avoid illicit behavior. In these ways anomie is prevented or avoided and a milieu is created in which society's members cannot see any fundamental conflict between themselves as individuals and society. There is set up, in their minds, a symbiotic interpenetration of individual and society.[63]

In contrast to the author of Colossians, the opponents supported many measures that would have enabled them to survive as a distinct group; they made use of Jewish practices that had a long history of serving this purpose. In fact, it is an interesting question whether the acceptance of the Colossian "philosophy" was related to the conviction that Paul's notion of a "new creation," "a community formed abruptly without the palpable, physical attributes of a distinctive religious observance," was "a bleak and homeless prospect."[64]

EPHESIANS

Unlike Colossians, Ephesians does not include a specific response to "false teaching" involving physical renunciation. In fact, the shape of the historical situation underlying Ephesians is very difficult to determine. Yet, the ascetic response to the world of the author of Ephesians is very similar to that of the author of Colossians: Believers "are in the world, but not of it." They are physically integrated within the dominant social environment, but their citizenship ultimately lies elsewhere. This is not to say, however, that Colossians and Ephesians carry identical implications for believers. In the following brief examination of Ephesians I highlight subtle, but important, differences between the patterns of life recommended in these documents.

Dealing with Outsiders

One of the most striking differences between Colossians and Ephesians is that Ephesians displays a much greater interest in how Christians should be distinguished from nonbelievers. Whatever may have been lacking with respect to the marks of distinctive identity in the stance adopted by the author of Colossians is seemingly compensated for by the author of Ephesians. In fact, all of Eph. 4:17–5:20 serves as a guide for life as children of God and for the rejection of the conduct of nonbelievers. The "Paul" of Ephesians is emphatic that believers should no longer live as the Gentiles do (Eph. 5:17ff.).[65] There is evidence in Eph. 5:15–16 of a stronger sentiment of being set apart from the evil world than in the parallel text of Col. 4:5–6. Ephesians lacks the specific concern for guiding exchanges between believers and nonbelievers that one finds in Colossians. Rather than being told to act wisely toward outsiders, the recipients are simply instructed to act as wise people. Caution is required not because of the delicate nature of the maneuvers that might be required to lead new members into the church, but simply because the days are evil. The most prominent feature of the type of world rejection demonstrated by Ephesians, however, is the sentiment that Christians are caught up in a battle against evil powers that penetrate even the heavenly realms (Eph. 6:11–12; cf. 2:1–3; 6:10–17). The expression in v. 12, "the heavenly places" (*epouraniois*)—an expression peculiar to Ephesians in Pauline literature—illustrates that, like Colossians, Ephesians has a cosmological focus (cf. Eph. 1:3, 20; 2:6; 3:10; 6:12). Believers are said to have been raised up with Christ and are seated with him in the heavenly places (Eph. 2:6). They have clearly gained access to the spiritual world that lies beyond the physical world.[66]

Long recognized as the most "ecclesiological" of the Pauline writings, Ephesians moves one step beyond Colossians in propounding a vision of the church as a spiritual, cosmic entity. Its lack of concern for the "local" dimension of the church in favor of a universalistic perspective works in conjunction with an ethos that rejects the battles of the physical world as being of any lasting significance (Eph. 6:12). Ephesians includes no reference to house churches (cf. Col. 4:15). Instead the church is referred to metaphorically in Eph. 2:14–22 as the household of God, the holy temple, and the body of Christ (implicitly; cf. 2:16). In the context of Ephesians, the fusion of the Pauline notion of the body of Christ with architectural metaphors suggests a critique of existing designations of sacred space and little interest in the institutional arrangements of meeting (cf. 1 Cor. 3:16–17). There is a sense in which believers, and indeed the universal church, are depicted as engaged in a journey of heavenly ascent. Paul's mission, for example, is described in terms of making "everyone see (*photisai*) what is the plan of the mystery hidden for ages in God who created all things; so that through the church the wisdom of God in its rich variety might now be made known to the rulers and authorities in the heavenly places" (NRSV, Eph. 3:9–10; cf. 1:18; 3:2ff.).

Heavenly Exaltation and Ritual

Given the critique of the visionary experiences of Colossian opponents, it is interesting to note the focus upon revelation, enlightenment, insight, and mystery that occurs throughout Ephesians (e.g., Eph. 1:3–14; 3:2–5, 8–10, 18–19).[67] As in Colossians, recollections of baptism figure prominently in an attempt to recall the experience of exaltation and to remind believers of their priorities (Eph. 1:11–14; 2:1–6; 4:4–6, 22–24, 30; 5:8–14, 25–27).[68] In Eph. 1:3–14 knowledge of the mystery of God's will (1:9) is connected with the experience of baptism, when believers were marked with the seal of the Holy Spirit (1:13–14). Comparing Eph. 5:18–19 to Col. 3:16, while keeping in mind the effort in Colossians to limit the rituals of the opponents, leads to an impression that Ephesians displays greater openness to periodic rituals that enabled early church members to affirm the experience of incorporation into Christ. As they sing psalms, hymns, and spiritual songs, believers are instructed to be filled with the Spirit. They are also told, however, to avoid the debauchery of getting drunk with wine (Eph. 5:18). This verse has sometimes been read as an attempt to distinguish the Spirit-induced ecstasy of the early Christians from the frenzies of pagan cults such as the cult of Dionysus.[69] If this reading is correct, an attempt to draw a boundary between believers and outsiders nevertheless allows for the continuation of rituals that, given the previous discussion, would in all likelihood have been judged by the author of Colossians as inopportune.[70]

Social Integration and Household Ethics

The very sharp, uncompromising distinction in Ephesians between those outside of the church and those inside has sometimes been judged to be a sign of introversion.[71] The pendulum may have swung in the direction of greater world rejection, but, in my opinion, to call Ephesians "introversionist" is to go too far. Perhaps to an even greater extent than Colossians, Ephesians understands the church as participating in a universal mission (e.g., Eph. 3:8–13; 6:19–20).[72] Moreover, the version of the household code in Eph 5:21–6:9 seems particularly well suited to encouraging church members to become integrated (at least physically) within Greco-Roman society. As Peter Brown puts it, by presenting relations between husbands and wives as a reflection of the relation between Christ and the church, the author of Ephesians was presenting "an image of unbreakable order that the pagan world could understand. In the church, as in the city, the concord of a married couple was made to bear the heavy weight of expressing the ideal harmony of a whole society."[73]

Given the integrative function of the body symbolism in Colossians discussed earlier, it is interesting to note that in Ephesians—which includes the same type of body symbolism (Eph. 1:22–23; 4:4, 15–16; 5:23, 30)—the church as body of Christ is incorporated within the household-code teaching on marriage (Eph. 5:23, 30). The exhortation concerning marriage in Ephesians is a dense composite that brings together scriptural allusions, traditional values, and central convictions. The use of Genesis in some ancient texts to refer to a kind of primordial unity[74] and the use of marriage as a paradigm for heavenly unification in gnostic literature[75] have led to much speculation about the background of Eph. 5:22–33. In particular, it has been suggested that the reference to Gen. 2:24 in Eph. 5:31, the reference to mystery[76] in Eph. 5:32, and the general sanctification of earthly marriage should be viewed as a response to an alternate understanding of sexual relations that may even have called for the avoidance of sexual relations altogether.[77] As early as 2 Clement we see an interpretation of the marriage metaphor that is much more conducive to physical renunciation than Ephesians is.[78] Later church literature makes it abundantly clear that the brides of Christ, spiritual mirrors of a pure church, were often perpetual virgins.[79] But arguments that see an attempt to respond to such tendencies in Ephesians must remain highly speculative, for the author of Ephesians tells us nothing about those who reject marriage. It is clear, however, that marriage lived out according to traditional patterns is viewed by the author of Ephesians as an indicator of the church's participation in the body of Christ. Given the importance of recollections of baptism in Colossians and Ephesians for establishing priorities, I think that the conflation of the image of the pure bride with the symbols of baptismal purification—the washing of water by the word—is enormously significant (Eph. 5:26–27). The sanctification of marriage is made even clearer in this passage by the interplay between allusions to baptism and allusions to the Jewish practice of purifying the bride with water in preparation for marriage (Ezek. 16:9).[80] Ephesians leaves little doubt that to be clothed in the new self, created according to the likeness of God, means embracing Christian marriage (Eph. 4:24).

In trying to understand the historical catalysts of this development, I have argued elsewhere that it is useful to examine how endogamy rules function within religious sects as defensive strategies against the outside world.[81] Already in 1 Thess. 4:4–5 marriage serves as an indicator of behavior that sets members apart from the evil world. Eph. 5:22–33 goes one step further than this text by sanctifying marriage between believers in the context of a document explicitly concerned with distinguishing Christians from nonbelievers. By the time Ignatius cites Ephesians 5:22–33 at the beginning of the second century, endogamy rules receive episcopal sanction. Marriages are to take place with the permission of the bishop (Ignatius, *Pol.* 5:1–2).

In exploring how teaching on marriage works to guarantee distinct identity, it is also useful to consider how Eph. 5:22–33 reflects Mediterranean values of honor and shame. To call the church a "pure bride" is to touch deeply rooted values in the ancient Mediterranean world that associated a woman's purity and circumspect behavior with the preservation of the reputation of the house. Rather than seeing the obedient wife simply as a static image of a pure church that keeps the evil world at bay, recent anthropological studies have invited exploration of how women's bodies function symbolically in the maintenance of household and group boundaries and in the mediation between realms.[82] In other words, the traditional marriage teaching of Eph. 5:22-33, so heavily infused with religious symbolism, not only may have been useful for communicating a particular vision of the sacred community, but also may have been viewed as integral to the process of making known the wisdom of God to even the heights of the heavenly places (Eph. 3:10).

CONCLUSION

Because the household code is introduced into Pauline Christianity via Colossians and subsequently taken up in Ephesians, these documents have frequently been judged as representing a major shift in the direction of accommodation to the standards of the world. But using asceticism as a central concept for analysis of these works has led me to the conclusion that what we have here is less a move in the direction of accommodation than a change of orientation in relation to the world. Integrated within the heavenly body, believers are to act on the historical plane like an invisible body. There is no doubt that this social invisibility, which includes living a highly conventional household existence, has important ethical consequences: The patriarchal structures of society are sustained. But it is also important to understand how this invisibility may function as part of a strategy for survival in a society that is being experienced as increasingly hostile. The heavenly body is one that might become secretly integrated within household quarters and, hence, carefully hidden from a householder who would resist such an invasion.

With its acts of physical renunciation and periodic rituals, the asceticism of the opponents of the author of Colossians resists such an "other-worldly" approach. In baptism the proponents of the Colossian "philosophy" may have been exalted with Christ, but their entrance into the heavenly realm needs to be symbolized physically and demarcated repeatedly. In response, the author of Colossians insists that acceptance of the gospel and baptism are the basis of a life that holds the dangers of the flesh at bay, rendering additional measures unnecessary. According to the author of Colossians, a Christian life is one that remains confident in heavenly citizenship. The vices of the outside world are shunned. Dealings with outsiders are cautious, and worship is conducted in such a way as to appear innocuous. Daily life takes its direction from the conventional wisdom of the household code. I have suggested, however, that the combined effect of pressures from the outside world and from internal opponents has led the author of Colossians to recommend a type of religiosity that is so devoid of the visible markers of identity as to make it very difficult to maintain the integrity of the group.

As is also true of Colossians, Ephesians offers heavenly citizenship and general conformity to earthly societal structures as the solution to the problem of the menacing powers of this world. But to a greater extent than Colossians, Ephesians articulates how this ironic predicament translates into patterns of life that allow for the maintenance of the boundaries of the body of Christ. With a keen sense of church identity, ethical distinctiveness, and convictions about the need to stand ready for an evil day (Eph. 6:13), the author of Ephesians prepares the way for the kind of argument we see in the *Epistle to Diognetus* (5.6–11, Loeb Classical Library):

> They [Christians] marry as all men, they bear children, but they do not expose their offspring. They offer free hospitality, but guard their purity. Their lot is cast "in the flesh," but they do not live "after the flesh." They pass their time upon the earth, but they have their citizenship in heaven. They obey the appointed laws, and they surpass the laws in their own lives. They love all men and are persecuted by all men.

NOTES

1. One very interesting study that pays significant attention to asceticism in Colossians, however, is Harold A. Attridge, "On Becoming an Angel: Rival Baptismal Theologies at Colossae," in *Religious Propaganda and Missionary Competition in the New Testament World: Essays Honoring Dieter Georgi*, eds. L. Bormann, K. Tredici, and A. Standhartinger (Leiden, The Netherlands: Brill, 1994), 481–98.

2. Vincent L. Wimbush, "Introduction," in *Ascetic Behavior in Greco-Roman Antiquity: A Sourcebook*, ed. Vincent L. Wimbush (Minneapolis, Minn.: Fortress, 1990), 2.

3. M. Y. MacDonald, *The Pauline Churches: A Socio-Historical Study of Institutionalization in the Pauline and Deutero-Pauline Writings* (Cambridge, England: Cambridge University Press, 1988).

4. Richard Valantasis, "Constructions of Power in Asceticism," *Journal of the American Academy of Religion* 63 (1995): 775–821, here 797. See also idem, "A Theory of the Social Function of Asceticism," in *Asceticism*, eds. Vincent L. Wimbush and Richard Valantasis (New York: Oxford University Press, 1995), 544–52.

5. Valantasis, "Constructions of Power" 800. For an illustration of how recent theoretical reflection on asceticism might shed light on Deutero-Pauline literature, see also Gail Corrington Streete (this volume, 299–316). Streete argues that although they are usually viewed as antiascetic, the Pastoral Epistles offer a model for "an active, social, 'householder' ascetic."

6. For discussion of the relation between Colossians and Ephesians, see W. G. Kümmel, *Introduction to the New Testament* (London: SCM, 1975), 358–60; Paul J. Kobelski, "The Letter to the Ephesians," in *The New Jerome Biblical Commentary*, eds. R. Brown, J. Fitzmyer, R. Murphy (Englewood Cliffs, N.J.: Prentice Hall, 1990), 883–90, here 884.

7. I believe that both Colossians and Ephesians are Deutero-Pauline. Colossians was probably written by a fellow worker or disciple of Paul's shortly after the Apostle's death. Ephesians is difficult to date, but the period 80–100 CE is often suggested. See MacDonald, *Pauline Churches*, 2–4.

8. The usefulness of the category "sect" for analyzing early Christian groups has been discussed extensively. See B. Holmberg, *Sociology and the New Testament: An Appraisal* (Minneapolis, Minn.: Fortress, 1990), 77–117. See also my response to Holmberg in "The Ideal of the Christian Couple: Ign. *Pol.* 5.1–2 Looking Back to Paul," *New Testament Studies* 40 (1994): 105–25, here 108, n. 16.

9. See, for example Philo, *Apology* 7.3, 5; Josephus, *Against Apion* 2.199. The apologetic function of household codes has been explored extensively by David L. Balch in *Let Wives Be Submissive: The Domestic Code in 1 Peter* (Chico, Calif.: Scholars, 1981). The connection made by some scholars between the adoption of the household code and the fear that "outsiders might perceive Christianity as a threat to the social fabric of the Roman Empire by corrupting households" has recently been critiqued by Sarah Tanzer. She argues that such explanations

are especially problematic for the household code of Ephesians "because it is part of a parenetic section exhorting Christians specifically to live in a way that is different from the non-Christian environment." But sociological studies of sects have alerted me to the possibility that calls to remain separate may be phrased in a way that simultaneously opens doors. In a group with a strong interest in winning outsiders, like Pauline Christianity, such ambivalence is especially likely to be found. See Sarah Tanzer, "Ephesians," in *Searching the Scriptures, Volume Two: A Feminist Commentary,* ed. Elisabeth Schüssler Fiorenza (New York: Crossroad, 1993), 325–47, here 330. I agree with Tanzer, however, when she points to the problematic nature of theories laying the "blame" on the influence of Jews or pagans for church teaching that appears to be patriarchal, such as Eph. 5:22–33 ("Ephesians," 329–32). Note that in contast to Tanzer, E. Elizabeth Johnson has recently argued in favor of an apologetic function of the Ephesian household code. See E. Elizabeth Johnson, "Ephesians," in *The Women's Bible Commentary,* eds. Carol A. Newsom and Sharon H. Ringe (Louisville Ky.: Westminster/Knox, 1992), 338–42, here 340–41.

10. For a detailed discussion, see MacDonald, *Pauline Churches,* 98–99.

11. On language of belonging and separation, see Wayne Meeks, *The First Urban Christians: The Social World of the Apostle Paul* (New Haven, Conn.: Yale University, 1983), 87ff.

12. Col. 4:5–6 has consistently been discussed in light of the missionary enterprise. See, for example, E. Schweizer, *The Letter to the Colossians* (London: SPCK, 1982), 233–34; Walter F. Taylor Jr. and John H. P. Reumann, *Ephesians, Colossians* (Minneapolis, Minn.: Augsburg, 1985), 158–60.

13. On the meaning of "seasoned with salt," see Eduard Lohse, *Colossians and Philemon* (Philadelphia: Fortress, 1971), 168–69.

14. See Lohse, *Colossians and Philemon,* 96–98.

15. See the summary of the evidence in Schweizer, "Slaves of the Elements and Worshipers of Angels: Gal 4:3, 9 and Col 2:8, 18, 20," *Journal of Biblical Literature* 107 (1988): 455–68.

16. Ibid, 464.

17. See Jerry Sumney, "Those who 'Pass Judgment': The Identity of the Opponents in Colossians," *Biblica* 74 (1993): 366–88, here 374–75.

18. See M. D. Hooker, "Were there False Teachers in Colossae?" in *Christ and the Spirit in the New Testament: Studies in Honour of Charles Francis Digby Moule,* eds. B. Lindars and S. S. Smalley (Cambridge, England: Cambridge University Press, 1973), 315–31. See also N. T. Wright, *The Epistles of Paul to the Colossians and to Philemon: An Introduction and Commentary* (Grand Rapids, Mich.: Inter-Varsity Press, 1986), 26–28, who combines aspects of Hooker's thought with the theory that in Colossians, Paul's polemic is aimed at Judaism.

19. To gain a sense of the wide range of theories about the identity of the Colossian opponents, consider the following articles: Randal A. Argall, "The Source of Religious Error in Colossae," *Calvin Theological Journal* 22 (1987): 6–20; Craig Evans, "The Colossian Mystics," *Biblica* 63 (1982): 188–205; F. F. Bruce, "The Colossian Heresy," *Bibliotheca Sacra* 141 (1984): 195–208; Roy Yates, "Colossians and Gnosis," *Journal for the Study of the New Testament* 27

(1986): 49–68. More recently, Troy W. Martin has identified the Colossian opponents as Cynics in *By Philosophy and Empty Deceit: Colossians as Response to a Cynic Critique* (Sheffield, England: Academic Press, 1996).

20. See Mary Rose D'Angelo, "Colossians," in *Searching the Scriptures*, ed. Fiorenza, 313–24, here 319.

21. See Sumney, "Those Who 'Pass Judgment,'" 366–67.

22. Note, however, that Wright (*Epistles of Paul,* 26) states that "it is easier to understand the reference to asceticism (2:20–23) as contemptuous and ironic, and the close parallel with Mark 7:5ff. increases the probability that the target of the polemic is the Jewish law." But, as will be made clear in what follows, the ascetic features of the teaching are too prevalent to support this theory. Martin (*By Philosophy*) pays significant attention to the ascetic features of the false teaching. However, this book appeared too late to have been considered in the present study.

23. To what extent the philosophy was actually Jewish has been the subject of debate. Lohse, for example, argues: "The 'philosophy' made use of terms which stemmed from Jewish tradition, but which had been transformed in the crucible of syncretism to be subject to the service of 'the elements of the universe'" (*Colossians and Philemon*, 116). Wright (*Epistles of Paul*, 118–19) argues the opposite.

24. For example, Dan 10.2ff. See Christopher Rowland, "Apocalyptic Visions and the Exaltations of Christ in the Letter to the Colossians," *Journal for the Study of the New Testament* 19 (1983): 73–83, here 74. Note, however, that it is possible that the reference to "humility" in Col. 2:18 concerns the activities of the angels and not human practitioners. For an explanation of this understanding of the Greek text, see ibid, 75. Note that Lohse (*Colossians and Philemon*, 118) prefers the translation of *tapeinophrosyne* as readiness to serve by means of cultic conduct. For further information about the debate concerning the meaning of the term, see Evans, "Colossian Mystics," 195–96.

25. See Fred O. Francis, "Humility and Angelic Worship in Col 2:18," in *Conflict at Colossae*, eds. Wayne Meeks and Fred O. Francis (Missoula, Mont.: Scholars, 1975), 163–95; Rowland, "Apocalyptic Visions," 73–83. On references to the "angelic" as a means of conceptualizing ascetical life in early Christianity, see Attridge, "On Becoming an Angel," 489–90; Robin Lane Fox, *Pagans and Christians* (New York: Knopf, 1987), 365.

26. See D'Angelo, "Colossians," 319. Ancient Jewish texts support this interpretation. The Enochic tradition (1 En. 71:1–17; 2 En. 22:4–7; 3 En.) is discussed in depth by Attridge, "On Becoming an Angel," 493–97. For the evidence from Qumran and other texts where human beings participate in heavenly worship, see Rowland, "Apocalyptic Visions," 77 and 81, n. 26. The reference to visionary phenomena contained in the phrase *ha heoraken embateuon* has been the subject of considerable debate. See Evans, "Colossian Mystics," 197–98; Summey, "Those Who 'Pass Judgment,'" 376–77; Rowland, "Apocalyptic Visions," 75–76. The use of the term *embateuein* in Col. 2:18 has invited comparison of the Colossian false teaching with initiation into the mysteries. See the important essay by M. Dibelius, "The Isis Initiation in Apuleius and Related Initiatory Rites," in *Conflict at Colossae*, eds. Meeks and Francis, 61–121. For a critique of Dibelius, see Francis, "Humility and Angelic Worship," 171–76.

Rowland, citing 1 En. 14:9 and building upon the work of Francis, suggests that *embateuein* is not so much a technical term as a general term for entry that is used here in connection with visionary ascent. See Rowland, "Apocalyptic Visions," 76.

27. See Robert Leaney, "Colossians II.21–23 (the use of [prov])," *Expository Times* 64 (1952–1953): 92.

28. On virginity and fasting, see Fox, *Pagans and Christians*, 373; A. Meredith, "Asceticism—Christian and Greek," *Journal of Theological Studies* 27 (1976): 313–32, here 319.

29. See Lohse, *Colossians and Philemon*, 124–27; Wright, *Epistles of Paul*, 127–28.

30. Lohse, *Colossians and Philemon*, 126–27.

31. On translating this term, see Summey, "Those Who 'Pass Judgment,'" 371–72.

32. The NRSV offers an alternate translation: "are of no value, serving only to indulge the flesh." But this alternate translation is probably the less likely one. See the discussion in Wright, *Epistles of Paul*, 127–28.

33. The values of honor and shame are communicated in the New Testament by means of several different terms. See Bruce Malina and Jerome H. Neyrey, "Honor and Shame in Luke–Acts: Pivotal Values of the Mediterranean World," in *The Social World of Luke–Acts: Models for Interpretation*, ed. J. Neyrey (Peabody, Mass.: Hendrickson, 1991), 25–65, here 46.

34. I discuss how the values of honor and shame shed light on Paul's treatment of ritual and asceticism in 1 Corinthians in my book *Early Christian Women and Pagan Opinion: The Power of the Hysterical Woman* (Cambridge, England: Cambridge University Press, 1996), 144–54.

35. Wayne Meeks refers to marriage as serving Paul's therapeutic concern. See Meeks, *The Origins of Christian Morality: The First Two Centuries* (New Haven, Conn.: Yale University Press, 1993) 144–45. See also my article, "Women Holy in Body and Spirit: The Social Setting of 1 Corinthians 7," *New Testament Studies* 36 (1990): 161–81, here 162–63.

36. For a fuller discussion of hymnic influences in Colossians, see MacDonald, *Pauline Churches*, 139–42.

37. On the role of baptism in the conflict with false teachers, see Attridge, "On Becoming an Angel," 481–98. Attridge believes that baptism is at the heart of the dispute over the false teaching: "I suggest that Colossians makes this appeal to baptism precisely because all of the other objectionable elements cohere within a certain kind of baptismal theory and consequent practice" (483). Attridge supports his argument on the basis of texts from Nag Hammadi, especially the tractate *Zostrianos* (NHC VIII, 1).

38. See Maurya P. Horgan, "The Letter to the Colossians," in *New Jerome Biblical Commentary*, ed. R. Brown, J. Fitzmyer, and R. Murphy, 876–82, here 881.

39. See Lohse, *Colossians and Philemon*, 130. The language of Col 2:11–15 has invited comparison of the practices of the false teachers with initiation into mystery cults. See ibid, 102. This is also true of Col. 2:18. See note 26.

40. Note that Clement of Alexandria here cites the "Gospel of the Egyptians," which should not be confused with its namesake from Nag Hammadi.

41. See Dennis R. MacDonald, *There is No Male and Female: The Fate of a Dominical Saying in Paul and Gnosticism* (Philadelphia: Fortress, 1987), 1–63. Similarly, but with a specific focus on Colossians, Attridge has pointed to an

interpretation of baptism that emerges especially strongly in the third-century gnostic text *Zostrianos*. In this text, a series of baptisms forms part of a mystical journey during which the seer is eventually transformed into a heavenly or angelic state. The practical implications of the mystical journey include celibacy: "flee from the madness and the bondage of femaleness, and choose for yourselves the salvation of maleness" (NHC VII, 1.130, 16–132, 5). See Attridge, "On Becoming an Angel," 483–86, esp. 486. It is surprising that Attridge does not discuss Col. 3:11, for it would have added further support to his case.

42. See MacDonald, "Women Holy in Body and Spirit," 161–81.

43. See, for example, Johnson, "Colossians," 346–48, here 347.

44. See D'Angelo, "Colossians," 321. On the interpretation of Genesis in terms of a perfect androgynous creation, see Dennis MacDonald's discussion of Philo in *No Male and Female*, 26–30.

45. There are significant similarities between the attitude of the author of Colossians and that of the author of the Pastoral Epistles. See Gail Corrington Streete, this volume, 299–316).

46. D'Angelo, "Colossians," 320.

47. Attridge, "On Becoming an Angel," 498.

48. Victor Turner, *Dramas, Fields, and Metaphors: Symbolic Action in Human Society* (Ithaca, N.Y.: Cornell University Press, 1974), 53. Turner's concept of liminality is drawn from the classic study of A. Van Gennep, *Les Rites de passage*, and refers to an unstructured, egalitarian condition on the peripheries or margins of everyday life (often a sacred condition).

49. Ibid, 56.

50. See my book *Early Christian Women*. Many studies relevant to this topic are cited there.

51. D'Angelo, "Colossians," 314.

52. See, for example, ibid, 314–15; MacDonald, *Pauline Churches*, 154. Unfortunately I have not had adequate opportunity to consider the recent study by Dale B. Martin, *The Corinthian Body* (New Haven, Conn.: Yale University, 1995). In his chapter on the body in Greco-Roman culture, Martin includes a discussion of the microcosmic body (15–21) and the hierarchical body (29–34). Among Martin's many insights that call for exploration in relation to Colossians and Ephesians is the following point: "[I]n the ancient world, the human body was not like a microcosm; it was a microcosm—a small version of the universe at large" (16).

53. Averil Cameron, *Christianity and the Rhetoric of the Empire: The Development of Christian Discourse* (Berkeley: University of California Press, 1991) 69.

54. Ibid, 69–70.

55. D'Angelo, "Colossians," 320.

56. Ibid, 322–23.

57. Ibid, 315.

58. Walter O. Kaelber, "Asceticism," in *The Encyclopedia of Religion*, ed. Mircea Eliade (New York: MacMillan, 1987), vol. 1, 441–45, here 442.

59. See Tanzer, "Ephesians," 330–31.

60. Kathleen E. Corley has linked conservative trends in the synoptic tradition to public perceptions about the visibility of early church women. See Kathleen E.

Corley, *Private Women, Public Meals: Social Conflict in the Synoptic Tradition* (Peabody, Mass.: Hendrickson, 1993).

61. See M. Y. MacDonald, "Early Christian Women Married to Unbelievers," *Studies in Religion* 19 (1990): 221–34. On the threat to the household of an unconverted paterfamilias caused by the conversion of women, slaves, and young people, see Elisabeth Schüssler Fiorenza, *In Memory of Her: A Feminist Theological Reconstruction of Christian Origins* (London: SCM, 1983), 262–66.

62. See the discussion of 1 Pet. 3:1–6 in MacDonald, *Early Christian Women,* 195–204.

63. Turner, *Dramas, Fields, and Metaphors,* 55–56.

64. Peter Brown, *The Body and Society: Men, Women and Sexual Renunciation in Early Christianity* (New York: Columbia University Press, 1988), 59. Brown speaks of Paul's position in terms of ritual invisibility, drawing upon the work of J. M. Gager, *The Origins of Anti-Semitism* (Oxford: Oxford University Press, 1983), 132, 206. Brown argues that this position eventually becomes untenable: "By the end of the first century, Christians found that they were forced to create for themselves the equivalent of the Jewish Law, if they were to survive as a recognizable group, separate from pagans and Jews." Drawing particular attention to Justin's *Apology*, Brown argues that strict codes of sexual discipline (with total chastity as the peak) were central in providing Christians with a distinctive code of behavior (*Body and Society,* 59–60).

65. The resemblance between this text and Jewish ethical exhortation has frequently been observed. Significant parallels have been noted with the Qumran material in particular. See Taylor and Reumann, *Ephesians, Colossians,* 73–76; Kobelski, "Ephesians," 885.

66. It is important to note that although Ephesians depicts the present heavenly enthronement of believers (Eph. 1:3; 2:6–7), it also stresses the future dimension of salvation to a greater extent than Colossians (Eph. 1:13–14; 4:30; 6:10–20). An "already/not yet" eschatological thread runs throughout Ephesians. See Tanzer, "Ephesians," 327.

67. Note that M. D. Goulder has argued that Ephesians was written to counter Jewish-Christian visionaries. See M. D. Goulder, "The Visionaries of Laodicea," *Journal for the Study of the New Testament* 43 (1991): 15–39.

68. The importance of baptism in Ephesians has figured prominently in theories concerning the occasion and purpose of the document. See N. A. Dahl, "Adresse und Proömium des Epheserbriefes," *Theologische Zertschrift* 7 (1951): 251–64; J. C. Kirby, *Ephesians: Baptism and Pentecost: An Inquiry into the Structure and Purpose of the Epistle to the Ephesians* (London: SPCK, 1968).

69. Taylor and Reumann, *Ephesians, Colossians,* 77; Cleon L. Rogers Jr., "The Dionysian Background of Ephesians 5:18," *Bibliotheca Sacra* 136 (1979): 249–57.

70. D'Angelo ("Colossians," 321) views the absence of encouragement of the more "dangerous charismata" by the author of Colossians as significant.

71. See, for example, Kirby, *Ephesians,* 142.

72. See the discussion in MacDonald, *Pauline Churches,* 97–102; Dahl, "Gentiles, Christians, and Israelites in the Epistle to the Ephesians," *Harvard Theological Review* 79 (1986): 31–39; here 34–35.

73. Brown, *Body and Society*, 57.
74. See the discussion in Fox, *Pagans and Christians*, 366.
75. See Fiorenza, *In Memory of Her*, 274–75.
76. The term "mystery" has a different significance in Ephesians than it has in the undisputed letters of Paul. See Tanzer, "Ephesians," 339–40; Taylor and Reumann, *Ephesians, Colossians*, 36.
77. See Taylor and Reumann, *Ephesians, Colossians*, 24, 80–81.
78. See *2 Clem.* 14:1–15:1. On asceticism in 2 Clement, see MacDonald, *No Male and Female*, 42–43.
79. On the virgin brides of Christ, see Fox, *Pagans and Christians*, 371.
80. See Tanzer, "Ephesians," 336.
81. MacDonald, "Ideal of the Christian Couple," 105–25.
82. See, for example, Jill Dubisch, "Culture Enters through the Kitchen: Women, Food and Social Boundaries in Rural Greece," in *Gender and Power in Rural Greece*, ed. J. Dubisch (Princeton, N.J.: Princeton University Press, 1986), 195–214, here 207–8. See also MacDonald, *Early Christian Women*, 240–43.

Askesis and Resistance in the Pastoral Letters

Gail Corrington Streete

INTRODUCTION

Resistant asceticism? The ascetic enterprise involves doing, action, reaction, and practice rather than fixture or closure. As Geoffrey Galt Harpham has observed, early Christian asceticism was marked by a constant struggle for self-refinement to become one's own text.[1] Further, as Richard Valantasis has noted, asceticism both requires and generates conflict and resistance in order to define "a new subjectivity and the alternative social relations" that mark it.[2] The technique of resistance that marks ascetic practice would thus initially seem inimical to the institutional authority promoted by the form of emerging Christianity exemplified in the Pastoral Epistles, which calls itself "right or sound" (*orthos*, cf. 2 Tim. 2:15) and insists upon a certain conformity in acceptable writings, behavior, and belief. Nevertheless, as Harpham has also suggested, the "chaotic" movement of asceticism can be harnessed in the service of community modeling through authoritative texts that themselves provide paradigms for "true" ascetic resistance.[3]

It is by using this "ascetic social hermeneutic," then, that one might understand the Pastoral Epistles—1 and 2 Timothy and Titus. These letters, more moral epistles than occasional missives, initially seem to be located in a realm far different from that usually thought of as ascetic social resistance. Indeed, the Pastoral Epistles constantly iterate the desire for social harmony, peace, and quiet, urging the avoidance of quarrels, arguments, struggles, and divisions, both within the congregation itself and between the congregation and the dominant "outside" world with which it is advised to be at peace (1 Tim. 2:2, 8; 2 Tim. 2:23–24; Titus 3:2, 9–11). Some passages, like 1 Tim.

4:1–3, which inveighs against the "liars" who "forbid marriage and teach abstinence from food," appear, in fact, to be actively antiascetic. Yet I propose to show that the Pastoral Epistles are not engaged in an attack upon asceticism per se, but rather in an attack on a kind of ascetic subjectivity and its concomitant social relations that the author[4] defines and challenges as illegitimate. By adopting the guise of a father's instructing a "true" or legitimate "child in the faith" (1 Tim. 1:2; 2 Tim. 1:2; 2:1; Titus 1:4), the author proposes a model of "true" asceticism, an active, social, "householder" ascetic that is based upon self-discipline in speech and conduct and upon "good deeds" (*erga kala*) appropriate to one's station or *taxis* in society (1 Tim. 5:10; Titus 2:7), rather than upon liberation from any social *taxis* in the name of a disciplined autonomy. What emerges is the kind of ascetic subjectivity that is, in Valantasis' terms, both "integrative," attempting to achieve transformation within a dominant culture, and "educative," one that centers on the teaching of a "master" to one who wishes to become an "adept" in the practice, against a "combative" asceticism that wishes to demolish existing social relations and perceptions of the world.[5]

Contrary to the way in which Bruce J. Malina defines early Christian asceticism, in which the individual's self-denial was "an escape from concern for group esteem and group honor," the asceticism of the Pastoral Epistles is one in which the individual denies his or her own honor for the sake of the group, a group whose leaders define the ascetic, or disciplined, position as a kind of a resistance to the antinomianism of ascetic "radical communitas" consisting of individual bodies "shorn of social concerns."[6]

The rhetorical strategy of the author of the Pastoral Epistles thus sets itself three tasks: first, to represent its ascetic opponents as "false" ascetics by showing that they lack or feign the hallmark of ascetical behavior, *sophrosyne*; second, to use the authority of Paul to assert an "authentic" or "master" tradition over the lack or deliberate distortion of Pauline authority among the opponents; and third, to construct an alternate asceticism that is as consonant with the prevailing social order as their opponents' is dissonant. The latter argument especially revolves around assertion of gender-appropriate behavior as the indication of good order. Overall, the author of the Pastoral Epistles attempts to show that his is not only the more legitimate, but ultimately the more natural and achievable *askesis*. In so doing, the author offers an ascetic model that, like all forms of "ascetical opposition," presents itself as "the [only] option for those capable of disciplined performance."[7]

"Bogus Asceticism": Branding the Other

The dispute over what constitutes "true" or "real" *askesis*, involving a distinction between true and false knowledge or gnosis (1 Tim. 6:20) and true and feigned piety or *eusebeia* (2 Tim. 3:5), can be seen to frame the discourse of the Pastoral Epistles. "True" or "sound" (*hygiainos*) asceticism, the discipline of the self in order to promote greater social harmony and consonance in doctrine, is dualistically opposed to the "false" asceticism that is characterized as antinomian individualism.

Self-discipline is opposed to self-indulgent passions and pleasures, peace and good repute to controversy, dispute, and "evil repute"; "good works" to "idle talk"; unity to dissent; healthy or sound teaching to infectious discord; scriptural and other written authority to speech that is "wrangling over words"; householder to itinerant (defined as "busybody" or "gadabout" if female, "invader" of the household if male); and "true" widows, who are pious, elderly, and poverty-stricken, to "false" widows, who have money and time to spend on their intellectual curiosity. To establish his norms for "true" asceticism, the author of the Pastoral Epistles must foster the assumption that "others" who lay claim to an ascetic mode of life do so mainly for show, as an "act," or out of delusion or deception. Way is thus cleared for the delineation of the true faith and the real ascetic practices that arise from and bolster that faith.

In 1 Timothy, the young disciple is advised to be on his guard against those who "forbid marriage and abstain from foods that God created to be received with thanksgiving by those who are faithful and know the truth" (1 Tim. 4:3). The would-be ascetics are characterized as "paying attention to deceitful spirits and the teachings of demons," who act "in the hypocrisy of liars, whose individual (*idian*) consciences are branded with a hot iron" (1 Tim. 4:1-2). Hence, the opponents are depicted as those who use simulated ascetic behavior based on beliefs that are likewise false. Similarly, in 2 Timothy, the author inveighs against those who follow their individual inclinations, "passions of every kind" (2 Tim. 3:7). Like the *idiotes*, who is characterized in Greco-Roman political theory as following personal and "private" needs and is opposed to the *politikos*, the public-spirited citizen, such persons militate against the good of the community. Their opposition is, however, partially undercut by making their performance a predicted part of the eschatological drama: The Holy Spirit that is opposed to these "deceitful spirits" says clearly that such behavior is to be expected "in the latter days."

Timothy is also warned against supporting "young widows," women who apparently are accused of "violating their first troth" to Christ out of a "sensual desire" to marry (1 Tim. 5:11). They do not really know what they want, a celibate marriage "to Christ" or a marriage to another husband, which they themselves had possibly rejected previously out of fidelity to the prevailing social ideal of a "one-man woman." These young women perhaps occupy a rather high position in the socially stratified Greco-Roman society, since they have enough leisure to go from house to house, "gossips and busybodies, saying what ought not to be said" (5:13), and thus give an opportunity for the community to be reproached by "the adversary," for "some have already turned away in Satan's direction" (5:15). These "widows" are therefore defined as "false," and suspicion is cast upon their chastity as both feigned and ephemeral (1 Tim. 5:3–15).

A "real" widow, by contrast, is one who has no family and thus is truly without a household (5:4–5). Her dedication to "prayer and supplications day and night" contrasts with the "idleness" of the "false" widows. Hers is, by implication, a "true" marriage to Christ, her spouse. The false widows, in their living for pleasure, are actually "dead," not really living (5:6). 2 Timothy continues the theme of an eschatological drama, in which the opponents are again merely playing parts. Timothy is again warned to expect "in the last days" many kinds of rebellious people, including "lovers of pleasure rather than lovers of God," who "keep the form of piety but deny its power" (2 Tim. 3:5). These are men who insinuate themselves into households and "take captive little women who are steeped in sins, driven by all kinds of desires, always being instructed and never being able to come to knowledge of the truth" (3:6–7). These belong to those with "itching ears" who seek teachers according to their own desires, and "wander away" from listening to the "truth." Again, "true" piety is contrasted to its "form," as true instruction in piety is against a craving to keep learning but never to know.

The emphasis in the Epistle to Titus is laid upon controlled behavior within the community rather than a specific attack on "false" asceticism. According to Martin Dibelius and Hans Conzelmann, the main concern in Titus is with the family structure and its duties in a "missionary church" that needs to remain stable and does not therefore tolerate dissent.[8] The author does, however, mention a group of opponents who are "rebellious, idle talkers and deceivers," including those Jewish Christians who are "overturning entire households," perhaps over the question of purity, which is rejected by the author as feigned and illegitimate. These persons claim to know God, but their actions deny him (Titus 1:10–16). Again, they are merely play-acting.

In attributing to the author of the Pastoral Epistles a characterization of asceticism as a dramatic illusion that dissuades its viewers and auditors from the truth, we are making two rather large assumptions: one, that the opponents in all three letters occupy the same general spectrum of belief and behavior, with a distinction, as Dibelius and Conzelmann put it, "only between the seducers and the seduced,"[9] and two, that the position held by the opponents was in fact a type of asceticism. If we follow the first assumption, those being attacked by the Pastoral Epistles exhibit behavior that encourages itinerancy, does not place any high value upon marriage and the family life of a structured household, restricts the eating of certain foods, perhaps out of a Jewish-Christian reliance on purity laws (Titus 1:10–15; cf.

1 Tim. 4:4–5), promotes or provokes disputations and discussions within households, and involves a number of women who are, by their own choice, not married. Finally, the opponents support their behavior with reference to a set of beliefs and teachings that the author of the Pastoral Epistles characterizes as "myths," "idle talk," "gossip," "random talk," "profane babblings," "a sick craving after disputes," the "godless tales of old women" (1 Tim. 4:7),[10] and a "falsely so-called knowledge" that "misses the mark" of the true faith (1 Tim. 6:10).

Are we able further to characterize the group or groups being attacked in the Pastoral letters as "ascetic"? Most of the commentators on the Pastoral Epistles assume so, attributing the combination of itinerant preaching, sexual asceticism, and the emancipation of women from domestic confinement characterized in the Pastoral Epistles as "false," either to gnostic asceticism or to the type of asceticism represented by the apocryphal Acts of the Apostles.[11] To return to Valantasis' definition of asceticism, most commentators would characterize the asceticism challenged by the Pastoral Epistles as "combative," one in which the ascetic pulls away from a "deconstructed identity" so powerful that it must be resisted by "constant warfare."[12] This point of view thus assumes that the Christian "householder" identity articulated in the Pastoral Epistles is the dominant one, against which the "rebellious" (*anypotaktoi*) struggle and from which they attempt to break away.

But we may be assuming, perhaps wrongly, that the Pastoral Epistles reflect the dominant paradigm for Christianity because in fact it was the paradigm that was ultimately the most successful. Hence, we tend to limit "asceticism" to the point of view of the opponents and to assert, contrariwise, that the author of the Pastoral Epistles and his presumed audience were not, or did not conceive of themselves as, ascetic. If that is so, then why the constant emphasis in these epistles on the fact that the opponents are representing themselves to be something that they are not, that is, "true" ascetics? Perhaps, as Dennis MacDonald suggests, the Pastoral Epistles are struggling against a widespread movement claiming to have apostolic sanction to defy civil and familial authority in the name of "true" Christianity,[13] and thus do not represent a dominant but rather a competitive tradition within the faith. Margaret MacDonald suggests that the Pastoral Epistles represent a protective reaction to a "severe conflict" within rival communities laying claim to differing versions of Pauline teaching.[14] Dewey even suggests that the Pastoral Epistles themselves may represent a "deviant" tradition in that they prescribe a norm for Christian congregations that in all probability neither had nor desired such a norm.[15] Or, as David C. Verner suggests, the Pastoral Epistles represent documents of a religious minority charged with "beguiling women and undermining the household" as the basis of society, and therefore make "exaggerated claims to orthopraxy in this area," thus branding their opponents as the "true" subversives.[16] Our task is thus to examine the strategies by which the author of the Pastoral Epistles first lays claim to "authentic" Pauline teaching and on that basis attempts to construct an ascetic subjectivity that undermines and opposes the power of the asceticism of his opponents.

"THOSE BASTARDS": THE ILLEGITIMACY OF THE OPPONENTS

The relationship between the author of the Pastoral Epistles, who is asserted to be Paul, and the named recipients, Timothy and Titus, is characterized in every case at the very beginning as that of parent to child (1 Tim. 1:2, 18; 2 Tim. 1:2, 3:1; Titus 1:4). Moreover, both Timothy (1 Tim. 1:2) and Titus (Titus 1:4) are addressed as "true child" (*gnesion teknon*), in "the faith" (Timothy) or "according to our common faith" (Titus). This is no mere rhetorical trope; according to Dibelius and Conzelmann, the term "true" denotes "the legitimate child, born in wedlock."[17]

The spiritual parent, by means of instruction, creates a "child" in his own image. According to Valantasis, "educative" asceticism employs just such a mechanism to create a new subjectivity.[18]

Dennis MacDonald claims that the author of the Pastoral Epistles constructed an image of Paul (and thus of those to whom he passed on his authority, including himself) as a "social conservative," in contradistinction to the Paul who fits the mold of the apocryphal Acts, an opponent of Roman social life and a proponent of radical asceticism. The "Paul" thus constructed was one who urged "social compliance" and passed that model of behavior on through "genealogical transmission" to his disciples, Timothy and Titus, who themselves are constructed as guardians of a tradition of "divine origin."[19] As Joanna Dewey further suggests, this divinely given tradition was characterized both by written scriptural authority and by teaching transmitted formally through the male line (as property was from father to legitimate male children), versus the oral and informal teaching that the Pastoral Epistles brand as female "gossip," inappropriate utterance (1 Tim. 5:13), and the "godless tales of old women" (1 Tim. 4:7).[20]

The Paul constructed in the Pastoral Epistles provides a model for the spiritual parent who, through instruction, creates a "true child," one in his own supposed image, who respects authority in the ecclesial household as well as the state, a respect that mirrors the reverence (*eusebeia*) to be shown to God. The worst fault, by contrast, is *asebeia*, which can only be corrected by the appropriate *paideia* that educates pupils to avoid the "worldly passions" associated with their youth toward self-control, righteousness, and respect (Titus 2:12; cf. 2 Tim. 2:23–24). Similarly, those who are leaders in the Christian congregation are to be exemplary leaders of others (1 Tim.

4:12; Titus 2:7–8), and those in positions of responsibility—bishops and elders—are to enforce the obedience and submissiveness of their own children (1 Tim. 3:4, 7, 12; 2 Tim. 3:2; Titus 1:6), while correcting adults and social equals under their charge with patience and gentleness (2 Tim. 2:24; 4:2).

In the Pastoral Epistles, what is written, and is thus orderly and uniform, is valued over speech. In Harpham's words, "Speech may be alive, but it represents a principle of kinetic disorder which it has always been the goal of philosophy (and writing, and ethics) to order and contain."[21] Where speech is allowed in the Pastoral Epistles, it is regulated and disciplined, proceeding from a single source; it is institutionalized, not charismatic. Otherwise, it becomes "profitless," "silly," "idle," "godless", and bad speech, or blasphemy, leading to further "bad speech" or ill repute; it is often associated with women who follow their own inclinations (1 Tim. 1:13, 20; 6:1). The addressee of 1 Timothy is advised to base his teaching, like his learning, on "healthy words," and to oppose "other," variant teaching that represents a "sick craving after disputes and battles about words (*logomachias*) from which arise hatred, strife, blasphemies, and wicked slanders" (1 Tim. 6:4). This kind of "random talk" and "profane babblings" (1 Tim. 6:20) is replete with orally transmitted "myths and endless genealogies" that purport to offer knowledge, but instead promote a "falsely named" knowledge that leads to endless and unregulated speculation rather than a single-minded, practical rather than intellectual, devotion to the faith. Timothy is urged to continue public readings, exhortations, and teachings, providing a unified source of instruction, until the arrival of the letter-writer (1 Tim. 4:13), the spiritual father and master, who communicates by means of the written, single and therefore, authoritative word.

2 Timothy continues to assert the authority of "the writings (scriptures)" as the means of ordering and controlling disorderly speech. "Healthy" (*hygiainos*) doctrine, contained in the scriptures and in the teaching that is passed from master to disciple, is also a sound remedy against the contagious "disease" of heterodoxy that is spread orally and enters through the ears. Again, the disciple is told to oppose the "charlatans" (*goetes*), those of "enchanting speech," who deceive and are deceived (literally, "cause to wander and are wandering"), by remaining firm "in what you have learned and in which you have believed, knowing from whom you have learned it," the "holy scriptures, which are empowered to instruct you for salvation," the scriptures that are both spiritual ("god-inspired") and practical ("profitable" for instructing others). This is the only true training for righteousness, and the equipment "for every good work" (2 Tim. 3:14–17). This adherence to education via the written word is a healthy defense against the "itching," perhaps already infected, ears of those who listen to "myths" and "wander off" from the truth, following their own passions (2 Tim. 4:3–4). Those who lis-

ten to debates, mere "warring over words" (*logomachein*), will not benefit, but will be completely ruined by what they hear. Such "profane, empty chatter" leads people away from the "straight-hewing word of truth" into greater irreverence (*asebeia*), and their errant speech (*logos*) will infect "like gangrene" (2 Tim. 2:14–17). Women are especially swayed by the itinerant preachers who "invade households"; they are always in the process of "being instructed," but never are capable of coming to ultimate "knowledge of the truth" (2 Tim. 3:6–9).

The teachers, according to Dewey, may be the kind of people represented by the apostles in the apocryphal Acts, who also are accused of "charlatanry," invading households and inducing women to abandon husbands, fiancés, and families.[22] Paul is also a hero in the legend cycle that goes under his name, one part of which supports the abandonment of the household and the assumption of authority from Paul, the *Acts of Paul and Thecla*. In this apocryphal document, the betrothed noble virgin of Iconium, Thecla, is "infected" by the teaching of Paul in the public square, to which she listens while sitting by the window, half-in, half-out of her mother's house. First in pursuit of Paul and later of his approval, she abandons her home and her fiancé, putting herself in direct opposition to her family and the governing norms of society. Paul himself is thrown into prison because of his alleged "seduction" of one of the leading women of Iconium, who might provide an example for other women to follow, as indeed Thecla ultimately does, cutting her hair and donning male costume, defying imprisonment, threatened sexual attack, and death to lead an anti-household, celibate, and itinerant life. It is this kind of teaching that, in the minds of the writers of the Pastoral Epistles, represents an unhealthy asceticism, as opposed to the God-given discipline, transmitted by the founder Paul, that supports marriage and "saves" women through childbearing and disciplined behavior, thus countering the "teaching of demons," condemned by 1 Tim. 4:1ff., that "forbids marriage."

Titus also is warned by the Paul of the Pastoral Epistles against "the many rebellious (*anypotaktoi*) people," those who have no *taxis* or do not recognize one, who are "empty talkers" and "deceivers," this time those who talk about circumcision and other "Jewish myths and commandments," who "turn people away from the truth," overturning "entire households" (Titus 1:10-14). The disorderly people "must be silenced" so that the Cretan congregation, prone as all Cretans are to lying, according to the proverb quoted in Titus 1:12, can be "healthy" in the faith. A bishop is to have the "healthy teaching" to combat "counter-speakers" (*antilegontas*) or challengers of the tradition (Titus 1:9). People who are contentious are to be avoided, since their controversies are "worthless" (3:9–11). The true "word of God" can be discredited through unregulated behavior, giving opponents an opportunity for evil speech, speech that is "out of control" (Titus 2:5–8;

cf. 1 Tim. 5:14; 6:1–2, 4–6). Thus, in all three letters, speech that is "contained" and "disciplined," either through the written word or transmission by approved authorities in parental fashion and through legitimate succession, is opposed to that which is "uncontained," having no unifying rule, no defined transmission, and is therefore illegitimate, a bastard child trying to claim an undeserved inheritance.

HOW TO ORDER A TAXIS: THE ASCETIC HOUSEHOLD

The author (and authority) of the Pastoral Epistles thus constructed as Paul, in the apostolic tradition that is passed on from spiritual "father" to "son," then proceeds to offer a counterasceticism to that of the so-called false asceticism of his opponents. As Lucinda Brown has pointed out, the author's advocacy of an "appropriate" or "proper" asceticism is centered upon "*sophrosyne* as a principal virtue."[23] In 1 Timothy, he urges his disciple, "Exercise (*gymnaze*) yourself towards reverence (*eusebeia*); for bodily exercise (*somatike gymnasia*) is of little value, but reverence is valuable in everything" (1 Tim. 4:7–8). Timothy's instructor also reminds him of his own exemplary struggle, his "contest" (*agona*, 1 Tim. 4:10). In 2 Timothy, the pupil is encouraged to adopt the God-given "spirit of power and love and self-discipline" (2 Tim. 1:7) and, like a good athlete, to win the crown by competing "according to the rules" (2 Tim. 2:4), again following the teacher, who has "finished the race" and won "the crown of righteousness" (2 Tim. 4:6). The competition, moreover, is paradoxically to be waged through a "quiet and peaceful way of life" that promotes "health" in the individual athlete and the church as well. Like a good athlete, one is to use self-control in obedience to and reverence for the proper authorities and instructors (1 Tim. 6:6).

As Alison Goddard Elliott has demonstrated in her study of early Christian hagiography, ascetic behavior is often described in the same terms as martyrdom.[24] While the *agones* of martyr saints were against the power of the pagan government, the agents of Satan, those of ascetic saints were against their own unruly inclinations. In the Pastoral Epistles, the contest is also against one's own inclinations (1 Tim. 6:12; 2 Tim. 4:5–6), rather than against the powers of the world. Instead, the level-headed bishop is to have a "firm grasp on the world" (Titus 1:5–6), echoing Paul's own voice in 1 Cor. 5:10, that to avoid the adulterers and the greedy and the robbers and idolaters of this world, one would have to be "out of this world."

Such advice, while using the metaphors usually associated with asceticism—training, physical discipline, athletic contests—wrests them from the realm of bodily denial, from the solitary struggle of the "spiritual athlete" usually thought of as the ascetic enterprise, and returns them to their original arena, that of a public contest, in a sphere where males dominate.[25] Within the household, an exemplary and model *kosmos* in dress, conduct, teaching, and speech is generated and offered as instructive of the larger society, which it mirrors to an extent in its "model citizenship," but from which it departs in its "more restrictive sexual ethics."[26] Although it might not appear so in its perceived anti-egalitarianism, this "householder" form of *askesis* is offered as a spiritual discipline that is accessible to and attainable by a greater number than that of the solitary champion of spiritual athletics. Everyone can compete; everyone who follows the rules can win (2 Tim. 2:5). This ascetic recommendation is like the Hindu *tapas* or ascetic practice, in which it is recognized that not everyone, and especially not women, can progress through the householder stage to that of the "forest-dweller" or anchorite and thence to that of the *sannyasin* or homeless "renouncer," but everyone can practice a kind of *tapas* through the appropriate performance of actions particular to one's station in life, without thought of or hope for personal reward. *Tapas*, originally the fire of the sacrifice, becomes the means by which one sacrifices oneself and one's desires on the fire of devotion.[27] In a similar vein, the author of the Epistle to Titus writes:

> For the saving grace of God has appeared to all persons (*pasin anthropois*), edu-
> cating (*paideuousa*) you so that, renouncing irreverence (*asebeia*) and the world-
> ly passions, you may live in the present age with self-control (*sophronos*) right-
> eousness, and reverence (*eusebos*). (Titus 2:11–12)

Relationships that require "good order" are "worldly" relationships in the sense that they are social ones: ruler to servant, master to slave, parent to child, and husband to wife. One feels certain that the author or authors of the Pastoral Epistles would have resonated positively to the Confucian teaching that harmony in the home, directed by the "noble man" whose heart is "pure" (cf. 1 Tim. 1:5), was the basis of a peaceful state and ultimately of a harmonious universe.[28] The *eremos kai hesychios bios* proposed by the Christian Pastoral Epistles also begins with the "rectification" of the individual soul, with this "rightness" (*dikaiosyne*) being manifest in the social arena through guidance of others.

The household itself represents that which is contained, controlled, and ordered, under the control of a model "head." The very church is God's *oikos*, of which he is the head. 2 Timothy employs the metaphor of a "great household" that contains equipment appropriate for different uses and of different values, "some for honorable uses and some for less honorable" (2 Tim. 2:20–26), but all to be "cleansed and useful to the master" (*despotes*) of the house. To be a useful and fitting vessel to contain the "truth," one must empty oneself by shunning youthful passions. The ascetic behavior advocated by the Pastoral Epistles employs the household as a metaphor for that structure which regulates and contains the individual soul. An individual must be "in control" or "master" of the potentially unruly passions of the soul, just as the "master" of the household controls and directs it at the command of God, the master of the "great house." Each person, therefore, is to practice self-control and self-discipline (*sophrosyne*) within his or her own station (2 Tim. 1:7). The "household management of God in the faith" that is the responsibility of the teachers and managers of the congregation (also a "household") is characterized by "love from a pure heart and a good conscience and a genuine faith," rather than by following one's own conscience (1 Tim. 4:2–5) or one's own "passions of every kind" (2 Tim. 3:7).

Both men and women are also expected to exhibit qualifications for office through their conduct in the heterosexual, paternal, male-dominated household, of which the foundation is marriage.[29] Sexual relations for men and women alike are characterized by terms that are often applied to celibate conduct—"pure" (*katharos/a*) and "holy" or dedicated to God (*semnos/e*). Christian males are to exercise self-control in praying, especially for those above them in authority, "without anger or argument" (1 Tim. 2:8). Bishops, who must be male, aim at a "noble work" and, therefore, must be "above reproach," "self-disciplined," and "temperate" (*sophrona*, 1 Tim. 3:2). Their sexual lives must be well regulated, as they should be married to only one wife. (Since in monogamous Greco-Roman society, even pagans married only one wife at a time, this injunction probably refers to the refusal of Christian bishops to remarry, thus marking them as different from the younger Christian widows.) They should be in charge of their own households, "keeping their children submissive in every kind of holiness" (1 Tim. 3:1–7), reputation among "those outside" being considered all-important. Deacons are to be similarly "holy" (*semnous*), having "a pure (*kathara*) conscience," and married to only one wife, managing their "own households" and children (1 Tim. 3:8–13). Female deacons (or "wives") must also be "holy" (*semnas*) and "faithful in everything," a phrase that may refer, as in other uses of the term, "*pistos/e*," to fidelity in marriage as well as to standards of "right" or proper teaching and belief. Indeed, the entire relationship of Timothy to his congregation in 1 Timothy is modeled upon a disciplined, holy, and sexually self-controlled household: He is to be to older men and women as a son, to younger men and women as a brother, but "in every purity" (1 Tim. 5:2), and to keep himself "pure" (1 Tim. 5:22).

In the letter to Titus, the author/authority encourages older men or "elders" to be "holy" (*semnous*), self-controlled (*sophronas*), "healthy" in faith, and older women or elders to be "similarly" behaved (Titus 2:1–2). Male elders must be "blameless" and "husbands of one wife"; their children are not to be rebellious. A bishop must also be "self-controlled" (*sophrona*), "holy" (*hosion*), and "self-disciplined" (*enkrate*, Titus 1:5–9). Younger men, like Titus himself, are to be likewise "self-controlled" (Titus 2:6). Younger women, taught by their female elders, are to be "self-controlled and holy," under the authority of "their own husbands" (Titus 2:5).

While speech in the Pastoral Epistles is the only area in which a severe *enkrateia* is to be practiced, to the extent of complete silence on occasion (1 Tim. 2:12), the watchword in "worldly" matters like food, drink, money, and sex is moderation. 1 Timothy inveighs against the hypocrisy of "deceitful spirits" and "teachings of demons" who enjoin complete celibacy (1 Tim. 4:3), but also against those who are "lawless" (*anomoi*) and "rebellious" (*anypotaktoi*) with regard to sexual behavior, since in his view they also show disrespect for "lawful" heterosexual marriage as God's institution (1 Tim. 1:10). Abstinence from certain foods that "God created," which the true believers should eat with thanksgiving, is likewise disrespect for God's authority (1 Tim. 4:1–3). Timothy is advised to "take a little wine" rather than to drink only water (1 Tim. 5:23; cf. 2 Tim. 4:5). Bishops must not be drunkards, and deacons should not drink too much wine (1 Tim. 3:3, 8), but they are not prohibited from drinking wine altogether. Older women should not be "slaves to drink" (Titus 2:3), but women "or anyone else" are not told to abstain completely.

With regard to money, which, according to Harpham, is "a crucial ascetic invention," a symbol that concentrates both "unworldliness" (through its rejection) and world transformation (with its use for "good works"),[30] the Pastoral Epistles advise the rich to "do good" with it, by their generosity becoming "rich in good works" (1 Tim. 6:18–19). A deliberate choice of poverty if one is rich is profitless, an unnecessary and perhaps even self-indulgent form of false asceticism, since how then can one share money with the poor?[31] Good money management, like good household management in a family, is a necessity for the community, although excesses—greed and ostentatious display of wealth on the one hand, stealing on the other—are to be avoided. In 1 Timothy, women are advised to adorn themselves with "shame," "self-control," and "good works" rather than with a display of braided hair, gold, pearls, and expensive garments (1 Tim. 2:9–10).

Bishops and deacons, in managing their own households, are to be "no lovers of money" nor "greedy for gain" (1 Tim. 3:3, 8), since the love of money is the root of all evils, leading believers astray in pursuit of their own individual pleasures (1 Tim. 6:10). The bishop as "steward of God's household" must also not be greedy (Titus 1:7–9). The appearance of people who are *philargyroi*, "lovers of money," is thus one of the signs of the chaotic "final days" (2 Tim. 3:2). Hospitality, on the other hand, is a particular service for widows (1 Tim. 5:9–15), and it is also a virtue for families to provide for their own widows (1 Tim. 5:8, 16). As appropriate to their own relationship to money and possessions, slaves must not steal, and their good conduct provides a public "ornament" to the doctrine (Titus 2:9–10). Believers in general are to devote themselves to "good works, in order to meet urgent needs," and not be "unproductive" by spending time in "profitless" controversies (Titus 3:9, 14).

There is also a social and ethical model for children envisioned by the Pastoral Epistles. The Paul of 1 Corinthians and Romans does not include children in his schema of appropriate relationships among persons living in the end time, but the Paul of 2 Timothy sees rebelliousness of children to parents being one of the signs of the "distress" and conflict of the final days (2 Tim. 3:2). "Entire families" can be upset by the wrong kind of teaching, that of the *anypotaktoi* (Titus 1:10), those who do not know their proper *taxis*, who may be teaching children to be similarly rebellious (*anypotakta*, Titus 1:6). The worst fault is *asebeia*, which can only be corrected by the appropriate training, one that educates pupils to avoid the "worldly passions" associated with their youth toward self-control, righteousness, and respect (Titus 2:12; cf. 2 Tim. 2:23–24). Those who are leaders in the Christian congregation—bishops and elders—are to enforce the obedience and submissiveness of their own children (1 Tim. 3:4, 7, 12; 2 Tim. 3:2; Titus 1:6), while correcting adults and social equals under their charge with patience and gentleness (2 Tim. 2:24; 4:2). It is worth noting that the deacons, whose very name—*diakonoi*—implies a position of "service," are not commanded to enforce obedience from their children, perhaps because their *taxis* in God's household is already one of "servant" rather than "master."

Naturally, there is also a *taxis* for slaves within the well-regulated household. Slaves, like parents and children, also are to offer a model of disciplined behavior within a Christian society. Like the utensils fit for a variety of uses in the "great house" of 2 Tim. 2:20–26, and like wives with their "own husbands," they are to treat their masters with "appropriate" honor and submission (1 Tim. 6:1–2a; Titus 2:9-10), not "disrespecting" believing masters if they are themselves unbelieving, giving satisfaction (their form of "good works"), and not stealing the master's goods. Like slaves, all Christians are subject to rulers and authorities and are to be similarly ready "for every good work" (Titus 3:1–2; cf. 1 Tim. 2:1–2). All believers, even those in "authority" over congregations, are actually to practice the chief virtues of slaves, who are to be obedient and "useful," not unlike Onesimus of Paul's letter to Philemon, who upon his flight from his master was deemed "useless," and afterward, upon his presumptive return, was to become truly "useful" (Phil. 10–11; cf. 1 Tim. 6:4–6; 2 Tim. 2:24; Titus 3:2–4, 8). The "slave of the Lord," Timothy, is likewise to be meek and gentle, even in correcting the rest of God's household who are under him as overseer (*episkopos*). All Christians are therefore to adopt the model of submissive slaves, obedient to, "reverent" toward, and respectful of those in authority over them in the state (1 Tim. 1:1–2; 2 Tim. 2:3–6; Titus 3:1–2). As Margaret MacDonald notes, "obedient servanthood" is the model for all Christian behavior throughout the Pastoral Epistles.[32]

EXCURSUS: CONTROLLING WOMEN

It must also be pointed out that the opposition between order and anarchy, discipline and laxity, in the Pastoral Epistles is frequently a gendered opposition. That is, "male" represents order and "female" tends to represent its opposite or "other," in direct resistance to control or providing the opportunity for it to be upset. Just as in the lives and writings of the ascetic male saints, the temptation against which self-control must struggle to define itself is represented by women,[33] so also in the Pastoral Epistles the threat of subversion is characterized as female and often as sexual. In 1 Timothy, married women are told to hold their peace with "total submission" (*pase hypotage*, 1 Tim. 2:12) because women are portrayed as more easily deceived by seductive talk and perhaps prone to deceive men also (1 Tim. 2:13–14). This reasoning appears to be based upon what seems to be a misreading of Gen. 3:6, that Adam was not deceived but that his wife was, and is interpreted by Dewey to mean that the author believed Eve was "seduced" by the serpent and that her "transgression" was sexual.[34] Whether one agrees with Dewey's interpretation of 1 Tim. 2:14 or not, female sexuality as a symbol of transgressing boundaries, of the unruly in need of control, is a constant trope in biblical literature. In the Pastoral Epistles particularly, great stress is laid upon directing female sexuality into the confines of a heterosexual marriage and within the household, to continue the Christian family as a stable and edifying model for "the world." Thus, 1 Timothy characterizes the "true" widows as those who have no household, in contrast to the "false" widows, the younger women, who can be led astray by "sensual desires" (1 Tim. 5:3–15). These "little women" (*gynaikaria*), steeped in their sins, are easily captivated by the itinerant, presumably male, teachers who invade households to promote an endless learning that never gets at the "truth" (2 Tim. 3:6–9). Women, especially those who are sexually active, are portrayed as providing "an occasion for the adversary" (1 Tim. 5:14), again like Eve, and hence as representing the potential for subverting order.

Although the sexuality advocated by the Pastoral Epistles appears not to be an ascetic sexuality understood as celibacy, for example, in 1 Corinthians 7, it is similarly "ascetic" in that it is disciplined within the bonds of marriage. As a means to resist temptation and unregulated passions, "appropriately" directed sexuality, especially in marriage, can lead to salvation (1 Tim. 2:16). "Lawless" behavior, on the other hand, is characterized not only by false asceticism but also by unregulated sexual conduct (1 Tim. 1:10). Silence, obedience, modesty in dress and demeanor, and childbearing are the marks of a "saved" woman, the characteristics of a "gender-based" *sophrosyne*.[35]

2 Timothy and Titus also are concerned with the ability of sexually mature, marriageable, fertile women to leave their male-directed households and ecclesial communities to form independent female-directed households

or to become itinerant, perhaps either converts of or even themselves "invaders" of households, who carry different teaching with them like a "disease" (2 Tim. 3:6–9). Titus is therefore instructed to make sure that older women lead a self-controlled life, practicing respect, not becoming addicted to drink, becoming models for younger women to lead a similarly "self-controlled" life, directing their energies to loving their husbands, raising their children, remaining chaste, and managing their households but being submissive to the heads of those households. Once more, these directions are predicated on authoritative teaching and are given "so that the word of God might not be discredited" (Titus 2:3–5). In short, the kind of self-control for women urged by the Pastoral Epistles is a regulation of sexuality, not in the direction of a voluntary celibacy leading to unrestricted freedom of movement, learning, and instruction, like that of the heroines of the apocryphal Acts, but in that of supporting a disciplined household, in which the woman as elder sets the example for other members of the household who are to lead a disciplined life that subjects the unruly individual will to that of the spiritual "father," "master," and "head of the household."

CONCLUSION

As we have seen, the great concern of the Pastoral Epistles is the prescription of right conduct for the purpose of inducing, rather than coercing, the rest of the world to adopt its *bios*, its way of life, which is nonetheless presented as the only true one. The behavior advocated in the Pastoral Epistles belongs to an asceticism that is not "combative," to use Valantasis' terminology, in that it resists not authority or society but the chaos produced by individual desire, and thus aims at the achievement of self-control both in those who are in positions of authority over others and in those whose only "triumph" is to turn their subordinate positions into models of self-sacrifice. (The success of this experiment still presents a problem for those whose positions of subordination in society have been consistently justified by those in authority by reference to the Pastoral Epistles.)

The author of the Pastoral Epistles is engaged in demonstrating an ascetic practice that creates not individual spiritual "champions" but a completely disciplined community of "households" within a household (the church) in which one does not follow one's individual conscience, but obeys the rules that promote the survival of the church as a corporate being. The major difference between this type of community and one that is cenobitic is that the community of the Pastoral Epistles does not withdraw to create its vision of the good society, but instead presents its vision as an achievable transformation of the existing society "of the present age" (*to nun aioni*, 1 Tim. 6:17). The ascetic subjectivity presented in the Pastoral Epistles is thus, again in Valantasis' terminology, "integrative."

This integration for purposes of social transformation cannot be accomplished, however, without the strenuous effort and self-discipline that are the chief elements of any *askesis*. "Paul," the "master," offers himself as the pattern to be followed, in the "educative" model of ascetic subjectivity: "I have competed in the good contest (*agona*), I have finished the course, I have kept to (*tetereka*) the faith" (2 Tim. 4:7). For this, he expects to be given the victor's crown, granted by the "just judge" (2 Tim. 4:8). He advises his disciples, his "children," to follow his example, but warns, "An athlete who does not compete by the rules does not win the crown" (2 Tim. 2:5; cf. 1 Tim. 6:12). The master offers other models to be followed: A good soldier, like the "soldier for Christ" (2 Tim. 2:3), does not fight on behalf of his own affairs, but to please his commander (2:4); only the farmer who "labors" has first claim on the crops (2:6); and the one who keeps the faith is a "worker who is not ashamed" before the master, God (2:15). Thus, self-discipline becomes social *askesis*, training to regard one's own *taxis* in the order (*kosmos*) created by God, not allowing it to be overturned by individual desire, passion, or inclination. Bending one's will to that of God, the project of Christian asceticism in general, is achievable in the Pastoral Epistles not by giving up such bodily actions as food, drink, sex, and familial interaction for the sake of individual devotion to God, but by giving up individual interpretations of that will, subject as they must be to variation and therefore disorder, for the sake of a single-minded, united, and controlled assent to God's authority. This is *askesis* as *eusebeia*. There remain the ascetic ideals of training, conditioning, subduing, and resisting, but the demonic powers that are to be resisted are demons that seek to represent God's will and authority as subjective, creating "wanderings" and debates over a single truth, in the name of the individualistic "falsely named" intuitive grasp of the divine that characterizes gnosis. As in other forms of Christian asceticism, the will is subdued, desire is fought, and God is honored in one's body, except that the individual body erases itself in the "greater" body of the community *qua* household, in which each member knows his or her "proper" place and function. If I may use a final analogy, it is an ideal exemplified by the root meaning of the Islamic jihad, the struggle that must occur first within the individual spirit before one can become truly "Muslim," a submitter to God's will. Only so will the world be re-formed into the Dar-al-Islam, the "house of submission (to God's will)."

Notes

1. Geoffrey Galt Harpham, *The Ascetic Imperative in Culture and Criticism* (Chicago: University of Chicago Press, 1987) 15, 27–28.
2. Richard R. Valantasis, "Constructions of Power in Asceticism," *Journal of the American Academy of Religion* 63 (1995): 813–15.
3. Harpham, *Ascetic Imperative*, 97, 134.

4. Following nearly all modern commentators on the Pastoral Epistles, I assume that they have one and the same male author, who claims the authority and the pseudonym of Paul.

5. Valantasis, "Constructions of Power," 803–4.

6. Bruce J. Malina, "Pain, Power, and Personhood: Ascetic Behavior in the Ancient Mediterranean," in *Asceticism*, eds. Vincent L. Wimbush and Richard Valantasis (New York: Oxford University Press, 1995), 168; see also Elizabeth Castelli's critique, "Asceticism—Audience and Resistance," in *Asceticism*, eds. Wimbush and Valantasis, 184.

7. Valantasis, "Constructions of Power," 815.

8. Martin Dibelius and Hans Conzelmann, *The Pastoral Epistles: A Commentary on the Pastoral Epistles*, trans. Philip Buttolph and Adela Yarbro, ed. Helmut Koester, Hermeneia (Philadelphia: Fortress, 1972), 159.

9. Ibid, 65

10. This is the translation of 1 Tim. 4:7 suggested by Joanna Dewey, "1 Timothy," in *The Women's Bible Commentary*, eds. Carol A. Newsom and Sharon H. Ringe (Louisville, Ky.: Westminster/Knox, 1992), 356.

11. Among these are Dibelius and Conzelmann, *Pastoral Epistles;* Steven Davies, *The Revolt of the Windows: The Social World of the Apocryphal Acts* (Carbondale: Southern Illinois University Press, 1980); Dennis R. MacDonald, *The Legend and the Apostle: The Battle for Paul in Story and Canon* (Philadelphia: Westminster, 1983); David C. Verner, *The Household of God: The Social World of the Pastoral Epistles* (Chico, Calif.: Scholars, Society of Biblical Literature Dissertation Series 71, 1983); and Margaret Y. MacDonald, *The Pauline Churches: A Socio-Historical Study of Institutionalization in the Pauline and Deutero-Pauline Churches* (Cambridge: Cambridge University Press, Society for New Testament Studies Monograph Series 1988). For a summary and analysis of these points of view, see Margaret Davies, *The Pastoral Epistles* (Sheffield, England: Sheffield Academic Press, New Testament Guides, 1996).

12. Valantasis, "Constructions of Power," 802.

13. D. MacDonald, *Legend and Apostle*, 14–15.

14. M. MacDonald, *Pauline Churches*, 158–59.

15. Dewey, "1 Timothy," 354.

16. Verner, *Household of God*, 79.

17. Dibelius and Conzelmann, *Pastoral Epistles*, 13.

18. Valantasis, "Constructions of Power," 803–4

19. D. MacDonald, *Legend and Apostle*, 14, 66–73.

20. Dewey, "1 Timothy," 359.

21. Harpham, *Ascetic Imperative*, 16.

22. Dewey, "2 Timothy," in *Women's Bible Commentary*, eds. Newsom and Ringe, 359.

23. Lucinda A. Brown, "Asceticism and Ideology: The Language of Power in the Pastoral Epistles," in *Discursive Formations, Ascetic Piety and the Interpretation of Early Christian Literature, Part I*, ed. Vincent L. Wimbush (*Semeia* 57; Atlanta, Ga.: Scholars, 1992), 88–94.

24. Alison Goddard Elliott, *Roads to Paradise: Reading the Lives of the Early Saints* (Hanover and London: University Press of New England/Brown University Press, 1987), 19.

25. See Harpham, *Ascetic Imperative*, 27–28.
26. Verner, *Household of God*, 145.
27. See Walter O. Kaelber, "Understanding Asceticism—Testing a Typology," in *Asceticism*, eds. Wimbush and Valantasis, 323–24.
28. See "The Root of Everything," in *The Great Learning,* trans. Charles A. Wong, in *The Portable World Bible*, ed. Robert O. Ballou (New York: Penguin, 1976), 509.
29. I am trying to eschew the term "patriarchal" where I can, since I believe that it has been so frequently and loosely employed as to be well-nigh meaningless.
30. Harpham, *Ascetic Imperative*, 62.
31. This line of reasoning is similar to Philo of Alexandria's invective against the "contrived poverty" of philosophers, who neglect or abandon their property without benefiting their relatives (*Vit. Cont.* 2.14–16).
32. M. MacDonald, *Pauline Churches*, 168.
33. Harpham, *Ascetic Imperative*, 54.
34. Ibid, 356.
35. Brown, "Asceticism and Ideology," 83–87.

Where is "This World" Headed?
Irony, World Renunciation,
and the Pauline Corpus

Will Love

The authors in this part deserve special thanks for leading us into the still virgin wilderness of Pauline asceticism. As all the contributors have made clear from their different vantage points, this wilderness is "virgin" more in spirit than in actual practice. For what is most commonly recognized as ascetic discipline, celibacy or retreat to the desert, is given no real place in the Pauline communities. While Paul himself maintained a celibate and itinerant lifestyle, he went to pains to discourage anyone else from following suit. Ancillary disciplines, beyond those required of specific members by their community, are generally denounced as contrary to the gospel of Christ. But it is in these same letters that we find for the first time in the early church the development of a language of world renunciation. As it is stated forcefully in Romans: "Do not be conformed to this world, but be transformed by the renewing of your minds, so that you may discern what is the will of God—what is good and acceptable and perfect" (12:2). The language of world renunciation continues into the more socially accommodating Deutero-Pauline letters, where the notion of renewal after the image and likeness of God (Col. 3:9–11, Eph. 4:22–24) deeply affected the subsequent development of the Christian ascetical tradition. How are we to address the deep ambiguity between word and deed in these letters in both their historical and interpretive frames?

The historical question raised by current wanderings in the Pauline wilderness is essentially one of how best to characterize the ethos of the Pauline community: Is it ascetical or nonascetical? Is it this-worldly (accommodationist) or other-worldly (transgressive)? Does the moral code promulgated in the community absolutize or relativize contemporary ethical standards? The great irony, of course, is that a given text can be used to support either side of such ethical antinomies, as many of the contributors to this part of the book have acknowledged.

Given that this is a book about asceticism and the New Testament, the weight of the arguments will tend to fall toward a reading of the letters as ascetical in some fashion. But we can now appreciate the irony that Pauline asceticism is located as much in the different understandings of asceticism brought to bear on the texts as it is in the social and historical context of the Pauline communities themselves. Avoiding such unsettling irony is perhaps one of the reasons why questions about asceticism in the Pauline corpus, despite its importance to the later Christian ascetical tradition, have been ducked in the past.

The principle of irony has become a standard rhetorical device employed in present-day literary, historical, and cultural-critical studies, encompassing both a literary device located externally in the text and a cast of mind employed by the critical reader in interpreting those texts.[1] Irony has proven useful in identifying subtle or long-suppressed meanings in a text. It is employed by many of the authors who write here to open up new possibilities for interpretation.

But irony can also be employed to show how contemporary scholarship is itself engaged in an unending play of difference. Elizabeth Castelli draws out the contemporary importance of difference in both history and asceticism in an article that itself stands out as markedly different vis-à-vis the other more traditional historical readings beside it. The irony between historical and literary-critical approaches to interpretation of the New Testament exists, however, not only between the different chapters in this book, but may also be seen to lie coiled serpentlike within individual contributions. There is a struggle within the reader both to deconstruct the rhetorical ploys of a text *and* to say something true about it at the same time. It would seem that the critical gaze cannot be directed back into its own sights, a dilemma that even the most deconstructionist reading does not entirely escape, if it is to argue anything at all (including "there is nothing to argue").

Rather than merely skim the surface of the many excellent chapters in this part, I propose instead to look more closely at a few of them to demonstrate in greater detail how irony plays itself out here on multiple and overlapping levels. Both Margaret MacDonald and Gail Corrington Streete employ irony in probing the ascetical contents of the Deutero-Pauline letters they investigate. In her chapter on Colossians and Ephesians, MacDonald speaks of the "ironic predicament," the "peculiar tension between symbolism that implies an ultimate rejection of standards and priorities of society and ethics that encourage acceptance of these same standards and priorities."[2] In both Colossians and Ephesians, world renunciation carries the paradoxical demand that the Christian become more, not less, conformed to society through strict adherence to the household code of ethics enjoined by Roman society. "Asceticism" enters into the equation, for MacDonald, as the thread that ties together the collection of practices and rituals associated with the "false teachings" in Colossians. The asceticism of these false teachings is deemed ineffective in freeing one from the self-indulgence of the flesh, and therefore from the world. From MacDonald's perspective, the message of Colossians and Ephesians is a-ascetical.

Streete also points us to the irony lying at the heart of the Pastoral Epistles, although for Streete the irony arises more from the nature of the texts than from their implicit social context. The Pastoral Epistles are depicted as bringing to written closure, and thereby into the realm of established authority, what was originally conceived as a mode of resistance to such authority. Streete refers us to Geoffrey Harpham's notion of the "ascetical imperative" located at the root of human culture, the idea that asceticism makes culture possible through the ambivalent tension it creates between the simultaneous expression of resistance and closure. With an enduring sense of irony, Harpham writes about the ascetic ground of early Christian culture:

> The durability of asceticism lies in its capacity to structure oppositions without collapsing them, to raise issues without settling them. Even within the ideological restraints of early Christian practice, asceticism exhibited a high-intensity comprehensiveness, a hyperarticulated ambivalence. Take for example the early Christian approach to culture, which often took radically anticultural forms, such as the retreat by the early monastic heroes to isolated caves in the desert. The often morbid or flamboyant deprivations and tortures they inflicted on themselves displayed a violence and self-loathing entirely incompatible with communal life or the family structure. But this apparent anticulturalism should not eclipse the fact that the Desert Fathers brought the Book to the Desert, and served as apostles of a textual culture in the domain of the natural. Asceticism neither simply condemns culture nor simply endorses it; it does both. Asceticism, we could say, *raises the issue* of culture by structuring an opposition between culture and its opposite.[3]

In a similar way, Streete argues that "the 'chaotic' movement of asceticism can be harnessed in the service of the community by modeling through authoritative texts that themselves provide paradigms for the 'true' ascetic resistance."[4] In contrast to MacDonald's a-ascetical reading of the "true" Christians at Colossians and Ephesians, Streete sees the Pastoral Epistles as providing evidence for the pervasiveness of ascetical discourse in the later Pauline communities.

For MacDonald, the resolution to the implicit irony of these letters that simultaneously reject and embrace the standards of the surrounding society lies in a sociological analysis of the particular community addressed by each letter. The movement by the Pauline communities to accommodate worldly structures through adherence to the householder code of ethics in Colossae and Ephesus conferred a substantial degree of protective invisibility on the Christian community, permitting it to grow in strength and numbers. The Christian community's invisibility acted as a kind of guerrilla tactic designed to overcome a more numerous and powerful opponent. By remaining indistinguishable from respectable families in the larger society, Christians were able quietly to go about their business promoting the gospel to the world.

The need for invisibility is also seen to provide a context for the suppression of the false teachings described in Colossians. The ascetic and visionary experiences attached to these false teachings attracted unwanted attention to the Christian community or to individuals within that community. Like a deer freezing at the slightest sign of danger, the Christian must resist the instinct for flight or to fight, which might expose the community to hostility; the community simultaneously rejects and is immersed in the world around it.

If indeed the Pauline communities at Colossae and Ephesus chose the path of least resistance in imperial Roman society, their relationship to the world takes on a distinctly relativist hue. Such a relativizing stance toward the world would seem to contradict the Christian celebration of the martyr who set an absolute standard of righteousness in Christian behavior. As found in Paul's genuine letters, the Christian is called to witness to the truth of the gospel in the face of persecution and even death (see, e.g., Phil. 1:12–26). Ultimately, for Paul in Philippians, the point is not to hide from the world, but to transform it into the body of Christ. So, while MacDonald's explanation resolves one irony of the tradition, a new one arises to take its place. Can this secondary tension between an absolute and a relative ethics in Paul be resolved?

If we break away from the Judeo-Christian mold for a moment, there may also be other ethical systems that support both an absolute and a relativizing standard of conduct. In Mahayana Buddhism, for example, the spiritual path of the *bodhisattvas* begins and ends with the imperative that they not escape from *samsara*, the round of birth and death, to enter *nirvana*, until all sentient beings have been enlightened. To effect the absolute good of *nirvana*, the *bodhisattva* is thus reborn lifetime after lifetime along the "six courses" (hell beings, hungry ghosts, animals, humans, titans, and gods). The *bodhisattva* conforms both to the outward form and to the manner of existence of the particular course into which they have been reborn to assist those beings in attaining enlightenment. I do not wish to suggest that Mahayana Buddhists and Pauline Christians share the same ethical standards. But both may seek to draw more attention to the intention behind the act than to the act itself, to a way of seeing the world rather than to the specific nature of the world as such.

For Streete, the resolution to the ironic textualization of the ascetic impulse in the Pastoral Epistles is found in what she calls "an active, social, 'householder' ascetic that is based upon self-discipline in speech and conduct and upon 'good deeds' appropriate to each one's station or *taxis* in society."[5] The different *taxeis* denote the specific social roles required of older and younger men, older and younger women, children, and slaves, as well as the specialized religious roles of bishops, deacons, and widows. The "true" asceticism of the Pastoral Epistles becomes a voluntary subjugation to one's particular *taxis* as determined by the proper authorities and set down in authoritative writings. While from a modern North Atlantic perspective this taxonomy supports an oppressively hierarchical social model, it nevertheless seems to have given everyone an opportunity to engage in a form of ascetic discipline as determined by their particular place within a given community. Unlike other-worldly forms of asceticism, this type is not limited to persons with extraordinary spiritual powers, higher knowledge, or a special role.

Thus for Streete, the real irony in the Pastoral Epistles does not occur between ascetical "false" and a-ascetical "true" teachings, but between competing rhetorics of asceticism, one fixed in writing and the other unstably fluid and presumably oral. Under this wider, linguistically defined model of asceticism, questions will inevitably arise among scholars regarding the ultimate intelligibility of the term "asceticism": Are all ethical systems, therefore, to be deemed ascetical? Has asceticism been so broadly defined in this case that it loses all coherence as a particular phenomenon? In terms of the later Pauline communities, can a Christian renounce renunciation of the world and still be considered a renunciant?

In considering how widely we should cast our net in defining asceticism, it may be helpful to consider another non-Western example. In the *Bhagavad Gita*, often called the "Hindu Bible," the great archer Arjuna, about to lead his clan into battle against his kinsmen and beloved teachers, suddenly decides that it would be better to renounce all action in the world and to be killed rather than to try to kill those so near and dear to him. But his chariot driver, the Lord Krishna, tells him that no one, not even a world-renouncing *yogi*, can renounce action in the world. It is Arjuna's *dharma*, his sacred duty as a member of the warrior class, to fight and to kill, or to be killed. Only by renouncing the fruits of his action in the performance of his rightfully appointed duties will he find freedom from the karmic burden that action in the world produces. At one point, using words not unlike Paul's counsel in 1 Corinthians to "remain where you are" (7:29–31), Krishna tells Arjuna that "Your own duty done imperfectly is better than another man's done well" (3.35).[6] Using the most extreme case possible—the text has been interpreted both literally to support armed revolt and metaphorically to support only passive forms of resistance (Gandhi)—the interests of the householder and the renunciant are merged in the single path known as *karma yoga*, the discipline of action in the world. Thus, despite championing the householder ethic, the *Gita* is replete with ascetic language and metaphor.

The fact that MacDonald and Streete have arrived at substantially different, even mutually exclusive, understandings of the role of asceticism in the Deutero-Pauline epistles gives a further ironic twist to their already irony-laden readings of these texts. The sense of irony does not arise simply from their methodological and definitional differences, however, but can be seen to begin deep within the ensuing memory of the Pauline writings themselves. A sharp divergence of opinion exists, for example, between traditional Protestant and Catholic views of asceticism. Martin Luther did not mince words in his assessment of monastic forms of asceticism in the Christian life. In his commentary on Genesis, Luther says of the "father of Christian monasticism":

> Of what concern is Anthony to us? Contrary to conscience, since he knew that nothing should be undertaken in life or doctrine apart from God's command, he hid himself in the desert. We know that there are three estates in this life: the household, the state, and the church. If all men want to neglect these and pursue their own interests and self-chosen ways, who will be a shepherd of souls? Who will baptize, absolve, and console those who are burdened with sins? Who will administer the government and protect the common fabric of human society? Who will educate the young and till the ground? ... The examples of the fathers, the prophets, and the apostles should be shown to them. These men did not despise the household, the state, and the church. Nor did they shrink from the works of farmers and slaves. Nevertheless, they were able to live in faith and God's commandments. In ordinary life they conducted themselves in such a way that to the eyes of the flesh no difference was apparent between Abraham, Isaac, and the other fathers, who were friends of God, and the heathen rulers who were ignorant of God and hated him. The flesh does not see the promise and the love of the saints, just as the papists and the jurists do not see these things.[7]

We hear here echoes of the Pauline letters, but especially of the Pastoral Epistles, although we must remind ourselves that Luther was in a very different position in his society than were the Pauline communities in their respective social contexts. Having ignored his superiors and renounced his community's vow of obedience, Luther soon wielded great political muscle throughout Europe.

Much closer in time to the Pauline communities are the early Greek Fathers who wrote extensively on Christian scripture from an ascetical point of view. Ironically, their writings also betray a strong dependence on Paul and specifically on the formula found in both Colossians and Ephesians demanding renewal after the image and likeness of God (Col. 3:9–11; Eph. 4:22–24). Christ, identified as the image of God in Col. 1:15, becomes the model after which a Christian is both created and renewed. In their interpretation of this formula, the Church Fathers drew a distinction between the meaning of *eikon* and *homoiosis* in the Septuagint version of Gen. 1:26. They imputed a dynamic movement from the "image," implanted in all persons from their beginning, to the "likeness," which can only be developed over time by a dedicated few. Humans are created in the image of God, so that one day, modeling themselves through *askesis* after Christ, they may become more like God. Thus, for example, Origen, in his exegesis of the two creation narratives in Genesis (1–2), distinguished between the "honour of God's image in his first creation" and its transformation into the "perfection of his likeness...reserved for the consummation":

> The purpose of this was that man should acquire it for himself by his own earnest efforts to imitate God, so that while the possibility of attaining perfection was given him in the beginning through the honour of the "image," he should in the end through the accomplishment of these works obtain for himself the perfect "likeness."[8]

In sharp contrast to Luther, then, the Church Fathers saw Anthony as providing the most perfect contemporary portrait of the Pauline notion of humanity reformed in Christ.

The fact that the Deutero-Pauline epistles could contribute to almost diametrically opposed ways of thinking about asceticism in Origen and Luther leads us to reconsider our assumptions about asceticism as a "new" category. The search for the grand definition of asceticism remains problematic in part because of lingering dogmatic biases. Instead of Origen and Luther, we now have Nietzsche and Foucault. Efforts to recognize both this-worldly and other-worldly forms of asceticism, as found in Max Weber's classic typology, tend to conceal as much as they reveal about asceticism.[9]

We may never resolve the anachronistic tensions lingering between narrow and broad definitions of asceticism. I would suggest, therefore, that we try building instead a definition of asceticism from the ground up, as it were, using the spatial imagery of flight from the world. What might be said to tie together many ascetical attitudes, at least within older societies, is the description of movement outside or above or beyond the world. By identifying the different senses of world and the direction(s) of movement adopted by the religious person to transcend them, we might create a grammar of ascetic terms that, when mixed together in different degrees and combinations, could help better to account for the infinite variations in ascetic behavior without falling into some all-inclusive, and hence not very informative, principle of culturation.

In its most celebrated form, world renunciation entails the intentional dislocation to a remote or otherwise inaccessible place—a desert, mountain, forest, or, alternatively, monastic enclosure, hermitage, or cell—what Karl Heussi called in his classic study of monastic origins a *Sonderwelt* or "world apart."[10] The geographical form of withdrawal has long been practiced by individuals and groups existing at the fringes of religious society. As long ago as the sixth century BCE in India, individuals began leaving their homes and villages to locate outside of towns or to wander in the forests, an ascetic practice that culminated in the two great ascetic orders of India, Buddhism and Jainism.[11] At least since the Han dynasty in China (206 BCE–220 CE), and a bit later elsewhere in East Asia, Taoist, Buddhist, and even Confucian sages left their social world behind to live in the sacred mountains.[12] Further west, around the time of Jesus, Jewish sectarians would remove themselves, at least for a time, from urban Jewish communities to form secluded religious retreats, as at Qumran. But not until the late third and fourth centuries CE in the circum-Mediterranean region do we find a permanent form of geographical withdrawal from ordinary human society in the Christian flight into the desert, a space perceived by contemporaries as existing beyond "the world" (*oikoumene*).[13]

Apart from such geographical dislocation, the ascetic's body, wherever located, also serves as a locus for movement beyond the world. At this physical level of world renunciation, the basic material conditions of human existence—the need for food, warmth, sleep, sex, and social recognition—are systematically suppressed and sometimes eliminated. Since the body is widely viewed as a microcosm of the world in traditional religious cultures, overcoming the body's ingrained habits is seen to lead to an overcoming of the same world. But unlike geographical flight, the direction of movement away from the surrounding world is inward. Basil the Great recognized this distinction when he said in a letter to his friend Gregory Nazianzus: "There is only one escape—withdrawal from the world. This withdrawal does not mean that we should leave the world bodily, but rather break loose from the ties of 'sympathy' of the soul with the body."[14]

Beyond physical mastery of the body's natural functions, the need to have one's body recognized as part of a legitimate social order might also be suppressed. This variation of body-based world renunciation is expressed as a return of the body to the instinctual level of the self-absorbed animal that must roam or scavenge for a living. Even open sexual conduct, as reputed among certain Cynics, can be seen to constitute a form of world renunciation. While the range of bodily forms of *askesis* varies widely, they all act to effect the body's displacement from the surrounding world through an inward movement of the senses.

One's standing in the social body, renounced by others, can paradoxically serve as another locus for world renunciation. Without fleeing from the larger community, without subjugating the body's physical functions or returning to the natural body, the ascetic may achieve a level of "outsiderhood" to the world by submitting his or her will to the spiritual authority of the community. The will, commonly identified as the seat of self, is displaced from its position at the center of the world, even as the ascetic remains physically and socially engaged within society. Generally, the will of the group as embodied in a particular spiritual guide becomes the center of one's being. Thus, the movement of the ascetic becomes a kind of self-dispersal within a body politic as embodied in a particular spiritual guide or community rule.

Since human interaction is necessary in order to deny one's will, social harmony becomes paramount for this sort of social training. Here we can locate such diverse forms of asceticism as cenobitic monasticism, modern Alcoholics Anonymous meetings, and the household code of the Deutero-Pauline epistles. What distinguishes these very different instances of one type of asceticism from each another is how they are all variously combined with other world-renouncing attitudes. The dispute in Colossians between "true" and "false" teachings might be explained as the argument between different factions in the community about whether bodily renunciation should be added to society-based forms of world renunciation practiced by the community.

As Valantasis' definition helps make clear, world renunciation has meaning beyond the negatively charged act of dislocation from the center to periphery, from a higher to a lower material condition, from self-will to other-will; it also involves a more positively understood revisioning of the world as a whole. Periods of intense geographical, bodily, and self dislocation are often accompanied by the claim that the renunciant, now "dead" to this world, has crossed over into another, higher world. Passing in spirit beyond the boundaries of the cosmos, the renouncer remains uncontaminated by mundane perceptions of reality.

This other world does not appear as a more perfect version of the one left behind, a view of heaven found in many sacrificial systems. Rather, it stands beyond the world, an extra-cosmic dimension that allows the ascetic to break free from more limited and limiting perceptions of the world. The forsaken world may then become the object of the ascetic's detached gaze. An expansive, because detached, vision of this world often marks the otherworldly gaze, making those who engage in such alternate sight the seers of hidden forces. It is this spirited search to transcend time and space that finally gives positive significance to the often negatively charged acts of geographical and bodily dislocation by the ascetic. Here we might locate the language of separation from the world found in the Deutero-Pauline epistles.

If at some level world renunciation contains the search for an expansive vision of world, it might be argued, as Castelli does, that the historian and literary scholar are engaged in a similar kind of world renunciation, albeit muted when compared to traditional religious counterparts. By "renouncing" the cultural viewpoint, the scholar searches for a vision of the world or worlds outside his or her own, attempting to grasp an overall logic from some higher plane of intellection. An analogy could be drawn between the scholar's "ivory tower" and the monk's retreat in the "desert": Each shares a sense of dislocation from the everyday world, a sense of isolation attending the dislocated self, and the search for an expansive or totalizing view of the world. In their own ways, the ivory tower and the desert equally connote inaccessibility, austerity, and freedom.

It must, however, be emphasized that modern and postmodern scholars do not remove themselves physically or socially to another world. They are not world renunciants in the geographical, bodily, or self-will senses of the term, despite cultivating a certain aloofness. Even those who are highly critical of their society seek through academic writing to enhance their position within the university and the encompassing community—do you know any scholars who do *not* want to be published? Like the members of the early Pauline communities, the contemporary scholar is tempered by domesticating forces that contain social behavior and thought within limits favorable to the maintenance of the status quo (if only by keeping radical thoughts securely between university walls). Like the *Bhagavad Gita*, the historian argues that it is impossible to escape the world, depending for this perspective not on a doctrine of *karma* but on standard sociology. While the Christian holy man was described in ancient literature as originating in a place beyond history and outside the world, the modern historian seeks to bring these figures back into conventional time and space. The premium for the scholar, as for other this-worldly ascetics, is placed on guiding others within the world.

The difficulty we as scholars have in distancing ourselves from this world brings us to the crucial irony raised by asceticism as a transhistorical and cross-cultural phenomenon. While efforts are inevitably made to transcend the limits of a particular world, and to see other worlds beyond our own, we get caught just as inevitably in the spatiotemporal web of our own spinning. As Nietzsche says:

> [I]n this analysis the human intellect cannot avoid seeing itself in its perspective forms, and *only* in them. We cannot see round our corner: it is hopeless curiosity to want to know what other modes of intellect and perspective there *might* be: for example, whether any kind of being could perceive time backwards, or alternatively forwards and backwards (by which another direction of life and another conception of cause and effect would be given).[15]

The world keeps pulling us back.

Like the discussion of Pauline asceticism, Anthony's flight into the desert as it has been portrayed in early Christian studies might be considered to reflect more accurately the wilderness of changing perspectives in late North Atlantic modernity than the perception of the desert in late antiquity. Like the simple monk in Luis Buñuel's ironic film *Simon du désert* (1965), the ancient ascetic has been whisked off his pillar in the desert and placed in the body of a worldly-wise modern intellectual caught in the jaws of historical time. When Simon tries to use the biblical retort, *vade retro*, against Satan, now his live-in girlfriend, she fires back, *vade ultra!* The ironic ending of the film is mirrored in the director's response to inquiries into his own religious proclivities—"I'm an atheist, thank God."

In a similar fashion, Anthony's star has been brought down into history and the world, where he is made to appear as little different in character and significance from those left working in the fields. Such a transformation from desert saint to village ascetic is perhaps what Nietzsche had in mind when he said that the human intellect is condemned to "seeing itself in its perspective forms, and *only* in them." But, perhaps, it is also possible to *imagine* these "facts" along more traditional lines. A good start was made by Peter Brown, whose emphasis on the holy man in late antiquity has caused us to rethink the very antimodern notion of "making [persons] into classics."[16] But Brown's reductive socioeconomic analysis of the holy man simultaneously subverts his own corrective. A more overtly self-critical analysis of modern spatiotemporal presuppositions in the study of early Christianity is required to take us beyond.

All ascetics implicitly recognize the world's attempts to domesticate their activities, often characterizing these pressures in terms of the malevolent forces at work in the world. Acts of geographical and bodily dislocation are designed to help guard against these "demonic assaults" on the renunciant's sense of integrity and self-sufficiency. But an ascetic can also choose to incorporate domesticating forces within an expanded worldview, admitting to the impossibility of escaping them completely. Such seems to have been the general attitude of the Pauline corpus. Such also is our attitude in studying that community.

NOTES

1. Alan Wilde, *Horizons of Assent: Modernism, Postmodernism, and the Ironic Imagination* (Baltimore: Johns Hopkins University Press, 1981).
2. Margaret MacDonald (this volume, 269–298).
3. Geoffrey Harpham, *The Ascetical Imperative in Culture and Criticism* (Chicago: University of Chicago Press, 1987), xii.
4. Gail Corrington Streete (this volume, 299–316).
5. Ibid.
6. It is commonly noted that while the *Gita* opened the door of salvation to all, including women and persons of low caste in Indian society, it reinforced the traditional inequality of the caste system. MacDonald (this volume, 284), quoting D'Angelo, also notes the "double consciousness" of women and slaves in the later Pauline communities, who "deny their subjected status in the religious realm while submitting to it in the social."
7. *Luther's Works*, Vol. 7, ed. Jaroslav Pelikan (St. Louis, Mo.: Concordia, 1965), 311, 312.

8. *Origen: On First Principles*, trans. G. W. Butterworth (Gloucester, Mass.: Peter Smith, 1973), 245.

9. Max Weber, "The Social Psychology of World Religions," in *Max Weber: Essays in Social Theory*, eds. H. Gerth and C. W. Mills (London: Routledge, 1970).

10. Karl Heussi, *Der Ursprung des Mönchtums* (Tübingen, Germany: Mohr, 1936), 53.

11. See the succinct discussion of the origin of Indian sramanic culture in Patrick Olivelle, *Samnyâsa Upanisads* (New York: Oxford University Press, 1992), 29–38.

12. For a discussion of world renunciation in Han Confucianism, see Aat Vervoorn, *Men of Cliffs and Caves: The Development of the Chinese Eremetic Tradition to the End of the Han Dynasty* (Hong Kong: The Chinese University Press, 1990). For a discussion of Japanese mountain men (*yamabushi*), see H. Byron Earhart, *A Religious Study of the Mount Haguro Sect of Shugendô* (Tokyo, 1970).

13. Peter Brown, *The Body and Society: Men, Women, and Sexual Renunciation in Early Christianity* (New York: Columbia University Press, 1988), 213–40.

14. Basil, *ep.* 2.

15. Friedrich Nietzsche, *Joyful Wisdom*, trans. Thomas Common (New York: Fredrick Ungar, 1960).

16. Peter Brown, "The Saint as Exemplar in Late Antiquity," *Representations 1* (1983), 1–25.

Part Four

UN-PAUL

The Virtue of Suffering, the Necessity of Discipline, and the Pursuit of Perfection in Hebrews

Pamela Eisenbaum

INTRODUCTION

In his thoroughgoing attempt to define asceticism, Richard Valantasis argues that "every asceticism becomes a performance"; asceticism constitutes a "highly complex performance genre."[1] Being an ascetic, however, is not a part-time job, at least not in the Christian tradition—it is a way of living one's life. Indeed, it is a way of constructing one's identity.[2] By stressing that the ascetic performs the regime that is his or her life, Valantasis highlights the self-conscious intention with which the ascetic carries out the facets of that life. Furthermore, in literate societies, the lives of exemplary ascetics are memorialized in narratives not only for the purpose of entertainment and admiration, but also for the purpose of mimesis, so that neophyte ascetics can imitate the masters. Thus, asceticism is a highly scripted form of behavior.

Although ascetic practices—both the spectacular and the everyday—were commonly narrated and prescribed early in Christian history, the believers in Christ who authored the documents of the New Testament were remarkably uninterested in offering adherents a detailed script for living the Christian life. There is a near total lack of distinctive Christian practices prescribed at the earliest stages.[3] While the message preached by the early Christians—Jesus died and was raised—was undeniably radical and distinctive, the implications for human conduct drawn by these same preachers look rather commonplace. Most readers of the New Testament are familiar with the unremarkable paraenetic demands Paul makes, the wholly unoriginal catalogs of virtues and vices, and the predictable exhortations scattered throughout the epistolary literature. In many ways, being a good Christian made one a better, more upstanding member of the greater society.[4] Paradoxically, an ancient convert could accept the radical message of Christ raised and look basically the same after the conversion as before. The problem this poses for the study of Christian origins is one of identity: How could Christians cohere as a group? How were they recognized by others?

The Epistle to the Hebrews reflects this paradox. Although this so-called epistle is really "a word of exhortation,"[5] very little verbiage is devoted to specific kinds of behavioral guidance. The author repeatedly goes back and forth between exposition of doctrine, which is devoted to christology, and paraenetic instruction;[6] only the former, however, is distinctively Christian. The author of Hebrews spells out very precise details of christology and its soteriological implications, while at the same time neglecting to tell his audience exactly how to live—*what to do*—in light of this knowledge. One finds slightly more concrete directions at the end of the text (chap. 13), but they still reflect typical, generic, Greco-Roman rhetoric of popular morality: Practice hospitality, show each other mutual respect, hold marriage in honor, do not crave riches, obey your leaders, and so on. Upon first reading, then, Hebrews does not appear interested in defining or scripting Christian behavior. It is certainly not designed to introduce Christians to new rules of behavior.[7]

Yet the intermittent parenesis of Hebrews is compelling because it is delivered with such vehemence.[8] Behavior befitting the Christian life is no trivial matter; in fact, it is of foremost importance, as evidenced in statements such as those found in 12:16–17:

> See to it that no one becomes like Esau, an immoral and godless person, who sold his birthright for a single meal. You know that later, when he wanted to inherit the blessing, he was rejected, for he found no chance to repent, even though he sought the blessing with tears.

Why, then, does the author of Hebrews, who no doubt sees himself as a moral pedagogue, not provide his students with the precise recipe for living the godly life that leads to eternal salvation? Why not tell them exactly what they need to do?

Although the study of asceticism once concentrated on distinctive practices, such as fasting and sexual abstinence, recent scholarship has instead focused on the implicit transformative goals, including the transformation of the self and the ability to effect social change, at work in ascetic practices (whatever they may be).[9] Yet, the texts scholars typically study are ones that either contain references to behavior of the standard ascetic fare or that already reflect a substantial degree of cultural acceptance and institutionalization.[10] It seems, therefore, that there are texts that stand to gain from reexamination in the light of this new approach to asceticism. This chapter aims to read a text not commonly deemed ascetical—Hebrews—by using some recent theoretical observations about asceticism.

The study of asceticism has uncovered manifestations of ascetic practice as technologies of religion and culture that effect and/or alter identity formation and social change. In another context I have written that the author of Hebrews "attempts to define what it means to have Christian faith *as distinct from* Jewish faith."[11] Despite the lack of distinctive Christian practices named in Hebrews, the author is actively engaged in shaping the identity, individual and collective, of his Christian audience. With this in mind, an ascetic reading of Hebrews can help us chart how such changes in subjectivity and community were being effected by the teachings of its author. There are three key elements by which the study of asceticism provides interpretive leverage for addressing this question in Hebrews.[12]

1. While ascetic practices are typically construed as acts of resistance to what are otherwise normal human inclinations, self-denial is not the goal itself; rather, such practices make up a disciplinary technology that allows one to achieve a higher goal.[13] Most of the literature we intuitively deem ascetical focuses on the *how-to*. Such literature either describes ascetical practices, usually in narrative (*Vita Antonii*), or prescribes the regime the ascetic must follow (as in manuals written for ascetic monasteries). The goal is often implicit or taken for granted and therefore left unstated. Nevertheless, the goal remains the primary motivation for ascetic practice. At its most fundamental, asceticism is a form of goal-oriented behavior.[14]

   Whether or not the goal is made explicit, spiritual goals remain elusive; in most cases they are unattainable during one's earthly life because of their intangibility. In comparison, training for an athletic event can indeed result in the attainment of the goal, for example, winning the race, which functions as a highly valued reward. A religious ascetic cannot experience the reward of eternal life directly but, by focusing on the means by which one can attain eternal life, he or she gains what sociologists call a *compensator*, an ersatz reward.[15]

2. The spiritual goals toward which ascetic practices are directed are communal as well as individual.[16] Ascetics create strong communal bonds among themselves, of course, but they also create bonds with their audience of admirers (conversely, they construct antagonistic barriers or points of friction against the dominant culture and the authority figures who represent that culture). As Kallistos Ware points out, even in the case of eremitical asceticism, where the monk flees communal life to attain his own personal salvation, some spiritual benefit accrues to the

community.[17] For example, often there is a return from the desert, where, after many years of solitary life, the ascetic has gained spiritual authority and power and can play the role of teacher, advisor, or healer. But even if the ascetic continues to live apart from the community, ascetic practice can still be understood as beneficial to the community, as in the case of prayer. Away from the cares of the world, the ascetic can concentrate on continual prayer—an activity that helps guard others from demons so that they can "carry on their daily activities in safety."[18] This kind of communal goal operates vicariously; those who are not ascetics share in the rewards the ascetic earns.

3. Since *askesis* naturally implies conscientious progress toward the spiritual goal, it requires education or at least some sort of socialization process. Thus, ascetic practice is developmental. The ascetic engages in *askesis* to perform better whatever the discipline, and the better one performs the discipline, the closer one is to achieving the goal. Whatever the ascetical practices are, they must be learned from mentors, teachers, and often texts.[19]

The ascetic's need for education means the ascetic's life is dynamic, progressive, and ultimately transformative. Even if an ascetic performs the same activity every day for years, he or she is not simply maintaining a spiritual order—although that might be an intermediate goal—but working toward some kind of transformation, which constitutes the ultimate realization of the goal.[20] Since spiritual goals typically remain elusive, there must be stages of achievement that are recognized by ascetic teachers and peers as marking progress toward the goal.

These three theoretical elements of asceticism—its being a form of goal-oriented behavior, its having communal ramifications, and its presupposition that transformation or spiritual maturation requires a deliberate socialization process—find embodiment in three themes in Hebrews: suffering (*pathema*), discipline (*paideia*), and perfection (*teleiotes*). By this I do not mean to correlate each aspect of asceticism described here with each theme in Hebrews. Rather, *all* these theoretical aspects of asceticism are embedded in these themes. In fact, applying ascetic categories reveals the intimate but previously undetected linkage of suffering, discipline, and perfection in Hebrews. Such linkage provides an interpretation that aids in solving the nagging problem alluded to earlier: the seeming disconnect between the discussions of distinctive christological doctrine and generic behavioral guidance.[21] It is no coincidence that suffering, discipline, and perfection are found in both the discussions of christology and the paraenetic material.

Thus I will first explicate the themes of suffering, discipline, and perfection in the text by means of the ascetic lens. This process will also demonstrate how the three are inextricably linked in Hebrews and how, in many ways, they break down the distinctions between exposition and exhortation that are so often seen to bifurcate the text of Hebrews. I will then explicate the relationship between christology and morality by means of this "ascetic" reading of Hebrews. I intend to highlight not only how Christ's life, death, and resurrection function to inaugurate a new world, but also how the portrayal of Christ models personal transformation for his followers. In other words, the extensive discussion of christology found in Hebrews is not present merely for the sake of doctrinal explanation, but also for the sake of mimesis. Christ inaugurates a new world; his followers facilitate the manifestation of this new world by following his example.

SUFFERING/PATHEMA

Consider the following passage:

> But recall those earlier days when, after you had been enlightened, you endured a hard struggle with sufferings (*pollen athlesin hupemeinate pathematon*), and sometimes being publicly exposed to abuse (*oneidismois*) and persecution (*thlipsesin*), and sometimes being partners with those so treated. For you had compassion (*synepathesate*) for those who were in prison, and you cheerfully accepted (*meta charas prosdexasthe*) the plundering of your possessions, knowing that you yourselves possessed something better and more lasting. Do not, therefore, abandon that confidence (*parresia*) of yours; it brings a great reward. For you need endurance (*hypomones*), so that when you have done the will of God, you may receive what was promised. (10:32–36)

The common interpretation of this text, grounded as it is in historical-critical presuppositions, asserts that the community being addressed has experienced, or may still be experiencing, some kind of violent persecution, and the rhetoric of the author is designed to encourage the addressees and embolden them to continue to endure. This reading implies that if the community did not have to face persecution, the author would not have to extol the value of suffering. In other words, on the face of it, the author of Hebrews does not glorify suffering per se; his statements are strictly situation specific, a necessary rhetorical strategy to avoid the embarrassment of believers' caving in under pressure. Scholars therefore have traditionally been more interested in dissecting, defining, and identifying the references to persecution (which persecution? Nero's burning of the Christians falsely accused of arson in Rome?) and what these references can tell us about pagan hostility toward Christians.[22]

No doubt the community has suffered some form of persecution, and no doubt the author tries to comfort his audience in this 10:32–36. Yet, while he encouragingly acknowledges their compassion for those who have suffered a worse fate, he does not exude much sympathy for them as sufferers. The rhetoric he uses to encourage them consists in praising their previous accomplishments and reminding them that greater rewards await them. The author does not need to express sympathy because suffering in his view can be efficacious, that is, as long as one rises to the occasion and endures it with dignity. The fact that the author says that the members of his audience "cheerfully accepted" (*meta charas prosdexasthe*; cf. 12:2) the plundering of their possessions indicates that suffering should be greeted felicitously, that it can be viewed as a blessed opportunity to demonstrate one's faithfulness.[23]

Asceticism, of course, is commonly associated with suffering. Usually, however, practices involving pain, humiliation, deprivation, or anything else that might constitute an ascetic form of suffering must be undertaken voluntarily for them to count as ascetic.[24] A victim of torture is not an ascetic. But the voluntary nature of suffering is not always so obvious, especially perhaps in the case of Christianity.

The author of Hebrews speaks of enduring (*hypomeno*) suffering (usually understood as inflicted upon the readers by others) repeatedly—but suffering is not something to be *passively* endured. Rather, it plays an active role in the spiritual journey of the adherent. In fact, the author's use of athletic language in 10:32 (*athlesin pathematon*) demonstrates his understanding of the Christian as an active contestant in a battle for the spiritual good.[25] The author's valuation of suffering represents more than a coping mechanism. Indeed, suffering as a Christian virtue follows almost inevitably from the christology so elegantly laid out in Hebrews.

For the author of Hebrews, like many other early Christians, Jesus is the quintessential sufferer. Although Jesus is portrayed in the gospel tradition as being at the mercy of malicious conspirers, he is hardly considered a victim of circumstance in the passion story—in any of its versions. Jesus freely gives himself up; indeed, in many ways Jesus chooses his tragic fate even if he himself did not manufacture the circumstances. The author of Hebrews does not say that Jesus actively sought the crucifixion—rather, he "endured" it (*hypemeinen;* 12:2), just as his followers are said to have endured their struggles in 10:32—but there is clearly a sense in which his acceptance constitutes a *choice*.

In two places the author forthrightly encourages members of his audience to experience suffering. In the first, he exhorts the people to "remember those who are in prison, as though you were in prison with them; those who are being tortured, as though you yourselves were being tortured" (13:3). This exhortation occurs in the midst of the paraenetic section in the last chapter of Hebrews. It is sandwiched between precepts about the practice of hospitality and fidelity in marriage. Because of its placement in the final paraenetic section, the motivation for this comment about remembering those in dire straits is only minimally to encourage sympathy for other sufferers, but more importantly to encourage people to experience the suffering of others vicariously.[26] In other words, if one does not have an actual opportunity to endure suffering, one should try to simulate the effect artificially.[27] This implies that suffering is not something simply incidental to one's spiritual life, but something a motivated Christian should experience, perhaps even cultivate. Furthermore, the communal value of suffering is emphasized here; even those who are not suffering are asked to share the experience. Suffering thereby becomes an identifiable Christian trait; community solidarity in suffering creates communal cohesion and identity over against those who are the source of suffering (i.e., the dominant culture).

In 13:11–13 the communal import of suffering can be seen as well, although from a different angle:

> For the bodies of those animals whose blood is brought into the sanctuary by the high priest as a sacrifice for sin are burned outside the camp. Therefore Jesus also suffered (*epathen*) outside the city gate in order to sanctify the people by his own blood. Let us then go to him outside the camp and bear the abuse he endured (*ton oneidismon autou pherontes*). (13:12–13)

Here the author explicitly draws a connection between the suffering endured by Jesus and that endured by believers, and in this case he urges them to go out and seek abuse deliberately. In this passage, like the previous one quoted, the sense of community solidarity in suffering is evident, only in this text it is not the solidarity among believers that is emphasized, but that between believers and Jesus.[28] Because Jesus' suffering ultimately constitutes a sacrificial act that vicariously atones for the sins of all who believe and because Jesus is the model sufferer, the author of Hebrews cannot help but incorporate a notion of shared suffering for believers in general. Like the cliché "misery loves company," the sharing of suffering somehow mitigates the pain.

Such passages suggest that believers should make suffering their personal choice. Although they might not have created the circumstances of persecution they face, believers are called upon to act with boldness (*parresia*; 10:35). Rather than shrink back and avoid pain—whether it be physical or social[29]—those who have faith deliberately embrace suffering when presented with the opportunity.[30]

Taking such a stand derives directly from the understanding of Jesus' suffering as a test (*peirasmos*) of fidelity. Besides the mention of crucifixion, there are two other references to the earthly Jesus in Hebrews: his confrontation with Satan (2:14–18) and the agony he experienced in Gethsemane (5:7–8). In the synoptic tradition both of these events are considered to be trials or temptations that tested Jesus' faithfulness to God (Matt. 4:1; Luke 4:2). Indeed, Heb. 2:18 makes this connection, too:

"Because he himself was tested (*peirastheis*) by what he suffered, he is able to help those who are being tested (*peirazomenois*)." Just as Abraham was tested, and when tested, made the decision to submit to God's will (11:17), so Jesus submits to God's will. It is important to emphasize that the author of Hebrews does not believe Jesus' submission was inevitable. This is not the place to digress into a theological discussion of free will and determinism, especially because the issue does not arise in Hebrews. For this author, there exists the possibility that Jesus could have sinned: "For we do not have a high priest who is unable to sympathize with our weaknesses, but we have one who in every respect has been tested as we are, yet without sin" (4:15). If Jesus was not genuinely tempted to disobey the will of God, or if he did not actually feel the pain of suffering and the sting of abuse, the incarnation would have been a meaningless charade for the author of Hebrews (see also 2:17–18; 5:7–8).[31] If Jesus was simply a player in a predetermined plan, his exemplary obedience, which is repeatedly emphasized in Hebrews, would hardly make sense.

The positive valuation of suffering for both Jesus and the Christian audience addressed by Hebrews—whatever the specific nature, be it martyrdom or physical or verbal abuse—functions as a kind of training on the path to salvation, not simply as a response to historical contingency. To understand the educational aspect of suffering, it must be explored together with the notion of discipline.

DISCIPLINE/PAIDEIA

As Harold Attridge has pointed out, "Hebrews uses the language of instructing children."[32] There are two places in the text where such language is striking: 5:11–14 and 12:5–13. In 5:11–14, a classical rhetorical device is used to get the audience's blood pumping:

> [Y]ou have become dull in understanding. For though by this time you ought to be teachers, you need someone to teach you again the basic elements of the oracles of God. You need milk, not solid food; for everyone who lives on milk, being still an infant, is unskilled in the word of righteousness. But solid food is for the mature (*teleion*), for those whose faculties have been trained by practice to distinguish good from evil.

Heb. 5:11–14 is an example of a teacher's motivational device: Badger the students by hurling insults at them. Such verbal chastisement gets their attention and has the added benefit of reverse psychology. Once they have been infantilized, he says to them, "[L]et us go on toward perfection, leaving behind the basic teaching about Christ" (6:1). Presumably the insults function to inspire them to make more of an effort.

Hebrews 12 uses the language of *paideia* explicitly and contains more substantive material for discussion. In 12:5–6, the author quotes from Prov. 3:11–12, which he introduces to his listeners as an "exhortation that addresses you as children":

> My child, do not regard lightly the discipline (*paideias*) of the Lord,
> or lose heart when you are punished by him;
> for the Lord disciplines (*paideuei*) those whom he loves,
> and chastises (*mastigoi*) every child whom he accepts.

The author of Hebrews follows the scriptural citation with his own exhortation:

> Endure trials for the sake of discipline (*eis paideian hypomenete*). God is treating you as children (*huiois*); for what child (*huios*) is there whom a parent (*pater*) does not discipline? If you do not have that discipline in which all children share, then you are illegitimate and not his children. Moreover, we had human parents to discipline us, and we respected them. Should we not be even more willing to be subject to the Father of spirits and live? For they disciplined us for a short time as seemed best to them, but he disciplines us for our good, in order that we may share his holiness. Now, discipline always seems painful rather than pleasant at the time, but later it yields the peaceful fruit of righteousness to those who have been trained (*gegymnasmenois*) by it. (12:7–11)

Hebrews 12 makes two important connections. First, painful trials are now explicitly described as divine *discipline* (*paideia*) that provides opportunity for spiritual *training* (*gymnazo*). By so doing, the author has equated experiences of suffering, such as physical beatings (*mastigoi*), with *paideia*. *Paideia* connotes the rhetoric of education and can indeed be used to refer to a system or philosophy of education, but it can refer to discipline in the simple or specific sense, as in punishing a child for bad behavior. Immediately preceding the quotations from Proverbs 3, in Heb. 12:4, the text reads, "In your struggle against sin, you have not yet resisted to the point of shedding your blood." This statement functions partly as a put-down (once again) to the audience, but, in any case, indicates that their training as sufferers has hardly achieved the highest level of accomplishment.[33]

Traditionally in Jewish wisdom literature, God's discipline can be either a test or a punishment for some minor infraction.[34] Does Hebrews' identification of suffering with *paideia*, then, in any way stand apart from either Hellenistic-Jewish ethical tradition or rhetoric? In recent discussions of asceticism, the question has been raised of whether we are in danger of so broadening the definition of asceticism that it might become synonymous with any form of goal-oriented education or social formation.[35] In the words of Kallistos Ware, "Asceticism...leads us to self-mastery and enables us to fulfill the purpose that we have set for ourselves, whatever that may be."[36] In other words, everyone makes sacrifices for long-term goals. Suffering is just the means, not the end. Is the understanding of suffering as part and parcel of *paideia* in Hebrews nothing more than this?

One would be hard-pressed to argue that the author of Hebrews has created an official system of social formation for adherents of the new faith, such as later Christians like Clement and Origen were to do.[37] Given the mention of "trials" in this immediate context, and the overall theme of suffering, it seems clear that *paideia* for this author evokes unpleasant, physical chastisement. On the other hand, the author nowhere seems to argue that his audience is being punished for sins previously committed.[38] The language of *paideia* in Hebrews looks exclusively toward the future. Thus, calling their trials *paideia* implies that the believers' sufferings are part and parcel of a process of spiritual development.

In other New Testament authors, the positive valuation of suffering appears frequently precisely because it is a means to an end. Paul, for example, sometimes views his suffering positively because it can lead to more success in his mission to the Gentiles (e.g., Phil. 1:12–26). In general in the New Testament, the exhortation to Christians that they endure suffering is motivated by a desire to uphold the reputation of the new religion and its claims—thus setting a good example to new and potential converts (1 Thessalonians). But in Hebrews (and in Paul sometimes, too), the experience of suffering itself has inherent spiritual value. Now in one sense suffering is still a means to an end in that suffering leads to a reward, that is, salvation, but at the same time, viewing the experience of suffering as educational training elevates the role of suffering to an active spiritual endeavor.[39] Suffering in this case is consciously practiced; it is not just an incidental experience to be endured with dignity so as not to embarrass the faith.

The ascetic function of educational suffering can be illustrated by its connotations of sonship. The comparison of God to a human father who disciplines his child out of love furthers the author's argument that suffering is not a sign of God's disaffection, but rather a sign of God's favor—a claim that is certainly not original.[40] But in 12:8, the author's logic works backwards from that typically found in wisdom literature: Instead of simply claiming that fathers are obliged to discipline their children and thus God naturally disciplines his children, Heb. 12:8 states that one needs to be disciplined to be considered a legitimate child of God. In this case, a stronger emphasis is placed upon the willing, even opportunistic, submission of the student to such discipline.

As with the case of the discussion of suffering in the previous section, submission and sonship once again link believers to Jesus. Jesus' suffering is heroic and exemplary not only because of its benefit to others, but also because it is a training mechanism for Jesus himself. The atoning of sins was not all that was achieved by Jesus' "sacrifice." For the author of Hebrews,

Jesus sacrificed his own immediate desires for the sake of a higher achievement, a divine reward granted to him by God. As Heb. 5:7–10 says:

> In the days of his flesh, Jesus offered up prayers and supplications, with loud cries and tears, to the one who was able to save him from death, and he was heard because of his reverent submission. Although he was a Son, he learned obedience through what he suffered (*emathen aph' hon epathen ten hypakoen*); and having been made perfect (*kai teleiotheis*), he became the source of eternal salvation for all who obey him (*egeneto pasin tois hypakouousin auto aitios soterias aioniou*), having been designated by God a high priest according to the order of Melchizedek. (5:7–10)

Thus, the suffering of Jesus, best exemplified in his passion and crucifixion (2:9), is the essential ingredient in Jesus' individual, personal, spiritual triumph;[41] "he learned obedience through what he suffered." Although 13:8 claims that "Jesus Christ is the same yesterday and today and forever," he achieved that eternal, divine, ecclesiastical status only after his earthly trials and tribulations. The earthly Jesus is transformed by his submission to humiliation and death. As such, Jesus is a model of what Christians should do as they progress toward their heavenly home; he is not merely their gateway to heaven.

As stated earlier, God created the circumstances by which Jesus was tested. In other words, Jesus' sufferings are the direct result of God's discipline insofar as God is Jesus' Father. The Father–Son relationship between God and Jesus constitutes one of the christological keys to Hebrews. Not only is the title "Son" used frequently throughout the whole text of Hebrews, but the opening chapter has been called a "private dialogue" between the Father and the Son.[42] What does it mean that God heard his "prayers and supplications, with loud cries and tears,...because of his reverent submission"? God did not save Jesus from his impending death; God did not "answer" Jesus' well-deserved plea for mercy. Rather, what God heard was Jesus' verbal submission to the trial he was about to face. According to gospel tradition, Jesus relinquished his plea immediately after making it. The Son remained obedient to his Father even in a time of distress. Furthermore, this Son is a kind of exemplary eldest child. Since Jesus lived on earth as flesh and blood, the same as any human being, both Jesus and humans are children of God who share "one Father" (2:10–13).

Hebrews' notion of suffering-as-*paideia* can further be seen in the use of the athletic language, metaphor, and imagery that pervade chapter 12.[43] As is commonly known, athletic symbolism strongly informed discourse about the ascetic life.[44] The twelfth chapter of Hebrews opens with the famous words, "[L]et us run with perseverance the race that is set before us (*trechomen ton prokeimenon hemin agona*), looking to Jesus the pioneer (*archegon*) and perfecter (*teleioten*) of our faith." Serious athletes undergo rigorous training to achieve rewards later, at the end of the competition. But, as many a modern athlete proclaims, the ultimate prize is the satisfaction of the athletic endeavor itself. Athletes often claim that they are competing against themselves, trying to do their best—which really means that they always desire to do better than they have done before, which is another way of speaking of self-transcendence.[45]

Thus, when suffering is spoken of in terms of athleticism and *paideia*, as they are in Hebrews, the implication is that suffering can be its own reward, not in the sense of masochism, but in the sense that it allows the individual to experience the transcendence of the earthly self. When the sufferer resists the natural urge to avoid pain and abuse, he or she attains the sense of having gone beyond himself or herself. So to say that suffering has inherent spiritual value in Hebrews means that the author thinks of the endurance of suffering as a holy act (12:10). In this sense, then, suffering constitutes a compensator, a proposal for attaining an otherwise unreachable goal. The designation of suffering as a compensator is not a case of mistaking the means (suffering) for the end (salvation); rather, the sufferer understands his or her suffering as a simulation of the goal, which brings with it a sense of self-satisfaction and accomplishment.

One can compare suffering in this sense to prayer, which the hearer of Hebrews is also exhorted to do (13:18). Prayer is often a means to an end in that people can pray for something or someone, but the practice of prayer—and, indeed, the ultimate meaning of prayer—lies in its being a spiritual activity in which an individual establishes a connection with a supernatural being (or beings) and attempts to discern its will. By so doing, one comes a step closer to a transcendent existence, which simulates the achievement of the reward and allows the individual to experience personal satisfaction.[46] Similarly, overcoming pain and persecution becomes an exercise in transcendence of the self that prepares the Christian for the ultimate spiritual accomplishment, entering the divine realm.

Perfection/Teleiotes

Perfection (*teleiotes*, as well its cognates *teleioo*, *teleios*, and *teleiosis*) is one of the author's favorite terms, and commentators on Hebrews have often found that it provides endless fodder for theological speculation. More recent commentators, however, stress that perfection terminology is most commonly used in ancient Greek in a formalistic sense, meaning to complete, to make whole, or, in the words of Aristotle, to bring something to its "contemplated end."[47] The term appears in so many different contexts in Greek literature—in discussions of ethics, philosophy, education, and so on—that its particular connotations can only be determined by the specific context. A few examples illustrate the variety of connotations: When a human being or an animal becomes a fully developed, mature adult, he, she, or it is said to be *teleios*;[48] an animal ready for sacrifice is *teleios*;[49] so is any person who is accomplished in a profession;[50] and in ethical philosophy, one can become morally *teleios* through the practice of virtue.[51] The term *teleiosis* can be used for the completion of a building,[52] a syllogism,[53] or for the enactment of marriage.[54] The verb is frequently used in the sense of carrying out an action, consummating an event, and fulfilling a prophecy, as well as in all the senses named already.

The endless variety of possible meanings has enticed many readers of Hebrews to fill in the formalistic meaning with a more substantial one,[55] but I will follow more cautious commentators who refrain from the substantivizing impulse.[56] Because the author of Hebrews possesses a large and sophisticated vocabulary base, his repeated use of perfection terminology no doubt reveals a preoccupation with the ultimate realization of a goal. The sheer number of possible connotations, however, makes denoting one meaning for the whole of Hebrews less prudent than analyzing individual texts—the immediate context thereby providing the substance of what is meant. Although there is not time to exegete every piece of text that uses the term "perfection" or one of its cognates, in keeping with the orientation of the two previous sections I will discuss those passages that reveal a connection between the perfection of Jesus and the perfection of believers. Once again, I hope to demonstrate that the theme of perfection is closely allied with suffering and discipline.

As David Peterson has convincingly argued, the perfection of Jesus in Hebrews includes three stages: his overcoming of struggles, temptations, and persecutions as a human being; his sacrificial death; and his exaltation to the heavenly realm.[57] The first use of "perfection" in Hebrews addresses stage one and perhaps stage two, describing Jesus' suffering as a means to his perfection. It also connects this means of perfection to believers:

> It was fitting that God, for whom and through whom all things exist, in bringing many children to glory, should make the pioneer of their salvation perfect through sufferings (*ton archegon tes soterias auton dia pathema ton teleiosai*). For the one who sanctifies and those who are sanctified all have one Father. (2:10–11)

A few verses later, in 2:18, one reads, "Because he himself was tested by what he suffered, he is able to help those who are being tested." It is important to observe that perfection in this context is explicitly achieved through an active process undertaken by the individual to be perfected, whether that person be Christ or anyone. Once earned, perfection takes on a permanent, static quality,[58] but any potential adherent must first consciously subject himself or herself to trials—the suffering and discipline discussed earlier—which then transform him or her into the state of perfection. The image modern readers of the New Testament often have of how an ancient person came to be a believer in Christ is that it happened in one insightful instant.[59] Stories of the disciples in the gospels or the story of Paul's conversion in Acts encourage this conception. Hebrews, on the other hand, has a dynamic understanding of the adherent's Christian faith. One is not a perfect or complete Christian from the time of baptism. There are stages of Christian faith, which involve both temporal and qualitative dimensions. If this were not a fundamental assumption in Hebrews, there would have been no reason for his paideutic approach, in which one learns certain doctrines at earlier stages and more sophisticated doctrines at later stages (5:11–6:6).[60] The result, of course, is a full-scale qualitative transformation, however, and not simply one of degree in improvement in learning or wisdom. Indeed, once transformation has happened, there is no going back.[61]

Following the process Jesus underwent as a man on earth, the existential meaning of Christ "having been made perfect" is typically understood in two ways. First, it means that Christ successfully achieved his mission as Savior and mediator; Christ's perfection in this case was accomplished for the sake of the believers. He plays the role of Savior not so much for his own glory (5:5), but because it enables others to achieve their "contemplated end," to bring "many children to glory" (2:10). Furthermore, Christ does not perfect himself but is said in Hebrews to have been perfected, presumably by God. In other words, the status of perfection is granted to him, and the significance of this status lies in the community of believers—not in his own achievement—insofar as the purpose of his achievement rests with its benefit to others, not himself.

The second understanding of perfection, and one that stands in contradistinction to the first, is that Christ was perfected personally because he was a man who did not sin. The author of Hebrews repeatedly stresses the authenticity of Christ's humanity; he was fully human (2:14–18; 4:15). As I argued earlier, although the doctrine of Christ's sinlessness is essential to the author's soteriology—Jesus must necessarily be unblemished in his sacrificial role (7:26–28; 9:11)—the *possibility* that he could have sinned must be real. Jesus' personal attainment of perfection as a man consists in his being fully human and at the same time unfailingly conforming himself to God's will.[62] In this sense, Jesus *earned* his perfection. The author's use of the terminology of testing Jesus, as well as the graphic description of Jesus' inner turmoil in the process of remaining steadfast, emphasizes the tremendous effort he put forth to achieve perfection (2:18; 4:15; 5:7–8).

The perfection of believers also plays out in these two ways, two ways that initially appear to cancel out each other. On the one hand, believers are perfected vicariously through Christ's perfection. "For by a single offering he has perfected for all time those who are sanctified" (10:14). In a statement such as this, it sounds as though perfection has already happened and believers passively partake of its benefits; their conscience is cleared of sin and guilt. On the other hand, the author of Hebrews also implies that perfection requires a conscious effort, which will necessarily involve trials and tribulations on the part of the believer. Jesus is not just an intercessor and provider of perfection; he is the example *par excellence* of how to become perfect. As the author says:

> [L]et us also lay aside every weight and the sin that clings so closely, let us run with perseverance the race that is set before us, looking to Jesus the pioneer and perfecter of our faith, who for the sake of the joy that was set before him endured the cross, disregarding its shame. (12:1–4)

That Jesus' struggle with human trials, sufferings, and ultimately death—all of which set the process to perfection in motion—is no doubt intended as a model for believers to imitate should already be evident from the discussions of suffering and *paideia* earlier in this chapter.[63] Although the author never explicitly uses an *imitatio Christi* formula, he does explicitly exhort believers to imitate the faithful (6:11–12). Scholars have long recognized the important placement of the text just cited, "looking to Jesus the pioneer and perfecter of our faith"[64]—it follows immediately after the famous list of biblical heroes in chapter 11.[65] Thus, most take 12:2 to mean that Jesus is the ultimate exemplar of faith. In fact, as David DeSilva points out, several early Greek Fathers assume the presence of the *imitatio Christi*[66] in Hebrews, as is the case with Origen:

> Jesus endured the cross, despising shame, and because of this, he sat down at the right hand of God; and those who imitate him by despising shame will sit with him and reign with him in heaven.[67]

Greg Riley, commenting on Hebrews in his book on christology and the concept of the hero in Greco-Roman antiquity, claims that "Jesus is the (quintessential) hero who secured the means of salvation for those who would follow him, and Christians are encouraged to do just that, to take up and hold that role themselves."[68] *Imitatio Christi* seems to be a central theme in Hebrews.

CHRISTOLOGY AND MORALITY

It is difficult to reconcile the author's use of Jesus as a model for *actively* living the Christian life with his portrayal of him as having already perfected the faith and therefore the vehicle through which one *passively* achieves salvation.

Must the author be understood in Pauline terms, namely, that right actions follow naturally from a believing heart? In other words, is the reader forced to accept the classic Augustinian-Protestant explanation for Hebrews that human effort and striving toward God actually accomplish nothing, but rather signify God's foreordained blessings upon human beings?

In the case of Hebrews, at least two criticisms can be leveled against this all-too-common view: First, such a view privileges the passive dimension over the active one. The two poles of attaining spiritual perfection are not held intact; one pole, namely, the active pursuit of perfection, is construed as disingenuous. If human efforts directed toward spiritual perfection are really signs of a perfection that has already been granted, then the only actual effort on the part of the believer is to recognize this fact. All behavior that follows this moment of recognition is really no effort at all, since the natural tendency of the genuine believer is to do the right thing. Second, if all ethical behavior flows naturally, without effort, from the fact that God approaches and perfects the human being, then all the ascetically oriented language of struggle, striving, weakness, temptation, and endurance, which pervades Hebrews, must be ignored or counted as mere rhetorical flourish. While the author of Hebrews does not often speak sympathetically to his audience, he recognizes that what he asks them to do is not easy; it takes tremendous effort. He in no way assumes that the Christians to whom he speaks are effortlessly inclined to endure suffering. He knows that everybody—including Christians—has an inclination toward the avoidance of pain and that one must exert fierce resistance to this inclination to overcome it. Furthermore, if Christ, who has the mind of God, had to struggle as a man to resist the temptation to avoid death—or conversely stated, to resist the will to live—and to achieve his own perfection, then surely humans, even those who possess the spirit of Christ, will have to struggle indeed to reach that ultimate state of perfection, that is, salvation.

As I have tried implicitly to demonstrate, Jesus' own life holds in tension the active and the passive dimensions of moral action. Jesus did not deserve to be crucified; he was innocent. Therefore, he cannot be said to have created the circumstances that lead to his crucifixion—others plot Jesus' ruin, thus enabling the possibility for him to demonstrate his faithfulness in the face of persecution and temptation. The crucifixion is something that happens to him. Jesus does not concoct it the way, say, a second-century ascetic might, completely of his own accord, by going out to the desert to live as a hermit. The crucifixion is, to a very great extent, Jesus' fate. In this way, Jesus incorporates the passive dimension of moral action; a moral agent is not just an actor, but also a *reactor*. Throughout the vicissitudes of his life, Jesus responds with integrity, and his response makes all the difference—it is deemed faithful and earns him his reward. It is, however, his *response*, and not his *initiative*, that is the measure of his faith. By describing Jesus' story as one of response and not initiative, it spotlights the contrast between Jesus and greater society.

Furthermore, as I already mentioned, Jesus does not—and presumably cannot—perfect himself; God perfects him. Similarly, believers cannot perfect themselves; Christ perfects them—even as they themselves must also struggle to achieve their reward. Neither the believer nor Jesus operates self-sufficiently. The actual enactment of perfection lies outside the individual self.

Since Jesus is the ultimate exemplar of faith, it is instructive to compare what is said of the biblical heroes of old listed in chapter 11. That salvation is impossible for any individual alone is evident from the concluding line of that chapter: "[A]part from us they should not be made perfect" (11:40). Although the heroes are exemplary, they cannot achieve perfection until believers in Christ also achieve it; thus their own merit is insufficient to bring their spiritual journey to completion. Furthermore, while each hero is introduced by the anaphoric word *pistei*, "by faith," the heroes are not entirely active agents of faith. In 11:23, Moses is said to have been hidden by his parents "by faith." Obviously, "faith" in this case does not refer to Moses' conscious faith, since he is only three months old at the time, and it is the action of his parents—not his own action—that saves him. An even more obvious case of the lack of personal intention with regard to faith occurs in 11:30: "By faith the walls of Jericho fell after they had been encircled for seven days." Surely, the walls of Jericho cannot be said to possess faith the way a believer possesses faith.[69] Such examples illustrate that God is at work in human history, too. The heroes experience faith as a transcendent force in which they participate; faith does not connote only an individual's self-generated response. In the anthropology of the author of Hebrews, human beings are partners with God in realizing the divine will.

Herein lies the key to understanding Hebrews' seemingly contradictory claims—between the tremendous effort that must be exerted on the part of believers if they are to achieve their desired goal and the perfection of believers having already been accomplished by the one-time salvific act of Christ. No individual can achieve his or her ultimate spiritual goal all alone. If that were possible, there would be no spiritual component, no sense of transcendence, only the self. Although it is imprudent to make universalist claims, all—or at least almost all—ascetics claim that their ability to perform ascetic practices comes from the divine. There exists some transcendent source of strength outside the self. The passive language in Hebrews about believers having already been perfected is not analogous to some oversimplified notion of Paul's message that one is saved by grace in which moral actions count for nothing. The passive dimension conveys, rather, the sense in which individuals are ultimately dependent upon something beyond themselves for their existence, whether that existence is divine or earthly.

People cannot entirely control many of the events in their earthly lives any more than they can control the divine will. Of course, by making certain choices or following a particular course of action, people do control some things about their lives. Persons must usually make choices within a given set of circumstances that are not of their making. Such circumstances may be due to nature, but just as often they are created by other human beings. Just as Jesus remained at the mercy of his persecutors and just as he also remained submissive to God, so, too, are believers at the mercy of their persecutors and are called to be obedient to God. In neither case, however, do the fated circumstances detract from the moral effort expended by Jesus and believers.

Thus, it seems to me that casting an ascetic perspective upon Hebrews provides a corrective to the avoidance among interpreters of seeing the pursuit of perfection as devoid of moral implications.[70] Both Jesus and his followers earn their divine reward through overcoming the trials and temptations set before them. Their moral action in pursuit of perfection in no way detracts from divine agency—divine agency is, in fact, the *sine qua non* for the ultimate attainment of perfection. Still, the believers must first align themselves with the divine will, which, in the case of Hebrews, means that they must resist the will of their persecutors—not in the sense of evading persecution, but in the sense of not capitulating to them. Such resistance is the substance of moral action for the author of Hebrews, and it serves to distinguish Christians from greater society. To be sure, as I said at the beginning of this chapter, the author offers no specifically Christian radical action in any of his explicit moral directives. Nevertheless, the call to endure suffering in a way similar to that of Jesus means—at least for those who heed the call[71]—that believers will aid in the social construction of the Christian community. There is never any confusion between persecutor and persecuted. By maintaining steadfast endurance with regard to their initial commitment to faith, these early Christians demonstrate their spiritual integrity and their constancy in the face of adverse circumstances, and thus they assist in carving out their collective identity.

Notes

1. Valantasis, "Constructions of Power in Asceticism," *Journal of the American Academy of Religion* 63 (1995): 798–99.
2. The construction of identity is also essential to Valantasis' definition, which reads: "Asceticism may be defined as performances within a dominant social environment intended to inaugurate a new subjectivity, different social relations, and an alternative symbolic universe" ("Constructions of Power," 797).
3. See Wayne Meeks, *The Origins of Christian Morality: The First Two Centuries* (New Haven, Conn.: Yale University Press, 1993), 14–15, 20–21. The two fundamental rituals of early Christianity, baptism and the eucharist, while no doubt important, receive little attention in New Testament documents. While Paul

makes mention of baptism numerous times, the topic never turns up as a central teaching; rather, it is incidental or is used as an illustration of some larger point. If it were not for the contentious members of the church at Corinth who had complained to Paul, we would never have heard anything from the Apostle about the celebration of the eucharist! And even on this occasion, Paul does not circumscribe the details of performing the eucharist.

4. This theme is explicitly there in writers such as Justin (see, e.g., *2 Apology*, 12), as Meeks mentions (*Christian Morality*, 20–21), but it is there implicitly in New Testament texts such as Rom. 13:1–8; 1 Pet. 2:13–17; 3:15.

5. The author himself uses this designation (*tou logou tes paraklaseos*) in 13:22.

6. For an overview of the structure of Hebrews, see H. Attridge, *Hebrews* (Hermeneia, Philadelphia: Fortress, 1989), 14–23.

7. Meeks, *Christian Morality*, 81.

8. As Attridge says, "The paraenesis is not a perfunctory afterthought to a dogmatic treatise, and the pastoral thrust of the work is clear" (*Hebrews*, 21).

9. See, for example, M. Foucault, *The Use of Pleasure. Volume 2. The History of Sexuality* (New York: Vintage Books, 1990), 72–77; G. Harpham, *The Ascetic Imperative in Culture and Criticism* (Chicago: The University of Chicago Press, 1987); Valantasis, "Constructions of Power," 794–97.

10. See, for example, the collection of texts in Vincent L. Wimbush, ed., *Ascetic Behavior in Greco-Roman Antiquity: A Sourcebook* (Studies in Antiquity and Christianity; Minneapolis, Minn.: Fortress, 1990). This volume is tremendously useful for scanning the wide variety of asceticisms in Western antiquity. In fact, it includes texts beyond the usual realm and itself has contributed to the expanded understanding of asceticism. Nevertheless, the majority of the texts chosen for the volume focus on typical ascetic behaviors.

11. P. Eisenbaum, *The Jewish Heroes of Christian History: Hebrews 11 in Literary Context* (*Society of Biblical Literature Dissertation Series* 156, Atlanta, Ga.: Scholars, 1997), 10.

12. I do not mean to imply that the following three elements constitute an exhaustive list of theoretical components in the study of asceticism; rather, these three best suit my purposes in interpreting Hebrews.

13. K. Ware, "The Way of the Ascetics: Negative or Affirmative?" in *Asceticism*, eds. Vincent L. Wimbush and Richard Valantasis (New York: Oxford University Press, 1995), 1–15. See also S. Fraade, "Ascetical Aspects of Ancient Judaism," in *Jewish Spirituality from the Bible to the Middle Ages*, ed. A. Green (New York: Crossroad, 1986), 253–88.

14. See A. Saldarini (this volume, 11–28).

15. According to R. Stark, a compensator can be distinguished from a reward "because the latter is the thing wanted, the former a proposal about gaining the reward" (*The Rise of Christianity: A Sociologist Reconsiders History* [Princeton, N.J.: Princeton University Press, 1996], 168). For a fuller theoretical discussion, see Stark and W. Bainbridge, *A Theory of Religion* (New York: Peter Lang, 1987), 36–42.

16. Again, as Valantasis argues, asceticism involves "the delimitation and restructuring of social relations" ("Constructions of Power," 796).

17. Ware, "Way of Ascetics," 4–13.

18. Ibid, 7.
19. Valantasis, in his typology of ascetic subjects, offers an educative model as one type ("Constructions of Power," 803–4). In highlighting the educative process, I do not mean here to evoke Valantasis' type, but rather to draw out the educational component inherent in all types of asceticism.
20. See Saldarini (this volume, 11–28).
21. Many scholars have recognized this problem for interpretation in Hebrews. For a recent, formalist solution, see Attridge, "Paraenesis in a Homily (*logos parakleseos*): The Possible Location of, and Socialization in, the 'Epistle to the Hebrews,'" *Semeia* 50 (1990), 211–26.
22. See the discussion in Attridge, *Hebrews*, 298–99.
23. Attridge's translation of *meta charas prosdexasthe* captures this sense better: "anticipated with joy" (*Hebrews*, 297).
24. W. Kaelber, "Asceticism," in *The Encyclopedia of Religion*, ed. Mircea Eliade (New York: Macmillan, 1987), vol. 1, 441.
25. The author expands his use of athletic language in chapter 12, particularly v.v.1, 4, and 12.
26. Cf. 10:34, where the word translated "compassion" is *synepathesate*, literally "to suffer with."
27. Aristotle pondered whether someone who never has the opportunity to fight in battle can be said to possess the virtue of courage—the point being that the circumstances of one's life affect the caliber of one's morality. Thus, it should come as no surprise that one would seek the opportunity to display one's virtue (see, e.g., *Nicomachean Ethics* 2.4, 3.6–7).
28. As Kaelber points out, in Late Antiquity and medieval Christianity, ascetic suffering meant that one not only suffered *like* Christ, but that one suffered *with* Christ ("Asceticism," 443).
29. The words *oneidismois* and *thlipsesin* in 10:33 refer, respectively, to verbal and physical abuse, according to Attridge (*Hebrews*, 298).
30. With regard to suffering in particular, it is useful to compare traditions about Heracles with the portrait of Christ in Hebrews, as D. Aune has done ("Heracles and Christ: Heracles Imagery in the Christology of Early Christianity," in *Greeks, Romans, and Christians: Essays in Honor of Abraham J. Malherbe*, eds. D. Balch, E. Ferguson, and W. Meeks [Minneapolis, Minn.: Fortress, 1990], 3–19). Although early legends about Heracles narrate the story of his twelve labors, which were forced upon him as a punishment for his notoriously uncivilized behavior, later tradition about the hero, particularly in Cynic and Stoic philosophy, "emphasizes the fact that his deeds were accomplished *voluntarily*" (Aune, "Heracles and Christ," 8).
31. See D. Peterson, *Hebrews and Perfection* (Cambridge, England: Cambridge University Press, 1982), 76–78.
32. Attridge, "Paraenesis in a Homily," 18.
33. The phraseology of "struggling against" (*antagonizomenoi*) evokes the language of martyrdom; see, for example, 4 Macc. 11:20 (where the sufferer's endurance of torture is called an *agon*) and the discussion offered by D. DeSilva, "Despising Shame: A Cultural Anthropological Investigation of the Epistle to the Hebrews," *Journal of Biblical Literature* 113 (1994): 450–57.

34. As in the quotation of Proverbs 3 discussed earlier; other examples include 2 Sam. 7:14 and Wis. 11:9–13.

35. The question posed by L. Vaage illustrates how closely linked education and asceticism are: "To what extent is all ascetic activity, whether Greek, Latin, Syrian, Indian, or any other, finally just one instance by *homo faber* for the education of his or her desire?" ("Ascetic Moods, Hermeneutics, and Bodily Deconstruction: Response to the Three Preceding Papers," in *Asceticism*, eds. Wimbush and Valantasis, 260).

36. Ware, "Way of Ascetics," 3.

37. For a discussion of Clement, Origen, and the beginnings of *paideia*, see B. McGuinn, "Asceticism and Mysticism in Late Antiquity and the Early Middle Ages," in *Asceticism*, eds. Wimbush and Valantasis, 58–74.

38. D. DeSilva, "Despising Shame," 457.

39. See C. H. Talbert, *Learning through Suffering: The Educational Value of Suffering in the New Testament and in Its Milieu* (Collegeville, Minn.: Glazier, 1991), 58–74; S. Garrett, "Paul's Thorn and Cultural Models of Affliction" in *The Social World of the First Christians: Essays in Honor of Wayne Meeks*, eds. L. M. White and O. L. Yarbrough (Minneapolis, Minn.: Fortress, 1995), 91–94.

40. Cf., for example, 2 Macc. 6:12–17. See Attridge, *Hebrews*, 361, for a multitude of references.

41. Peterson, *Hebrews and Perfection*, 66–67.

42. M. Barth, "The Old Testament in Hebrews: An Essay in Biblical Hermeneutics," in *Current Issues in New Testament Interpretation*, eds. W. Klassen and G. F. Snyder (New York: Harper, 1982), 62.

43. For a full discussion of athletic imagery in Hebrews 12, see Attridge, *Hebrews*, 353–65.

44. See Harpham, *The Ascetic Imperative*, 26, 28; also Meeks' discussion of the *Tablet of Cebes* (*Christian Morality*, 23–25).

45. See C. E. Thomas, "Sports," in *Spirituality and the Secular Quest*, ed. P. H. Van Ness (New York: Crossroad, 1996), 498–519.

46. See the discussion by Ware of Arsenius the Desert Father, who prayed so intensely that he looked as though he were on fire ("Way of Ascetics," 6). Similarly, in Eastern religious traditions, meditation helps simulate self-transcendence; see the discussion by P. Olivelle ("Deconstruction of the Body in Indian Asceticism," in *Asceticism*, eds. Wimbush and Valantasis, 193–94) about the Indian ascetic's meditative practices on the disgust of the body, which have the goal of freeing the ascetic from its desires and cares.

47. See Aristotle, *Metaphysics* 4,16,1021b (as referred to in Peterson, *Hebrews and Perfection*, 21).

48. Plato, *Laws*, 929C.

49. Thucydides, *History of the Peloponnesian War*, 5.47.

50. Plato, *Cratylus*, 403E.

51. Plato, *Laws*, 2.653A; for Stoic philosophy, see Diogenes Laertius, *Vit. Phil.* 7.128 (on Cleanthes). These citations are taken from Attridge, *Hebrews*, 84.

52. 2 Macc. 2:9.

53. Aristotle, *On First Philosophy*, 29a.16.

54. Jer. 2:2.

55. See, for example, B. Lindars, who, while making exegetically sensitive comments on some perfection passages, ultimately reduces the meaning of perfection in Hebrews to one thing: "[P]erfection in Hebrews means the completion of God's plan of salvation" (*The Theology of the Letter to the Hebrews* [Cambridge, England: Cambridge University Press, 1991], 44).

56. As in Peterson, *Hebrews and Perfection*.

57. Ibid.

58. When perfection is used to describe things, such as the "perfect tent" in 9:11, it is naturally static. In regard to people, however, there first needs to be a transformative process, but insofar as the result of that process is a state of perfection, it appears that once it has been obtained, it cannot be lost. Thus, the Son "has been made perfect forever" (7:28).

59. Such a conception of the early Christians has in turn informed notions of the conversion experience in general. But cf. Lewis Rambo (*Understanding Religious Conversion* [New Haven, Conn.: Yale University Press, 1993]), who argues that conversion is always a process.

60. As Peterson says, "It cannot be denied that 5:11–6:3 puts the emphasis on progress in understanding the Christian faith as the pathway to maturity" (*Hebrews and Perfection*, 185).

61. The author does not seem to believe in the efficacy of repentance for "those who have once been enlightened" (6:4)—a theological juggernaut for many interpreters of Hebrews, who often explain it away as referring only to the sin of apostasy. I think the author literally means what he says, namely, that there is no going back, but I do not think it is necessarily due to a severity of attitude, but rather that it derives naturally from his understanding of how the believer is qualitatively transformed. Like Christ, once the process of transformation is complete, it need never be repeated—it happens once and for all and remains forever.

62. R. Williamson, "Hebrews 4:15 and the Sinlessness of Jesus," *ExpTim* 86 (1974–1975): 4–8. Cf. the discussion by Peterson (*Hebrews and Perfection*, 188–90), who essentially agrees that it was possible for Jesus to have sinned but tempers this interpretation by—it seems to me—diminishing the force of Jesus' humanity.

63. This conclusion resembles that of A. Wikgren ("Patterns of Perfection in the Epistle to the Hebrews," *New Testament Studies* 6 [1959–1960]: 164), but stands in contrast to the peculiar comment made by Peterson that "believers are perfected by the very actions and accomplishments that perfect Christ, not by any actions of their own" (*Hebrews and Perfection*, 175). I could agree but for the words following the comma.

64. According to Greg Riley, the term *archegos*, translated in the NRSV as "pioneer" but which also means leader or chief, is a common designation for Greco-Roman heroes (*One Jesus, Many Christs: How Jesus Inspired Not One True Christianity, But Many* [San Francisco: HarperSanFrancisco, 1997], 201–2).

65. Jesus is also called a "pioneer of salvation" in 2:10. The placement of these two references, 2:10 and 12:2, is such that they structurally complement each other.

66. In addition to the quotation from Origen that I have included here, DeSilva quotes from Chysostom and Macarius ("Despising Shame," 447–48).

67. Origen, *Exhor. ad Mart.* 37.11–14 (translation mine).
68. Riley, *One Jesus, Many Christs*, 200.
69. For a discussion of the impersonal connotations of faith in the hero list of Hebrews, see Eisenbaum, *Jewish Heroes*, 166–67.
70. The case of Lindars (*Theology of Hebrews*, 44–45) is typical.
71. As Riley reminds us, "persecution worked"—it caused many intimidated Christians to forsake their faith (*One Jesus, Many Christs*, 196).

An Asceticism of
Resistance in James

Alicia Batten

INTRODUCTION

The term "asceticism" may immediately conjure up the image of a starving
hermit, crouched in his cave, but as recent scholarship has shown, asceticism
is a multifaceted phenomenon and has appeared in so many different guises
that it is not easily defined.[1] In a cross-cultural perspective, it seems impossible to isolate one specific type of praxis or motivation that could characterize asceticism, especially when we are conscious that our own "situatedness"
complicates the issue even more.[2]

Yet despite the difficulties, we still likely have a "default setting" definition of asceticism that may be linked with our own particular contexts.
Growing up in a liberal Protestant environment in which Christianity was
intimately joined to what Charles Taylor calls the "affirmation of ordinary
life,"[3] I tended to associate asceticism with the stereotypical medieval monk
who whipped himself or the emaciated yogi lying on a bed of nails. Yet after
entering university, I was fortunate enough to encounter various individuals
who were by no means as exotic as the monk or the yogi, but who could be
described as "ascetic." Of course, they denied themselves various pleasures,
which for some included the renunciation of possessions, sexual relationships, and types of food, but not because they hated these things or abhorred
their bodies (as far as I could tell). Rather, their renunciation was conducive
to focusing on larger theological and social visions. As Kallistos Ware has
written:

> [A]skesis signifies not simply a selfish quest for individual salvation but a service rendered to the total human family; not simply the cutting off or destroying of the lower but, much more profoundly, the refinement and illumination of the lower and its transfiguration into something higher.[4]

Thus, while some ascetics may seek to subdue their bodies and imaginations out of self-loathing or perhaps a need to draw attention to themselves, others engage in ascetic practices because they aid in achieving larger social, political, or spiritual goals.

Exposure to the latter type of ascetics has thus considerably altered my understanding of asceticism. However, whether they are motivated by positive or negative forces, I would argue, as L. William Countryman does,[5] that ascetics must choose to be ascetical. Both the medieval monk and the contemporary "worker-priest" choose their lifestyles; asceticism is not forced upon them. Secondly, although the intensity, type, and duration will vary, ascetics must engage in some form of self-discipline. Such discipline will often require the regulation of the body, but it seems to me that the body does not always have to be the central focus. James Francis notes that for Marcus Aurelius, "[T]he essence of ascetic training lies in love, aversion, fear and desire. The focus is more on the disposition of the mind (or soul, [*psyche*]) and less on that of the body ([*soma*])."[6] The renunciation of possessions, for example, requires resistance to material gratifications, not necessarily to bodily desires. One has only to think of some of the ancient Cynics, who wandered around with a few meager possessions but freely indulged their physical appetites.[7]

The Cynics are good examples of the third component of my definition of asceticism, namely, that its practitioners are different from most people. Countryman also includes this criterion when he states that asceticism "sets those who adopt it apart from and, in some sense, above the ordinary run of people in their world."[8] The ascetic views his or her world from a different perspective. This sense of difference is also apparent in Richard Valantasis' definition of asceticism as "performances within a dominant social environment intended to inaugurate a new subjectivity, different social relations, and an alternative symbolic universe."[9] The ascetic monk, for example, practices forms of behavior that will inevitably distinguish him from the larger group, both in the way in which he sees the world and how he is viewed by it. Asceticism is nonconformist.

Nonconformism often invites conflict, but not always. Francis argues that Marcus Aurelius "simultaneously manifests respect for ascetical ideals and dogmatic adherence to the political and social status quo."[10] Aurelius' embodiment of personal self-control was in itself extraordinary, but rather than upseting the social order, it served as a conservative force that further entrenched the structures of authority. Alison Keith has made a similar observation about Augustus: "Augustus, as the master of his own sexual appetites, models the self-mastery that has eluded his inferiors among Roman aristocrats (notably Antony) and can therefore be the legitimate master of the Roman empire."[11] Exercised in particular ways, asceticism can strengthen the preexisting systems of power and domination.

Conversely, many ascetics and ascetic communities challenge those systems. Celsus, for example, considered early Christianity to be a threat to the social order because of its ascetical tendencies. Early Christian practices like the renunciation of sexuality, the acceptance of women in leadership roles, prophecy, and charismatic authority "lay outside of the *nomos* of the received culture and, therefore outside the control of its social norms. As such, they constituted a threat, especially since they subverted society at its very foundations."[12] Thus, although it may not always explicitly intend to do so, asceticism often functions as a resistant force against the status quo, as a cultural and political critique.[13] To take a modern example, one has only to think of Gandhi, whose asceticism was integral to his civil disobedience.[14] Progress in virtue and the practice of self-restraint and endurance are therefore aids in resisting what are perceived to be oppressive and possibly even corrupt forces.

JAMES

These three components of asceticism—that it is voluntary, requires self-discipline, and is nonconformist—are all operating in the letter of James. Although James does not discuss issues often associated with asceticism, like fasting and sexual ethics, he incorporates entreaties to reform and discipline the self, to remain patient, to defy the love of the world, and perhaps most compelling, a pungent critique of wealth and patronage, all into this compact document. James represents a choice to resist larger social forces; the instructions to the audience are politically nonconformist in light of the status quo.

Using the lens of asceticism magnifies the fact that James is highly unusual among early Christian letters. On the one hand, the document draws on traditional wisdom and demonstrates attitudes and concerns comparable to such texts as the Pastoral Epistles. Yet at the same time, James makes difficult demands, more characteristic of sayings collections like Q and the *Gospel of Thomas*. James, as we'll see, is an interesting blend of conventional wisdom and social radicalism.

Social Situation

It is important to begin, however, with a brief discussion of a possible social situation behind this text. Such a discussion is fraught with speculation, for James mentions no specific names or places. However, the genre of the letter, paraenesis, aids in positing, albeit to a very limited degree, a social context. Paraenesis consists of "admonitions of general ethical content" that can address a variety of situations,[15] thus making it difficult to determine the nature of the community or all of the concrete issues with which it struggled. Yet despite the letter's preservation of many unoriginal sayings and examples, Leo Perdue has observed that "it is rather odd to suggest that [James] would not choose admonitions and other traditional materials to address real issues in the life of the community itself."[16] Perdue goes on to show that one can suggest general characteristics of the social setting, although they must be "inferential and analogical,"[17] based upon the genre of paraenesis itself.

One consistent feature that Perdue discovers in paraenetic literature is that it involves a mature teacher who is instructing a novice or a community as that person or group either undergoes initiation into a new group or achieves "group membership or a new status."[18] He suggests a scenario for James in which the writer, who has recently been separated from the group or is about to leave them (death may be approaching), exhorts them to endeavor toward greater moral perfection. Such a relationship between the author and audience is impossible to prove, but Perdue's point about the letter's recipients' having achieved a new status is a compelling one, for James wants the community to think of itself as different in comparison with the rest of society; it should be at odds with the "world" (4:4).

Perdue states that some of the members of the community possess more wealth than others and are being enticed by the world.[19] That some people are tempted by the "world" is clear in 4:1–10, although it is difficult to determine to what extent this community is a combination of rich and poor. Luke Timothy Johnson notes:

> [I]t is easier to affirm that the author and his readers shared the *ideology* of the poor than it is to deduce from that a realistic appreciation of the actual economic conditions within which they lived.[20]

It could be that some of the poor are seeking the support of the affluent and even that a few of these rich are beginning to enter the community (for example, the wealthy man who enters the assembly in 2:2).[21] New wealthy members would deflect the community's emphasis from the poor to the rich, and thus James may be writing to guard against such events from happening.

Whatever its precise economic status, however, this is a community facing difficult issues and requiring some assurance of its own identity and legitimacy. The rich, be they within the group or outside, are mistreating the poor (2:6; 5:1–6). Thus James encourages his audience to have "patience" (*hypomone*, 1:3–4) and to be joyful in its trials (1:2, 12). James also establishes strong lines of distinction between the poor and the rich, which is another social function of paraenesis. Like the cohesive theme of the *parousia* (5:7) and the promise of God's kingdom to the "poor in the world" (2:5), this poor/rich characterization can fashion group identity. Moreover, by using familiar traditional materials—for example, references to scripture and famous examples (Abraham, Rahab, Job, Elijah)—James contributes to the legitimation of his audience's social world,[22] another example of a social function of paraenesis.

Perdue's discussion of the setting and function of paraenetic materials reinforces the notion that the recipients of this letter were facing conflicts within their community and/or with surrounding social and economic forces. Whatever the precise scenario, this was a tense situation. Such tension is possibly linked to the morally rigorous admonitions that pervade the letter.

Resist Yourself

Although he does not elaborate in great detail concerning the "inner" compulsions of which he disapproves, James does not hesitate to make uncompromising demands upon the moral life of his audience. He calls for resistance to personal vices, that is, vices for which the individual can be ultimately responsible. There is no preoccupation with the body, although many of James' exhortations would have bearing on what one does with one's body.

"Lured and Enticed by His Own Desire"

The most explicit of these is James' command not to succumb to desire. Resistance to desire, especially sexual desire, was a common theme among ancient philosophers and moralists.[23] The word *epithymia* has many meanings, depending upon its context.[24] Plutarch associates it with a variety of things, including sexual desire and the yearning for wealth,[25] the latter being the most detestable form of desire.[26] Among the Stoics, *epithymia* has a negative meaning without regard to its object; it is another example of a passion that must be eliminated for the sake of achieving virtue.[27] *Epithymia* also took on a negative connotation in Hellenistic Judaism[28] and in other texts of early Christian literature.[29]

Such a negative connotation is evident in James. In 1:13–15 a contrast is made between God, who tempts no one, and *epithymia*, which "lures" (*deleazein*) the person and then, once it has "conceived" (*syllambanein*), "gives birth" (*tiktein*) to sin. This sin, when fully grown, then "bears" (*apokuein*) death. Although James does not discuss sexual ethics in his letter, he has personified *epithymia* as a woman who seduces people and then conceives and gives birth to destructive sinfulness, which in turn leads to death. Such an association of "female" with desire or other such threats of disorder appears regularly in ancient literature. Gail Corrington Streete observes that "in the Pastorals the threat of subversion is characterized as female and often as sexual."[30] Such a characterization is likely linked to these letters' insistence on keeping women under control, that is, married and within the household. Gillian Clark, moreover, comments that among male ascetics

> the construct of woman as sexual temptress, as desire personified, was apparently so powerful that even men committed to a life of prayer could not think of women as fellow human beings with the same commitment.[31]

Perhaps it is not incidental, therefore, that when Abba Sisoes was asked about the passions, he responded by recalling the words of Jas. 1:14.[32]

In Jas. 4:2, *epithymia* is again destructive. Here, the result of desiring without gratification leads to killing. In this chapter, desire is connected with *hedone* ("pleasure" or "desire for pleasure"[33]) which causes wars both within human beings (James refers to the passions warring in the "members" [*melesin*]) and among people. *Hedone* can also be a neutral word, as Plutarch attests,[34] although it is understood pejoratively in James, as it is in Hellenistic Judaism[35] and the three other times that it appears in the New Testament.[36]

The connection of *epithymia* or *hedone* with social turmoil, moreover, is common throughout the writings of Greek and Hellenistic writers.[37] Xenophon describes the degeneration of Critias and Alcibiades, who, upon leaving Socrates, were no longer able to control their *epithymia* and fell into lawlessness and corruption.[38] Many realized that the unbridled pursuit of pleasure, be it in the form of food, drink, wealth, or sex, must be resisted so that human beings might live together harmoniously. This is clearly the case in James, in which succumbing to desire leads to fighting and death.

"Quick to Hear, Slow to Speak, Slow to Anger"
Stern warnings about speech and anger also appear in James, although the emphasis is upon the former. These subjects are discussed widely in moral and ascetic literature, often in connection with each other. Plutarch, for example, states:

> [C]ontrol over the tongue ... is something which it is impossible to keep always in subjection and obedience to the reasoning faculties, unless a man by training, practice and industry has mastered the worst of his emotions, such as anger, for example.[39]

Many desert monks considered anger to be the worst of passions and thought that it should be avoided at all costs. So easily could angry words inflict pain that, as is widely appreciated, many of these monks made lifetime vows of silence.[40]

Some traditions connected taciturnity with wisdom and philosophical insight. Even fools, as Prov. 17:28 makes clear, are considered wise when they keep silent. A quiet person was the sign of a good listener, and a good listener was one who would gain in wisdom. Prov. 19:20, for example, gives the instruction, "Listen to advice and accept instruction, that you may gain wisdom for the future." Silence is thus a requirement for gaining wisdom.

In other non-Christian circles silence acquired a religious significance. No talking was allowed during the initiation rite of the Mysteries, for example, and Pythagoras received accolades from Philostratus for inventing the discipline of silence.[41] Philostratus goes on to express great admiration for the Pythagoreans, who remained mute for a period of five years after initiation into the religious community.[42]

In contrast to quiet, wise people, however, the incessant babbler was generally considered irritating, untrustworthy, and lacking in self-control. It comes as no surprise to learn that some writers thought noisy, lying, gossipy people were threats to the social order, especially when they became doubly verbose and fraudulent due to intoxication or anger.[43] In the apocryphal and pseudepigraphical literatures, for example, William Baker explains that "the tongue can be a help or a deterrent to the goal of a peaceful society and all too often is the latter."[44] We find a similar view in Greco-Roman literature. Theophrastus' study of the garrulous person reveals how destructive the incessant talker can be. He depicts a rather terrifying individual who, among other things, goes around disrupting the classroom, preventing people from eating their meals, thwarting the judicial process, and interfering with the audience at the theater.[45]

Babblers are always annoying, but what really concerned many ancient Mediterranean cultures was dishonesty. Without verbal integrity, societies thought that they would fall apart.[46] Plutarch explains how friendship would not be possible,[47] as true friends must be completely honest with one another. Members of the ascetic Qumran community, moreover, had to promise to be "forever lover[s] of truth and to expose liars."[48]

Baker suggests that controlled speech and verbal integrity "is even more vital within subcultures" such as the people at Qumran and the early Christian communities.[49] The Pastoral Epistles display a definite anxiety about uncontrolled speech. Streete observes that "[s]peech in the Pastorals is in fact the only area in which a severe *enkrateia* is to be practiced, to the extent of complete silence on occasion (1 Tim. 2:12)."[50] The desert monks, moreover, were particularly concerned about speaking with integrity. They were acutely aware of the threats of reckless talk and thus, according to Burton-Christie, developed "a spirituality in which integrity or purity of speech was highly valued."[51]

James clearly recognizes the futility and wickedness of anger when he states that "the anger of man does not work the righteousness of God" (1:20) and his instruction about listening and being slow to speak and slow to anger (1:19) mirrors the attitudes of many ancient Mediterranean cultures.[52] However, he is much more preoccupied with speech. The need to control the tongue is a recurrent theme in the letter, leading one to suspect that useless, boastful, and nasty chattering was a concrete problem for James' audience. He explicitly tells his audience not to speak evil against one another (4:11) and at one point goes so far to say that if a person cannot control his or her tongue, he or she is not religious (1:26). This latter statement indicates to what degree James considers unchecked speech to be wicked.

James reserves chapter 3 for a more elaborate critique of the tongue. He begins by stating that not many in the community should become teachers (like him), as teachers will be judged more harshly.[53] Teachers in antiquity generally had the responsibility of training the young in virtue. They thus not only had opportunities to stimulate and promote the pursuit of virtue but to corrupt their students or seek admiration through flattery.[54] Thus teachers would be judged with greater strictness because they were more likely to cause damage with their speech.

James then goes on to describe the evil powers of speech in what Baker calls a "bold exposé on the negative, destructive capabilities of the tongue."[55] Although many Hellenistic moralists had a deep mistrust of the tongue, they thought that it could be mastered. James, however, states that the tongue stains the body (3:6) and that "no human being can tame the tongue" (3:8); he is this much more pessimistic.[56] Like the unstable "double-minded" person in 1:8, the tongue can both bless and curse. For James, this should not be so (3:10).

Whether or not the critique of the tongue in chapter 3 is addressing a concrete situation in the community, James' comments still indicate the importance he placed on the impact that false and seductive teaching could have on his audience, a concern that is equally apparent in the Pastoral Epistles.[57] This may be another reason why James and others so vociferously preached control of the tongue: so their readers will learn to distrust anyone who attempts to persuade them with the wiles of speech.

Imperfect and incorrigible as the tongue is, however, James offers positive examples of how to speak (2:12; 4:15; 5:12). For James, there is a connection between proper speech and community living. This is most perceptible in 5:13–20, the closing verses of the letter. Here, James gives examples of how speech can build and reinforce the community.[58] The author exhorts the suffering to pray, the happy to sing praise (5:13), and the "elders" to pray over the sick (5:14). The members are to confess their sins to one another and to pray for each other so that they may be healed. Finally, James encourages his audience to reprove one another if they stray from the true path (5:19–20). Thus, despite James' deeply skeptical attitude toward the tongue,[59] he has granted that speech, that is, *controlled* speech, can perform important functions for the strengthening of the community.

In addition to wild speech, anger, and desire, there are other vices mentioned by James. Envy, jealousy, and selfish ambition, for example,[60] are to be avoided, as they inevitably lead to destruction. Again, these vices receive regular castigation in other moral literatures.[61]

James is fairly typical, therefore, in his emphasis upon resistance to human failings. Writers and communities often commanded their audiences to defy desire, to relinquish meaningless or cruel talk, and to refrain from falling into anger or envy. These were common themes among many sorts of communities, including those represented by Jewish wisdom literature, Greek and Roman moralists, and the later Christian monastic figures.

James is not an extremist, however. On the basis of the moral exhortations discussed here, I do not think that he would necessarily stand out as an asectic. His interest in self-control and self-improvement is not exceptional, as compared to, say, the vegetarian Pythagoreans; the stern, hard figure of Marcus Aurelius; or the celibate and solemn desert monks. Aspects of James' attitudes, especially toward speech, are typical of wisdom literature, which generally counsels the proper way to live, but not a radical asceticism.[62] James' concerns also have much in common with texts like the pastoral epistles, which in many ways uphold the status quo with their emphases on the control of women and the household.

Resist the World

Yet there are aspects of this letter that would, it seems to me, characterize the writer and possibly the readers (if they heeded James' words) as distinct. First, it is clear that James possesses a deep mistrust of the world. In 1:27 he states that "[r]eligion that is pure and undefiled before God and the Father is this: to visit orphans and widows in their affliction, and to keep oneself unstained from the world." Then in 4:4 he states that "friendship with the world is enmity with God." James is again typical of biblical traditions in his concern for widows, orphans, and the poor in general,[63] but he is more like the *Gospel of Thomas* in his negative attitude toward the world. Logia found in Thomas, such as "Be passersby" (*Gos.Thom.* 42) and "If you do not fast from the world, you will not find the kingdom" (*Gos.Thom.* 27), support Patrick Hartin's claim that Thomas shares James' suspicion of the world.[64] The world is of no value to them. The two documents represent a person or people who think of themselves differently in comparison with the rest of society.

"Is It Not the Rich Who Oppress You?"

Thomas' and James' rejection of the world are connected, argues Hartin, to their comparable attitudes toward rich and poor. Firstly, both texts espouse poverty over wealth. A few examples from the *Gospel of Thomas* include the beatitude "Blessed are the poor, for yours is the kingdom of heaven" (*Gos.Thom.* 54), a series of parables criticizing wealth (*Gos.Thom.* 63–65), and Jesus' advice to give money away (*Gos.Thom.* 95). James contains vari-

ous passages about the evils of the rich and the hope for the poor. The letter decrees that the lowly brother will boast in his "high rank" (*hupsos*)
(1:9–10) but that the rich person will boast in his humiliation. He then compares the wealthy to the flower of the grass, which, although once beautiful,
will quickly die and fade away. In 2:6–7 the rich are those who exploit members of the community, haul them into court, and blaspheme their good
name. Finally, in 5:1–6, he describes wealthy landowners who exploit their
workers, live in luxury, and who have condemned and killed the righteous
one.

In the *Gospel of Thomas*, the saying "Let one who has found the world,
and has become wealthy, renounce the world" (*Gos. Thom.* 110) renders the
connection between the world and wealth quite explicit. James also makes
the link when he states that pure religion requires one to help the poor (widows and orphans) *and* to keep oneself unstained from the world (Jas. 1:27).
When James equates friendship with the world and enmity with God, it is
directly after his criticism of covetousness and greed for more (Jas. 4:1–4).
Clearly for both authors, the world and the pursuit of wealth are bound
together and thus both must be rejected.

Yet as Hartin points out, Thomas and James emerge from different
social situations. The *Gospel of Thomas*, like the sayings source Q (with which
James shares many traditions)[65] may represent a group of "itinerant social
radicals"[66] who actually identify with the poor. There is no evidence of such
itinerancy in James. Although it is unclear as to what degree James' rhetoric
is reflecting the facts, he does make the point that his readers have "dishon-
ored the poor man" (Jas. 2:6) when they force the pauper to stand aside or
sit at their feet, giving the best seat to the rich person.[67] Although they are
not rich, James' audience may be at the "stage where the previous concern
for the poor is now fading."[68]

"Show No Partiality"

If James' audience needed reminding that they should give more alms, the
author could have limited his instructions to such. But James goes further
and takes a much stronger stance. Like Thomas, he praises and reassures the
poor, but he also challenges the scheme of power relations based upon status distinctions. This system was pervasive throughout the ancient world and
was supported by the institution of patronage, defined as an exchange of
goods and services between unequals. Patronage promotes "a potentially
unstable relationship which, because of the unequal bargaining position
of the two parties, can easily slide into overt exploitation."[69] That James
viewed the system as exploitative is clear. The angry attack on the wealthy
landowners (5:1–6) describes the laborers and harvesters, who cry out to
God because their patrons have kept back their wages by fraud. Clearly the
rich are not only condemned for their affluence, but because they cheat their
workers.

Yet it is in 2:1–26, as John Kloppenborg points out, "that James' alternative to patronage most clearly emerges."[70] Here, James criticizes the standard custom of bestowing honor upon the rich patron. By attending to the wealthy man and offering him the best seat while simultaneously ordering the poor man to sit at their feet, James' readers are making distinctions among themselves and judging with evil designs (2:4).[71] Showing such partiality is sinful (2:9), for it honors the rich who exploit and drag people into court (2:6), while it dishonors the poor man (2:6a). For James, this system of patronage should be turned upside down so that it is the poor, the humble, who will boast and the rich who will be humbled (1:9). This turning of the tables is echoed in 5:1, in which the rich are to undergo the humiliation that the poor have traditionally suffered. As Claus Wengst states, "The invitation to be wretched, mourn and weep is here given to those who behave in the way the world behaves, namely the world of the rich and powerful."[72]

For James, a new reality must be central in the minds and hearts of his audience. This is a reality that opposes wealth and patronage and all of the accompanying behaviors that assist in the perpetration of such evils. James is not the sole ancient writer, however, to oppose status distinctions based upon wealth. In his criticism of the rich and championing of the poor, he has drawn upon the literary traditions of prophecy and wisdom, some of which are quite comparable to those found in the *Gospel of Thomas* and Q. Moreover, some Greek moralists, at least in theory, disapproved of this constant concern for social and economic standing. Plutarch, for example, opposes the value system based upon hierarchy with one grounded in friendship of character, in which honesty, trust, and frank speech are paramount.[73] Certainly these virtues are important for James, but he goes further in that the evils created by status distinctions will not be solved by human merit, but by a radical reordering of humanity's relationship to God. Honesty, loyalty, submission—all of the things that one would hold sacred in a friendship—must, for James, be maintained in relationship to God. As he says, "Do you not know that friendship with the world is enmity with God? Therefore, whoever chooses to be a friend of the world is established as an enemy of God." It is only through resistance to and denunciation of this sinful world and its manipulative institutions that one can embrace the new reality, that of friendship with God (4:7–10).

"And Let Steadfastness Have Its Full Effect"

To criticize the rich and confront the system of patron-client relations would not have been easy within the ancient Mediterranean economy. If community members were rejecting relationships with patrons, for example, they were resigning themselves to difficult lives, as they would receive neither funding nor favors from the prosperous. A consolation for this suffering would certainly have been the knowledge that Jesus would soon return, and James is sure to remind his audience of this (5:7–9). Yet the promise of the *parousia* does not mean that the community should simply wait, as if life on this earth is of no importance. James' calls for patient endurance should not be interpreted as demands to be passive, wherein the community simply languishes in anticipation of its Savior's return. Rather, patience is productive; it literally yields a perfect work (1:4), which in turn, can lead to perfection. Elsa Tamez calls it an "active, working patience"[74] and suggests that James may have realized the "difficulty of [the audience's] situation and the need for valiant perseverance, that is militant patience."[75]

The assertive nature of this patience is borne out by other themes in the letter. The community members must vigorously resist their own inclinations to desire, grumbling, and anger, but they must also complete their faith through works. James' famous phrase, "Faith without works is dead" (2:17, 26) resounds throughout the letter as he repeatedly gives examples of how faith and works must be coexistent (2:14–17; 2:18–26). The author does not want his audience to quietly retreat into a corner in expectation of the *parousia*, but to uphold their faith through their actions, even if it risks further suffering.

CONCLUSION

In my view, the letter of James can be described as ascetic. There is no evidence that the author is under some sort of duress as he writes, and thus I think it fair to say that James represents a *choice* to relinquish various vices. Although James is not an ascetical zealot, he exhorts his audience to self-discipline: There are admonitions to resist the lures of desire, false talk, and wealth, and counsels to embody integrity of speech, action, and faith, all themes that appear later, in some form, in other ascetic communities.[76] Merged together, these exhortations produce a text that evinces a new subjectivity, particularly evident in the hostile attitude toward "the world" and wealth. James wants his audience to maintain a disciplined nonconformism.

Using asceticism as a framework for studying James has highlighted what it shares with other texts. For example, some of the letter's concerns about proper speech and desire are common themes in many kinds of literature including early Christian texts like 1 and 2 Timothy and Titus. Yet unlike the Pastoral Epistles, which Streete has described as "a kind of controlled experiment in a 'good' society, a society that is 'good' in that it resists, not authority, but the vagaries of individual desire,"[77] James defies authority. Like the *Gospel of Thomas* and Q, the letter evinces a deeply critical attitude toward wealth, even to the point of directly attacking the rich and the system they uphold, namely patronage.

James is a mixture of conventional teachings characteristic of established communities and the radical ethos of wandering itinerants. As discussed here, that there were tensions both among the audience and with the surrounding society is probable. James may thus be a witness to a settled group, but one torn between the craving for security and the unruly spirit manifest in the early sayings traditions. Whatever happened to James and his audience, it was precisely this need for security that eventually triumphed.

NOTES

1. See the papers and responses in Vincent L. Wimbush and Richard Valantasis, eds., *Asceticism* (New York: Oxford University Press, 1995).
2. See Elizabeth A. Clark, "The Ascetic Impulse in Religious Life: A General Response," *Asceticism*, 505–10.
3. By "ordinary life," Taylor (*Sources of the Self: The Making of the Modern Identity* [Cambridge, Mass.: Harvard University Press, 1989], 211) refers to "those aspects of human life concerned with production and reproduction, that is, labour, the making of the things needed for life, and our life as sexual beings, including marriage and the family."
4. Kallistos Ware, "The Way of the Ascetics: Negative or Affirmative?" *Asceticism*, 12.
5. L. William Countryman (this volume, 371–391).
6. James A. Francis, *Subversive Virtue: Asceticism and Authority in the Second-Century Pagan World* (University Park: Pennsylvania State University Press, 1995), 12.
7. See Francis, *Subversive Virtue*, 65.
8. Countryman (this volume, 371, 383).
9. Richard Valantasis, "Constructions of Power in Asceticism," *Journal of the American Academy of Religion* 63 (1995), 797.
10. Francis, *Subversive Virtue*, 181.
11. Alison Keith and Leif E. Vaage (this volume, 411–420).
12. Francis, *Subversive Virtue*, 174.
13. Vincent L. Wimbush, "The Ascetic Impulse in Ancient Christianity," *Theology Today* 50 (1993), 420–21.
14. "For [Gandhi] a precondition of 'seeing truth' was self-purification from baser desires; while the preliminary to exercising 'truth-force' was to strengthen oneself through self-discipline and persistent adherence to non-violence" (Judith M. Brown, *Modern India: The Origins of an Asian Democracy* [Delhi, India: Oxford University Press, 1985], 206).
15. Martin Dibelius, *James* (rev., Heinrich Greeven; trans., Michael A. Williams (Philadelphia: Fortress, Hermeneia, 1976), 3, 46.
16. Leo G. Perdue, "Paraenesis and the Epistle of James," *Zeitschrift für Neutestamentliche Wissenschaft* 72 (1981), 247.
17. Ibid.
18. Ibid, 250. See also, Leo G. Perdue, "Liminality as a Social Setting for Wisdom Instruction," *Zeitschrift für alttestamentliche Wissenschaft* 93 (1981), 114–26.
19. Perdue, "Paraenesis," 250.
20. Luke Timothy Johnson, "The Social World of James: Literary Analysis and Historical Reconstruction," *The Social World of the First Christians: Essays in*

Honor of Wayne A. Meeks, eds., L. Michael White and O. Larry Yarbrough (Minneapolis, Minn.: Fortress, 1995), 185, n. 31.

21. Patrick J. Hartin, "The Poor in the Gospel of Thomas and the Epistle of James," paper delivered at the annual meeting of the Society of Biblical Literature, Philadelphia, 1995, 13.

22. Perdue, "Paraenesis," 254.

23. See K. J. Dover, *Greek Popular Morality in the Time of Plato and Aristotle* (Oxford: Basil Blackwell, 1974), 208–9.

24. *Epithymia* can also be used in a neutral sense. See for example, Phil. 1:23.

25. Plutarch, *On Love of Wealth* 525B; 524F.

26. Edward N. O'Neil, "De Cupidate Divitiarum (Moralia 523C–528B)," *Plutarch's Ethical Writings and Early Christian Literature*, ed. Hans Dieter Betz (Leiden, The Netherlands: Brill, 1978), 332.

27. See Martha C. Nussbaum, *The Therapy of Desire: Theory and Practice in Hellenistic Ethics* (Princeton, N.J.:Princeton University Press, 1994), 359–401.

28. Wis. 4:12; Sir. 23:5.

29. For example, Rom. 1:24; 7:7; Gal. 5:24; 2 Tim. 2:22; 3:6; 1 Pet. 4:3.

30. Gail Corrington Streete, (this volume)

31. Gillian Clark, "Women and Asceticism in Late Antiquity: The Refusal of Status and Gender," *Asceticism*, eds. Wimbush and Valantasis, 37.

32. Douglas Burton-Christie, *The Word in the Desert: Scripture and the Quest for Holiness in Early Christian Monasticism* (New York: Oxford University Press, 1993), 193.

33. In this case it likely means the latter as James is "tracing out the logic of envy" (Luke Johnson, *The Letter of James: A New Translation and Commentary* Garden City, N.Y.: Doubleday, The Anchor Bible 37A, 1995), 277.

34. For example, Plutarch (*Advice About Keeping Well* 126C; 127A) values pleasure in moderation.

35. See 4 Macc. 1:25–26.

36. Luke 8:14; Titus 3:3; 2 Pet. 2:13. See Ralph P. Martin, *James* (Waco, Tex.: Word Books, Word Biblical Commentary 48, 1988) 145.

37. For example, Plato, *Phaedo* 66C; Philo, *On Joseph* 10–11; and 4 Macc. 1:20–29.

38. Xenophon, *Memorabilia* 1, 2, 23–24.

39. Plutarch, *How to Profit by One's Enemies* 90C. See Johnson, *James*, 199–200 for other examples from moral literature.

40. See Burton-Christie, *The Word in the Desert*, 146–50; 267–73.

41. Philostratus, *Life of Apollonius of Tyana* 1,1; 6,11. This control of the tongue was represented by the phrase "An ox sits upon it."

42. Diogenes Laertius 8, 17. For a discussion of the Pythagoreans and Orphics as "protest movements against the established polis," see Walter Burkert, *Greek Religion*, trans. John Raffan (Cambridge, Mass.: Harvard University Press, 1985), 301–4.

43. Plutarch, *Concerning Talkativeness*, 4.

44. William R. Baker, *Personal Speech-Ethics in the Epistle of James* (Tübingen, Germany: Mohr [Siebeck], 1995), 149.

45. Theophrastus, *Characters*, 7.

46. See William R. Baker, "'Above All Else': Contexts of the Call for Verbal Integrity in James 5:12," *Journal for the Study of the New Testament* 54 (1994) 57–71.

47. Plutarch, *How to Tell a Flatterer from a Friend.*

48. Josephus, *Jewish War* 2, 8, 7. See Baker, "'Above All Else,'" 61.

49. Baker, "'Above All Else,'" 61–62.

50. Corrington Streete (this volume, 299–316).

51. Burton-Christie, *The Word in the Desert*, 144.

52. Luke Timothy Johnson, "Taciturnity and True Religion: James 1:26–27" *Greeks, Romans and Christians: Essays in Honour of Abraham J. Malherbe*, ed. David L. Balch, Everett Ferguson, and Wayne A. Meeks (Minneapolis, Minn.: Fortress, 1990), 330.

53. The use of *krima* in this case might indicate that teachers will be judged by a higher standard (see Johnson, *James*, 255), however, the fact that James later says that the tongue is evil and cannot be tamed (3:8) indicates that anyone who uses speech in his or her profession, like a teacher, will thus be judged with greater severity (see Baker, *Personal Speech-Ethics*, 136–37).

54. Johnson, *James*, 263.

55. Baker, *Personal Speech-Ethics*, 126.

56. Johnson, *James*, 264.

57. For example, 1 Tim. 4:3.

58. Johnson, "Taciturnity and True Religion," 339.

59. James 3:6–12 gives one the impression that the author would prefer his audience to remain mute.

60. Jas. 3:14–16; 4:2.

61. Plutarch (*How to Tell a Flatterer from a Friend*, 54C), for example, thinks jealousy (*zelos*) is inimical to friendship. For James' use of the topic of envy, see Luke Timothy Johnson, "James 3:13-4:10 and the *Topos [peri zelou]*, *Novum Testamentum* 25 (1983), 327–47.

62. See Patrick J. Hartin, *James and the Q Sayings of Jesus* (Sheffield, England: Journal for the Study of the Old Testament, Journal for the Study of the New Testament Supp. 47, 1991), 35–40; 62–65.

63. See F. Charles Fensham, "Widow, Orphan, and the Poor in Ancient Near Eastern Legal and Wisdom Literature," *Journal of Near Eastern Studies* 21 (1962), 129–39.

64. Hartin, "The Poor in Thomas and James," 10.

65. For a chart of the correspondences between James, Matthew, Luke, and Q, see Hartin, *James and the Q Sayings of Jesus*, 141–42.

66. Stephen J. Patterson (this volume, 49–70)

67. Hartin, "Poor Thomas James," 17.

68. Ibid.

69. Peter Garnsey, *Famine and Food Supply in the Graeco-Roman World: Responses to Risk and Crisis* (Cambridge, England: Cambridge University Press, 1988), 58.

70. John S. Kloppenborg, "Status and Conflict Resolution in Early Christian Groups" (paper delivered at the Toronto School of Theology Biblical Department Seminar, September 1995), 16.

71. Johnson (*James*, 224) translates *dialogismos* as "designs" both because the word has a negative connotation throughout the New Testament and because of "the *calculation* that is built into favoritism toward the rich; in the ancient system of patronage there would have been a *quid pro quo.*"
72. Claus Wengst, *Humility: Solidarity of the Humiliated*, trans. John Bowden (Minneapolis, Minn.: Fortress, 1988), 44.
73. See Troels Engberg-Pedersen, "Plutarch to Prince Philopappus on How to Tell a Flatterer from a Friend," *Friendship, Flattery and Frank Speech: Studies on Friendship in the New Testament World*, ed. John T. Fitzgerald (Leiden, The Netherlands: Brill, 1996), 61–79.
74. Elsa Tamez, *The Scandalous Message of James: Faith Without Works Is Dead*, trans. John Eagelson (New York: Crossroad, 1990), 53.
75. Tamez, *The Scandalous Message*, 54.
76. Burton-Christie, *The Word in the Desert*, 144–66; 217–19.
77. Corrington Streete (this volume, 299–316)

Asceticism or
Household Morality?
1 and 2 Peter and Jude

L. Wm. Countryman

DEFINING ASCETICISM

Given the diversity of possible meanings for the term "asceticism," it is probably wise to begin by specifying how I am using it here. By asceticism, I understand *a relatively demanding bodily praxis, voluntarily undertaken, that sets those who adopt it apart from and, in the view of some, above the ordinary run of people in their world.* This definition emerges from my own perspective as a social historian. The element of social contrast is as essential to it as the demanding character of the praxis. And I include also the element of personal choice to distinguish ascetical behavior from simple cultural differences between neighboring groups. I would not, for example, label Anglo-Saxon culture "ascetical" merely because it is more prudish than French culture is.

The rejection of alcohol can serve as an illustration. It has certainly been an ascetical act at many times in history, yet growing up in a Protestant home in Oklahoma in the 1940s and 1950s, I did not perceive the rejection of alcohol as ascetical. It was less a matter of personal choice than an acceptance of the dominant mores of that world. It was the use of alcohol, if anything, that set a person apart from the ordinary run of people in that world, yet such use would not qualify as ascetical because it was not perceived as a "more or less demanding bodily praxis." It seems to me that three qualities are requisite to make something ascetical: a relatively *demanding* bodily praxis, *voluntarily undertaken*, that sets those who adopt it *apart* from and, in the view of some, above the ordinary run of people in their world.

One need scarcely say that there are other possible definitions of asceticism, many of them represented in this book. Whether one finds asceticism in any given ancient document will depend partly on how one defines the term. From my own perspective, there are three key advantages of my definition: It is clear, it is related to the traditional use of the term, and it is heuristically useful. It regards asceticism as an aspect of social relations, not as a Platonic idea. It encourages the observation of behavioral phenomena and their public, social interpretation. And it defines asceticism as an exceptional activity, one that distinguishes the ascetic from the run-of-the-mill, everyday sort of person on the street—precisely what has normally given asceticism its interest.

I am not suggesting that the exceptional is inherently more interesting or important than the everyday, but that exceptional behavior is more readily identifiable and more subject to comment than what is submerged in daily life and taken generally for granted. Because of its visibility and its distinctiveness, the exceptional behavior therefore serves to highlight not only itself but also its background. The ways in which it is interpreted, whether by those who practice it or by those who object to it, will then tell us much about both ascetical self-understanding and about how the larger society related to ascetical practice and identity.

The larger society may—broadly speaking—object to ascetical practices, ignore them, or incorporate them by defining them as a special category within the larger society. Thus, traditional Protestants have often objected to ascetical practices as "Romish," while liberal Protestants may view them as a matter of purely individual choice to be ignored by the larger community unless they cross certain ill-defined boundaries and become something categorized as bad (e.g., anorexia). Catholicism, on the other hand, has tended to incorporate asceticism by making it the particular preserve of a specialized and perhaps superior monastic class.

I make these observations, not just because it is generally desirable to have a definition of one's subject, but because they are crucial to what follows. We shall find some texts that could be seen as ascetical or not, depending on our understanding of the category itself and our analysis of the social context suggested in the texts. The texts in question come from three somewhat disparate documents: 1 and 2 Peter and Jude. Though they are grouped together as Catholic Epistles, they are related to one another only incidentally—1 and 2 Peter by common ascription to the same author, 2 Peter and Jude by the fact that the one incorporates a substantial portion of the other.

JUDE

I begin with Jude, the briefest and, although it is singularly difficult to date, quite possibly the oldest of the three.[1] Because of its brevity and the fact that the author chooses to slam his opponents rather than argue with them point by point, it is difficult to feel confident that we know much about what was at issue on either side. Indeed, many discussions of Jude assume that the author's collection of insults is miscellaneous and has no precise application to those he attacks. If, however, we begin by treating the selection of insults as deliberate, it is quite possible to construct a coherent sketch, if not a detailed map, of the central issue. Jude is particularly exercised about inter-action between angels and human beings—especially sexual interaction.[2] Consider the core sequence of "bad examples" that Jude offers:

1. Some of the exodus generation did not believe and were destroyed (v. 5). Since the exodus generation is often a type of the early Christian community itself in New Testament writings, this establishes the Christian community as the locus of danger.
2. The angels who left their place in heaven to have intercourse with human women are being held for punishment (v. 6). This, in itself, might merely be a way of reinforcing the preceding: Not even angels are exempt from punishment. But it is followed by a monitory example that also deals with sex between humans and angels.
3. Sodom and Gomorrah were destroyed because the men there went out "after strange flesh" (AV), a phrase that points to the angelic nature of Lot's visitors, not their maleness (v. 7).
4. Even Michael kept a respectful distance in his dealings with Satan over the body of Moses (v. 9), not daring to "level a judgment of blasphemy" (or, perhaps, a "blasphemous judgment").

Of all the elements in his argument, Jude develops these four images most fully. If we connect them with one another, they suggest that Jude felt that the Christian community to whom he wrote was in danger of judgment because some of them claimed to have sexual relations with angels and were therefore violating the angels' honor ("blaspheming" them). Jude, in fact, makes this point relatively explicit in v. 8: "And yet, likewise (i.e., like the men of Sodom), these people are actually polluting the flesh in their dreams and nullifying lordship and blaspheming glories." Given the reference to Sodom, "polluting the flesh in dreams" suggests a sexual emission of some sort. The term *kyriotes* ("lordship" or "dominion") appears elsewhere in ancient Jewish and Christian Greek (including the Greek remains of 1 Enoch, which Jude regarded as scripture) with reference to angelic beings.[3] It is not difficult to think that "glories," given the peculiar use of the plural, has a similar meaning here. Jude is concerned, then, about Christian teach-ers who claim to have sex with angels.

Jude's presentation of these teachers is, of course, hostile. What were they really proposing? Some kind of religious practice, presumably, leading to an experience that was interpreted as intercourse with angels. In all prob-ability, they understood this praxis as setting them apart from the common run of humanity—or even of the Christian community. But was it the kind of demanding bodily praxis assumed by my use of the term "asceticism"?

Jude, it seems, would say "no." He describes these persons as "reefs in your love-feasts"—where the word for "reef" is etymologically connected to the word meaning "blotches," which, in turn, suggests uncleanness (v. 12). He speaks of them as "wild waves of the sea foaming up their own shames"—language rife with sexual connotations, as the reference to the sea and the verb "foaming up" (*epaphrizonta*) both evoke the legend of the birth of Aphrodite (v. 13). He calls them "mockers proceeding according to their own impious passions," suggesting insincerity and disorder (v. 18). In other words, they are really doing all this for the sake of sexual pleasure, not advancement in faith. Hence, however much they present themselves as religiously superior, there are no grounds for such a claim. They are charlatans, not ascetics; they are not distinct from the run-of-the-mill person except in being more dissolute.

We cannot know, of course, whether Jude's assessment was accurate. Since the ancient Mediterranean world was as well supplied with religious charlatans as the modern, his accusations are plausible. On the other hand, let us suppose for a moment that these now nameless and voiceless teachers were demanding of their disciples a praxis that involved fasting, sleeplessness, and the avoidance of sexual intercourse with other humans as preparation for the moment of angelic intercourse. And let us further imagine that this moment itself was not so much physically orgasmic as it was a moment of spiritual illumination. Would such a teaching be ascetical, according to my definition? Yes, it would. And the suggestion that its teachers were really motivated by nothing more spiritual than ordinary lust might well be the ideal way for Jude to attack it. What better way to attack ascetical teaching than by suggesting that, however self-denying it may appear, it is really nothing more than a form of self-indulgence? Yet, the mere fact that Jude felt it necessary to attack these teachers suggests that there were some in the Christian communities he addressed who thought of them as being above, not below, the ordinary run of people.

I reiterate that this reconstruction is an act of imagination. I have no reason to argue that such an early Christian sexual practice ever existed. Jude may just have been describing with perfect accuracy a little group of talented charlatans. The mere fact that most modern readers do not much like the Epistle of Jude should not blind us to the possibility that its author is telling the truth. His attack may be accurate, even if it is impassioned and rhetorically shaped. I merely suggest, by this imagined alternative reading of Jude, that much will always remain hidden in the New Testament writings.

In the case of Jude's opponents, we can say that they were engaged in exceptional behavior, that they invited others to participate in it voluntarily, and that their behavior set them apart. But we have no details of the actual praxis in question. Jude argues that they are charlatans. He denies any claim they might have made to honor as ascetics. Yet Jude does not appear to be an advocate of asceticism, either. He does not argue for a "counterasceticism" as his response to their libertinism. Insofar as one can identify his own parameters of social behavior, they are the conventional presuppositions of well-ordered households of the first century: sobriety, decency, and piety. In this case, then, we remain uncertain about the presence of asceticism because of a lack of decisive evidence. In other cases, our difficulty may arise rather from our uncertainty about the relevant social context within which a practice should be assessed.

2 PETER

2 Peter, almost certainly the last of these three texts to be written, probably dates to the first half of the second century and is, therefore, surely pseudonymous. I take it up next because of its close relationship with Jude. The author of 2 Peter mined the Letter of Jude for insults, but not to any great effect. He took Jude's pointed and well-aimed missiles and turned them into blunt instruments for clubbing a more miscellaneous group of enemies. It has long been recognized that the principal aims of this letter are to reassert the expectation of an imminent parousia and to put a certain spin on interpretation of the developing Christian canon.[4] It has also been pointed out that the rhetoric the work uses against its opponents is closely related to that used by both Jewish and Gentile authors against Epicureanism.[5] The author declares that those who do not expect an imminent end of the world have also become dissolute, and he uses Jude's insults, minus the elements that referred specifically to sex with angels, to paint a broad picture of moral collapse in the Christian community.

The persons under attack are clearly part of the Christian community. Because they are Christians, the author accuses them not simply of dissolute living, but of moral apostasy (2:20–22). Their failure of belief has led to and is manifest in moral failure. In a neat twist, "Peter" argues that the very tardiness of the parousia that they mock is, in fact, God's kindness to people like them, giving them time for conversion (3:9). There is still time for them to be found "spotless and undefiled" (3:14).

Was asceticism a feature of 2 Peter's opposition? The opponents here, unlike those in Jude, do not seem to have any religious praxis peculiar to them. Even their possible Epicurean leanings do not emerge as a clear profile. For the author, their identity consists in what they do *not* take seriously, both in belief and in morals. If there is any specific religious program in view here, it is probably implied in the author's effort to counter the authority of certain unspecified interpretations of the writings of Paul (3:14–16). We can only guess what these might have been. Were the opponents defending their relatively relaxed version of Christianity with reference to Paul's doctrine of justification by grace rather than works? Or were they perhaps appealing to 2 Thessalonians 2 as evidence for an indefinite postponement of the parousia?

And what does "Peter" propose as an alternative for the congregation? *Eagerness* (*spoude*—a term that appears repeatedly in the work). For 2 Peter, eagerness is composed of equal parts eschatological enthusiasm and moral rigor. This letter is a coach's pep talk, focused less on ideas than on emotions and commitment. It uses a rhetoric of return to older, more rigorous standards. A Christian advocate of asceticism could, of course, use such a rhetoric by presupposing that the earliest Christians were themselves ascetics whose legacy had been corrupted by their lax and debased successors. Much of 2 Peter would not be inappropriate in the mouth of such a teacher, but there is nothing concrete to suggest such an identification for its author. The rhetoric is equally appropriate in the mouth of one who wants to recall a group to a more rigorous observance of ordinary, preexisting community standards. Would his audience become superior, then, to normal expectation? No, they would merely cease being inferior to it. "Peter" could be an ascetic, but he could also just be a social conservative in an era of what he sees as collapsing standards.

I tend to opt for the latter interpretation—2 Peter as conservative manifesto. Why? Partly because of the absence of unambiguously ascetic expressions and the very conventionality of the author's moral standards, but also partly because the image of Peter, which this letter exploits with its claim to Petrine authorship, is not otherwise an ascetic one in the New Testament literature. Peter failed to stay awake at the Garden of Gethsemane (Mark 14:37 and parallels). Peter was married and took his wife with him on apostolic journeys (1 Cor. 9:5). 1 Peter, as we shall see, upheld the structure of the ancient Mediterranean household, the most conventional of contemporary social structures. Peter functioned as a symbol for the mainstream of the emerging Christian community. He was not portrayed as someone who set himself apart by distinctive practices. If the author of 2 Peter were seeking to make an argument for asceticism, as I have defined it, I suspect he would have chosen a different pseudonym. In any case, I see nothing that can specifically serve as evidence for an ascetic stance, either on the part of the author of 2 Peter or on the part of those whom he admonishes or attacks.

1 PETER

This, the longest of the three documents treated in this chapter, is perhaps the most difficult to assess in relation to asceticism. Without doubt, there are phrases in 1 Peter that could be and no doubt have been cited in support of Christian ascetical practice—language, for example, about incorruption, the avoidance of fleshly desire, and the value of sobriety and wakefulness. The first question is whether the letter as a whole supports an ascetical reading of such phrases. The second question is a larger one—whether a norm of Christian community life (not something intrinsically ascetical as I am using the term) might at the same time function as or be perceived as ascetical in relation to the broader culture in which Christians, willingly or not, were enfolded.

Some later Christian apologists certainly did describe the Christian community as being set apart from and superior to the common run of non-Christian humanity in their world. The terminology employed to justify this superiority was that of "philosophy," understood as a way of life (as in ancient Stoicism) and not just an intellectual discipline. Tertullian, for example, described the Christian ethos as more rigorous, more abstemious, and more demanding than that of the environing Gentile world. At the same time, Tertullian could easily turn around and berate his Christian readers for their laxness. Is the identification of asceticism, then, partly a matter of audience? Undoubtedly so. The definition I have offered of asceticism implies that there is always an element of social comparison involved in it. Accordingly, the average Christian might be claimed as an ascetic in comparison with the Gentile context or berated as lax when seen as the standard from which more ascetical Christians (like Tertullian himself) distinguished themselves.

But, first, does 1 Peter as a whole encourage us in an ascetical reading? It begins with language evoking the atmosphere of the Jewish diaspora, of a subject people living scattered among their overlords and trying to maintain themselves with some degree of dignity and security (1:1). In other words, it addresses established communities in a more or less alien environment.[6] Like Jude, 1 Peter is difficult to date with any confidence, but the consensus placing it in the 70s or 80s is probably not far off.[7] There is at least a threat of persecution on the horizon—the vaguely ever-present kind of threat that hung over Christian communities for the second half of the first century—leading the author to write about ways of understanding and enduring it. It has been suggested that a portion of the letter was based on baptismal or catechetical materials, which might account for the letter's interest in conversion.[8]

1 Peter summons its readers to a high standard of behavior that we might at first assume is meant to distinguish them from the surrounding society. From the start, the author uses terms such as "sanctification of spirit" and "obedience" (1:1–2). He speaks of "an inheritance incorruptible, unspotted and undecaying" (1:4). He offers a catalog of social duties (a kind of expanded *Haustafel*) beginning with an exhortation to "avoid fleshly desires that war against the *psyche*." (The contents of the section suggest that he means not so much sexual desire as the generally disruptive tendency toward self-seeking [2:11–17].)[9] Like Christ, the one who suffers in the flesh is to put away sin and is no longer led by human desires; the past is time enough for indulging in "Gentile" behavior (4:1–6). Sobriety is necessary for prayer (4:7). "Be

sober," says 1 Peter. "Stay awake" (5:8). The observant reader will recognize here many watchwords of later Christian monastic writing.

As with 2 Peter, however, we have to ask in what sense the language is meant. While it is language with which later Christian asceticism was comfortable, we would do well to ask whether 1 Peter, like 2 Peter, might be more at home in the world of the conventional Jewish or Christian household. Again, we have to ask what is the standard of comparison. While Jewish and Christian apologists might present their households as more moral or righteous than their pagan neighbors, internally their praxis will have functioned primarily as an inherited norm, not as something newly or voluntarily chosen to distinguish them from the larger culture. Since the audience of 1 Peter is Christian, some of its members may certainly have been adult converts. For such converts, we can perhaps speak of the deliberate adoption of exceptional norms and therefore of a kind of asceticism here. But for those born in the community, 1 Peter can be read more readily as expressing a relatively conservative household morality—something reflecting the ancient Mediterranean mainstream (albeit constituting a subculture of it) more than the self-differentiation characteristic of asceticism.

Several elements in 1 Peter support this sense of the settled Mediterranean household as the context for the rhetoric. Note the section of the letter devoted to affirming existing structures of authority in state and household (2:11–3:12). Here the author returns to the imagery of diaspora (2:11–12): "resident aliens," "sojourners," "among the nations/Gentiles." He acknowledges the vulnerability of the minority community to the opinion of its dominant neighbors. The "day of visitation" in 2:12 may have connotations of judgment day, but it also seems to be the threatened day of persecution or martyrdom.

In this context of threat, our author urges his audience to live up to the ideals of the larger society even better than the majority group around them, always showing obedience to the constituted authorities (2:13–14, 18). Yes, as Christians they have a dignity that is entirely their own, yet their Christian freedom is not to be a cloak for vice (2:15–16). This sounds less like an ascetic dictum than one intended to rein in possible "excesses" in existing Christian behavior. 1 Peter always keeps an eye on public opinion (2:15). The exhortation to obey the political authorities is designed not so much to distinguish Christians from the other people of their world as to make them exemplary inhabitants of that world. Perhaps one could call this a kind of asceticism, but would its practitioners be seen as set apart from the ordinary social expectations—or simply as an exemplary version of what they inculcate? 1 Peter's goal is the latter.

The address to "servants" that follows (2:18–25) is a special case of the command to be obedient to political authorities and speaks particularly to those who had a legitimate complaint against such duly constituted authority. Again, the "problem" the author is countering is that Christians may expect too much on the basis of their self-understanding in relation to God. The author urges them to seek not the difference that asceticism leads to, but a kind of "fitting in" with the society as a whole—even a disappearance into the environing society. This external conformity, to be sure, is an ironic mask for those who know themselves to be, in truth, free persons in God's eyes (2:16, 19). But the visible end result is conformity, not difference. The address to wives (3:1–6) is explicitly designated as parallel (*homoios*) with that to servants. It, too, is primarily an address to those who might have some complaint against the authorities over them—in this case, husbands who were not believers.

Finally, husbands (3:7) are advised to eschew threatening conduct and to treat their wives as coheirs of the grace of life. Even this does not break too sharply with the conventions of the environing society, although it does manage to reaffirm the early Christian perception of women as believers in their own right. The conclusion of this whole long passage on social duties emphasizes that Christians should preserve harmony among themselves (3:8; cf. 2:17) and avoid conflict with outsiders. The point is not to establish difference so much as to practice an ironic assimilation.

Much of the author's concern seems to be motivated by the threat of persecution. He holds out the hope that, if Christians' behavior is sufficiently unexceptionable, no one will harm them (3:13). But, even so, he immediately goes on to provide an extended explanation of how the audience can make sense of the coming persecution and steel themselves to survive it (3:13–4:19). They are to remember Jesus' innocence and what his death gained them through baptism. They are to suffer like Christ, putting away sin and no longer being led by human desires. The past is time enough for indulging in Gentile behaviors: "debaucheries, passions, drunkenness, revelries, drinking bouts, and lawless idolatries" (4:3). Perhaps 1 Peter hints at a kind of ascetical superiority for Christians here. And yet, one might easily avoid all these things without being an ascetic; indeed, the average householder of the period, Jewish or Gentile, probably prayed to the appropriate divinities that his sons would be strangers to all of these.

The focus of the author's argument is again apparent in the conclusion of this section (4:7–19). If Christians are facing persecution and, by implication, the end of all things, they should continue to practice the gifts given them. They should think of themselves as sharing Christ's sufferings in order to share his life also. They should be sure not to suffer as criminals, but only for "the name." Yet, for all these high standards, 1 Peter does not assume that the behavior of his Christian audience is perfect. He holds Gentiles up as a bad example. But he seems prepared to accept that there are things in the Christian community that are less than perfect. Love, after all, is held up as "covering a multitude of sins" (4:8). The perfection the author desires is not absolute or heroic or even dramatically distinctive. Its purpose is simply to undercut the charges of opponents.

Finally, the letter concludes with advice to various groups within the church, including the familiar passage advising the young to "be sober, be watchful. Your adversary the Devil goes about like a roaring lion, seeking someone to gulp down" (5:8). It is an ideal image for later ascetical Christianity—the devil as the tempter, seeking to turn the ascetics from their purpose and so devour their souls. But in this particular case, the image refers rather to the threat of persecution and embodies an apocalyptic more than an ascetical notion of temptation (5:9). While the two are not, of course, mutually exclusive (as witness Tertullian), one should not merely equate them, either.

However much individual phrases of 1 Peter, then, might lend themselves to an ascetic interpretation, the work as a whole appears to belong to a rather different world. The communities addressed were already organized in households of a relatively traditional sort. Even the relatively positive attention to women is not entirely unexampled among the more philosophical of contemporary Greek writers. But the author felt a need to reemphasize the importance of the broadly accepted cultural values embodied in this structure because the majority population was beginning to view Christians with suspicion and alarm. It was a situation that opponents of the Christian communities could exploit to stir up persecution. The author believes that the first line of defense is to appear as unexceptional and unexceptionable as possible. If the Christians are "different," it is only in that they are soberer, quieter, and more obedient than most other people. They excel in meeting the common standards. They do a better job than their neighbors of meeting the norms of behavior they share with the environing society. What household would not be happy to have a Christian slave or a Christian wife?

If 1 Peter made any substantive contribution to the further development of Christian asceticism—something more than the mere reuse of specific images and phrases—I suspect that it consisted of its emphasis on conversion, a point introduced as early as 1:13–21. Christians have *changed*; they are children of obedience now and must not go back to their old ways. This emphasis on conversion and on distancing oneself from the past establishes a basic pattern of removing oneself from the world in which one grew up—a pattern that would encourage later Christian ascetical behavior. Its call would continue to resound in the ears of people who were already Christians and perhaps no longer threatened with persecution. For them, Christianity had become the basic social and cultural order—the baseline, as it were. What would conversion mean for them? Not becoming Christian, since they already were, but becoming something more than an ordinary Christian—perhaps ascetics.

I suggest, then, that the ascetic "sound" of some of 1 Peter's phrases is exactly that, only "sound": The phrases later were filled with ascetical meaning, but they do not incorporate asceticism itself. As with later Christian apologists who, following in the footsteps of their Jewish predecessors, claimed moral distinctiveness and superiority for their community, the author of 1 Peter presents a high standard. Yet the contents of that standard are closely related to the ideals of the larger community. 1 Peter's basic message is not "Distinguish yourselves," but "Blend in so that you won't be noticed. Be just like everyone else—only a little better in order to shame your accusers." At the same time, there is a potential engine here for later asceticism in the repeated call for conversion and for leaving behind one's old life. Perhaps one might say that the Christian audience of 1 Peter sounds mildly ascetical in comparison to the larger society, but even that claim is muffled at best.

SUMMARY AND CONCLUSION

One cannot expect three such disparate texts to yield common results. Their being grouped together is a result of largely accidental factors. The two Petrine letters do, however, share a common tendency to reaffirm a conservative household moral standard, which implies no highly distinctive praxis. It does not concentrate on contrasting the Christian group with the larger society except by saying, "We do better at fulfilling their own ideals than they do." 1 Peter's emphasis on conversion, however, keeps alive for subsequent Christian generations the importance of the voluntary and personal choice that was critical for the first Christian converts and would also be essential to later Christian asceticism.

The Letter of Jude opens a window on a rather obscure landscape in which one might perhaps see some vestiges of asceticism. But perhaps they are merely canals on Mars. What is clear is that Jude is branding his opponents as self-indulgent and libertine, the very opposite of ascetics. He expects such a characterization to undermine their credibility, but that does not tell us how he evaluated asceticism. "Ascetic" may or may not be good, in his rhetoric, but "libertine" is definitely bad. In this, he would probably have found agreement from almost any first-century Mediterranean householder. Perhaps Jude's own moral location was not too far away from the conservative householding milieu that the Petrine correspondence reflects.

NOTES

1. For a convenient summary of the argument for a relatively early date, see Richard Bauckham, "Jude, Epistle of," *The Anchor Bible Dictionary*, s.v.
2. At present, I am aware of only three observers who have noted this as a significant issue in Jude: G. H. Boobyer, "Jude," in *Peake's Commentary on the Bible*, eds. Matthew Black and H. H. Rowley (London: Nelson, 1962), 912c; Victor

Paul Furnish, *The Moral Teaching of Paul* (Nashville, Tenn.: Abingdon, 1979), 56; and myself, *Dirt, Greed, and Sex* (Philadelphia: Fortress, 1988), 133–34.

3. In this sense, *kyriotes* is usually translated "dominion" rather than "lordship." Interestingly, some ancient authorities, including Codex Sinaiticus, read the plural of *kyriotes* in this verse, which would make the reference to celestial beings even more obvious.

4. Thus, for example, the author deletes Jude's references to *Enoch* and to the *Assumption of Moses* and warns that much of Paul is difficult to understand and is, therefore, potentially dangerous (3:14–16).

5. For references, see John H. Elliott, "Peter, Second Epistle of," *The Anchor Bible Dictionary*, s.v.

6. Pliny's famous letter (*ep.* 10) about Christians in Bithynia, probably written somewhat later than 1 Peter, speaks of them as an old and settled community. My thanks to Richard Ascough for this observation.

7. See Elliott, "Peter, First Epistle of."

8. Ibid; cf. Edward Gordon Selwyn, *The First Epistle of St. Peter* (London: Macmillan, 1949), 18–23.

9. This is also Paul's normal use of the term "flesh"; cf. John A. T. Robinson, *The Body* (London: SCM, 1952), 17–26.

Asceticism in the Johannine Letters?

L. Wm. Countryman

INTRODUCTION

This chapter assumes the definition of asceticism laid out in my chapter on 1 and 2 Peter and Jude in the previous chapter of this volume: "a relatively demanding bodily praxis, voluntarily undertaken, that sets those who adopt it apart from and, in the view of some, above the ordinary run of people in their world." This is a social definition that treats asceticism as a kind of cultural interaction, by which some persons claim superiority through their bodily practices, while the larger society debates the merits of those claims and eventually accepts, rejects, or ignores them.

There are many possible variations of asceticism. The distinctiveness that asceticism creates is not necessarily permanent. Like the Greek physical training whose name (*askesis*) is the root of the word "asceticism," it may be limited to particular persons, a particular period of life, or particular locations and events. At the other extreme, it may represent a lifelong commitment, as in traditional Christian monasticism. The environing society may so far accept the ascetical life into its norms as to offer asceticism as an accepted option for some. But if a particular practice associated with asceticism ceases to be truly exceptional—if, for example, it becomes so much an expectation that most people practice it without any sense of having chosen it—it ceases to be ascetical in the way that I am using the term.

There are, then, no inherently ascetical practices or disciplines. Asceticism is always a stance relative to societal and cultural norms. From within the ascetical perspective, asceticism is a kind of subtraction by which the ascetic gains or hopes to gain particular access to the holy and/or a sense of moral and religious worth. In some cases, this positive evaluation of the ascetic practices will be limited to the ascetic, either individually or as part of a small, ascetic group. In other cases, at least some part of the larger, nonascetic public will also accept the claims and therefore offer the ascetic confirmation of the value of the undertaking, even though they may not join in it themselves in any substantial way.

The topic of asceticism in the Johannine letters is difficult in that I find no reason to suspect that it was a significant issue either for those who come under attack or for the person or persons standing behind the letters. Perhaps the great question about asceticism in relation to these letters is: Why, in a world where asceticism was becoming a significant cultural element, does it make no appearance here?

Ultimately, of course, such a question is unanswerable from a historical perspective. But we can at least ask what other elements may have occupied the space that asceticism here leaves vacant. For there is indeed a social *space* here, waiting to be occupied—a space defined by a widespread human need to approach the holy and to distinguish oneself in relation to it. Not everyone is satisfied with being one of the ordinary folk in the presence of what is ultimately valued, whether it be called "God" or some other name. There is a desire on the part of some to draw closer. There is also a desire, sometimes on the part of the same persons, to be seen to draw closer. In other words, the distinctiveness that asceticism produces fills a particular religious and social need, but the need in question can be filled in other ways as well. What one may achieve, under appropriate circumstances, by means of asceticism may be better achieved, under other circumstances, by means of ritual roles, learning, nonascetical expressions of piety, and so forth.

This chapter will return to these questions later. First, however, it will be wise to look at the three letters individually to see with what they *are* concerned.

WHAT ISSUES ARE IMPORTANT IN THE JOHANNINE LETTERS?

In the exposition that follows, I draw my basic understanding of the Johannine community from the work of Kenneth Grayston,[1] who argues that the letters of John are older than the Gospel of John and that the letters represent a response to a teaching that effectively substituted the Spirit/Paraclete for Jesus as the source and guarantor of authentic Christianity. The opposition teachers were thus primarily prophetic persons who claimed that their anointing with Spirit gave them an authority superseding that of the elder who wrote the letters. To them, the authority of the elder was based on mere physical, historical contact with the human Jesus; the authority of the prophets was like that of Jesus himself, derived directly from the Spirit.

1 John

The author of 1 John (or authors—there is a shift from first-person plural to first-person singular at 2:1) begins by stressing the material origins of the tradition the readers had originally received from him and his colleagues. The joy of the addressees depends on a tradition—the elders' verbal report of what they not only saw, but also heard and handled, regarding the logos of life (1:1–4). After this relatively clear and pointed proem, however, the argument of the work becomes more difficult to unravel. I understand 1:5–2:27 as constituting a kind of discrete structural element in the letter, characterized by language of sin and forgiveness, light and dark, Father and cosmos. The rhetorical goal of this segment is to define the audience as persons who are at least growing in love of one another, as opposed to those who claim anointing but do not manifest love toward other members of the community or may even have left it.

The author rejects emphatically the notion that anyone can be sinless (1:5–10). Even though he claims that his goal in writing is to keep the audience from sinning, he points to Jesus as the *one* Paraclete and expiation if anyone does sin (2:1–3).[2] What defines sin in this situation is whether one loves the *adelphos*, the Christian sister or brother: This is what divides light from darkness (2:3–11). The author can write to the addressees because they are already in the light (2:12–14). The cosmos, the realm that has rejected the light, is represented by the *antichristoi*, the "anti-anointed" or "those with an opposite anointing." But the readers are not to be misled, for they have their own anointing and do not need another one from these false teachers (2:15–27).

It appears that the *antichristoi* are committing certain acts that they would not see as sinful but that seem gravely sinful to the author of the letter (cf. 1:10). Given the author's repeated emphasis on loving the *adelphos* and the information that some of the opponents have in fact left the community, we may further suspect that their "sins" consisted of a failure to live up to the author's standards of care for other members of the community. Were the *antichristoi* claiming that they did not need to give alms or to share with the needy? Were they perhaps limiting their generosity to people of their own subgroup?

In any event, the next section (2:28–3:34) continues the theme of sharp distinction between the two groups (now called "children of God" and "children of the Devil"). The author claims that you can tell the two apart by their behavior. Those who love the *adelphos* will have *parrhesia* before God in the day of reckoning. *Parrhesia* is the boldness and freedom of speech that comes from having a clear conscience and being sure of where one stands. By contrast, the author claims that the *antichristoi* are prefigured biblically in the figure of Cain, who killed his *adelphos*. The commandment for all is to believe in Jesus and love the *adelphos* (3:17–24).

In the next section (4:1–5:12), the author reprises a number of themes and pulls them together more tightly. Ultimately, it is not spirit that is decisive, but flesh. Only the spirit that confesses Jesus as having come in the flesh is from God. (This, of course, sustains the authority of the letter's author[s], who claim[s] a tradition that goes back to the fleshly Jesus.) We can tell the difference between spirits because we, unlike the opponents, are from God and not from the cosmos; across that boundary, there is no communication (4:1–16a). Love creates *parrhesia* before God by casting out fear (4:16b–21). The believer is born of God. And what is born of God overcomes the cosmos. What is it to overcome the cosmos? It is to believe that Jesus is God's son, coming through water and blood. Spirit, water, and blood agree in bearing witness. The material elements are as important as the spiritual (5:1–12).

In the concluding summary (5:13–21), the author affirms that we (i.e., the author and his adherents) know who we are and who God is, and we can ask for what accords with God's will and get it. Specifically, we can pray for forgiveness of the sin of an *adelphos* and, if it is not beyond forgiveness, it will be forgiven (5:13–17). The distinction between us and the more "spiritual" teachers is that we belong to the true God (5:18–20).[3]

2 John

2 John, a much briefer letter, is also concerned with the *antichristoi*. It is not surprising, given the letter's brevity, that it adds nothing substantive to the picture in 1 John. But it confirms the outlines of 1 John, as sketched earlier in this chapter, by combining its distinctive points is a very brief and direct way. The critical issues are loving one another (vv. 4–6), confessing Jesus as coming in flesh (vv. 7–8), and staying with the community (vv. 9–11).

3 John

3 John is different from its two companions, being addressed rather to a situation where rivalries over control of local congregations appear to be causing a schism. There is nothing in the letter to suggest any divergence of belief or practice between the elder and Diotrephes. Diotrephes is simply cutting his house-church off from the larger network of churches connected with the elder.

ASCETICISM AND ITS ANALOGUES IN THE JOHANNINE LETTERS

There is nothing in this short survey (nor, I think, elsewhere in the letters) that suggests an ascetical perspective on the part of the author.[4] The first two letters have a strong emphasis on body, but not in terms of a "demanding bodily praxis." It is a positive emphasis, framed in terms of the senses of "touching," "hearing," and "seeing," which grounds the tradition, in terms of Jesus as coming in the flesh, in terms of the a*delphos* in need, in terms of the water and blood that witness along with the Spirit. The opponents are accused of not loving the *adelphos*, perhaps meaning that they do not give to the needy. Asceticism does not appear to be a living option in the tradition represented by the author, which focused rather on charity as the criterion of Christian behavior.

If we want to find some ascetics here, it will have to be among the *antichristoi*, who must in some respects have represented the opposite of the author's position. If they were indeed, as Grayston suggests, people who exalted their experience of Spirit above everything in the material realm, they could conceivably have made this the theoretical foundation for an ascetic manner of life. Yet, there is nothing to suggest that they did. In the absence of positive evidence for ascetical practice, it is perhaps more prudent to envisage them as charismatics who exalted a certain sort of spiritual (probably prophetic) experience almost to the exclusion of any bodily praxis, whether charitable or ascetical. Grayston even suggests that they were relatively "worldly" in the sense that they rejected the elder's admonition that one should separate oneself from the world and hoped, through their prophecy, to rescue it.[5]

If neither the author nor the author's opponents can safely be described as ascetics, is there any other way of asking these letters questions that might at least illuminate the issue of asceticism? One possible way might be to look at the internal dynamic in religion and spirituality that draws people to try to distinguish themselves religiously in socially discernible ways. At its best, this dynamic may help produce saints (although some might say it is the saint's enemy rather than the saint's motive); at its worst, it produces what is variously called "pride" or "works righteousness." Either way, the drive to distinguish oneself through a distinctive, observable religious excellence seems to be inherent in human religion. It is satisfied in various ways in different cultural and historical contexts. If asceticism is the means under particular consideration in this book, we may think of other means of satisfying this drive as functional analogues of asceticism.

Through most of Christian history, monasticism, which usually involves some degree of ascetic practice, was the primary means of pursuing exceptional religious standing, as it may still be in most Christian communities. Protestantism largely rejected monasticism during and after the Reformation and found other means for the Christian to distinguish himself or herself—for example, through learning, through doctrinal precision, through certain emotional experiences, through certain expressions of piety, through gifts of the Spirit such as speaking in tongues, and so on.

We might describe the general religious and social dynamic in question as operating in terms of a basic, "unmarked form" of religion that is common to a larger community and somewhat contrasting "special exercises" that serve to distinguish the more serious few. Anglo-Catholicism, as it existed in the first half of the twentieth century, may serve as an example. Liturgy in accordance with The Book of Common Prayer served to define the basic, unmarked form of Anglican religion, while a large and complex array of special exercises in the form of additional rites and ceremonies distinguished Anglo-Catholics. The unmarked form of Anglicanism was not absolutely uniform. The Book of Common Prayer allowed for some variety in the way its rites were performed. But there was a general and broadly accurate expectation that the service would everywhere follow the same general order. In Anglo-Catholic parishes, however, the uninitiated worshiper was likely to find a number of rites and ceremonies that were unfamiliar in the unmarked form of the religion, including such elements as missals (service books) that "enriched" the Prayer Book with elements from the Roman rite, additional prayers, the singing of liturgical lessons, noncommunicating High Masses at 11 AM on Sundays, Stations of the Cross, and Benediction of the Blessed Sacrament.

As often happens with groups that distinguish themselves from the unmarked form of their religious community, Anglo-Catholics often regarded themselves as religiously superior to those who practiced only the unmarked form of Anglicanism. They were apt to see their practice as purer, more historical, more catholic, truer to Anglicanism's real identity, and more pleasing to God. Those who practiced the unmarked form of Anglicanism, in their turn, sometimes regarded those dedicated to the special exercises of Anglo-Catholicism as absurd, subversive, peculiar, and excessive—or, in some ways, as genuinely superior in religious terms because of their devotion and rigor.

The relationship between "unmarked form" and "special exercises," in this case, has undergone an ironic historical shift in the latter half of the twentieth century—at least within the American manifestation of Anglicanism. There has been a fairly decisive rejection of some aspects of Anglo-Catholic distinctiveness (for example, its rejection of the ordination of women) and a wholesale embrace of others (for example, the centrality it accorded to the Eucharist). This is a useful reminder that special exercises remain such only as long as they are the preserve of a minority group. If they are adopted by the majority, they can no longer serve to distinguish a religious elite. Anglo-Catholicism is by no means dead in the Episcopal Church, but it is looking for a new raison d'être.

In the Johannine correspondence, the writer certainly maintains high standards of Christian conduct, but he is careful to represent his stance as the *unmarked* version of the religious tradition to which he belongs. He presents it not only as the original version but also as the one that will require the least rethinking or change of basic beliefs for the average member. The opponents, by contrast, he represents as distinguishing themselves through special exercises. They have attained an observable religious excellence through spirit possession and prophecy. Apparently the community to which "John" writes has accepted this claim or is at least impressed by it. As a result, the spirit-filled teachers find they can use their religious superiority over the community at large to supplant the traditional leaders and the unmarked form of the community's religion. They question the importance of the fleshly Jesus and withhold charitable gifts. Even Diotrephes in 3 John has found that control of charity (in his case, hospitality) is a convenient way to define authority in the community.

This sketch of the situation, of course, is derived from a one-sided source: the letters of the elder written in response to the perceived challenges. There is no reason to suppose that the elder has given us a completely accurate account. Doubtless the pneumatic figures under attack could have given a more presentable account of themselves. Even so, it is possible to say that a large part of the contest surrounded the question of who was to be seen as particularly religious and pleasing to God. The elder claims that his connection with the communities addressed goes back to their beginning and therefore is implicated in the unmarked form of their religious life. He insists that there is and was nothing lacking in that unmarked form. Accordingly, the special exercises of the "spiritual" teachers are not an improvement in their faith, but a denial of it.

If this sketch is anywhere near on target, it may help us to situate the Johannine conflict in relation to asceticism, not because asceticism as such is at issue here, but because the opponents have in effect accomplished one of the goals of ascetical behavior, without resorting to asceticism itself, through use of a charismatic analogue to asceticism. They have other, charismatic, special exercises that serve to distinguish them from the unmarked form of their community's religion and to ground their claims to religious worth and authority. We might go further to ask why they chose this route (or why it chose them) rather than the ascetical one, but such a question is probably unanswerable on the historical level alone. It is enough to acknowledge here that the enormous importance of asceticism within the Christian tradition from the fourth century onward had not yet asserted itself in the first century and that asceticism was, at that time, merely one option among many.

Asceticism, then, was not the only means to the particular end of religious distinction in first-century Christianity. In the first century, other special exercises coexisted with it: the charismatic enthusiasms mentioned in

Paul's writings as well as those of John, the apocalyptic excitement wide-spread in the New Testament writings, the path of martyrdom that is just beginning to show itself in 1 Peter and the Revelation of John, perhaps also the learned study of scripture one finds in Hebrews and the rigorism of that same letter and of some other early Christian sources. These were not, of course, mutually exclusive. Few, if any, will have felt an obligation to adhere to one of them alone. A century or so later, a distinguished (in both senses of the word) Christian like Tertullian could demonstrate affinities with most or all of them by being a rigorist, charismatic Christian, learned in scripture and intent on martyrdom.

Perhaps a full exploration of asceticism in earliest Christianity would profit from looking broadly at the religious and spiritual dynamics by which individuals seek to move closer to the holy and to establish distinctiveness and superiority within religious communities. Did asceticism's growing importance within the Christian tradition come at the expense of other ana-logues? And why? Because it was able to subsume the alternatives? Was it because the temper of late antique culture was shifting significantly toward the ascetical mode? Quite possibly, all of these elements were of impor-tance—and others besides.

Whatever the answers may be to such long-term questions, we may con-tinue to ask why asceticism was not an option in use within the Johannine communities at the time of the writing of the Johannine letters. Was the idea of asceticism not meaningful in their cultural context? Was it foreclosed by the importance in earliest Christianity of spirit-filled phenomena such as prophecy, which already offered a convenient and accessible model for reli-gious distinction? Is its absence merely accidental, resulting from the fact that the limited resources of these small communities were already monop-olized by the partisans of charismatic phenomena and the defenders of the unmarked version of the Johannine tradition? I have no answers to these questions. And, given the relatively abstract and allusive style of the letters, we may never have answers to them. Still, the questions themselves are worth holding in mind because they remind us that asceticism is always a social phe-nomenon, that aims at this-worldly as well as other-worldly goals and is sub-ject to the vagaries of history.

NOTES

1. See Kenneth Grayston, *The Johannine Epistles*, The New Century Bible Commentary (Grand Rapids, Mich.: Eerdmans, 1984). This is not the place to justify this choice over the wider consensus represented by the writings of D. Moody Smith or Raymond Brown. Suffice it to say that Grayston's approach succeeds in giving a more straightforward, comprehensive, and unified inter-

pretation of the letters. Udo Schnelle offers a somewhat comparable analysis in *Antidocetic Christology in the Gospel of John*, trans. Linda M. Maloney (Minneapolis, Minn.: Fortress, 1992).

2. The Gospel of John, by contrast, adopts a mediating position between the elder and the opponents on this issue at least and accepts the Spirit as "another Paraclete" (John 14:16).

3. The concluding line ("Children, guard yourselves from the idols," 1 John 5:21) remains difficult to relate to the rest since it uses a term ("idols") that has not figured earlier in the work. Rudolf Bultmann's exegesis suggesting that the false teachers are here being equated with idolatry is perhaps as persuasive as one can make it: See Rudolf Bultmann, *The Johannine Epistles*, trans. Philip O'Hara et al. (Philadelphia: Fortress, Hermeneia, 1973), 90–91.

4. David Rensberger (this volume, 127–148) suggests that there may be an ascetical intent behind 1 John 3:16–18. The text does invoke the pattern of Jesus' laying down his life for the *adelphoi*, but then uses it to encourage sharing on the part of those who have the goods of this world. Whether this is ascetical or not would depend, of course, on the extent of such sharing—whether it is meant to eventuate in a radical divestment of wordly goods or simply a sharing of abundance. The text can be read in either way, but there is abundant material in 1 John to support reading it as a reference to the practice of charity, and nothing else to encourage reading it as ascetical.

5. See Grayston, *Johannine Epistles,* 16–19.

The Ascetic Way: Reflections on Peace, Justice, and Vengeance in the Apocalypse of John[1]

William Klassen

INTRODUCTION

It has been customary to view the ascetic life as focused on a certain joyless commitment to austerity. Is not asceticism normally defined as a "systematic self-denial for some ideal"?[2] This book contains other definitions, all worthy of consideration. In a classic treatment Ernst Troeltsch defined it thus: "The word 'asceticism' originated in philosophy, from the Cynics and Stoics, and signifies in the first instance the systematic training of the will and the virtues, similar to the discipline of the body and the will applied in military and athletic training."[3]

Where religion flourishes, said Troeltsch, so does asceticism. According to Troeltsch, Christianity brought a type of asceticism with it. In the gospel of Jesus himself lie certain intimations of a Christian asceticism—denial of self, humility, suffering, and self-sacrifice, which is closely tied to the love command—all of which are closely tied to the kingdom of God and in opposition to the kingdom of Satan. But Troeltsch concludes:

> It is especially the arousal of hope, a healing strength, the message of joy, the impetus towards the kingdom of Heaven, the power which is manifested in weakness and the suffering—naturally not only among the poor and the oppressed—changed into strength—wherein lie the seeds of asceticism.[5]

For Christian asceticism and glorification of suffering, the idea of substitution has critical bridging importance.[6] In a community of love such substitutionary suffering was a way of reaching out to others.

The word "renunciation" is commonly associated with asceticism, and most treatments of this theme in the Apocalypse deal, therefore, with the 144,000 referred to in Rev. 14:4 who "did not defile themselves with women, for they had kept themselves chaste (*parthenoi*)." Viewed from this side of the history of celibacy and monasticism, we assume that we know to what this chastity refers. Only seldom is it recognized that the sexual symbolism used everywhere in the book of Revelation "is metaphorical, signifying that these pure ones have not participated in the idolatry of the imperial cult."[7] It does not often occur to us that perhaps the early Christians, including those in apocalyptic communities, and not only the author of Hebrews (13:4), saw the marriage bed as honorable for everyone and coitus as undefiled and undefiling. Therefore, the reference in Rev. 14:4 could be to those who have been faithful to their spouses by refusing to commit adultery.

It is especially striking that few have observed that one New Testament writer, the Apostle Paul, makes a shocking observation, totally consistent with some trends in the Judaism of his day, which radically changes all standard definitions of asceticism. It is in conjugal union, Paul affirms, that a Christian spouse can make holy the unbelieving one (1 Cor. 7:14).[8] It would totally transform the view of asceticism that has dominated Christian history if this point were observed.

My approach to the Apocalypse and indeed to the entire New Testament owes a lot to the many feminist interpreters who have built their careers on this book, including Elizabeth Schüssler Fiorenza, Adela Yarbro Collins, and Josephine Massyngbaerde Ford. I am indebted, above all, to the finest feminist interpreter, Luise Schottroff, especially her treatment of the eschatological dimension for women in the first century CE and the affirmation of hope.[9]

We intend to use a more specific definition of asceticism and focus our discussion on the issue of peace and justice. We pick up on the broader meaning of *askesis* as training for the good life, and even though the word never appears in the Apocalypse[10] in any form, the book makes sense only when viewed as an attempt to train the readers to pursue justice and peace, especially at a time when there is much provocation to renounce a nonviolent way to deal with conflict. Moreover, vengeance is a central motif in the book, but the Apocalypse specifically rules out vengeance for all followers of the Lamb. Only God can exact vengeance and will do so in a way and at a time that remains outside of human manipulation or control. In the meantime, the book invites us to "The Stature of Waiting," those periods in life when we seem not to be in control and everything that happens seems to be done to us. Canon Vanstone has dramatically portrayed that as happening during the last week of Jesus' life, and the Apocalypse invites the ones who hear it to do the same.

To the question: How long until God hears and establishes divine sovereignty? the Apocalypse answers repeatedly: "Not yet"; that "not yet" is meant to delay the hour of reckoning as long as possible so that opportunity for repentance is offered to those who resist God's sovereign rule (9:21; 16:11).[11]

My inquiry is based on the conviction that the New Testament commands to "seek peace and pursue it"—found in four different layers of the literary tradition of the early church—is, at its core, a Jewish community value, but one that, historically, neither Judaism nor Christianity has been particularly good at living out or communicating to a larger world. There is, in addition, the new call for discipline and asceticism in our time that has made a strong impact even though it has not been easy to translate consistently into action as far as one's own personal lifestyle is concerned.[12] The place that peace and peace research have had in this area is especially praiseworthy.[13]

THE APOCALYPSE IN ITS CONTEXT

We detect a similarity between what Musonius and Epictetus—broadly speaking, contemporaries of the author of the Apocalypse—sought to do and what the Apocalypse sets out to do. All three authors assume that life is a struggle, indeed, a battle; thus, training at least as rigorous as that of the soldier is needed, and there are models of behavior one can follow. They all take advantage of certain models of discipleship, of "following after" an example that has been left behind (for Epictetus and Musonius, this is Socrates; for the author of the Apocalypse, it is the Lamb[14]). All three accept the ideal of joyous denial or abstention. Moreover, they all extol a model of living that goes against the grain of the one espoused by their contemporaries. All place a very high premium on peaceful living together and see violent conflict as either demonic (Apocalypse) or bestial (Musonius and Epictetus). They all urge their followers to avoid violence, revenge, and retribution at any price. All three were rejected by the ruling power of the day. Finally, all three place justice as a very high desideratum, although the contexts in which this value emerges differ. Both Musonius and Epictetus, as Stoics, address middle-class concerns, while the Apocalypse is obviously written to a poorer class and perhaps even to people under severe persecution.

THE APOCALYPSE AND THE EARLY
CHRISTIAN COMMUNITY

It is often asserted, by respected teachers, that the Apocalypse has strayed from the Christian fold—some would argue that the book never made it inside. We question, however, whether the Apocalypse has really bid farewell to such central Christian affirmations as "love your enemies" and, above all, "seek peace and pursue it." Is it really the "Judas of the New Testament," as Elizabeth Schüssler Fiorenza has called it?[15] Or is it possible, as we shall suggest here, that the form in which hope is expressed in this book is a highly developed schema in which an *askesis* is practiced whose closest analogues are both some Jewish apocalyptic sources and the works of Epictetus and Musonius Rufus?[16]

A review of the theme of peace in critical early Christian sources shows how they are indebted to Jewish apocalyptic writings prior to the beginning of the early Christian movement. The early Christian apocalyptic materials themselves did not, however, simply repeat what was found in the sources to which they are indebted.

The uniqueness of the Apocalyptic view of peace is easy to miss. Ulrich Mauser borders on a misreading of apocalyptic in his otherwise excellent book on peace.[17] Although he provides what is clearly the most comprehensive, thorough, and competent study of this theme in the New Testament, when comparing Jesus and Paul, Mauser nevertheless argues:

> [I]n Paul's letters peace is associated with wide-reaching concepts that appear to have lost touch with concrete and individual problems and needs...[T]he time in whose perimeter peace is made is no longer datable...rather it is immeasurably expanded to cover the whole aeon from the inception of human history to the Christ event. The problems and needs to which peace brings resolution are no longer the identifiable realities of sickness, depravity, and destitution; peace is now determined by the internal struggle between spirit and flesh which overshadows every individual concretion.... [I]n Paul's apocalyptic modes of thought the peace of God is still relegated to its disclosure in the future. And the immediacy of Gospel narratives that tell of acts of messianic peacemaking gives way in Paul to admonitions for peace that, in comparison to the Gospels, appear pale and abstract.[18]

Most of Mauser's discussion of Paul, even his discussion of Rom. 5:1, does not support Mauser's own observations. Mauser deals ably with the ways in which Paul brings in peace when he deals with such very concrete issues as what to eat and with whom to eat it (Romans 14–15), whether to marry and whom to marry (1 Corinthians 7), quarreling and divisiveness, and so on. "You are called to peace," Paul writes to the couples in which one partner is an unbeliever, and seems to suggest that in such instances the rule of Jesus against divorce may be relaxed.

Fortunately, when Mauser deals with the critical apocalyptic text, Rom. 16:20, he recognizes that for Paul the concept of Satan being crushed under the feet of the Roman believers through God's initiative does not exclude some very profound changes that can come to their lives even now as they allow the peace of Christ to rule over them. In short, Mauser has done us a great service in seeing this text as related concretely to the problems of the Roman church even though its audience may have been broader. Moreover, Mauser sees that in the notion of peace perhaps more than most others, the uniqueness of the Jewish way of viewing peace as a concrete reality of history is maintained by the early Christians.[19]

As a historical footnote, we may add that the Christian idea of peace was not futurized, internalized, and individualized until Augustine, who apparently owed his distortion of the idea of peace to the Stoics.[20] For Paul's readers, there would have been a clear idea that while they were encouraged to make peace with God (Rom. 5:1), that peace had profound implications for their life together in the Spirit.

The writings of Adela Yarbro Collins, J. J. Collins, and Elizabeth Schüssler Fiorenza—all of whom place apocalyptic writings into their historical and social context—but perhaps most importantly the very careful study of the political nature of ancient apocalyptic writings and the patent commitment of many ancient apocalyptic writers to nonviolence by Klaus Wengst and Ulrich Luz, enable us now to see Rom. 16:20 as a call to concrete engagement in history rather than a wistful hope projected into the future. As expressed here, there is in the mind of Paul a significant tie between the work of God through God's community crushing the work of Satan and the work of unmasking and neutralizing those who would break up the unity of the church. Satan is the source of all fighting and disharmony and must be "crushed." The Apocalypse is an elaborate commentary on this fundamental affirmation of Paul, which he shared with other early Christians.

One important aspect of the message of peace of the Hebrew scriptures is that the person or community living under Yahweh's covenant will be at peace. Isaiah puts it particularly strongly in chapters 24–29. We need to review especially the oft-quoted lines: "You have kept in perfect peace, the one whose mind is stayed on you" (Isa. 26:3). The apocalyptic context in which this appears is worthy of note.

AN ASKESIS OF PEACE IN THE APOCALYPTIC COMMUNITIES

The standard assumption about apocalyptic writings is that the theme of peace is missing but that the theme of war reverberates throughout the literature; as one writer put it, the Johannine Apocalypse portrays Christians as "tormented and unhappy," not "peaceful and happy,"[21] and that any interest in peace is seldom to be found among apocalyptic writings. Because peace is mentioned over ninety times in the New Testament and because the ethical command "Seek peace and pursue it" (Mark 9:50; Rom. 12:18; 14:19;

Heb. 12:14; 1 Pet. 3:11) is so important to the Christian way, we are tempted to greet the absence of the term "peace" in the Apocalypse by labeling
the book with demeaning epithets like the "Judas in the New Testament."

I should like in this chapter to test that point of view and try to ascer-
tain what Jewish and Christian apocalyptic sources say about this theme and
how they approach it. In the large body of literature that over the last two
decades has addressed the New Testament views of peace, the Apocalypse
appears to be an embarrassment, if it is treated at all.[22]

My starting point is that the Hebrew concept of *shalom*—wedded as it is
on the one hand to a view of God as one who favors prosperity and peace
and on the other to a concept of justice and, above all, anchored as it is in
God's will and purpose for the people but rooted in the present world—is
one of the essential aspects of Hebrew and early Christian *askesis* and one of
the most distinguished and noblest contributions to human history. The
hope for peace is perhaps universal, and there may have been earlier
expressed convictions that a time would come when the nations of the world
would turn their swords into ploughshares and study war no more.
Nevertheless, the hopes and expectations of Isaiah (2:1–4; 9:5–7)[23] and
Micah (4:1–4) in this regard stand out as singular and impressive.[24] Certainly
there were many voices in the ancient world as in ours that seek to convince
us that war is inevitable and even part of God's plan. Likewise the way in
which the prophets sought to promote peace and justice by refusing (as true
prophets) to endorse the wars of the kings and stood their ground makes for
fascinating reading; for centuries, it has motivated and continues to inspire
many activities for peace among both Jews and Christians.

Furthermore, if Paul Hanson is correct, apocalyptic literature was born
precisely out of the tension between prophet and king.[25] Apocalyptic literature is accordingly a form of communication that emerged out of the repression of the prophets. It may well have emerged as underground literature,
written from what Elizabeth Schüssler Fiorenza calls a "jail-house perspective."[26]

There is a tendency to view it as literature born of despair. It is far from
that. Pinchas Lapide has it right when he says that apocalyptic literature is
"an offshoot of an irrepressible power of faith" For Lapide, apocalyptic has
three distinguishing features:

1. The expectation of the ultimate demise of the present world
2. An absolutizing of the Messianic time of salvation
3. The overcoming of death, war, and Satan through the establishment of
   a new ideal world on earth[27]

What interests us now is whether the idea of peace, so important to the
Israelite prophets and also, we shall argue, to the Jewish apocalyptic writers,

is still retained as part of the vision of the Messiah's role in the future of the world. Not much attention has been paid to this matter. To speak, then, of the Apocalypse as a form of weak or Judaized Christianity, or of a "Judaized Gospel,"[28] is to do both religions a disservice.

Egon Brandenburger does justice to the Apocalypse in his book on peace in the New Testament because, like Richard Hayes in his book on the moral vision of the New Testament,[29] he begins with christology, namely, with the central role of Christ. He sees the christology of the Apocalypse as linked with the pre-Pauline christology of the sonship of David, according to the flesh, and, on the level of the Spirit, declared son of God (Rom. 1:2–4). Brandenburger traces the following motifs of the royal ideology found in the Apocalypse:[30]

1. The eschatological Messiah-King does battle against the enemies—seen primarily as enemies of God and thus of God's people, the believers—and overcomes them (12:5; 17:14; 19:11ff.; cf. 20:7); and he rules in justice (19:11).
2. Closely related is the victory over and destruction of Satan along with his angelic powers (proleptic, 12:7; eschatological, 20:1,10).
3. The completed victory over the enemies and the anti-godly chaotic powers allows *shalom* to come to expression and to work (20:4–6; 21:1–22:5). This is guaranteed for the duration of the rule (=image of the Throne: 3:21; 20:4; 21:5; 22:1–3) of the Lamb, who moves from chapter 5 progressively to occupy the Throne. The theme of war is not in contradiction to the motif of peace; indeed, the Messiah struggles against the powers of chaos, and his victory over them is what makes peace possible.[31]
4. The domain or the essence of the state over which the eschatological king rules is Jerusalem as the city of David. In the Apocalypse it is the heavenly transcendent Jerusalem that has descended to the newly transformed earth (21:2–9). Gone is the motif of Paradise (22:1), so that now from both Jerusalems the blessed working of *shalom* proceeds: fullness of fruits (22:2), water of life, and fruit of the tree of life (2:7; 7:17; 22:1–14; cf. T. Levi 18:10f. and 8:52). They provide eternal life; tears, suffering, and death are no more (7:17; 21:4).
5. Alongside of this, there are also cosmic changes: Sun and moon are no longer needed (21:23), and there will be no night there (22:5). In their place the *doxa* of God and the light of the heavenly Messiah-King will provide light. True to his Jewish roots, the writer envisions a spiritual existence without a temple.[32] The first creation will disappear and will be replaced by a new heavenly world (21:1–4).
6. Doing evil is ruled out (21:27).
7. The nations and their kings come with their treasures into the city of the

eschatological king (21:24–26); that is, they carry out their homage as a sign of their subordination to the justice that rules in this kingdom of God established by the Messiah-King. That justice will guarantee peace. That is the meaning of "they shall walk in his light" (22:5).

As an attempt to find meaning in the book itself, others have tried to interpret the war language and terminology as Messianic war talk.[33] It is clear that the Messiah as warrior had an important role, especially in pre-70 CE Judaism. Whether it ever had any significant role after Bar Kochba (135 CE) is highly doubtful. At the same time, some very valuable work has been done in this area, and the way in which conflict is defined and seen is an important issue. Critical for our understanding of the Apocalypse is a correct under-standing of Pseudo-Philo,[34] again roughly a contemporary of the author of the Apocalypse. It has been often observed (by Ragnar Leivestad, among others) that the concept of victory is critical to our understanding of the book. So, of course, it is to Epictetus, except that he describes the Stoic as "the invincible One," an idea that does not occur in the Apocalypse. In fact, it could be argued that the Apocalypse is written to assist its readers to achieve victory and treats them as vulnerable to defeat.

The triumphalism in the book that upsets modern liberals should be placed into context. It is hard to endure persecutions if you have no reason to think you will eventually conquer. What kept Nelson Mandela sane over many years in prison and Martin Luther King active was the firm conviction that they were on the winning side; eventually that conviction brought about a phenomenal victory over hatred against white regimes.

THE TRANSPOSITION OF THE WAR MOTIF[35]

Charles Giblin in his brief commentary on the Apocalypse proposes that the Holy War thematic "is reborn in John's Christian perspective and according to his own creative genius."[36] Building on the work of R. Bauckham, Giblin suggests that "Revelation deliberately transposes physically belligerent con-duct or preparedness in order to enunciate a spiritual thesis of suffering wit-ness,... The triumph of God's army and that of the Lamb lies through its participation in Christ's death and resurrection, not in any physical combat of a destructive nature."[37] He suggests that the theme does not just appear here and there. Rather, in the major vision (chaps. 4–22), "the Holy War theme in all its essential institutional features *structures the entire course of events.* Its various components also cohere strikingly with the literary struc-ture of Revelation."[38]

Giblin provides a succinct summary of the key elements of the Holy War and, like Bauckham, sees certain critical elements of this theme in the

Apocalypse. The War Scroll from Qumran is seen as evidence that this kind of thematic portrayal of the Holy War was alive and well in the first century.[39]

The essential clue to understanding it is the "transposing" or "transforming" that John does with the material. Giblin has used the best of recent research into the book of Revelation and has made an important contribution toward understanding the book in its setting. In doing so, he has also made a contribution to our study of the *askesis* of peace in the Apocalypse. For once we have overcome the hurdle of thinking that the theme of peace can only be addressed where the word appears, we are free to see it as symbiotically related to the cause of justice.

We do well to view the Apocalypse in the context of other transformations of militant and even violent language, such as the call, attributed to Paul, in Ephesians 6 to put on the armor of God, among which the boots of peace make a strange and unprecedented appearance. The practice of this kind of "transposition" goes back far into ancient Greek ethical thought,[40] particularly in *askesis*; it is standard in both Musonius and Epictetus and is very common in Jewish ethical thinkers as well.[41]

The starting point for Jews and Christians attributing martial language to God were texts from the Hebrew Bible and most likely the idea of a Messianic war. That idea had to be reinterpreted by Christians when it became clear that Jesus had himself rejected that manner of bringing God's kingdom. Indeed, in the Holy War Jesus fought, God did not hand over the enemy to Jesus but rather "handed Jesus over" to evil ones and allowed them to do with the Lord's Anointed as they pleased.

Unique in the Apocalypse is the combination of such symbolic use of battle imagery with the literary genre of apocalyptic, and its evocative and consistent appeal to a nonviolent model, Jesus, the Lamb as if slain. The combination of *askesis* and the literary form of ethical battle, but not the model of behavior, finds a precedent in the War Scroll. At the same time it has been suggested that the theme of vengeance is thoroughly changed in some of the Qumran sources and that for one Qumran writer vengeance takes the form of repentance, or dramatic change, of the evil one.[42]

My hypothesis is that the Revelation of John when properly read contains a profound theology of peace; it is perhaps, next to that of Ephesians, the most profound theology of peace in the New Testament. Although it avoids the precise terminology of peace almost entirely, no doubt because of the terrible mockery of the idea brought about by its misuse by Rome,[43] it establishes a foundation for peaceful behavior that served the church well. Above all, it avoided all cheap rhetoric about a "last war," "inner peace," "eternal and universal peace," and "a new age" and addressed the most important ingredient to make peace: Someone has to stand against the violence and paganism of the times and in an act of resistance follow the Lamb. Faithfulness in following the Lamb may mean death, but ultimately God will vindicate the Lamb and wipe away all tears. Suffering under the lordship of Christ will not be in vain. The Apocalypse as a worship manual provides hope for the reader and the listener and a foundation for endurance by doing the following:

1. John sought to curtail revolutionary activity through exaltation of the Lamb, who chose to be slaughtered rather than slaughter others. Just as the words of Jesus and his example in rejecting all violent zealotry had been able to keep Christians from joining the revolt against Rome in 66 CE, so the Apocalypse achieved that goal in the Bar Kochba revolt. But most important, the ascetic model is in place. Introduced with high drama in chapter 5, this model, image, or symbol—the Lamb as if slain—controls and directs all the action for the rest of the book. No character in the book of Revelation is more decisive for history than this one, and nothing is more important for this writer's *askesis* than to "follow the Lamb."

2. By focusing on victory, the victory that Christ had achieved, was achieving, and would ultimately achieve, our author could nurture the flames of hope. It is despair that leads to violence. Those who have hope have the strength to suffer, for they know that love, patient love, love capable of waiting, can overcome hatred.

3. The stress that John lays on worship and celebration has the potential of keeping the community of faith strong, for through worship they affirm the presence of God among them.[44] They relate to the omnipotent one, whose nearness to them in all things forms the basis for their faith.

4. In the clash of loyalties between Caesar and Christ, the writer admonishes his people to remain firm and faithful to their Lord. It is not an easy thing when this has economic and social consequences. But, and this point is made most strongly by Peter Lampe, the author does not project peace into some distant future, nor does he individualize it. Rather, the future victory is already available here[45] and while inner peace may be offered to the martyred souls under the altar, "the thesis of 'inner peace' would have been energetically resisted by John." Instead, he offered a deeply communal concept of peace to his readers. The hierarchical-institutional model is replaced by a familial one.[47]

5. John does not present a view of peace as passivism. The community of Christ is a resisting community. Her refusal to bow the knee at Caesar's shrine or at the economic temples defies the structures where she lives. Our author shares with most Jewish apocalyptic literature a direct engagement with political powers, even though, given his situation, it seemed wise to use a highly coded language.[48]

6. Finally, the concern for justice is very strong in this community. Not only the cry of the martyrs who want assurance of the sovereignty of

God, but each member must have assurance that justice can be done and will be done. Otherwise God is not God. And to this writer God is often the *pantokrator*.[49] As in the Holy War, the victories are called "the righteous acts of Yahweh," so here the Holy War brings justice.[50]

The discussion of the Jewishness of the Apocalypse is often raised. Behind it lies the quite erroneous assumption that Judaism is more violent as a religion than is Christianity. A large body of evidence can be provided to prove otherwise. Judaism greatly emphasizes peace; it is a religion of peace. For Jews who are in touch with their tradition, peace is the highest value, and it is inextricably united with justice and high regard for the creation that God has made. Indeed, since the quest for peace and justice go hand in hand, peace can never be relegated to some future world or to the Beyond by either Christians and Jews. It is impossible for Jews to consider Jesus the Messiah, given their belief that the Messiah will bring peace and they see so little evidence of that peace among those who claim to follow Jesus.

And yet Jews and Christians are joined in their quest for peace and justice; both affirm that the creation in which we live is a trust given to us by God. And both are convinced that suffering in the created order can bring forth the new life God wishes for this world.

One ancient Jewish text focuses the issue well and can also be affirmed by Christians. It is the call of the dying Maccabean youth:

> Fight a holy and honorable warfare on behalf of righteousness, through which may the just providence that watched over our fathers become merciful unto his people and take vengeance on the accursed tyrant. (4 Macc. 9:24)

This call to Holy War, to an honorable warfare on behalf of justice, will meet all calls for vengeance. Tempted as we may be to issue such calls, they are best left in the hands of just providence. Leave vengeance to God, the author seems to say.

The early Christians were Jews, and it is only logical that their views on peace were built on their own heritage. In any case, Jews and Christians share far more with each other than either shares with any third group in their views on peace and their commitment to pursuing it. It is especially in early Christian apocalyptic sources that both the similarities and differences come into sharp focus.

Some Jewish writers called for their people to renounce both violence and their desire for revenge.[51] So did some Christians. Above all, the biggest difference between the two groups lay in the desire of both the zealots and the Qumran sectaries to assist God, indeed to act as God's agents of vengeance. Both believed firmly that God's sovereignty could be established as they took matters into their own hands and used the sword to establish

God's rule. That Christians too were tempted by this option is clear from the warnings placed on the lips of Jesus in Matthew. The other group waited for God to act and believed that their martyrdom and death would move God to action (e.g., in the Testament of Moses; Apocalypse of John).

The Johannine community rejected all forms of violence. Instead, they urged their people to endure suffering and to follow the Lamb in steadfastness and faithfulness. Only in that way could the Lamb continue to open the seals of history and only then could the Lamb join with the One on the Throne and defeat the enemies arrayed against them. G. B. Caird is correct, theologically and exegetically, when he suggests that God's victory is seen as the victory of love over hate. When that happens, the peace of God that surpasses all human understanding can come into the community's midst. G. B. Caird's commentary was the first to assert boldly that the book was fundamentally nonviolent in that "the only weapon the Lamb wields is his own cross and the martyrdom of his followers" (2:27; 12:5; 19:15).[52] He sees the "repeated attacks upon the ungodly world order by all the armament of heaven, which occupy so large a part of John's book, as designed not to destroy or to punish, but only to penetrate the defenses which the world has erected against the rule of God."[53]

Klaus Wengst concludes his study of the relation of the Pax Romana to the peace of Christ with a reminder that the liturgy and the singing of a new hymn is of critical importance to the author. For in the worship of the church God is installed as king anew and therefore Caesar's throne becomes less stable:

> Recollection of the liturgy therefore becomes a subversive recollection. So the reading of the book of Revelation leads not least to celebrating the liturgy as training in resistance. Should that not be a specifically Christian contribution to a peace which includes justice?[54]

John Collins puts the ascetic dimensions of the Apocalypse succinctly when he writes:

> The legacy of the apocalypses includes a powerful rhetoric for denouncing the deficiencies of this world. It also includes the conviction that the world as now constituted is not the end. Most of all it entails an appreciation of the great resource that lies in the human imagination to construct a symbolic world where the integrity of values can be maintained in the face of social and political powerlessness and even in the threat of death.[55]

NOTES

1. I acknowledge the contribution made to my thinking by the participants of the Seminar on the Apocalypse at the annual Society for New Testament Studies meeting, Bethel bei Bielefeld, July 1991, where I was first invited to explore this

topic. I am grateful for Vincent Wimbush and Leif Vaage's invitation to present my conclusions in a more refined way to the conference on asceticism at Emmanuel College in the fall of 1996.

2. *Webster's Unabridged Dictionary*, s.v. "asceticism," adds a second meaning: "The religious doctrine that one can reach a higher spiritual state by rigorous self-discipline and self-denial."

3. Ernst Troeltsch, "Askese," first published in 1916; reprinted in *Askese und Mönchtum in der alten Kirche*, ed. K. Suso Frank (Darmstadt, Germany: Wissenschaftliche Buchgesellschaft, 1975), 69–90.

4. The *Encyclopedia of Religion and Ethics* has a series of excellent articles on the topic and notes that some world religions have virtually no ascetic strain in them.

5. Troeltsch, "Askese," 78.

6. Ibid, 84.

7. See Elizabeth Schüssler Fiorenza, *Revelation: Vision of a Just World* (Minneapolis, Minn.: Fortress, 1991), 88; also idem, *The Book of Revelation, Justice and Judgment* (Philadelphia: Fortress, 1985), 190: "To assume that either the heavenly or the eschatological followers of the Lamb are a class of exclusive male ascetics seems to be unfounded in the overall context of the book."

8. The Greek verb *hagiazo*, as an active verb applied to what people do to each other, is used only in this connection in the whole early Christian literary corpus.

9. See Luise Schottroff, *Lydia's Impatient Sisters: A Feminist Social History of Early Christianity*, trans. Barbara and Martin Rumscheidt (Louisville, Ky.: Westminster/Knox, 1995), 152–73. Tina Pippin, *Death and Desire: The Rhetoric of Gender in the Apocalypse of John* (Louisville, Ky.: Westminster/Knox, Literary Currents in Biblical Interpretation, 1992), seems to ignore the historical context of the Apocalypse, appears blithely unaware of the Greco-Roman context in which the Apocalypse was written, and ignores some fundamental guidelines of interpretation. See Gregory Linton's review of Pippin's book in *Critical Review* (1994): 248–50. Judgments such as: "In the Apocalypse women are disempowered in every way" (Pippin, *Death and Desire*, 70) or that Rev. 17:3b–6 is "the most vividly misogynist passage in the New Testament" (ibid, 58) reveal only how little Pippin has been able to enter into the apocalyptic world. Let us at least compare such supposed "misogynism" with materials in the Greek world, beginning, say, with the poem "How God Made Woman," written in the seventh century BCE by Simonides. Or consider how the Apocalypse has empowered modern feminist interpreters. Throughout Pippin's book, there is confusion between what the author of the Apocalypse actually portrayed and what later writers thought that he had portrayed. Sharon Welch, *A Feminist Ethic of Risk* (Minneapolis, Minn.: Fortress, 1990), is an excellent treatment of the theme of resistance and especially of the joy of celebrating victories as they are achieved—modest and transitory as they may seem. Is not the Apocalypse such a song of celebration of victory?

10. See Bernard Lohse, *Askese und Mönchtum in der Antike und in der alten Kirche*, 115–29: "Apart from Paul—if we ignore Luke's communistic ideal—we encounter no ascetic tendencies in the New Testament. That could also apply to

the Apocalypse" (127); "More than a tendency to a stronger emphasis on asceticism cannot be derived from the Apocalypse" (129).

11. The repeated call to repent (twelve times in Revelation, more than any other book of the New Testament), which is given also to the churches, indicates that God's community must respond to the same invitation that the "outsiders" receive. Those who seek to move history forward have to learn that God's patience is meant to allow humans more time to respond to the invitation to join the wedding party. Repentance, as we have seen ourselves so dramatically in the case of Mikhail Gorbachev and of South Africa's Frederick de Klerk, can lessen bloodshed and allow the strength of forgiveness and restitution to flow. There is a divine way in which justice is done and wrongs avenged. It remains to be seen in our day whether Northern Ireland, the tortured people of Bosnia, and the Palestinians and Israelis can learn this lesson. Or for that matter the successive presidents of the United States of America, who have their cruise missiles ready (after testing them in Canada's north) to use at the slightest provocation and who seem to think it their divine mission to tell the rest of the world how they are to conduct themselves. Only thirty years later some, like Robert MacNamara, have the courage to repent. Otherwise, repentance is rare among politicians—and academics.

12. See especially Roger L. Shinn, "Asceticism for our Time," *A.D.* (December 1974): 42–46. He reports that the World Council of Churches, in the summer of 1973, held a conference in Romania on the theme "The Ambiguous Future and the Christian Hope." That conference proposed a new asceticism: "An appropriate 'asceticism' for our time will not be a punishing of the body for the sake of the soul or worldly denial for the sake of an otherworldly reward." Instead: "This reclaimed tradition recognizes the futility of the scramble for unlimited wealth and calls for the recovery of some of the simple joys that have delighted people through the centuries" (45). While noting that major changes have to be made in the area of consumption, Shinn also concludes: "I have no great confidence that [our society] will even [sic—ever?] give up war, which—in addition to all else that can be said about it—is the activity most wasteful of human and natural resources" (46).

13. See the detailed essay by one of the leaders in this research, Willard Swartley, "War and Peace in the New Testament," *Aufstieg and Niedergang der römischen Welt* II.26.3 (1996): 2293–389 (with bibliography, 2389–408).

14. See the extensive bibliography on this subject in the able treatment of this theme by Nikola Hohnjec, *Das Lamm—"to arnion" inder Offengarwig des Johannes: eine exegetisch—theologisch Untersuchung* (Rome: Herder, 1980)

15. Schüssler Fiorenza, *Book of Revelation*, 198: "Critics of Rev. have pointed out that the book preaches vengeance and revenge but not the love of the Sermon on the Mount. It is therefore sub-Christian, the Judas of the New Testament." On "poor old Judas" as a subject of vilification, perhaps even by some writers in the New Testament, see William Klassen, *Judas: Betrayer or Friend of Jesus?* (Minneapolis, Minn.: Fortress, 1996). In addition, the article "Love (NT and Early Jewish)," Anchor Bible Dictionary 4 (1992): 381–96, addresses this issue, especially 394–95.

16. See Ben Hijmans, *[ASKESIS]: Notes on Epictetus' Educational System* (Assen, The Netherlands: Van Gorcum, 1959). On the changing ways in which the word is used in Greek literature, see H. Dressler, *The Usage of [askeo] and Its Cognates in Greek Documents to 100 A.D.* (Washington, D.C.: Catholic University of America, 1947). On the central role of *askesis* in Musonius Rufus, the teacher of Epictetus, see [Lutz, 52–57]; Delbert Wiens, "Musonius Rufus and Genuine Education" (Ph.D. diss., University of Chicago, 1970), 74–85.

17. Ulrich Mauser, *The Gospel of Peace: A Scriptural Message for Today's World* (Louisville, Ky.: Westminster/Knox, 1992).

18. Ibid, 130.

19. We lack a thorough study of *shalom* from a Jewish perspective. This gap, however, has been filled by Shemaryahu Talmon's essay "The Signification of and its Semantic Field in the Hebrew Bible" in *The Quest for Context and Meaning: Studies in Biblical Intertextuality in Honor of James A. Sanders*, ed. C. A. Evens and S. Talmon (Leiden, The Netherlands: Brill, 1997).

20. Specifically, to Varro, as argued by Harald Fuchs, *Augustin und der antike Friedensgedanke* (Berlin: Weidmann, 1965; orig. pub. 1928); but strongly opposed by Joachim Laufs, *Der Friedensgedanke bei Augustinus* (Wiesbaden, Germany: Steiner, 1973).

21. See D. H. Lawrence, *Apocalypse* (London: Penguin, 1931), 124–25. Two decades later, C. G. Jung, *Answer to Job* (Cleveland, Ohio: World Book, 1955; orig. pub. 1952), sees the book as presenting "a terrifying picture that blatantly contradicts all ideas of Christian humility, tolerance, love your neighbour and your enemies, and makes nonsense of a loving father in heaven and rescuer of mankind" (see also 161). It is a profound irony that two writers of our century who have done so much to help us appreciate imagery and symbolism could not appreciate the rich imagery of apocalyptic literature. Biblical scholars have also been in favor of rejecting the apocalyptic genre and, in particular, the Apocalypse of John. For illustrations, see my article, "Vengeance in the Apocalypse," *Catholic Biblical Quarterly* 28 (1966), 300–12. One could add the philosopher Friedrich Nietzsche, who described the Apocalypse as "that most obscene of all the written outbursts, which has revenge on its conscience." Nietzsche comments on "the profound logic of the Christian instinct" when this very book of hate is attributed to the disciple of love! "Therein lies a portion of truth, however much literary forging may have been necessary." See Friedrich Nietzsche, *The Genealogy of Morals—a Polemic*, trans. Horace B. Samuel (New York: Boni and Liveright, The Modern Library 12, 1900), 54.

22. Note the treatments of this question by Dinkler Hastings and G. Zampaglione in *The Idea of Peace in Antiquity*, trans. Richard Dunn (Notre Dame, Ind.: Notre Dame University Press, 1972), 237. Notable exceptions are Klaus Wengst, *Pax Romana* (Philadelphia: Fortress, 1987), 118–36, and especially Egon Brandenburger, *Frieden im Neuen Testament* ([Gutersloh] Gutersloher Verlagshaus G. Mohn, 1973) 17–28. There is also that most insightful contribution made by Peter Lampe, "Die Apokalyptiker—Ihre Situation und ihr Handeln," in *Eschatologie und Friedenshandeln*, U. Luz et al. (Stuttgart: KBW, Stuttgart Bibelstudien 101, 1981), 59–114.

23. See Hans Walter Wolff, *Friede ohne Ende: Eine Auslegung von Jes. 7:1–7 und 9:1–6* (Neukirchen-Vluyn: Neukirchener, 1962), 70–81, especially the importance of the term "Prince of Peace." Wolff notes that according to Isaiah's view "this new King will not himself ever wage war" (72). He sees the fulfillment of this word in Jesus of Nazareth, "The nonresistant Jesus, the crucified, who intercedes for the godless, must just as the newborn child in Isaiah's vision, and just as the word of his witness who is being attacked be seen together with the actual world ruler. In the same way Jesus and his new coming kingdom, indeed Jesus and the end of history are inseparable from the password, peace. In brief, now Isaiah's hymn of hope for the people in darkness becomes a helpful model of confidence in the zeal of God whose ultimate will is liberation and pacification. This zealous God has, in Jesus, become our God. Without him people cannot be people at peace in history. People do violence to themselves when they seek on their own to establish a kingdom of peace" (80–81).

24. Talmon argues that these texts cannot be used to describe the Hebrew view of peace, since the word does not appear there. In this case, he, too, is a victim of a mistake made frequently by scholars of confusing one word for a reality.

25. See Paul Hanson, *The Dawn of Apocalyptic* (Philadelphia: Fortress, 1975).

26. See Schüssler Fiorenza, "Visionary Rhetoric," in *Book of Revelation*, 198. Cf. Lampe, "Apocalyptiker," 65, 69.

27. See Pinchas Lapide, "Apokalypse als Hoffnungstheologie," in *Apokalypse: Eine Prinzip Hoffnung?* Eds. R. W. Gassen and Bernhard Holeczek (Heidelberg, Germany: Brausdruck, 1985), 10–14.

28. See H. Windisch, *Der messianische Krieg und das Urchristentum* (Tübingen, Germany: JCB Molar, 1909) 89: "eine judaisierung des Evangeliums."

29. See Richard Hays, *The Moral Vision of the New Testament* (San Francisco: HarperSanFranscisco, 1996).

30. See Brandenburger, *Frieden im Neuen Testament*, 23–24.

31. Ibid, 23, n. 46.

32. David Flusser has shown this motif to be present in pre-Christian Jewish sources.

33. See Windisch, *Der messianische Krieg*. See also my article, "Jesus and the Messianic War," in *Early Jewish and Christian Exegesis: Studies in Memory of William H. Brownlee*, eds. Craig Evans and W. F. Stinespring (Atlanta, Ga.: Scholars, 1987), 155–75. Cf. Brownlee, "From Holy War to Holy Martyrdom, " in *The Quest for the Kingdom of God: Studies in Honour of George Mendenhall*, eds. H. B. Huffmon et al. (Winona Lake, Ind.: Eisenbrauns, 1983), 281–92. Brownlee's article did not come to my attention until after I had written my own.

34. See the excellent work of Frederick J. Murphy, *Pseudo-Philo: Rewriting the Bible* (New York: Oxford University Press, 1993); idem, "The Martial Option in Pseudo-Philo," *Catholic Biblical Quarterly* 57 (1995): 676–88.

35. See especially T. R. Yoder Neufeld, *God and Saints at War: The Transformation and Democratization of the Divine Warrior in Isaiah 59, Wisdom of Solomon 5, 1 Thessalonians 5, and Ephesians 6* (Sheffield, England: Sheffield University Press, 1997).

36. See Charles Giblin, *The Book of Revelation* (Collegeville, Minn.: Liturgical Press, 1991), 28.
37. Ibid, 29.
38. Ibid.
39. See also the excellent essay summarizing the treatment of the theme of Holy War in the Old Testament by G. H. Jones, "The Concept of Holy War," in *The World of Ancient Israel*, ed. R. E. Clements (Cambridge, England: Cambridge University Press, 1989), 299–322.
40. See Hilarius Edmonds, "Geistlicher Kriegsdienst: Der Topos der *militia spiritualis* in der antiken Philosophie," in *Heilige Überlieferung: Ausschnitte aus der Geschichte des Mönchtums und des Heiligen Kultes*, ed. I. Herwegen (Münster, Germany: Aschendorff 1938), 21–50, reprinted in A. Harnack, *Militia Christi* (Darmstadt, Germany: Wissenschaftl Buchgesellschoft 1963), 133–62, but unfortunately not translated into English by D. M. Gracie in A. Harnack, *Militia Christi* (Philadelphia: Fortress, 1981). More recently, on this topic, see A. J. Malherbe, "Antisthenes and Odysseus, and Paul at War," *Harvard Theological Review* 76 (1983): 43–73.
41. On this reconstituted view of war in Judaism, see my article "War (NT)," Anchor Bible Dictionary 6 (1992): 867–75. On *askesis* in Judaism, see Efraim Urbach, *The Sages: Their Concepts and Beliefs* (Jerusalem: Magnes, 1975), 447–48.
42. See Johann Maier, *Die Schriften vom Toten Meer* 2:30; also Hendrik George Laurens Peels, *The Vengeance of God: The Meaning of the Root NQM and the Function of NQM-texts in the Context of Divine Revelation in the OT* (Leiden, The Netherlands: Brill, 1995). Peels deals with the theories of Klaus Koch, Paul Volz, and George Mendenhall on vengeance and finds them wanting. He treats the concept of revenge at length (145) and cites Maier, who argues that "atonement" (*söhneschaffen*) does not take place through eschatological vengeance but through uniting or union (*yahad*).
43. It is striking how very popular the notion of *eirene* was in the period 50–150 CE both in Rome and elsewhere in the Roman Empire. See, e.g., Wengst, *Pax Romana*, but for the personification and deification of the idea of peace in literature and cult, see especially the article by Waser in Pauly-Wissowa, *Real-Encyclopädie der Classischen Altertums Wissenshaft* 5.2 (1915): 2128–34.
44. See T. Holtz, "Gott in der Apokalypse," in *L'Apocalypse johannique dans le Nouveau Testament*, ed. J. Lambert (Leuven, Belgium: Leuven University Press, 1980), 261.
45. See Lampe, "Apokalyptiker," 104–6.
46. Ibid, 112.
47. Ibid, 102.
48. E. [KoHis], "Apokalyptik und politisches Interesse im Spätjudentum," *Judaica* 27 (1971): 71–89. He concludes correctly: "Both the thinking and the action of the apocalyptists had nothing in common with the attitude of lovely neutral people (*neutrale Schöngeister*)" (71, n. 1).
49. See Holtz, "Gott in der Apokalypse," 256. The term appears nine times in the book of Revelation and only once elsewhere in the New Testament (2 Cor. 6:18).

50. See Jones, "Holy War," 303.
51. See especially *Assumption of Moses*; also Jacob Licht, "*Taxo*, or the Apocalyptic Doctrine of Vengeance," *Journal of Jewish Studies* 12 (1961): 95–103.
52. See G. B. Caird, *The Revelation of St. John the Divine* (New York: Harper & Row, 1962), 293.
53. Ibid, 300. See also C. F. D. Moule, "Punishment and Retribution: An Attempt to Delimit Their Scope in New Testament Thought," *Second Century* 30 (1966): 21–36.
54. See Wengst, *Pax Romana*, 135; also Lampe, "Apokalyptiker."
55. See John J. Collins, *The Apocalyptic Imagination: An Introduction to the Jewish Matrix of Christianity* (New York: Crossroad, 1987), 215.

Imperial Asceticism: Discipline of Domination

Alison Keith and Leif E. Vaage

SUBVERSIVE ASCETICISM

It will be evident by now that for many of the authors in this book, including the editors, the topic of asceticism and the New Testament is appealing especially because of its subversive or transformative potential. Subversion would be at hand, or underhand, wherever the practice of (ancient) asceticism might be seen to represent a particular form of social resistance to different (ancient) cultural hegemonies. The same is also true insofar as the question itself of (ancient) asceticism helps to unravel and to reorient prevailing assumptions and analytical habits of contemporary (modern) New Testament scholarship. Hence all of the chapters presented herein under the aegis of "Paul" and "Jesus" that claim, forthrightly or cautiously, to have found evidence of "asceticism" in their respective New Testament text(s) tend to understand by the term "asceticism" a disciplinary practice that would stand in significant opposition to one or more aspects of the surrounding dominant culture. The same practice would also ideally and simultaneously struggle to articulate an alternative, countercultural, previously subjugated social sensibility. Those chapters which claim to find *no* evidence of "asceticism" also do so, it seems, on the basis of a similar understanding of what the term "asceticism" properly designates.

In this chapter, we will not discuss any further whether or not and if so, to what degree such subversive asceticism may indeed be found in the different canonical gospels—including the Acts of the Apostles—or the various

Pauline writings of the New Testament. Although it should be noted that already within this discussion there are signs, albeit less pronounced, of another, correlative, less-than-countercultural assessment of what ascetic practice actually is and does. Thus, for example, Ronald F. Hock suggests, regarding the discourse of 1 Thessalonians, that in view here is "an *askesis* not in conflict with dominant values, but rather one that saw itself as the best way of achieving these values." And in the Pastoral Epistles, Gail Corrington Streete has proposed that we find "an asceticism that is not 'combative,'" precisely because it "aims at the achievement of self-control both in those who are in positions of authority over others and in those whose only 'triumph' is to turn their subordinate positions into models of self-sacrifice."

In what follows, we shall seek to underscore how the practice of "asceticism"—without failing to be, like the subversive variety, a matter of choice, by definition conflictual, rigorous, costly, and even utopian—may nonetheless be "co-opted" or harnassed as a means of pursuing and imposing strategies of domination, namely, "effective leadership." Insofar as this is true, it will then be requisite to inquire not only whether or not "asceticism" is part of a given textual field, for example, the New Testament, but also, if so, what kind of "asceticism" there is in view. Is it the discipline of subversive resistance and the construction of an alternative social identity? Or is it the discipline of determined domination and conventional control over a given social body? Or, perhaps, we have at hand a strategy of accomplished accommodation—the difficult middle path or proverbial balancing act—between two oppositions.[1] These questions, of course, apply equally well to the discursive field of New Testament scholarship itself.

DOMESTIC ASCETICISM

That the practice of asceticism may serve to maintain a conventional social order—thereby contradicting, although not invalidating, the definition(s) of asceticism developed by Richard Valantasis[2]—is made clear, for example, in the traditions of Brahmanical renunciation or Indian "Hindu" domestic asceticism studied by Patrick Olivelle.[3] An enduring problem faced by students of the Vedic literature has been to explain the relationship that exists here between a discourse focused on the proper performance of sacrifice, namely, one's social duty and a discourse of thoroughgoing renunciation, which would seem to register the desire for full release from all aspects of conventional social existence. Different explanations have been given for the apparent tension in Brahmanical teaching. According to Olivelle, the practice of renunciation as it is articulated in Vedic scripture would represent the means by which a direct challenge, by Buddhists and Jains, to the dominant civilization of the Indian subcontinent, an order supported by Brahmanical theories of sacrifice, was integrated, domesticated, subsumed, and suppressed by the sacerdotal class. By establishing renunciation as a particular phase—the final one—in the "normal" passage of a proper Indian householder's life, an earlier refusal to acknowledge the ethical imperative of such a life was effectively discounted and undermined. One wonders to what degree something similar does not occur in a number of writings of the New Testament.

We have already made reference to Streete's description of a certain "householder" asceticism in the Pastoral Epistles. Although neither Pamela Eisenbaum nor Alicia Batten uses such language in their chapters to account for the specific asceticism of Hebrews and of James, respectively, the final assessment of both writings by the two authors effectively describes a form of domestic asceticism, in the same sense that both Olivelle and Streete employ this terminology.

For example, in a broad generalization meant specifically to introduce Hebrews, Eisenbaum writes: "In many ways, being a good Christian made one a better, more upstanding member of the greater society. Paradoxically, an ancient convert could accept the radical message of Christ raised and look basically the same after the conversion as before.... The Epistle to the Hebrews reflects this paradox." The "vehemence" of the work's paraenetical rhetoric, not to mention the "very precise details of christology and its soteriological implications," stands in notable contrast, both at the beginning and at the end of Eisenbaum's analysis, to the fact that "the author offers no specifically Christian radical action in any of his explicit moral directives. Nevertheless, the call to endure suffering in a way similar to that of Jesus [this phrase essentially summarizes Eisenbaum's three analytical foci of suffering or *pathema*, discipline or *paideia*, and perfection or *teleiosis*] means—at least for those who heed the call—that believers will aid in the social construction of the Christian community."

In other words, the abstractness of Hebrews' rhetoric of suffering, discipline, and perfection both permits and promotes the pursuit of greater spiritual heights without ever rocking the social boat. The "social construction of the Christian community" undergirded by this kind of ascetic practice amounts to self-conscious participation in a model ancient household—this is another way of saying that "being a good Christian made one a better, more upstanding member of the greater society." Like the dutiful and learned Brahmanical renunciant, the implied ascetic of the Epistle to the Hebrews disturbs no one else in his daily round, as the same ascetic wends his exegetically intricate way out of this world.

Similarly in Batten's chapter, despite what the title "An Asceticism of Resistance in James," seems to suggest and the author herself appears to seek, the result of her analysis is decidedly moderate: "James is a mixture of conventional teachings, characteristic of established communities, and the radical ethos of wandering itinerants." Batten believes that the original audience of James is "a settled group, but one torn between the craving for security and the unruly spirit manifest in the early sayings traditions."

While Batten knows that "it was precisely this need for security that eventually triumphed," she seems to underestimate the degree to which she herself has shown that, in James, the scale has already tipped significantly in this direction. Thus, for example, Batten writes: "James is not an extremist, however. On the basis of the moral exhortations discussed earlier, I do not think that he would necessarily stand out as an ascetic.... Aspects of James' attitudes, especially toward speech, are typical of wisdom literature, which generally counsels the proper way to live, but not of a radical asceticism. James' concerns also have much in common with texts like the Pastoral Epistles, which in many ways uphold the status quo with their emphases on the control of women and the household." Even when Batten is sure that James is decidedly more countercultural in resisting the customary valuations, in antiquity, of the perogatives of wealth and the practice of patronage, such resistance ends, at least as Batten describes it, in a strangely abstract realm. James is said to "go farther" than the usual Greco-Roman moralists by insisting that "the evils created by status distinctions will not be solved by human merit, but by a radical reordering of humanity's relationship *to God....* It is only through resistance to and denunciation of this sinful world and its manipulative institutions that one can embrace the new reality, that of friendship *with God*" [italics mine]. Although Batten claims to find in James "a text that evinces a new subjectivity, particularly evident in the hostile attitude toward 'the world' and wealth," urges "a disciplined nonconformity," and "defies authority," it seems as though this new subjectivity, namely, reality, has primarily to do with *God* and not, as one might have anticipated, a radical reordering of human beings' relationships to one another or friendships with more and/or different persons.

The point here is simply to observe that not everything that shines ascetic necessarily gets you very far from home and business as usual, perhaps especially when the rhetoric of another superior reality is most strident and pitched in a universal key and therefore is short on mundane detail, making no immediate difference.[4]

IMPERIAL ASCETICISM

An even more striking example of asceticism in the service of the established social order, specifically in the context of the ancient Mediterranean world, is the imperial asceticism depicted in the work of the Roman poet Virgil; most especially in the *Aeneid,* his great unfinished masterpiece. We will consider this work in some detail because, apart from intrinsic interest, it represents the governing perspective of the larger sociopolitical context—*pax romana*—within which all the texts of the New Testament were first written. Insofar as this perspective entails a certain *askesis* of power—the exercise of personal restraint and self-mastery in order better or more "rightfully" to master others—a further vantage point will have been gained whence to assess the presence of asceticism in the writings of the New Testament. In certain instances, it may be that the evidence of an ascetic practice registers neither resistance to prevailing cultural hegemonies nor assimilation of such discrepancy—"begging to differ"—to the conventional order but precisely a mode of participation in, or emulation of, the very discipline of domination.

Born in 70 BCE, Virgil lived through much of the century-long collapse of the political structures of the Roman Republic, which led to the establishment of the Principate under Augustus in 27 BCE. Virgil seems to have been educated at Rome and in Naples (after early schooling in Cremona). An especially intriguing notice, found in *Catalepton* 5, a short poem attributed to Virgil, alludes to a school the young Virgil attended in Naples run by the Epicurean philosopher Siro. The poem characterizes the Epicurean project as one of renunciation—the abandonment of rhetoric, of poetry, of age-mates, and of cares—while the Epicurean community is represented as a blessed haven presided over by the master's teaching. Like the community depicted in Batten's study of James, the Epicurean association led by Siro in Naples had turned its back on the contemporary society of Roman Italy in order to seek the tranquillity promised by Epicurean training. While the poem does not answer the question of whether or not Virgil and other members of the community adhered, as Countryman's definition of asceticism suggests that a proper ascetic would, to "a relatively demanding bodily praxis"—although the language of the poem does hint at a rejection of rich food and of sexual indulgence—we can certainly see that Virgil's participation in the same community was "voluntarily undertaken" and that it set "those who adopt it apart from and, in some sense, above the ordinary run of people in" the greater encompassing world.

The evidential value of this poem for Virgil's life is ambiguous, however, for it is possible that *Catalepton* 5 was the work of a forgerer. Nevertheless, the first work that Virgil undoubtedly wrote, the *Bucolics*, likewise reveals a deep familiarity with and a strong sympathy for the Epicurean project, albeit now also with some growing uncertainity.[5] And, in fact, at the end of his life, Virgil transformed the uneasy Epicureanism of the *Bucolics* into a complete rejection of Epicurus' tenets. In the *Aeneid*, as Julia Dyson has shown, Virgil's portrait of Dido entails a comprehensive critique of the Epicurean life.[6]

As Carthage is opposed to Rome in the *Aeneid* and Dido to Aeneas, so is Dido's Epicureanism opposed to Aeneas' quasi-Stoic asceticism. The portrayal of Aeneas in the poem has usually been interpreted in the light of Augustus' character and career, with whom Augustus was held to be related, but scholars both ancient and modern have recognized the important contribution of Roman notions of the Stoic wise man to the characterization of Aeneas as well.[7] At Rome, Stoic ethics had long held considerable appeal for elite male citizens—active statesmen and soldiers—of the classical Republic who justified their competition for the spoils of the empire (at the heads of Roman armies) and their rule over most of the Mediterranean (through control of the Senate) with the claim of embodying exemplary virtue. Ancient Roman historians, all upper-class male citizens, frequently represent Roman national identity "in terms of the moral superiority of Romans"[8] as revealed through their frugality, military discipline, and austere lifestyle, particularly in comparison with the luxury and avarice of other peoples in the ancient world, especially those living in the richer eastern Mediterranean. In Virgil's portrait of Aeneas, we find a typically Roman elite male concern with the moral training and conduct of the ruler articulated through a matrix of Stoic ethical ideals.[9]

The proem to the *Aeneid* characterizes Aeneas' project as one of risk and toil, entailing "so many dangers and so many labours" (1.9–10), "so great a struggle it was to found the Roman nation" (1.33). Critics have frequently interpreted the mission of Aeneas as a course of training in virtue and wisdom. We are first given the opportunity to observe Aeneas' schooling in the fortitude of will that he requires to accomplish his imperial destiny early in the first book of the poem, when Juno incites Aeolus, the king of the winds, to overwhelm the Trojan ships in a storm at sea. Having lost many men and ships, the Trojans finally make landfall near Carthage in North Africa, where Aeneas addresses his despairing men with words of comfort (1.198–207) despite his own even greater cares: "Such words he spoke, and sick with huge cares he feigned hope with his face, and stifled his grief deep within his heart" (1.208–209). One of the most prominent precepts of Stoic philosophy is the eradication of the passions, a state that Aeneas is far from achieving here, but toward which his character struggles by repressing anxiety and simulating equanimity.

Aeneas learns a second valuable lesson about self-control and self-mastery during his winter at the court of Queen Dido in Carthage. Invited by Dido to join her in ruling Carthage, Aeneas neglects his duty toward his son and the proto-Roman nation (the fulfillment of one's obligations is another prominent theme of Roman Stoicism) and abandons himself to a winter of sexual indulgence and physical luxury in the form of feasting, drinking, fine clothes, and jewelry (4.193–194). Mercury, sent by Jupiter (the benevolent god of Stoic providence)[10] to remind Aeneas of his duty, discovers him resplendent in purple, gold, and jewels: "[Aeneas'] sword was studded with yellow jasper, and a cloak hung from his shoulders ablaze with Tyrian purple—a gift that wealthy Dido had made, interweaving the web with gold thread" (4.261–264). Pointing out that Aeneas is founding the wrong city, the god bids him to abandon the fleshpots of Carthage and to refocus his energies on his mission, the foundation of Rome (4.265-276). As a result of his encounter with Mercury, Aeneas "burns to be off and to leave behind the land of luxury" (4.281). In his subsequent interview with Dido, Aeneas presents an impassive and emotionless demeanor to the lovelorn Dido, renouncing their passion and articulating instead a love purged of any of the appetites of the flesh: "But now Grynean Apollo and the Lycian lot have bidden me to seek Italy, great Italy; here is my love, here is my country" (4.345–347). In the face of Dido's tears and protestations, Aeneas masters his instinctive emotional response, refrains from any further speech with the distraught queen, and prepares to fulfill the will of the gods (4.393–396). Aeneas here gives evidence of a new taciturnity,[11] a mastery of his tongue remarkably akin to the one recommended by James.

A scene in Book Six, in which Aeneas successfully undertakes a descent to the underworld, illustrates his continuing progress in virtue. In response to the Sibyl's detailed prophecy of the great labors awaiting Aeneas in Italy (6.84), Aeneas says without a trace of complaint or faintness of heart: "For me, maiden, no form of labours arises strange or unexpected; I have already anticipated and traversed all this in my own mind" (6.103–105). The younger Seneca will quote these lines as exemplifying the attitude the Stoic wise man holds when threatened by the onslaught of fate (*ep. mor.* 76.33). The rewards of this training in self-mastery and moral virtue are then depicted in characteristically Roman terms of value at the triumphal climax of Aeneas' visit to the underworld: "Others, I trust, will beat out the breathing bronze with softer lines, and will lead living features from marble, better plead cases at law, trace the heavens with a rod and tell of the rising stars: Roman [man], you remember to rule peoples in empire, (these will be your skills), to impose custom on settlement, to spare the conquered, and to battle down the proud" (6.847–853).

Like other later Republican and early imperial Roman authors, Virgil (through the mouth of Anchises) is exclusively concerned here with the behavior of the upper classes, for it is their behavior as the rulers of empire that matters. Any tendencies toward asceticism in Aeneas' character must therefore be balanced by a deep concern with the social order as a whole, for "the Roman elite justified their privileged position by pointing to their superior morals. Their capacity for self-control legitimated the control they exercised over others who were, it was implied, unable to control themselves."[12]

The tension that this generates is well illustrated in the famous scene at the end of Book Eight when Aeneas shoulders the shield his mother has procured for him. Finding Aeneas alone in a remote valley apart from his troops, Venus bestows on her son the weapons crafted by Vulcan for him at her request (8.608–610). Elsewhere in the poem, Aeneas characteristically withdraws from his followers, only to consider how best to fulfill his obligations to them; even the descent to Hades (6.237–900) can be viewed in this light.[13] Similarly, Aeneas' withdrawal from the world in Book Eight is the setting for his receipt of the weapons by which he will conquer it. Vulcan decorates Aeneas' shield with a parade of heroes drawn from Roman history in a pageant that stages the relentless rise of Roman imperial power from the foundation of Rome to Augustus' victory in the Battle of Actium (8.625–728): These scenes document the empire that Aeneas' introspection serves. Rejoicing in his descendants, although without understanding the specific references of individual episodes on the shield, Aeneas lifts the shield to his shoulders in a gesture that vividly dramatizes the link between his labors and his will to rule (8.729–731). Aeneas' physical and spiritual fortitude legitimates and quite literally underpins his imperial mission.

Comparison with a contemporary poetic account of the civil war that brought Octavian to sole power suggests a series of similarities between the mythological hero Aeneas and Aeneas' supposed historical descendant Augustus.[14] Suetonius supplements the verse portrait of Octavian's self-control in battle with a picture of Augustus' self-restraint in private life. Suetonius relates that the first Roman emperor lived in a modest house of neither size nor elegance and used the same bedroom for over forty years in both summer and winter, although he suffered from ill health when wintering in the city (*Aug.* 72). Even the bed he slept on testifies to Augustus' plain mode of living, for the bed was low and simply made up (*Aug.* 73). Indeed, Suetonius comments approvingly on the frugality of all of Augustus' household furnishings, many of which, he says, were scarcely worthy of a private citizen, let alone an emperor (*Aug.* 73). The emperor dressed plainly, too, habitually wearing the humble domestic clothing woven for him by his womenfolk (*Aug.* 73). He was extremely sparing in his consumption of wine (*Aug.* 77), and although he constantly gave dinner parties on state business (*Aug.* 74), he himself ate abstemiously and only plain food (*Aug.* 76). Suetonius adduces much interesting evidence of Augustus' preference for plain fare from his correspondence, including a letter in which the *princeps* boasts to Tiberius that "not even a Jew observes his fast on the sabbath as scrupulously as I did today" (*Aug.* 76). Augustus is also reported to have voluntarily assumed a demanding schedule to fulfill his offical obligations in the courts, temples, and other imperial public fora (*Aug.* 33; 78). The first *princeps*, as the master of his own physical appetites, models the self-mastery that had eluded his inferiors among the Roman aristocrats (most notably, Anthony) and therefore legitimately assumed control of the Roman empire.

One wonders to what extent "the ascetic way" depicted in the book of Revelation does not envision (*pace* Klassen) a comparable project, albeit one not initially articulated from the same position of elevated social privilege and pervasive political power as Virgil's *Aeneid*. Without wishing to support a view of the book of Revelation as "the Judas of the New Testament," the evident "militarism" of its language, even when transposed from the killing fields of actual mortal combat to the bloodless peace of anticipated divine intervention, places the text squarely within the standard discourse(s) of empire. In the chthonic struggles that must be undergone, in the book of

Revelation, before "a new heaven and a new earth" may appear (21:1), only those (144,000) who, like Aeneas rejecting Dido, have learned to resist the evident allure of "Babylon the great, the mother of whores and earthly defilements" (17:5) with whom "all the kings of the earth have whored and those inhabiting the earth have gotten drunk from the wine of her whoredom" (17:2); who "have not soiled themselves with women, for they are *parthenoi*"; who "follow the lamb wherever he may go"; in whose mouth "was found no lie; they are without blemish" (14:4), will be able to inhabit the new Jerusalem, again like Aeneas acceding resolutely to the challenge of imperial destiny, shouldering in Book Eight of the *Aeneid* the weighty panorama of Roman history that begins with the foundation of the eternal city. The study of the *Pax Romana* and early Christianity, including the book of Revelation, by Klaus Wengst, to which Klassen occasionally refers and cites approvingly in conclusion, deserves to be pursued, although the evident conviction by both of these authors that a clear contrast exists between the two projects, at least regarding Revelation, seems much less an assured result. Not infrequently, when something wholly other is promised, to wit, the rule of "the Lamb that was slain" and his martyred minions, there occurs the return of the oppressed.

NOTES

1. Cf. Margaret Y. Macdonald (this volume, 269–298), who suggests for Colossians that it "recommend[s] subservience while...legitimating subversion of the traditional household," and a strategy of "social invisibility...carefully hidden from a householder who would resist such an invasion."
2. See Richard Valantasis, "A Theory of the Social Function of Asceticism," in *Asceticism,* eds. Vincent L. Wimbush and Richard Valantasis (New York: Oxford University Press, 1995), 544–52; idem, "Constructions of Power in Asceticism," *Journal of the American Academy of Religion* 63/4 (1995): 775–821. In this present essay on Galatians, Valantasis (this volume, 211–230) speaks of a "traditional" ascetic subjectivity that would seem to be now a form of asceticism at the service of the dominant social order.
3. See Patrick Olivelle, *The* Asrama *System: The History and Hermeneutics of a Religious Institution* (New York: Oxford University Press, 1993).
4. I take the reference in James 1:1 to "the twelve tribes in the diaspora" as effectively a claim to universality. Differently, but to similar effect, the lack of any introductory remarks that might specifically situate the Epistle to the Hebrews pitches it in the same universal key.
5. The "woodland Muse" (*siluestrem musam, Buc.* 1.2), whom Virgil's shepherds study appears first in Lucretius' scientific account of the acoustical phenomenon of echo (*DRN* 4.589), while the "leisure" (*otia, Buc.* 1.6) in which they live has overtones of the tranquillity sought by the Epicureans.
6. See Julia T. Dyson, "Dido the Epicurean," *Classical Antiquity* 15 (1996): 203–21.

7. On Aeneas as a figure for Augustus, see the ancient commentaries by Servius and Ti. Claudius Donatus, *passim*; cf. A. Powell, "The *Aeneid* and the Embarrassments of Augustus," in *Roman Poetry and Propaganda in the Age of Augustus*, ed. A. Powell (London: Bristol Classical Press, 1992), 141–74. On Stoic traits in the characterization of Aeneas, see R. Heinze, *Virgil's Epic Technique*, trans. Hazel Harvey, David Harvey, and Fred Robertson (London: Bristol Classical Press, 1993; orig. pub. 1903), 227, 240–41; C. M. Bowra, "Aeneas and the Stoic Ideal," *Greece & Rome* 8 (1933–1934): 3-21 (repr. in *Oxford Readings in Vergil's* Aeneid, ed. S. J. Harrison [Oxford: Oxford University Press, 1990], 363–77); V. Pöschl, *The Art of Vergil*, trans. G. Seligson (Ann Arbor.: University of Michigan Press, 1962; orig. pub. 1950), 45, 54–55; M. Edwards, "The Expression of Stoic Ideas in the *Aeneid*," *Phoenix* 14 (1960): 151–65.

8. See C. Edwards, *The Politics of Immorality in Ancient Rome* (Cambridge: Cambridge University Press, 1993), 20–21.

9. See Heinze, *Virgil's Epic Technique;* Bowra, "Aeneas and the Stoic Ideal"; M. Edwards, "Expression of Stoic Ideas in the *Aeneid*." For the view that the king-ship ideal exemplified by Aeneas is Cynic, see F. Cairns, *Virgil's Augustan Epic* (Cambridge: Cambridge University Press, 1989).

10. See Heinze, *Virgil's Epic Technique* 236–41.

11. See D. C. Feeney, "The Taciturnity of Aeneas," *Church Quarterly* 33 (1983): 204–19 (repr. in *Oxford Readings in Vergil's* Aeneid, ed. Harrison, 167–90).

12. See C. Edwards, *Politics of Immorality*, 25.

13. Cf. *Aen.* 1.180–93; 1.305–13; 5.721–46; 8.18–78; 10.159–60.

14. Fragments of a poem about Actium were found in the charred remains of the library in the Villa dei Papyri at Herculaneum, but no consensus exists among scholars about the identity of the author. Quintilian (*Inst. Or.* 10.1.10) mentions a poem about Actium by a certain Rabirius, whose work is praised by both Ovid (*ex Pont.* 4.16.5) and Velleius (2.36.3). For discussion of the fragments from Herculaneum with text, translation, and further bibliography, see H. W. Benario, "The 'Carmen de bello Actiaco' and Early Imperial Epic," *Aufstieg und Niedergang der römischen Welt*, ed. A. Temporini and W. Haage. II.30.3 (1983) 1656–62.

The New Testament in Asceticism

Leif E. Vaage and Vincent L. Wimbush

In writing the epilogue to a book, the temptation exists, as every ascetic (editor) knows, to impose one's own a priori imagination of how things ought to be or might have been on the material (texts) at hand. It is a temptation to be resisted, as every ascetic (editor) also knows, for nothing will be accomplished thereby but the endless return of the same. The practice of asceticism (including editing) is undertaken not for the sake of control but, rather, as the effort to create a certain social space—in the body (of the book)—where something other than the current regime of knowledge and set of expectations or "what we already know" might be glimpsed and elaborated. In this regard, the chapters in this book have successfully explored the topic of asceticism and the New Testament, insofar as they now serve to loosen governing presuppositions of what, in fact, might constitute the proper meaning of these texts.

As already noted in the Introduction, the chapters attest to the continuing difficulty of adequately defining the category of "asceticism." Although many of the authors in this book have used, in one form or another, the definition of asceticism developed by Richard Valantasis, it is evident that few find it a sufficient or complete definition as such. Nor does Valantasis himself pretend with his definition to have exhausted or corralled the phenomenon of asceticism. Nonetheless, it is plain that the effort to define asceticism in a manner that goes beyond both abstract generalization and merely listing the different things that so-called ascetics have said or done, if not absolutely necessary, will be increasingly desirable in order for the category of asceticism to serve as a methodological wedge in interpreting different (ancient) texts, including those of the New Testament. This is so, if only because implicit and focused in the category of asceticism is a particular theory of religion.

Although shifting from the definition of asceticism to a theory of religion may effectively mean jumping from the frying pan into the fire, it is important to bear in mind this larger frame of reference in the discussion about asceticism and the New Testament. One of the main reasons for the continuing debate about what exactly asceticism "is," and whether or not it has anything to do with the New Testament, derives from this encompassing sphere of strong conviction and critical distance. For whatever else (ancient) asceticism may be, it plainly presupposes and therewith proposes that (ancient) religion—whatever else it may entail—is, first of all, as Kloppenborg has underscored, a bodily matter, and, therefore, necessarily a fleshly, deeply material, this-worldly social practice. Whatever else (ancient) religion may be, as (ancient) asceticism it would remain primarily focused on those problems that attend the (ancient) human effort to exist and the concomitant desire to be somehow *more* than one presently is: that is, more fully, more completely, more plainly, more purely, more transparently, more enduringly, more utterly human.[1] "More" does not mean "other" but it does mean "different"; not "alien," but "satisfied" in a way that the experience of recurring appetites and shifting circumstances routinely undermines and dishevels.

It is, in fact, this implicit challenge to other understandings of the nature of religion, including the writing of religious texts, that accounts for why the question of asceticism can serve as a methodological wedge for rereading the different works of the New Testament. As already noted in the Introduction, the question of asceticism, when used as a methodological wedge, does not provide or itself represent a new method of interpretation, in the sense that one would now know to look for x, y, or z = *asceticism* in a given writing and thereafter be able to catalog it within a particular taxonomy of ascetic manifestations. At least, such a reduction of the question of asceticism to a specified set of linguistic markers and discursive ploys would fail to maintain, at the level of textual analysis, the constitutive insight of an ascetic theory of religion.

The chapters in this volume do not represent ascetic readings of the New Testament. They do suggest, however, in keeping with the theory of religion that attends the question of asceticism, another—perhaps ascetic—understanding of what a text is, including those of the New Testament. Of course, by reconfiguring what we understand a text to be, the practice of interpretation would itself be realigned and, therefore, methods of interpretation must follow suit.

In the Introduction, it was suggested that the question of asceticism shifts the bottom line of interpretation from simply rehearsing one or more aspect(s) of the self-contained world of the text toward describing and assessing the complex and fluid constructions of social texture that the text attests as partial instance. In searching for signs of asceticism in the New Testament, in order to see them there, the interpreter must first regard the text neither as an independent aesthetic object that the reader may enjoy and rearrange at will nor as an inscriptionally suspended act of "communication," sending forth a "message" that still awaits reception. Rather, the text—when approached under the aegis of the question of asceticism—should be seen as a residue or trace of—and only in this sense as an enduring testimony to—a particular,. larger, textually uncontained, and ultimately unfinished life project.

Using the question of asceticism as a methodological wedge, the text—for example, the New Testament—would register an almost "incidental" effort of a certain form of being in-and-against-and-alongside, or beyond, a given—social—world further to articulate itself. The text would belong and should be read as an extension or projection—and only in this sense as an objectification or representation—of singular human strivings to enjoy more broadly and more profoundly—more deeply, more intensely, more easily, more continuously—an always singularly embodied life. The goal of textual interpretation becomes thereby not entrance into or, as it were, the losing of oneself within the world of the text, but rather, via the text, the catching sight of the particular project of human life enhancement, some traces of which are at hand. Such a goal does not presume on the part of the interpreter either a priori agreement or a fortiori affirmation of the project in question, but it does demand at the outset at least a certain entertainment of the ethical possibility now enshrined *as* the text.

At this point, the requirements for responsible textual interpretation—including of course, interpretation of the New Testament—become remarkably akin to the social and political skills and commitments needed for the textual scholar to play a significant role in the ongoing cultural construction of his or her own immediate social environment. The discipline of textual—New Testament—interpretation and other contiguous modes of rewriting the governing script(s) of an encompassing social world begin to appear as activities closely related to one another. Historical reconstruction is not uniquely or primarily about a time, a place, and other people "way back when." It is as much and more about the present construction of our own historical moment and "us here and now." The question of asceticism is, we believe, an especially auspicious, because adequate, frame of reference within which to pursue such a self-conscious, socially critical, life-enhancing intellectual disciplinary practice, especially for scholars of the New Testament and early Christianity.

In the Introduction, we suggested that among the benefits of taking the question of asceticism and the New Testament to heart would be significant changes in the conduct of New Testament scholarship. In conclusion, we name a few of the changes that we would happily foresee. As already noted, scholars will cease to interpret the New Testament primarily as (a collection of) *texts*, that is, as a deposit of religiotheological ideas or independent aesthetic object. The focus on asceticism makes the question of (social, cultural, political, and/or economic) *texture* far more poignant and relevant. Issues of worldview and response to the encompassing social "world," of formation, power and hierarchies, representation, gender, and ethnic identity, among other issues, will become irresistible, indeed haunting (if rightly approached), for interpretation.

Paying attention to asceticism and the New Testament will force a scrambling of conventional scholarly boundaries and categories. At least, it raises the stakes for reconsidering what exactly it might mean to argue that, as far back as we can follow the developing traditions of early Christianity, they may be characterized as "ascetic." In this case, Nietzsche and Weber and Troeltsch, not to mention many of our own teachers and other scholars of the New Testament and early Christianity, and the paradigms that they respected and translated, will need to be revisited and critiqued on different terms.

For the study of asceticism and, specifically, studies of early Christian asceticism, the focus of this book on texts of the New Testament suggests that it will no longer be appropriate to presume either the "figure of the Desert Father or the aristocratic male church prelate as the "normal" model of asceticism. Evidence of asceticism in the New Testament raises serious questions about all of the traditional scholarly and popular notions and assumptions regarding the origins, language, and social character of early Christian asceticism. A little probing in the New Testament has served to demonstrate that, in fact, there were many different and conflicting rhetorical forms, social practices, privileged sites, configurations of power, models, and motivations at work in early Christian asceticism. The particular face, gender, activity, politics, immediate goads, and ultimate aspirations of early Christian ascetics all need to be reassessed in the light of the fact that one can and must take seriously the possibility that the New Testament, too, is "ascetic."

Finally, the question of asceticism and the New Testament provides a case study in the social psychology and politics of professional North Atlantic scholarly interpretation. If this book has been at all successful in establishing the issue of asceticism as pertinent to the meaning of not a few texts of the New Testament, how, then, should we account for the long history of scholarly inattention to, if not flat-out denial of, this very possibility? What is at stake in previous "canonical" (North Atlantic) portraits of a decidedly nonascetic Jesus and, occasionally, insecurely ascetic Paul? Why has it been so important in both scholarly historiography, viz., hagiography and popular ecclesiastical and cultural thinking—to spare the New Testament, its heroic figures, traditions, and erstwhile communities—the label of "ascetic"? In answering these questions, by beginning to ask them, it may become possible for New Testament scholars better to understand their own work and, we suggest, more creatively to deploy themselves as trained readers, writers, intellectuals, and teachers within our own cultural context: namely, late, still fervently imperialistic, capitalism.

NOTE

1. Hence the angelic life that later Christian ascetics identified as the goal of their asceticism was not a life they sought to know after death, but, often, precisely before death, while still very much defined by the human body.

Index